I I I

TRW

*Pioneering Technology
and Innovation
since 1900*

I I I I I

Davis Dyer

HARVARD BUSINESS SCHOOL PRESS

Boston, Massachusetts

02 01 00 99 98   5 4 3 2 1

Library of Congress Cataloging-in-Publication Data
Dyer, Davis.
    TRW : pioneering technology and innovation since 1900 / Davis
Dyer.
        p.   cm.
    Includes bibliographical references and index.
    ISBN 0-87584-606-8 (alk. paper)
    1. TRW, Inc.—History.   2. Industrial equipment industry—United
States—History.   3. Automobile supplies industry—United States—
History.   4. Electronic industries—United States—History.
5. Aerospace industries—United States—History.   I. Title.
HD9680.U54T73   1998   97-30659
338.7'621'0973--DC21   CIP

The paper used in this publication meets the requirements of the American National
Standard for Permanence of Paper for Printed Library Materials Z39.49-1984.

To the memory of

Frederick Coolidge Crawford,
1891–1994

Contents

PREFACE

I I I

TRW Inc. commissioned this book. The company had long sought to capture its story and had even launched history projects in the 1960s and 1980s. In the earlier effort, William Crowell, a member of TRW's Public Relations Department, gathered many files and records based primarily on the voluminous papers of Frederick C. Crawford, who led the company (then Thompson Products) between 1929 and 1958. Crowell apparently made little headway in writing, however, and the company eventually donated the papers to the Western Reserve Historical Society in Cleveland, where they are now housed.[1]

The history project of the 1980s, also carried out by TRW's Public Relations Department, was more modest in scope. It consisted of extended oral history interviews with leaders of the company, starting with Crawford and continuing with J. David Wright (chairman and CEO, 1958–1969), Horace Shepard (president, 1962–1969; chairman and CEO, 1969–1977), Dean E. Wooldridge (president, 1958–1962), Simon Ramo (executive vice president, 1958–1961; vice chairman, 1961–1978), and Ruben F. Mettler (president, 1969–1977; chairman and CEO, 1977–1988). The intention was to create a history of the company based on the edited recollections of these leaders. That project slowly metamorphosed into the present one, when TRW's top management agreed on the need to expand the oral history program to a much wider range of past and present employees and to set the company's story in a broader context. Accordingly, the company engaged The Winthrop Group, Inc. to produce this work.[2]

Two principal factors motivated TRW to commission an outside historian. First, the company sought an objective record of its growth and change, both for its own sake and as a way to capture learning with potential present and future value. Although it bears a proud tradition as a technology leader, TRW had no interest in glorifying its past. Rather, it wanted to honor and understand past achievements as preparation for meeting the challenges of tomorrow. Second, the company was eager to record the experiences of many employees whose memories stretched back a long way. At the start of this project, every chief executive of the company since 1929 was still alive, a circumstance that permitted the creation of a continuous oral history record of unusually long duration. In addition, the launch of this project represented an opportunity to interview while their memories were relatively fresh many employees and retirees in the company's space and defense operations, which had begun during the mid-1950s. Many of these individuals retired during the 1980s, and waiting much longer to gather their recollections would have increased costs and risks.

In engaging The Winthrop Group, TRW agreed to adhere to professional standards of historical research and writing. Although the company was generous in support of the project, it placed only two restrictions on me: a general concern to avoid disclosing competitive and trade secrets and a refusal to disclose or discuss information about classified work on behalf of the United States government. The little I have written about TRW's work in classified areas is based entirely on public sources or on information gleaned outside the company. In addition, I have chosen to make the final two chapters, which deal with TRW since 1985, different in approach and tone from the other historical chapters in the book. The concluding chapters concentrate on narrating—as opposed to explaining—TRW's recent history. Despite an author's wish to reach a crescendo at the end of a book, this anticlimax is inevitable in a biography of a living subject. The book ends, but the story continues to unfold in ways that are presently difficult to anticipate but bound to be surprising. Five or ten years from now, a historian considering TRW during the 1980s and 1990s will doubtless see patterns and arrive at conclusions that are not evident to me.

To oversee the project, TRW and The Winthrop Group agreed to establish a History Advisory Committee, which included both representatives of the company and outsiders. The company members included Arden Bement, formerly corporate vice president of technology and now professor of engineering at Purdue University; Howard Knicely, executive vice president of human resources and communications; Ruben Mettler, retired chairman and CEO; James Roosevelt, vice president, assistant general counsel and assistant secretary; and Alan Senger, director of community affairs.[3] The outside members were Alfred D. Chandler, Jr., Straus Professor of Business History emeritus at Harvard Business School, and Carroll W. Pursell, Jr., Adeline Barry Davee Distinguished Professor of History at Case Western Reserve University and a specialist in the history of technology.

Although the History Advisory Committee and other TRW officials reviewed the plan of research, the outline, and all or part of the manuscript and provided many critical comments and suggestions, the organization, themes, interpretations, and conclusions of the book are entirely my own. TRW provided no subvention to Harvard Business School Press, which followed its customary review procedures before agreeing to publish the manuscript.

Disclaimers aside, of course, commissioned corporate histories have an inherent bias: companies that fail or that have dark episodes in their past typically do not invite outsiders in to dig and probe. TRW is an old and successful company with a basically good story to tell and the self-confidence to have it told. Within that context, however, this is a portrait, warts and all. The focus is on TRW's performance and accomplishments, but the book also considers projects, businesses, and actions that failed or backfired. How it has responded to challenge and adversity is an important element of the company's character.

The primary audience for a history of a company consists of people who already possess some connection with it: employees, retirees, customers, suppliers, competitors, specialists in the industries it serves, citizens of communities where it maintains operations. But TRW's story may also engage a broader group of readers, for several reasons.

First, the history of TRW is really the history of many companies, but especially of two—Thompson Products, Inc., and the Ramo-Wooldridge Corporation—and of the protracted process of their becoming one. Each of these subjects carries an interest and significance of its own.

The story of Thompson Products—the "T" in today's TRW—affords an unusual perspective on the development of the automobile industry in the United States. Although the histories of Ford, General Motors, and, to a lesser extent, Chrysler, are well known, we have lacked comparable portraits of automotive suppliers, which together constitute a major industry in the economy. Companies such as Thompson Products accounted for many innovations and improvements in the automobile industry in engine performance, steering and handling, safety, so-called creature comforts, and other areas, although these contributions have been largely anonymous. Thompson Products' story sheds light on the role of automotive suppliers in technological innovation, as well as in other distinctive characteristics of the automobile industry such as purchasing practices and behavior, production methods, and the evolution of the huge independent automobile repair market.

Similarly, the company's main product line, engine valves, positioned it to supply another important but unheralded industry: aircraft engines. Like the aircraft industry, the aircraft engine industry shares common roots with the automobile industry, although it followed a more independent course after World War I. The history of Thompson Products helps illuminate this story, as well as the role that suppliers have played in the development of aviation generally.

A second reason why TRW's history may interest the random reader lies in the story of the "RW" side of the company. Formed by two of America's most outstanding scientist-engineers, Ramo-Wooldridge played a crucial part in the evolution of the defense industry in the United States. The company proved profitable and started growing rapidly within weeks of its incorporation in September 1953. This performance reflected its key role in the development of one of the most significant technologies of the twentieth century, the intercontinental ballistic missile (ICBM). Suddenly, nuclear weapons became even more frightening because they could be delivered anywhere on the planet within thirty minutes. There is still no proven defense against these weapons. The ICBM stimulated enormous changes in world politics. It also stimulated important innovations in electronics, communications, computers, software, and spacecraft for both military and commercial applications. In all of these new areas, TRW made significant contributions. The company's experiences offer important insights into the development and spread of high technology during the second half of the twentieth century.

Third, the history of TRW enables examination of how two very different companies merged and managed the process of becoming one. The 1958 union of Thompson Products and Ramo-Wooldridge proved anything but simple and straightforward, except in legal and financial terms. The merger created a corporation that shared the characteristics of a new kind of company that appeared in the United States after World War II: an organization that combined the ability to mass produce for industrial and commercial markets with the ability to engineer complex systems using a variety of advanced technologies, primarily for military applications. Companies such as TRW, Martin Marietta (now Lockheed Martin), ITT, Rockwell International, Emerson Electric, Allied Signal, Gencorp, and others expanded and diversified by adding defense-related businesses to traditional manufacturing or processing operations. Integrating such diverse businesses proved extraordinarily difficult, however, because of major differences in organization and markets.

From time to time TRW sought to transfer learning across the gap between military and commercial operations and often experienced frustration. Methods of mass production proved difficult to apply in advanced electronic and aerospace systems; similarly, the skills and capabilities characteristic of these R&D-intensive businesses, where most research and development was funded by customers and conducted at the frontiers of technology, proved too advanced and expensive in the highly competitive world of automobile and aircraft supply. In TRW's case, geographical separation—Cleveland and Los Angeles—as well as perceived differences in background and education of personnel, types of business, growth prospects, and other considerations compounded the two-cultures problem that has persisted for decades. How the company approached this problem and what it has learned in the process is a major theme of the book.

A fourth reason to ponder TRW's history is its pioneering role in corporate management and in the management of technology, which the business press long ago noted and continues to celebrate. One tradition, for example, harkens back to Crawford, who presided over the transformation of Thompson Products from a struggling supplier to the automobile and aircraft engine industries into a diversified and stable corporation.[4] During his tenure—and well beyond—he demonstrated remarkable qualities of leadership on both a local and a national scale. He played a leading role in local and national business organizations, including a term during World War II as president of the National Association of Manufacturers. Much of his fame outside Cleveland reflected Thompson Products's distinctive employee management practices. They proved controversial at the time—and ever since—because they kept at bay industrial unions, which were heavily represented elsewhere in Cleveland and in the industries in which Thompson Products competed. The company was one of a handful of large American manufacturing corporations to remain independent of industrial labor unions during the 1940s, a fact that drew lightning both to it and to Crawford. This book offers a detailed explanation of these practices and a pointed contrast to much of American business and labor history during this period.

Similarly, Ramo-Wooldridge (and then TRW) developed distinctive practices for organizing and managing large-scale, complex projects such as missiles and spacecraft. Although the concept of "systems engineering" has roots in the development of the great electrical power and telephone networks of the late nineteenth and early twentieth centuries, TRW promoted the term and formalized techniques to help the company develop the ICBM. TRW also pioneered the use of computer modeling, matrix organization structures, new types of graphical aids for managing and scheduling projects, and other management innovations.

Finally, the history of TRW during the postwar period affords an opportunity to consider the evolution of large U.S.-based industrial corporations generally. We do not have many detailed studies of such companies in this period, although some patterns and themes are becoming evident.[5] Soon after the war, for example, Thompson Products adopted a decentralized, multidivisional organizational structure characteristic of other leading companies, including the later TRW. This organizational structure and supporting policies facilitated rapid growth and diversification during the 1960s. Like many other companies, TRW expanded its overseas commercial businesses and, heavily influenced by U.S. antitrust law, branched into new areas, most often via acquisition. For TRW, the result was that by 1970 the company included more than fifty separate divisions and many more distinctly different businesses. At the same time, the company's corporate headquarters staff grew increasingly specialized as new technologies, the increasing volume of foreign transactions, problems of managing employee relations in many different countries and settings, the need for rigorous planning, and challenges of communicating TRW's distinctive strategy to investors and the public characterized the company's business. During the late 1970s and early 1980s, however, TRW encountered many operating and financial problems at least partly rooted in the rapid expansion and broad scope of its activities. In the past decade the company undertook two painful restructurings to divest businesses that it no longer considered essential. As of the mid-1990s, TRW is focused on core businesses in automotive and space and defense.

TRW's pattern of rapid growth, rapid diversification, and slow, painful retrenchment and refocusing is characteristic of many leading companies in the United States during this period. The specifics and details of this sequence at TRW provide insights into the evolution of strategy, structure, and management in the modern corporation.

After a brief introductory chapter profiling TRW in the mid-1990s, this book is organized in three main parts. Part I (Chapters 2–4) deals with the history of Thompson Products and its forebears from the founding of Cleveland Cap Screw Company in 1900 through the outbreak of World War II. During this period, the company became successful as a precision manufacturer of parts and components for the automotive, aircraft, and aircraft engine industries. The company's function as a supplier to these industries determined its essential character: it filled an important role in the development of emerging transportation industries in the United States; it worked at the frontiers of materials science and manufacturing technology; its fortunes were tied closely to those of a small number of large, powerful customers; and it struggled constantly and eventually successfully to diversify its business, reduce its dependence on a few customers, and seize control of its own destiny.

Part II (Chapters 5–9) covers the emergence during World War II and the two following decades of a new and complementary role for the company. To its ongoing business as a supplier, the company also added government defense contracting. This new work flowed both to Thompson Products and to Ramo-Wooldridge, the new venture that it helped launch and its eventual partner in merger. As we have already noted, the peculiar economics of defense contracting had profound implications for the company and its forebears, helping to keep separate and isolated the evolution of the military and commercial parts of the company. The military side of the house featured a much higher proportion of employees with advanced degrees in science, technology, and management. They worked on products and systems with high technology content and produced in small quantities; they also developed new approaches and techniques to managing complex problems. The skills, capabilities, and experience developed in defense contracting proved transferable to similar kinds of projects, such as government-funded space programs during the 1960s, but transferring its military technology and program management skills to commercial sectors also proved a constant struggle for TRW.

Part III (Chapters 10–15) considers TRW since 1965. As we noted earlier, during the past thirty years the company has passed through a cycle of expansion, diversification, restructuring, and refocusing that characterized virtually every large U.S.-based manufacturing corporation. Supported by a buoyant national economy, antitrust concerns in the United States, and the nation's leading role in global political and economic affairs, TRW grew rapidly by expanding its traditional commercial businesses around the world and by diversifying into new areas such as electronic components, industrial and commercial tools, energy products, and information systems, among others. During the 1970s and early 1980s, however, a series of shocks and disruptions in the international economy—the demise of the gold standard as the basis of Western currencies, two energy crises (each followed by a severe recession), and a prolonged period of high inflation and high interest rates—called such corporate strategies into question. During the mid-1980s, TRW began a decade-long process of pruning its portfolio and concentrating on activities and developing capabilities that it understood best. By the mid-1990s, the cycle of expansion and diversification had rolled around full circle, with flattened growth and heightened focus on supplying and contracting some traditional and some new products and services to industrial, commercial, and government markets.

Many people contributed to the making of this book. My thanks start with TRW's chairman and CEO, Joseph T. Gorman, who sponsored the project, submitted to several long interviews, furnished several key documents, and made many valuable suggestions. I wish also to thank the members of the TRW History Advisory Committee. Their guidance and tough, good-natured criticism of research plans, outlines, and chapter drafts helped smooth an inherently bumpy process of writing a book and saved me from egregious errors.

As my principal point of contact with TRW, Al Senger proved a great support: encouraging, resourceful, patient, and understanding. Marianne Fortunato attended cheerfully and promptly to myriad details. Several former TRW employees, including Mike Johnson and Bill Oliver, helped to get the project under way and direct its early going. Mike Jablonski of the company's PR Department gave drafts of the final chapters a tough review. Several present and former members of the company's PR Department, including Julian Levine, John Booth, Gary Kious, Montye Male, and Jack Powell, gave generously of their time to open doors and answer a historian's curious (in both senses of the word) questions.

I benefited from the enthusiastic cooperation of many current and former TRW personnel who were interviewed (often more than once) for the project. (Their names are listed after the Note on Sources at the back of this book.) All gave generously of their time and patiently answered whatever questions I could fire at them—except, of course, when my interest strayed into classified territory. Many of these people, including John Armbruster, Budd Cohen, Harry Hayes, Jack Irving, Don Kovar, and Bob Rupert proved to be squirrels of the kinds of records and documents that historians prize. Ray Livingstone kindly arranged for me to consult the important collection of his papers at Florida Atlantic University in Boca Raton. At the Ballistic Missile Division, Markné Wright had gathered a mountain of information about TRW's efforts in ballistic missiles that she made accessible to me. Many other TRW employees and retirees, whose names unfortunately I failed to get or record, helped by giving plant tours, arranging interviews, providing access to documents and publications, and making photocopies. It was a great pleasure to work with these people and a great help to enjoy such support.

I also came into contact with a wide array of historians, librarians, archivists, and interested students of TRW who answered questions and provided assistance. I want particularly to thank Kermit Pike, John Grabowski, and Ann Sindelar at the Western Reserve Historical Society; Martin Collins at the National Air and Space Museum at the Smithsonian Institution; Florence Lathrop at Harvard Business School; and Cargill Hall, Tim Hanley, and Ray Puffer of the U.S. Air Force History Office. Dr. Puffer's assistant, Barbara Giles, also responded promptly to many requests for information and photocopies of key documents. Tom Ball of Telos Video in Cleveland, with whom I collaborated on a video biography of Fred Crawford, arranged for me to access recordings of Crawford's wartime speeches by transferring them to modern cassettes; Tom also shared with me his considerable knowledge of TRW's recent history.

Present and former colleagues at The Winthrop Group, Inc., were also supportive and patient with a project that grew very big and at times unwieldy. George Smith, Margaret Graham, and Bettye Pruitt shared ideas, insights, and considerable expertise about the development of twentieth-century corporations. Paul Barnhill provided excellent research assistance early in the project. Suzanne Spellman, Susan McWade Surapine, and Pamela Bracken produced excellent transcripts of taped interviews.

At HBS Press, director Carol Franco steered the manuscript through the approval process, and managing editor Barbara Roth helped guide it through production. Reviewers of the manuscript, including Thomas P. Hughes and Lawrence J. Reeves, as well as several anonymous critics, offered useful advice and suggestions. A veteran of the aerospace industry, Reeves made many detailed and significant comments on the later chapters especially. HBS Press copy editors Pat Denault and Carol Beckwith suggested many significant improvements to the text.

Three other people rendered important contributions to the project. My Cleveland-based friend and former colleague Virginia Dawson helped with research in local records, especially pertaining to the early part of the book and subjected early chapter drafts to close scrutiny. Budd Cohen, a veteran scientist, engineer, and manager at Space Park, guided me through the ins and outs of TRW's complicated initiatives in space and defense and helped arrange interviews with key personnel. His privately printed account of the evolution of TRW's space and defense business is an essential source for anyone attempting to understand this part of the company. Budd also gave the manuscript a close critical reading.

The biggest source of support and encouragement—and most important, the inspiration for this project from the outset until his death in December 1994 at age 103—was Fred Crawford. It may seem odd to view the passing of a centenarian as untimely, but in this case it was. I have never met a figure as full of fun, energy, and vitality as Fred—and I met him when he was 98! He recruited me as TRW's historian, gave inordinate amounts of time for interviews and questions, and prodded me forward with a steady stream of correspondence. With his delightful wife, Kay, he hosted me on many occasions at their homes in Cleveland, in Vermont, and on Cape Cod. Fred had astounding recall of long-ago events, and, for a business historian, meeting with him represented a once-in-a-lifetime opportunity to connect with someone who knew personally Henry Ford, Walter Chrysler, Alfred Sloan, Boss Kettering, Pierre Du Pont, Glenn L. Martin, Dutch Kindleberger, Donald Douglas, and many other pioneers of American business. More important, Fred had remarkable human qualities: great warmth, a lively intellect, a far-larger-than-life presence, an unmatched ability to make those around him feel at ease and at home, and a puckish (and occasionally ribald) sense of humor. Although he sometimes used expressions that grate on the modern ear, I never found him to be unreasonable, uncharitable, or uncaring toward any individual or group—except, perhaps, the Democratic Party. Whenever I saw him—unfortunately with decreasing frequency after his back operation in 1993—he always greeted me warmly and with the question, "Are you having fun?" His enthusiasm for TRW's history and his blunt and funny comments and stories always helped keep things in perspective.

Finally, I wish to express my deepest appreciation to my family for their help during this long endeavor. My brother and sister-in-law Daniel and Joyce Dyer, of Hudson, Ohio, were gracious hosts during many research trips to Cleveland. My wife, Janice McCormick, and my children, Ricky and Bella, endured my time on the road and in front of the word processor with remarkable understanding and respect. I couldn't ask for anything more, and I couldn't be more grateful.

Chapter 1

House of Technology

▶   ▶   ▶

I N ITS 1996 ANNUAL REPORT, TRW ATTEMPTED TO DISTILL ITS ESSENCE INTO TWO SENTENCES, as

> a global manufacturing and service company strategically focused on supplying advanced technology products and services to the automotive and space and defense markets. TRW is recognized for providing products and services that create exceptional value for its customers—from automotive occupant restraint systems, automotive electronics, steering systems, and engine components to spacecraft, software, defense systems, and complex systems integration.[1]

Like most business definitions, this one is packed with content and meaning, the nature of which is understandably less obvious to outsiders than to those familiar with the company. The key phrase is "advanced technology products and services": TRW is a house of technology—as it has been since its beginning nearly a century ago.

During its long existence, the company has produced a steady stream of technological innovations and achievements, not only in its present core industries of automotive and space and defense, but also in many other areas. The following achievements provide a glimpse of TRW's broad and diverse capabilities and expertise in technology management.

- In 1905, the company's oldest direct ancestor pioneered the manufacture of two-piece valves for internal combustion engines. Fashioned with new electrical welding technology, the two-piece valve enabled marked improvements in engine performance at significant savings in cost and helped stimulate the mushrooming demand for automobiles.

- In the 1920s, the company used new alloys and designs to achieve breakthrough performance in aircraft engines. Its precision-engineered sodium-cooled valves in Wright's J-5 engine powered Charles A. Lindbergh's historic transatlantic flight in 1927.

- During World War II, the company mass produced hundreds of thousands of precision-engineered aircraft engine valves for the American defense effort. The company also engineered critical components for the interior of the first turbojet engines.

- In the 1950s, the company oversaw the development of the first intercontinental ballistic missiles—a complex feat of systems engineering and program management that rivals World War II's Manhattan Project in conceptual difficulty and strategic significance.

- In 1958, TRW became the first private enterprise to build a spacecraft—*Pioneer 1*, which climbed about eighty thousand miles into space (briefly a distance record) before plunging back to earth. This was the first of nearly two hundred spacecraft that the company fabricated, including the Vela satellites that helped monitor nuclear test-ban treaties; *Pioneer 10*, the first spacecraft to leave the solar system and, at a distance of more than 6 billion miles, the farthest-flung work of humanity; the Defense Support Program satellites, which over three decades monitored missile launches and played a significant role during the Gulf conflict of 1991; the tracking and data relay satellites essential for communications between the earth and satellites, including the Space Shuttle, in low-earth orbit; and the *Compton Gamma Ray Observatory*, the second of NASA's four great observatories designed to map the heavens from various perspectives on the electromagnetic spectrum.

- TRW produced hardware to perform in the harsh environment of space, including the lunar module descent engine that enabled six Apollo missions to land safely on the moon and, along with the TRW-developed abort guidance and command system, that played a key role in the safe return of the astronauts from the aborted *Apollo 13* mission (chronicled in a popular American movie of 1995); the biological instrument package and meteorological instruments for the Viking spacecraft that in 1976 landed on Mars to search for evidence of life; and the electronics payloads for the Milstar military communications satellites, among the most complex, sophisticated, and capacious communications satellites ever launched and the essential building blocks in the global defense communications network for the twenty-first century.

- In the 1970s and 1980s, the company popularized rack-and-pinion steering systems for automobiles. Much lighter, cheaper, and more reliable than conventional systems, rack-and-pinion steering proved an essential ingredient in the conversion to front-wheel drive automobiles.

- In the 1980s and 1990s, TRW pioneered the development of automotive occupant restraint systems, including active and passive seat belts and air bags. The company is presently working on the next generation of smart occupant restraint systems, which will tailor their performance according to the dynamics of particular crashes and help protect the occupants of a vehicle, regardless of their height, weight, or position, in a wide variety of circumstances.

- In the 1990s, the company successfully demonstrated high-energy laser systems as a viable countermeasure against tactical missile threats. Under development for more than two decades, such systems have potential to defend not only against ground-to-ground missiles, but also against other weapons, including air-to-air missiles, ground-to-air missiles, fighter planes, helicopters, short-range rockets, and, eventually, ICBMs.

- In the 1980s and 1990s, TRW played a leading role in transferring techniques of systems engineering, program management, and information management from military to civilian government applications. In 1996, for example, the company served as the architect and integrator of an "intelligent transportation system" in Atlanta that helped visitors to the Olympics move with remarkable freedom, ease, and safety throughout a region notorious for congestion and traffic delays.

SNAPSHOT

The company responsible for these illustrations of technology at work, Cleveland, Ohio-based TRW Inc., posted 1996 net income of $480 million on revenues of nearly $10 billion and employed approximately sixty-eight thousand people.[2] About two-thirds of the company's sales originated in North America, which also accounted for about two-thirds of its employment. TRW's sales total earned it 135th place in the *Fortune* 500 listing of the largest public corporations based in the United States. *Business Week,* which ranks in various ways the Standard & Poor's 500 (a group that includes utilities, banks, insurance companies, and other service businesses, as well as industrials) places TRW 125th by sales and 220th by market value. *Industry Week* ranked TRW as one of "the world's 100 best-managed companies" and 144th in sales among the world's largest publicly held manufacturing companies."[3]

TRW's 1996 totals for both sales and earnings continued a three-year string of strong results that followed nearly a decade of struggle. Losses in 1985, 1991, and 1992—the first losses since the Great Depression—reflected restructuring charges that the company absorbed as it, like most big U.S.-based manufacturing and engineering corporations, came to terms with a new competitive reality. For TRW, this meant a more focused strategy, divestitures, heightened emphasis on quality and productivity, and considerable downsizing. In 1996, the company completed its last piece of restructuring by selling its Information Systems and Services unit to a buyout group for just over $1 billion.[4] Included in this transaction was one of the few TRW-branded businesses familiar to the public: consumer credit reporting, a local cottage industry that TRW had modernized and brought into the information age. Following the sale of this and other units in the 1980s and 1990s, TRW employed only slightly more people than it had thirty years before, when sales in nominal terms were about one-tenth of those today.

Presiding over TRW in the mid-1990s was a two-person chief executive office supported by a management committee consisting of the top dozen general managers and corporate staff heads. Joseph T. "Joe" Gorman was forty-nine years old late in 1988 when he became TRW's chairman and CEO. A former collegiate basketball player, Gorman is tall and energetic. His glasses give him an owlish aspect befitting his formidable intellect. Bearing a law degree from Yale University and experience at one of Cleveland's leading law firms, Gorman joined TRW in 1968. He rose within a decade to become vice president, general counsel, and corporate secretary. In 1980, Chairman and CEO Ruben F. Mettler appointed Gorman to his first general management position as executive vice president in charge of the industrial and energy sector, a miscellaneous assortment of businesses that Gorman eventually proposed for divestiture. TRW has a long tradition of grooming its leaders for several years before they move up to the top job. In 1984, the board of directors elected Gorman assistant president, and the following year he became president and chief operating officer as well as Mettler's heir apparent.

Ten years later, a similar situation unfolded. In February 1994, the board elected forty-three-year-old Peter S. Hellman assistant president and promoted him to president and chief operating officer on January 1, 1995. Hellman's strong background in corporate finance began with an MBA from Case Western Reserve University. He climbed swiftly through the ranks at Cleveland-based BP America (formerly Standard Oil of Ohio) before joining TRW in 1989 as vice president and treasurer. Among many achievements, he helped to engineer the early 1990s restructuring that saw TRW divest marginal operations, pay down long-term debt, and triple the value of its common stock.

In 1996, TRW organized its business in two major segments or areas: Automotive and Space & Defense. The oldest and largest segment is Automotive, which accounted for $608.5 million in pretax operating profit (before special charges) on revenues of $6.5 billion. The sales total represented two-thirds of all corporate revenues, a ratio that more than doubled during the past decade as the result of rapid growth in this segment relative to the performance of the company's other businesses. TRW is the fourth-largest independent manufacturer of automotive components in the world (after Nippondenso, Bosch, and Aisin Seiki) and the largest based in the United States, where it ranks just ahead of AlliedSignal and Dana Corporation. TRW competes globally as an automotive supplier, with about half of its segment revenues originating overseas. The company is especially strong in Europe, where it serves most of the region's motor vehicle manufacturers. (Volkswagen is the company's second-largest commercial customer after Ford.) TRW also serves Japanese original equipment manufacturers, and its sales to those customers rose nearly tenfold during the previous decade to approach $750 million annually. The company also has a growing presence in many emerging markets and in the 1990s established operations or participated in joint ventures in China, the Czech Republic, Poland, India, Thailand, Turkey, and other countries.

In 1996, TRW's automotive groups included Occupant Restraints; Steering, Suspension, and Engine; and Automotive Electronics. That year the company manufactured 13 million air bags, 55 million seat belts, 7 million air bag crash sensors and electronics modules, more than 300 million engine valves, 9 million power rack-and-pinion steering gears, and 400,000 integral gears for commercial vehicles.[5] These 1996 totals made TRW the world's biggest supplier of most of these products. At the same time, the company had in development several promising new automotive technologies: side air bags; dual-stage air bag inflators; single-point crash sensors that from one location can discriminate front, side, and rear crashes; and electrically powered steering systems that can assist maneuverability and improve fuel economy up to two miles per gallon. Two acquisitions negotiated late in 1996 also extended TRW's capabilities. The addition of the steering wheel and air bag cover business of Long Island–based Izumi Corporation Industries, Inc., enabled TRW to supply its customers with integrated steering wheel and air bag modules. The company enhanced its position in the European market by purchasing majority interests in two occupant restraints facilities in Germany previously owned by Magna International, a supplier of seating systems, door panels, and other interior vehicle parts, components, and modules. In addition, TRW and Magna International agreed jointly to finance a technical center that will focus on total vehicle safety system integration.

TRW's operations in Space & Defense accounted for the remaining third of TRW's corporate revenues during 1996, when the segment reported pretax operating profit (before special charges) of $247.1 million on sales of $3.4 billion. The company ranked in the top fifteen defense contractors in the United States, although it was dwarfed by the mammoth producers of military hardware, including Boeing-McDonnell-Douglas, Lockheed Martin, United Technologies, General Dynamics, and Northrop Grumman. After a prolonged, gradual decline that had started in the mid-1980s, when the Department of Defense and NASA began passing on their shrinking budgets to suppliers, TRW's sales in Space & Defense resumed growth in the mid-1990s. For government customers—primarily U.S. government customers—TRW built spacecraft and electronic hardware (some of it classified); wrote software; and provided engineering, project management, and systems integration services for scientific, military, and administrative purposes. Its 1996 groups in this segment were Space & Electronics and Systems Integration.

TRW Space & Electronics was engaged by its customers in several thousand projects ranging from small analytical research studies to prime contracting and "strategic teaming" with partners on big-ticket programs. Among the group's most visible efforts were

- NASA's Advanced X-Ray Astrophysics Facility (AXAF), the third component of the Great Observatory program and scheduled for launch in 1998;
- the Advanced Milsatcom, a multibillion-dollar program involving TRW and Lockheed Martin to develop the next generation of military communications satellites;

- the Airborne Laser program, in which TRW teamed with Boeing and Lockheed to develop high-energy laser systems carried aloft Boeing 747s for theater antimissile defense. Initial funding for the multiyear program was $250 million but the technology held multibillion-dollar revenue potential; and

- the Space-Based Infrared System-Low, in which TRW paired with Raytheon to develop the low-orbiting component of a sophisticated system for detecting and tracking missiles.

Purportedly, the company also made equipment, perhaps including satellites, for classified programs that presumably involved surveillance and reconnaissance. Under penalty of law, no one at TRW will confirm, deny, or even acknowledge the existence of such programs.

TRW Systems Integration worked both for military and civilian government customers and sought especially to expand business among the latter. Its many projects included engineering "intelligent transportation systems" such as that used to manage traffic during the Olympic Games in Atlanta and

- a multiyear program to upgrade the computer system at the heart of the U.S. Internal Revenue Service;

- a prime contract to oversee and manage the U.S. Department of Energy's Civilian Radioactive Waste Management Program;

- computerized security systems for airports and other public venues and electronic identification systems for police agencies in the United States, the United Kingdom, and other countries;

- a nationwide electoral registration and enumeration system to help ensure fraud-free elections in Jamaica; and

- significant contract awards for information and management systems integration services with the U.S. Department of the Treasury, Federal Aviation Administration, and other federal, state, and local agencies.

As a result of these and other "civil systems" initiatives, the proportion of TRW's space and defense sales devoted to nonmilitary customers soared from less than 10 percent in the late 1980s to nearly 35 percent in 1996.

M<small>OVING</small> P<small>ICTURE</small>

TRW's capabilities are the result of a long and complex evolution. How the company became a house of technology is the subject of this book.

Viewing the evolution of an organization as old, as huge, and as diverse as TRW requires flying at a high altitude—much like the advanced surveillance and reconnaissance satellites the company is reputed to build but never acknowledges. The perspective from such a height necessarily obscures details. TRW produces thousands of products ranging from items as straightforward as fasteners to those as sophisticated as spacecraft. It serves many different customers and operates in many different nations. It has completed several dozen acquisitions and later spun off a number of them. Over its lifetime, TRW has employed several hundred thousand people, some of whom stayed a brief time but many of whom remained for decades. No work of history—not even a volume as hefty as this one—can render full justice to the many facets and accomplishments of such an organization.

However, certain themes and patterns in TRW's history are clear even when viewed from afar. Some are implicit in the preceding overview of the company's operations or stem from the 1958 merger between Thompson Products, a supplier to the automobile and aircraft industries, and Ramo-Wooldridge, a specialist in defense electronics and the emerging technology of systems engineering, that created the modern TRW. Such themes include the role and constraints of a supplier; the impact of the economics of defense contracting on organization and management; the company's pioneering role in corporate and technology management; the struggles to transfer military technology to commercial realms; and the interdependency of the company and its business environment, which led TRW to follow a general pattern of growth and change common among other big American companies.

Other themes should be noted. One is the company's long-time service as a supplier to transportation industries. Almost from its beginning, TRW linked itself to innovation in transportation—from the automobile, through aircraft, to spacecraft. Usually it either led or followed quickly the progression into new areas. At the same time, the company played a key partnership role in the reinvention and renewal of older industries, such as motor vehicles, that today feature advanced technology and management practices that TRW helped to pioneer.

The company's work on the frontiers of technology is a closely related theme and follows a pattern similar to that of other highly successful manufacturing companies. At the outset, TRW made its mark by exploiting a new process for manufacturing a traditional product, the cap screw. From there it developed new and advanced products and applications for the automobile, aircraft, and aircraft engine industries, as well as a steady stream of process innovations and improvements. It gained mastery of advanced and nearly intractable materials designed to perform under the extraordinarily harsh conditions inside automobile and advanced aircraft engines. It ventured into wholly new technologies such as chemical propulsion and electronics. These in turn opened new and sometimes unexpected vistas in spacecraft, chemical lasers, electronic systems, complex integrated circuits, software and information management, and avionics.

Another important theme is the company's role in the shaping of U.S. national defense policy. During World War II, Thompson Products became a key supplier of critical parts for aircraft and aircraft engines. At the end of that war and during the Korean War, it took the lead in developing and producing the key components of turbojet engines and emerged from the second tier of suppliers to become a prime contractor to the U.S. Air Force. During the 1950s, Ramo-Wooldridge's role in systems engineering and technical direction for the U.S. Air Force ICBM program dramatically increased the company's influence on defense policy. Thereafter, TRW was intimately involved in many strategic military technologies that shaped the world's political map during the second half of the twentieth century: missile systems, satellite communications networks, and other complex hardware and software systems that promoted and protected American interests.

TRW's high visibility in industrial, scientific and technical, military, and general economic affairs is another related theme. This prominence is out of proportion to TRW's size and position in the U.S. economy or in most of the industries it serves. This theme can be traced back a long way and owes much to the colorful personalities of the company's leaders. C. E. Thompson became a senior officer of the first national trade association of automotive suppliers. Fred Crawford served as president of the National Association of Manufacturers and was active in countless local, regional, and national industrial, scientific, and defense-related organizations. Si Ramo and Rube Mettler also held (and hold) many significant positions on national industrial, educational, and scientific committees and advisory boards. Joe Gorman is well known in international economic circles and is a frequent spokesperson on issues of trade, especially between the United States and Japan. Below the office of chief executive, personnel occupy leadership roles in countless scientific, technical, business, and community service organizations. TRW also has many distinguished alumni, including two heads of NASA, the director of NASA's Apollo program, several senior officials in the U.S. Department of Defense, and past chairmen and CEOs of Hughes Aircraft, General Dynamics, and Gencorp. Such connections proved good for business and positioned the company to identify and respond to many emerging opportunities.

A final main theme emerges in the long view of TRW's history. Continuous transformation and renewal mark the company's experience. At different moments, distinctly different businesses have been more or less important to the company's outlook and performance. Thompson Products rose to prominence by making engine valves and selling them to American automakers. Although TRW remained in 1996 the world's largest independent supplier of automotive engine valves, this business accounted for much less than 10 percent of total revenues. By 1970, sales to automakers overseas exceeded those in the United States. In the 1970s, when total automotive business represented about one-third of total corporate sales, steering and suspension systems, which had been part of the company since the second decade of this century, surpassed engine components in revenues. In the mid-1990s, when the automotive segment again produced more than half of total revenues, occupant restraint systems became a bigger business than steering and suspension systems.

During World War II, parts and accessories for aircraft and aircraft engines produced 90 percent of sales. A decade later, about two-thirds of total revenues depended on sales of components for turbojet engines. A decade after that, these components produced less than one-fifth of total revenues. In the mid-1980s, when TRW finally divested its aircraft components businesses as part of a major strategic shift and restructuring, the effect was momentary.

On the Ramo-Wooldridge side of the house, the pattern of transformation and renewal is also evident. In 1958, about 90 percent of R-W's business depended on the U.S. Air Force's ballistic missile program. By the late 1960s, no single product or program accounted for as much as 10 percent of revenues generated at Space Park. TRW's revenue stream was broadly diversified in a variety of industrial, commercial, and defense markets. During the 1960s and 1970s, several ventures in commercial electronic components were integral to the company's strategy and performance. In the 1980s, these businesses all but disappeared. Industrial and energy products, once also key contributors to TRW's fortunes, likewise vanished a decade later.

TRW consciously sought to manage the transitions from dependence on one business to dependence on another (or many others). Since C. E. Thompson's time, it has always looked forward. At first the process was informal, engaging a few top managers on an episodic basis. In the early 1950s, however, TRW's planning became more structured and widespread, the subject of annual conferences and reviews in which managers of the company's various divisions participated. In the 1960s and 1970s, at Ramo's instigation, planning grew ever more sophisticated, embracing computer modeling, technology forecasts, peer and competitor analysis, and other leading-edge techniques. Most of TRW's successful major transitions—entry into defense electronics, spacecraft, energy products, information systems, and occupant restraints—resulted from intentional and deliberate effort. Of course, the same processes also yielded some stubbed toes: nuclear energy, civil systems (in the 1960s and 1970s), and several unsuccessful ventures in commercial and consumer electronics and energy systems.

Luck also played a part in ensuring the company's long-term success. Cam Gears, a foreign licensee in suspension systems that TRW bought in the mid-1960s, brought with it capability to produce rack-and-pinion steering systems, a pivotal technology in the downsizing of the automobile during the 1970s and 1980s. Similarly, a 1972 investment of just over $10 million in Repa Feinstanzwerk GmbH, a small, young German company that stamped the metal parts of seat belts for Volkswagen, became a far more significant part of the corporation than ever imagined, the foundation of a multibillion-dollar business in occupant restraint systems.

Throughout its long history, TRW has proven resourceful as well as fortunate in anticipating and adapting to change. It has succeeded by capitalizing on particular capabilities in engineering, manufacturing, information technology, and management. Near the end of its first century, TRW's fundamental identity is based on these capabilities rather than on specific products, services, or markets served. To describe TRW as a technology-based company is more meaningful than to label it, say, an automotive supplier, a government contractor, a diversified corporation, or a conglomerate. It has been all of these things, and doubtless more labels will attach to it as time goes on. An understanding of the roots and development of TRW's capabilities provides the best basis for predicting what kind of company it will be in the future.

PART ONE

Supplier

▮ ▮ ▮ ▮ ▮

1900–1938

The endpoints of Part I bracket a period of enormous economic and social change in the United States. In 1900, most Americans still made their homes in rural areas, moved about on foot or by horse, and communicated at a leisurely pace through the mail. Four decades later, most citizens lived in cities, traveled by motor vehicle, and used the telephone with increasing frequency.

Many factors catalyzed this transformation: innovations in transportation and communications; new sources and types of energy; the widespread availability of key materials such as steel, aluminum, rubber, glass, and many chemicals; new technologies based on electrical, mechanical, and chemical engineering; government policies that encouraged economic growth and favored the development of infrastructural industries; and new ways of organizing and conducting business. Indeed, the modern business corporation was both a cause and a consequence of economic development during these years.

In 1900, the big public corporation had only recently arrived, taking advantage of new technologies to pioneer techniques of mass production and of evolving networks of transportation and communication to develop methods of mass distribution. Companies rose and fell in spectacular fashion, competing in a Darwinian world of unregulated, free-market capitalism that government or organized groups of employees influenced little. By 1938, big public corporations dominated the industrial sector of the economy, yet they also faced countervailing powers in government and organized labor. The federal government employed nearly nine hundred thousand people—more than four times the number it employed in 1900—and federal government expenditures totaled $6.7 billion—more than twelve times the total in 1900—as President

Franklin D. Roosevelt's New Deal accounted for a mushrooming population of agencies and regulatory bodies. At the same time, the national Congress of Industrial Organizations (CIO) included scores of industrial unions that represented (or clamored to represent) millions of workers in many of the economy's largest industries.

Social and economic transformation provided the backdrop against which the progenitors of TRW Inc. organized and grew. The company descends from several different companies, the oldest of which, Cleveland Cap Screw Company, formed in 1900 to exploit a new electric welding process to make products for the general hardware trade. One of the most vibrant and economically diverse cities in America's industrial heartland, Cleveland provided fertile ground for entrepreneurs such as those who established Cleveland Cap Screw. Electricity was revolutionizing industrial production and residential life. The metalworking industries—bicycles, carriages, machine tools, and machinery of all kinds—were booming. The automobile industry was in its infancy, with a few thousand units built in the United States, many of them in Cleveland, and all of them assembled by hand. Waves of immigrants formed an abundant pool of skilled and low-cost labor.

It was, in short, a time of optimism and opportunity. It was also a time when many young companies faltered and failed. Cleveland Cap Screw narrowly escaped this fate, a near-casualty of insufficient capital, weak management, and a business based on a product that few customers wanted, at least at the prices the company could afford to offer (Chapter 2). Three factors helped turn Cleveland Cap Screw around. The first was fortuitous: the same patented process for making cap screws applied also to automobile engine valves, a highly promising new opportunity. Second was the arrival in 1905 of new owners, including Alexander Winton, one of America's leading automakers. Winton and his partners provided a fresh infusion of capital and helped guarantee purchases of the company's valves. And third was the rise of a new management team headed by C. E. Thompson, a resourceful and ambitious electrical tradesman. With Winton's encouragement—and to his eventual chagrin—Thompson built a healthy company and combined it with several other operations and interests to establish a leading supplier to the automobile industry.

Known after 1926 as Thompson Products, the company prospered initially by exploiting its patented manufacturing process as well as by establishing close informal and personal ties between its leaders and executives in prominent automobile companies. Later, as new technologies superseded its patented process, the company scrambled to improve both its products and its production processes, learning to compete successfully on the basis of price, quality, and reliability (Chapter 3). At the same time, it branched into new territory, selling valves and other automobile parts not only to the original equipment manufacturers, but also to the "replacement" (automobile repair) market. It also developed related products for aircraft engines, an entry point into another promising transportation industry.

The company's rise, however, was hardly smooth (see Exhibits I-1 to I-3). Its fortunes followed the boom-bust-boom cycles of the American industrial economy generally and the automobile industry in particular. Once it focused on making valves, and until its patents expired, the company all but printed money. It continued to prosper during World War I, but nearly foundered during the postwar recession. It roared back during the middle and late 1920s, spurred on by product and process improvements and Americans' love affair with their automobiles. Then it nearly crashed again during the Great Depression before showing signs of restored health in the late 1930s.

A pivotal moment for Thompson Products occurred in 1929, when Fred Crawford succeeded Thompson as general manager. Crawford's initial achievement was to fuse the company's various lines of business with a coherent strategy implemented under the direction of an energetic and creative management team (Chapter 4). As it emerged from the Great Depression, Thompson Products focused explicitly on three lines of business: parts and components for the automobile industry, parts and components for the replacement market, and engine valves for the aircraft engine industry. As a supplier to the automobile companies, it concentrated on hard-to-make parts such as engine valves, pistons, and forged chassis components, supported by continuous investment in research and development and constant improvement in manufacturing processes. To serve the replacement trade, the company augmented its own products with others such as water pumps and other engine-related parts and components distributed through its own warehouses and, after a 1935 acquisition, under a second well-known brand name, Toledo Steel Products.

For the aircraft engine companies, a small but promising market before World War II, Thompson Products developed sodium-cooled valves to withstand the intense

EXHIBIT I - 1

THOMPSON PRODUCTS, INC., AND PREDECESSOR COMPANIES GROSS REVENUES AND NET INCOME, 1901–1938

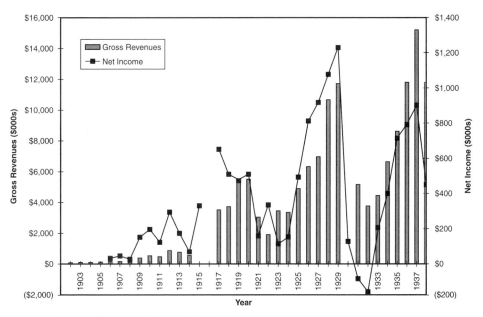

SOURCE: WRHS 3942 and annual reports.
NOTE: Data for 1916 not available; revenue data for 1930 not available.

heat and stresses of high-performance engines. Although aircraft engine valves constituted a small business, representing less than 10 percent of the company's sales, it was
highly visible in part because of the public's fascination with aviation. In 1927, the
company achieved a public relations coup by supplying the engine valves for Charles
A. Lindbergh's historic nonstop flight between New York and Paris. Two years later, it
again captured attention by awarding the Thompson Trophy to the pilot of the fastest
plane during the National Air Races. Thereafter, the Thompson Trophy became a highlight of the annual competition.

Although Thompson Products' fortunes dipped again in 1938 during the decade's
second downturn, the company was far more balanced and resilient than at any other
time in its history. It also operated in an increasingly complex business environment.
The Great Depression whittled the number of automobile manufacturers in the United
States from several hundred to fewer than fifty, with the top three—General Motors,
Ford, and Chrysler—accounting for 80 percent of the market. As a result, Thompson
Products found itself supplying a few big and powerful companies that were well
aware of their purchasing clout and their ability to manufacture key parts and compo-
nents themselves. To remain successful and independent, the company had to pour

EXHIBIT I - 2

THOMPSON PRODUCTS, INC., AND PREDECESSOR COMPANIES MEASURES OF PROFITABILITY, 1901–1938

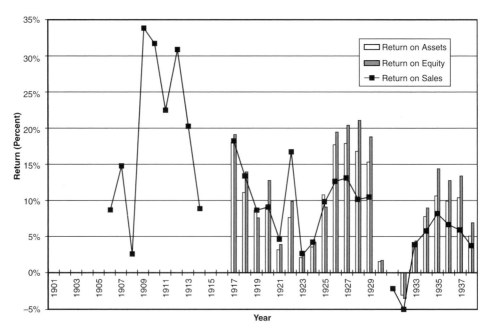

SOURCE: WRHS 3942 and annual reports.
NOTE: Data for 1916 not available; revenue data for 1930 not available.

resources into research and development and remain fast afoot. It also redoubled its efforts to cultivate the independent aftermarket and to diversify into new areas such as aircraft engine components.

The threats that Thompson Products faced during the 1930s extended well beyond its dependence on the big automakers. In the aftermath of the depression came the New Deal and a vast expansion of government employment and intervention in the economy. The government also facilitated the rise of industrial unions that gathered under the banner of the CIO. The new business environment brought challenges in the forms of legislation, regulations, and union organizing drives that clashed with Crawford's fundamental values of independence and self-reliance and jeopardized management's traditional autonomy. In 1938, the outcome of these challenges was anything but clear.

EXHIBIT I - 3

THOMPSON PRODUCTS, INC., AND PREDECESSOR COMPANIES EMPLOYMENT, 1901–1938

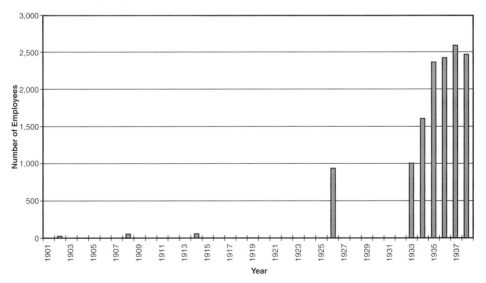

SOURCE: WRHS 3942 and annual reports; data for many years not available.

TRW started out—and later resumed after a long hiatus—in the business of fasteners. Pictured here: A cap screws price list that doubled as promotional literature.

*The company manufac-
tured its first products in
this factory on Clarkwood
Road in Cleveland.
Although the building has
since been demolished,
TRW still operates a pis-
ton plant on the grounds.*

Courtesy of The Western Reserve Historical Society, Cleveland, Ohio.

Top Left: *The Savior: In 1905, Alexander Winton kept the company out of bankruptcy by providing a fresh infusion of capital and a guaranteed market for welded engine valves. Pictured here: Winton behind the wheel of a Winton Bullet in 1903, shortly before he invested in Cleveland Cap Screw.*

Top Right: *By 1910, C. E. Thompson had already embarked on the course that would enable him to acquire the company from Winton six years later. Thompson also had already displayed a taste for the high life.*

Left: *Under the protection of its welding patents and licenses, the company proved extremely profitable during its early years. Pictured here: The Welding Department about 1908. Note the maze of belts and pulleys.*

THE
THOMPSON SILCROME VALVE
A Distinct Achievement in the Motor Field

THOMPSON SILCROME

This steel at one time considered the highest grade valve material.

This steel the highest priced valve material, and for a long time considered the finest valve steel.

A comparison of three valves, built with equal care and subjected to the same Heat Conditions.

THE THOMPSON SILCROME VALVE DOES NOT BURN OR SCALE

The Steel Products Co.
Cleveland, Ohio

Left: *During the 1920s, the company regained lost ground by perfecting ways to forge valves from hard-to-work alloys such as sil-crome—"the Devil's steel."*

Above: *A beleaguered and declining C. E. Thompson presents the Thompson Trophy to Lowell Bayles, pilot of the fastest plane in 1931's closed-course speed race.*

Courtesy of The Western Reserve Historical Society, Cleveland, Ohio.

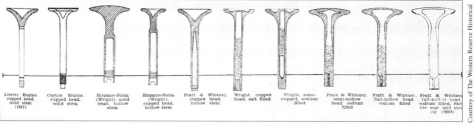

Courtesy of The Western Reserve Historical Society, Cleveland, Ohio.

Top: *In the 1930s, the company manufactured a growing line of products for automobiles, including valves, pistons, pumps, and chassis parts.*

Above: *Far from a low-tech, humdrum product, the engine valve has been a marvel of precision engineering since its earliest days. Pictured here: Chapters in the history of the*

aircraft engine valve between 1918 and 1934, a particularly fertile period for innovation.

Right: *Under Fred Crawford, Thompson Products organized itself to serve three major markets: the automobile makers (including the replacement trade), the aeronautical manufacturers, and the industrial manufacturers.*

DIVERSIFICATION OF THE BUSINESS OF THOMPSON PRODUCTS, INC. AND SUBSIDIARIES

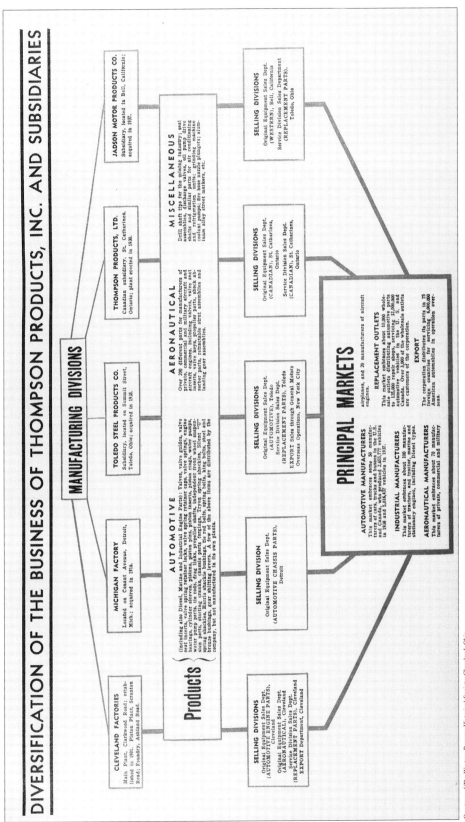

Courtesy of The Western Reserve Historical Society, Cleveland, Ohio.

The Great Communicator: Crawford honed his skills as a speaker by meeting regularly with employee groups such as this address to the Old Guard Association in 1935. Note his use of graphical aids to explain the economics of the business.

Chapter 2

Cap Screws, Poppet Valves, and a Cast of Characters

▶   ▶   ▶

1900–1916

MOST YOUNG COMPANIES FAIL BEFORE THEY REACH THEIR FIFTH BIRTHDAY. THE REASONS vary: an ill-conceived product or service; underestimation of the competition; lack of capital; excessive dependence on a single individual or a few people who depart or prove unreliable. The list is easy to extend. In the young life of any company, certain owners, managers, or customers arrive at key moments of decision and change. At such moments the choices these actors make determine the company's prospects for years to come.

At the Cleveland Cap Screw Company, ancestor of today's TRW, the first such moment arrived in its fifth year, as the company teetered on the brink of bankruptcy or merger. The crucial day was September 21, 1905, and it brought new owners to the company: automaker Alexander Winton and his partners, Thomas Henderson and George Brown. President of one of the nation's largest automobile companies, Winton had embarked on a quest that has engaged his competitors and their successors ever since: the development of lighter, mightier, and more efficient engines to power each generation of cars. The Cleveland Cap Screw Company, Winton believed, offered a partial solution to his problem.

By 1905, the fundamental principles of the internal combustion engine were well understood. Combustible gases, ignited under heat and compression in a closed environment, produced a massive burst of thermal energy that could be converted into mechanical energy. Most automobile engines made the conversion by means of a piston in a closed cylinder, and most delivered power in a four-stroke cycle: intake, compression, power, and exhaust. In 1905—and throughout the history of the internal combustion engine—a critical constraint on engine power and reliability was the performance of the intake and, especially, of the exhaust valves during the cycle.[1]

Called "mushroom valves" because of their shape, or more commonly "poppet valves" because of the distinctive clicking noise they made in operation, these engine parts were a nemesis to automakers and more than a nuisance to auto buyers. They were hard to install, prone to pit, warp, or break, and expensive to replace. For maximum engine performance, valves had to open reliably and seal tightly; withstand intense pressures, corrosive gases, and a wide range of temperatures; and endure thousands of explosions per minute, hour after hour, without fail. It was not unusual for engines to expire of valve disease after only a few hours of operation. To unhappy carmakers who struggled to persuade the public that automobiles were more reliable than horse-drawn carriages, and unhappy car owners who were obliged to budget for frequent, expensive, and invariably inconvenient engine overhauls, a better engine valve seemed a prize worth pursuing.

The object of Winton's attention that day in 1905, Cleveland Cap Screw, held promise of delivering better valves, manufactured in a better way. Organized in 1900, the company had licensed a new process for making cap screws (big, heavy-duty bolts used principally in industrial applications) by welding the cap and the stem together. This process, Winton and other entrepreneurs believed, could easily be adapted to making automotive engine valves. Indeed, several automobile companies and suppliers had already begun to experiment with welding to make valves. Whichever among them succeeded seemed likely to enjoy a bright future supplying the phenomenal appetite of the U.S. automobile industry—though Winton and his partners could not have foreseen then that their modest investment in Cleveland Cap Screw would become the basis of a major diversified corporation that remains the world's largest independent producer of automotive engine valves as the twentieth century draws to a close.

Humble Origins

Cleveland in 1900 was an ideal place and time for founding a manufacturing company. The city teemed with foundry workers, machinists, mechanics, toolmakers, and mechanical engineers. It was also accumulating an enormous population of immigrant laborers arriving from southern and eastern Europe. The city occupied a strategic location between sources of energy and metallic ores around the Great Lakes and fast-growing markets for metals, machinery, and industrial products in the Midwest and East. With a diversified industrial base and a population of nearly four hundred thousand, Cleveland was the seventh-largest city in the United States, and it was adding citizens at the rate of twenty thousand a year.[2]

At the turn of the century, Cleveland was a leading producer of women's and children's garments, highly refined gasoline (the city is the birthplace of John D. Rockefeller's Standard Oil empire), paints and varnishes, druggists' preparations, industrial chemicals, and electrical equipment. Visitors were especially impressed by the range and quality of the city's metalworking trades, which together accounted for the biggest share of its manufacturing activities. Cleveland was one of America's largest producers of iron and steel. Its manufactured metal products included wire and wire nails, nuts and bolts, twist drills, pipes, rails, springs, and other hardware; small machinery such as electrical apparatus, sewing machines, bicycles, and astronomical instruments; and large machinery and metal objects such as machine tools, printing presses, carriages, "self-propelled vehicles," ships, and bridges.

In 1900, one of the most dramatic signs of progress in the city was visible in its downtown area, where electric streetcars delivered employees to the large office buildings that began to ring Public Square and to radiate eastward down Euclid and Superior Avenues. The newest of these structures was the eighteen-story Williamson Building, located on the Euclid side of the square, which opened in the spring. Here, in Room 1215, TRW's ancestor, Cleveland Cap Screw Company, was born in late December.

On December 28, five men—David J. Kurtz, H. Verner Bright, Frederick E. Bright, John E. Morley, and William F. Carr—gathered "to form a corporation for profit" called the Cleveland Cap Screw Company. Carr and Morley, attorneys with the firm Kline, Carr, Tolles, and Goff, hosted the meeting.[3]

These were not struggling entrepreneurs, and this was not a start-up on a shoestring. The lawyers represented one of Cleveland's most successful firms, which numbered Standard Oil among its clients. Morley would eventually become one of the city's most distinguished attorneys. Frederick Bright, a resident of Philadelphia, would soon help establish the Hess-Bright Manufacturing Company, a leading maker of ball bearings for carriages and industrial uses. His brother Verner owned a machine shop on Seneca Avenue in Cleveland.[4]

The central figure of the group was the thirty-eight-year-old Kurtz. Little is known of his early life, although as a teenager in the late 1870s he appeared in Cleveland as a salesman and "travel agent" for W. Bingham & Co., one of the region's largest distributors of hardware and industrial supplies. His travels evidently took him to Warren, Ohio, where, in 1883, he married well, taking as his bride Illa W. Park, daughter of a prominent businessman and banker. The young couple settled in Cleveland, where Kurtz held several different positions, including secretary and treasurer of the Parkin File Company. By the late 1880s, he was back at Bingham, where he rose eventually to become manager in the retail department. In 1900, he appeared to be a man of means. He was a director of City Trust Company, a small bank, and would soon become vice president and treasurer of the Independent Stone Company, a mining operation also headquartered in the Williamson Building. In addition to carrying out these responsibilities, Kurtz was about to assume the presidency of Cleveland Cap Screw.[5]

The founders capitalized Cleveland Cap Screw at $250,000, consisting of 2,500 shares with a par value of $100 each. The company immediately issued 1,562 shares, of which Kurtz subscribed 1,000, Frederick Bright 400, Verner Bright 16, and each of the lawyers a single share. The first capital was actually paid in during February 1901, by which time another key figure was involved: Samuel M. Mathews, an associate of Kurtz at W. Bingham & Co.[6]

These men defined the company's business broadly as "the manufacture and sale of cap screws, machinery, tools, and any and all products manufactured from iron, steel and other metals."[7] Compared with the major innovations and inventions that occurred in America at the turn of the century, the prospect of manufacturing cap screws appears mundane, to say the least, but Kurtz and his colleagues addressed a perceived market need. The opportunity lay in developing a new way to make cap screws of a standard size at a cost significantly below that of conventional methods.

The issue of standard size was central to the opportunity. During the 1860s and 1870s, the Franklin Institute of Philadelphia, a private and prestigious association of machinists and manufacturers, had specified standard dimensions for screws, nuts, and bolts of all sizes, including cap screws. These standards won general acceptance in American industry by "eliminating the necessity for more than one size of wrench for similar products of all manufacturers . . . and also improving the appearance of the products on which nuts, bolts, and cap screws were used." The standards, moreover, were necessary prerequisites for the interchangeability of nuts and bolts and hence also manufacturing on a large scale.[8]

As was well known throughout industry and the hardware trade, however, cap screws of standard size were expensive. In the 1894 W. Bingham catalog, for example, a cap screw one inch long and one-quarter inch in diameter listed for 2.6 cents, compared with 1 cent for a flathead or machine screw of comparable dimensions. The premium reflected difficulties related to both the dimensions of a cap screw, which called for the head to be significantly larger than the stem, and traditional production methods. These methods, a contemporary observer complained, resulted in "costs out of all proportion to the value of the finished product." The traditional process started with a metal bar, the diameter of which corresponded to the head of the screw, and then milled away metal below the head to form the stem. To make the screws precisely not only required careful attention by skilled workers, but also generated a lot of scrap. Given the high costs, most machinists and mechanics simply used cheaper flathead or machine screws.[9]

Kurtz and his colleagues believed they had found a better way to make standard cap screws. Their idea was to make the caps and stems separately and then weld them together, using newly available automatic welding equipment manufactured by Thomson Electric Welding Company of Lynn, Massachusetts. This company held a thicket of patents on electrical resistance welding, a process that applied high-amperage electrical current to the abutting surfaces of pieces to be joined as they were held together under pressure. The resulting high temperatures produced strong, homogeneous welds at a fraction of the time and cost of traditional or alternative methods of joining metals. The process, moreover, proved amenable to automation, and it permitted mass production of metal products of all kinds, ranging from wire fence and steel chain to filing cabinets and metal furniture to wheel rims and structural parts of bicycles, carriages, and eventually automobiles. By automating the manufacture of such products, notes a leading historian of technology, the Thomson process superseded "what had always been one of the most difficult tasks of blacksmithing."[10]

During the 1890s, electrical resistance welding spread quickly across the metalworking industries. Published accounts of the process attracted the attention of Kurtz and his associates, who saw a promising application in the manufacture of cap screws. Welded properly, they reasoned, the two-piece cap screw would be strong enough for most applications and significantly cheaper to make than those made by traditional methods.[11]

On December 22, 1900—a week before the incorporation of Cleveland Cap Screw—Kurtz, Mathews, and Frederick Bright licensed Thomson's patents for electrical resistance welding and arranged to purchase machinery and equipment to make two-piece cap screws. Terms of the deal included a down payment of $9,175 and an equal amount to be paid once the equipment was fully operational. In addition, Cleveland Cap Screw agreed to pay an annual fee of $500 for an exclusive license on the Thomson process for making screws and bolts. A subsequent agreement between the two companies provided for Cleveland Cap Screw to pay Thomson Electric Welding a royalty ranging between fifty and seventy-five cents per thousand welds, with the higher amount due for welds of large diameters. Cleveland Cap Screw guaranteed a minimum royalty of $1,600 a year.[12]

On February 14, 1901, Kurtz, Mathews, and Frederick Bright sold their license for the Thomson welding process to Cleveland Cap Screw in exchange for $100,000 in stock. They also arranged to sell to the company "the property known as The Grant Ball Company's plant, located at Nos. 66 to 72 Clarkwood Avenue in Cleveland" for $40,000 in stock. (The location is the present site of TRW's main plant, which makes pistons for high-performance engines.) Finally, Verner Bright sold his business "for the manufacturing of light machinery and specialties, including all of his machinery, tools, and goodwill" to Cleveland Cap Screw for $16,000 in stock.[13]

This transaction essentially accounted for the entire first issue of Cleveland Cap Screw's common stock. During 1901 and 1902, the company collected paid-in capital of about $80,000, mostly in the form of small investments from individuals in Cleveland and Philadelphia who were probably friends and associates of the founders. Several of these investors, including Carr, Herbert Wright, and William G. Dietz, were elected directors of the corporation.[14]

The new business occupied a two-story factory situated close to a rail line on Cleveland's East Side. The factory had been in existence since at least 1898, when it housed the Grant Ball Company, a maker of antifriction bearings and automatic screw machine products, and the Grant Tool Company, a manufacturer of tools and dies. The officers of Cleveland Cap Screw undertook negotiations to buy the property early in 1901, completing the purchase in September via a mortgage loan for about $39,000 from City Trust Company—the bank of which Kurtz was a director (and Herbert Wright president). During the spring and summer, Cleveland Cap Screw began to install machinery and equipment and built a new power plant on the site. Production commenced during the late summer or early fall, and by the end of the year net revenues amounted to about $225. Office and factory personnel totaled twenty-nine people, most of whom apparently worked part-time or on speculation.[15]

Among the early recruits was thirty-year-old Charles E. Thompson, who was destined to become a legendary figure in the history of Cleveland Cap Screw Company and its successors. Known variously as "Charlie" or "C. E.," Thompson was hired to help install and oversee the operation of the equipment purchased from Thomson Electric Welding.

Thompson was born on August 9, 1871, on a farm in McIndoe Falls, Vermont, a crossroads near the small village of Barnet. During his childhood, his parents moved to Lynn, Massachusetts, and he attended schools in Lynn and Boston. Of his education he later recalled, "I don't think that I showed any great brilliance and I don't think I was the kind of boy who would win a prize in [a scientific] contest, although I was interested in electricity. Put it down that I was just an average boy and let it go at that." After graduating from high school, Thompson took a job with the Thomson-Houston Company in Lynn, where he learned electrical resistance welding and completed a trade course in electrical engineering. In 1892, he moved to Cleveland to work for the Cuyahoga Telephone Company. He started as a lineman and rose through the ranks until 1899, when, to support his wife and infant son, he took a job as a manager with the Bell Telephone Company in Dallas, Texas. He spent just one year in Texas before returning to Cleveland, where he found employment with Cleveland Cap Screw.[16]

Thompson may have considered himself "an average boy," but, as related by his later protégé, friend, and successor, Fred Crawford, he was possessed of above-average ambition. During his years as a telephone lineman in Cleveland, for example, Thompson one day was working on a pole near the Union Club, a gathering place for the city's leading businessmen and professionals. Peering through the window into the club, he watched the comings and goings of Cleveland's economic elite and vowed to join them someday.[17] One day, he would.

Fʀᴏᴍ Cᴀᴘ Sᴄʀᴇᴡs ᴛᴏ Vᴀʟᴠᴇs

Although it took several years for Cleveland Cap Screw to perfect its manufacturing process, the two-piece welded cap screw proved a technological success. The company boasted that its process yielded "absolute uniformity in the length of the screw, height of the head, and in the alignment of head and body." In 1905, a delegation from the Franklin Institute visited the company and came away impressed: compared with cap screws made the traditional way, these experts reported, "an electrically-welded head and body . . . is apparently a great gain in both economy and strength." "We believe this is an important item," the visitors added, and they recommended that Kurtz be awarded a prize as the originator of the method.[18]

Unfortunately, the new cap screws were not successful in the marketplace. Business grew slowly, and the company posted revenues of nearly $40,000 in 1902, more than $75,000 the following year, but only about $74,000 in 1904. Costs climbed steeply, leading to a frantic scramble for cash. The firm's troubles stemmed from various sources. First, few customers apparently wanted standard cap screws, at least at the prices Cleveland Cap Screw could offer, and cheaper alternatives continued in common use. Second, initial costs ran higher than anticipated. According to a contemporary account, the company experienced particular problems with its machinery for making cap heads, and it was forced to consider buying the heads from outside vendors. Third,

Kurtz's limited background in engineering and manufacturing and his lack of experience as an operating manager proved to be handicaps that Verner Bright and other employees could not overcome. Within a few years the board of directors entertained a plan whereby Kurtz would have devoted his "undivided attention to the sales and purchase of supplies, with a reliable working superintendent in charge of the works."[19]

Cleveland Cap Screw's most pressing problem, however, was lack of capital: it had no reserves on which to draw while it struggled to perfect its process and develop the market. Facing high costs and low sales, the company found its loan obligations, including the mortgage on the plant and notes payable of $25,000 used to acquire machinery and tools, increasingly worrisome.

In the summer of 1903, management launched a search for new investors. Relief soon appeared in the form of Alexander Winton and his partners Thomas Henderson and George Brown, owners of the Winton Motor Carriage Company, one of the largest manufacturers of automobiles in the United States. In August, Kurtz sold $20,000 worth of his own stock to the Winton group. Five months later, Henderson was elected a director of Cleveland Cap Screw.[20]

Today Winton is remembered primarily by business historians. During the first decade of the twentieth century, however, he was one of the most flamboyant and storied entrepreneurs in the fledgling automobile industry. Until about 1910, for example, his name was better known in automotive circles than Henry Ford's. (Several automotive historians assert that Ford once applied for a job at Winton's factory but was turned down because the owner was "unimpressed with Ford's training and skill.") A friend who knew Winton well used crisp phrases to summarize him: "a tireless worker, a real inventor, lacking education, possessed with a violent temper, moderately addicted to 'wee drap' which made him ill natured. Disposed to deal fairly in business, and was able to keep very capable men around him."[21]

Born in Scotland in 1860, Winton had emigrated to the United States around 1880. He worked as a machinist and marine engineer in New York for several years before settling in Cleveland at the behest of his brother-in-law, Thomas Henderson, a blacksmith. In 1884, Winton hired on with the Phoenix Iron Works in Cleveland, a maker of furnaces, and soon was appointed superintendent. His abiding passion, however, was personal transportation. During the "bicycle craze" of the late 1880s and early 1890s, he patented several key inventions, including improved ball bearings and a spring-supported saddle, that made for a smoother, more comfortable ride. In 1891, he established the Winton Bicycle Company, which produced six thousand bicycles the following year.

About 1893, Winton began experimenting in his basement with gasoline-powered vehicles, an activity that generated controversy in his East Side neighborhood. According to a later account, these experiments "almost asphyxiated [Winton] and his family to say nothing of the neighbors." Winton only ceased some years later, when "the neighbors complained to the police that a lunatic was making their lives miserable," and he became "a bit more circumspect."[22]

Four years later, with Henderson and Brown, he founded the Winton Motor Carriage Company. To demonstrate the reliability of his "horseless carriage," Winton conceived an audacious stunt. He and his shop foreman drove a prototype vehicle from Cleveland to New York, a journey of about eight hundred miles over primitive roads that Winton described as "outrageous." The trip consumed nine days, including nearly seventy-nine hours of running time. Nonetheless, it helped establish the durability, reliability, speed, and economy of the new form of transportation. The following year, 1898, Winton claimed—probably erroneously—to have sold the first automobile purchased in North America. At a price of $1,000—including a profit of $400—the transaction was a milestone in the birth of the automobile industry in the United States, as well as the high-water mark for the profitability of Winton's businesses.[23]

Winton sought to build the market for motor carriages through racing and heavy spending on advertising. In 1899, he again motored from Cleveland to New York, this time as the result of a bet with Charles B. Shanks, a reporter from the *Plain Dealer,* who accompanied him on the trip. Shanks's dispatches from along the way generated considerable publicity and, among other effects, helped popularize the term "automobile," a jauntier and more forward-looking expression than contemporary alternatives such as "horseless carriage" or "self-propelled vehicle." When Winton rumbled down the streets of New York toward City Hall, it was said that more than a million residents cheered him on. After the trip, Shanks joined Winton's firm as advertising manager, and he continued to blitz the media with stories about Winton and his vehicles. In October 1901, Winton lost the only race in which he competed with Henry Ford, but two months later, a car built and driven by Winton established a world land-speed record of 57.8 miles per hour. The legendary race driver Barney Oldfield won many prizes behind the wheel of a Winton, and in 1903 a Winton was the first automobile to cross the North American continent.

By that year, Winton claimed to operate the largest automobile factory in the United States, annually building about 850 cars targeted at affluent buyers. His company was responsible for many innovations, including "two-drum braking systems," improved batteries, the steering wheel (an honor shared with Packard), a pedal-operated throttle (assisted by compressed air), and four-, six-, and eight-cylinder motors designed for ease of manufacture and maintenance. Winton also pioneered in the use of interchangeable standardized parts, and he was a founding member of the Association of Licensed Automobile Manufacturers, the industry's leading trade organization. During his thirty years as an automaker, Winton earned more than a hundred patents, which he freely provided to his competition. "Inventors share things," he once declared, "tools, ideas, equipment, or entire patented inventions."[24]

How Cleveland Cap Screw attracted Winton's notice is not definitely known, although he undoubtedly was familiar with both cap screws and electrical resistance welding from his days as a bicycle maker. In addition, between 1897 and 1902 (toward the end of the period in which Winton was annoying his neighbors by tinkering with motors in his basement) he lived not far from Kurtz. Winton was also known to invest in enterprises in which he took no management interest. At about the same time as he acquired stock in Cleveland Cap Screw, for example, he invested in a start-up venture, Lindsay Wire Weaving Company, which manufactured wire screens and materials for the papermaking industry.[25]

But Winton's interest in Cleveland Cap Screw was more than casual. His automobiles required cap screws. A fastidious personality and a devout believer in standardization, perhaps Winton shared Kurtz's wish to eliminate nonstandard cap screws. He might also have supposed that the welding equipment could be adapted to making other automobile parts, including engine valves. If so, his investment would yield only experimental results, unless the terms of Cleveland Cap Screw's license agreement with Thomson Electric Welding could be expanded to cover new products.

Despite Winton's initial investment, Cleveland Cap Screw continued to struggle. In the spring of 1904, Kurtz's bank, City Trust Company, merged with State Banking & Trust Company, which began to reexamine its acquired portfolio of loans. In July, Kurtz arranged to borrow an additional $5,000 from State Banking & Trust, which approved the loan but pointed out that a director of Cleveland Cap Screw had neglected to sign a bond covering the original loan. When asked for his signature, that director refused and resigned his seat on the board. Another director balked at signing the new bond. The crisis was temporarily averted in August, when the company arranged to borrow an additional $30,000, with signatories to the loan, including not only all the directors, but also Winton and Brown.[26]

Although sales began to pick up during 1905, Cleveland Cap Screw remained in desperate financial straits. In the spring, the board authorized Kurtz and Frederick Bright to open discussions with Russell-Burdsall & Ward Bolt and Nut Company of Port Chester, New York, about a possible coalition or combination.

As reported to the Cleveland company's board, the talks went well, although the unfortunate Kurtz missed a meeting in May, "confined to home as result of injuries received in a railroad wreck." Bright subsequently carried on, and on June 14 reported "a very satisfactory meeting" with Mr. Ward, who stated "that in his opinion we have one of the best propositions in the screw business and that the advantages to his concern of an alliance with ours would warrant hearty co-operation on their part." The proposed arrangements apparently called for Cleveland Cap Screw to distribute a broad line of screws, nuts, and bolts from Russell-Burdsall & Ward, while that company would gain access to the Cleveland company's manufacturing technology, which Ward regarded as the basis of "a unique monopoly."[27]

Ward concluded the meeting by promising to give "all possible practical aid in improving [Cleveland Cap Screw's] manufacturing facilities toward doubling or trebling [its] output," and by suggesting that "by reducing costs . . . and increasing output to meet the demand which he had no doubt would follow an alliance of our Companies, we should become a snug successful concern." Ward promised to continue discussions when he returned from a six-week trip to England. In the meantime, he dispatched an engineer to assess the Cleveland company's plant and urged its management to meet its short-term obligations by issuing additional bonds.

In July, the stockholders of Cleveland Cap Screw approved a plan to raise between $100,000 and $150,000 by selling gold bonds that would yield 6 percent interest annually. Kurtz and the Brights formed a committee "to dispose of and place these bonds to the best advantage of the company." State Banking & Trust agreed to purchase some bonds in return for a seat on the board of directors.[28]

The fate of these bonds and the course of subsequent discussions between Cleveland Cap Screw and Russell-Burdsall & Ward are unknown. It is probable, however, that few bonds were actually sold and that by the time Ward returned and received his engineer's report, his ardor to create "a snug, successful concern" had cooled. In any event, on September 21, 1905, time ran out for the founders of Cleveland Cap Screw. Winton and his partners seized control of the company by acquiring shares from the Brights and other stockholders with smaller holdings. Winton replaced Kurtz as president of Cleveland Cap Screw, with Henderson as vice president and Brown as secretary and treasurer.[29]

The timing of this transaction reflected another factor: the desire of Winton and some people at Cleveland Cap Screw to steer the company in new directions. In particular, these people saw that the process for making cap screws could be applied to a much more promising product, poppet valves for gasoline engines.

Among the advocates of change was Charlie Thompson, who, like many of his coworkers, moonlighted to help make ends meet. After his first wife's death in 1903, Thompson shared quarters with a friend, Edwin L. Russell, proprietor of Russell Motor Vehicle Company, a small company that built several automobiles in 1903 and 1904. Thompson served as treasurer of Russell's company and apparently spent many evenings tinkering in its shop. The Russell cars featured an unusual engine design that included a single, tapered rotary valve for each cylinder. Its engines, it was said, ran "after a fashion" before encountering a familiar problem: the valves warped under "the heat and back force of the explosions." After 1904, Russell's company disappeared, but the experience, Thompson later recalled, "was sufficient to start him to think in terms of automotive valves."[30]

"The same large head, the same small stem, and the same great strength," Thompson observed, "were all required for the valve, as they had been for the standard cap screw." Winton, who was on the eve of offering his new six- and eight-cylinder engines, evidently shared this realization. So did several other automobile manufacturers, suppliers, and machine shops, including the Olds Motor Works of Lansing, Michigan, which had already licensed or were about to license the Thomson process for the purpose of welding valve stems.[31]

Electrical resistance welding had several advantages over the conventional approaches to manufacturing valves. The earliest engines used two-piece valves consisting of a cast-iron head screwed or riveted to a cast iron or steel stem. Although such valves could be produced at low cost, the joint between the two metals broke down frequently under the constant hammering endured in operation. In addition, cast-iron heads proved too heavy for the new high-speed engines that affluent buyers began to prize after about 1905. The alternative was to forge or machine one-piece valves from a steel alloy (usually nickel steel) that stood up well to operating temperatures and pressures. Such valves, however, carried the same production problems as the one-piece cap screw: they were expensive to manufacture because they generated a high volume of scrap and required significant amounts of labor in finishing and grinding. In addition, the entire valve had to be designed to accommodate the pressures on the head, although the stem operated in a much less demanding environment and could be made from less expensive materials. By using electrical resistance welding to attach a head of nickel steel to a carbon steel stem, for example, manufacturers could combine the advantages of both conventional types of valves: high performance and a low-cost manufacturing process.[32]

In February 1906, acting on behalf of Cleveland Cap Screw, Charlie Thompson negotiated a nonexclusive license from Thomson Electric Welding to apply electrical resistance welding to products including "valve stems used in engines," lap rods used in textile machinery, propeller shafts, and transmission rods for motor carriages. The terms of the license were similar to those for cap screws, with royalty payments contingent on the size of the weld.[33]

Soon thereafter, Winton and his partners, who remained preoccupied with making automobiles, appointed Thompson general manager of Cleveland Cap Screw with a salary of $1,800 per year. The company now advertised that in addition to screws and bolts it made "gas engine valves from nickel and machinery steel."[34]

THE MAKING OF A MONOPOLY

When Winton and Thompson decided to focus on making poppet valves, they touched off extraordinary changes at Cleveland Cap Screw. Sales and profits soared, except for brief dips following the Panic of 1907 and recessions in 1910–1911 and 1913–1914. In an action symbolizing the new era, the company changed its name to Electric Welding Products Company early in 1908 "for the purpose of removing any possible inference that the company was engaged only in the manufacture of cap screws and related products."[35]

Signs of prosperity were evident throughout the decade after 1906. As business expanded, employment soared from fifty-five employees in 1908 to more than six hundred in 1916. Thompson watched his salary rise to $3,000 in 1909 and to $10,000 two years later. The company acquired parcels of adjoining real estate seven times between 1909 and 1915. Electric Welding Products started to pay handsome dividends: 10 percent in 1911 and in 1914 and 20 percent in 1912 and 1913. In the latter year, the company also retired the last of the ill-fated bonds floated in Kurtz's desperate final months as president. The culmination of the company's prosperity was a special dividend of $200 per share, payable in common stock, in June 1915. At about the same time, the company's total capitalization was raised from $250,000 to $1 million, and its name was changed once more, this time to Steel Products Company.[36]

The source of this bonanza was the two-piece welded valve, which clearly demonstrated its superior performance and economy compared with valves manufactured by other methods. By 1916, according to "a conservative estimate," Steel Products produced or licensed the manufacture of "90% of all valves used in the automobile industry," with the significant exception of Ford, whose Model T used heat-treated cast iron valve heads and stems that were screwed together.[37]

Credit for the transformation of the struggling Cleveland Cap Screw into the very profitable Steel Products belongs primarily to Charlie Thompson and his colleagues

William D. "Billy" Bartlett, factory superintendent, and J. Albert "Pete" Krider, sales manager. These leaders sought to grow and enrich the company in two ways. First, they secured patent protection on welded two-piece valves. Second, they cultivated close ties with the largest automakers, including many of Winton's fiercest competitors.

Prior to joining Cleveland Cap Screw in 1904, Bartlett had been a machinist and toolmaker. Fred Crawford, who knew Bartlett well, recalled him as "a great machinist" and a man who "loved machinery." Despite a limited education, Bartlett possessed high native intelligence, and his ingenuity enabled him to solve production problems and improve factory operations as the company expanded. "A little fat fellow," Bartlett maintained a very quiet life, devoting himself almost entirely to work: "He was the kind of fellow who would wake up at night and think there might be a fire at the factory. He would get up and dress and go to the factory. He loved that place." In addition to being an effective engineer, Bartlett was popular with employees. "He knew all the workmen by name," said Crawford, adding, "He maintained excellent relations with the workers because he was the workman's worker."[38]

Krider had joined Cleveland Cap Screw in 1905 as sales manager, although he had trained as a bookkeeper and his previous employment had been as chief clerk of the Atlas Bolt and Screw Company, a business located down the street from Kurtz's residence. Krider was "a very quiet man," Crawford recalled. "He couldn't sell anything. He couldn't make anything. But he was pretty good with money." Fortunately, Krider's position at Cleveland Cap Screw included the assignment to keep the books, a task he performed so well that in 1910 he was elected a director of the company.[39]

Thompson, Bartlett, and Krider combined to form an effective management team that would remain intact at the head of Cleveland Cap Screw and its successors for the next quarter-century, broken apart only by the deaths of Bartlett in 1931 and Thompson in 1933. Krider remained a board member until his death in 1945. "Not one of them would have succeeded alone," Crawford believed, but "[t]he three of them so completely supported each other and complemented each other that they were a success. Whenever they were busted, Krider could dig up a little more money. When Charlie took an order that was hard to make, Billy could make it."[40]

Under these leaders, the company modified the Thomson welding process in ways that yielded a significant competitive advantage over other licensees. These modifications had their origin in improvements that Thompson and Bartlett had engineered in the process for making cap screws. In 1907, for example, Cleveland Cap Screw had applied for several patents that eventually resulted in the company's domination of the independent market for poppet valves.

The first patent pertained to an improved clamping device that held the abutting pieces to be joined. The device precisely centered the stem with the head and significantly reduced the amount of metal consumed in the welding process or machined off afterward. Indeed, the stem required no machining at all, and the only labor performed on the valve after welding was to grind it. The clamp was also designed to accommodate rapid production. "So great were the savings effected by this clamp device," the company later boasted, "that it soon became apparent that without the use of the device no one could successfully compete . . . in the manufacture of welded products."[41]

The second key patent covered a method of welding two dissimilar metals with different rates of heating. Thompson and Bartlett had encountered this problem in trying to make cap screws with brass heads and steel stems for use in electrical switchboards. Their solution applied equally well to welding metals and alloys for other kinds of products, including poppet valves. Indeed, the patent proved extremely valuable for valves, because it permitted "the manufacture of a valve with head of one kind of steel, designed to resist the action of gases in the cylinder, and stem of less expensive material." The process enabled Electric Welding Products to manufacture valves from many different metals and alloys.[42]

The patents for the clamping device and the process for welding dissimilar metals were awarded to Electric Welding Products in 1909 and endowed the company with a significant advantage in welding poppet valves. It manufactured better products, using lower-cost materials, less labor and scrap, and fewer operations than its competitors. The company even helped develop an alloy of low-chromium nickel steel called EWP (after the company's initials), which it used for valve heads that were welded to carbon steel stems.[43]

The company's success also reflected a mushrooming customer base. In this respect, Thompson and Krider benefited not only from the phenomenal growth of the the automobile industry during the first two decades of the twentieth century, but also from Winton's generous spirit in sharing innovations with his competitors.

Between 1903—when Winton was one of the biggest producers in the industry—and 1916, automobile production in the United States climbed from about 11,000 units to about 1.5 million units per year. Much of this increase came after 1913, when Henry Ford introduced the moving assembly line at his Model T factory in Highland Park, Michigan. But growth was rapid even during earlier years; more than two hundred companies organized to produce cars before 1910. In Cleveland alone, more than eighty makes appeared on the market.[44] The vast majority of the nation's car companies were ephemeral enterprises, founded by mechanics who built one or two vehicles a year, and most soon flickered out of existence. Among them, however, were companies that survived for decades and some that remain in business today.

The birth and rapid growth of the automobile industry created obvious opportunities for independent suppliers, which also formed a rapidly growing industry. No manufacturer could afford to make every part in a product as complex as an automobile. In addition, because most automakers started with minimal capital, they relied heavily on suppliers not only for parts, but also for credit. Therefore, the financial health and viability of suppliers were important to their customers. Later the automakers welcomed capabilities that suppliers provided, including standardized, interchangeable products and focused engineering services. The automakers also recognized the scale economies achieved by suppliers' production runs, which were larger than would have been needed to meet the demand of any single manufacturer.[45]

In addition to the explosive growth of its customer base and the opportunities for independent suppliers, Electric Welding Products profited from the development of bigger, mightier engines. One-, or more commonly, two-cylinder engines had powered the first automobiles. During the first decade of the twentieth century, a few automakers, including Winton, began to produce four-, six-, and eight-cylinder engines. The growing popularity of these large engines multiplied the demand for valves. The new engines also raised valve performance requirements, aiding a handful of suppliers, including Electric Welding Products, capable of incorporating advances in metallurgy into their products.

Although the Winton group controlled Electric Welding Products, it did not restrict the company from selling valves to other automakers. Indeed, Winton apparently encouraged the practice. In part, this policy reflected his antipathy to patent litigation, as manifested by his willingness to license his own inventions freely. By itself, moreover, the Winton company constituted a small market; rather than building inexpensive cars for the general public (which many makers thought was impossible), Winton, like many other small producers, chose to concentrate on making a relatively small number of high-quality, classic cars for aficionados. In 1908—the year that Ford first sold the Model T, his car for the masses—Winton built just five hundred vehicles. Electric Welding Products supplied valves or licensed its patents to most of the substantial automakers of the era, with the conspicuous exceptions of Ford and several units of General Motors. In addition to Winton, the biggest customers included White Motors, Packard, Studebaker, Willys-Overland, and Weston-Mott.[46]

THOMPSON'S TAKEOVER

The success of Electric Welding Products provided Thompson, Bartlett, and Krider with security and the satisfaction of building a growing business. It also netted them a small fortune. Nonetheless, Thompson remained dissatisfied and restless. As remembered by Crawford, Thompson was "always thinking about how to promote his affairs. Many a man just goes to work for a company and works for it, but Thompson from the start was figuring out how the hell could he get control and become owner."[47]

Certainly Thompson proved resourceful in managing his own affairs, and he had an entrepreneur's nose for opportunity. While general manager of Electric Welding Products, he continued to moonlight as the treasurer of Edwin Russell's company. In 1910, he founded another company in Cleveland to weld broken castings and gears using oxyacetylene torches. This small concern, incorporated as Metals Welding Company, was started with an investment of $5,000. Thompson served as president and director, with Edward C. Reader as general manager. Other backers of Electric Welding Products, including Herbert Wright, also served on the board of the Metals Welding Company.[48]

Thompson also played a pivotal role in the emergence of still another business, this time in Detroit. In 1907, a Michigan farmer named George Agnew had approached licensees of the Thomson process, claiming to have developed a resistance-welding machine that did not infringe on the Thomson patents. Cleveland Cap Screw was obviously interested, but declined to manufacture the Agnew machines for fear of "complications that would arise" with Thomson Electric Welding.[49]

Undeterred, Agnew applied for a patent on his process on March 3, 1909. Although the value of this patent was doubtful at best, Thompson decided to back the inventor personally, apparently using surplus funds from Electric Welding Products to do so.[50] Thompson probably saw nothing unusual in the action, which may have had the company's unofficial support.

The Agnew Welding Company was organized in Detroit on August 11, 1909, with a capitalization of $25,000 and with Agnew and Thompson as trustees. Bartlett and Krider subsequently acquired small stakes in Agnew Welding, which made "only such machines as it required for its own use, and entered into the manufacture, in Detroit, of welded propeller shafts, starting cranks, and brake rods." Later, it made drag links, tie rods, automobile frame cross members, and other products that were welded or forged.[51]

Agnew Welding Company was not an immediate success. It had few orders and apparently made most of its products in small job lots. In June 1910, Agnew sold his interest to Electric Welding Products for $10,200, and the company was renamed Michigan Electric Welding Company, with Thompson as president and Krider as vice president. In that year, the company reported total assets of $31,446.06 and posted a loss of $3,389.95. The situation began to improve almost immediately, however. In 1911, Thompson appointed Carl F. Clarke general manager and compensated him with an incentive based on increasing sales. At the same time, Michigan Electric Welding acquired a small competitor, the Detroit Electric Welding Company. By 1914, Michigan Electric Welding's assets totaled $164,204.13, and it reported a gross profit (excluding salaries and payroll) of $134,196.70 on sales of $252,882.32.[52]

The Agnew patent apparently contributed little to Michigan Electric Welding's earnings. According to Crawford, the Agnew machines failed to work, so to meet its orders the company simply borrowed Thomson welders from Electric Welding Products in Cleveland. In 1913, when the Michigan company manufactured most of its products by forging, the Agnew patent was dropped from its balance sheet as "being more or less questionable in value."[53] By then, however, the Agnew venture had performed valuable services both for Electric Welding Products and for Thompson, Bartlett, and Krider. In particular, although the value of the patent was still in doubt, Electric Welding Products was able to use the threat of the Agnew patent to secure release from additional royalty payments on the Thomson process in exchange for a flat fee of $2,500.[54]

To Thompson, Bartlett, and Krider, Michigan Electric Welding represented not only a growing sideline in Detroit, but also a significant source of income. Metals Welding Company was also evidently successful; in 1916, an appraiser valued its tangible assets as worth nearly $50,000, about ten times its subscribed capital six years earlier. But the greatest benefit of these investments was yet to come: the success of the Michigan company and of Metals Welding gave their principal owners the means to help wrest control of Electric Welding Products Company from the Winton group.[55]

Early in 1915, Thompson and his associates were ready to make their first move. At the annual meeting of Electric Welding Products in February, several noteworthy events occurred. First, the company increased its capitalization and paid a three-for-one stock dividend, thereby further enriching the owners. Second, the stockholders voted to change the corporate name. As of April 1915, the company was known as Steel Products Company. The effect of this move was to emphasize the company's products, including those made in Detroit as well as those made in Cleveland, rather than the welding process used in the operations. At the board of directors meeting on the same day, the Thompson group replaced the Winton group as the elected officers of the company. Thompson succeeded Winton as president, Bartlett was elected a director and vice president, and Krider replaced George Brown as secretary. No reason was given for the change, although the Thompson group may well have argued that the company's titles ought to reflect actual operating responsibilities. Brown continued as treasurer, however, and the Winton group still controlled a majority of the common stock.[56]

The next step was to acquire control of Michigan Electric Welding. In May, Thompson acquired Steel Products' stake in the Michigan company for $300 a share. Once again, he apparently used surplus funds from Steel Products that had been transferred into his personal expense account. This transaction placed Thompson and his partners firmly in charge of the Michigan company. At its next annual meeting, in February 1916, the company raised its total capitalization from $25,000 to $250,000. At the same time, Steel Products Company reported a surplus of $250,000 and declared a dividend of 33.3 percent on its common stock.[57]

The remaining step was to confront Winton and his partners. In May 1916, Thompson met with the Winton group and offered to acquire its majority shares at par value—just over one-half million dollars in cash. As Thompson later recounted (in a version confirmed by Winton), he observed that Winton, Henderson, and Brown had "devoted but a negligible amount of their time" to Steel Products yet "had received a very satisfactory return on their stockholdings." Thompson also pointed out that the majority owners held more than three times as much stock as the company's managers, and that he believed Winton and his partners should sell their stock to the Thompson group at par value. Finally, Thompson "candidly stated" that if the Winton group refused, then he, Bartlett, and Krider would "withdraw from the company, organize a new company and . . . engage in a similar line of business."[58]

Thompson's threat was not idle. He and his partners were prepared to use Michigan Electric Welding and Metals Welding Company as springboards to independence. Recognizing the situation, Winton and his associates promptly accepted Thompson's offer. Although Steel Products and its affiliates and predecessors had enriched them, they were in fact consumed with other matters. In particular, Winton's automobile company was falling far behind its competition. The company's troubles stemmed from Winton's reluctance to follow Ford and General Motors in adopting techniques of mass production, as well as from his persistent investment in unpopular technologies such as an automatic starting mechanism using compressed air. Winton's classy cars enjoyed favorable reviews, but in the era of the Model T they were fast becoming high-priced curiosities. In 1915, Winton reorganized and renamed the business Winton Motor Car Company, and he directed efforts to launch a new, small model targeted at middle-income buyers. The Winton partners were also engaged in the affairs of another company they had established in 1912, Winton Gas Engine & Manufacturing Company, a maker of heavy-duty engines for marine use. The prospect of receiving more than one-half million dollars in cash on a much smaller initial investment a decade earlier probably seemed too good to pass up, especially given Thompson's threat.[59]

To secure the money to acquire Steel Products, Thompson and his associates hatched a clever plan. First, they persuaded the Winton group to accept a short-term note payable for its stock. This note was apparently convertible back to stock if the Thompson group failed to raise the cash by a specified date. By early June 1916, then, Thompson and his associates owned voting control of Steel Products Company, with Thompson holding about 47 percent of the shares and Krider and Bartlett holding about 24 and 23 percent, respectively.[60]

Second, the Thompson group arranged to establish a new corporation, also called Steel Products Company, capitalized at $4 million, consisting of 25,000 shares of common stock and 15,000 shares of preferred stock. Each class of stock had a par value of $100 per share, and the preferred stock guaranteed an annual yield of 7 percent.[61] On June 27, 1916, the new Steel Products Company issued 18,756 shares of common and 9,000 shares of preferred stock, which it used to acquire the property and assets of three companies: the old Steel Products Company, for 10,000 shares of common stock and 7,500 shares of preferred, which was offered as a dividend to holders of the old common stock; Michigan Electric Welding, for 7,350 shares of common stock; and Metals Welding Company, for 1,406 shares of common stock.

Directors of the new company, in addition to Thompson, Bartlett, and Krider, were Carl Clarke of Michigan Electric Welding, Samuel Mathews of the original Cleveland Cap Screw group, and three others: Edward Reader, who had managed Metals Welding; Herbert Wright; and Charles A. Morris, a lawyer. Thompson was elected president and general manager of the new Steel Products at an annual salary of $30,000; Bartlett served as vice president and Krider as secretary and treasurer, each at a salary of $15,000.[62]

The final step was for the Thompson group to sell their preferred stock, which they arranged to do through Borton and Borton, a Cleveland brokerage firm. Successful placement yielded $750,000 in cash, which was used to pay off the notes held by the Winton group. Henceforth, Steel Products was securely in the hands of Charlie Thompson and his close associates.

As for Thompson's predecessors, fate proved unkind. Misfortune continued to plague David Kurtz's career after he left Cleveland Cap Screw in 1905.[63] (He remained a stockholder until 1909 or 1910, when he sold his stock shortly before its great increase in value.) He retired briefly, then re-emerged in 1907 as president of Mitchell Company, a Cleveland firm that made and distributed stoves, ranges, furnaces, specialties, and hotel kitchen outfits. This enterprise failed almost immediately during the Panic of 1907. In 1909, he attempted to capitalize on another emerging technology by establishing Kurtz Refrigerator Company, which designed and built cold-storage rooms. This business collapsed by 1915, and Kurtz then listed his occupation as salesman. In 1917, he was Cleveland district manager of the United Security Company, a securities firm based in Canton. He died in Cleveland on August 29, 1919.

Setbacks and reversals also punctuated Winton's later career.[64] His small, low-priced vehicles failed to regain ground lost to Ford and General Motors, while his magnificent touring cars struggled in competition with Cadillac and Packard. The recession that followed World War I delivered a fatal blow, and Winton liquidated the company in 1924. By then his personal fortune, estimated to be between $4 million and $5 million at its peak, had dwindled to about $750,000, most of which was tied up in his heavy-duty engine company. A 1927 marriage (his third) to Marion Campbell, "a local theatrical personage" forty years his junior, further depleted his fortune. The new Mrs. Winton "had a passionate love for Indian affairs," and she composed an opera, *The Seminole*, which was staged at great expense on the grounds of Winton's Lakewood estate. Guests at the gala affair included the governor of Ohio and most of Cleveland's "high society." In 1930, she filed for divorce in order to marry a Native American chief and was said to have received a $200,000 cash settlement from Winton. That year—probably not by coincidence—the seventy-year-old Winton sold his engine business to General Motors. He died two years later. At the time of his death, Winton's estate was valued at just under $50,000.

Chapter 3

Peaks and Valleys

▶   ▶   ▶

1916–1933

C. E. THOMPSON IS REMEMBERED FONDLY BY EMPLOYEES WHO WORKED FOR HIM. AS FRED Crawford put it, "He had a quick mind. He was aggressive. He was an extrovert. He loved people. And he was a dreamer." Thompson was "very colorful, very charismatic," adds J. David Wright, who, as a young lawyer, served as executor of Thompson's estate. "He didn't have college training, but he was very, very bright," according to Wright. "He would come up with all sorts of ideas. He was creative."[1]

As president of Steel Products (and its post-1926 successor, Thompson Products) from 1916 until his death in 1933, Thompson continued to display the qualities that marked his rise: the positive attributes of ambition, salesmanship, a knack for making friends, and an ability to recognize talent, as well as the less appealing traits of avarice and opportunism. During these years, Thompson's abilities as a leader were stretched to the fullest as his company embarked on a wild and bumpy ride through the financial peaks and valleys of World War I, the postwar recession, the Roaring '20s, and the Great Depression.

The endpoints of Thompson's tenure as president bracket two distinctly different eras in the evolution of the company he led. In 1916, to all outward appearances, Steel Products was a very profitable business. Patents protected its manufacturing processes, and its primary products—valves and steering parts for automobile engines—were in increasing demand. The company's fate no longer depended on a few key accounts, and Steel Products served scores of customers. The competition consisted of a group of small garages and machine shops that served regional markets. Thompson and his partners had broken away from this pack through a combination of patent protection, savvy deal-making, and plain good luck.

The remainder of Thompson's presidency would highlight the fragility of this initial success. During the next seventeen years, the fortunes of the company and its owners changed dramatically. Thompson Products (as it was known after 1926) barely survived the boom-and-bust rhythms of the era. In 1933, it reported a modest profit after two consecutive years of losses, and demand for most of its products fell well below the rising levels of the previous decade. The company faced stiff competition in its principal product lines, not only from big, technologically sophisticated rivals, but also from major customers such as Ford and General Motors, which increasingly became vertically integrated. As a supplier to the automobile and aircraft industries, the company watched helplessly as the balance of power in its relationships with customers shifted sharply in the customers' favor. Thompson Products' business was significantly more complicated and diverse than it had been in 1916, and the company was engaged in a constant struggle to find new ways to make its products, new products to offer, and new markets to serve. Its universe was populated with large institutions, rising technological requirements, and the competing demands of owners, lenders, managers, employees, customers, and lawmakers.

Yet through all these changes, important continuities helped to carry the company forward: the genial leadership and entrepreneurial instincts of Thompson and his partners, the hard work and resourcefulness of employees, and the company's adaptability as a manufacturer. Thompson Products survived its double ordeal of expansion and retrenchment because it diversified, retained good personnel, proved willing and able to revamp its plants when it had to, and forged important technological alliances with key suppliers.

SALAD DAYS—BRIEFLY

Fred Crawford remembered vividly the occasion of his job interview at Steel Products in 1916. A twenty-five-year-old engineering graduate from Harvard, he had just completed two years as a tutor to young men preparing for college, and he had arrived in Cleveland after a long period of travel with the son of a prominent local clergyman. At a dinner party he met Herbert Wright, who suggested that Crawford visit Steel Products and talk to Thompson, which Crawford arranged to do the next day. When Crawford declared his interest in a job, however, Thompson snorted, "We can't use you. We don't want any college loafers around this place. We're self-made men." Taken aback, Crawford made an effort at small talk. At one point, he expressed admiration for an inkwell on the president's desk. Thompson's eyes twinkled, and he said, "You like it? Well, when you get to be general manager here, I'll give it to you." With that, Crawford was hired as a millwright's helper.[2]

Thompson—who at this juncture preferred to be called "C. E."—was then in the prime of life, basking in recognition he had long sought. He had become a figure of standing in industry, elected to the position of second vice president of the Motor and Accessory Manufacturers Association, a nationwide trade organization of automotive parts suppliers. He had also risen to prominence in the Cleveland business community.

In 1917, for example, he joined with other local investors to persuade the aircraft maker Glenn L. Martin to set up shop in the city. During its early years of operation, Thompson served as president of the Martin company—forerunner of the aerospace giant Martin Marietta (now Lockheed Martin). In this capacity he built relationships with many aviation pioneers, including Martin and employees such as Donald Douglas, Lawrence Bell, and J. H. "Dutch" Kindleberger, who went on to found or lead major aircraft companies.[3]

Thompson also continued to invest in more closely related projects. In 1917, he joined with his partners Billy Bartlett and Pete Krider to establish Ross Manufacturing Company (also known as Ross Tool Company), a business that supplied tools to Steel Products and was housed in the Clarkwood Road plant. Two years later, Thompson and several backers of Steel Products acquired controlling interest in Lewis Steel Products Company, a maker of valves for automotive engines in Toledo, Ohio. The new owners bestowed a new name on the business, Toledo Steel Products, but they made few other changes and no effort to integrate its operations with those of Steel Products. (Thompson sold his controlling stake in Toledo Steel Products in 1925, but Thompson Products, then under Fred Crawford, acquired the company ten years later.)[4]

Thompson reveled in the fortune he had made. He and his second wife, Alberta "Polly" Brown, whom he married in 1919, moved into an expensive home, replete with a stable and horses, on the West Side of Cleveland. They also purchased "Johnny-cake Ridge," a large, picturesque farm on Ridge Road, east of Painesville, as the site of their country estate. In his ongoing quest for respectability, Thompson even pulled Fred Crawford out of the factory for six months in 1917 to serve as a personal tutor to Thompson's son, Edwin, who was hoping for admission to Cornell University.

Steel Products was managed with an easy informality befitting the owner's genial personality. Billy Bartlett remained nominally in charge of operations in Cleveland until December 1917, when Clarence W. "Doc" Miller was named general manager. Bartlett continued to act informally as a personnel manager and to immerse himself in projects on the shop floor. Both Bartlett and Miller delegated a great deal of authority to engineering superintendent William H. Spire and production superintendents Al Gorris, Eugene McBride, and John Kerwin. Carl Clarke ran the Detroit factory until 1917, when he had a falling out with Thompson and was replaced by H. A. Garman, who had been Clarke's assistant. Edward Reader, who had managed the old Metals Welding Company, remained until 1919, when Steel Products sold the gas welding business to him and several partners. Pete Krider served as corporate secretary, treasurer, and, in effect, chief financial officer.[5]

In 1919, the company hired its second and third college graduates: Lee Clegg, who moved into sales, and Richard E. Bissell, a trained metallurgist. Another key appointment followed in 1922, when Arch T. Colwell, an engineering graduate of West Point (where he had roomed with Crawford's cousin) joined as a sales engineer. In these young hirees, as well as others including Len W. Reeves, Raymond S. Livingstone, and Dave Wright who joined several years later, Steel Products possessed the nucleus of its next management team.

For its first few years, life was bountiful for Steel Products. In 1917, revenues approached $3.5 million and soared to nearly $5.5 million three years later. During this period, profits hovered at around $.5 million declining relative to sales but nonetheless providing ample returns to shareholders. Steel Products distributed more than half of its net income as dividends to investors. In paying out big dividends, the company followed a common financial policy of the era. After covering expenses, most industrial corporations set aside small amounts of cash from earnings as accumulated surplus or reserves, then distributed the balance to stockholders. Conventional financial wisdom held that most stockholders were looking for regular cash returns rather than long-term capital appreciation or a mixture of the two.

The good times did not last long, however. Revenues plummeted to $1.9 million in 1922 and would not surpass the 1920 peak until 1926. Profits also tumbled, despite a spike in 1922, until the mid-1920s (see Exhibits I-1 and I-2 in the introduction to Part I). Several factors started this roller-coaster ride, but most significant was the health of Steel Products' customers, which in turn reflected the state of the U.S. economy. A dramatic surge in industrial production during World War I provided the initial boost. Between 1916 and 1920, U.S. gross national product doubled. Over the same period, output of motor vehicles rose nearly 40 percent, from 1.6 million to 2.2 million vehicles, an impressive performance considering that many automakers diverted production capacity to serve military needs during the period of U.S. participation in the conflict.[6]

This boom came to an abrupt halt in 1920, when the United States entered one of the deepest recessions in its history. Between 1920 and 1921, wholesale prices plunged by 40 percent, while over the two years unemployment among nonfarm workers nationwide soared from 2.4 to 19.5 percent. The automobile industry was hit particularly hard, as the recession provided the first real check to its extraordinary growth. To stay afloat, Ford cut prices by 20 percent, closed its factories for six weeks, and offloaded inventory onto dealers, many of whom went bankrupt and all of whom bitterly resented the action. General Motors narrowly escaped bankruptcy, saved only by a Du Pont–J. P. Morgan syndicate that supplied a huge capital investment and new management. The recession devastated smaller automakers; between 1919 and 1923, the number of producers fell from more than two hundred to about fifty.[7]

Poppet Valves: New Materials and Production Methods

Although the recession accounted for much of Steel Products' misfortunes during the early 1920s, the company also proved vulnerable to competition in its major business, poppet valves. The source of its vulnerability was the ongoing quest for more powerful engines for high-performance automobiles and aircraft, a quest that rendered Steel Products' patented manufacturing processes all but worthless.[8]

World War I and its aftermath constituted a fertile period for engine design. The new engines required valves that had to endure hotter temperatures, higher compression, faster operating speeds, and more volatile fuel mixtures. The demands were especially great on exhaust valves, which must cope with more hostile conditions than do intake valves. The incoming flow of the fuel-air mixture cools the intake valve, but the exhaust valve must survive the blow-torch effect of a concentrated flow of extremely hot exhaust gases. Metals sufficiently strong to withstand the new requirements proved difficult or impossible to weld using the electrical resistance process. To remain competitive in valve manufacture, therefore, Steel Products had to upgrade its capabilities in forging and work with new steel alloys.[9]

The first factor to disturb Steel Products' comfortable domination of the independent valve market was the meteoric rise of a new competitor, Rich Tool Company of Chicago, the founder of which, George Rich, had in 1913 developed a one-piece exhaust valve made from an alloy of tungsten and steel. The Rich valve proved capable of withstanding very high temperatures and showed remarkable resistance to pitting. Although it was costly to manufacture, it immediately won over makers of high-performance engines such as Packard, and from there it filtered down to the makers of less sophisticated cars. At the low end of the market, Steel Products could compete with Rich Tool by offering discounts and package deals on both intake and exhaust valves. As engine performance requirements continued to rise, however, Steel Products had no alternative but to follow Rich Tool's lead into forged valves.[10]

The development of new engines for aircraft during World War I also raised demands on valves. The most sophisticated aircraft motor of the period was called the Hispano-Suiza (so named because it was designed by a Swiss engineer working in Barcelona), a water-cooled V-8. In 1915, Pierre Gillet, an agent for the French military, which used the Hispano-Suiza motor in its Spad fighter planes, arranged to purchase valves from both Steel Products and Rich Tool. These valves consisted of "solid-forged tungsten steel, had a solid head with a slightly convex top, a partly hollow stem with an inside thread and an adjustable tappet." The valves, moreover, had to be finished to extremely close tolerances.[11]

The experience of making valves for the Hispano-Suiza motor provided a considerable technical boost to Steel Products, which gained expertise in forging and machining tungsten steel. In 1917, the company acquired additional property on Clarkwood Road and invested in new forging equipment. Steel Products further upgraded its forging capabilities after the United States entered the war that year, once again under the stimulus of rising performance requirements for aircraft engine valves. To power its aircraft, the U.S. military chose a new engine, the Liberty motor. A water-cooled L-12, this engine at first used forged tungsten steel valves developed by Rich Tool. Very late in the war, problems with burning of the valves led Rich Tool to experiment with stainless steel alloys. As production geared up in the fall of 1918, the government enlisted Steel Products as a second supplier. The company acquired still more property and added a new forge shop.[12]

Although demand for aircraft engines nearly ceased after the Armistice, lessons learned from the experience transferred quickly to the automobile industry. Engine designers specified forged valves of tungsten steel and stainless steel for high-performance engines. These ever-rising requirements, along with fierce competition from tough, sophisticated competitors such as Rich Tool, posed unprecedented techni-

cal challenges to Steel Products. The company made some headway when Billy Bartlett oversaw development of semiautomatic equipment to gather metal at the end of a
blank to form the head of a forged valve. It was during this period, in 1919, that the
company hired Dick Bissell, its first trained metallurgist. At the same time, Steel Products began searching for ways in which it could reclaim its leading position in the
independent valve business.[13]

Sᴀᴠᴇᴅ ʙʏ Sɪʟᴄʀᴏᴍᴇ

Steel Products did not have to wait long to regain technological leadership in poppet
valves. During the early 1920s, a key supplier provided the means of recovery: a new
alloy of silicon, chromium, and carbon steel that satisfied the technical demands of
engine designers at a cost significantly below that for tungsten-steel or stainless-steel
valves.

Credit for development of the new alloy belongs to Percival A. E. Armstrong of
Ludlum Steel Company. During 1914 and 1915, Armstrong, a specialist in arc welding, had encountered problems of rusting and scaling of steel alloys under the heat of
welding. While searching for alloys that would better withstand high temperatures, he
observed remarkable properties in alloys containing silicon. At the time, most metal-
lurgists supposed that "silicon when used in more than the least possible quantity"
resulted in an alloy that was "brittle, less desirable, and less available for most purposes." Armstrong, however, found that alloys containing a relatively high percentage
of silicon and specified amounts of chromium and carbon possess remarkable surface
properties, including resistance to rust, scaling, and corrosion, freedom from cracks,
fissures, or blemishes, and durability at high temperatures. Armstrong also claimed
that such "silcrome" (silicon-chromium) alloys could be forged readily and that heat
treatment would yield virtually any degree of hardness. No alloy previously known
possessed all these properties. Best of all, silcrome was less expensive to produce than
other hard steel alloys.[14]

In 1919, Armstrong filed two patent applications for stable-surface alloy steels
containing a high proportion of silicon. Among the first envisioned applications were
exhaust valves for internal combustion engines, and Ludlum Steel made the alloy
available to automakers, aircraft engine builders, and independent valve suppliers,
including Steel Products and Rich Tool. Most recipients were unenthusiastic about the
alloy, reflecting "the deep seated prejudice against any steel with more than a minimum
silicon content." Rich Tool, for example, apparently believed that the material was
unworkable and perhaps dangerous to manufacture. The company declined to pursue
silcrome and continued to focus on valves made from tungsten-steel and chromium-
steel alloys. This decision would prove costly.[15]

Initially Steel Products was also reluctant to investigate silcrome, but eventually it
agreed to collaborate with Ludlum on some experimental valves. Armstrong's claims
about ready workability notwithstanding, the alloy proved extremely difficult to handle. The very qualities that rendered it desirable for high-performance exhaust valves

also rendered it problematical to cut, drill, or forge. In frustration, Steel Products employees christened silcrome "the devil steel." Part of the problem was the company's manufacturing equipment, which, one executive noted dryly, was "not the best and the latest" of its type.[16]

With assistance from Ludlum researchers, however, Steel Products engineers learned "from the ground up" processes for working, cutting, heat treating, and finishing the silcrome alloy. Once produced, the finished valves demonstrated yet another remarkable quality. When heated to operating temperatures, the valves turned a bronze color from oxidation. The new surface coating was so dense that, in Crawford's words, it acted like "a magic paint" to inhibit further corrosion and accounted for extraordinary durability.[17]

Use of silcrome in valves grew slowly until the spring of 1922, when the U.S. Bureau of Aeronautics sponsored comparative endurance tests of aircraft engine valves at Anacostia Field in Washington, D.C. The goal was to achieve fifty hours of continuous use at full throttle in an improved Hispano-Suiza motor. Tungsten-steel valves burned out after about 10 hours. Valves of chromium steel were destroyed after about 30 hours. The first set of silcrome valves supplied by Steel Products ran for 387 hours before the test was halted—with the valves found still to be in good condition. The company came away from the tests with a substantial order for silcrome valves from Wright Aeronautical (successor to Wright-Martin).[18]

A bigger breakthrough followed another test soon afterward. Engineers from an unidentified "large automobile manufacturing company" equipped test vehicles with Steel Products' silcrome valves. The cars were driven around the clock for 25,000 miles, stopping only for fuel, oil, and minor adjustments. At the conclusion of the tests, the valves were found to be "in splendid condition." The automaker adopted the valves as "standard equipment."[19]

Silcrome's success arrived at a timely moment for Steel Products, which was still feeling the effect of the postwar recession as well as intense competition from Rich Tool and other rivals. Morale at the company was poor. Despite the results from Anacostia Field, Bartlett was pessimistic about manufacturing silcrome valves on a large scale because of inherent difficulties in working with the alloy. Even Bissell, the metallurgist, was reluctant to proceed with silcrome, apparently because he was not convinced that it could meet all the design specifications for valves. Crawford, on the other hand, was an enthusiastic proponent. As a sales engineer, he had witnessed the valve trials at Anacostia Field. He also had in his pocket a tentative order for silcrome valves from Daniels Motor Company of Reading, Pennsylvania, a maker of high-priced cars with powerful engines.[20]

The debate about whether to proceed with silcrome came to a head in the summer of 1923. By that time, Armstrong had applied for a third patent on a specific formula for a silcrome alloy for use in exhaust valves. One Sunday morning, Crawford traveled to C. E. Thompson's farm near Painesville for a routine meeting. As Crawford described, Thompson "was lower than hell. His second wife had just walked out on him, and he felt that life just wasn't worthwhile. And to cheer the old man up, I said, 'Now, wait a minute. Everything isn't so bad, Charlie.'" Crawford proceeded to give "a helluva sales talk about how we were on the verge of a wonderful expansion," adding that "if we didn't get out and sell silcrome, [then we'd] be missing a chance to build the company." Crawford was characteristically persuasive. The next morning, Thompson appeared in the plant and announced, "We're going to take on silcrome. We had better go find out how to machine it and how to treat it." By September, the company was confident that volume production of silcrome valves was feasible. The following February, Steel Products licensed the Armstrong patents and began producing silcrome valves in earnest.[21]

Steel Products quickly found itself in the enviable position of offering better products at lower cost than its competitors. Silcrome valves created a sensation among automakers and engine designers, and orders flooded into Cleveland. The engineers who designed the first Chrysler engine, an enormously successful high-compression model based on advanced aircraft engines, specified silcrome valves. Under pressure from their dealers, who had been dazzled by Steel Products' sales representatives, Dodge Brothers converted its entire production from cast-iron head valves to silcrome. Buick soon followed suit. By 1925, more than fifty makes of cars, trucks, buses, and tractors were using Steel Products' silcrome valves, and the company had recovered its leading position in the market.[22]

Rich Tool, meanwhile, faced several lean years as it persisted with tungsten-steel and stainless-steel valves until about 1926. By then, it had moved from Chicago to Detroit and changed its name to Rich Steel Products. In 1928, it merged with another independent valve supplier, Wilcox Motor Parts & Manufacturing, to form Wilcox-Rich Company.[23]

PURLOINED DRAG LINKS AND AN EXPERIMENT IN HUMAN RELATIONS

The shift from welded to forged parts also occurred at Steel Products' Michigan plant. In 1916, the principal products of Steel Products' factory on Hart Avenue in Detroit were drag links and brake rods, although it also manufactured starting cranks, lap rods, blow pipes, and other miscellaneous items. (Drag links were long, hollow tubes with a ball-and-socket attachment at each end; they were used to connect the steering column with the front wheels. Brake rods were also metal connecting pieces, between the foot pedal and the brake drums.)[24]

The Michigan plant had begun making drag links, by far its most important product, some time before August 1915, when it applied for a patent on a model for heavy-duty trucks and tractors. It is not clear how the company chose to make this product, though it was familiar with a similar device made by another Detroit business. In 1914, Schweppe & Wilt Manufacturing Company had obtained a patent for "steering reach rods" (another term for drag links), and it used Michigan Electric Welding as a subcontractor to weld the constituent pieces together. The Schweppe & Wilt patent, Crawford later testified, "was basic in its particular field and extremely valuable because it afforded economies that were possible with no other type of drag-link, and because it was mechanically better than all other types of drag-links."[25]

Relations between Michigan Electric Welding and Schweppe & Wilt soon soured. As Crawford later stated, once the Detroit plant became familiar with the manufacture of drag links, it also became "tempted by the great profits which had been the reward" of Schweppe & Wilt, and the plant "engaged somewhat on its own account in such manufacture."[26]

When Schweppe & Wilt discovered what was going on, it obtained several cease and desist orders that Steel Products ignored. Finally, in 1917, Steel Products arranged to license Schweppe & Wilt's patent under terms that fixed prices and limited production. These terms proved "far from satisfactory" to Steel Products, however, because expansion was impossible, and the profits enjoyed by Schweppe & Wilt remained "extremely tempting." Steel Products' customers, moreover, "chafed under the tribute" that they had to pay to get drag links. As a result of these pressures and concerns, Steel Products in June 1919 arranged to purchase "a large part of the assets" of Schweppe & Wilt, including its factory on Conant Avenue. Crawford considered the price, slightly more than $432,000, "exorbitant" but necessary to acquire the key drag link patents.[27]

Almost immediately thereafter, Steel Products arranged to buy a second factory adjacent to the Schweppe & Wilt building from the Parker Rust Proof Company for $190,000. The old Michigan Electric Welding Products plant on Hart Avenue was abandoned, and Steel Products consolidated its Detroit operations in its newly acquired properties.[28]

Unfortunately for Steel Products, these moves occurred at the worst possible time, just as the postwar recession hit the automobile industry with full force. During its first several years, the plant suffered "alarming losses." Thompson dispatched Doc Miller, general manager at Cleveland, to oversee the plant, but that arrangement was temporary. By the summer of 1922, losses were so bad that Thompson was inclined to consolidate the Detroit operation with the main plant in Cleveland. To prepare the way for the move, he sent Crawford to Detroit as plant manager.[29]

Crawford's experiences in Detroit are legendary in the lore of TRW. As he recounted events, what he found when he got there was worse than a business suffering a momentary downturn. "The place was operating without discipline, so everything was careless. People came late and loitered in the restrooms. We produced as much scrap as finished product." Worse still, "I spent a lot of time talking to the employees, and I was surprised to find that they had no idea that anything was wrong." Crawford continued:

Well, my interests being human, I felt so sorry for these people that I decided to tell them what my orders were. The only place large enough for all of us to meet was the parking lot out front. I rented some undertaker's chairs and got some canvas to hang over the fence to keep the public from looking in, and then I got up on a soap box and I told the employees the condition of the plant and what I was supposed to do about it. When I said the company wanted to close the plant, I'll never forget the look of shock and disappointment on their faces.

Then, on impulse, I said, "If I disobey orders and try to save this plant, how many of you will go all out to help me?" Every hand went up. Then I said, "Wait a minute. Do you know what you're voting for? If you vote yes that means you'll be here on time and work a full day. No making scrap. No smoking breaks in the toilet room." They all voted yes again. Then I said, "Wait a minute. I want to vote again. Will you come in here—everyone—and work as if you own the business and you were fighting for yourself?" Everyone voted yes again. It was like a religious revival.

Crawford's speech stirred a remarkable reaction among veterans of the plant:

In the days that followed, those people looked different. They walked different. They talked different. They were in early, and they were working when the bell rang. The response was amazing. Fantastic things . . . began to happen.

For example, there was a machine in the plant that was water-cooled. The water was discharged through a hole in the floor and it splashed everything; the floor was a hell of a mess. A week or two after that meeting, the operator of that machine came to me and wanted me to see his invention. He had rigged an awning over the machine from canvas and wire that he had bent himself. The awning channeled the water so that it dropped down neatly into a pan. He had solved the problem. For the first time, that fellow had begun to think about the efficient operation of the business.

Crawford held mass meetings of employees periodically during his tenure at the plant. He also relied heavily on a small staff of handpicked associates, including as manufacturing manager Matthew P. Graham, a college-trained engineer with more than a decade of experience in factory operations; Arch Colwell as sales engineer; and George Hufferd as "experimental engineer." Graham, moreover, brought with him a talented group of factory hands, including C. H. "Smoker" Ledinsky, George Herkimer, and John Seeholtzer.[30]

The willingness of these managers to listen to employees paid many dividends. One worker who "could barely speak English" contributed a design improvement to the plant's second-leading product, tie rods (devices to link the front wheels of a car so that they turn together) that yielded a savings of five cents per unit. On another occasion, employees helped cement strong relations with a key customer. One Friday afternoon, Crawford received a phone call from a purchasing manager at Packard, who

said it had a rush order to build some cars by Tuesday, and [asked] could we get them parts by Sunday night. I said, "Gosh, it's Friday. We're going home, but let me ask the gang." I called in the workers and told them the story. I said, "I think that if you fellows will give up your weekend and build these parts, Packard will be awful happy. They might be so happy that they'll give us a lot more business. You fellows can be our sales department."

You know what happened? Those people organized themselves to get the job done. The forgemen came in Friday night and worked all night. The machinists worked all day Saturday and Saturday night. Then the assemblers came in and worked through the night and all day Sunday. That night, we delivered our sets to Packard. After that, we never had any competition at Packard. They just sent us orders.[31]

The plant also set to work to develop new and improved products. In 1924, the growing popularity of four-wheel brakes with inclined kingpins caused Steel Products to engineer its first significant modification to the old Schweppe & Wilt design for steering rods. Vehicles using the new brake systems no longer had enough clearance to accommodate the old drag link. Accordingly, the Detroit plant developed the so-called Indian pipe or vertical socket to connect the drag link to the wheels. The company further improved the Indian pipe design in 1926, when it marketed the product as the Thompson Eccentric Tie Rod, which became a bestseller until the introduction of independent front suspensions in 1934.[32]

The result of these and many more efforts was the rejuvenation of the Detroit plant. In 1922, the plant had managed to achieve only $450,000 in revenues while posting a net loss of $300,000—a performance that Crawford thought "must be some kind of record." After the turnaround, although no subsequent profit figures survive, revenues skyrocketed, reaching $1.9 million in 1925 and $4.6 million three years later. The plant supplied drag links and tie rods to virtually all of the major automakers, including Hudson, Nash, Buick, and Ford.[33]

To Crawford, the postwar failure of the Detroit plant was "a failure of management," and its resurgence reflected what he calls "an experiment in human relations": common working people teaming up under inspirational leadership to achieve above-average performance. The story, moreover, "illustrates what happens when you stir men up, win their loyalty, make them understand what the problem is. They were fighting for their jobs. That's where I learned that job security is the biggest worry that the worker has."[34]

The Detroit plant's comeback heralded the growing significance of personnel management at Steel Products, as well as the mounting importance of quality and service as competitive weapons. The plant's turnaround also reflected the economic recovery of its customers and the emergence of new markets.

Roots of the Replacement Business

Between 1923 and 1929, Steel Products experienced another boom as sales soared from $3.3 million to $11.8 million, and profits from $85,339 to $1.2 million. Profitability was high, with returns on sales averaging over 10 percent and returns on assets over 30 percent. In 1926, the company resumed paying dividends, distributing, as had been its earlier custom, an average of about two-thirds of its net income to stockholders.

The recovery and vast expansion of the automobile industry was the principal reason for the company's good fortune. Automobile production soared from 1.9 million units in 1920 to 4.5 million in 1929. Another trend in the automotive market proved highly beneficial to Steel Products: between 1920 and 1929, passenger car registrations nearly tripled, from 8.1 million to 23.1 million—one car for every six people in the nation. (In 1928, Herbert Hoover, in accepting the Republican Party's nomination for president, proclaimed the famous objective to put "two cars in every garage.") These numbers reflect the growth in the sales of used cars, and to help maintain them, a vast market for repair parts and services opened up during the 1920s. The replacement market for poppet valves was particularly promising, although Steel Products initially had to take care lest it antagonize its principal customers, the automakers, who sought to channel replacement products through their own dealers.[35]

Steel Products began serving the replacement market surreptitiously through intermediary firms, with which it enjoyed close working relationships. In 1915, several of Thompson's friends and business associates had organized the first such partner, the Ford-Clark Company, which occupied a facility on Perkins Avenue near the old Metals Welding Company. Ford-Clark stated its business as manufacturing bolts and studs, but it was "not long" before it started making replacement valves for automobiles, apparently using Steel Products' expertise.[36]

In 1919, two more firms in the replacement market appeared in Steel Products' orbit, this time as sales and distribution organizations. Parts Service Company organized in Cleveland "for the purpose of dealing in automobile replacement valves and parts," most of which it purchased from Steel Products or Ford-Clark. Steel Products accountant Wesley M. "Weck" Albaugh kept the books for Parts Service. At the same time, Garage Service Company was established to serve the over-the-counter demand from dealers and independent garages in Cleveland. Garage Service also obtained its inventory from Steel Products or Ford-Clark.[37]

Parts Service evidently struggled, and in 1922, thirty shares of its stock were acquired by Steel Products in "settlement of accounts." (As one of the company's first historians noted, "In the early days of automobile parts merchandizing, it was more or less common practice to permit certain customers to liquidate their delinquent accounts by accepting stocks or bonds of that particular company in payment.") During the following year, Steel Products upped its stake in Parts Service. Finally, in December 1923, Steel Products took control, placing its own employees in several key management positions. At the same time, Steel Products also arranged the merger of Parts Service, Garage Service, and Ford-Clark, which by then was headed by Steel Products production manager John Kerwin. The new partners then consolidated operations in "space provided in buildings owned by the Steel Products Company on Clarkwood Avenue."[38]

The close relationship between Steel Products and its partners in the replacement business was gradually formalized and made public. In April 1924, Ford-Clark was renamed Thompson Products Incorporated, with Albaugh as president and C. E. Thompson's son Edwin as vice president. At the same time, Thompson Products became a charter member of the National Standard Parts Association. Steel Products continued to acquire the outstanding stock of Thompson Products, a program completed in May 1925.[39]

These actions caused considerable friction with vehicle makers, who wanted to control distribution of replacement parts on their own terms. Arch Colwell recalled visiting a customer whose engineering department wanted silcrome valves. When he was referred to a purchasing agent, however, he met a chilly reception. "This fellow threw a magazine [containing an advertisement from Parts Service Co.] across the table to me and said, 'What is this? . . . Anybody who sells our valves in service will not get orders from us.'" Lee Clegg, sales manager for the main plant, claimed that at least two principal automotive customers canceled business with Steel Products because of its subsidiary's activities in replacement markets.[40]

Steel Products persisted, nonetheless. As Clegg put it, "We felt that unless we established our own jobber outlets throughout the nation, it wouldn't be long before the 'gyp' manufacturers would come into the field and capture it, and then not only would we be denied the business, but the car manufacturer himself would also lose out to the so-called pirate parts people." Crawford recalled making exactly this argument to Ford:

> I went up there with some gyp parts made from plain, cheap steel by some other firm. They wouldn't stand up to normal use. I put them down on the desk of a Ford manager and said, "Now, *this* is what people are going to use if you don't let us supply the market you can't get." Then we showed the Ford people that they couldn't possibly get over half the replacement parts business through the dealers. They couldn't, because the dealer is more interested in selling new cars. Dealers don't take the interest in repairs that they do in selling new cars. We showed Ford that it would not get half of the replacement business and that if we weren't permitted to supply our parts, the gyps will. And those parts will fail, and Ford will lose its reputation for quality and reliability because of the way it was handled.[41]

Such reasoning ultimately carried the day, and Thompson Products embarked on an aggressive growth strategy in replacement parts. The subsidiary operated as an autonomous unit of Steel Products, and employees routinely referred to it as "the Jobbing Division" or "the Service Division." According to one of its early employees (and later general manager), Jim Syvertsen, "the trials and tribulations of launching the new venture were serious and numerous." Syvertsen and two other employees produced the first trade catalog, which consisted of a price list of Steel Products items manufactured in Cleveland or Detroit. The catalogs were mailed to car dealers and garages whose addresses were provided by the automotive marketing firm R. Polk. Thompson Products carved the United States into four sales territories, assigned veterans of Parts Service to each, and gave them the goal of signing up one hundred jobbers across the country.

Among the unit's "tribulations" were arrangements in Boston and Chicago granting local distributors exclusive rights over very large markets. The deals went sour almost immediately when the distributors proved incapable of serving their assigned territories. Within a year, three of the four sales reps had proved inadequate to the task, so Albaugh, Ed Thompson, and sales manager Burke Patterson went outside the company to hire new talent. The company gradually added more sales reps, supported by advertising and sales aids around the theme, "We at Thompson do not consider the sale completed until the parts are sold and removed from the jobbers' store." By mid-1925, Thompson surpassed its goal of obtaining a hundred jobbers and set its sights on five hundred.[42]

Enjoying the Fruits

The success of its silcrome valves, steering parts, and replacement business during the mid-1920s presaged further transformations of Steel Products. At their annual meeting in April 1926, the stockholders recommended changing the corporate name to Thompson Products, Inc. (hereafter referred to as TP). "The purpose back of this move," it was stated, "was to secure a larger amount of the growing automobile replacement business which was being handled by the recently acquired service and sales company which had operated under the name of Thompson Products Incorporated." The move also recognized the value of C. E. Thompson's name in the trade, the company's health and expansion under his leadership, and the size of his ego.[43]

The appointment of new officers and the election of additional board members accompanied the change of identity. The new officers included Ed Thompson, vice president of the Service Division; Doc Miller, vice president and general manager of the main (Cleveland) plant; Fred Crawford, vice president and general manager of the Michigan plant; and Weck Albaugh, who replaced Pete Krider as corporate secretary. All four men became eligible for bonuses based on the contributions of their operations to the total net profits of the company. Finally, all four were elected to the board of directors.[44]

By the middle of 1926, business had picked up sufficiently that the stockholders voted to distribute to owners a special dividend of one-quarter share of common stock for each share held. The following spring, stockholders approved a much more significant change in the company's capital structure. In recognition of TP's great expansion and growing positions in new markets, the owners approved a twelvefold increase in common stock capitalization, from $2.5 million to $30 million. Stockholders received a ten-for-one stock dividend, with the remaining shares held as treasury stock. This transaction made multimillionaires out of the owners, including Crawford, who had earlier borrowed money to acquire substantial blocks of Steel Products stock.[45]

C. E. Thompson remained president, but he was beginning to manifest the erratic behavior and questionable judgment that would characterize the remainder of his life. At age fifty-six in 1927, Thompson "was tending to spend less and less time on company business," Crawford recalled. "He'd come in late. I had great trouble getting him to call on the customers. By then, he was mixed up in all kinds of things and really didn't concentrate too hard on the business."[46]

Thompson's new business activities included establishing two new companies. The first, C. E. Thompson, Inc., was a Delaware corporation that served as kind of a trust or personal holding company to control all of his and his family's business interests. The second, Thompson Research, Inc., was founded to conduct "engineering and research on methods, processes, and devices of mechanical, chemical, and electrical nature for the automobile industry and internal combustion engines." This entity consisted of TP's small research department, and it came as a surprise to Crawford and other managers that it was formed as a separate corporation. It started out with a focus on alloys, hoping to reproduce the success of the silcrome valve. Lightning did not strike twice, however, and the research company quickly settled into its familiar role of providing applications engineering services to TP. Thompson Research, Inc., was liquidated in 1934.[47]

Thompson's conduct outside business was a source of greater concern to his partners and colleagues. A well-known womanizer, he contracted syphilis, which left him chronically debilitated during the remainder of his life. In 1927, for example, he spent several months at Johns Hopkins University Hospital in Baltimore for treatment. To the extent possible, Thompson was also enjoying his riches. In 1924, he and Krider had paid "a somewhat extended visit to France and Switzerland." The trip was justified when the two men reported that they had "acquired the right to a new valve gathering process" in France, where they were hosted by Pierre Gillet, the former purchasing agent for the French government, whom they had met during World War I. This trip was the first of many lengthy visits to Europe, especially to Paris and the south of France, where Thompson enjoyed gambling in the casinos of the Riviera.[48]

"Charlie was an admirable person in many ways," said Crawford, "but he was also a great spender. As the company became more successful, he was mainly concerned with getting dividends. In fact, his main motivation—and Bartlett's and Krider's—in running the company was to take money out of it."[49] Although Steel Products paid no dividends on common stock between 1921 and 1925, it more than made up for the money forgone by resuming payouts as high as 78 percent of net income during the next several years.

By 1928, Thompson's personal fortune was estimated at about $7 million. His appetite for cash grew exponentially after his third marriage in November 1927 to Gloria Hopkins, a colorful character whose checkered past included several previous marriages and, reportedly, a stint as a call girl. (At the time of this ceremony, Thompson was not divorced from his second wife, Polly, who had left him in 1923. Crawford, who stood up with Thompson at his marriage to Gloria, thus became "best man at a bigamist's wedding." When Gloria discovered the second marriage, she forced Thompson to arrange a divorce from Polly. During the course of these proceedings, Polly died, and Thompson and Gloria were wed a second time on April 15, 1929.)[50]

With his new wife at his side, Thompson consumed on a grand scale, acquiring new real estate, automobiles, furnishings, clothes, and jewelry, and spending freely on travel and entertainment. He purchased a second home in Cleveland (a fashionable penthouse apartment on Cedar Hill) and a townhouse on 64th Street near Fifth Avenue in New York City. Ostensibly to facilitate moving back and forth between these properties, he had the company buy him a $25,000 Duesenberg automobile (at a time when a Cadillac sold for less than $2,000), which he rarely used. His most extravagant investment, however, was a chateau at Cap Ferrat on the Riviera. Each of his homes was lavishly furnished, but his American properties paled in comparison to "Chateau Gloria," which featured a $10,000 oriental rug, an entire library of leather-bound books purchased from Brentano's, and gold fixtures in the bathrooms. Sparing no expense, Thompson even ordered a sunken swimming pool built off his second-floor bathroom, so that he could plunge in with a minimum of preparation or effort.[51]

Thompson fed his hunger for cash by collecting a high salary and generous dividends or simply by appropriating expense-account money from his company—a practice that the board of directors discouraged but did not stop until the depth of the Great Depression. He also financed purchases by borrowing heavily from Union Trust, a Cleveland bank, against the value of his stock.

CONSTRAINED CHOICES

By the mid-1920s, indulging its president's passions entailed significant costs to TP. The environment in which it now competed had changed dramatically from the days in which Thompson and his partners first came to prominence. The company's products and manufacturing processes were much more sophisticated. So, too, were the needs and expectations of its principal customers, the automobile manufacturers.

During the 1920s, the American automobile industry settled into an oligopolistic structure and developed patterns of competition that endured for decades. The industry's rapid growth after the post–World War I recession benefited the biggest producers at the expense of their smaller rivals. The demands of large-scale manufacturing, frequent model changes, nationwide advertising and distribution, and installment financing were simply too great for small automakers to bear. By the end of the decade, the three largest producers—General Motors, Ford, and Chrysler—accounted for nearly 90 percent of all new-car sales.

The automobile industry's growth and maturity helped create a growing and mature supplier industry. Between 1914 and 1925, the number of companies producing "motor vehicle bodies and parts" in the United States rose from 971 to 1,358; the wholesale value of their products increased from about $130 million to more than $1.5 billion; and employment soared from just under 50,000 to more than 225,000. Many standards and standard practices characterized the supplier industry. The Motor and Accessory Manufacturers Association (MAMA) supplied members with credit and trade information, as well as lobbying support. The Society of Automotive Engineers (SAE) became a vigorous champion of technical standardization throughout the industry, dealing with such matters as the dimensions of parts and accessories, specifications for purchasing materials, and engineering practices. SAE standards applied to basic matters such as the design of screw threads, the composition of metal alloys, and the dimensions of specific products such as poppet valves, rod and yoke ends, steering-wheel hubs, and throttle ball joints.[52]

The consolidation of the automobile industry and the development of product standards helped to formalize the relationship between the automakers and their suppliers. As one supplier put it, the automakers got "better deliveries, higher quality; ability to buy out of stock for rush orders; less danger of accumulating year by year dead stock due to . . . ordering special sizes and making changes; [and] . . . possibly better prices." Suppliers also benefited from the reduction in the number and variety of parts, which lowered tooling and setup costs, enabled longer production runs, and reduced dependence on specific customers.[53]

The relationship between automakers and suppliers also became more bureaucratized. Crawford noticed the change during his period as a sales engineer during the early 1920s. In the industry's early days, he recalled, "most of the big deals were forged at the bar of the Pontchartrain Hotel in Detroit," a watering hole for purchasing agents and suppliers. As a teetotaler, Crawford felt at a severe disadvantage. The crisis of the early 1920s brought an end to "friendship buying," however, and the automakers became much more receptive to formal terms on price, quality, and on-time delivery.[54]

Not all trends favored independent suppliers, however. For example, the automakers insisted on having at least two sources for key components. They also found various ways to limit suppliers' bargaining power, including pressuring them to license innovations to at least one strong competitor. The ultimate threat was backward integration. During the early 1920s, General Motors acquired many parts makers, and Ford sought to manufacture as much of the content of its cars as possible, including basic materials such as steel, glass, and wood. Between 1922 and 1926, the proportion of purchased parts in U.S.-produced automobiles dropped from 55 to 22 percent.[55]

TP was well aware of its dependence on a few key customers, and company leaders repeated a quotation attributed to C. E. Thompson: "We must make our parts so good and at such low cost that the car manufacturers won't want to make their own." Nonetheless, the major automakers manufactured at least some of the products that TP made. Several GM divisions produced valves, for example. Ford made all of its own exhaust valves, and Chrysler operated a valve plant to supply some of its needs. In steering products, several GM car divisions and Chrysler made tie rods.[56]

Given the investments necessary to remain competitive in its major product lines, TP suffered by adhering to its policy of paying out large dividends. The tension between allocating funds for growth and making cash payments to stockholders was evident throughout the late 1920s, when the company encountered more opportunities than it could fund. Both the main plant and the Michigan plant, for example, required significant investments to serve booming markets in automobiles and aircraft. These investments entailed acquiring additional property, erecting new buildings, and installing new equipment at both locations.[57]

The company's policy of paying generous dividends also constrained opportunities to diversify. During the fall of 1927, for example, C. E. Thompson approached the board with a proposal for "developing manufacturing capacity" for valves in Europe, preferably in his beloved France. Thompson believed that although the company "could to a limited extent compete with European manufacturers in the production of the highest grade articles, it could not expect to compete in quantity manner without actually manufacturing on the Continent." The board authorized Ed Thompson, who was about to visit his father in France, to investigate acquiring control of a company there, but to spend no more than $50,000 in the effort.[58]

The following spring, C. E. Thompson cabled the board that a $50,000 investment would gain controlling interest in a company that Pierre Gillet had found: S.A. des Établissements Mécaniques Monopole, "the largest maker of high grade engine valves, pistons, and piston rings in France." Headquartered in Poissy, near Paris, the Monopole company had earlier licensed TP's process for forging silcrome valves, and it supplied original equipment makers in France, as well as replacement markets in southern Europe and northern Africa. When it came to approving the investment, however, the TP board rejected the request, citing two reasons. First, members pointed out that the Monopole factory "was not equipped for quantity production, being operated substantially as a jobbing factory," and hence could not supply vehicle makers without additional investment. And second, the board preferred to allocate its scarce investment capital elsewhere. C. E. Thompson proceeded to make the investment anyway, using his own money and apparently harboring the hope that TP would eventually buy him out.[59]

Ed Thompson encountered a similar reaction from the board when he sought funds for another venture. In July 1927, using $15,000 put up by TP, he had established Thompson Aeronautical Corporation (TAC), a concern organized around the broad intent to "manufacture, sell, and operate aeronautical machines, parts, and accessories." TP had justified this initial investment "in view of the advertising and publicity benefits, especially due to the fact that [it] was a large producer of valves for aeronautical motors." TAC began operations by acquiring several airplanes, leasing space at Cleveland airport, and ferrying passengers between Cleveland and Detroit. Later in 1927, TAC borrowed $20,000 from TP to acquire more aircraft. TAC then bid successfully on airmail contracts for service between Cleveland, Chicago, Detroit, and several small cities in Michigan.

In May 1928, at the same TP board meeting that rejected the Monopole investment, Ed Thompson asked to borrow another $70,000 to help fund additional expansion for TAC. The board not only refused the loan, but also voted to sell its stake in TAC, citing potential liability issues and pleading insufficient capital to support its own projects.[60]

The principal drain on investment capital was the continuing rapid growth of the Service Division. In 1927, acting on the "realization that you can't render service at long distance," the division opened its first branch warehouses in Newark, Chicago, Kansas City, and San Francisco. It also established an export division to market replacement products abroad. During the next four years, additional branches were opened or acquired in Atlanta, Dallas, St. Louis, Minneapolis, Boston, Seattle, and Los Angeles. These facilities sold not only parts manufactured by TP, but also items such as bushings, shackles, and valve guides purchased from other producers.[61]

In 1929, the company further augmented the Service Division by acquiring Cleveland Piston Manufacturing Company and its "subsidiary," Cox Tool Company, for a total of $350,000. To finance the transaction, as well as additional expansion of the Michigan and main plants, TP authorized the sale of 15,000 shares of treasury stock at $55 per share.[62]

The same energetic entrepreneur, John R. Cox, had started both companies. A high school dropout with "a penchant for fooling with machinery," Cox had acquired what training he possessed as a mechanic at an apprentice school run by Warner & Swasey. He worked his way up through a series of manufacturing jobs in Ohio and Indiana before founding (in Cleveland) his own business in 1922 to make cast-iron pistons for the replacement market. He started out by dividing his time in an unusual manner: he dedicated one week to fabricating pistons and the next week to selling them. After repeating this cycle for several months, he was ready to pursue more conventional business practices. He hired a friend as vice president, opened a factory on Scranton Road, and transacted business under the name Cleveland Piston Manufacturing. Several years later, Cox added to his product line cast-aluminum pistons, which he bought from another firm. He also established a second factory to make piston pins. This operation, located on Detroit Avenue, was called Cox Tool Company. By 1928, combined revenues from Cox's businesses surpassed $1 million.[63]

When Cox declared his intention to sell, TP's Service Division was eager to deal. After the acquisition, Cox stayed on to run the plants. He was "an excellent mechanic" with "a lot of gumption," said Crawford, who also remembered Cox as "feisty, a rough guy . . . and not easy to get along with." His plants, Crawford added, were "not very good at making pistons, but the pistons were all right for the replacement trade and at lower levels. It was better for us to buy a piston shop and build on it than to cut new cloth. We bought him out simply to have a head start and have on board some people experienced in the business."[64]

MANUFACTURING TRIUMPHS AND MARKETING COUPS

TP also poured much of its limited investment capital into expanding capacity to make valves for aircraft engines. After its success with silcrome valves during the early 1920s, the company continued to seek customers among aircraft engine builders. Several factors rendered the business attractive. First, it was growing rapidly. Between 1925 and 1929, aircraft production accelerated from less than one thousand to more than six thousand units per year. Many of these aircraft, moreover, carried more than one engine. Most engines featured at least nine cylinders, and some were designed to operate with four valves per cylinder.[65]

Second, the competition, though brisk, was also familiar. TP's major rival was Rich Steel Products, whose chief engineer, Robert Jardine, was highly regarded by engine designers. Nonetheless, TP enjoyed a superior reputation as a manufacturer, which stood the company in good stead against Rich Steel Products. Finally, unlike the situation in the automotive businesses, TP faced little backward integration by aircraft engine builders. Designs and technical requirements were changing too fast. The new engines were no longer simple adaptations of automobile engines, but rather were designed specifically for use in aircraft. Such characteristics as weight, shape, power, and reliability were far more critical for aircraft than for automobiles. Although some automakers such as Ford and GM continued to make aircraft engines, pioneering advances came from companies that focused on the product, such as Wright Aeronautical and, after 1925, Pratt & Whitney (now a unit of United Technologies).

The development of air-cooled engines for aircraft further escalated technical requirements for valves. For the new aircraft of the 1920s, water-cooled engines were problematical because of the extra weight of radiators, pumps, hoses, and other necessary apparatus. In addition, some military customers, including the U.S. Navy, were concerned about difficulties in operating water-cooled aircraft in cold-weather climates.

Work on air-cooled engines had begun during World War I, but progress was impeded by a familiar problem: exhaust valves that overheated, cracked, and warped.

The high temperatures and compression of air-cooled engines meant that even the most advanced alloys were inadequate for exhaust valves. The engineer most familiar with this problem was an Englishman, Sam D. Heron of the Royal Aircraft Factory. A prickly character—contemporaries described him as "forthright to the point of bluntness" and "a sour puss"—Heron once observed that the British Jupiter aircraft motor, the most popular air-cooled engine of the war, should have had its efficiency rated "in terms of pounds of exhaust valves, rather than in pounds of fuel, per horsepower-hour!"[66]

At the end of the war, the problem of how to keep valves in air-cooled engines from overheating remained unsolved. Heron and his colleagues tried filling hollow-stemmed valves with several liquids, including mercury and water, to no avail. In the United States, renowned researchers Charles F. Kettering and Thomas R. Midgely of Dayton Electric Company (later GM's Delco Division) spent months on the problem, but fared no better. The solution came to Heron in 1922, when he was working as a civilian engineer with the U.S. Army Air Corps at McCook Field, near Dayton.

Heron was searching for a suitable liquid coolant when one day he suddenly focused his attention on a pot containing a solution of chemicals used for heat treatment. The solution had wet the pot so thoroughly that liquid crept up over its side. In this mundane observation, Heron saw an answer to the problem of cooling valves. He then tried the solution—a mixture of potassium and sodium nitrates—in a hollow-stemmed exhaust valve. The results were evidently unimpressive. At that point, he recalled reading about use of the salts in their liquid metallic state in thermometers. When he filled a valve with the metallic salts, he found the result he had hoped for. Under high operating temperatures, the salts liquefied, sloshing up and down the inside of the valve "like a cocktail shaker" to draw heat away from the head. Commenting on an experiment that had caused many earlier valves to fail, Heron observed that this "salt-cooled" valve not only survived but in operation ran "black"—as opposed to red hot.[67]

In 1922, Heron applied for patents on both the salts and the metals as coolants. In subsequent work, he found that the valves ran at even lower temperatures when he filled them with a mixture of lithium nitrate and potassium nitrate. Finally, in 1925, a friend pointed out that sodium or a sodium alloy would thoroughly wet a surface without the use of a salt, and when he tried liquid metallic sodium in the valves, he indeed achieved the best results.[68]

Development of the salt-cooled, and then of the sodium-cooled, exhaust valves represented complex technological achievements. Manufacturing these valves in volume, reliably, was also a demanding challenge. Heron credited Jardine and Rich Steel Products with the early lead in commercializing the valves, but TP also licensed Heron's patents and plunged into development. It made its first salt-cooled valves from silcrome and simply drilled the stems to create the cavity for the salts. In subsequent designs, it used a chromium-nickel-silicon steel alloy known as CNS, which possessed higher heat-strength and resulted in stronger stems, but which also required a specially hardened tip of cobalt-chromium steel to be welded to the stem.

The manufacturing process for hollow-stemmed valves was itself extremely complex. In 1930, a trade journalist visited TP's main plant and described more than forty separate operations between handling and inspection of bar steel and final packing of finished valves. Most of these steps involved automatic or semiautomatic equipment, with inspectors stationed "at all machines to check all dimensions at all times." The valve heads were machined or ground four separate times and the stems, six. "From this lengthy series of operations," concluded the journalist, "it is seen that utmost care is taken in production of airplane valves, but these valves are necessarily a quality product and must be unceasingly inspected."[69]

Loading the salts or sodium into the valves also required particular care. The salt mixture was toxic, while metallic sodium was volatile and prone to spontaneous combustion, and it could even explode under some conditions. Automatic equipment injected the filling into the stem, which was promptly sealed by a steel plug. The operation to weld the hardened tip provided additional protection from leakage.[70]

Although Rich Steel Products sprinted to an early lead in developing advanced valves, TP quickly established a stronger position in the marketplace. Three reasons accounted for its success: First, in Lee Clegg the company employed a resourceful and well-connected technical sales representative. Second, TP was aggressive in promoting the technical features of its products. And third, once it developed an advantage, the company exploited it vigorously.

Clegg possessed all the requisite skills of an effective technical sales rep. A graduate of the Case School of Applied Science, he spoke easily to engineers. He was also a believer in "plain damned hard work." Contemporaries described him as "genial, capable, quick, frank, obdurate, kindly, forceful, energetic, fearless, and sincere." Others noted that "he speaks well" but "chooses [words] with the care of an engineer working on blueprints." Although "carefully groomed on all occasions," Clegg was also an avid sportsman, adept at fishing, golf, and bridge, and a good traveling companion. "It is a legend in the company," observed the author of a flattering profile, "that some of [the company's] most important contracts and best customer relations have been negotiated by him before a sizzling log fire in his Canadian lodge at Gatineau, P.Q."[71]

During the early 1920s, after replacing Crawford as the company's traveling sales rep, Clegg became friends with Donald Brown, a purchasing agent for Wright Aeronautical. Later, when Wright was seeking to place an order for five hundred salt-filled valves, Clegg and Brown worked together to persuade Wright management to use TP valves. In 1925, the relationship between the two men yielded further benefits when Brown left Wright Aeronautical to become one of the founders and first president of Pratt & Whitney. Pratt & Whitney's "Wasp" engine, noted a contemporary expert, was "the first large radial air-cooled engine of what may be called 'modern' design." The expert also praised the Wasp, which used Thompson valves, for setting "a high standard for future radial-engine development."[72]

The second factor in TP's success—nerve—was displayed during the following year, when Charles A. Lindbergh, Ryan Aircraft, and Wright Aeronautical prepared for the first successful transatlantic flight. Wright had sixty days to build the engine for the *Spirit of St. Louis,* a modified J-5 Whirlwind. At the time, Wright often used Rich Steel Products as its valve supplier, in part because TP was closely affiliated with Pratt & Whitney. During preparations for Lindbergh's flight, however, Wright engineers voiced skepticism about the J-5's ability to run continuously for as long as forty hours using its conventional salt-cooled valves. At the last minute, recalls Crawford, Thompson sales engineers intervened and offered to provide experimental sodium-cooled valves for the flight. The Wright engineers discussed the offer with Lindbergh, then decided to accept it. As a result, eighteen Thompson valves accompanied Lindbergh on his historic flight.[73]

Many years later, Fred Witt, the long-time advertising manager at TP, obtained a copy of the original blueprint for the exhaust valve for Lindbergh's engine. Scribbled on the document was the notation: "Purchase from Wilcox-Rich or Thompson Products, Inc."

"By golly, we were lucky," reflected Witt. He had taken "a special nostalgic interest" in the flight, and he recalled "quite well the Saturday afternoon [May 20, 1927] when Lindbergh was somewhere over the Atlantic, on his way." Witt was at his desk writing an advertisement announcing that TP valves were in the *Spirit of St. Louis*. "Boy," he exclaimed, "was I praying for a lot of reasons he'd make it!" That spring, by coincidence, C. E. Thompson was in Paris on an extended visit. On May 21, he joined the excited throng that greeted Lindbergh at Le Bourget airport.[74]

Lindbergh's achievement provided an obvious boost to TP, lending credibility to its self-promotion as a technological leader. Curiously, however, the company gained little publicity from the episode. For one thing, Wilcox-Rich clouded matters by making the technically accurate but misleading boast in its promotional literature that its valves were "used in the Wright J-5 engine which powered the historic 'Spirit of St. Louis.'" For another, TP was learning the distinction between advertising, which it did passably, and public relations, which it knew little about. In August 1929, Clegg addressed the issue by hiring Raymond S. Livingstone as the company's first publicity manager. A former newspaperman, a pilot, and another genial, people-oriented person, Livingstone made his mark at TP almost immediately.[75]

In 1929, several aviation-minded executives in Cleveland had persuaded the National Aeronautic Association (NAA) to bring the National Air Races to the city's new municipal airport. At that point, the NAA was just three years old and still unsure of how best to promote aviation. It had sponsored previous races in cities around the country but had not attracted the attention it had hoped to receive. The Cleveland backers proposed an exciting new approach. To organize and publicize the races, they hired flamboyant show promoter Clifford Henderson, who planned an extravaganza for the 1929 races. Local politicians and business leaders rallied behind the cause, offering a package of facilities, events, and prizes that the NAA found irresistible. More than 100,000 people—a total far exceeding previous attendance records—appeared at the 1929 races, which were held over eleven days in late August and early September.[76]

A week or so before the competition was set to begin, a volunteer worker from the races visited Clegg to ask whether TP would provide an inexpensive trophy for the winner of one of the events. At the time, seven of the sixty races on the schedule lacked a sponsor. Clegg called in Livingstone, who had been on the job only a few days, and the two men proceeded to scan the list of unassigned races, which had been "pretty well picked over." As Livingstone later recounted, "suddenly [our] eyes popped," for, from their perspective, the most appealing race of the entire competition was unclaimed: the International Land Plane Free-for-All. The race, which consisted of ten laps around pylons on a five-mile closed course, was open to "any type plane, powered with any type engine or engines," with "superchargers and special fuels permitted." Both military and civilian aircraft were eligible. TP quickly agreed to sponsor that race, and Livingstone purchased from a downtown merchant a large, silver plated loving cup for $25, plus $10 for engraving—the original Thompson "trophy."[77]

The first Thompson-sponsored race caused a sensation. Flying a commercial sport monoplane powered by a Curtiss-Wright (successor to Wright Aeronautical) Whirlwind engine, Doug Davis cruised to an easy win, averaging 191.1 mph. His victory proved significant for several reasons. First, the race was the media event of the entire eleven days. Not only was it intrinsically exciting—spectators could actually follow much of the action—but Davis was also the only winner to receive a prize on the spot. Immediately after the race, Livingstone thrust the loving cup into Davis' hands and arranged for a local photographer to snap a picture that became front-page newspaper material around the country. Second, because Davis easily defeated the fastest military aircraft, which were traditional biplanes, the race drew much comment from politicians and editorial writers who were alarmed about the state of military preparedness.[78]

The publicity generated by Davis's victory proved a bonanza for TP, and the company pressed its advantage home. Soon after the race, Livingstone proposed to Clegg and Crawford that the company establish a permanent Thompson Trophy, which would go to the winner of the free-for-all, closed-course speed race each year. The executives agreed and successfully negotiated terms with the NAA. Before the 1930 race, Crawford and Livingstone arranged a national competition among sculptors to design the trophy, which Crawford believed should represent something more than "another naked lady waving a flag." Judges in the competition included Orville Wright. Winner of the design competition was Walter A. Sinz of Cleveland, who produced a thirty-inch-tall bronze sculpture of Icarus reaching for the sun—a peculiar theme in view of Icarus's fate.[79]

The National Air Races paid handsome dividends to TP after 1929, generating publicity far out of proportion to the company's investment or its position in the aircraft industry. "It was amazing the amount of publicity that was generated," Crawford confirmed; "the race put us on the map." The race also became an important occasion for entertaining customers and for meeting with other significant figures in politics and industry. Finally, the race bestowed prestige on TP. "It got us tangible good will for the company, our products, and our sales people. We squeezed a hell of a lot of mileage out of the Thompson Trophy Race."[80]

By the early 1930s, TP's combination of skilled manufacturing, aggressive selling, and periodic promotions had helped the company develop a commanding lead in the market for aircraft engine valves. According to one estimate, TP produced 95 percent of all airplane valves used in 1933.[81]

INTO THE ABYSS

The first National Air Races in Cleveland kicked off an unusually hectic fall for TP in 1929. In September, the board of directors authorized several moves aimed at expanding the business. Crawford negotiated with Dunning Manufacturing Company, which possessed the American rights to a new type of shock absorber invented in Germany, for an exclusive license to make these products at the Michigan plant. At the same time, the board voted to purchase a nine-acre parcel of land in St. Catharines, Ontario, for the location of a new plant to serve automakers in Canada. To administer the new operation, the company formed a wholly owned subsidiary, Thompson Products, Ltd. The board also approved another international expansion, at last agreeing to acquire C. E. Thompson's personal stake in the Monopole company, the French valve maker. In a significant step, the board approved plans to amend the corporate bylaws to permit the company's stock to be listed on the New York Stock Exchange.[82]

That fall, Thompson also raised two other important issues with the board. First, he announced that he was engaged in negotiations with the Eaton Axle and Spring Company of Cleveland about a possible merger. In late September, he reported that "the matter was being considered with an open mind by both sides." In talking merger, Thompson was in tune with the times. The late 1920s witnessed the biggest flurry of merger activity in U.S. history between the turn of the century and the conglomerate movement of the 1960s. Conditions were ripe for combining companies: the breakdown of geographically distinct markets, excess capacity, and heavy demand for industrial securities. In the automobile supply industry, for example, Borg-Warner, Bendix Aviation, and Eaton were active acquirers during the late 1920s.[83]

A merger between TP and Eaton had obvious appeal. Headquartered down the street from the Thompson main plant, Eaton had become a leading independent producer of springs, bumpers, axles, and other automobile parts, and it was eager to diversify into engine components. The deal must also have seemed attractive from Thompson's perspective. The merged entity would have become a formidable competitor, especially in under-the-car parts, and C. E. Thompson would have become a significantly wealthier man. Talks between the companies soon broke off, however. Thompson declared himself dissatisfied with the valuation of Eaton's shares. He also stated that no agreement could be reached "with respect to the official personnel of the proposed new company"—a clue that both parties probably insisted on providing the chief executive.[84]

A few months later, Eaton satisfied its wish to combine its steering and axle business with an engine components company by acquiring Wilcox-Rich, thereby becoming TP's most significant competitor in valves. For its part, TP continued to weigh other merger opportunities, including the acquisition of Columbus Auto Parts, a maker of steering and suspension parts, and a blockbuster combination with Midland Steel Products and Motor Products of Detroit. None of these deals was consummated before their potential dissolved amid uncertain economic times.[85]

The collapse of the Eaton deal perhaps explains the timing of the second significant issue Thompson raised with the board in the fall of 1929: he sought the appointment of a new general manager of the company. Although he was just fifty-eight, Thompson was in no condition physically or emotionally to run the company. Perhaps he gave consideration to Doc Miller and to his own son, Ed, but the obvious choice was Crawford. Only thirty-eight years old, Crawford had proved himself as an operating manager through the remarkable resurgence of the Michigan plant. Indeed, after obtaining a big order to make forged steering parts for the Ford Model A, the Michigan plant contributed more to sales and earnings in 1929 than the main plant. By then, too, Crawford had become the company's largest stockholder after Thompson, Bartlett, and Krider.[86]

In late October or early November 1929, Thompson summoned Crawford for a chat. During the conversation, Thompson excused himself for a moment, then returned bearing the inkwell Crawford had admired at his interview thirteen years earlier. Thompson handed over the inkwell, saying "you're in charge now." A few days later, the board elected Crawford as first vice president and general manager of the company. Thompson retained the title of president, but subsequently he appeared in the office even less frequently. Krider also edged closer to retirement by relinquishing the office of treasurer to Weck Albaugh.[87]

At the moment of these transitions, the economy was already displaying very troubling signs, including falling industrial output, increasing unemployment, and rising interest rates. The worst sign of all was the stock-market crash of October 29, which wiped out in one day the entire gains of the previous year. The value of TP's stock plunged from the year's high of nearly $70 to $18. Although at year end the company reported record earnings of $1.2 million on record sales of $11.8 million (paying out nearly half of its net income in dividends), this performance represented a high water mark that would not be matched again for nearly a decade (see Exhibits I-1 and I-2 in the introduction to Part I).

Although few people then recognized its long-term significance and consequences, the stock-market crash triggered more than a decade of economic turmoil. At its low point in 1931–1932, the Great Depression brought a 30 percent drop in U.S. gross national product, a 32 percent plunge in wholesale prices, roughly nine thousand bank failures, and a national unemployment level of 25 percent. Most of the markets that TP served were severely distressed. In 1929, more than 5.3 million cars, trucks, tractors, and buses had poured out of American factories; three years later, total output of motor vehicles reached a low of 1.3 million—a decline of 75 percent. Over the same time, aircraft production plummeted from 6,193 units to 1,396—a drop of 77 percent.[88]

TP suffered terribly during these years. By 1932, sales hit a low of $3.7 million— a drop of 70 percent from its peak three years before. The price of the company's common stock hit bottom in 1932, when it traded for $2.75. TP recorded a slender profit of just over $100,000 in 1930 before delivering two years of losses. Only the relatively strong performance of the Service Division kept matters from being even worse. The replacement market did not, as Thompson and Crawford had hoped, prove countercyclical to the original equipment market, except that when the latter "went all to pieces" replacement sales fell off somewhat less dramatically.[89]

Service Division sales dipped by about 20 percent during the depression, nonetheless accounting for slightly more than half of TP's total revenues in 1932 and 1933. The arrival of a new sales manager and a small acquisition kept the situation from growing worse. The new manager, Tom Duggan, joined TP in 1931 from an executive position in the National Standard Parts Association, where he had impressed Crawford with his "great knowledge of the jobber's and independent garage man's problems," as well as his "good experience, a convincing manner, and much enthusiasm." The acquisition, which occurred early in 1933, consisted of a small distressed business, Cleveland Packless Pump Co., which brought the capability to produce water pumps, a promising product for the replacement market. By then, the Service Division channeled replacement parts through a dozen warehouses and 650 dealers in the United States and Canada and through another 150 dealers elsewhere around the globe.[90]

TP's principal problem was the steep decline of sales to the automakers. The company took strong actions to deal with the crisis, including slashing employment levels and overhead. Selling and general and administrative expenses plunged by more than 80 percent between 1929 and 1933. The new Canadian plant, which had been scheduled to open in 1930, did not start production until two years later, when changes in tariff policy justified a modest start-up. Even then, the plant operated with used equipment from Cleveland, including "an array of machine tools all showing signs of wear." TP continued to pay high dividends from accumulated reserves through 1931. Thereafter, in actions that must have been especially painful to C. E. Thompson, the board eliminated dividends on both common and preferred stock. The board also entertained several merger proposals, including deals that would have combined TP with bigger and healthier companies, such as Electric Auto-Lite, Midland Steel Products, and Motor Products of Detroit. Although none of these possibilities came to pass, TP's leaders were ready to consider almost any alternative.[91]

Despite its desperate circumstances, TP managed to invest funds to protect key markets or develop new ones. In 1932, for example, GM announced the closing of its Muncie products division, a unit that had supplied between 30 and 45 percent of GM's total valve consumption. When Crawford learned that GM intended to move equipment from Muncie to a Buick facility in Flint, Michigan, where it would be combined with an existing operation and new equipment, he was alarmed. If such a plan were carried out, he believed, then it would be "only a matter of time" before GM could supply virtually all of its own valve requirements. To forestall this possibility, Crawford arranged for TP to purchase the Muncie equipment and inventory for roughly $150,000.

Because it was strapped for cash, however, the company financed the purchase creatively. TP borrowed the purchase price from GM, promising to repay it by returning 10 percent of the value of each order GM placed with TP for valves until the balance was paid off. As a result, the company acquired the equipment without any outlay of cash and also provided additional incentives for GM to buy Thompson valves. Second, acquiring the Muncie assets enabled TP to send surplus equipment from Cleveland to its new Canadian plant, thereby reducing the start-up costs of that operation.[92]

To help offset the declining performance of its established lines, TP launched a search for new product opportunities. Although the company pushed hard to find customers for its shock absorbers, these devices were not competitive with alternatives already in the market. TP's effort to sell shock absorbers was abandoned by 1931.[93] Much more significant business resulted from the company's research and development efforts, which were spared the deep cuts that affected most operations. When Crawford became general manager, the company's chief engineer, Dick Bissell, had recently met an untimely death in the Cleveland Clinic disaster—a fire that claimed 123 lives. To replace him, Crawford brought Arch Colwell from Detroit. This appointment proved to be very important because it gave TP a technical leader to rival Wilcox-Rich's Robert Jardine. A hard-working, careful engineer, Colwell was also something of a Renaissance man. He taught himself to play the classical guitar and to play golf, a sport in which he excelled. He also became an accomplished sales rep on behalf of the company, knowledgeable about technical matters and adept at expressing himself in plain language. A prolific writer, he published many papers in technical journals and in publications of the Society of Automotive Engineers.[94]

Despite the company's financial straits, Colwell insisted on spending to acquire cost-saving and labor-saving equipment. For example, in 1931, TP purchased photo-electric equipment, which engineers attached to several machines used in making valves. The new equipment precisely determined critical temperatures for performing certain operations such as gathering the valve heads and hardening the tips of stems to resist wear. When coupled with automatic or pneumatic controls, the photoelectric equipment resulted in significant savings of time in the work flow, reduction in scrap, and increases in productivity.[95]

Colwell also launched efforts to develop new products, particularly those "necessitating special metallurgical, engineering, and production skill, or unique patented designs." Colwell and metallurgist Harry Bubb, for example, worked closely with Ludlum Steel to review more than a thousand valve steels, one of which, an improved silcrome alloy designated XB, became the standard material for high-performance automotive engine valves during the following decade. Colwell also focused research and development on ancillary products such as valve seat inserts and valve retainer locks. These "valve train parts" and others added subsequently met the company's criteria for new products: they generally featured patent-protected designs and required a high level of engineering and manufacturing skill to produce in volume. They also represented a product line related to valves and helped increase the content of TP parts inside engines built by its customers. Best of all, the parts were extremely profitable, both in sales to engine builders and to the replacement market.[96]

Not all of Colwell's efforts yielded success. For example, he led a crash program to develop copper-cooled valves for high-performance and heavy-duty engines, hoping to achieve some of the temperature resistance of a sodium-cooled valve at a fraction of the cost. Many automotive engineers had worked on techniques to fill valves with copper or aluminum to conduct heat away from the head. Most approaches involved drilling out the valve and inserting a rod of copper or aluminum, but air pockets formed between the metals and greatly impeded thermal conductivity. A team led by Colwell developed a technique of forging copper symmetrically inside the valve stem, resulting in "a perfect bond" between the two metals and valves twenty times more efficient in transmitting heat than solid silcrome. The copper-cooled valve was introduced to the trade with fanfare in August 1931. By the following January, however, the bond proved less than perfect, and the company was forced to recall the valves because of a tendency of the stems to crack or burn. Colwell continued to work on the valves, but the project eventually withered away. "It was a difficult thing to make, to maintain the [proper] wall thickness," he later observed. "I think, had we stayed with it longer we could have made it a success. It was a difficult thing to do."[97]

Other executives also contributed new product ideas. While still at the Michigan plant, for example, Crawford and several employees—including experimental engineer George Hufferd—had launched a search for products to "level out production hills and valleys in the manufacture of automobile parts" and help maintain employment. In particular, the group hoped to find "gadgets and specialty items which could be made in a few minutes and be sold throughout the year." The group explored making such items as roller skates, "trick tricycles which steered with the rear wheels," as well as "various accessories." One day Hufferd happened to be collecting rent from his mother's tenants when he found one of them, an elderly man named Owen L. Dautrick, fiddling with an overhead garage door. Dautrick had already patented several hardware devices for overhead doors, and Hufferd was intrigued by the notion of making them in the Michigan plant. He brought the idea to Crawford, who agreed to support the project.[98]

As Crawford remembered events, after about three months of development work on the overhead door, C. E. Thompson visited the plant. He spotted the door activity and inquired about it. Crawford said, "We're going into the building business." Thompson responded, "Like hell we are! Get that stuff out of here!" To Crawford, the project "looked too good to kill," so he relocated it to an unused shed on the plant grounds.[99]

In February 1930, Crawford, his secretary, Cathryn Newey, Hufferd, Matt Graham, and several other employees of the Michigan plant joined with Dautrick to incorporate Crawford Door Company. The initial capitalization was $5,000, of which half was paid in. Crawford served as president, but the company had only one full-time employee, R. Torrey Foster, who resigned from TP to run the new business. Crawford Door contracted with the Michigan plant to manufacture hardware and to provide other business services. During the depression, the new venture limped along, surviving only on TP's credit. When business picked up later in the decade, Crawford Door moved to its own quarters and became a moderately successful enterprise.[100]

Although C. E. Thompson was cool toward overhead doors, he suggested another new product idea that provided an entertaining diversion, if not much business. During his visits to Paris, Thompson had noticed metal pieces embedded in the streets to mark off pedestrian areas. In 1931, he championed a plan for TP to make such traffic markers by melting down scrap silcrome and casting them into small rods. These rods would be driven into street pavements as a substitute for the painting of white lines.

On the face of it, the notion seemed reasonable: special rubberized paints required for road use were expensive, and painting required significant traffic delays or premium rates for labor performed at off hours.[101]

The first test of Thompson's idea came early in 1932, when Raymond Livingstone, who had been given charge of developing the business, appeared with city traffic department officials on Cleveland's High Level Bridge. Problems began, Livingstone later recounted, when "a burly street laborer" swung his sledgehammer at the first markers. The first two markers broke on impact. The third entered the pavement successfully, "but the head cracked off when the first car passed over, and [it] flew into the windshield of the car immediately behind." The fourth marker ricocheted from a passing car and hit a nearby pedestrian on the arm. At this point, Livingstone noted sheepishly, "The test was called off on the grounds of 'sales resistance.'"

A switch from cast silcrome to forged aluminum pieces yielded much better results, and TP went on to sell markers to about fifty cities for trial installations at pedestrian crosswalks. Pittsburgh with 30,000 markers and Mexico City with 20,000 were the largest purchasers. Nonetheless, the operation never became profitable, and it was eventually abandoned in 1936. As summed up by Livingstone, "it was a miserable business."

In the spring of 1933, TP's fortunes began to show modest improvement, particularly in the Service Division. As a bonus, the company received nearly $60,000 from the government as settlement of a disputed tax case dating back to the First World War. (The lawyer responsible for achieving the settlement, Dave Wright of the firm Garfield, Cross, MacGregor, Daoust and Baldwin, was soon to join TP as Crawford's assistant, and he would eventually become TRW's chairman and CEO.) Despite these encouraging signs, the company remained in serious trouble, and the board of directors voted to cut executive salaries for the second time in two years. By fall, the company was so desperate for cash that it sold on the open market 9,500 shares of stock that it had accumulated prior to the depression as part of an executive bonus plan.[102]

The company's financial struggles proved disastrous for C. E. Thompson. By 1932, his $7 million stake in the company had dwindled to less than $500,000, and he was in serious trouble with his creditors, including Union Trust. Suspension of dividend payments and executive bonuses, salary cuts, and crackdowns on the use of expense accounts further compounded his troubles. The chateau on the Riviera was repossessed, and, to keep his creditors at bay, he was forced to put his New York City home on the market and to sell off part of his stake in TP. In 1933, he returned to live fulltime in Cleveland. Back at the main plant, Colwell remembers that Thompson, desperate to save money, "would run all over the building at noon and turn out the lights."[103]

Thompson never got the opportunity to rebound from his misfortune. Early in October 1933 he traveled to Washington, D.C., to meet with representatives of other automobile parts manufacturers. The purpose of the gathering was to fashion a cooperative response to the depression under the watchful eye of the federal government's newly created National Recovery Administration (NRA), and Thompson was prepared to lobby for a national "buy a car week" as a cure for the depression. On October 4, at a luncheon with General Hugh Johnson, head of the NRA, Thompson was stricken with a heart attack. He died several hours later. It was an event fraught with symbolism. The occasion portended great changes unfolding in relations between business and government, and it foreshadowed TP's coming struggles with government intervention.[104]

So too, Thompson's funeral in Cleveland was an event of symbols. Thompson had asked to be cremated and to have half of his ashes interred, with the remainder scattered from the air over downtown Cleveland. It was a nice sentiment, and it made good copy in the newspapers. Unbeknownst to the media, however, Thompson had specifically requested that his ashes be dumped on the Union Trust building. Jimmy Doolittle, winner of the 1932 Thompson Trophy Race (and later national hero destined to become an important recurring figure in TRW's history), was asked to fly a plane containing Crawford and Livingstone, who would honor Thompson's last request. When the passengers attempted to discharge their duty at the appropriate moment, however, backwash from the propeller scattered the ashes back into their faces and around the cockpit, where they proved impossible to recover.[105]

The passing of C. E. Thompson marked the conclusion of a distinct era for his company. He had presided over the transformation of the struggling Cleveland Cap Screw Company into Thompson Products, a leading independent supplier to two of the country's most exciting industries, automobiles and aircraft. His friendships with the pioneers of those industries and his instincts for—and relish of—the limelight were essential ingredients of TP's success. Although the company's fortunes were at a low ebb when he died, it possessed the technological and human resources, as well as the market position, to fare well in more prosperous times. What the company now needed was something that Thompson was temperamentally and professionally unsuited to deliver: a strategy and an organization to succeed in the long term. These elements would be the legacy of the next generation of young, ambitious, professional managers, who were interested in building a business rather than in accumulating—and spending—a fortune.

Chapter 4

Fred Crawford's Company

▶   ▶   ▶

1933–1938

DURING THE FIRST FIVE YEARS FOLLOWING THE DEATH OF C. E. THOMPSON, THE COMPANY that bore his name underwent profound changes. Its businesses remained the same: automotive parts for both the original equipment and replacement markets, and aircraft engine parts. The differences occurred in the way the company was managed and operated. Thompson Products (TP) pursued a clear strategy of balanced growth. As it recovered from the Great Depression, it poured money into new products. It revamped its manufacturing processes to make them more efficient; it increased market coverage through direct investment and acquisition; it developed and acquired valuable brand names in the replacement market; and it placed young, energetic, hard-working managers in charge of the plants and of key corporate functions such as engineering, law, and personnel. In the space of five years, Thompson Products rose from the abyss to become a consistently profitable company with a growing reputation for engineering excellence and progressive management.

The catalyst for this transformation was Fred Crawford, who at age forty-two was elected president of TP in November 1933. During his first five years at the top, he left a strong imprint on the company. He also acquired a growing reputation as a champion of the business community at a time when it felt besieged by increasing government regulation, the demands of national labor unions, and the mounting hostility of public opinion.

Before Crawford could assert control of TP, however, there was one more act to unfold in the tragicomic saga of the Thompson family.

ED THOMPSON'S LAST STAND

Soon after his father's death, Ed Thompson approached Fred Crawford with a proposition. According to Crawford, Thompson asked for support in his bid to become TP's president in return for a promise to leave Crawford alone in his role as vice president and general manager with day-to-day responsibility for running the company. Thompson also outlined a scheme that would make both men rich. "What we would do," Crawford recalled Thompson proposing, "is put out unfavorable financial statements and the stock would go down. Then we'd put out a good statement, and the stock would go up. We'd play the market that way."[1]

Crawford had no intention of accepting Thompson's offer and every intention of becoming TP's leader himself. The two men, who had once been good friends, became bitter rivals in a contest for control of the company. In pursuing the presidency, Thompson faced significant obstacles. Not only did Crawford possess more experience and far better credentials, but the Thompson family no longer controlled a majority of shares in the company. Ed Thompson's personal fortunes, moreover, were also dwindling. His sideline business, Thompson Aeronautical, had limped into the Great Depression only to collapse when a pilot for a subsidiary, Thompson Transatlantic Airline, crashed his plane into the English Channel. In 1932, Thompson was forced to sell the venture to a syndicate for a paltry amount. (The business recovered under new owners and eventually merged into American Airlines.)

The confrontation between Thompson and Crawford came to a head on November 29, 1933, when TP's board of directors gathered to elect a new president. At the meeting, Thompson proposed that the company be run by a "management committee" consisting of himself, Crawford, and Clegg. According to the understated language of the official account, a discussion followed, "wherein it appeared that Directors were in accord that such a form of management would not be to the best interests of the company." At that point, Crawford was nominated for the top position and elected by the vote of all directors, with one abstention (his own) and one dissenting voice: Ed Thompson's.[2]

Although he lost this battle, Thompson was not prepared to surrender. During the next several months, he attempted to rally stockholders friendly to himself or his father in a proxy fight for control of TP. Crawford knew that the balance of C. E. Thompson's stock holdings—about 40,000 shares—was held by Union Trust as security against personal loans. At the time, the stock was trading at about $8 per share, but Crawford offered to buy it at $10 per share. The bank agreed, but stipulated that Crawford place the $400,000 in an escrow account for a stated period during which the Thompson family could reclaim the stock for the same price. Crawford raised $400,000 from family and friends (including $100,000 from Thomas Henderson, Alexander Winton's partner and brother-in-law, who wanted back into the business) and placed it with the bank. About an hour before the expiration of the deadline, a bank officer called Crawford to come get the stock. With about five minutes to go, as he was sitting in an office at the bank, Crawford was startled to see Ed Thompson arrive in the company of two investment bankers from the New York firm Burnham & Co. Thompson and the bankers produced a check for $400,000 and claimed the stock.[3]

The next confrontation occurred at TP's annual meeting in March 1934. Thompson again appeared with two Burnham bankers, Oscar A. Krieger and W. A. Ditmars, to challenge the management of the company. But Crawford and his associates had not been idle during the intervening months. In waging its side of the proxy fight, the management group relied on an obscure provision in the preferred stock agreement that had helped finance the organization of Steel Products back in 1916. That agreement stipulated that, if the company should default on four consecutive quarterly dividend payments, then "the Preferred Stock shall as a class have equal voting power with the Common Stock as a class." In other words, at the end of 1933, the company had outstanding 263,000 shares of common stock and 3,500 shares of preferred; the default provision made each share of preferred stock worth 75.14 shares of common stock in voting power.[4] Because TP had suspended dividends on the preferred stock during the depression, this provision was invoked. To retain control of the company, therefore, management needed to persuade a small group of preferred stockholders to support it, while keeping dividend payments at least one year in arrears, a task all too easily accomplished given the company's perilous financial condition.[5]

During the early months of 1934, Thompson managers divided responsibility to explain the situation and their goals for the company to the preferred share owners, most of whom were prominent Clevelanders well known to Crawford. Although circumstances favored management, the proxy fight provided moments of tension and humor. For example, Tom Duggan, the recent recruit as sales manager in the Service Division, was sent to Washington, D.C., to meet with Republican congressman Chester Bolton, who owned a big block of the preferred stock. (Bolton's estate in Lyndhurst, Ohio, is now the site of TRW's corporate headquarters, and Bolton's home is the company's guest house.) After the meeting, Bolton spoofed—and alarmed—Duggan by saying that though he had already sent his proxy to management, "after listening to you, I'm going to change it!"[6]

The annual meeting itself proved anticlimactic. TP's directors, led by Frank Ginn, a prominent lawyer with the firm Tolles, Hogsett & Ginn (a forerunner of today's Jones, Day, Reavis & Pogue), produced the proxies and easily defeated the Thompson-Burnham challenge. In recognition of their stake in the company, however, two members of the Burnham group, Krieger and Ditmars, were elected directors. Ed Thompson remained a director and a vice president without portfolio until he resigned and severed his connections with the company in September 1934.[7]

The story has an epilogue. The battle lost, Thompson moved to New Mexico, where he listed his occupation as aviator and rancher. He bought and operated Rancho Real, a thirty-five-hundred-acre dude ranch near Albuquerque, "said to be one of the finest in the Southwest," that had fallen on hard times. In the summer of 1935, Thompson found himself embroiled in a feud with J. Bryson Corbett, a small, sickly man who had visited the dude ranch with his wife. Soon afterward the wife sued for divorce, and Corbett held Thompson responsible. Bad blood between the two men resulted in at least one altercation.

For what happened next, we have only the breathless reporting of a local journalist who pieced together the story. On August 23, Thompson, who possessed an evil temper, allegedly phoned Corbett several times to threaten more harm. Although warned to stay away, Thompson appeared at Corbett's house wearing his rancher's garb, "high-heeled shoes, gay coat, and gayer neckerchief, and four-gallon Stetson." The two men apparently exchanged threats, whereupon Corbett produced a .38-calibre Smith & Wesson handgun and shot Thompson in the chest. He then called the police. When they arrived, "they found the little man [Corbett] calmly sitting at the top of the porch steps, smoking a cigarette and looking complacently down upon the playboy, who, in his high-heeled boots and other picturesque paraphernalia, lay sprawled at the bottom of those steps—and very, very dead." Thompson was thirty-eight years old. Corbett was later released on bail and acquitted on a plea of self-defense.[8]

HAVING FUN

Management's victory in the 1934 proxy fight confirmed a new generation at the top of TP. The new president, Fred Crawford, proved quick to make his mark, aided by a team of young, energetic, and highly capable managers.

Crawford himself was well bred, well educated, and well connected. He was born in 1891 on a farm in Watertown, Massachusetts, a town founded by his maternal ancestors in the 1630s. His father, a Harvard-educated lawyer, descended from Scots-Irish immigrants who had settled in rural Vermont during the 1720s. His mother, Matti Coolidge Crawford, was an artist and a distant cousin of Calvin Coolidge. Crawford attended high school in Watertown and college at Harvard, earning a bachelor's degree in engineering in 1914 and a master's of civil engineering the following year. He was a good student. During these years he revealed other enduring traits, including a high energy level, an athletic bent, an ability to make friends easily, and an unfashionable disdain for alcohol.

Following graduation, Crawford spent two years as a private tutor, helping to prepare sons of well-to-do people for college. One of his charges, William Z. (Bill) Breed, was the son of Rev. Walter Breed, rector of St. Paul's Episcopal Church in Cleveland, where many of the city's leading citizens worshiped, perhaps because they were impressed by the rector's principle of never exceeding eighteen minutes in a sermon. It was through the Breeds that the twenty-five-year-old Crawford met Herbert Wright, who in turn persuaded him to meet C. E. Thompson, who in turn hired him as a mill-wright's helper at the Steel Products Company in 1916.[9]

Crawford's rise to the top of Steel Products and Thompson Products was swift. Within ten years he was a plant manager, a major stockholder, and a board member. He became general manager at thirty-eight, and president at forty-two. As head of the company, he gathered around him a like-minded, hardworking crew of managers. Most of the new management team came from inside the company, with the notable exceptions of Tom Duggan in the Service Division and Dave Wright, who joined in 1933 as Crawford's assistant. Arch Colwell served as director of engineering, with college-trained metallurgist Harry Bubb as chief engineer. Within a matter of months of taking over the company, Crawford handed Ray Livingstone, still occupied with winding down the traffic-marker business and some miscellaneous sales tasks, the assignment of becoming an expert on personnel management. The lone executive holdovers from the Thompson years besides Crawford were Weck Albaugh as secretary (and treasurer after Ed Thompson's defeat in 1934) and Lee Clegg as vice president of sales. Crawford appointees Eugene McBride (nicknamed "the Gray Eagle" because of his silvery gray hair and fine features), Matt Graham, and George Stauffer served as managers of the main, Michigan, and Canadian plants, respectively. The average age of the top group was thirty-seven.[10]

TP's executives found Crawford easy to work for, partly because of his strong belief in open communications and his great skill as a communicator. An uncommonly clear thinker and forceful speaker, Crawford had a common touch with people. He enjoyed mixing with employees and working a crowd. Gifted at small talk and a brilliant raconteur, he was equally at home with small groups and huge audiences. He also possessed a terrific sense of humor, which he considered an essential tool of management.[11]

In his first days as president, Crawford assembled the management staff of the main plant to hear dismal news about the company's financial position. It was a repetition in miniature of his performance at the Detroit plant in 1922. "Things didn't look good," he recalls telling the staff. "I won't cut your wages. I want to raise them— you're not paid enough as it is. But if you fellows are as smart as I think you are, you'll take a ten percent cut voluntarily." He then asked for a vote in favor of the pay cut, and every hand went up. At that point, Ed Riley, a new hire in the engineering department, entered the meeting late, saw the hands in the air, and raised his own, too. Later, he asked what he had voted for and was given the news. "It was awful funny," Crawford remembers, "except to Ed Riley." Riley, who eventually became a top executive at TRW, later laughed about the incident, too.[12]

At the start of his presidency, Crawford assembled his staff for daily 8 A.M. meetings to talk about what TP could do to improve its prospects. As a sign of how important he regarded these sessions, Crawford was usually the first person present. As fortunes improved, the staff met less often, although Crawford insisted that the departments work together closely. To foster better communication, for example, he had the partitions removed from most of the offices of the main plant. Thereafter, most middle managers worked in one big room, where they could interact with each other spontaneously. Crawford and other senior executives continued to work in private offices, but they kept their doors open and most answered their own phones.[13]

Stories of Crawford's restless energy were legion among his friends and coworkers. He often entered meetings with a flourish and an acrobatic stunt, tossing his hat on a distant coat rack, bounding over chairs, or hopping up to perch on a table or desk. His secretary (and second wife), Kay, remembers him entering an elevator and leaping up to push the buttons with his foot. To help channel his energy in meetings, he generally brought colored pencils and paper so that he could doodle and draw. "He was so good at it," says Dave Wright, "I think he could have been a professional cartoonist." He also kept colored pencils on his desk for use during smaller meetings or phone calls. The doodles often took off from the name or initials of people with whom he met. One time he showed an unusually elaborate design to Fred Witt, the company's advertising manager, saying, "See. That fellow stayed too long!" Later on, Crawford applied his graphic skills for speeches and employee communications, and some of his drawings appeared in company publications.[14]

As a businessman, Crawford also had a steely side that was fully revealed in his confrontations with the federal government and national unions. "Free enterprise is not a charity," he pointed out. "It's a goddamn tough fight. . . . Business is a struggle between human wants, and the manager is the guy who has got to satisfy those wants." His desk featured a framed motto: "Hard work is the only prayer that is answered." He gave long hours to the job, often staying at the plant to speak with employees on the late shifts. On occasion, he even slept at the office. He kept himself fit with daily yoga exercises.[15]

Although he disliked reading reports and delegated this sort of work when he could, Crawford had a nose for significant details or troubling omissions. He paid especially close attention to overhead expenses. During one episode of the 1930s, for example, he ordered the plant managers to employ "economy men," or efficiency experts, to find ways to save money, and he recommended especially that they find ways to trim indirect labor costs. When he heard that the economy man in Detroit had requisitioned $700 worth of office furniture, Crawford fired off an angry memo to Matt Graham. "We do not want to become unreasonably picayune on expenditures," he wrote, but he reminded Graham that the company was in debt and "straining every possible cash reserve" to keep going and growing. He would have preferred to see the new man "begin on a $10 kitchen table with a box to sit on and a nail keg for a waste basket." He also reminded Graham of orders to slash his payroll and concluded the memo on an ominous note: "You show this letter to [the economy man] and tell him he is up there to find ways to save money—not spend it. I repeat—the period of free lancing is over for the Michigan Plant. You fellows are on the band wagon or out the window."[16]

Such missives were the exception, however. Crawford preferred to motivate people by using the carrot rather than the stick, by his own energetic and flamboyant example, and by humorous prods. The favorite picture in his office showed a very fat, tired, balding, and scantily-clad old businessman seated on a bench in the hereafter. Behind him was Father Time, pointing at a page in a large volume. Under the picture was the inscription, "'This,' said the Ancient, 'is the most important precept of them all.'" Bending forward, the businessman read in golden script, DON'T TAKE YOUR-SELF TOO DAMNED SERIOUSLY.[17]

"You can't imagine how much fun Crawford was to be around," recalls Wright. "We always had time for fun. Always."[18]

CRAWLING OUT OF THE GUTTER

"A wonderful time to get to the top is when things couldn't be worse," Crawford later remarked, looking back on his early years as TP's president. "If you manage to crawl out of the gutter and up on the curb people think you're a genius." Genius or not, Crawford began to re-energize the company almost immediately.[19]

At the same meeting that elected Crawford president, for example, the board of directors commissioned the Cleveland accounting firm Ernst & Ernst (now Ernst & Young) to carry out an "efficiency study" of TP's operations. The study, which was completed within six weeks, proposed many specific changes in the company's management practices and included a strong recommendation to adopt more rigorous forecasting and budgeting procedures. The board accepted most of the advice without comment, apart from Crawford's understatement that the company's "previous experience in the operation of a budget . . . had not been successful."[20]

Ernst & Ernst apparently also suggested ways to improve the company's routine financial reporting. Since the late 1920s, top management had customarily received monthly reports including a balance sheet, general operating statement, and statements of sales, inventories, and expenses for each plant and the company as a whole. After September 1934, these statements became longer and more comprehensive, providing not only more detail but also enabling new types of analysis. The old reports, for example, broke down sales by plant; as revised, they supplied analysis of sales by product as well. The new data enhanced management's ability to spot trends in demand, not only for traditional breadwinners such as commercial valves, pistons, tie rods, and drag links, but also for newer products and experimental items such as valve guides, street markers, and water pumps.[21]

Under Crawford, new methods also prevailed on the shop floor, where TP redesigned its operations for making precision parts such as valves and pistons. For most of its existence, the company had carried out such operations in "colonies," in which a supervised unit of workers performed one type of activity such as grinding and polishing before passing the work along to the next station. During 1934 and 1935, detailed engineering studies under Colwell's assistant Emil Gibian enabled the company to reorganize high-volume valve and piston production into "line" operations, in which machines of the same type and character were grouped together. This change enabled a single supervised unit to carry out a long series of successive operations, and it resulted in significant increases in productivity, with a savings estimated at four cents per unit on some low-cost valves.[22]

TP's management initiatives occurred at a propitious time. By early 1934, the worst of the Great Depression was over, and sales of new autos and replacement parts climbed once more. In March, TP received a critical loan of $100,000 from National City Bank to make new capital investments, acquiring a new extrusion press for valves and equipment for plating pistons. At the same time, it restored pay cuts taken by salaried employees in 1932 and 1933 and began rehiring factory workers. In June, the board resumed paying dividends on the preferred stock, which had been suspended more than two years before, and repaid five quarters of the dividends deferred. By the end of the year, the company had appropriated another $60,000 for capital improvements and added new Service Division warehouses in Boston and Portland, Oregon. For the year, TP earned nearly $400,000 on sales of $6.6 million. Crawford was particularly pleased to note that "relatively new products" such as knee-action spring sets for Chevrolet, retainer locks, valve seat inserts, water pumps, and piston castings accounted for more than $800,000 of the revenue total.[23]

The company's expansion continued until a recession near the end of the decade. (See Exhibits I-1 and I-2.) Sales climbed to $14.5 million in 1937, a total still below the peak of 1929 but a definite sign of renewed health. The stock price rebounded from a low of $2.75 in 1932 to a high of nearly $29 in 1937. The plants filled up again with orders and enabled TP to expand operations in Cleveland several times and to purchase a warehouse as headquarters for its burgeoning Service Division.[24]

TP paid off the last debts on the preferred stock in 1936, at the same time beginning a program to restructure its capital base by expanding its authorized issue of common stock from 300,000 to 500,000 shares and replacing the old preferred stock with a new issue of prior preference stock. The company resumed paying dividends on common stock in 1935, initially allocating more than half of net income in this fashion before gradually lowering the payout ratio. This policy was adopted, management later observed, so that earnings could be plowed back into the business to retire debt, develop new products, and expand market coverage. "The old-fashioned step of putting most of the earnings back into the business was the backbone of our program," said Wright. Such measures warmed the hearts of the Burnham & Co. directors, who in 1936 sold their stake at a tidy profit and relinquished their board seats. Thereafter, management faced no serious challenges from the Thompson family or from any other disaffected parties.[25]

The Two-and-a-Half-Legged Stool

Crawford did not immediately make his strategy explicit, but its outlines were clear enough. He sought to make the company grow in all of its principal markets through internal expansion, related diversification, and occasional acquisitions. Or, as he put it in 1938, "the planned expansion and diversification program" that began with his presidency had two aspects: "first, a diversification of the markets to which the Company's products might be sold, and second, a diversification of the products to be sold to each of the various markets." In practice, TP sought to balance its business on three legs: products sold to vehicle manufacturers, to the automotive replacement market, and to the aircraft industry.[26]

The first two legs of the stool proved longer and stronger than the third. Between 1933 and 1937, the production of motor vehicles more than doubled, and the number of motor vehicle registrations rose by 25 percent. TP first responded to reviving opportunities by focusing on improving existing products such as valves, pistons, and other items it had made for years. During the 1930s, new alloys tailored for specific uses dislodged Silcrome No. 1 from its position of universal acceptance as a material for exhaust valves. Silcrome XB, for example, was used for many automobile and light-truck engines; Silcrome X-10, an austenitic steel (temperature- and corrosion-resistant but not hardenable with heat treatment), was for heavier duty engines; and Silcrome XCR, an unusual and expensive alloy, found application in high-performance and heavy-duty engines where cost was not a concern. For TP, these developments meant continuous monitoring and testing of new alloys as well as engineering new ways to work with them efficiently.[27]

In 1933, Colwell created a development staff to pursue new product opportunities. On Crawford's recommendation, the group purchased several cars and stripped them down, looking for parts that TP might make. Colwell directed more focused research on parts related to the valve such as seat inserts, retainer locks, and other similar items. A fruitful area of research involved ways to extend a valve's operating life. A common problem was that any area of leakage around the valve seat caused a hot spot to develop. The hot spot would progressively worsen and eventually cause the valve to "blow by" or leak. By rotating the valve slowly, however, TP engineers appreciably reduced the risk that a hot spot would form. At the same time, valve rotation helped keep the valve seat clean and prevent carbon and other harmful deposits from building up on the stem. In 1938, TP introduced the Roto-Valve, a spring-actuated device that lifted the valve and relied on engine vibration to initiate rotation. This approach, Colwell later admitted, "was not a good one," but continued work eventually yielded a very successful product introduced in the 1940s: the Thompson Rotocap.[28]

TP's ongoing research on valve technology continued to forestall the threat of backward integration by the automobile manufacturers. The threat was nonetheless a constant concern to TP management, and it led to a 1937 merger with Jadson Motor Products Company, a producer of valves and pistons for high-performance and heavy-duty engines based in Bell, California. This company had originated in 1898 as a blacksmith shop in Traver, California, owned by J. A. Drake. During the early years of this century, Drake brought his six sons into the business, and J. A. Drake & Sons was contracted into "Jadson." In 1923, E. M. Smith, an oil field entrepreneur, acquired a major stake in the company, which he moved to Bell five years later. By the mid-1930s, Jadson manufactured principally for the replacement market, although it also made original valves for race car, aircraft, truck, bus, stationary, and heavy-duty engines. According to a contemporary account, Jadson products outfitted "ninety-five per cent of all Indianapolis racing cars finishing in the money."[29]

At some point in 1935 or 1936, Crawford heard a rumor that Chrysler, a major TP valve customer, was seeking new sources for valves. At the time, he knew, Jadson had recently obtained a license on the silcrome patents. If Chrysler were somehow to acquire Jadson, he reasoned, not only would TP lose a big account, but it would also face a formidable new competitor with access to key metallurgical patents. A major product line would be at risk. In the summer of 1936, Crawford approached E. M. Smith with an offer to buy Jadson. At first Smith refused, saying that he was not interested in selling. During the late winter of 1937, however, Smith called Crawford and asked him to meet in New Orleans within a week. Smith had been caught cheating on his income taxes and was about to serve time in a federal penitentiary. To pay his fines, he needed to sell Jadson, which TP promptly arranged via a merger agreement involving an exchange of stock worth about $260,000. (Like many other episodes at TP during Crawford's presidency, the Jadson deal resonated with comic overtones. About a year later, Smith called Crawford from prison to say that he was enjoying the best year of his life. He had lost weight and improved his health. He had gotten a job as the warden's chauffeur and spent much of his sentence playing golf with the warden and his friends. "Book me a room," was Crawford's reply.)[30]

Although TP merged with Jadson for defensive reasons, the deal brought with it a useful facility on the West Coast and incremental sales opportunities in new markets. The factory was far removed from most automotive and aircraft engine builders, but it sat near the heart of the aircraft industry, an advantageous location in the coming years.

The rebound in new car sales in the United States during the mid-1930s boosted TP's sales dramatically. Its strategy for competing in the replacement market helped to raise the company's fortunes still further. Between 1933 and 1938, TP's sales to this segment soared from $2.1 million to nearly $5 million, placing the business on a par with direct sales to the automobile companies. TP's strong performance in the replacement business resulted in part from effective management by Tom Duggan and his colleague, E. T. "Jim" Syvertsen, leaders of the Service Division. They developed a clear strategy to increase TP's geographical coverage, signing up new retail outlets and opening new warehouses every year. TP's export department, a unit of the Service Division, also expanded swiftly: by 1938, TP replacement parts were available in more than seventy-five countries.[31]

Duggan and Syvertsen also sought to increase the dollar value of TP products in each car on the road. To achieve this goal, they arranged to bundle TP parts with items purchased on the outside into "service packages." One package, for example, included TP valves and valve retainer locks as well as valve springs and related parts made by other manufacturers. The package appealed to buyers, because in a single transaction they could obtain a complete set of parts needed for a common engine repair job. During the 1930s, the Service Division also mounted a nationwide advertising campaign to build awareness of the TP brand. The division created a new logo—the TP teepee—that adorned advertisements and packages. Finally, the division began publishing specially prepared service aids for jobbers and mechanics. Not only did these items carry useful advice, but they also provided additional support to the TP brand name.[32]

The opportunistic acquisition of a key competitor also helped TP to expand its position in replacement markets. During the fall of 1935, Crawford learned of the sudden availability of the Toledo Steel Products Company (TSP), a once-strong maker of automotive replacement valves brought low by the Great Depression. Negotiations to purchase TSP proceeded swiftly. The deal was completed in December for about $190,000 in cash—an excellent bargain, since TSP's assets, which included a factory in Toledo, a network of more than 650 distributors, and an established trade name, were valued at more than $400,000.[33]

The transaction marked TSP's return to the TP family, for C. E. Thompson and his associates had held a controlling stake in TSP between 1919 and 1925. When they sold it back to local interests, TSP was tiny, but it embarked on an aggressive growth strategy. In 1929, it purchased the Fostoria Screw Products Company, a maker of chassis bolts and bushings in Fostoria, Ohio. During the next few years, TSP expanded its product line to include valve guides and other valve train parts and built up nationwide distribution. Under Thompson Products, TSP operated as a separate subsidiary, keeping its own manufacturing capability, sales organization, warehouses, and headquarters staff. It continued to market its own product line, as well as TP-made products such as pistons and chassis parts, under its distinctive Toledo brand name.[34]

Of the lines of business inherited from the 1920s, only products for the aircraft industry—the hoped-for third leg of the stool—posted disappointing results during the mid-1930s. The principal problem was the unexpectedly slow growth of the market after the Great Depression. Put simply, aircraft makers enjoyed no rebound from the crisis: between 1933 and 1938, U.S. manufacturers built fewer than 15,000 airplanes, and not until 1940—under a program of defense mobilization—did they make more aircraft than they had built in 1929. TP's total sales of aircraft valves in 1934 amounted to about $500,000—less than 10 percent of total revenues, a relative performance that remained constant until the end of the decade.[35]

Expanding the Third Leg

The slow growth of the aircraft business line did not reflect lack of effort on the part of TP and its managers. The National Air Races, for example, continued to provide both Crawford and the company priceless exposure. Crawford's annual appearances to award the Thompson Trophy made good newsreel footage and front-page photo material, especially in the company of famed aviator Roscoe Turner, the dapper, mustachioed three-time winner (1934, 1938, and 1939). Each Labor Day weekend, Crawford and other TP managers hobnobbed with movie stars, politicians, leading corporate executives, and heroes like Charles Lindbergh and Amelia Earhart. Starting in 1931, the races were immortalized in paintings by artist Charles Hubbell, whose work TP reproduced in calendars that it gave to its best customers and sold profitably to the public.[36]

Behind the scenes, Crawford and other TP managers worked tirelessly to promote aviation and to position Cleveland as a center of the industry. Crawford served successively as vice president, director, and president of the National Air Races of Cleveland, Inc., as well as governor of the sponsoring National Aeronautic Association. He lobbied successfully for the races to be held in Cleveland in 1934 and 1935 and for the city to become the permanent site of the races starting in 1937. The friendships and connections formed and strengthened during the races would serve TP well in future years.[37]

Although the slow growth of the market constrained TP's efforts, other trends in aircraft technology provided opportunities. In particular, the development of more powerful multicylinder engines, the growing popularity of multiengined airplanes, and the need for spare engines enabled successful valve makers to earn profits on low volume. During the 1930s, aircraft engine manufacturers such as Curtiss-Wright and Pratt & Whitney continued to upgrade air-cooled engines, while the U.S. military funded the development of higher-horsepower liquid-cooled engines that they hoped would yield better performance at high speeds and altitudes. Both types of engines placed heavy demands on exhaust valves and required innovative responses from valve makers. As Colwell put it, the challenge in making automotive valves was "working to a budget"; in making aircraft valves, it was using "any means available to get dependable performance."[38]

The major technical achievements of the 1930s involved improved forging techniques, which enabled hollow-stem and hollow-head valves to be made "exactly to print contour," and "tremendous strides" in cylinder head design and fabrication, including new materials, better lubrication, and improved cooling techniques. By the close of the decade, aircraft valves had become far more sophisticated than predecessors of the 1920s. The exhaust valve for the powerful Curtiss-Wright Cyclone air-cooled engine, for example, was not only sodium cooled, but also featured a nitrided (hardened) and honed stem, a seat faced with "stellite," an exceptionally hard alloy of cobalt, chromium, and tungsten, and a cobalt-chrome welded tip. Such valves typically sold for about $20 apiece, about a hundred times the price of a typical automotive poppet valve.[39]

During the 1930s, innovations in aircraft valve technology continued to emerge from varied sources, including engine designers and builders in Europe and the United States, as well as valve makers like TP and Wilcox-Rich. Many important advances originated in Great Britain, where Rolls Royce developed high-performance liquid-cooled engines for the Royal Navy during the 1930s. The British, for example, pioneered the use of TPA austenitic steel for aircraft valves, which quickly became a standard alloy also in the United States. Colwell praised TPA steel for its "excellent hot strength, good corrosion resistance, and high impact value." British engineers also extended valve wear by welding stellite to valve seats and making seat inserts from a new silcrome alloy designated X-9. TP proved adept at working with these metals, as well as in manufacturing valves reliably and efficiently. The company developed, for example, an economical way to treat valve stems that resulted in less susceptibility to corrosion and longer life.[40]

TP's work on aircraft valves also spilled over into its automotive businesses, sometimes in unexpected ways. During the 1930s, the British and American governments pursued development of flat engines that could be housed inside the wing of an aircraft, thereby reducing drag and enabling higher speeds. A promising design for such an engine called for sleeve valves to replace traditional poppet valves. (In reciprocating engines, a sleeve valve consists of a second cylinder, or sleeve, fitted inside the piston cylinder in such a way as to move freely up and down. The sidewalls of the piston cylinder contain ports to admit fuel and expel exhaust that are alternately opened and closed by the action of the sleeve.) In addition to enabling more compact engines, sleeve valves had several other advantages over poppet valves: they could be made from cheaper alloys and were simpler to manufacture, operate, and cool. The key disadvantage, however, eventually proved fatal: sleeve valve engines were considerably heavier and less efficient than engines using poppet valves.[41]

In 1937 and 1938, with the ultimate fate of the technology still in the balance, Pratt & Whitney negotiated development contracts with the U.S. military to build aircraft engines with sleeve valves. These programs undoubtedly got TP's attention. In 1938, Crawford and Colwell made "a hurried trip" to Great Britain, where they licensed several patents pertaining to cylinder sleeves. "We were not convinced that the sleeve valve would replace poppet valves," Colwell later wrote, "but taking no chances, we had an understanding that we could have the American rights on the production of sleeve valves in America, if they were used." The British patents covered a process for nitriding sleeves. To gain manufacturing experience, TP applied the process to making cylinder sleeves for heavy-duty truck engines. Several thousand units later, the company discovered that it had an attractive product line for the replacement market.[42]

A PROGRAM OF HUMAN RELATIONS

In 1988—more than fifty years after TP climbed up from the depths of the Great Depression—Dave Wright claimed that the company's situation was never desperate, in large measure because of Crawford's vision. "We never really worried about going broke," he said. "We figured we were on solid ground, that we were doing things right. We were building a real company here; I was very excited about that. I was excited that Fred Crawford was willing to go ahead and *do* things. Some people are bright, but they're unwilling to take the initiative, to actually set things in motion. Fred had both qualities."[43]

Crawford led TP to recovery by articulating a clear strategy for growth and developing a pool of talented managers to carry it out. If that were all he had done, he would be remembered in the industries TP served as a good businessman, a leader of a moderately successful enterprise. But he did much more than that. By the close of the 1930s, Crawford was fast attracting notice in management circles as an articulate spokesman for the interests of business. And as his own reputation mushroomed, so did that of TP.

The basis of this renown was TP's approach to industrial relations—or "human relations," as Crawford later preferred to call it. TP's personnel policies mirrored its president's personality, reflecting his genuinely warm feelings toward employees and a determination to be a fair employer, his faith in frank and open communications as a means of bridging differences, and his fierce streak of Yankee independence. From the interplay of these factors with time, place, and circumstance emerged a program of industrial relations destined to be widely admired in management circles and just as widely distrusted among partisans of the national labor movement.[44]

Crawford became president of TP during the first year of Democratic president Franklin Delano Roosevelt's first term—a turbulent time in the United States. In 1932, the electorate, discouraged by more than two years of severe economic distress and impatient with the decentralized and voluntaristic remedies of Republican president Herbert Hoover, had sanctioned the New Deal, a vast escalation of government intervention in the economy. During a hundred-day period in the spring of 1933, guided by Roosevelt and his advisers, Congress enacted nearly a score of statutes creating public agencies to monitor, support, or regulate agriculture, the banking system, securities and commodity markets, welfare, utilities, and public corporations. Although Roosevelt at first slashed the federal payroll, his policies soon produced an enormous expansion of government services and employment, much of it financed by debt.[45]

One of the most controversial programs of the New Deal was the National Industrial Recovery Act (NIRA), which created the National Recovery Administration (NRA). Under the NRA's guidance, competitors in industries were encouraged to associate and develop industry codes for pricing, competitive practices, and industrial relations. Section 7(a) of the NIRA stipulated maximum hours and minimum wages for work and granted employees the right to organize and bargain collectively through representatives of their own choosing, "free from interference, coercion, or restraint" from their employers.[46]

Among its other effects, the statute emboldened national unions in the United States. Organizing drives erupted across the country, especially in manufacturing industries such as automobiles, steel, aluminum, communications, electrical equipment, and chemicals, where the traditional craft unions of the American Federation of Labor (AFL) had left masses of "unskilled" production workers without representation. Employers responded by encouraging the formation of employee representation plans—later reviled by labor sympathizers as "company unions" because they were influenced by management—while AFL militants sought to establish national industrial unions representing all the workers in a given industry regardless of their employer or level of skill. At issue, the proponents of the national industrial unions believed, was the solidarity of labor: if all workers in the automobile industry could be organized, for example, then their combined bargaining power would be much greater than that of separate unions at each auto company or of many different craft unions that crossed company borders. Only through industrywide unions that included unskilled workers could wages, hours, and working conditions become standardized across all employers, thereby removing labor cost as an element of competition.

The views and activities of labor militants were controversial not only among employers, who believed that wages should be a function of the market for labor and a company's ability to pay, but also in the AFL, where the growing power of the mass production unions unnerved leaders of the old-line craft unions. In the workplace, the battle lines were drawn, and a wave of strikes broke across the country. In 1934, according to one estimate, nearly 1.5 million workers—7 percent of the total U.S. labor force—were involved in serious industrial disputes.[47]

To Crawford, who as a young man had met and disliked Roosevelt, the New Deal was an anathema, an unjustified and unnecessary intrusion of government into an economic system that was basically sound and would heal of its own accord. (For many years, Crawford kept a portrait of FDR in his office; the picture hung from a string, upside down.) The rise of industrial unions, apparently supported by federal legislation, particularly alarmed him, because it introduced a third party into the relationship between employer and employees and institutionalized conflict in the workplace. He joined with many other business leaders in opposing the NIRA, and he sympathized with challenges to its constitutionality.[48]

Crawford's upbringing and his experiences in business made him deeply suspicious of government regulation and other forms of third-party intervention. A descendant of New England Puritans and Yankee pioneers, he espoused traditional virtues of individualism, hard work, thrift, discipline, and self-reliance. Adherence to these virtues, he believed, had made America great, and had certainly helped his own family prosper through the generations.

As a day laborer at Steel Products in 1916, Crawford had met and mingled with factory workers and observed close at hand Billy Bartlett's informal style and fondness for employees and the respect Bartlett commanded in return. At the Detroit plant during the 1920s, Crawford came to appreciate workers' concerns for job security as well as the contributions they were capable of making. Although there is no evidence that he continued to hold regular mass meetings of employees in the first years after he moved back to Cleveland in 1929, it is important to note that TP's total employment (in all locations) was about fourteen hundred people, that many of these people had been with the company for years, that its administrative offices were attached to the main plant, and that by dint of personality and the nature of his business Crawford spent many hours on the factory floor. He knew many of his employees by name, liked them, and shared a common history with them. They, in turn, liked him, and they responded enthusiastically to his leadership.

The coming of the New Deal marked the beginning of a decades-long struggle between TP and the national union movement, a struggle made all the more intense by the apparent support the unions enjoyed from the government and in the court of public opinion. TP's strategy for maintaining its independence reflected Crawford's faith in the reasonableness of employees and his own extraordinary gifts as a communicator. In 1937, he explained TP's labor policy in a letter to an executive of another company who sought his advice. "For four or five years we have been giving a great deal of time to labor relations," Crawford wrote, adding:

> More and more we are coming to the conclusion that complete frankness on all subjects is the best method. We like to turn the limelight on everything the laborer is interested in, such as the labor issues of the day and particularly the financial story of our Company. More and more we are coming to believe that the average workman is a pretty reasonable fellow if he understands the facts and develops trust in the management. Results seem to indicate that there is nothing that need be excluded from our frank discussions with labor. We show them contracts, discuss earnings, salaries, dividends and all the subjects which many consider dynamite. To our surprise our employees do not consider high executive salaries unreasonable if the executives are doing a good job, nor do they seem to question that the stockholder is entitled to a good return. Of course, it is necessary to lead up to such a relationship gradually, building confidence slowly.[49]

Crawford's ability to break down complicated economic questions into plain language without patronizing his audience and his blunt, forceful, and humorous style made him a favorite speaker to employee audiences. He addressed such groups often, generally stressing themes of mutual understanding and cooperation between employers and employees. A talk from February 1935 is typical and worth quoting at length because it conveys both the substance and the style of his speech. Crawford chose human relations as his topic. He began by asking, "What is Management and what is Labor?" He continued:

All of us in this room are friends. We are all workmen. We all come in in the morning and punch a clock and go to work and we all go home at night. None of us do that because we love work. Let us not kid ourselves. We come here because we have got to eat; we have got to pay the rent; we have got to support ourselves and our families. . . . You come; we come, those of us you call Management. We both want the same things. We both want lots of business; we both want lots of money; we both want the plant fixed up; we both want success for Thompson Products; we both want our pay raised; we both want our working hours shortened. None of us is wholly satisfied. There is no man that works in this entire organization including Management that gets as much as he thinks he is worth. We are all in the same boat, and apparently there seems to be no difference whatsoever between us on that.

After noting that many people in the government and the labor movement persisted in drawing distinctions between labor and management, Crawford offered his own views on the point. "I am going to try and tell you what I think is the key difference":

Labor has a job to do, and it has it to do every day. Management has its job to do, and does that every day. But Management has an added responsibility, an added duty, to perpetuate the institution.

[That is] My key word tonight: Perpetuity. You know what that means. To carry on and keep going. To keep the organization going, not to let it die. That is today the only difference between your viewpoint and the Management's viewpoint. Every day you come and do your work and go home. Each day Management comes and does its work, but all the time it must worry about whether we will be here next year, whether we are running this year so that we won't go down in defeat, whether our product and whether our money is such that we can carry on. If you will keep the thought in mind that, so far as I can find, there is no difference between our viewpoint[s] except that, I think it will be easier for us to go forward with this little talk and understand each other. In your negotiations and in your talks with us remember that Management must always take out this yardstick of Perpetuity and examine the problem with it. This responsibility is ours. We must carry on; we must be here next year and the year after next. So everything you ask for, everything we ask for, and everything that we do, Management must stop and think, "How will it affect this great responsibility of perpetuating this institution and carry on this organization?"

. . . I might say to you fellows, "What thing in the world do you want today from this company more than anything else?" I know what you would answer: "A steady job and more pay." I would answer the same with you. But if you are the thinking, intelligent chaps that I know you are, there is a second answer to that question, and that would be that you want a steady job next year and fair pay next year and not do something this year that is going to harm the chances of carrying the company on next year and the years after.[50]

Later in his career, Crawford often repeated similar views in speeches and publications before outside audiences. The comments became almost a litany: "The working man is a great American, no different from you or me. He wants three things, in this order. First, job security. Second, he wants to be treated fairly, with dignity and respect. And third, he wants all the money he can get, consistent with the first two." Crawford boiled his approach to human relations down to two points: "observe the Golden Rule" and "maintain constant communications." In following these principles, he believed, lay the success of any program of human relations.[51]

Organizing Workers, Independently

The specific elements of TP's personnel policies, as well as the timing of their introduction and implementation, resulted from the interaction of Crawford's independent views and the march of events. Some innovations came about because management applied the same common sense, energy, and emerging professionalism to personnel matters as it did to other aspects of its business. Other actions arose more immediately from management's response to, or anticipation of, government policies and the efforts of national unions to organize the company. Finally, TP's policies played out differently in different plant locations. Although the company attempted to standardize its personnel practices, enforcement was left to local management. Crawford himself paid greatest attention to affairs in the main plant, which accounted for about 60 percent of TP's total employment.

Soon after Crawford assumed the presidency, at a time when AFL organizers were active in Cleveland, the company authorized formation of a new employee association. A committee consisting of members of the Old Guard, an informal group of veteran employees with at least five years of service and including managers such as Lee Clegg, drafted a constitution for the Thompson Products Employees Association (TPEA). A joint council of fourteen members, including seven representatives elected by employees and seven management appointees, governed the TPEA. Among other provisions, the constitution stated that decisions of the joint council were binding on all employees. It also barred strikes or "other independent action taken by the employees or their representatives," providing instead for arbitration and ultimate appeal to the company's board of directors. The initial meeting of the TPEA joint council took place in February 1934. Soon thereafter, Crawford signed an agreement recognizing the association as a bargaining agent for employees. Although representatives of the AFL and other outside labor groups protested that management inspired and controlled the TPEA, the Cleveland Labor Board held that it was a valid association under the terms of the NIRA.[52]

The joint council met monthly from February 1934 until it was disbanded in July 1937. From all indications, employees accepted its actions and decisions, and there is no evidence of widespread dissatisfaction with its work. During this period, the joint council dealt with many issues affecting wages, benefits, and working conditions. It negotiated annual increases in wages and salaries (generally approving management offers), premiums for overtime pay, and terms for vacations. It also approved and monitored a multistage process for handling grievances. It even approved and helped administer a profit-sharing plan, including a procedure for evaluating jobs and determining rates. In May 1934, at Clegg's suggestion, the joint council named Ray Livingstone as its executive secretary, inviting him to attend all meetings but withholding the privilege of voting. His duties involved administering the affairs of the TPEA and working with employee representatives, "coordinating ideas and gathering data for the formulation of their plans."[53]

Elsewhere in the company, employee representation plans fared less well. At the Michigan plant, Matt Graham continued to manage as though his elected plant council did not exist. At the Cleveland pin plant, presided over by John Cox, matters were more serious still. Cox's feisty temperament and rough-edged management style provoked a discontent that was exacerbated by ethnic divisions in the plant. The TPEA represented a majority of the plant's 150 workers (most of them Irish-American), but about one-third of the employees (most of them Polish-American) joined the International Association of Machinists (IAM) of the AFL. During the summer of 1935, Cox laid off several employees, including two IAM members, citing lack of business. The IAM local representative protested that his members were let go because of their union affiliation, and he called a strike. On July 24, some IAM members began picketing and blockading the plant, which Cox promptly closed and placed under armed guard. As the strike wore on into its third week, the TPEA majority grew increasingly restive about lost income and questioned the grounds for the strike. In early August, TPEA representatives collected signatures from more than one hundred employees approving plans to return to work. On August 12, with management's cooperation (including protection provided by security personnel) these employees gathered early in the morning in Cleveland's Public Square and boarded streetcars that stopped directly across from the plant's entrance. When the doors opened at the plant stop, the group rushed en masse through the gates, surprising the picketers, and resumed work.[54]

By these and similar episodes of gamesmanship, the strike was effectively broken, although picketing lingered on for several months. The situation never exploded, although tensions ran high. On one occasion after the return to work, recalls Livingstone, some AFL sympathizers attacked three TPEA members walking toward the plant on Cleveland's High Level Bridge. One of the TPEA men was a highly skilled amateur boxer, however, and he made short work of the AFL assailants. After this story made the rounds, some AFL picketers lost heart, and picketing ceased altogether during the fall.[55]

The strike produced several lasting effects at TP. None of the AFL militants was rehired, and the IAM never again attracted many TP workers. Moreover, the company accelerated plans to consolidate the piston and pin plants into the main plant, steps completed in 1936.[56]

Professionalizing Personnel Management

A preference for working with employee representation plans rather than dealing with national unions was only one particularly vivid aspect of Crawford's approach to industrial relations. Much less publicized but equally important were his efforts to improve personnel management in the company. These efforts started with sponsorship of the Old Guard and other social and recreational activities. An annual series of

Old Guard banquets and picnics began in 1934. At each occasion, Crawford appeared to congratulate new members, hand out pins and other awards—always with a warm and personal touch and usually with humor—and speak openly about the state of the business. He and his young first wife, Audrey, also turned up faithfully at company athletic and social events.

Crawford also took significant actions to improve communications between management and employees, as well as to provide formal policies and administration of personnel matters. In April 1934, for example, the company began twice-monthly publication of an employee newsletter, the *Friendly Forum.* The periodical appeared initially as a publication of the TPEA, but by the end of the year was taken over by management and included news of the Michigan and Canadian plants as well as operations in Cleveland. The *Friendly Forum* carried editorials (including many signed by the employee chairman of the TPEA joint council) supportive of management policies and actions, news of company business, personnel changes, personal items, and coverage of athletic activities and other company events.[57]

During 1934, Crawford made a highly significant appointment, naming twenty-seven-year-old Ray Livingstone as director of personnel and assistant to the president for all personnel functions in the Cleveland and Detroit plants.[58] Livingstone's assignment was nebulous. As he recalls the occasion, he was primarily engaged in selling and visiting customers when one day he was summoned to Crawford's office, where he found the boss along with Wright and Clegg. Crawford told Livingstone, "'We're going to set up a personnel department, something we've never had in the company before, and we've decided you're the fellow to take on the job.' When I recovered from my surprise," Livingstone recalls, "I remember answering, 'But I don't know anything about personnel work.' Fred replied, 'I know it, and neither do we. But we'll learn together. This is tremendously important, and we're willing to take our chances on a young fellow who'll put his heart into the thing, and work [at it].'"[59]

Crawford's faith in Livingstone proved well founded. During the ensuing months, Livingstone read widely on personnel management, visited local companies such as Ohio Bell and Standard Oil of Ohio that were regarded as model progressive employers, and soaked up information at personnel seminars sponsored by the National Association of Manufacturers (NAM) and the American Management Association. He gleaned much from his role as executive secretary to the TPEA joint council, as well as from "innumerable conversations with employees from all shifts, departments, and occupations." This sampling of employee attitudes was initially informal. During the mid-1930s, however, the company took a more scientific approach, becoming one of the first in the United States to make systematic use of surveys of wage data and employee opinion.[60]

Livingstone learned that progressively managed companies focused on the training of foremen. The main plant was typical of a traditional manufacturing plant, in which foremen wielded enormous power. They hired and fired employees at will and assigned all work in their departments. Employees who felt unfairly treated had little recourse. In the worst cases, some foremen abused their power or performed their duties poorly; in any case, their behavior had a disproportionate effect on employee morale. In November 1934, TP launched its first program to train foremen and paid special attention to personnel issues. The program featured a local expert from the Cleveland Board of Education, who offered a series of classes that included "The Why of a Foreman," "Handling Men," "Supervision," "Job Analysis," and "The Placement of Men." Soon afterward, Livingstone organized foremen's clubs at each plant to provide ongoing training, development, and support.[61]

Livingstone also followed the example of progressive companies by developing systematic and formal policies toward hiring, transfers, promotions, training, arbitration of grievances, and compensation. One of his first acts, for example, was to strengthen the employment office, which was then a sinecure for Sam Naff, C. E. Thompson's brother-in-law. Livingstone gave Naff final authority for hiring new employees and urged him to become more organized in his approach to the issue. This entailed developing specific criteria for selection, and processes for interviewing and reference checking. Criteria included a high school education and traits related to particular assignments, such as physical fitness or carefulness for demanding or hazardous work, as well as more qualitative assessments about "friendly, congenial" dispositions and people "who respect order and the principles of this country." (Company guidelines never mentioned candidates' attitudes toward national unions, but it is safe to assume that if potential hirees revealed such sympathies, it did not help their cause; national labor organizers frequently alleged, but never proved conclusively, that TP discriminated on this point in hiring.) To humanize the hiring process, Livingstone insisted that interviewers be friendly and supportive and that interviews take place, not at the traditional "bullpen" employment window near the entrance to the plant, but in a private room. He obtained funds from Crawford to expand the employment office and to provide comfortable furnishings.[62]

The staff in the employment office also devoted attention to improved record keeping and developed guidelines for promotion and transfer of employees. Employment records included "a complete set of job specifications for jobs in all three Cleveland plants, detailed application blanks, periodic rating of all employees, and a personnel inventory to be consulted in the promotion and transfer of employees."[63]

Livingstone and his colleagues also developed guidelines for training and development. In September 1935, the company established an apprentice training program in the tool room of the main plant. The following year, this effort was expanded into a more general four-year program to develop production managers. To the customary shop training, the company added classroom work on production control, time study, costs, tool design, and related subjects. Twelve employees joined the program each year. TP also established cooperative training programs with Fenn College and Cleveland College (both now part of Cleveland State University) that enabled employees who could afford to reduce working time to pursue degrees in engineering or business administration.[64]

In many aspects of its work, the Personnel Division supported and depended upon good working relations with the TPEA. With respect to grievances, for example, the association's constitution had stipulated a general procedure, on which Livingstone elaborated in a bulletin to foremen in March 1936. The bulletin urged foremen to be careful to "check all facts" through separate interviews with the affected parties as well as with pertinent witnesses. Foremen were encouraged to provide answers within one week of the request, including specific explanations of the decision to each affected party. Foremen were also required to provide documentation to Livingstone in his capacity as executive secretary of the TPEA joint council. In cases of dispute, foremen were directed to discuss the matter with a TPEA representative; if a decision still could not be reached, then appeal could be made to the joint council. In speeches and writings, Livingstone also stressed the importance of prompt handling of grievances and noted that individuals who reported grievances "should be regarded as trouble finders rather than trouble makers."[65]

The Personnel Division's involvement with compensation issues also entailed working closely with the joint council. Once again, Livingstone's efforts resulted in better-informed and more comprehensive policy decisions. In December 1934, for example, the joint council commissioned a wage survey of Cleveland-area manufacturers to help evaluate the company's pay policies. The findings showed that TP paid average rates for the area, but it also identified certain classes of work for which the company's rates seemed low. The TPEA sought, and got, an explanation for the discrepancies. A company policy manual published soon afterward stated that TP

> guarantees to pay each employee a fair, honest wage. In determining what constitutes a fair, honest wage we take into consideration these factors: the skill required for the job, the wage paid by similar or competitive companies for the same job, and the financial condition of the Company. Effort is made to give the cost of living consideration. It is not our policy to make blanket increases or decreases. We believe it fairer to give constant study to our rates and make adjustments on the basis of individual merit, or conditions.[66]

This policy was soon borne out. In the summer of 1935, at the request of several employee representatives, the company instituted periodic wage surveys, carried out under the joint supervision of the TPEA and the Personnel Division. A more comprehensive survey revealed, for example, that TP's base rates for certain skill occupations were lower than those of comparable employers. Accordingly, a subcommittee of TPEA representatives recommended increases, a request endorsed by the joint council and ultimately approved by management.[67]

A final significant area of Livingstone's responsibilities involved employee communications. In addition to the *Friendly Forum* and many notices and news items posted on billboards in each department, the Personnel Division produced handbooks for supervisors, employees, and TPEA representatives. The company's thirty-six-page *Industrial Relations Manual,* for example, published in January 1935, was designed for foremen. It relied extensively on publications of the National Association of Manufacturers and General Motors, and it described at length appropriate behavior toward employees and the proper handling of grievances. The manual also echoed Crawford's views about the company's right to manage relations with employees without interference from the government or other outside agencies. It pointed out that "enlightened employers and enlightened employees realize that they have a mutuality of interests" and that good relationships depend on open and honest communications. A key passage dealt with management rights:

> . . . some employee representatives might attempt to usurp some of the functions of management. In the event that such a situation arises, arbitrary refusal to discuss a given point will only complicate matters but a firm denial with supporting reasons will convince employee representatives that management functions remain intact. At the same time some members of the management may mistake questioning of their rulings or actions as an infringement on their rights, and such persons must be made to understand that they have nothing to fear if their actions are based on correct procedure but that any hasty or ill advised practices are subject to review by employee representatives.[68]

The company expressed similar views in another important publication issued in March: its first *Employee's Handbook,* a thirty-two-page pamphlet that described policies regarding promotion, compensation, and grievances, as well as the role of the TPEA. Crawford wrote the introduction, in which he once again stressed the theme of mutual cooperation.[69]

As he had been in Detroit in the 1920s and with his top management staff in 1933, Crawford proved willing to speak openly with employees about the state of the business. The annual banquets of the Old Guard Association provided an ideal platform. A correspondent for the *Friendly Forum* reported his speech to the Old Guard in February 1935 in glowing terms. Crawford, he wrote,

> held the undivided attention of the group for more than 40 minutes while he dealt with the company's most vital workings. Driving his points home with spirited oratory, he used brilliantly colored blocks to illustrate the proportion of the total earnings coming from each of the several plants. . . . He used similar blocks to show how the money was spent—there were blocks representing taxes, wages, machinery, research, and finally a very thin wafer-like block on the top which represented profit—the margin between success and failure.

The correspondent noted that "a burst of applause featured the conclusion of [Crawford's] talk, with all rising in respect."[70]

Starting in 1935, TP began using the *Friendly Forum* to publish "a simple digest in every-day language" of its annual report to stockholders. Later on, the company published a separate annual report to employees, which broke down the company's revenues and expenditures into basic categories and made the point vividly that more than 95 percent of total revenues remained in the business to cover payroll expenses, plant and equipment, and capital investment, with less than 5 percent returned to stockholders as dividends. Senior managers also discussed the company's financial position in detail during wage negotiations with TPEA representatives. In 1936, for example, Clegg and Wright provided the joint council with a detailed analysis of the company's cash position, its tax, loan, and dividend obligations, its investment needs, and its profitability projections for the coming year as a background to granting a 5 percent wage increase.[71]

In carrying out its duties, TP's Personnel Division adopted many practices that were becoming widespread in large manufacturing corporations of the era. By themselves, few of TP's policies were distinctive: many other employers modified the role of foremen, launched training programs, and became more systematic about hiring, firing, compensation, and grievance practices. TP was unusual among employers, however, in three important respects. First, it placed a distinctive emphasis on both the substance and the form of communications with employees. Crawford and other TP managers apparently shared more vital information with employees, more often, and in more ways than did most other corporations of the period. Second, the scale and scope of TP's personnel activities were highly unusual for an employer of its size. TP used many tools such as training programs, social activities, and policy manuals that much larger employers felt were unnecessary, even to deter national union organizers.[72]

Third, and perhaps most important, the motives behind TP's policies were genuine. It is not credible that the company would have invested so much and carried out its programs with such zeal only to keep out the national unions. Many other employers abandoned the struggle after token resistance, believing that accommodation with the unions was the rational, more economical course. TP management believed that its program of human relations was worth the investment not only because it preserved management's independence, but also because it was the right thing to do. This conviction was rooted both in morality—the Golden Rule—and in an economic ideology that insisted on the mutuality of interests among employers and employees.

TP's personnel policies and the resolve behind them were put to the test soon enough.

THE CIO'S OPENING SALVO

In May 1935, the U.S. Supreme Court ruled that the NIRA was unconstitutional, and soon thereafter Congress passed the National Labor Relations Act—known more commonly as the Wagner Act in recognition of its sponsor, Senator Richard Wagner, a Democrat from New York. The new statute provided another boost to the national labor movement by restricting employers' ability to influence employee associations and by guaranteeing the rights of employees to engage in collective bargaining about wages and the terms and conditions of work and to receive redress from certain unfair practices by employers. The act created the National Labor Relations Board (NLRB) to conduct union representation elections, investigate and settle labor disputes, and enforce the act's provisions through the regular judicial process.

The Wagner Act had a number of immediate consequences for American industry. The first was to spark another wave of strikes across the manufacturing sector, perhaps including the IAM strike at TP's pin plant in July 1935. The statute also encouraged labor militants inside the AFL to break with the organization and establish a rival national labor organization, the Committee (later Congress) of Industrial Organizations (CIO) in 1936. Under the leadership of John L. Lewis, president of the United Mine Workers, the CIO campaigned aggressively to organize mass-production industries such as automobiles, rubber, steel, textiles, electrical equipment, and communications.

Most employers opposed the Wagner Act, but they chose to bide their time until the U.S. Supreme Court could review the statute. At TP, for example, management held that the act required no significant changes in its personnel practices, while chief legal officer Dave Wright "expressed considerable doubt as to the constitutionality of the power given to the National Labor Relations Board." During the first eighteen months following the passage of the act, the company continued to support the TPEA and to oppose efforts of industrial unions to organize its plants.[73]

Several factors forced TP to change its ways. First were the vigorous organizing tactics of the CIO unions, including the fledgling United Automobile Workers (UAW-CIO; this cumbersome designation is necessary because of the existence of a conservative rival, the UAW-AFL). Soon after the CIO parted ways with the AFL, northeastern Ohio became a hotbed of CIO activity, with major sit-down strikes in Akron and Cleveland. In December 1936, the UAW-CIO fixed its sights on the main quarry, General Motors. Rather than target the company's headquarters in Detroit, the union chose to strike at the Fisher body plants in Flint, Michigan, and in Cleveland. The tactic proved effective, and on February 11, 1937, GM recognized the union as a legitimate bargaining agent for many of its plants. Less than three weeks later, U.S. Steel recognized the Steel Workers Organizing Committee of the CIO as the bargaining agent for most of its workers.

The capitulation of such major employers as GM and U.S. Steel further bolstered the CIO unions, which then targeted selected automobile parts suppliers in Michigan, including TP's Michigan plant. On March 5, three days after the U.S. Steel settlement and following a brief sit-down strike of about fifty employees, Matt Graham signed a six-month contract with the UAW-CIO, said to be the first contract ever negotiated by the union in the automotive parts industry. Graham acted without consulting Crawford, who was furious when he learned what had happened. He ordered Graham to ignore the agreement, which the company regarded as having no force because employees never voted formally to join the UAW-CIO or to ratify the contract.[74]

TP's clash with the UAW-CIO at the Michigan plant was the opening salvo in a protracted struggle that would resurface again and again for decades. The next skirmish followed soon enough, however. In early April, spurred by its initial success in Detroit, the union started an organizing drive at TP's main plant in Cleveland. Unable to sign up enough TP employees to make a strike effective, the union's young organizer, Bert Cochran, unleashed a flurry of handbills and leaflets attacking management and proclaiming the gains the union had won at the Michigan plant and at GM. TP responded in kind, using the *Friendly Forum* and its own bulletins and handbills to present its side of the story.[75]

On April 12, as the antagonists hurled leaflets and memoranda at each other and at undecided employees, a bombshell dropped. The U.S. Supreme Court finally rendered its opinion on the Wagner Act, upholding its constitutionality. The verdict in *National Labor Relations Board v. Jones and Laughlin Steel Company* was a watershed event in the American labor movement, and it forced employers across the country to reevaluate their tactics in opposing national union organizing drives. Within months major corporations in the electrical equipment, communications, textile, and garment industries joined General Motors and U.S. Steel in recognizing CIO unions.

At TP, the *Jones and Laughlin* decision made it clear that the TPEA was no longer a legal association: among other things, Livingstone wielded enormous influence on its operations as executive secretary. It was also clear that employees would have to be represented by an alternative organization of their own choosing. Accordingly, Livingstone abandoned his involvement with the TPEA, and the association's employee-elected officers soon followed with their resignations.

In May 1937, a committee of TPEA employee representatives met to revise the association's constitution, but they concluded that it could not be salvaged. Instead, they determined to establish a new union free from both management involvement and the CIO. To help them organize the new entity, the Automotive and Aircraft Workers Alliance (A&AWA), the employee representatives engaged Milton A. Roemisch, a Cleveland labor attorney notably unsympathetic to the CIO. By the end of June, the A&AWA claimed more than eight hundred members, and Crawford and Livingstone recognized its "exclusive bargaining rights" to represent TP employees in Cleveland. The TPEA was disbanded, and by July the company and the A&AWA had agreed on a basic contract confirming wage increases recently negotiated by the TPEA, as well as seniority rights. Among its other provisions, the contract established a labor relations council and an executive committee, each consisting of an equal number of A&AWA members and management representatives, to continue bilateral discussions between the parties about matters of mutual interest. Together, these groups performed essentially the same tasks as had the TPEA joint council in earlier years. During 1937, similar independent labor organizations were established at the Michigan, TSP, and Jadson plants.[76]

The *Jones and Laughlin* verdict touched off one other train of events at the main plant, signaling the pugnacious and independent course that Crawford would follow in dealing with the NLRB. A week after the verdict, the UAW-CIO petitioned the NLRB, charging that TP had unfairly dismissed three main-plant employees who had joined the union. In response, the company argued that the three men were bad employees who had been discharged for "just and sufficient reasons." The resolution of this case would consume more than a year, as TP exercised every procedural and appellate option at its disposal. Although an NLRB trial examiner upheld the UAW-CIO complaint and ordered reinstatement of the three employees, the company declared that "it would reinstate the three workers only if forced to do so by an order from the federal district court." The NLRB sought exactly that remedy, petitioning the 6th Circuit Court of Appeals to enforce its order. The court finally took up the case in the spring of 1938, when it ruled on the company's behalf. Speaking for the majority, Judge Elwood Hamilton no doubt pleased Crawford by holding that the NLRB's findings tended "to promote discord among employer and employee," that the board had not proved its case with "substantial evidence," that the board "had acted without 'due process of law' and beyond the authority given to it under the Wagner Act," and that TP "would have been justified in discharging the three had there been no effort to organize employees in a union."[77]

Although TP beat back the UAW-CIO's initial challenge under the Wagner Act, the struggle would soon be reenacted in a much more public way at the height of World War II. By then, the stakes for both parties would be much higher.

PART TWO

Supplier and Contractor

❚   ❚   ❚   ❚   ❚

1939–1965

DURING ITS FORMATIVE YEARS, THOMPSON PRODUCTS DEVELOPED AND MASTERED KEY TECH-nologies related to engine valves and chassis components, acquiring renown for its understanding of the internal combustion engine, expertise in metallurgy, and ability to mass produce items from intractable alloys. The company also displayed a progressive approach to human relations, as well as a flair for marketing its products. By the close of the 1930s, Thompson Products was securely established as a key supplier to the most successful automobile manufacturers and to the leading producers in the much smaller, but still promising, aircraft engine industry.

During the next quarter century, Thompson Products made notable advances in its traditional markets. For the automakers, for example, the company developed a new kind of piston ring, a new suspension ball joint (in collaboration with Ford) that swept through the industry, and more durable steering linkages. The 1950 acquisition of Ramsey Corporation, a maker of piston rings and other products for the automotive aftermarket, and the subsequent merger of the Thompson Products and Toledo Steel Products brand names expanded the company's position in that business. And Thompson Products played a central role in the development of the revolutionary turbojet engine by fabricating key metal components to perform in an extraordinarily hostile environment.

But during these years, Thompson Products' business also changed dramatically as it grew rapidly, developed and acquired new skills and capabilities, and diversified into new areas (see Exhibits II-1 to II-5). World War II served as the initial catalyst for change. The war had many obvious and far-reaching effects, including massive impacts on world order and the world economy—much to the benefit of American corporations. In the United States, the war brought to an end a decade of economic distress and turmoil as public resources poured into industry, underwrote new technologies, raised employment, subsidized new facilities, and helped wipe out corporate debt. In the war's aftermath, American corporations enjoyed a preeminence in the world economy unrivaled before or since in their history.

The war also helped establish the U.S. government as a colossal consumer of goods and services, especially of military technology. Although U.S. defense spending dropped immediately after the war, the nation quickly assumed a leadership position in world politics. With new responsibilities came new appetites: the dawn of the Cold War in the late 1940s, the conflict in Korea, and the escalation of military and technological rivalry with the Soviet Union during the 1950s and especially after 1957, when the Soviets launched the first man-made satellite, saw huge surges in federal spending on defense technology.

The emerging defense industry represented a major source of opportunity for established companies such as Thompson Products as well as for its new venture partner in 1953, the Ramo-Wooldridge Corporation (R-W). Government spending stimulated activity in new areas ranging from aircraft propulsion and fuel systems, to the extremely advanced technologies of missiles, to electronic components and systems,

EXHIBIT II - 1

TRW INC. AND PREDECESSOR COMPANIES NET REVENUES AND NET INCOME, 1939–1964

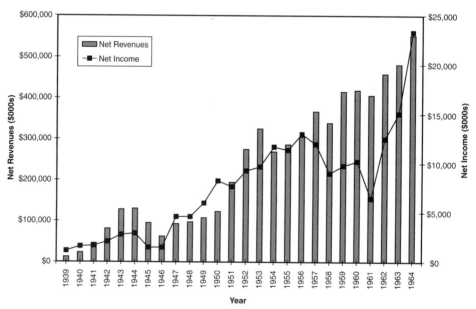

SOURCE: Annual reports.

to spacecraft and space-borne equipment. During periods of rapid expansion, however, the defense industry also posed challenges and concerns, skewing the company's sales mix dramatically and raising questions about how it would manage the inevitable downturns.

The peculiar economics and procedures of defense contracting, moreover, profoundly affected the characters of Thompson Products, Ramo-Wooldridge, and their eventual union as TRW. The new business of defense contracting—especially as R-W practiced it—contrasted in many ways to Thompson Products' traditional business as an industrial supplier. The defense industry embraced a world of big and extremely complex projects and programs, new and advanced technologies, highly credentialed and accomplished employees with concomitant egos and ambitions, and a market defined by politicians, bureaucrats, and international politics. The industry offered many attractions, such as customer-funded R&D, huge long-term contracts with guaranteed returns, and repeated opportunities to push back the frontiers of science and technology. But it also posed major risks: sudden and unpredictable swings in government support, the limited applicability of much military technology to commercial markets, and increasing public scrutiny of contracts and performance. In recognition of these distinctive opportunities and threats, TRW adopted and developed an unusual

EXHIBIT II - 2

TRW INC. AND PREDECESSOR COMPANIES MEASURES OF PROFITABILITY, 1939–1964

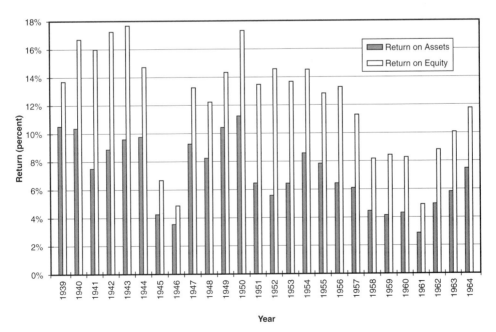

SOURCE: Annual reports.

organizational structure and supporting policies. It managed itself as both a supplier and a contractor, isolating its commercial and military activities, and becoming in the process a new kind of corporation.

TRW entered the world of defense contracting during World War II. One of the greatest and most immediate beneficiaries of the war was the aircraft industry: in 1938, manufacturers built about thirty-six hundred planes; at the peak of wartime production in 1944, they built more than ninety-five thousand. For Thompson Products, as for other key suppliers to the aircraft industry, the vast wartime expansion brought transformation: sales soared by a factor of fifteen, and employment by a factor of five (Chapter 5). The company built and operated a mammoth facility in Cleveland, becoming the largest employer in the region. It also developed new capabilities in precision manufacturing for advanced aircraft engines and auxiliary product lines such as high-altitude fuel systems and pumps. To help manage its growth, train and organize its burgeoning work force, and ensure its independence from the national labor movement, the company continued to refine and develop its pioneering program of human relations.

Although during the war Thompson Products served as a subcontractor to other industrial manufacturers, the strategic significance and huge volume of its business gave it unusual visibility. Its achievements and its success in fending off the national

EXHIBIT II - 3

TRW INC. AND PREDECESSOR COMPANIES EMPLOYMENT, 1939–1964

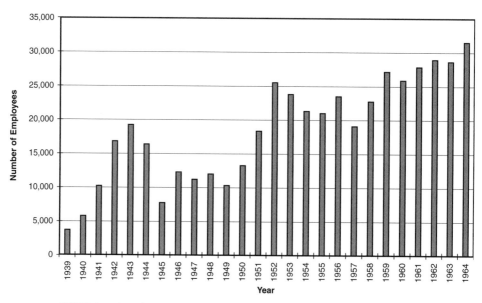

SOURCE: Annual reports.

unions contributed to its—and Fred Crawford's—growing national reputations. During 1943–1944—the peak of national defense production—Crawford served as president of the National Association of Manufacturers and figured prominently in many industry–government advisory committees and panels. His close contact with leading officials in government, industry, and the military would prove immensely valuable after the war.

In 1945, Thompson Products' postwar challenge was the same as that facing every other defense contractor: reconversion to peacetime activity and identifying new opportunities to build on the skills, experience, and financial and human resources accumulated during the war (Chapter 6). Pursuing an organic strategy of growth, the company added new products to the markets it already knew and served well: the automobile, automobile replacement, aircraft engine, and aircraft industries.

The onset of the Cold War and another rapid escalation during the Korean War particularly stimulated the market for aircraft. During these years the company distinguished itself as producer of high value-added components for turbojet engines, such as turbine wheels, compressor blades, and airfoils—a business that accounted for as much as 70 percent of total revenues. Under Crawford and his close associate and

EXHIBIT II - 4

TRW INC. AND PREDECESSOR COMPANIES SALES BY LINE OF BUSINESS, 1935–1962

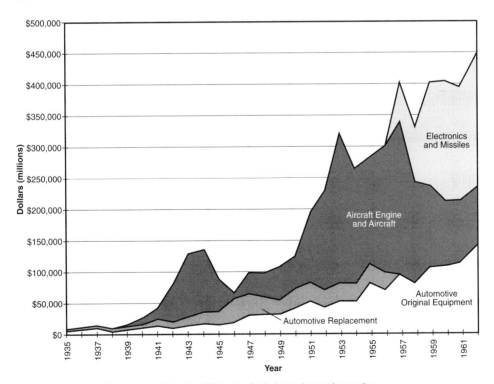

SOURCE: Annual reports. Data after 1962 not available due to changes in reporting.

eventual successor, Dave Wright, Thompson Products also established principles of decentralized management and organization that would later facilitate a strategy of growth and diversification. The company began formal planning for demobilization in 1951. Two years later, it took its first tentative steps into new areas of commercial and military electronics and nuclear power.

Of its new areas of interest, only military electronics yielded lasting success. Thompson Products' investment in Ramo-Wooldridge (R-W) proved the foundation of a major segment of TRW's modern business in space and defense (Chapter 7). But first, the challenge to develop the intercontinental ballistic missile (ICBM) almost wholly diverted the attention of R-W's founders, Simon Ramo and Dean Wooldridge. As contractor to the U.S. Air Force for systems engineering and technical direction (SETD), R-W took charge of the nation's highest-priority defense initiative, helping to solve innumerable complex technical problems in guidance, propulsion, electronic control and communications, and reentry. At the same time, R-W took its first tentative steps into commercial electronics businesses, introducing electronic test equipment, digital computers, and other electronic products and systems.

As SETD contractor for the Atlas, Thor, and Titan missiles, R-W occupied a privileged position in shaping the U.S. Air Force's technical capabilities and long-range

EXHIBIT II - 5

TRW INC. AND PREDECESSOR COMPANIES PERCENTAGE SALES BY LINE OF BUSINESS, 1935–1962

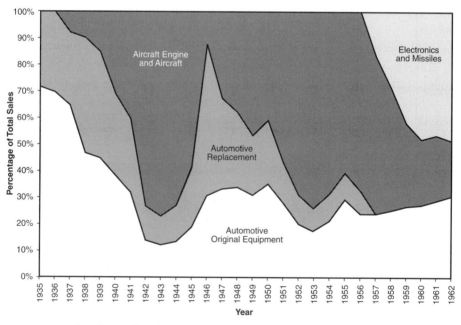

SOURCE: Annual reports. Data after 1962 not available due to changes in reporting.

plans. To avoid problems of conflict of interest, the company accepted a ban on producing hardware for the Air Force missile program—a ban that also extended to Thompson Products. These arrangements proved a source of increasing irritation: to other industrial contractors, who resented R-W's favored position; to Thompson Products, which met frustration in its efforts to offset the decline of its jet engine components business by making parts and components for missiles; and to R-W itself, which saw its long-term future as a producer of electronic hardware for both military and commercial markets as opposed to a provider of technical and analytical services to the Air Force.

Several factors converged to resolve these tensions and to stimulate a merger between Thompson Products and R-W (Chapter 8). The beginnings of a next-generation ICBM—the Minuteman—raised the stakes for both companies because the government's intention to deploy the missile in large numbers offered attractive prospects to hardware producers. In addition, the October 1957 flight of *Sputnik* galvanized Congress and Dwight Eisenhower's administration to commit massive investments to the American space program, as well as to science and technology generally. And by late 1957, R-W planned to capitalize on its capabilities in space-related hardware and systems. As Thompson Products endured a cyclical downturn in its automotive business and forecast a long and probably irreversible decline of its major business in aircraft engine components, its best hope seemed a merger with R-W. Similarly, with ambitious plans for growth, R-W needed access to the greater pools of capital that Thompson Products possessed.

The merger between the supplier and the contractor created a new corporation, Thompson Ramo Wooldridge, Inc. (TRW), with a new chairman, Dave Wright, based in Cleveland, and a new president, Dean Wooldridge, based in Los Angeles. The merger also created an entity comprised of very different pieces (Chapter 9). The former Thompson Products businesses continued to focus on precision manufacturing and mass production of parts and components for the automotive and aircraft industries. The erstwhile R-W businesses included an array of divisions concerned with commercial and military electronics as well as ongoing missile development work. TRW initially managed these diverse businesses as two disconnected parts under Thompson Products' decentralized organization and management policies. In 1960, the company finally resolved the long-standing tension over the hardware ban by divesting part of R-W's operations concerned with long-range planning for the Air Force.

During the next few years the company successfully managed the transition from an adviser on the missile programs to a producer of spacecraft and electronic systems for scientific, commercial, and military applications, including some projects that remain classified. The early 1960s, however, brought a crisis to the former R-W electronics businesses that triggered a change of management personnel and philosophy at TRW. Dean Wooldridge and several other former R-W leaders left the company or shifted into new assignments. At the same time, Horace Shepard, a former Air Force general with a decade of service in senior management at Thompson Products and TRW became president and maintained his office next to Wright's in Cleveland. Under

Wright and Shepard, TRW continued to function as a decentralized company but under tighter financial and operating controls. TRW divested several electronics divisions, including the computer business, and refocused others on specific military markets. At the same time, management sought to grow the corporation in new areas unrelated to defense. In 1964, the company completed two big mergers, joining with Marlin-Rockwell, a manufacturer of bearings for transportation and general industrial applications, and Ross Gear, a leading producer of steering systems for trucks. Yet another sign of new times was the formal and official truncation of the corporate name from Thompson Ramo Wooldridge, Inc., to TRW Inc.

Courtesy of The Western Reserve Historical Society, Cleveland, Ohio.

Designed for mass production and bristling with the latest manufacturing technology, the mammoth Tapco plant accounted for many significant achievements during World War II. Bright, open, and airy, it proved a highly desirable place of employment and housed nearly ten thousand workers in round-the-clock operations.

Thompson Products applied its pump technology in timely fashion to help manage fuel delivery in high-altitude bombers. Pictured here: Female workers assemble aircraft fuel pumps. By 1944, about a third of the company's Cleveland-area employees were women.

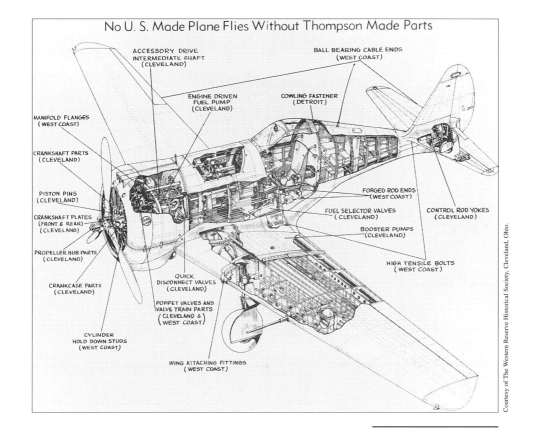

Courtesy of The Western Reserve Historical Society, Cleveland, Ohio.

Thompson Products developed this schematic of a generic airplane to illustrate its contributions to the aircraft industry during the war.

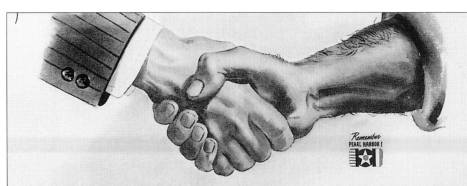

We're seeing this through *Together!*

WE, the workers and the management of Thompson Products, have learned how to *work together.* It is all so simple when there's square-dealing, tolerance and cooperation on BOTH sides of the conference table!

Such harmony is the key to all-out production. With it, we'll do more than our share to put Uncle Sam in first place.

There are 9,500 of us now in Thompson plants. We'll be 14,500 early next year when our new RFC subsidiary in Euclid, Ohio, is in full swing on aircraft parts.

We are proud and jealous of our record as an *"Arsenal of Democracy."* We've taken those words to heart.

In Thompson plants we have wasted not one single day because of strikes!

In two years we've stepped up our total defense production 400%—our aircraft parts production *1500%.* We're turning out over 1,000 different vital parts for bombers and fighters. Our automotive parts are going into military cars, trucks and tanks, and are helping to keep 32,000,000 American motor vehicles on the highways. By the end of 1942 we'll be shipping at the rate of $70,000,000 a year.

Over 3,000 of us have completed our company's industrial training courses. More of us are in training today.

We've added 600,000 square feet of productive floor space by reclaiming old, abandoned buildings—and 750,000 square feet of new construction. We're subletting lots of work.

We've subscribed heartily to National Defense Bonds, offered through our company. The company is paying Uncle Sam four times the taxes it paid two years ago—and paying gladly. It has borrowed $4,500,000 to speed national defense production.

Our wages are kept at highest possible levels through intelligent negotiation. Our working conditions are as good as we can make them these abnormal times. We're guarding our health and safety at work.

We're working three shifts, seven days a week, harder and faster than we've ever worked before.

Tension, strain, pressure, privations? *Sure!* But we can take it, and *we'll out-produce the world!*

We, the workers and the management at Thompson Products, are seeing this war through TOGETHER. We want to produce, and *produce to the limit,* for America and the American Way of Life.

We're getting RESULTS. We'll do more than our share to WIN THIS WAR!

THE MANAGEMENT *Pledges*

1. All our time, energy and resources to win this war.

2. The highest possible wage scale consistent with sound management.

3. A fair and square deal to our men in all negotiations.

Signed by the following officials of THOMPSON PRODUCTS, INC. and its subsidiaries:

F. C. CRAWFORD
L. M. CLEGG
R. S. LIVINGSTONE
G. A. STAUFFER
A. F. SEUBERT
M. P. GRAHAM
P. D. HILEMAN

THE EMPLOYEES *Pledge*

1. Every possible piece, every day, from every machine. We're in earnest!

2. The full use of our experience in improving quality, reducing waste, and teaching the *"know how"* to new men.

3. Intelligent bargaining, man to man —The American Way.

Signed by:

JOHN A. KENNA, *Pres.*
Automotive and Aircraft Workers Alliance, Inc., Cleveland
CHARLES G. DeVOS, *Pres.*
Society of Tool and Die Craftsmen, Detroit
IRVIN HESS, *Pres.*
Pacific Motor Parts Workers Alliance, Los Angeles
A. F. BERG, *Pres.*
Automotive Parts Workers Alliance, Inc., Toledo
R. T. LETOURNEAU, *Pres.*
Thompson Products Employees Association, St. Catharines, Canada

The Workers and Management of

Thompson Products

and Subsidiaries

Factories in Cleveland, Detroit and Los Angeles; *Subsidiaries:* Thompson Aircraft Products Company, Euclid, Ohio; Toledo Steel Products Company, Toledo, Ohio; Thompson Products, Ltd., St. Catharines, Ontario.

"A Different Kind of a Company"
Manufacturers of Automotive and Aircraft Parts

Remember PEARL HARBOR!

Courtesy of The Western Reserve Historical Society, Cleveland, Ohio.

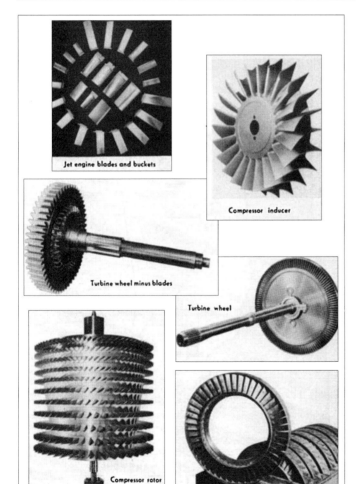

Jet engine blades and buckets

Compressor inducer

Turbine wheel minus blades

Turbine wheel

Compressor rotor

Nozzle diaphragms

Facing page: *The hand-shake between manage-ment and worker reflected Crawford's fundamental beliefs about human rela-tions, which helped the company prevail in its extended struggle with organized labor during the war.*

Above: *The Spellbinder: The secret of a good speech, said Crawford, is "Be yourself: that was my first rule. Second, nothing stirs up an audience like a good belly laugh." Pictured here: Crawford addresses a mass meeting at the Tapco Plant in 1942.*

Left: *Thompson Products played a central role in the development of the turbo-jet engine by fabricating highly complex compo-nents to extremely precise dimensions from hard-to-work alloys.*

Above: *Team at the top: The management team that led Thompson Products shared decades of common experience. Pictured (left to right): Arch Colwell, Jim Coolidge, Fred Crawford, Dave Wright, and Ray Livingstone.*

Right: *Under Crawford and Livingstone, Thompson Products became renowned as "A Good Place to Work." Pictured here: An employee checks the bulletin board at the Tapco plant in 1951.*

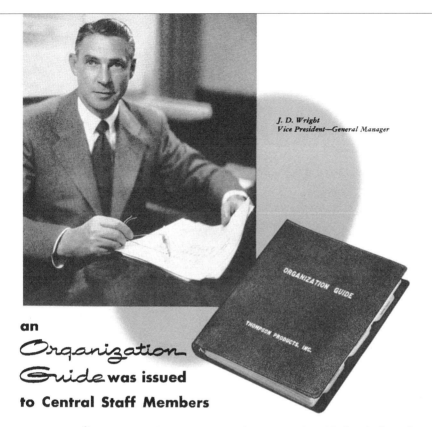

J. D. Wright
Vice President—General Manager

an *Organization Guide* was issued
to Central Staff Members

● In October the forty-two members of the company's Central Staff received a newly compiled Organization Guide—"a plan of organization that involves centralized control of overall policy and decentralization of operations into operating divisions." A page in the Organization Guide lists these thirteen

RESPONSIBILITIES COMMON TO ALL MEMBERS OF MANAGEMENT

1. *Live up to a high code of personal honor; follow the Golden Rule and obey the law.*

2. *Understand and follow sound principles of organization.*

3. *Fill all positions with the best qualified personnel; make promotions from within the organization whenever practicable, and maintain a sound replacement program.*

4. *Make plans for the discharge of your responsibility.*

5. *Keep yourself informed on all overall corporate policies and on such specific*

policies as affect your particular responsibilities.

6. *Offer suggestions and criticisms for consideration by the General Policy Group.*

7. *Keep yourself abreast of developments relating to your particular responsibility by following a personal program of study and observation of the activities of others.*

8. *Establish a two-way communications system by which you keep your organization fully informed on all matters of specific or general interest and by which your organization keeps you informed on such matters.*

9. *Constantly inspect and appraise the activities and results of yourself and your organization.*

10. *Know by personal contact the morale, the problems, and the achievements of all members of your organization.*

11. *Maintain an annual calendar and follow-up system to make certain no duties are overlooked.*

12. *Conduct sound human relations both inside and outside the company.*

13. *Follow common sense. Recognize when and where exceptions to rules should be made.*

The Organization Man: As vice president and general manager (1949–1953), president (1953–1958), and chairman and CEO (1958–1969), Dave Wright developed the organization structure and administrative policies that positioned Thompson Products and TRW for rapid, profitable, and sustained growth.

Above: *Ramo and Wooldridge started out modestly, first conducting business from a former barbershop. Later, the company took off like a rocket.*

Right: *Although the demands of the ICBM stretched R-W's capabilities nearly to the limit, the company also sought to develop other military and commercial businesses. Pictured here: A reconstructed organization chart from 1955.*

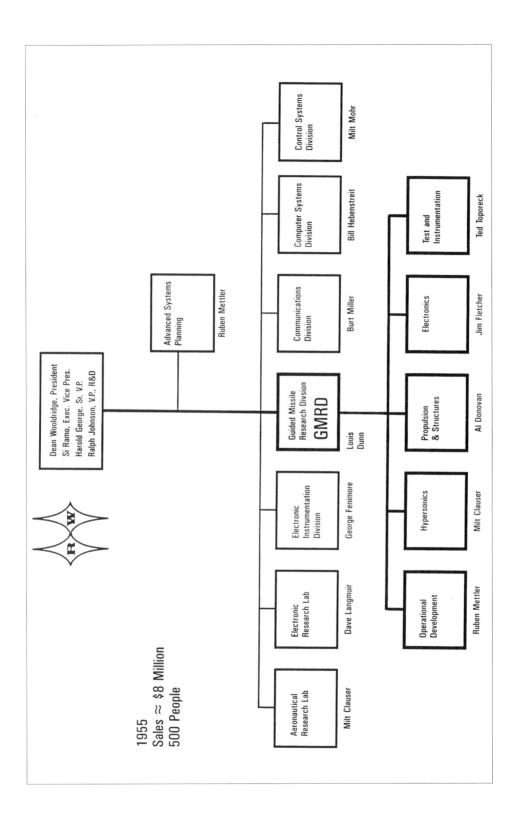

The close partnership
between the Air Force's
Western Development
Command and Ramo-
Wooldridge extended to
co-location as well as
mutual admiration.
Pictured here: General
Bernhard Schriever greet-
ing Ramo, his counterpart
as technical head of the
ICBM program, in 1954.

Rising Star: Rube Mettler was still in his early thirties when Ramo asked him to run the Thor program. Mettler later oversaw development of the Minuteman missile and the company's successful transition from missiles to space. As TRW's president (1969–1977) and chairman and CEO (1977–1988), he guided the company's expansion into many new areas.

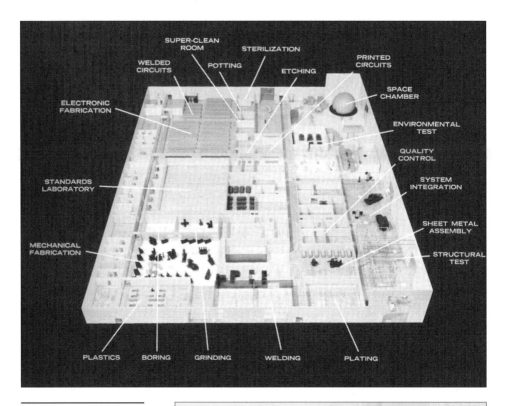

SUPER-CLEAN ROOM
STERILIZATION
WELDED CIRCUITS
POTTING
ETCHING
PRINTED CIRCUITS
ELECTRONIC FABRICATION
SPACE CHAMBER
ENVIRONMENTAL TEST
QUALITY CONTROL
STANDARDS LABORATORY
SYSTEM INTEGRATION
SHEET METAL ASSEMBLY
MECHANICAL FABRICATION
STRUCTURAL TEST
PLASTICS   BORING   GRINDING   WELDING   PLATING

Above: *Big Bet: TRW designed and started construction on its manufacturing complex before it had won any spacecraft awards. The facility defined the state of the art in building spacecraft and greatly enhanced the company's capabilities.*

Right: Pioneer *1, the first privately produced American spacecraft, proceeded from the drawing board to the launch pad in fewer than six months. The vehicle measured twenty-nine inches in diameter and thirty inches long. Aimed at the moon, it fell far short of its target but nonetheless established a short-lived distance record of 70,717 miles in space.*

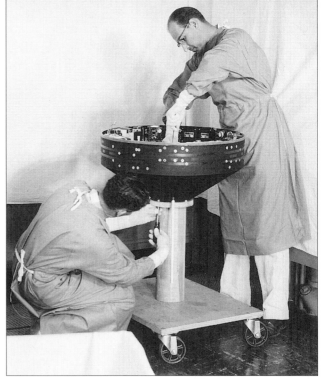

By the spring of 1957, Wooldridge and Ramo had become two of the most famous aerospace engineers in the United States.

Above: *The board of directors convenes around a model of the Orbiting Geophysical Observatory, a highly versatile and successful NASA program during the 1960s. Clockwise from lower left: Dave Wright, Jimmy Doolittle, Fred Crawford, Dean Wooldridge, Ralph Johnson, Jim Coolidge, Arch Colwell, Harold George, Si Ramo, and Horace Shepard.*

Right: *The youngest general in the U.S. Air Force, Horace Shepard moved to Thompson Products in 1951, rising to become president between 1962 and 1969 and thereafter, until his retirement in 1977, chairman and CEO. Under his leadership, TRW became a global competitor in automotive supply.*

Chapter 5

Transformation

▶   ▶   ▶

1939–1945

IN 1946, A REPORTER FOR *FORTUNE* MAGAZINE PENNED A FLATTERING PROFILE OF THOMPSON Products and its president. The article crackled with positive but nonetheless astute observations of Crawford, whom the reporter portrayed in colorful terms: "the only human thing around Thompson Products that runs faster than a turbine wheel, hotter than a valve head and noisier than a drop forge." The writer described Crawford as "a compact gentleman," noting that he seemed to move "with such restless energy that he eats and sleeps only for want of anything else to do. He is broad shouldered, slim-hipped, erect, and sublimely self-assured. Even his enemies do not deny that he has some grounds for confidence, for he is a good engineer (Harvard M.C.E.), a crack manager, a born showman." The reporter went on to discuss Crawford's political views, calling him "an uncompromising advocate of rugged individualism," who maintained "a religious faith in the private-enterprise system" and ranked "among the most eloquent evangels of modern conservatism."[1]

All of these qualities were on display at TP during Crawford's first five years as president. After 1939, they were on display for the entire nation, as TP became a major defense contractor and Crawford himself became a celebrity in business circles for his passionate defense of free enterprise and his sharp criticisms of big government and big labor.

Supplying the Arsenal of Democracy

The primary force that propelled both TP and Fred Crawford to center stage was their response to the vast expansion of business during World War II. The buildup transformed TP from a middling producer of automobile parts that also dabbled in aircraft engine valves into a significant defense contractor and a major supplier to the aircraft and aircraft engine industries. It also required TP to develop and master new techniques to organize, motivate, and manage people and production on a large scale.

During the war, TP experienced tremendous growth: between 1939 and 1944, sales soared by a factor of eight, skyrocketing from $15.6 million to $130.8 million. At the same time, net income climbed from $1.2 million to $2.9 million. At first glance, these profit figures may not seem striking, but the $14.2 million the company reported as operating profit before taxes in 1944 totaled more than the entire sales of the company just six years earlier. Before the war, the company had employed about four thousand people, two-thirds of them in Cleveland; at its wartime peak in 1943, TP employed nearly twenty thousand, more than 80 percent of them in Cleveland (see the exhibits in the introduction to Part II).

The defense buildup affected every TP plant and operation and included major expansions at the main plant and at TP factories in Toledo (Ohio), Bell (California), and St. Catharines (Ontario), as well as the construction of a huge new facility in the Cleveland suburb of Euclid. In the Cleveland-area plants, the company manufactured both traditional items for military vehicles and aircraft engines, and entirely new products for the aircraft industry. Elsewhere, TP plants took on special ordnance contracts for the U.S. and Canadian governments. The Detroit facility, which specialized in the forging of hollow metal tubes, for example, produced fuse adapters; at the Canadian plant, TP, Ltd., manufactured special ordnance items, including the six-pound armor-piercing shells that helped stop Rommel's tanks in North Africa.[2]

Most of TP's output during the war derived from its conventional products. As Dave Wright put it, "By and large, Thompson Products has been a shoemaker sticking to its last." The company enjoyed rapid growth in every line of business. Although the automobile manufacturers made no passenger cars between 1942 and late 1945, they built millions of jeeps, trucks, tanks, ambulances, and other motor vehicles, and TP's traditional customers continued to purchase items such as valves and chassis parts. The company also brought to market new products from the development efforts of the 1930s: hardened cylinder sleeves for trucks, aluminum pistons with steel belts to control expansion, and various mechanisms to rotate valves. Between 1939 and 1945, TP's sales to manufacturers of automotive original equipment rose from $7.3 million to $16.9 million.[3]

TP's replacement business grew even faster during the war, more than tripling in sales from $6.5 million in 1939 to $21.5 million in 1945. This demand stemmed not only from the need for spare parts for military vehicles but also from the cessation of new car production in the United States early in 1942. Car owners had little alternative but to pay any price to keep their vehicles on the road. In these circumstances, the work begun before the war by Tom Duggan and Jim Syvertsen paid handsome dividends. The Service Division continued to add new wholesalers and jobbers, blanketing the country with "Thompson" and "Toledo" service packages.

In 1941, the Service Division introduced its *Thompson Repair & Tune-Up Manual,* a fat volume that ran to more than fifteen hundred pages, included six thousand illustrations, and weighed nine pounds. The manual provided technical data and specifications for practically every car, truck, tractor, and diesel engine in use, and it was a smash hit. It sold for $25 but was given away free to any distributor who ordered more than $100 worth of TP or Toledo parts. Other sales aids included trade paper advertising, calendar and display material, motion pictures, trade meetings, and a fleet of roving "M" (for missionary) cars that carried the TP display line to warehouses and garages across the nation. The division also provided "a business and technical counselor service" consisting of experts "trained in the operation of a distributor's business, to aid in the repair of a car, to lay out a new store, and to set up an efficient machine shop." By such means, the value of TP and Toledo parts per car on the road rose from nine cents in 1938 to twenty-eight cents in 1943.[4]

By far the biggest increase in TP's sales resulted from the enormous expansion of aircraft production after 1940. To supply this burgeoning market, the company made not only sodium-cooled valves, but also entirely new products such as booster pumps and other elements of high-altitude fuel systems. This work led to many other opportunities throughout the war, including the chance to participate in the revolutionary development of turbojet engines at the war's end.

The Factory in the Vineyard

Signs of a pickup in the market for aircraft engine products first appeared in 1938 with the arrival of British and French military purchasing commissions to the United States and an upsurge in interest by the American military. In 1938, Pratt & Whitney received a $2 million order from the French for aircraft engines, which was raised the following year to the staggering backlog of $85 million. These orders rippled down to TP, which expanded its capacity to make sodium-cooled valves at the main plant several times, starting in early 1939.[5]

U.S. military spending on aircraft also began to soar, rising to the record total of $68 million in 1939, a level 50 percent higher than three years earlier. This was merely a prelude of things to come. On May 16, 1940, after watching the devastating impact of the German Blitzkrieg and the Nazi invasion of France, President Franklin Roosevelt astounded—and pleased—the aircraft industry by calling for production of fifty thousand airplanes a year. This goal was extraordinarily ambitious, representing a nearly tenfold surge in production and a fivefold expansion of capacity. As the war proceeded, Roosevelt raised the goal first to sixty thousand, then to one hundred twenty thousand planes a year.[6]

To plan this enormous increase in capacity, in 1940 Roosevelt created the National Defense Advisory Commission and persuaded General Motors president William S. Knudsen to become its director. At this organization and its successors, the Office of Production Management and the War Production Board, Knudsen presided over the conversion of much of American heavy industry to defense production. Early in 1941, the federal Reconstruction Finance Corporation—a New Deal agency—established a subsidiary, the Defense Plant Corporation, to finance new production facilities and lease them to manufacturers.[7]

These events provided the backdrop to a late-1940 telephone call from Knudsen, who now bore the rank of general, to Fred Crawford. Knudsen invited Crawford to visit Washington, which he shortly did, accompanied by Dave Wright, TP's thirty-five-year-old treasurer. As recalled by Crawford and Wright, Knudsen announced, "We're going to have to make a hell of a lot of valves." (In fact, each four-engine airplane built during the war required 144 valves.) He then handed out a schedule calling for production of several hundred thousand aircraft engines a year, and invited his visitors to manage a new valve factory that would be built at government expense. The government would provide funds for construction and to purchase most of the equipment, but TP would have responsibility for design, layout, and operation of the plant, including recruitment and training of personnel. TP was also expected to invest capital in the project, transferring some equipment from the main plant, in return for which it would receive an equity position, a guaranteed return, and first option to buy the plant after the conclusion of the defense emergency.[8]

Crawford delegated the details of organizing the new operation to Wright, who conceived the notion of managing the new business through a separate subsidiary corporation. This stratagem, Wright believed, had several advantages. First, it limited the financial risks to TP. "Because the increase in orders for valves for the war was so big," he recalled, "if the war would suddenly end and the demand would suddenly stop, we'd go bust." But, he pointed out, "if the subsidiary goes bust, [we would] be able to just walk away from it, without having to absorb any of the debts." The subsidiary arrangement also made it easier to audit use of government funds, a major concern both to the government and to defense contractors who were well aware of the scrutiny paid after World War I to profitable munitions suppliers.[9]

On January 10, 1941, Wright filed papers to incorporate Thompson Aircraft Products Company (Tapco) in Ohio as a wholly owned subsidiary of TP. From there, matters moved swiftly. Drawing on an initial outlay of $18 million from the Defense Plant Corporation, Tapco purchased an abandoned 120-acre vineyard in Euclid, Ohio, eleven miles east of downtown Cleveland. This property would house a 565,000 square-foot, one-story factory fronted by a two-story office that would employ about five thousand workers. To design the plant, TP engaged Albert Kahn, the famed industrial architect who had designed many factories for General Motors and Pratt & Whitney. Kahn's facilities were noted for their massive size, sawtooth roofs, and wooden floors—all features of the new Tapco plant. The Sam W. Emerson Company of Cleveland served as general contractor, breaking ground on April 14. By June, underground work—water mains, sewers, concrete piers, basements, machinery foundations, and electrical conduits—was virtually completed. The first structural steel girders arrived, appropriately, on Independence Day. Construction of the roof began in October. On December 2—five days before the Japanese attack on Pearl Harbor and the U.S. entry into the war—with the north end of the building still open to the elements, a chilled group of workers produced the plant's first sodium-cooled valve.[10]

The rapid scale-up of the plant testified vividly to the managerial skills of Wright, who served as vice president and general manager of Tapco, and of Gene McBride, who moved over from the main plant as factory manager. In November 1941, McBride brought with him seventy-five engineers, supervisors, and workers from the main plant, who started production. This was the initial complement of about eighteen hundred main-plant employees who formed the nucleus of a Tapco work force that grew to more than ninety-five hundred within two years. By then, a $12 million expansion program had increased the production area to more than a million square feet.

At its peak operation, the Tapco plant was a showcase of 1940s American manufacturing know-how—"a far cry from the old conception of factories as places of clangor, dust, and gloom," as a company publication put it. It featured more than seven thousand tons of steel, fifteen and one-half miles of fluorescent lighting, fifty-nine miles of pipes for plumbing, heating, and ventilation, two air-conditioned cafeterias, individual lockers for employees, and parking for thirty-five hundred cars. The larger of the two cafeterias doubled as an auditorium for business and social gatherings.

All production took place on the ground floor in a vast open area with few partitions; the plant's high ceilings provided ample room for overhead machinery, plumbing, electrical conduits, and ducts. Nine production lines, each performing about 180 separate operations, totaled more than 1.5 miles. Between them were wide aisles, used "to accommodate the flow of work and the busy traffic of personnel 'taxis' and traveling refreshment stands." The ventilation system was so efficient that ovens for heat treatment of metal parts that were traditionally placed in separate "hot rooms" could be installed directly in the production line.[11]

By the middle of 1943, the plant was capable of turning out four hundred thousand sodium-cooled valves per month—between 80 and 90 percent of all Allied valve requirements. Behind this remarkable performance lay TP's success in developing machinery and automatic processes for handling valves as they worked their way through the plant. During the 1930s, the sodium-cooled valve had evolved into a sophisticated product. The basic valve material, TPA austenitic steel, served as a carrier onto which various alloys and materials were added: stellite on the valve seat, another hard material on the tip, and a special surface coating on the stem. Manufacturing tolerances were extremely close. Some parts of the valve had to be machined to within 3/10,000 of an inch—about one-tenth the diameter of a human hair. To make these valves in such volume, TP engineers devised automatic equipment to weld stellite to the valve seats, a step that resulted in significant cost savings, although some work continued to be done by hand. They also improved processes for handling sodium and developed many other time- and labor-saving techniques.[12]

For all their complexity, TP's sodium-filled valves proved highly reliable in service. On one mission, a damaged U.S. warplane returned to base where mechanics discovered that one of its valves had been shot clean through. Even so, it continued to function as an air-cooled valve, enabling enough engine power so that the plane could limp home. The heroic valve became the focus of a popular TP advertisement, as well as a source of consternation at Wilcox-Rich, which also claimed to have manufactured it.[13]

The Tapco plant's achievements earned it an Army-Navy "E" (for Excellence) production award, which was presented to Crawford and Wright at a massive public event on September 5, 1943. Nearly forty thousand people, including employees and their families, a crowd said to be the largest gathering of its kind in Cleveland during the war, jammed into the Tapco parking lot for the presentation ceremony.[14]

The pressures of managing Tapco proved so great that early in 1942 Wright resigned as treasurer of TP to devote himself full time to the job. As his successor, Wright recommended that the board of directors elect James H. (Jim) Coolidge, an executive vice president and partner in the Cleveland investment firm McDonald, Coolidge & Co. Coolidge, who was also Fred Crawford's first cousin and a brother of Arch Colwell's roommate at West Point, accepted the assignment, joining the company in January 1942. Two months later, he was elected a director of TP. During the next several years, he worked closely with Crawford, Wright, and other top executives to finance the company's impressive wartime expansion.[15]

Into Accessories

Its vast increase in defense work provided occasion for TP to develop entirely new products for the aircraft industry. From a financial perspective, the most important was fuel booster pumps. This story began in 1938, when Curtiss-Wright, which was unhappy with another supplier, asked Arch Colwell whether TP could manufacture aircraft fuel pumps. Colwell promised to look into the matter and briefly considered acquiring a pump company. The price was prohibitive, however, and TP instead licensed patents for aircraft fuel pumps from Curtis Manufacturing Company of Dayton, Ohio. During the next two years, the proprietor of that company, William H. Curtis, worked closely with TP as a consultant and "resident engineer."[16]

Late in 1940, just as the fuel pump business was beginning to expand, a much more promising opportunity appeared. The U.S. Army's Materiel Procurement Division at Wright Field near Dayton sponsored a conference to investigate the alarming tendency of bomber engines to sputter and stall at altitudes above eighteen thousand feet, well below optimum cruising altitude for high-level bombing. It was quickly learned that at high altitudes, vapor pockets formed in the feed lines leading to the fuel pumps, which were situated near the engines, and disrupted the flow of fuel, often with catastrophic results. The solution was far from obvious, however, and engineers from several companies, including Curtis Manufacturing and TP, began to study the problem intensively.

Early in 1941, Curtis had a flash of inspiration. Relaxing on a cross-country train ride, he played with the swizzle stick in his drink. He noticed that a swirling action caused bubbles in the liquid to rise to the surface. More specifically, Curtis realized, the stick's action separated the lighter bubbles from the heavier liquid. The same general principle, he reasoned, could be applied to the problem of high-altitude fuel vapor locks. On his return to Dayton, he designed an electric fuel booster pump that could be attached directly to a fuel tank. In operation, it would agitate the fuel, cause bubbles to rise to the surface of the tank, and push the heavier liquid directly into the fuel lines. On April 4, 1941, a B-24 bomber equipped with the booster pump cruised uneventfully at its service altitude of thirty-one thousand feet.[17]

TP obtained an exclusive license from Curtis to manufacture the pump, and production began at the main plant in the summer of 1941. The following year, after the U.S. Army's Eighth Air Force set up command in Britain, American bombers equipped with the new pumps and the famed Norden optical gunsights launched a sustained and devastating series of daylight raids into Germany. Later in the war, the Eighth Air Force—by then under the command of Generals Carl Spaatz and Jimmy Doolittle—was flying more than a thousand missions into enemy territory each day. To support this effort, TP manufactured twenty thousand pumps a month at peak output. As early as the spring of 1943, demand was so great that TP had arranged for the Crawford Door Company to become a second-source supplier. Thompson engineers continued to refine the pump, developing more efficient immersible versions, and to work on other products relating to aircraft fuel systems, such as fuel transfer pumps, water-injection pumps, "foam breakers," selector cocks, shut-off valves, quick-disconnect couplings, and other similar items.[18]

In 1943, the company organized all work of this kind into an Accessories Division at the main plant. At the same time, it opened a small R&D laboratory in Inglewood, California, near one of the centers of the American aircraft industry, to work with manufacturers on the design and engineering of high-altitude fuel systems. The laboratory housed refrigeration equipment and pressure chambers that enabled researchers to test components and systems to altitudes well above thirty thousand feet and to investigate the combined effects of high altitude, high speeds, and various rates and angles of climb and descent. "For the first time," claimed Colwell, "a fuel system could be set up and its performance at altitude predicted before it was installed in the plane."[19]

TP's work in fuel systems yielded several spin-offs. The most promising was a device to inject a mixture of water and alcohol into fuel just prior to ignition as a means of preventing engine "knock," the tendency of fuel in high-performance engines to detonate rather than burn. Over time, the cumulative effect of the shaking and vibration placed key engine parts and components under severe stress that could result in catastrophic failure.

During the war years, engine manufacturers, oil and chemical companies, and other research organizations all sought solutions to the problem, including techniques to cool the fuel and improved fuel chemistry and processing. At first the most promising approach relied on an old principle of cooling via water injection. Engineers had known since the nineteenth century that blending small amounts of water into fuel inhibited engine knock, but the technique was never widely used in practice. In the 1930s, however, government researchers working on supercharged aircraft engines at Wright Field discovered that injecting a mixture of water and alcohol not only prevented detonation, but also provided an added benefit: a big, temporary surge of power—important, say, for aircraft taking off under heavy load or for enabling use of cheaper, lower-octane fuels. In September 1942, engineers at Pratt & Whitney were looking at the impact of severe rain storms on supercharged engines when they "redis-covered" the surge effect noted at the Wright Field laboratories. The researchers soon identified a water-alcohol mixture that when injected into the fuel yielded a 20 to 30 percent boost in power.[20]

In 1943, Pratt & Whitney worked with TP to develop a pilot-controlled injector to blend the mixture with fuel on takeoff or when emergency conditions demanded a burst of power. This equipment became a standard feature of Allied fighter aircraft and of some bombers. Colwell was particularly interested in the device and saw eventual commercial applications in automotive engines. Late in the war, he directed a research effort that resulted in an improved injector that used a diaphragm to sense changes in engine pressure. When the engine labored, the injector automatically mixed water and alcohol with the fuel to provide a power boost, "much the same as if the gasoline had been stepped up fifteen octane numbers." Colwell also claimed other benefits, includ-ing increased engine efficiency and longer engine life. In 1945, TP began limited advertising of its automatic injector under the trade-name "Vitameter," targeting own-ers of high-performance automobile engines and heavy-duty trucks.[21]

Roots of a Revolution in Propulsion

Another and much more promising opportunity emerged from TP's work on aircraft engine performance and fuel systems during the war. In 1940, Curtiss-Wright had asked the company to manufacture hollow-bucket turbine wheels for a turbosuper-charger. By then, the principle of this device was already well established: energy in the exhaust of an internal combustion engine could be used to drive a turbine wheel, which in turn would drive a compressor, which in turn would supply compressed air to the engine, where it would allow more fuel to be burned, resulting in higher tempera-tures and a significant power boost. In practice, a limiting problem in building turbo-superchargers was finding materials able to withstand hellish operating conditions: searing blasts of exhaust temperatures well above one thousand degrees Fahrenheit and enormous stress from centrifugal force and engine vibrations. Early turbosuper-chargers were made of silcrome, then of more exotic alloys such as Hastelloy B (nickel and molybdenum) and Vitallium (a variant of stellite also used, curiously, in dentures).

By the early 1940s, the most popular material for turbosupercharger turbines was a stellite alloy designated No. 21. Given its expertise in making products from hard-to-work, temperature-resistant alloys, TP was a logical source to manufacture these tur-bines, especially since the engine builders and turbine companies lacked capacity to supply the huge demand. Throughout the war, the company forged stellite No. 21, Hastelloy B, and other alloys into components for turbosuperchargers for Curtiss-Wright and other manufacturers.[22]

Its experience in this area prepared TP to participate in the development of one of the most revolutionary technologies of the war: turbojet engines for aircraft. The fun-damental principles of the turbojet engine had been known for decades before the war.

The basic concept was simple. Flight propulsion consists of moving air backward so that by reactive force an aircraft moves forward. To create this backward force and forward thrust, conventional aircraft rely on propellers to capture and accelerate air backward. An alternative method of propulsion is to focus the flow of air through a turbojet or gas-turbine engine. The turbojet engine operates by sucking air into the engine, compressing it greatly, and mixing it with fuel. This mixture is then ignited, and the resulting extremely hot gases pass through a turbine wheel and nozzle before blasting out as exhaust. The extremely high velocity of the exhaust gases pushing backward accounts for the engine's forward thrust.[23]

In the 1940s, these principles were well understood. The problem was to manufacture a reliable turbojet engine. Critical constraints were the availability of metals that could function reliably under unbelievably hostile conditions and of techniques to fabricate such resilient materials into extremely precise shapes. During the war, the British and Germans accelerated development of turbojets, but work proceeded at a slower pace in the United States, as the major engine manufacturers concentrated on producing internal combustion engines for current-generation military aircraft. Between 1940 and 1945, U.S. manufacturers built only about 1,300 turbojet engines, and nearly all of those appeared in the last year of the war. By way of comparison, during the same period, output of conventional aircraft engines totaled more than 812,000 units.[24]

In the United States, manufacturers of industrial gas turbines, including General Electric, Westinghouse, and Allis-Chalmers, carried out most of the development work on turbojets. GE established an early lead, based on an engine design acquired from the British firm Power Jets Limited. In October 1942, America's first jet-powered aircraft, using a GE engine that delivered about thirteen hundred pounds of thrust, flew a successful test mission. (A typical turbojet engine of the 1990s delivers about one hundred thousand pounds of thrust.) In the ensuing months, GE made significant improvements to the British design, including a new casing and a turbine wheel fitted with buckets forged from Hastelloy B. Early in 1943, while at work on a new model, the I-16 (so named because it could deliver sixteen hundred pounds of thrust), GE apparently ran into difficulty in making the turbine buckets. As recounted by Colwell some years later, GE's lack of progress troubled a U.S. Army officer, who happened to be a West Point classmate of Colwell's, assigned to the project. The officer called Colwell, complaining, "I've got a job that has to be done right, and it isn't being done right." He arranged for Colwell to visit the GE factory in Lynn, Massachusetts, and for TP to receive a small order for forged turbine wheels. The assignment to manufacture these turbine wheels fell to Harry Bubb, Tapco's chief engineer, and the company relied on its proven techniques of precision forging to make a handful of units for the GE I-16 jet engine.[25]

A much greater opportunity surfaced at the end of 1944, when the U.S. Army Air Force placed a large order for more advanced turbojets, the I-40 (J33), a derivative of the original British design, and an independently developed J35 (TG-180) engine, which used an original American-designed compressor. Demand for these four-thousand-pound thrust turbojets was so urgent, in fact, that the military required GE to license its technology to two divisions of General Motors for manufacturing. GM's Allison Division built both engines, while the Chevrolet Division concentrated on the J35.[26]

During the Christmas holidays in 1944, Dave Wright received an urgent phone call from his friend Hugh Dean, general manager of the Chevrolet Division. Dean pressed Wright to suspend his holiday plans and meet him as soon as possible at Chevrolet's engine factory in Tonawanda, New York, near Buffalo. The meeting, Dean added, could not wait. Wright dutifully journeyed to Buffalo, accompanied by Colwell. There Dean met them with a proposition. He had received an order to manufacture two thousand jet engines, but he had no intention of keeping Chevrolet in that business after the war. Rather than create the capacity to forge key components, therefore, he preferred to buy them. He asked the TP executives whether their company could take on an order for $40 million to $50 million worth of compressors, turbine wheels and shafts, and other components. Wright, who had never before seen a turbojet engine, was staggered by the complexity of the product, as well as the magnitude of the request. "The amount of business was hard to believe," he recalls, but he wasted no time in saying yes.[27]

During the early part of 1945, TP geared up to make jet engine components for Chevrolet. In February, Wright established a separate manufacturing division for jet propulsion at Tapco under Harry Bubb. At peak production, estimated for the fall of 1946, the company committed to supply a thousand turbine wheels in a single month. Although the business did not yield much dollar volume until after the war, TP gained valuable experience in fabricating complex components and enhanced its growing reputation for solving particularly difficult engineering problems. It also prepared the way for the company to become a major supplier to the turbojet engine builders after the war.[28]

WORKING TOGETHER

TP's wartime buildup and expansion required the company to recruit, train, and organize thousands of new employees under intense time pressure. The company's responses to these challenges, as well as to continuing organizing drives by the UAW-CIO, involved many changes and improvement to its program of personnel management. The program became more formal and highly organized. What did not change, however, was the company's emphasis on providing "a square deal": competitive wages, fair treatment, and good working conditions in return for a day's labor. TP also continued to stress close personal contact between supervisors and employees, dealing quickly with grievances, and maintaining a constant stream of communications about the progress and concerns of the business. These policies and actions helped the company meet or exceed its production targets as well as triumph over the UAW-CIO in several spirited and highly publicized union representation elections during the war.

In terms of employment, the magnitude of the defense buildup was staggering. In 1938, twenty-five hundred people had worked for TP in five separate locations. By early 1940, a greater number than that toiled in the main plant alone. By 1943, nearly twenty thousand people worked for TP, the vast majority of them at the main and Tapco plants. Most of the new hires lacked factory experience before signing on.

The company's personnel department attacked the problem of rapid growth in several ways. The first was a heightened effort to upgrade the skills of "the key management employee," the foreman. "The increased demand for production for national defense makes it more not less necessary that good labor relations be maintained in all plants," an official publication pointed out. "Primarily the success or failure of the labor relations program rests with the foremen and supervisors, the first line of management."[29]

In addition to holding monthly meetings of the Foremen's Club, early in 1939 the company began publishing the *Foremen's Bulletin.* This mimeographed document appeared frequently and featured news of company affairs, digests of government laws and regulations, and general advice about personnel matters such as hiring, communicating with and listening to employees, contract administration, and prompt handling of grievances. The *Foremen's Bulletin* urged foremen to resist lax practices in hiring, for example, and to work closely with the employment office to find "the cream of the crop," workers "of good, dependable habits." A potential hire's lack of experience should not be a drawback, the policy ran, so long as he or she seemed "capable of learning quickly."[30]

The foremen were also reminded frequently of the importance of attending to paperwork, especially in documenting employee performance. This work was necessary so that the personnel department would have accurate records on which to base promotions and transfers, as well as to provide evidence for disciplinary action. The foremen were urged to be diligent and fair in the application of company policies: "Above all, be careful of your actions. Don't let even the suspicion of discrimination creep in on any of the decisions you make. Have good, sound, defensible reasons for every disciplinary action you take."[31]

At the end of 1940, the personnel department retained Harry Newton Clark, "a trained conductor of courses in foremanship and a man of long experience in the industrial field," to direct a redesigned Foreman's Training Program. As a *Foremen's Bulletin* explained, the course was designed "to bring about a uniform understanding and interpretation of all company policies, a pointing up of procedures necessary to good, efficient department management and a greater appreciation for the need of sound organization." Later on, training for supervisors became "a constant activity," with forums and regular meetings "scheduled constantly" to cover "all of the problems of supervision from psychology to cost control."[32]

Ray Livingstone was also concerned about the increasing scale of TP's operations and employment. Early in 1940, he established a new management post in the personnel department: personnel supervisor. The model in his mind was that of a branch bank, which rendered services closer to customers. In general, the personnel supervisors were responsible for taking the company's personnel policies to the floor and being available both to department supervisors and to employees. As the first occupants of the job, he promoted two burly production supervisors. It was no accident that both men were former football stars—one had played professionally as a halfback for the Canton Bulldogs, and the other had been a three-year starting guard for Notre Dame and a Golden Glove boxing champion. Livingstone wanted employees—and union organizers—to see that personnel managers were powers to be reckoned with.[33]

By August 1940, the experiment had proved a success, and Livingstone received permission to hire additional personnel supervisors to cope with the company's mushrooming employment. He divided each plant into "districts" with a maximum size of one thousand employees and stationed a personnel supervisor in each one. He charged them "to be entirely familiar with and to be able to advise supervision and employees of all policies" and "to know all the men in the division as intimately as possible." Once again, the new managers came from the ranks of production workers, and they were stationed "right out in the production area." Livingstone's plan recognized that "the best individual to see that fellow workmen received square dealing, and that the company's interests too were settled on an equitable basis, would be an employee who had worked in the plant himself, knew the organization and its policies, and had demonstrated qualities of leadership." Livingstone sought, moreover, to keep "the personnel program where he believed that it belonged—right out on the factory floor."[34]

With this personnel organization in place, the recruitment and orientation of factory workers was seldom a problem, despite the fact that many experienced employees volunteered for military service and most able-bodied males were subject to the draft. Like other Cleveland-area employers, TP advertised openings in the newspapers and other media, and applicants besieged its employment office every day. During the war, the composition of its work force changed dramatically with growing employment of blacks and women.

Although TP had employed a few black workers in unskilled jobs since World War I, it mounted a conscious effort to increase opportunities for blacks. In part, the company was simply reacting to the changing demographics of the labor market: blacks migrated into northern cities such as Cleveland and Detroit in increasing numbers after the Great Depression. In 1939, at the request of a local minister, the company hired a small group of blacks for jobs in the heat treatment area and in maintenance at the main plant. These efforts expanded in 1941, when officials of the Urban League of Cleveland, an organization dedicated to promoting economic opportunities for blacks, met with Livingstone to discuss hiring policies at the new Tapco plant. The officials were evidently persuasive, and Livingstone agreed "to employ Negroes in approximately the same percentage in which they existed in the greater Cleveland community." As a result, TP became one of the first big employers in the area to hire large numbers of blacks and to advance them to semiskilled and skilled jobs.

In announcing its intention to hire increasing numbers of blacks, the company acknowledged that it might "not be a popular move with present employees." A *Foremen's Bulletin* directed supervisors to have little patience with opponents of the policy, however, and declared that "virtually all objections to the employment of colored people are based on prejudice" and that "prejudicial arguments don't stand the light of reason." Another official publication gave more pragmatic reasons to promote racial harmony: "Tapco is a War plant. A War plant is a place to work. A War plant is not the proper place for individuals who want to crusade for race, nationality, or religion."

Tapco management arranged for officials of the Urban League to address its foremen on "the psychology of the Negro worker" and to help plan the integration of blacks into the Tapco work force. The program was evidently successful: at the peak of war-time production (1943), more than two thousand blacks, representing between 10 and 15 percent of TP's total employment, worked in the Cleveland plants.[35]

TP was initially more reluctant to hire women, but by early 1942, it had little choice. Accordingly, the company conducted a survey of job classifications to determine which could be filled by women. During the next eighteen months, TP and Tapco placed growing numbers of women (including, after January 1943, black women) in jobs as draftsmen, machine operators, finishers, inspectors, time keepers, and in other semiskilled and skilled positions. Somewhat to their surprise, reported the *Friendly Forum,* foremen were "fairly well pleased" with the performance of women in these assignments. By 1944, about a third of TP's Cleveland-area employees were women, with a higher percentage at the main plant, where operations such as assembly of booster pumps consisted of light manufacturing, than at Tapco, where the production of sodium-cooled valves entailed many dangerous and heavy-duty operations. But even at Tapco, women were "scattered all over the factory, working side by side with men."[36]

The shortage of skilled tradespeople was a serious problem, especially because TP found itself in competition with many other Cleveland-area producers in the defense effort. In October 1939, the company offered a Learner Training Program to qualify employees on new precision machinery purchased to meet the rising tide of business. The initial program ran for two weeks and focused on grinders and screw machinery used to make aircraft engine parts. By the spring of 1940, more than 250 employees had enrolled. Still TP suffered from the shortage of skilled workers, and the program was opened to scores of additional employees and expanded to cover a broad base of factory operations, including an intensive curriculum for toolmakers.

As the Tapco plant neared completion, the company established an ambitious Preliminary Trade Training Program to prepare workers for a modified Learner Training Program. Classes for the preliminary program ran every other day after work for two weeks and concentrated on "such elementary subjects as blue print reading, use of micrometers and measuring instruments and standard practices and [the] machine shop." At the same time, the Learner Training Program was expanded to accommodate at least three thousand employees at the rate of six hundred employees per month. The object of the program was to prepare workers in advance to operate new machinery as soon as it arrived. The program started with a day of classroom work, followed by a day of observation in the factory, and then up to eight weeks of after-hours classroom work covering machine demonstrations, the physics of grinding and cutting metals, use and care of measuring devices, and other related subjects.[37]

The company's apprenticeship training program, in operation since 1938, was also intensified and expanded. This program ran for four years and covered comprehensive training in the trades as well as in general factory management topics such as production control, time study, and cost control. Graduates were accorded "high honor accompanied by suitable financial recognition."[38]

TP and Tapco management also developed a wide array of techniques to improve communications in the plants. To the *Friendly Forum* (which began publishing separate editions for each TP plant in 1942), the big bulletin boards located in each factory department, and its bulletins to foremen, the company added many specific occasions, events, and publications in an effort to keep employees abreast of operations and to present its side of the ongoing struggle with national unions. Crawford, Wright, Livingstone, and other top managers spoke regularly at Old Guard banquets, picnics, cafeteria meetings, and other company-sponsored events.

As circumstances warranted, top corporate and plant managers addressed open mass meetings of all employees on company property and on company time. These meetings were frequent—in one wartime year, there were twenty-two such occasions—but they were seldom scheduled far in advance. The meetings dealt principally with production issues and the company's financial performance, although, as TP's struggle with the national unions wore on, they also addressed labor issues. Crawford most often used the occasion to deliver homilies about archetypal characters—Tony the laborer, Joe the umbrella maker, and the old prospector. Or he would invoke simple analogies—comparing a business to a coffee-grinder—to educate employees about the workings of the capitalist economy. In addition to these mass meetings, management representatives met with supervisory personnel as a group every four to six weeks. At Tapco, Wright and Livingstone held monthly dinner meetings with randomly selected employees to explain company objectives and field questions.[39]

During the early 1940s, the personnel department produced a stream of manuals, handbooks, booklets explaining particular programs and benefits, bulletins on topical subjects, and even a forty-five-minute orientation film about the company's employment philosophy and practices. In 1940, the company issued a thoroughly revised version of its *Employees' Handbook* containing an introductory letter from Crawford stressing the familiar theme of the mutuality of interest between the company and its employees. The new handbook replaced many of the generic, boilerplate passages derived from the National Association of Manufacturers and other sources that had filled the 1935 edition with specific discussion of TP's own "time-tested policies." The manual was designed to be read and reread as a reference tool on such basic matters as wages and hours, overtime, seniority rights, shift preferences, and other rules and regulations. The film *Men, Management, and Production* (May 1943) was intended for new employees, and it preached TP gospel: "There are no secrets between men and management in the Thompson organization. We want company members to know the story on everything and we go to great lengths . . . to provide employees with information."[40]

TP management also communicated frequently with workers outside of the workplace. In 1940, the company started the tradition of printing special annual reports to employees, which were mailed to employees' home addresses. Like the financial digests previously published in the *Friendly Forum*, the annual reports to employees focused on how the company divided the money it received during the year. They invariably showed that more than 95 percent of revenues remained in the business to cover payroll, operating expenses, and capital expenditures, and that less than 5 percent was paid out to shareholders. TP and Tapco management also frequently sent letters to employees at their homes. These letters, which arrived on average about every six to eight weeks, dealt with such matters as changes in production schedules, congratulations for meeting or exceeding production goals, and management's views of union organizing activities. Letters sometimes included reprints of articles by TP managers or by experts on aspects of production and labor relations.

Personnel supervisors were particularly exhorted to maintain frequent communications with employees. Livingstone prepared a checklist for these managers that, among other duties, urged them to make regular rounds on all three shifts. They were expected to pass by each employee's machine at least twice a week; to catch the employee's eye and smile each time they passed; to meet and make friends with all new employees; to make an effort to tell employees something about the business each time they talked, using material drawn from the *Foremen's Bulletin;* to make each meeting with employees a "two-way affair"; and to contact independent union or employee representatives daily to keep incipient grievances from festering. Livingstone's advice concluded with a general summary of TP's approach to "good labor relations," which depended on

> reasonable policies, friendly and frequent personal contact, prompt elimination of unnecessary irritants, and explanation of all matters, which if allowed to continue to be misunderstood, would result in fear or uneasiness. . . . The aim should be PREVENTION of grievances before they occur. This requires constant diligence, resourcefulness and often intuition.[41]

The sheer volume of regular contact between managers and workers increased in one other way during the war. Early in 1942, Donald M. Nelson, Knudsen's successor as head of the War Production Board, called for "unprecedented" cooperation between labor and management to ensure rapid mobilization of America's industrial capacity. Given all their efforts at constant communications, TP management might well have taken the position that they had already met Nelson's objective. Nonetheless, management responded by taking out a full-page advertisement inside the front cover of *Time* magazine around the theme "Working Together." The design for the ad showed two hands clasping, one emerging from a manager's suit, the other from a worker's blue shirt. The handshake image adorned many TP publications throughout the war. More important, TP supervisors at all TP plants scheduled intimate weekly production meetings with employee representatives from April 1942 until the end of the war.[42]

By the middle of the war, TP operated a large, efficient, and comprehensive personnel organization with nearly six hundred employees stationed at various plants. The company's investment in personnel management reflected growing awareness of its strategic importance in ensuring continuous improvement in production and productivity, as well as in fending off potential labor difficulties. In recognition of the function's importance, in November 1942 Raymond Livingstone was elected vice president in charge of personnel, a position in which he met regularly with Crawford and joined other top executives in charting the company's overall strategy.[43]

The significance of Livingstone's promotion was more than symbolic. As he put it, "Finance, Sales, Engineering and Manufacturing have long been recognized as the four major activities in an industrial organization, and the wisdom of filling top posts in these divisions with the most competent men available is unquestioned."

"Today," Livingstone added, "we are witnessing the addition of a fifth function—Personnel Administration—as a major activity of top management." He defined this activity as

> the OBTAINING and MAINTAINING of an EFFICIENT, HAPPY working force. The capitalized words establish personnel administration as a *dynamic* function of business, contributing to the production of better goods at lower prices, with greater income and satisfaction on the part of the working force, rather than a paternalistic, soul-saving, welfare activity designed to temporize or gloss over real or imagined agonies of workmen.[44]

"The chief executive of a business or plant, whether he likes it or not," Livingstone pointed out, "is inevitably the chief personnel officer of the organization." In Crawford, he had a boss who heartily agreed. "No activity of our company is more essential," Crawford wrote in 1944, "than personnel. It is the new, dynamic function of modern industry—permanent and indispensable as engineering, research, production, selling, or finance."[45]

CRAWFORD ON THE NATIONAL STAGE

In Crawford's mind, TP's ability to achieve impressive production records was intimately connected with its program of personnel administration. The program also reflected his determination to be a fair employer and to manage the company free from outside interference of any sort. During the late 1930s and early 1940s, Crawford displayed qualities of showmanship, leadership, and industrial statesmanship that, added to his infectious enthusiasm and impressive reserves of energy, vaulted him to the forefront of the American business community.

Glimpses of Crawford's flamboyant personality first appeared outside the confines of the company at public occasions like the National Air Races. After the late 1930s, he abandoned the conservative suits and pince-nez that had made him resemble an Edwardian clerk in favor of more stylish and even outlandish dress. He seldom wore glasses in public. Decked out in a checkered sport coat, spats, and saddle shoes, he appeared more like an entertainer or sportsman than a corporate executive. On clear days, he drove an ancient, uncovered Hupmobile to work. These changing habits had an explicit purpose. "It's good business," he later said, "to create situations in which the employees could have a good laugh at the boss's expense." His actions also imprinted in the public mind the image of an original character.[46]

Crawford also became more active generally in Cleveland philanthropic, business, and civic affairs. By the late 1930s, he was already a member of the city's most prominent business clubs, a trustee of St. Luke's Hospital, and a director of several local banks, companies, and industry associations, including the Cleveland Chamber of Commerce. Starting in 1939, he served two consecutive terms as president of the

chamber, a position in which he lobbied long, hard, and successfully to create and promote opportunities for business in Cleveland. For example, he helped to persuade the
National Advisory Committee for Aeronautics (NACA—the forerunner of NASA) to
build a major research and development laboratory for aircraft engine technology in
Cleveland. The winning bid drew not only on Crawford's connections with NACA
officials, but also on his ability to mobilize support among the "80 to 90" local companies catering to aviation, the Cleveland chapter of the Society of Automotive Engineers, Case Institute of Technology, Western Reserve University, and even the local
electrical utility.

Ground was broken for what would become the Lewis Flight Propulsion Laboratory in January 1941. Three months later, the chamber awarded Crawford its Cleveland Medal for Public Service, noting his "intelligent and constructive public service,"
as well as his company's "scientific research resulting in important contributions to the
safer and speedier operation of aircraft." The following spring, Case Institute
bestowed upon him an honorary doctorate of engineering, calling him "an admired
exemplar of young engineers, pioneer in aeronautical industry, inspiring civic leader
and fearless defender of free institutions."[47]

An avid collector of vintage automobiles and aircraft, Crawford proved willing to
share his hobby with the public. In August 1943, he presided at the opening of the TP
Auto Album and Aviation Museum in a former Service Division warehouse in Cleveland. The collection, one of the most extensive in the United States, included many
rare vehicles owned personally by Crawford, as well as scores of old automobiles that
Service Division sales reps had purchased on behalf of the company starting in 1935.
Advertising manager Fred Witt took charge of the design of the museum, which first
exhibited the cars in period settings. Early in 1945, the design changed to the backdrop
of "Thompsonville," an imagined, turn-of-the century small town. Along Thompsonville's Main Street, Witt named shops after company executives, generally with
tongue-in-cheek. "Crawford's Saloon," for instance, played on the fact that Crawford
was a teetotaler, while "Albaugh's Elite Grocery" made sport of the longtime TP director's portly physique. The museum proved a popular diversion to Clevelanders during
and after the war, at one point attracting several thousand visitors a week. (In 1963,
TRW donated the collection to the Western Reserve Historical Society, which displays
it under the rubric of the Frederick C. Crawford Auto-Aviation Museum.)[48]

His role in the National Air Races, the Cleveland Chamber of Commerce, and in
local civic and philanthropic affairs earned Crawford growing national recognition.
His great skills as a speaker and writer also helped. In 1938, he adapted a speech on
the workings of the economy that he had given to various employee groups into an
article for *Investment Banking* magazine. The article was called "The Triangle of
Industry and the Production of Wealth," and it was destined both to attract great notice
and to cement Crawford's reputation as a champion of free enterprise. Alfred Sloan,
the legendary chairman of General Motors, somehow obtained a copy of the article,
which he greatly admired. In November 1940, he invited Crawford to give a version of
the article as the keynote address at the annual convention of the National Association
of Manufacturers.[49]

The speech, which was later printed in the trade magazine *Steel,* played off the notion that the economy works by satisfying the conflicting needs of three groups—hence the triangle: the marketplace of consumers, which wants "more products, better products and lower prices"; the providers of capital, who seek "reasonable security and greater return"; and labor, which pursues "higher wages and shorter hours." Crawford pointed out that the demands of the three groups were in conflict and that it was management's job to mediate among them. The only long-term answer to the conflicting goals was through increased production; otherwise, he argued, "the triangle becomes a poker game, in which if one wins, another must lose."

To show how the triangle was "a device for producing wealth," Crawford told a simple parable about an umbrella maker named Joe, who saw his output increase and prices fall but wages rise as a result of time-saving equipment. Crawford's point was that automation was not a threat to workers, as Eleanor Roosevelt, among other prominent people of the day, had argued, but an enabler of increased production, lower prices, and higher employment and wages. He went on to claim that barriers to increased production, such as "arbitrary controls imposed by Capital or Labor in any field of industry or by Government on the whole industrial system," represented serious obstacles to the efficient operation of the capitalist economy.[50]

"The Triangle of Industry" and many other speeches of the period reaffirmed Crawford as an articulate and adamant foe of "unnecessary" government regulation and taxes, as well as of the demands of organized labor. A 1941 speech entitled "Plowshares into Swords," for example, so impressed S. S. McClure, publisher of *McClure's* magazine (a conservative national periodical that covered political and economic subjects) that he labeled it "a great article—very, very great. . . . This man sees through to fundamentals." Crawford's addresses struck a responsive chord with management audiences. In 1941, NAM elected him a vice president, with the presumption that he would become president the following year. His duties as an officer of NAM included major responsibilities to lobby in the cause of production, to speak before business and community organizations around the country, and to serve as a business representative on many national committees and associations, all of which he performed with characteristic flair and zest. At NAM, he helped revive a flagging organization, shaping it into an effective voice of the business community, especially with regard to industrial relations issues. His election as president of the organization in November 1942 gained him for the first time the cover of a national magazine, *Business Week.*[51]

By the mid-1940s, Crawford was on the road constantly, spending as much time in Washington or elsewhere on NAM or other national commitments as he did at TP. By one count, in 1943 he made 130 speeches and traveled fifty thousand miles, most of it on behalf of NAM. "He is like the volcano which is creating itself in Mexico, constantly sending out heat, light, fire, steam, and sometimes brimstone," wrote an admiring *Plain Dealer* reporter. "He feeds on work and activity and grows by what he feeds on." The same enthusiasm and rhetorical gifts that endeared him to employees won over many audiences around the country.[52]

Most of Crawford's speeches and articles dealt with the theme of how to increase production, and they were usually hits with his audience. A 1943 address to

the Economic Club of Detroit enabled Crawford to meld the need for increased production with implied criticism of the New Deal, a task he accomplished, typically,
with humor:

> My main thesis is that you've got to produce something before you have it or can share it.
> It seems almost ridiculous to attempt to refute that, but that's the whole difference between
> two schools of economic thought.
>
> Some people would split up the horse to get more abundance of horseback riding. The in-
> dustrial way would be to produce more horses—whole horses ride better than horse meat.

In April 1943, Crawford's old speech on the triangle of industry was reworked again
into an article for *Reader's Digest.* The article attracted widespread notice, and during
the next several years the magazine distributed more than four million reprints.[53]

Crawford's notoriety thrust him into many positions of national prominence,
including some by presidential appointment. Twice he traveled to the European front
with delegations of American business leaders to gain firsthand knowledge of the
progress of the war. He also served on President Roosevelt's War Advisory Council of
Businessmen, the War Manpower Commission, the Management-Labor Policy Committee, and several other national industry groups. In each instance, Crawford viewed
his role as an opportunity to present the producer's point of view and increase its
influence.[54]

Crawford's growing fame and outside commitments had important implications
for TP. His frequent absences left the day-to-day responsibilities for managing the
company in the capable hands of Wright, Colwell, Clegg, Coolidge, and Livingstone.
Many of these executives basked in growing local and national recognition in their
own right. In 1940, for example, the Cleveland Junior Achievement awarded Livingstone its accolade as the city's most outstanding young man. The following year, Colwell was elected to the very prestigious position of president of the Society of
Automotive Engineers, one of the nation's most influential engineering associations.

Crawford's growing prominence also raised TP once more into the crosshairs of
the UAW-CIO sights.

THE WAR OF INDEPENDENCE

Thompson Products contributed significantly to the Allied cause during World War II
through its skills in precision manufacturing, its efficient operation, and the tremendous expansion of its output. The company and its management became famous during the war, however, not simply because they achieved production records, but
because they achieved them while simultaneously defeating national unions three
times in representation elections in the Cleveland plants. The last vote, which came
just months after the end of the war, represented a victory not only over organized
labor, but also over the administrative reach of federal regulators. TP's repeated suc-

cesses owed much to Crawford's ability to frame the struggle as a contest between the company and outside forces rather than between management and workers. The votes also provided ample testimony to the effectiveness of Livingstone's personnel policies and administration in preventing internal dissension and satisfying employees' concerns. (For a chronology of labor relations at TP between 1940 and 1945, see the appendix to this chapter.)

By the early 1940s, when TP's struggle with the UAW-CIO heated up once more, the circumstances of the company, the national union, and the climate for organizing had changed dramatically since the first go-around in 1937. TP and Tapco were big operations, staffed by seasoned managers and supported by an elaborate system of personnel management. Crawford, moreover, was both popular inside the company and a rising star in the larger American business community. The CIO had racked up successful drives at major employers in virtually every manufacturing industry, and the UAW-CIO, which organized all of the major automakers and many suppliers, had become one of the biggest, wealthiest, and wiliest of the industrial unions. During the period between the U.S. Supreme Court's 1937 affirmation of the Wagner Act and the Japanese attack on Pearl Harbor, the national unions generally benefited from government initiatives and enjoyed favorable public opinion.

Cleveland was a particularly important battleground in the struggle between big employers and the national unions. The economies of Detroit, Pittsburgh, and Akron were dominated by single industries—cars, steel, and rubber, respectively; by toppling the biggest employer in each city, the national unions gained entry into entire industries. In cities like Cleveland, Chicago, and St. Louis, which had diversified manufacturing economies, the situation was subtler and more complex. The national unions scored successes at some major Cleveland employers—Alcoa, Republic Steel, Fisher Body, and Eaton—but were repeatedly frustrated by others such as TP and Lincoln Electric Co. These companies not only resisted unionization, but also earned national recognition for progressive employee relations. The independent employers generally enjoyed the support of the city's major newspapers. They could also rely on a vigorous local employers' organization, Associated Industries of Cleveland, whose president, William Frew Long, was an uncompromising foe of the industrial unions and himself a prominent national figure.[55]

The coming of World War II helped to tip the scales back in favor of employers. In 1939, Hitler's nonaggression treaty with the Soviet Union put Communists and leftists in the United States on the defensive. Many CIO unions, including the UAW-CIO, began to purge or disempower radical members, even though many of them had excellent track records as organizers. The priority given defense mobilization also hurt the national unions because it allowed employers to portray them as unpatriotic when they sought to disrupt production. The UAW-CIO was particularly vulnerable to such criticism after federal troops intervened to halt a June 1941 strike at North American Aviation, a major aircraft producer. After Pearl Harbor, the national unions' predicament grew worse. The national officers of the CIO joined with representative business leaders to back a three-point program to ensure steady production: no strikes or lockouts for the duration of the war; peaceful settlement of all industrial disputes; and creation of a new federal agency, the National War Labor Board, consisting of equal numbers of members from the national unions, employers, and the government, to rule on such disputes. This "no-strike pledge" weakened organizing activity by disarming the national unions' major weapon in the struggle with employers.

The Battle of '42

TP made an inviting target for the national unions during the war: not only was Crawford a high-profile adversary, but the company was also the largest employer in metropolitan Cleveland. The Tapco plant was the second-largest manufacturing facility in the region. (Only the Fisher Aircraft Assembly Plant No. 2, located at the municipal airport, had more floor space. That plant produced components for B-29 bombers and entire P-57 tanks; it is presently the site of Cleveland's International Exposition and Trade Center.)

Skirmishes between TP and the UAW-CIO resumed early in 1940, when the union mounted a fresh organizing drive on the main plant. For many months, the two sides merely sparred, using a steady stream of handbills, notices, and other forms of propaganda. Several events during 1941, however, gave matters a decidedly nastier turn. First, on August 1, the National Labor Relations Board finally ruled on an old UAW-CIO charge that TP had violated Section 8 of the Wagner Act by recognizing the independent labor organization, the Automotive and Aircraft Workers Alliance (A&AWA) as the exclusive bargaining agent for employees at the main plant. The NLRB held that the A&AWA was an outgrowth of the outlawed Thompson Products Employees Association and, as such, a company-dominated union. The NLRB ordered immediate disestablishment of the A&AWA. Although officers of both TP and the A&AWA appealed the decision in the courts, the ruling nonetheless bolstered the UAW-CIO, especially after it was eventually upheld and enforced by the 6th Circuit Court in August 1942.[56]

The second event of 1941 followed in September, when UAW-CIO representative Ed Hall took over the organizing drive at TP, assisted by Wyndham Mortimer. The two men were natives of northeast Ohio. They had been founding officers of the UAW-CIO and strategists behind the 1936–1937 sit-down strikes at General Motors that established the union as a force in American industry. Prior to focusing on TP, Mortimer, an activist in the Communist Party, had led the union's drive on the aircraft industry in California. There he achieved success at Vultee Aircraft Company but also earned opprobrium for the failure of the strike at North American Aviation. The assignment of Hall and Mortimer to TP was a sign of the UAW-CIO's serious intent to organize the company.[57]

The third event of 1941 was "the spontaneous move on the part of employees in the TAPCO organization" during the fall to form a new and independent labor organization separate from the bargaining unit at the main plant. The constitution of the new union, the Aircraft Workers Alliance (AWA), bore a strong family resemblance to that of the A&AWA, and its first contract provided terms virtually identical to those in effect at the main plant. This coincidence was not accidental: many of the founders of the A&AWA, including anti-CIO lawyer Milton Roemisch, helped to launch the AWA. In December, Roemisch produced proof, certified by a local accounting firm, that 201 of the 265 hourly rated employees then at Tapco—a clear majority—had signed membership cards with the AWA. Accordingly, Tapco management recognized the new union, thereby flaunting both the UAW-CIO and the NLRB. Given that TP management handpicked the first wave of employees to move from the main plant to Tapco, it seems clear that the UAW-CIO had little chance to organize the new plant's work force. And indeed, the UAW-CIO immediately appealed to the NLRB to have the AWA disestablished and the main plant and the Tapco plant considered as a single bargaining unit.[58]

The clash of strong personalities and principles on both sides of the organizing drive made for many anxious, some unsavory, and some unintentionally amusing moments during the fall of 1941 and the spring of 1942. The UAW-CIO mobilized support from other Cleveland-area CIO locals and launched a weekly newspaper, *TP Organizer*, to woo workers, allege unfair practices or unfavorable conditions in the plant, and challenge management's version of events. The union even hosted a weekly radio show on Wednesday evenings. The broadcast repeated news and interpretations of events from the newspaper and gave employees sympathetic to the union a chance to speak out. The company counterattacked with a series of bulletins bearing the title *Let's Have the Truth*. These bulletins sought to refute union claims point by point.

To Ed Hall, this was no ordinary organizing campaign. The main plant, he pointed out, was "one of the few remaining big factories in Cleveland in which workers have not yet been able to obtain full organization and the benefits of CIO wages and conditions." The UAW-CIO was also pressing for victory at TP to further its national drive to organize the aircraft industry, and it saw the Tapco plant as an essential building block. Finally, Hall regarded Crawford as both a public and a personal enemy: the "No. 1 Fascist in America," a man who "has no regard for the law and doesn't hesitate to say so." "As long as I have been with the UAW," he thundered, "I have never encountered a management that so openly and arrogantly flaunted the rights of workers. We have accepted his challenge. We will be here for one year or forty years until his plant is organized under a CIO contract."[59]

Hall even wrote a letter to President Roosevelt, which he released to the press, charging that Crawford was "un-American, subversive, Pro-Axis and an enemy of our country." In support, he cited TP's refusal to disestablish the A&AWA despite the NLRB's ruling. He also alluded to Crawford's notorious contempt for the New Deal. "It is no secret and it is well known in the city of Cleveland," Hall wrote, "that for years Mr. Crawford had your [FDR's] picture hanging in his office up-side-down and Mrs. Roosevelt's picture with a pipe stuck in her mouth!" Concluded Hall, "Only a man bordering on degeneracy, such as Hitler, would conduct himself in this manner." In response, Crawford took the high road, throughout the campaign describing "the Company's labor policy as being merely the Golden Rule." The authors of *Let's Have the Truth* were less scrupulous, alluding to Hall's rumored drinking problems and Mortimer's Communist leanings, internal dissension in the national union, and making explicit charges that both organizers were unpatriotic.[60]

The UAW-CIO also sought to marshal support in Washington, D.C. In January 1942, the union persuaded U.S. Secretary of Labor Frances Perkins to certify the UAW-CIO's dispute with TP to the tripartite National War Labor Board (NWLB). The action incensed Crawford and Livingstone, who accused the UAW-CIO of "attempting to make an organizing tool" of the board. Nonetheless, in February 1942, the NWLB sent a team of investigators to Cleveland to assess the situation, including UAW-CIO charges that the company had wrongfully dismissed nine workers for union sympathies. Five of the workers had allegedly posted pro-UAW-CIO stickers in plant lavatories, actions that exposed them to the charge of defacing company property. The offense was petty, but it violated a stated company policy and provided grounds for dismissal. Crawford vigorously defended the actions in a letter to the NWLB, claiming that

> a competent, impartial investigation would show that in every case the material statements [of the accusers] are either wholly untrue, falsely colored, full of half-truths, properly and legitimately explainable, or the result of the individual's attempt to avoid the application to him of rules relating to conduct, production and efficiency which are indiscriminately enforced by this company against all employees alike.[61]

An NWLB team soon investigated the case, conducting hearings in Cleveland and Washington. The team exonerated TP from most of the UAW-CIO's charges and found the remainder inconclusive. Nonetheless, they described the situation as "tense" and "with danger of interference with all out war production."

Soon after, Frank P. Graham, head of the NWLB, summoned Crawford and Livingstone to Washington. The executives' recollections of this meeting portray a strange and strained session. Graham apparently "gave an eloquent sales talk on the satisfaction of dealing with international unions," remarking "how reasonable and cooperative they can be." He encouraged Crawford and Livingstone to use their influence to have the UAW-CIO recognized, stating that "the nation faced 'stark revolution if we were to enter another depression without strong international unions.'" Graham seemed surprised when the executives pointed out that to use their influence in this way would constitute an unfair labor practice, although he acknowledged that "ways can always be found." Graham then startled his visitors by inviting R. J. Thomas, president of the UAW-CIO, to join the meeting. Thomas warned the executives that he could shut down TP's Cleveland plants on twenty-four hours' notice and demanded that the dismissed workers be reinstated. The executives refused, and the meeting broke up. As Livingstone recalled much later, Graham seemed resigned at the end: "He said something to the effect that he had done all that he could for us," and he added, darkly, that "he was afraid we were headed for serious trouble."[62]

The NWLB eventually referred the dispute back to the NLRB, with a request to hold a representation election as soon as possible. At an NLRB hearing to determine whether such an election was warranted, the UAW-CIO was joined by an unexpected ally, the IAM-AFL, which had not mounted a serious attempt to organize skilled workers at TP since the ill-fated pin plant strike in 1935, and which failed to produce enough signatures to guarantee a place on the ballot. Nonetheless, the NLRB allowed the IAM-AFL to be listed, along with the UAW-CIO and "Neither," which was the only alternative available at the main plant to supporters of management or the A&AWA independent union. At the Tapco plant, the AWA appeared on the ballot in a three-way race with the UAW-CIO and the IAM-AFL. The election was scheduled for May 1 and 2.

To TP management, the appearance of the IAM-AFL was no accident but rather a deliberate tactic designed to influence the outcome of the proposed election at the main plant. Under NLRB rules, the winner of a representation election had to collect more than 50 percent of the votes. This represented an ambitious goal for supporters of "Neither," considering that they had to contend with two national unions. More worrisome for opponents of the national unions was a controversial NLRB requirement regarding a run-off election should none of the three choices attain a majority. In that event, should the two national unions together attain a plurality, then the "Neither" option would be dropped from later balloting. Main plant employees would face a second election between a CIO and an AFL union, a choice wholly unpalatable to TP management and supporters of the A&AWA. Crawford and Livingstone considered the NLRB's decision to add the IAM-AFL to the ballot as evidence of the board's tacit support for the national union movement. In one key respect, however, the timing of the election proved favorable to management. The campaign coincided with annual wage bargaining between the company and the independent unions. Less than two months before the vote, management approved a significant wage increase, including a special year-end bonus agreement, at both Cleveland-area plants. To employees, these actions appeared to affirm the real bargaining power of the independent unions.[63]

The election campaign itself was spirited and intense, with the parties using all media at their command to present their cases. The national unions published handbills and newsletters, made frequent radio broadcasts, and gave daily speeches outside the gates of both Cleveland plants. TP management answered with its own bulletins, editorials in the *Friendly Forum,* and letters to employees at their homes. The A&AWA, which had not yet exhausted its appeal of the NLRB's disestablishment order, campaigned vigorously for "Neither" at the main plant; at the Tapco plant, the AWA waged its own animated campaign.[64]

In the end, the balloting on May 1 produced a decisive defeat for the national unions. At the main plant, "Neither" received 65 percent of the vote, while at Tapco the AWA won 63 percent of the total. The national business press took note, calling it "one of the most serious election losses in years" for the CIO. Ed Hall did not take the results quietly, charging that the outcome reflected "the most vicious campaign in the history of labor. Every labor law ever written by the government legislators was broken through [TP's] coercion, intimidation and bribery of their employees, and other illegal acts." The results, he concluded, "show that it is a physical impossibility to hold a fair, democratic election in the Thompson plants."[65]

A measure of the significance of the 1942 election to the victors was that soon afterward Livingstone was promoted to vice president of personnel and Crawford was elected president of the National Association of Manufacturers.

A Case of Free Speech

The 1942 representation election was the first and most important of a series of elections at the main and Tapco plants during the 1940s, all of which resulted in decisive victories for management. The 1942 election established themes and patterns that would recur often in TP's conduct: its determination to stand and fight; its success in portraying the struggles as "us versus them"; its willingness to invest heavily to present its case; its hard-nosed approach to enforcing company rules; its cooperative stance toward the independent labor organizations; and its belligerence toward NLRB orders. The entire series of elections showed that a resourceful employer could remain free of an aggressive national union, even one supported by public policy and strong public sentiments. But it was never easy for the company. In fact, early in 1943, the UAW-CIO succeeded in winning NLRB elections at TP's plants in Toledo and Detroit, where local management never fully embraced Livingstone's personnel innovations. These victories gave the UAW-CIO representation of about 10 percent of the company's total work force.[66]

In Cleveland, the main battleground, the aftermath of the 1942 election was anything but peaceful. During the next several years, the company continued to spar with the UAW-CIO, the NWLB, and the NLRB around the validity of the election results and new charges of unfair labor practices. Over time, the company succeeded in portraying itself as a victim of political harassment by the combined forces of organized labor and federal administrative agencies. The confrontation came to a head in October 1945 over a legal dispute that pitted New Deal labor policy against the Bill of Rights—exactly the sort of constitutional confrontation that Crawford had long hoped for. To management, TP's ultimate success was no mere victory; it was a triumph. Before that happened, however, there were several twists and turns in the story.

The first twist occurred in August 1942, when the 6th Circuit Court of Appeals in Cincinnati finally upheld the NLRB's order disestablishing the A&AWA. TP workers were suddenly left without a labor organization to represent them. The UAW-CIO attempted to move in quickly, while many of the adherents of the A&AWA sought to establish still another independent labor organization, the Brotherhood of Independent Workers (BIW). Although its sympathies lay with the BIW, TP refrained from recognizing it pending the outcome of the UAW-CIO's continuing procedural challenges, which came thick and fast during late 1942 and early 1943.

The national union's attack centered on charges that the AWA and BIW were company-dominated unions and that management and the now-outlawed A&AWA had interfered with and prejudiced the outcome of the 1942 representation elections. The national union also alleged that TP and Tapco had wrongfully dismissed another dozen workers because of their UAW-CIO sympathies. The UAW-CIO even went so far as to issue a strike call at the main plant on April 13, 1943, to protest the dismissals. The strike fizzled after one day, however, when nearly 95 percent of workers remained on the job and the head of the Regional War Labor Board in Cleveland declared the action a violation of the CIO's national no-strike pledge.[67]

Although the strike attempt failed, the UAW-CIO once again got the attention of federal labor regulators. The NWLB ordered that seven of the dismissed workers be reinstated and that four others be given access to TP's grievance mechanisms if they wished to seek reinstatement. The NLRB also reentered the dispute and held hearings in Cleveland during much of the spring of 1943. The testimony and supporting evidence ran to more than ten thousand pages. Not surprisingly, the regional trial examiner took several months to issue an intermediate report. When his report finally appeared in August 1943, it supported the UAW-CIO charges, but TP immediately filed a protest. Through procedural tactics, the company was able to delay a final NLRB ruling for a year. On August 4, 1944, however, the board backed the UAW-CIO, finding that TP had used illegal tactics in the first representation campaign, including the conduct of officers (Crawford and Livingstone among them) who disparaged the UAW-CIO in verbal comments to employees by "issuing and posting derogatory bulletins" against the UAW-CIO, by showing favoritism to the A&AWA and AWA, and by permitting "unnecessary disorder, confusion, and campaigning in the plants." The board also held that the company had interfered in the organization of the AWA at the Tapco plant and that it had wrongfully discharged the dozen employees. Finally, the board voided the May 1942 vote and ordered new representation elections in both the main and the Tapco plants to be held within thirty days.[68]

The company followed standard practice in response to the orders, challenging them in the court of appeals. It nonetheless agreed to hold the new representation election on August 31, 1944. Once again, TP management and the UAW-CIO pulled out the stops. The company published a glossy booklet, *Thompson Products: A Decade of Achievement,* which reviewed the company's growth and health under the leadership of Crawford and his management team. It prepared for the press leather-bound scrapbooks under the title *The Thompson Products Organization and Outside Unions.* The scrapbooks contained representative company publications and samples of UAW-CIO campaign literature, along with an introductory note reviewing TP's seven-year struggle with the national unions.

One item in the scrapbook was a published opinion survey, which the company had commissioned earlier in the year through Fenn College. The survey covered sixteen thousand employees at the main and Tapco plants, and it reveals many interesting statistics about the composition and outlook of the work force. Thirty-seven nationalities were represented in the TP plants. Twelve percent of employees were black, and 32 percent were women. As for employee opinions, the survey painted an overwhelmingly positive picture of the company. Results showed that by large majorities TP and Tapco workers liked their jobs, regarded earnings and hours of work as satisfactory, found their working environment friendly, preferred their present employment to previous experiences, held management and fellow employees in high regard, believed that they had "a dependable future" with TP and Tapco, and hoped to remain in their jobs after the war. Favorable ratings of foremen and supervisors were particularly striking. By amounts ranging from 75 to 92 percent, employees believed that these first-level managers were fair, "knew their stuff," and set good examples as leaders.[69]

Also during August, Crawford composed an eight-point "Thompson Creed," which was displayed prominently in company publications, bulletins, and billboards. The creed offered a crisp summary of his views: the only way to create more and better jobs, higher pay, and greater job security, he stated, was through "understanding, harmony, decency, and teamwork between worker and management." The creed cited the Golden Rule, stressed the importance of open communications between management and employees, and declared "that it is not only our right but our duty to resist with all our power any effort by outside forces to drive a wedge between labor and management." A five-point pledge that Livingstone drafted and all senior operating managers signed promised that "as long as the affairs of this company are in our hands," TP would pay fair wages, treat employees with friendly respect, deal promptly and fairly with grievances, and offer benefits that equaled or exceeded prevailing standards in the community. The pledge concluded with the commitment that "we will devote our best efforts and thinking to the building of a growing business within which will prevail an atmosphere of friendliness and harmony with steady jobs and opportunity for all."[70]

On August 24, Crawford addressed all three shifts of the main plant and four days later did the same at the Tapco plant. In each instance his message stressed the success of the company under present management, reinforced its principles of fairness and square dealing, and took issue with UAW-CIO claims to the contrary. He appealed to employees to vote as they pleased but urged them to get the facts first, to think carefully about the decision, and to discuss it at home with their families. The issue to him was simple: did employees want "a leadership that will build a larger company, employ more people, get more business and more orders, and more capital, and continue to build job security in here, and settle all the little squabbles that come up every day," or did they want "to change this thing and bring in some outsiders, and go through all the brawls that seem to follow where outsiders come in?"[71]

Such methods and such reasoning again proved persuasive. The vote on August 31 produced an outcome similar to that of the first election two-and-one-half years earlier. The UAW-CIO collected 36 percent of the vote at the main plant and only 22 percent of the vote at Tapco. Once more, the UAW-CIO protested the result, this time objecting to Crawford's speeches to employee audiences on company time. The NLRB agreed, and on March 21, 1945, invalidated the 1944 election on the grounds that management had improperly interfered with the election by delivering "captive audience" speeches to employees during regular working hours.[72]

The board's order prepared the way for the test case between administrative agency rulings and the U.S. Constitution that Crawford had long sought. That case came together during the late summer and early fall of 1945. On August 28—less than two weeks after VJ Day—the NLRB scheduled a new election at the main plant for October 23. The company tried unsuccessfully to delay the election because its timing coincided with the reconversion of the plant, postwar layoffs, and much uncertainty about future business. Nonetheless, it proceeded to campaign for employee support using accustomed tactics such as mass meetings and a blizzard of publications. A week before the scheduled election, the NLRB petitioned the 6th Circuit Court of Appeals for an injunction and restraining order against TP officers that would prevent them from "participating in any campaign with respect to the October 23rd election."

If upheld, the NLRB petition would block Crawford from speaking again to mass meetings of employees on company time prior to the vote. TP immediately filed an objection to the petition on the grounds that it violated Crawford's right of free speech. Crawford himself was outraged. As he saw it, the constitutional issue was clear: whether a "dictatorial, arrogant agency of government can get a court in this land to order an American citizen to shut up." He thought not, and the Circuit Court apparently agreed. It dismissed the NLRB petition without comment on October 19.[73]

Two days later, Crawford appeared before mass meetings of each shift at the main plant, each time brandishing a striped convict's garb on his arm. He opened his comments with lines like, "I wasn't sure I would be here, so I brought this along!"; "It's all right, boys, I don't have to go to jail—the Constitution still stands!"; and "Well, this is still America. The boss can talk with his men, and you can tell the boss to go to hell if you want." Each time he got a good laugh. At the election on October 23, the UAW-CIO once again lost by a wide margin.[74]

To Crawford, the victory was doubly sweet: not only had TP again vanquished a long-time foe in the UAW-CIO, but it had shown the limits of the NLRB's reach into the company's personnel practices. "For many years a colossal bluff has been pulled on the country by the NLRB," Crawford observed the day after the dismissal of the board's petition. "This bureaucratic agency has sought by bullying and threats to intimidate American business management." No more, he exclaimed: "We have called this bluff. . . . By its decision the court has made it clear that members of American management have the right to talk with their employees at any time, anywhere, on any subject, including NLRB elections, so long as no coercion or intimidation is used." "It is my humble belief," he wrote to employees, "that together we have made some kind of a mark in American history."[75]

Crawford's claim was no idle boast. The Circuit Court's action in the TP free-speech case was one of the first of a stream of events including investigations of national labor union conduct, the expulsion of Communists and other radicals from the CIO, the Taft-Hartley Act, and the onset of the Cold War that pushed back the tide of industrial unionism in the United States and reasserted employers' rights.[76]

Closer to home, the ruling added to Crawford's growing fame and contributed to a spate of favorable publicity that he and the company received in the immediate postwar years, including the profile in *Fortune* cited at the beginning of this chapter. The ruling also capped an extraordinary period in TP's history, helping to seal its transformation from a middling producer of automotive parts into a large enterprise with diverse interests, including major roles in support of the aircraft industry and the emerging defense industry.

In many respects, TP came of age during the war, acquiring a national reputation for precision engineering and manufacturing as well as for independent business leadership and progressive management. The great expansion of business posed many challenges and triggered creative responses. By 1945, the company had greatly expanded and extended its traditional capabilities. It had developed new skills and expertise in metallurgy, large-scale manufacturing, aircraft fuel systems, and advanced aircraft engine design. At Tapco, the company not only operated an enormous state-of-the-art manufacturing facility, but also possessed a young management team that had demonstrated the ability to organize and manage effectively thousands of employees. The company's well-oiled program of personnel management supported steady and efficient production while helping to minimize disputes and disruptions, and it became a model for other industrial corporations.

These achievements and assets reinforced Crawford's natural optimism as he and his management team faced new challenges in the postwar world.

Epilogue: Human Relations at TP and TRW

TP's victory over the NLRB in the free-speech case did not end its struggles with the national labor movement. During the next few years, the UAW tried several more times to organize TP's Cleveland-area plants, although each effort proved futile. The Tapco plant remained organized by the AWA until sold by TRW in 1986; at the main plant, management formally recognized the AWA as sole bargaining agent in 1948, and the UAW-CIO lost votes in 1947, 1948, and 1967. But Ed Hall's prophecy that the plant would eventually be organized bore out. In the fall of 1991—forty years after his prediction—the UAW finally won representation elections at the main plant and at a sister valve operation in Collinwood (an eastern area of Cleveland). By then, however, the circumstances of the company and the UAW were vastly different and the consequences of the vote were distinctly local in scope.

TP's repeated successes against organized labor starting in the 1930s and 1940s drew much comment from contemporaries, as well as occasional later scrutiny from industrial relations specialists searching for lessons in the story. Commentary has generally focused on two questions: first, why and how did TP succeed in fending off the national unions? And second, was the company's investment in its personnel program worth it—that is, would the company have been better off in the long run by following the examples of most of its competitors and customers in recognizing a national union?[77]

How these questions have been asked and answered generally betray normative biases in the persons asking them. Those observers who believe that TP *should have* recognized the union argue that the company "got away with it" through "questionable" tactics, a willingness to spend extravagant sums to keep its work force independent, and the blunders of union organizers. Those who believe that TP *should not have* recognized the union point to Crawford's charismatic leadership, as well as to the company's effective personnel initiatives, the positive role of the independent local unions, and the national union's blunders.[78]

The question of what TP should have done, of course, can never be answered to everyone's satisfaction. Putting that question aside, there is merit to most of the explanations for the company's success. Crawford was an able and popular leader; the company pioneered many innovations in personnel management, which contributed to labor harmony; the AWA proved capable of delivering attactive wage settlements and otherwise of meeting the needs of employees; and the national union organizers did commit blunders such as the personal attacks on Crawford and the abortive strike in 1943.

As to whether TP used "questionable" tactics, if by that is meant breaking the law as the law was interpreted at the time, evidence is meager, although accusations are not. Moreover, some "findings" that ostensibly neutral parties such as the NLRB or the courts made were at least partly motivated by politics and ideology, complicating any examination of what really happened. Clearly TP screened job applicants thoroughly; just as clearly, these screens let through a big, diverse, and productive work force, a third of whom voted for national union representation. Clearly the company pounced on minor offenses (such as producing political graffiti in the bathrooms) to dismiss union activists; just as clearly, union activists committed these offenses and violated company policies. (The number of dismissals alleged as unfair labor practices during the war was about twenty, which needs to be considered in the context of the nearly fifteen thousand workers in the Cleveland plants at the peak of employment.) Clearly the company preferred working with independent employee associations to working with national unions and stacked the deck when it could, as happened in the choice of employees to start up the Tapco plant and establish the AWA; just as clearly, a substantial majority of TP's employees were satisfied with representation by independent labor associations. Clearly the company expressed contempt for many NLRB rulings; just as clearly, it abided by them when so ordered by the courts after all appeals were exhausted. TP proved a tough and resourceful opponent to union organizers and their allies. The company found ways to remain independent that had little to do with alleged violations of law or other questionable tactics.

In my view, what kept TP independent was the same thing that made it a good employer not only in the eyes of pro-business partisans, but also—and more important—in the eyes of most employees. By focusing so much on conflicts such as the representation elections, many commentators have missed the much bigger story of the absence of conflict most (indeed, virtually all) of the time. By the mid-1930s, when the national unions began to stir at TP, managers and employers shared a common history and mutual trust that presented a significant barrier to outside forces. Crawford convinced most employees of what he really believed: that managers and workers were partners in the enterprise. Crawford expressed the point bluntly: "If employers are bastards, then employees might need a union. We were not bastards."[79]

Most employees and potential hires regarded TP as a good employer, and for readily apparent reasons. TP offered an attractive deal: in return for a specified number of hours of labor, the company provided compensation at prevailing rates for the type of job and local economy, immediate resolution of grievances, protection against arbitrary dismissal, a friendly atmosphere, regular communications about the state of the business, and opportunities for training and advancement subject to the growth and health of the company. The deal did not include one other point that employees might have wished for: job security. TP recognized that its ability to maintain employment was a function of its business, and it never promised to guarantee jobs. Nonetheless, one of the express goals of its strategy to diversify its product lines and base of customers was to permit stable employment.

This discussion, of course, raises the question of whether TP would have been such a good employer in the absence of the threat of unionization.[80] Based on the record of Crawford and his management team, I believe the answer is yes, but clearly not in the same way. The core of TP's policies—observing the Golden Rule and maintaining constant communications—was characteristic well before the appearance of union organizing drives. In this sense, TP was a good employer during the 1920s and 1930s. The Great Depression, which discredited management and employee representation plans in many companies for failing to maintain wages and employment, neither detracted from Crawford's popularity nor forced him to rethink his ways.[81]

On the other hand, during the late 1930s and early 1940s, the company went to great lengths to develop a system of personnel management that was more formal and elaborate than those in place at much larger companies and perhaps anywhere else in American industry. Some of TP's policies, especially its aggressive techniques of communication and immediate handling of grievances, were either direct responses to organizing drives or reflected a general desire to chart an independent course. Other policies, such as its terms for compensation or use of foremen, reflected good management practice to retain productive workers and ensure steady increases in production. And still other policies, such as its training programs and use of personnel supervisors, were developed to meet the great business challenge of the era: staffing up and organizing to produce during the World War II defense buildup.

Finally, some of TP's policies were direct responses to changes in U.S. labor law. The company's program became more systematic and comprehensive in part because the Wagner Act enumerated unfair labor practices that required management vigilance to avoid and prevent. Crawford opposed the Wagner Act because its effect, he believed, was to institutionalize conflict between employers and employees. Nonetheless, TP's compliance with the statute necessitated expansion of the personnel department and vigorous enforcement of personnel policies.

Did TP overinvest in human relations? The question is impossible to answer satisfactorily, because, once again, it betrays normative biases. To some, any investment that kept out unions would have been worth it. To others, the company built up a program far too complex for the needs of a company its size. TP probably spent more per capita (including investment of top executive time) on the personnel function than most of its competitors or customers. The company's program of human relations was often compared to those at far bigger companies such as Du Pont, AT&T, Esso (now Exxon), and Procter & Gamble. On the other hand, TP's overall profitability compares favorably with that of other companies with a similar size and type of business. Crawford justified the expense of the human relations program as a good business investment. "Profit is in the hands of employees," he noted, adding:

The difference between winning and losing in companies is often very small. A company is on a razor's edge. In a good year, net profit is 10% of revenues. Now think about the contributions employees make. If those people are disgruntled or bored or just unconsciously slow, if they come to work a little late or leave a little early or go to the water cooler a little too often, then your business will fall off maybe 5%. On the other hand, if those people are fired up and have confidence in the company and they're proud of their jobs, you'll get that extra effort, that extra 5%. In the distance between those two points lies the whole success of the company.

That's why I never worried about the expense of our human relations program. We never lost a day of work to a strike or any other industrial dispute.[82]

The philosophy and practice of human relations that evolved at TP during the 1930s and 1940s remained characteristic of the company for decades, even as its circumstances changed dramatically. TP and its successor TRW, for example, continued to stress open communications and immediate handling of grievances. The company developed a technique called "one-in-five" meetings, in which supervisory personnel at all levels met periodically with five randomly selected hourly employees for a frank exchange of views. It also relied on employee attitude surveys and other sensing mechanisms that were used both in measuring and tracking morale in the plants and in evaluating management personnel. Later TRW acted early to adopt other progressive personnel techniques such as job enrichment, employee involvement and participation plans, and team-based and pay-for-knowledge incentives.[83]

Later changes in business mix, geographical scope, and management eventually diminished TRW's need to work with independent labor organizations in the United States. Until about 1960, independent unions represented employees in most domestic TRW locations, although some businesses that the company acquired included facilities organized by national unions. The 1958 merger between TP and the Ramo-Wooldridge Corporation altered the nature and balance of the company's work force, introducing many employees with advanced degrees in science, engineering, and management. These employees tended to resist unionization of any sort. Most of the company's newer manufacturing facilities in the United States, moreover, were situated in southern and western states where organized labor was weak. Many of these operations, especially those in electronics, employed relatively small concentrations of people and did not represent fertile ground for independent or affiliated union organizers. Finally, in 1962, several years before his scheduled retirement, Livingstone moved to a new corporate job in government relations. His successor as vice president in charge of personnel matters, James Dunlap, had made his career in the nonunion environment of Ramo-Wooldridge, and he worked hard to ensure the union-free status of TRW's operations.[84]

TRW's experience also reflected a national trend as the U.S. economy grew away from dependence on heavy-duty manufacturing, with the resulting steady decline in national union membership as a percentage of the total labor force. By 1983—near the peak of its manufacturing activity in the United States—TRW operated eighty-four domestic plants. Of these, fifty-six were nonunion, nine had independent unions, and nineteen were affiliated with national unions. The company proved adept at managing in these various settings and experienced few strikes or significant disruptions of work in any of its locations. Among specialists in industrial relations, the company remains a highly regarded exemplar of effective personnel management.[85]

Appendix: Industrial Relations Chronology, 1940–1945

1940

January	UAW-CIO renews drive to organize workers at TP's main plant.
	Livingstone appoints first personnel supervisors.
March	TP publishes its first separate Annual Report to Employees.
August	TP appoints personnel supervisors for every one thousand employees.
October	UAW-CIO files charge of unfair labor practices against TP, alleging that A&AWA is a company-dominated union.
December	NLRB holds hearing on UAW-CIO petition.

1941

January	TP announces contract to build and operate Tapco plant.
March	NLRB trial examiner issues intermediate report finding TP in violation of the Wagner Act.
August	NLRB agrees with trial examiner and orders disestablishment of the A&AWA independent union. Both TP and the A&AWA vow to appeal the decision in court.
September	UAW-CIO organizers Ed Hall and Wyndham Mortimer take charge of organizing drive at main plant. Activity intensifies.
November	AWA independent union forms at Tapco plant.
	TP begins practice of writing to employees at their home addresses.
December	The United States enters World War II after Japanese attack on Pearl Harbor.
	Tapco plant begins production.
	CIO adopts no-strike pledge for the duration of the war; National War Labor Board created to settle disputes affecting defense production.
	NLRB asks 6th Circuit Court to enforce order disestablishing the A&AWA.
	Tapco management recognizes AWA as exclusive bargaining agent.
	Ed Hall writes to President Roosevelt attacking Crawford and urging immediate disestablishment of the A&AWA and AWA.

1942

January	UAW-CIO petitions NLRB to disestablish AWA at Tapco plant and to consider main and Tapco plants as a single bargaining unit.
	U.S. Secretary of Labor Frances Perkins certifies dispute between TP and UAW-CIO to NWLB.
February	NWLB begins hearings in Cleveland.

MARCH	Crawford and Livingstone summoned to Washington by Frank Graham, head of NWLB. NWLB asks NLRB to schedule representation election.
APRIL	NLRB orders representation election at main and Tapco plants for May 1 and 2. UAW-CIO and IAM-AFL listed on ballot. A&AWA not permitted on the ballot but campaigns for "Neither."
	TP begins weekly management-employee production meetings in all plants.
MAY	Representation election results in decisive repudiation of UAW-CIO at both Cleveland plants.
	UAW-CIO files objections to the conduct of election.
AUGUST	NLRB orders hearing on conduct of May representation election.
	Sixth Circuit Court of Appeals disestablishes A&AWA at the main plant as a management-dominated union.
NOVEMBER	Livingstone promoted to vice president of personnel.
	Crawford elected president of National Association of Manufacturers.

1943

JANUARY	UAW-CIO wins representation election at Michigan plant.
FEBRUARY	NLRB conducts hearings of labor relations at main and Tapco plants.
APRIL	UAW-CIO wins representation election at Toledo Steel Products.
	UAW-CIO strike attempt fizzles at Tapco plant.
AUGUST	NLRB trial examiner files intermediate report overturning May 1942 election results at Cleveland Plants.

1944

AUGUST	NLRB endorses findings of trial examiner in August 1943; orders new representation elections at both Cleveland plants.
	Massive TP communications plan includes brochures, film, bulletins, and handbook for the press; Crawford addresses mass meetings of all three shifts at both plants.
	Second NLRB election at Cleveland plants results in another decisive defeat for UAW-CIO.
SEPTEMBER	UAW-CIO protests second election, alleging that TP officers exerted undue influence in preelection speeches.

1945

MARCH	NLRB agrees with UAW-CIO petition of September 1944; invalidates August 1944 elections at both plants.

APRIL   V-E Day marks end of World War II in Europe.

AUGUST   V-J Day marks end of World War II in the Pacific.

OCTOBER   NLRB orders third representation election at main plant; petitions 6th Circuit Court of Appeals to enjoin TP officers from speaking to employees before election.

Sixth Circuit Court of Appeals rejects NLRB request for injunction as violation of First Amendment right of free speech; brandishing prisoner's garb, Crawford addresses three shifts at main plant.

Election results in third decisive defeat for UAW-CIO at main plant.

NOVEMBER UAW-CIO protests the election result, citing management efforts to influence employee opinion prejudiced the outcome.

NLRB regional director recommends that election results be set aside. NLRB finally rejects that advice in January 1947 and certifies the October 1945 election.

SOURCES: Harvey Shore, "A Historical Analysis of Thompson Products' Successful Program to Discourage Employee Acceptance of Outside Unions" (Harvard Business School, DBA diss., 1966), esp. pp. 576–582; Frank K. Dossett, A Chronological Record of the Physical and Economic Development of Thompson Products, Inc., typescript in TRW WRHS 3942, boxes 20–21; Statement of Raymond S. Livingstone to The Committee on Education and Labor of the House of Representatives, February 24, 1947.

Chapter 6

Taking the Next Step

▶ ▶ ▶

1945–1953

R AY LIVINGSTONE RECALLS A MEETING OF TP'S TOP BRASS IN THE EXECUTIVE DINING ROOM at Tapco during the late summer or early fall of 1944. As he tells the story, Fred Crawford had called the meeting to consider whether to buy the gigantic Tapco plant, a question that by extension raised the bigger issue of the company's plans for the postwar world. Crawford sketched out two scenarios. The first entailed buying the plant, building on traditional opportunities as a supplier to the automobile and aircraft industries, and finding new markets to conquer. In the short term, this option was fraught with risk: it would mean operating a factory that was vastly bigger than the company's expected volume of business warranted and scrambling to find business in an aircraft market likely to be saturated with war surplus material for years to come. But if it succeeded, TP could continue on its path toward becoming one of America's biggest industrial corporations.[1]

The second option Crawford outlined was retreat. TP could concentrate on prewar business, consolidate operations in the main plant, manage prudently, and grow along with its traditional customers. This was a business the company understood well. There would be little strain on executives, who could take long vacations in places like Cape Cod—where Crawford owned a beachfront property. In fact, Livingstone recalls that Crawford called this strategy "Cape-Codizing" the company: "It would be a nice comfortable life, and we'd be well paid."

The ensuing discussion was "thoughtful" and "not emotional at all," but did not take long, because most of the participants knew the outcome. Only Lee Clegg expressed reservations about buying the Tapco plant, arguing that it was much too big for TP's needs. Dave Wright spoke for the majority. As he recalls the meeting, he pointed out that the Tapco plant was the only modern, efficient factory the company had and that it would be a mistake to pass on the opportunity to buy it. He stated that he didn't think he would be interested in going back to business as usual; in fact, he recalls saying, "If we just return to the old main plant, I'd rather go back to being a lawyer with a law firm. I'll resign." The challenges lay ahead, and he was looking forward to meeting them.[2]

Wright knew his boss well. Crawford weighed in on the side of expansion, and the question was settled. The decision to push forward, however, did not imply that TP's leaders knew what the future held in store for them. But they were optimistic about the recovery of prewar markets, and they believed that TP's growth would resume there. They foresaw not only a booming business for new automobiles, but also continuing steady expansion of the replacement business, especially given the venerable average age of vehicles still on the road. They had especially high hopes for new products in development such as the Vitameter, U-Flex piston rings, and a new type of suspension system. In assessing demand for aircraft, TP's leaders were more cautious, although they believed that turbojet engines held revolutionary potential and that the company would benefit enormously by building on a foundation already laid.

The debate in the dining room was the first of many discussions of the growth problem that would characterize the postwar years. TP reentered the peacetime economy by building on the three-legged stool of the 1930s: sales to the motor vehicle industry, to the automotive replacement trade, and to the aircraft industry. Yet the limitations of this strategy became apparent soon enough. As a supplier to bigger, more powerful customers, TP found it a struggle to expand its product offerings and improve its profitability. The replacement market, which had boomed during the war and the first years after, grew saturated and increasingly competitive. The onset of the Cold War renewed opportunities for TP as a defense contractor, but that business manifested disturbing cyclical tendencies: when business boomed, it really boomed; when it crashed, it really crashed. By the early 1950s, TP's leaders saw the need for diversification, a fourth leg to the stool. Its most promising opportunities surfaced in new and potentially glamorous industries of the era: electronics and nuclear power.

Preparing for the Postwar World

In 1952, the economist John Kenneth Galbraith coined the term "depression psychosis" to convey the prevailing mood of American business leaders immediately after World War II. Most of these executives had vivid, bitter memories of the Great Depression, and many also recalled the deep recession that had followed World War I. They were concerned about finding customers to replace the lost volume of wartime production. They worried about raw material shortages and finding jobs for returning veterans. They fretted about continued price controls in the near term and the specter of rapid inflation once controls were lifted. They forecast a decline in real income and foresaw a turbulent era of relations with organized labor. To many experts who contemplated such issues in 1945, the future seemed bleak and full of doubt.[3]

To Fred Crawford, however, the future seemed bright and full of promise. "We are confident," he wrote early in 1946, "that America will solve its present ills and move forward, ultimately, into a period of sustained industrial progress." He added that "to share in this growth we are applying everything we learned during the war of new machines, new materials, new methods, and improved organization." And, he boasted, "we enter the postwar period with the finest organization and facilities in our company's history, and our peacetime markets are greater than ever."[4]

Both the pessimists and the optimists proved partly right about the economy of the immediate postwar period. The pessimists could point to declining GNP totals in 1946 and 1947, as well as a recession in 1949—a soft economy in three of the first four years after the war. This was a rocky start to the new economic era. But optimists like Crawford could also find evidence to support their views. Led by the motor vehicle industry, the manufacturing sector of the U.S. economy recorded steady and solid gains in output and productivity, as the pent-up demand for consumer goods during the war and its immediate aftermath was released after 1946.

There were still more reasons for manufacturers such as TP to look forward to the postwar era. First, the great influx of wartime investment, much of it guaranteeing a positive return, allowed many producers to reduce or eliminate long-term debt. After the war, these companies could plan ahead with a clean balance sheet. Second, the government's willingness to sell defense plants at fire-sale prices provided many manufacturers with state-of-the-art facilities and equipment for extremely low capitalization and investment. Third, the government itself, especially the armed forces, remained a hungry consumer of manufacturing output. Annual appropriations for defense during the mid-1930s had averaged just over $1 billion per year; between 1946 and 1950 they averaged more than $12 billion per year. The government's appetite for hardware increased markedly after two events in 1948 that are commonly considered to mark the start of the Cold War: the Communist coup in Czechoslovakia and the Soviet blockade of Berlin.

Against this background, TP resumed its quest for business as a specialist in precision engineering and manufacturing.

A Halfway Reorganization

Victory over Japan and the end of World War II brought a rapid winding down of TP's defense production. During the month following V-J Day (August 14), the company saw cancelled more than three thousand contracts, representing a total value of more than $50 million. At Tapco, a work force that had totaled nearly 12,000 at the peak of production was slashed to 650 by the end of August. The cutback, management believed, was only temporary, and it announced plans to employ 3,600 workers at Tapco by the spring of 1946. The basis for this cheerful forecast was renewed demand for automotive valves and parts, as well as continuing orders for aircraft engine components and aircraft accessories. As Crawford put it, "These three great fields, for which we manufacture a wide variety of products, give us unusual diversification of outlet. In years ahead we expect that our business will be divided about equally between the three markets. For each of them we are constantly developing new or improved products."[5]

During the fall of 1945, TP restructured and reorganized its operations to make them more efficient. On September 20, the company announced an agreement to purchase the Tapco plant, which would henceforth serve as the corporate headquarters. The price was $5 million, between one-third and one-half of replacement value. This was a bargain-basement deal, but the transaction nonetheless gave the company pause. It had little hope in the short run of filling the plant's cavernous 1.5 million square feet of capacity. Indeed, before the board of directors voted to purchase the plant, Crawford arranged to lead them on a tour, and he arranged to have machinery and equipment scattered around so that the plant would not seem so empty.[6]

Five days later, Crawford announced a reorganization of Cleveland-area operations into five divisions grouped along product lines. Four of the five units—Light Metals (aluminum foundry operations), Piston Ring, Parts and Accessories, and Valve and Jet Propulsion—were housed at Tapco, with only the Special Products Division (automotive replacement parts and miscellaneous forged-metal products) located at the main plant. Each division was intended to be "a complete business organization headed by a manager solely responsible for its operations."[7]

To provide general direction to the new divisions, Crawford announced the creation of a Staff Policy Committee, an "over-all policy-making" body consisting of himself, Clegg, Colwell, Wright, Coolidge, and Livingstone. In addition, Wright was named "Co-ordinator" of the Cleveland divisions and chairman of a committee of divisional managers.[8]

These organizational changes resulted from an extended series of conversations between Crawford and Wright during the late stages of the war. On the long train rides between Cleveland and the West Coast, the two had spent many hours discussing their hopes and plans for TP. Both believed that the company had a sound basic strategy as a supplier to the automotive and aircraft industries and as a manufacturer of differentiated, hard-to-make parts. They also believed that TP's abilities to make precision products cost-effectively and to maintain production without disputes or strikes would keep its business profitable and deter its customers from taking over the business themselves. These customers valued suppliers that could deliver dependably. But both executives worried about TP's ability to continue to execute this strategy as the big company that it had become as a result of wartime expansion. TP was not only roughly ten times larger than it had been in the 1930s, but it was also increasingly diverse: in 1944, it sold more than 1,400 different products, including subassemblies and subsystems, as well as make-to-print parts.[9]

To learn to cope better with pressures of size and diversity, Crawford and Wright investigated how other large, diverse companies organized their businesses. Through his connections in the National Association of Manufacturers, Crawford had become friendly with Lammot du Pont and Alfred Sloan, and he arranged briefings on how Du Pont and General Motors had decentralized their operations. Wright focused on General Electric and its Cleveland-based Lighting Division: "I'd visit their plants all around and make notes on their organization—ideas that we could use to run our own company. I had a lot of respect for GE. I thought it was very well run, with a good organization."[10]

To outward appearances, the new organization that TP adopted in 1945 resembled the multidivisional structures of larger companies like GM, Du Pont, and GE. However, Crawford and Wright followed these examples only part of the way. They did not endow division managers with full responsibility for profit and loss, nor did these managers direct all of the major functional departments that affected their business. Rather, TP's new divisions consisted of manufacturing departments whose managers were responsible for production, but not for R&D or sales. Those functions remained centralized at headquarters, where Colwell's engineering staff and Clegg's large sales department continued to handle business for all of the Cleveland-area divisions. These arrangements were undoubtedly made in deference to the authority of Colwell and Clegg as well-established and productive senior officials. But the new structure tended to breed conflict among engineers, production managers, and sales reps over the pricing and profitability of TP's products. During the next several years, these conflicts became increasingly worrisome to senior management.[11]

The 1945 reorganization also had little impact on TP's operations outside Cleveland, most of which remained autonomous organizations. The Michigan plant returned to its prewar focus on automotive chassis and suspension parts. The old Jadson operation in Bell, California, made parts for large reciprocating engines such as marine and railroad diesels. The Canadian plant produced miscellaneous automotive parts, as well as specialty items such as drill shaft tips for the Canadian oil industry.

Only at the Toledo replacement parts plant was significant change in the offing. In November 1945, the UAW-CIO committed a disastrous blunder by calling a strike at the plant to protest job assignments for returning servicemen. Almost immediately, TP announced plans to close the facility indefinitely and to consolidate replacement parts manufacturing in Cleveland. The decision cost about four hundred jobs in Toledo, although the company later remodeled the factory into a parts warehouse. The Toledo Steel Products Company, a wholly owned subsidiary of TP, retained responsibility for marketing the Toledo line of replacement parts.[12]

"A GOOD PLACE TO WORK"

TP reentered the competitive marketplace with a healthy financial condition, a modern facility at Tapco, a new, decentralized organization, and a proven management team still in its prime. Another key asset was the company's battle-tested program of human relations, which continued to reflect the personality and beliefs of its nationally renowned president.

During the postwar years, Crawford's considerable abilities and restless nature continued to draw him into outside commitments: director of the National Association of Manufacturers; several officer positions, including president, of the Automotive Parts Manufacturers Association; president of the National Air Races (which resumed in 1946); and member of various national commissions and associations, including the

Munitions Board of the Aircraft Industries Advisory Committee, the Industry Advisory Committee on Military-Contractor Relations (U.S. Department of Defense), and the Industrial Advisory Committee (U.S. Department of the Treasury). These assignments proved valuable to TP because they helped the company maintain relationships with high-level government officials and other leading industrialists and provided insights into evolving technologies and government policies.[13]

In all of these positions, Crawford remained an articulate spokesman for free enterprise and a controversial foe of government and industrial unions. He was pilloried in the pro-labor press and even cast as an unsympathetic character in a book by a UAW-CIO partisan, Elizabeth Hawes. In her fictionalized memoir of the 1945 representation election, *Hurry Up Please Its* [sic] *Time,* her characters portrayed Crawford as "no fool" and at the head of "a really potent management," but also as a liar, a scofflaw, and a master at duping employees. The book was not kindly reviewed and achieved only modest sales. It did help to keep Crawford's name near the top of the list of the national labor movement's enemies.[14]

Crawford enjoyed more favorable press in management circles. In December 1945, for example, the National Industrial Conference Board profiled "personnel organization" at Thompson Products in one of a series of case studies of model companies. The profile highlighted various aspects of TP's approach, including the importance attached to human relations by senior management and the company's competence in employee communications and supervisory training. The author of the report quoted a recent visitor to a TP plant as being

> convinced that one of the requirements for holding a personnel job in that organization was that the applicant be a good walker. The example is set by the President of the company, who spends every moment he can on the factory floor, and by the Personnel Vice President [Livingstone], whose wide acquaintance with individual workers is little less than astounding.[15]

One management expert even coined the term "Crawfordism" to describe an ideal type of industrial relations in which the aggressive, personal intervention of the CEO minimized conflict in the workplace. In 1951, at a time of industrial turmoil in Japan, a delegation of Japanese employers visited TP to study its program of industrial relations. Their goal was to understand better how to maintain peace in the factories as a means of increasing production.[16]

For their part, TP's employees continued to view their boss fondly. It was common, for example, for employees to call the Tapco plant "the joy factory," while the company adopted a new motto in the postwar years: "TP—A Good Place to Work." The ultimate expression of good feeling came at an Old Guard banquet in 1952, when employees recognized Crawford's thirty-five years of service with a remarkable gift: a 150-foot scroll bearing the signatures of virtually all of the eighteen thousand men and women who worked for the company. A plaque accompanying the scroll hailed Crawford as a "job-maker whose genius for leadership has made our company great . . . whose unyielding insistence on equal rights and respect for every individual among us has made us proud to be a part of the Thompson organization."[17]

PERFORMANCE

TP's strengths in manufacturing and management helped propel its fortunes upward during the postwar period. The company's financial performance showed steady improvement after 1946, building up to gross sales of nearly $110 million in 1949, a total well below wartime highs but nearly eight times the company's prewar peak. From there, sales shot upward, almost tripling by 1953 as a result of TP's business with the military during the Korean War. Profits were razor thin in 1945 and 1946, but soon built up to respectable margins, especially as measured by returns on assets and equity (see Exhibits II-1 to II-5).

TP's overall performance concealed wide swings in the fortunes of its various businesses and was a tribute to its strategy of diversification. During the 1930s, Crawford had theorized that the replacement business would be countercyclical to the original equipment market. The experience of the early postwar years bore him out. When the automakers built few cars in 1945 and 1946, for example, the Replacement Division (the new name for the old Service Division) posted record years. In 1946, the division produced nearly $40 million in revenues, accounting for almost 60 percent of TP's total sales.

This boom did not last long, however. Signs of a slowdown became evident as early as April 1947, when orders for TP replacement parts tumbled by nearly half "almost overnight." The apparent explanation was that jobbers had restocked inventories depleted during the war and henceforth were prepared to buy only to meet current demand, but that diagnosis concealed more disturbing trends at work. As growth slowed, competition began to heat up. Jim Syvertsen, who succeeded Tom Duggan as head of the Replacement Division after the war, complained that TP's rivals were "forever trying to steal our accounts by offering customers greater sales helps, better prices, [and] longer rebates." Several of the automakers, moreover, were making "fancy deals with their dealers" to keep prices low and to increase share in the replacement market. He cited GM, in particular, for "practically making automotive parts jobbers out of every dealer." Finally, he observed that TP's own outside suppliers for such items as water pumps, pistons, pins, and bolts were also competing for business. These small rivals generally operated with lower overhead and labor costs than TP.

Such forces added up to a gloomy picture for the Replacement Division. Indeed, after 1947, its fortunes declined, both absolutely and relatively, and sales hovered at about $30 million for most of the next decade.[18]

During the late 1940s, however, TP's sales to the automakers, which soared along with the increase of car, bus, and truck production, made up for the decline of the replacement business. Following a brief period of readjustment, motor vehicle production climbed past prewar production milestones and roared onward to record years in 1949 and 1950. By the time demand for motor vehicles began to soften—a result of market saturation combined with a recession—TP's sales to the aircraft industry began to pick up, more than compensating for the struggles of the other lines of business. During the Korean War (1950–1953) TP found itself in a position similar to the one it had occupied during World War II: a major defense contractor as a producer of components for aircraft engines. This time, however, the company's fortunes depended not on sodium-cooled valves but on the key interior parts of turbojet engines.

THE BUSINESS OF ENGINEERING

During the postwar period, TP derived the vast majority of its revenues from three concentrated industries—motor vehicles, aircraft, and aircraft engines. Its position as a supplier to powerful customers had many implications for how TP conducted its business. In general, its customers wanted the company to make parts and components to print specifications at acceptable quality and at prices as low as possible. The actual buyers of TP products were middle managers and purchasing agents whose compensation and likelihood of promotion depended on obtaining lower prices from suppliers. Contracts were typically made for one year; if they were renewed, the supplier's price was almost always lower than the year before. Its customers did not necessarily want or expect TP to develop entirely new products or to become a profitable source of innovations. Most of TP's customers insisted on having at least two sources of supply for key components, and the strongest were reluctant to use suppliers who also sold to their competitors. Finally, many of these customers were partly backward integrated themselves.[19]

TP's management was acutely aware of its vulnerability in such circumstances. As Dave Wright put it, "Our principal competitive threat comes from our own customers, who are all good mechanics and well able to produce the parts we make." He added that TP would retain this business "only so long as we can do the job better and cheaper than the people to whom we sell can do it themselves."[20]

TP managed to offset these unattractive industry conditions in several ways. It relied on close personal contacts with key customers at many levels of organization, starting at the top. At the very end of the war, for example, Crawford attended a NAM meeting at which his friend, GM chairman Alfred Sloan, spoke about the need for the automakers to cooperate closely with their suppliers during the period of reconversion. Soon thereafter, Crawford heard a rumor that GM's Chevrolet Division was planning to build a new factory to forge engine valves. He promptly arranged to meet Sloan and noted the contradiction between the NAM speech and Chevrolet's plans. Sloan saw the point and suggested a strategy for Crawford to adopt. He advised TP to make a low bid for Chevrolet's business. When Chevrolet's management appeared before GM's executive committee to ask for capital for the proposed new plant, Sloan would question the request closely. If Chevrolet could not show that the investment was justified on the basis of competitive prices for valves, then GM's executive committee would reject the request for funds. According to Crawford, exactly this scenario played out. For TP, this was a close call: the company retained a major customer, but at the cost of a very low margin—which, of course, was exactly what Sloan wanted.[21]

The concentration of the industries TP served made it possible for senior managers to spend a good deal of time with their customer counterparts. For example, Crawford and Wright, separately or together, made it a practice to visit the chief executives of major customers several times a year, either at the customer's headquarters or at industry association meetings. Clegg continued to work his contacts in the industries TP served, often inviting executives to join him on hunting and fishing expeditions to Quebec. Through the Society of Automotive Engineers and other engineering and technical organizations, Colwell maintained a wide circle of friends in customer organizations. And, of course, it was a standard TP practice for its salesmen to be on very familiar terms with their customers' purchasing agents. TP general managers and sales personnel spent a lot of time on the road. As a result, TP gleaned good intelligence about its customers' activities and plans and positioned itself as a friendly and responsive supplier.[22]

TP also stressed to its customers its own record of reliable production. Although strikes and industrial disputes plagued many big manufacturers after the war, TP maintained harmonious relations and steady output in its plants. "The greatest selling pitch in our business," recalled Crawford, "was, 'Buy from us and you'll get your stuff on time. We don't have strikes.'"[23]

Finally, in addition to its strengths in customer relations and personnel management, TP highlighted its expertise as "an engineering services organization—not merely filling orders, but pioneering the field with superior products tailored to meet our customers' exacting requirements." This strategy was born of TP's long experience as a valve maker. The company sought to find other products like valves in which it could establish a defensible position. This meant avoiding commodity items and striving constantly to lower costs, master new materials, and improve manufacturing processes.[24]

TP's emphasis on cost reflected the ascendancy of Dave Wright as coordinator of the Cleveland divisions. In November 1945, he established an Industrial Engineering Department for the main and Tapco plants headed by Emil Gibian, who had been chief industrial engineer at Tapco during the war. The reasons given for creating the department were that "even with recent price increases the company is losing money on virtually all products" and that "our manufacturing methods and controls have not kept abreast of the advances in modern factory management."[25]

As managed by Gibian, the department attempted to replace the traditional guesswork and occasional sloppy procedures of "cut-and-try" engineering with scientific analysis. As he described it, the department had six areas of responsibility: standards engineering, job evaluation, budgetary control, cost engineering, plant layout, and methods improvement. "We have had all these functions in the past," he noted, "but since they all interlock with each other, they have been brought together into one integrated organization." Gibian paid particularly close attention to determining correct standards for direct labor, machinery, materials and scrap, and other costs. This task entailed "an all-out effort towards reliable yardsticks," including the latest techniques in standards engineering and time-study analysis. Once set, the standards became the basis of an information system that tracked daily every fixed and variable expense in the factories. This information, in turn, formed the core of monthly reports to general foremen and division general managers, with comparisons of actual versus budgeted performance.[26]

Lowering and controlling costs were the department's prime objectives. The next most important task was methods improvement. Before 1946, Gibian observed, "methods improvement was performed informally by all mechanically minded people in the organization, including foremen and [certain] ingenious workmen." In the new order, methods engineers searched for new processes and equipment to lower manufacturing costs or improve quality. They worked closely with production engineers and shop-floor employees to simplify operations and find more cost-effective methods. Finally, the methods engineers oversaw a suggestion program to improve factory methods.[27]

During the next several years, the Industrial Engineering Department extended its reach into TP's factories outside Cleveland and assumed additional responsibilities, including capital expenditure control, inventory control, and statistical quality control. The department brought the same rigorous engineering approach to bear on these areas. Its study of the company's inventory practices, for example, resulted in better-controlled stocks of parts and a savings of $4 million "without affecting efficient production." Gibian was particularly fond of statistical methods, which he compared to radar's ability to "see through fog and reveal the significant facts concerning a situation." TP applied statistical analysis especially to quality control, adopting and adapting techniques developed for industry during the war, including detailed monitoring of operations coupled with frequent random sampling and statistical analysis of the results.[28]

The "D" in "R&D"

TP also placed great emphasis on process improvement and product development, which remained Colwell's major responsibilities as vice president of engineering. Although he was a prolific author and frequent speaker, Colwell seldom expanded on his philosophy of engineering, preferring instead to offer a few simple dicta. In 1951, for example, he described his specialty to a reporter for a trade magazine in these words: "Before you have anything to sell, you have engineering. Once you have a product, you have to improve it, you have to meet competition, you have to keep costs down—that's engineering."[29]

Colwell seldom waxed more philosophical than that, but he viewed engineering as a continuous development activity and TP as an engineering development company. "In many companies," he noted, "it is easy to define where research ends and development begins, and where production takes over from development, but the lines are almost impossible to draw for Thompson Products." He was particularly proud of the company's basic concept that "any design engineer is, in the long run, limited to designing components which can be manufactured on an economically feasible basis. Not the new product alone, but the means of making it in quantity and at low cost is the goal." This attitude, he argued, had not inhibited TP's growth at all. On the contrary, TP's "emphasis on the practical—on production as the goal of all research and development—has led to constant growth . . . ."[30]

On another occasion, he asserted that "an original worth-while idea is about 5 per cent of the total development, important as that idea may be." The other 95 percent—the process of development—consisted of "working out the most satisfactory and simplest design, extensive laboratory testing, followed by field tests, always redesigns and further testing, followed by exhaustive customer testing, both laboratory and field." For production, "the necessary machine tools must be supplied and tooled, personnel trained, and working capital supplied." In the markets TP served, Colwell said, production was "a long step from the starting point of the original idea."[31]

In concrete terms, development engineering at TP followed a definite procedure. New product ideas came from three sources: customers who wished TP to develop a particular item; TP's "sensing the market need for a new or improved product"; or the spontaneous submission of a proposal by an inventor or designer from inside or outside the company. The first screen for the new idea was study by a project group under the director of development, a senior manager on Colwell's staff. If the prospect seemed promising, it then proceeded to an engineering panel composed of the three senior officers in the engineering department. From there, it was assigned to a project group in one of the divisions to produce and test prototypes. Field tests typically ran from nine to twelve months, during which time cost engineers developed estimates of manufacturing cost and the sales department conducted market studies to determine the extent of demand for the product and a tentative selling price. At the end of the field tests, TP made a decision whether to move to production. If analysis showed that the product had little hope of paying an acceptable return, it was either cycled back to the engineers for redesign or killed outright.[32]

No detailed record of new product development at TP survives from this period, but case studies of the company's most visible new products can be reconstructed. Taken together, these case histories reveal patterns of an engineering development company at work. These patterns include long development cycles, high levels of expense and risk, and the benefits of close collaboration with customers when possible.

Piston Rings, Ball-Joint Suspensions, and Vitameters: A Single, a Home Run, and a Strikeout

During the postwar period TP offered the automotive original equipment and replacement markets many products that had been in development since before the war; these included sodium-cooled valves, steel-belted pistons, chromium-plated cylinder sleeves, a self-adjusting valve tappet, a new device to rotate valves, and a new type of mechanical shock absorber. The company had particularly high hopes for several products long in development, including the U-Flex piston ring, a new type of suspension system, and the Vitameter, the water-alcohol injection device to boost engine power and performance.

TP's involvement with piston rings began in the 1930s with a search for products other than valves and related parts that TP might make for builders of internal combustion engines. (Piston rings are metal rings that encircle a piston in a cylinder; they serve several functions, the most important of which is to prevent oil in the crankcase below the cylinder from entering the combustion chamber at the top: mixing oil into fuel causes engines to consume oil, run roughly, and eventually fail.) At that time, most piston rings were made from cast iron, and they were not sophisticated items. They were manufactured to be slightly larger than the cylinder so that when squeezed into place, they would fit snugly. A nagging problem, however, was that it was impossible to bend cast-iron rings exactly, and they would eventually leak at one or more points under pressure. Engine designers often specified several rings per piston to compensate for this problem. Even so, rings tended to be the first part in an engine to fail, and their replacement was an awkward and time-consuming operation that involved tearing the engine apart and rebuilding it.

During the 1930s, several manufacturers investigated making piston rings from steel alloys. These rings had superior durability and other advantages, but they proved costly to make. The challenge for a new entrant such as TP, then, was to produce steel piston rings that were demonstrably superior to their cast-iron counterparts at a comparable cost.[33]

Elmer Siegling, an engineer on Colwell's staff who specialized in patents, took charge of TP's efforts to make a better piston ring. He focused on product design, investigating both solid steel and flexible steel rings, as well as on issues of manufacturability. Although his work was interrupted and delayed during the war, Siegling benefited from TP's wartime studies of the dissipation of heat in automotive engines. This research again confirmed the tendency of cast-iron piston rings to leak after extended operation and underscored the desirability of making rings from materials more versatile than cast iron. Moreover, flexible rings could be made to fit new and unusual engine designs featuring tapered or noncircular cylinders. Siegling experimented with several flexible ring designs before settling on one patented by Thomas Bowers, an independent inventor. The Bowers ring resembled a string of parallel "U"s. When wrapped around the piston, the ring's spring-like tension made it flex into a tight, reliable seal between the piston and the cylinder. In addition to its tight fit, the new ring lasted longer, provided superior lubrication, and weighed far less than conventional piston rings. A single flexible ring, moreover, could do the work of two or more cast-iron rings. It offered so many advantages that Colwell hailed it as "the most novel piston ring development of the last 25 years."[34]

In 1945, TP christened the Bowers ring "U-Flex" and began small-scale production and field testing. Believing that prospects for the U-Flex ring were "exceptionally good," Wright named Siegling head of the Piston Ring Division, one of the new postwar operating units at the Tapco plant. Several big customers, including Buick and International Harvester, showed interest in the U-Flex. The next problem was to find ways to manufacture the new piston ring economically so that TP could sell it for a profit amid tough price competition from producers of cast-iron rings. Siegling gave Harry Norton, a specialist whose background included the engineering of zippers, the assignment of building an automatic machine capable of stamping out more than four thousand U-Flex rings per hour. "This was a long and difficult development," recalled Colwell. It involved an investment of more than $1 million over seven years as Norton continually tinkered with and improved his machine. By the fall of 1947, the equipment was reliable enough for TP to take an order from Buick for four hundred thousand rings per month. In 1949, TP began producing U-Flex rings for the replacement market, and it offered a related line of Z-Flex and Strut-Flex piston rings for heavy-duty engines. By then other customers such as Nash, Continental, and Mack had become customers. Still TP was losing money on the investment, and it was not until October 1950 that its piston ring business finally reported a profit.[35]

The development of another successful new automotive product, ball-joint front suspension, was also a long and expensive process, but TP's payback came much more quickly. Developed between 1947 and 1952 at a cost of more than $2 million, TP's new system, proclaimed TP engineers, amounted to "the first basic improvement in front-end suspension in 20 years." The ball-joint design combined suspension action and steering motion "at one point into a neat package" and replaced the traditional mechanism of king pins and spindle support forgings. The new product offered impressive advantages: smaller size and weight, which allowed more room under the hood to accommodate bulky V-8 engines; better steering and handling characteristics; simplified lubrication and longer service life; and much greater ease of installation, repair, and maintenance.[36]

TP developed the ball-joint front suspension at its Michigan plant under chief engineer Jim Booth, with the assistance of Barney Ricks, Tinse Kennedy, and Barney Fountain. It also collaborated closely with engineers from Ford, the division's largest customer. As Booth admitted, there was nothing new about the idea of applying ball joints to front suspensions; TP's approach to the problem, however, was novel. Automakers and other suppliers had long known that ball-joint suspensions offered many advantages over conventional suspensions, but they were troubled by the stiffness of the steering that resulted from requiring the ball surfaces to perform the dual role of bearing the weight of the front end and acting as a pivot point for steering. The TP design separated the two functions, using an upper ball joint to bear weight and dampen directional instability and a lower ball joint supported by a ring of ball bearings to enable free movement of the wheels for steering. This approach reflected TP's work on steering-linkage ball joints as well as its investigations of the steering and suspension systems of European and American automobiles.[37]

Once TP established its basic design, it worked with several automobile manufacturers, but especially with Ford, to test the new system under a wide variety of driving conditions. Cars traveled thousands of miles over rough roads, through mountainous terrain and deserts, and through extremes of heat and cold. Each test provided valuable data about the performance and endurance of the system and resulted in changes to materials, lubrication seals to keep out moisture and grit, the shape of the joint sockets, and other design elements. TP engineers also addressed problems of manufacturability, focusing on ways to control scrap and to lower cost. In the end, TP concluded that its system was more costly by itself than conventional suspensions, but that it was competitive when analysis took account of "weight savings, eliminated operations, part reductions, and design improvements made possible by the ball-joint adaptation."[38]

TP's ball-joint suspension was an immediate hit in the marketplace. The collaborative tests with Ford paid off: Ford's Lincoln Division adopted the ball-joint front suspension for its 1952 model year and promoted heavily the "smoother, more comfortable ride." A favorable review in *Popular Mechanics* quoted a satisfied owner who praised "the roadability and maneuverability" of his car. By September 1952, interest in the product was so great that Matt Graham, Michigan general manager, forecast $10 million in revenues for the coming year. At the same time, TP earmarked $2 million to refit and modernize a plant in Fruitport, Michigan, to be wholly dedicated to fabricating ball-joint suspensions. Less than a year later, "bursting at the seams" with increased orders, the Michigan Division acquired a new, modern factory in Portland to house additional production.[39]

Of TP's most promising postwar developments, only the Vitameter, the water-alcohol injection device, proved a major disappointment. In 1945, Jim Syvertsen, sales manager for the project, forecast "an annual business of not less than $28 million even with a half-hearted job of selling," once bugs in the product could be worked out. He turned down an order of fifty thousand units from a distributor in Oklahoma City because the system was not yet ready. Syvertsen also planned to market alcohol-water mixtures under the brand name "Vitol." He predicted that this ancillary business would account for $18 million in annual revenues. According to his calculations, the Vitameter-Vitol system could save a truck $277 a year in operating expenses by permitting use of lower-octane gasoline. Syvertsen expected the device to appeal particularly to trucking companies, taxicab owners, and other businesses that operated fleets of motor vehicles.[40]

Despite this optimistic scenario, the TP project engineers for the Vitameter—Arch Colwell, J. N. Cole, and Dave Anderson—encountered many serious obstacles. The first was manufacturing cost for the injection device itself. As originally designed, the basic structure of the unit was cast from brass. Late in 1945 or early in 1946, TP started a simultaneous program of road tests to evaluate performance and of market research to determine the extent of demand and an optimum selling price. The market research concluded that the best price for the Vitameter system was about $30, including installation. When that number filtered back to the project engineers, however, it was obvious that the manufacturing cost was too high. The Vitameter was sent back for redesign, while the engineers conducted a long search for alternative materials and manufacturing methods. They eventually settled on die-cast aluminum as the basic structure. Once they were confident of this approach, the engineers scheduled another nine to twelve months of road tests.[41]

Results of these tests were encouraging, and Colwell believed the device was "soundly engineered" at last. In May 1947, TP created a new subsidiary, the Thompson-Toledo Vitameter Corporation, with Colwell as president, to manufacture and market the device. The new entity planned to push the Vitameter and Vitol in both the original equipment and replacement markets. After a delay occasioned by a search for the best types and sources of alcohol for Vitol and problems in developing noncorrosive coatings for the Vitol storage tank, the Vitameter finally made its public debut amid great fanfare in September 1948 in a major market test in Columbus, Ohio. The price of the system, including a five-quart tank for Vitol, was $29.95, plus installation, which the company calculated could be accomplished in less than an hour. TP sold Vitol for 30 cents a quart and estimated that its five-quart tank would hold enough of the water-alcohol mixture to last between five and seven hundred miles.[42]

By the time of the Columbus trials, other problems with the Vitameter were fast becoming apparent. These problems pertained to the Vitameter's role in two systems: the fuel management system inside an engine and the fuel distribution system that controlled the types and availability of fuels sold at gas stations and garages. For the Vitameter to succeed, TP not only had to make a reliable automatic injection device cheaply; it also had to convince automakers and car owners to purchase the system, owners of garage and repair shops to install and repair it, and the oil companies and owners of gas stations to support the system by making Vitol universally available. On all these counts, TP faced insuperable obstacles.

The automobile manufacturers, for instance, believed that the way to produce better engine performance was to design better, more powerful engines such as the increasingly popular V-8 rather than to adopt an add-on device like the Vitameter. A handful of automakers, including Cadillac and Crosley, recommended the Vitameter to their customers, but none of them agreed to install the device as factory equipment. Owners of garages and gas stations proved more willing to support the Vitameter, but TP ran into enormous and very expensive difficulties in creating a distribution system for Vitol. The company's approach was to build up distribution city by city, starting with the trials in Columbus.[43]

TP lacked the time and the money to succeed in supporting the Vitameter in the field. By the late 1940s, the key assumption behind the program was quickly eroding. At the outset of development, Colwell had sought and received assurances from the oil companies that they had no plans to make high-octane gasoline widely available. He even calculated an extravagant cost—about $4.25 billion, or nearly $300 million per octane number—that the oil industry would have to bear to carry out research on high-octane fuels, increase production capacity, and expand distribution to duplicate the technical performance of the Vitameter. These assurances and analyses notwithstanding, the growing popularity of the V-8 compelled the oil companies to develop and distribute high-octane fuels. By 1950, "super," "premium," and "high-test" gasolines were available at pumps across the country. When that happened, demand for the Vitameter all but evaporated.[44]

The Vitameter lingered on in production for several more years. In 1950, the Thompson-Toledo Vitameter Corporation was downgraded into a division of TP. Although the company sought to find markets for the Vitameter overseas, it abandoned production altogether in 1954. Its passing saddened Colwell, who declared it to be one of the two biggest disappointments of his career—the other being the failure of the copper-cooled valve. Like the U-Flex piston ring and the ball-joint front suspension, the Vitameter represented a very significant investment, probably in the millions, and consumed many years of development time. Its ultimate failure pointed up the high barriers and great risks facing automotive suppliers that attempted to develop entirely new products. TP fared much better when it focused on manufacturing process improvements for products designed by its customers.[45]

Blades, Buckets, and Vanes: Another Home Run

The constraints on TP as a supplier to the automobile industry were also apparent in the aircraft and aircraft engine industries, but to lesser and different degrees. The pace of technological change in both those industries created many opportunities for suppliers to develop entirely new accessory products as well as to make expensive critical components.

During the postwar period, TP maintained a profitable business in aircraft accessory products such as fuel pumps and other components of fuel systems, and it continued to produce sodium-cooled valves for aircraft with conventional reciprocating engines. Such aircraft remained dominant until the early 1950s, when turbojet-powered aircraft came to the fore. By then, TP was poised to benefit from its accumulated expertise in fabricating hard-to-make engine components such as compressor stators and rotors, turbine wheels and buckets, and nozzle diaphragms and vanes.

TP's immediate problems after the war reflected the obvious problem of the aircraft industry's overcapacity. After V-J Day, orders for aircraft plummeted, and for several years the major aircraft manufacturers struggled to retrench, reorganize, and stay afloat. After building more than 300,000 airplanes during World War II, the industry produced just 1,417 military aircraft in 1946, and no more than 2,680 units in any year before the Korean War expansion of 1951. This situation would have been disastrous but for a partly offsetting trend: postwar aircraft were bigger, heavier, more sophisticated, and more expensive than their predecessors. The new aircraft used new materials, incorporated new propulsion technologies, and contained more complex equipment for communications, navigation, and weapons control.[46]

Several events of the late 1940s converged to improve the industry's condition. The first was a series of organizational changes in the federal government resulting from the National Security Act of 1947, which established a unified military command under the Joint Chiefs of Staff in the Department of Defense, recognized the U.S. Air Force as an independent branch of the service, and created the National Security Council and the Central Intelligence Agency. This action recognized the strategic significance of air power and helped reawaken public interest in the health of the U.S. aircraft industry. That year, the industry's fortunes received a further boost from two national commissions, one appointed by President Harry Truman and the other by Congress, which independently recommended significant increases in federal appropriations for aircraft procurement. The Communist coup in Czechoslovakia and the Berlin blockade provided the final stimulus to the industry's revival. Military aircraft appropriations grew from $750 million in 1947 to $900 million in 1948, and a healthy percentage of those funds was earmarked for turbojet-powered fighter aircraft.[47]

TP was well positioned to profit from expanded funding for turbojet engines. In 1946, the company supplied subassemblies that together accounted for more than half of the value of a finished jet engine to more than 90 percent of the nation's jet engine projects. TP boasted a backlog of $50 million in orders for turbojet engine components.[48]

TP's success in this business reflected its remarkable ingenuity in fabricating complex shapes from alloys that were extremely difficult to work with. Each turbojet engine typically required several thousand separate airfoils classified as blades, buckets, and vanes. TP's terminology for these items reflected their different applications and specifications: a *blade* is a rotating member used to compress gas; a *bucket* is a part rotated by hot gas, as attached to a turbine wheel; and a *vane* is a stationary part used to change gas direction, as in a nozzle diaphragm. For the engine to achieve rated performance, each of these airfoils had to meet exacting requirements for size, shape, and durability. The tips and edges of turbine wheel buckets, for example, were often hardly thicker than heavy wrapping paper, with allowable variances of between one-thousandth and five-thousandths of an inch. After polishing, the final variance was one-twenty-millionth of an inch. Yet the buckets had to endure, reliably, centrifugal pull of almost thirty thousand pounds per square inch while red hot and spinning at rates from eight thousand to thirty thousand revolutions per minute. In most instances, buckets were forged or cast from exotic cobalt-chromium alloys, and they sold for as much as $5 apiece. Completed turbine-wheel assemblies sold for about $4,000.[49]

TP's skills and experience in precision forging provided the company's original point of entry into the manufacturing of turbojet engine components. To stay ahead of the competition, however, the company continually investigated new fabricating techniques. For the early J-35 (TG-180) engine built by GM's Chevrolet and Allison divisions—the power plant for Lockheed's P-80 "Shooting Star," the most successful of the early turbojet-powered airplanes—TP engineers perfected a method of welding turbine buckets to a wheel using automatic equipment instead of attaching them mechanically, as accomplished on the first turbine wheels.[50]

Later, TP engineers pursued wholly new approaches to making airfoils in response to demands for more powerful and efficient engines. The most important change involved the development of more efficient compressors. The first American turbojets followed the British example in using centrifugal compressors, in which the blades acted like those of a large electric fan. They channeled air outward and relied on the tapered design of the engine housing to contain and compress the air and channel it through to the combustion chamber. These engines resembled an inverted cone lying on its side, with a big leading edge that tapered off to a narrower exit nozzle. The design created a great deal of aerodynamic drag.

By 1948, however, American engine builders showed a marked preference for axial compressors, which moved air directly along the axis of the engine. Each compressor looked somewhat like a porcupine, with as many as twenty-five hundred different blades or "quills" of different shape and length jutting out from a metal cylinder. Axial compressors permitted sleeker and more compact engine housings, more efficient movement of air, and higher compression ratios than were obtainable with centrifugal compressors. However, axial compressors also created complex internal aerodynamic problems and posed formidable manufacturing challenges.[51]

Not the least of these was to produce extremely high-precision blades in volume. In wartime, for example, Colwell calculated that it might become necessary to make as many as fifty million blades per month. This kind of output raised basic questions about both the availability of critical alloys and the capacity of conventional methods of precision forging. In 1946, TP launched a research program to develop a way to make blades that would "save critical material, reduce cost, and have less die work than in forging." The researchers quickly discovered that these goals could be met by working with powdered metals, although success would require making parts of greater strength and density than ever before achieved with such materials.[52]

In February 1947, TP obtained an exclusive license on "certain powder metallurgy processes" from American Electro Metal Corporation. At the same time, it retained several engineers from this company as consultants and worked closely with GM's Allison Division on a new process for manufacturing small precision airfoils. The result, after two years, was the TP-1 process for making compressor blades and stator vanes from powdered metals. As described by Colwell, "the process resembles the making of buttered toast. The powder is compacted (dough), sintered (baking), and then infiltrated (butter seeping into hot toast)." That is, iron oxide powder was purified and mixed with lubricants and other materials, then molded into the shape of a blade in a mammoth hydraulic press. Next, the blade was sintered in a furnace at two-thousand degrees Fahrenheit, then further compressed and shaped to impart twist and contour. From there, it was infiltrated with a copper alloy in a specially designed controlled atmosphere furnace. The final steps involved surface treatments and coatings. In all, the process not only saved on critical materials like chromium but also required less direct labor and floor space and resulted in few rejects and virtually no scrap.[53]

The manufacture of turbine buckets was also replete with engineering challenges. Indeed, like exhaust valves in a reciprocating engine, turbine-wheel buckets were subjected to the most extreme operating conditions in a turbojet engine. The first turbine buckets were forged, but engine designers recognized that buckets would stay cooler if ways could be found to make them hollow but with internal ribs to provide strength, specifications that were nearly impossible to meet with precision forging. The best alternative technique of fabrication was investment or "lost-wax" casting. In this process, liquid metal was poured into ceramic molds of precise dimensions. The tricky part was to make the molds. This was done by pouring hot wax onto metallic dies and allowing it to solidify. The wax was then removed from the dies and used as a pattern for making ceramic molds. This was usually accomplished by dipping the wax pattern into a series of successively coarser ceramic baths. When the ceramic material hardened, the mold was heated to melt and burn off the wax, leaving behind a cavity of precise dimensions. In making turbine buckets by lost-wax casting, it was extremely difficult to hold the patterns to the specified contours. Buckets made in this way, moreover, tended to suffer fatigue under the stress of engine vibration.[54]

By the late 1940s, an alternative casting process was available, one that used mercury instead of wax to form the pattern for the mold. TP began investigation of this process by working with New York-based Mercast Corporation, whose research laboratory it eventually acquired in August 1949. The process relied on several unique properties of mercury. At room temperature, the metal was so fluid that it would fill around even the most abrupt section changes and deepest crevices of precise metallic dies. At that point, another property of mercury came into play. When frozen to a temperature of minus 125 degrees Fahrenheit, mercury held its shape exactly. In addition, at this temperature, the frozen metal easily formed a strong weld when two pieces were brought into contact under light pressure.

The frozen-mercury process—called "Intricast" by TP—permitted the design and production of more complicated shapes than did conventional investment casting. The process had other advantages, too: it allowed fabrication of larger parts with better surface finish and closer tolerances, and it could be used to make hollow pieces with exceptionally intricate internal cavities. Finally, as Colwell noted, the process was not called "lost mercury," because all the mercury could be recovered when poured from the mold. The process was costly, but justifiable for products with extremely precise dimensional requirements.[55]

TP's investments in new fabricating technologies and metallurgical research paid off in several ways. When new entrants such as Westinghouse and Pratt & Whitney appeared in the turbojet engine industry, TP occupied an entrenched position as a supplier of key components. The company's expertise and ongoing investment deterred its customers from attempting to make these components themselves; and TP's new casting expertise prepared the way for making a wide variety of industrial and commercial products. In 1950, the company organized a new unit at Tapco, the Metallurgical Products Division, to pursue such opportunities.

THE ORGANIZATION MAN

On March 29, 1949, Crawford announced the promotion of Dave Wright to the new position of vice president and general manager of Thompson Products. This action confirmed what many had long suspected: Wright was Crawford's heir apparent. The promotion apparently disappointed some rivals for the top spot, but Wright merely shrugged: "We have a spirit of teamwork in this company that makes this job fun," he said at the press conference announcing the change. "I just hope to be able to use what I've learned from Fred Crawford."[56]

The new general manager was forty-four years old, fourteen years Crawford's junior. Despite some gray hairs, Wright still appeared much younger than his age. His boyish looks, slight build, and reserved manner often created first impressions quite at odds with a tough-minded and disciplined approach to management. Years later, Crawford paid him high compliments: "Dave had a quality that a lot of people don't have: . . . the ability to brush the unessentials away and get at the heart of a problem. Napoleon said [that] Alexander Hamilton was the greatest American because he had perception; he could ignore the less important things and focus on the important ones. Dave had a good deal of that ability."[57]

"Dave and I worked well together," Crawford added, "because we thought alike. We had the same values, the same ideas." The two men were best friends and frequent companions, not only on business trips but also on vacations. They often dined together and would stay up long into the night talking over business. They joined the same clubs, shared the same friends, and played golf together frequently. Both were officers and directors of the National Air Races. They even invested together; among other ventures, the two were the principal backers and dominant board members of the Crawford Door Company. (Both men retained major interests in Crawford Door until the mid-1950s when, for estate-planning reasons, they transferred ownership to their wives; their family holdings in the company ceased altogether with the sale of Crawford Door to the Jim Walter Company in 1962.)[58]

In many respects, Wright was Crawford's alter ego. Whereas the older man was flamboyant, spontaneous, at ease and at his best in crowds, and in love with the limelight, the younger man was a private person, meticulous and analytical, an effective but unremarkable speaker, and content to work behind the scenes. Although he lacked Crawford's marvelous common touch with people, Wright was nonetheless friendly and approachable. He left his door open and continued to answer his own telephone until near the end of his career as chairman and CEO of TRW in the 1960s. "I don't think I'm a big shot," he later said. "I never thought that. I resented people in business who would say, 'I did this, and I did that.' In a big company, it's almost never 'I,' it's 'we.' I would always say that 'we' did something. Almost every achievement in business is the result of a collective effort, not the effort of just one person."[59]

Wright's concerns for efficiency and detail were legendary inside the company. "He would wear shoes that you slip on and off, so he wouldn't have to tie them," recalled Crawford, noting also that "he wore shirts without cuffs, so he wouldn't have to put in cuff links. Anything to eliminate the waste of time." Wright later recalled, "I guess I had a reputation as something of a penny-pincher," adding that he might have acquired it because he "used to review the subscriptions for the magazines that were in the lobby and cut them back." Such stories indicated Wright's style as a manager. "I was always very organized," Wright later admitted, "maybe too much so. . . . When I'd call a meeting, I'd always start it on time. When I worked for the law firm, I would write a letter and correct it maybe ten or eleven times." Why the focus on order? "I don't like messes," he said. "I wanted things together—orderly, consistent, systematic. I wanted the reports to be regular. I tried, above all, to make things systematic."[60]

During the immediate postwar years, as Crawford increased his outside commitments, Wright remained dedicated to running TP, and his concern for organization and detail proved valuable to the company. The timing of his promotion reflected a recognition shared by Crawford and the board of directors that the company needed better organization. "We recognized that we had been building volume, good products, good labor relations, but without building proportionate profit," Crawford explained, adding:

> We had been going on this way for fifteen years as we built the company from a little business to a big business. This spring we decided to get out of the little business class into the big business league. For years we had run the company by hunch and instinct, by guess and by gosh. You might have called us a "hunch company." We set out this spring to become a modern, analytical company; to run our affairs by cold self-discipline rather than by emotional decision or hunch.

As general manager, Wright had two main responsibilities. The first was "to bring us through to a profit balancing [of] all the factors that bear upon the business." The other involved "continuing cold analysis of all the functions of the business."[61]

Much in Wright's career prior to 1949—his experiences in organizing and managing Tapco; his role in decentralizing TP into divisions; his interest in industrial engineering; his positions on the board of directors, the staff policy committee, and the committee of divisional managers—amply prepared him for his new role. As general manager of TP, he became not only its chief operating officer, but also its architect of organization.

From Hunches to Cold Analysis

Wright wasted little time before making significant changes to TP's organization and management systems. As he had during the war, he drew on his study of other big, successful manufacturing companies. This research revealed to him what he considered were three secrets of success: "decentralization, coupled with delegation of authority, divisional dealings on an arm's-length basis, and payment of those who are in a position to control profit on the basis of return on investment." Accordingly, TP implemented "a sweeping program to strengthen our organizational structure" to achieve "more effective control of sales, production, capital expenditures, inventory, and other major activities of our business."[62]

Wright's initial step was to complete the half-way reorganization of 1945. He delegated to the Cleveland division managers responsibility not only for operations, but also for engineering and sales, "and above all the profit" of their business. These divisions thus became full-fledged business units like the decentralized operations in Detroit, Bell (California), and St. Catharines (Ontario). Wright also directed each general manager to appoint an assistant general manager, a position designed to create opportunities for promising young executives.[63]

Wright also made existing policy structures more formal. The staff policy committee, for example, began to meet more regularly on board meeting days and more frequently by arrangement. This group was charged to think on "a corporation-wide basis," which meant taking "responsibility for future planning and strategic thinking— making decisions based on fact and controlled by budget, studying developments on a companywide basis, determining policies and implementing them throughout the organization." The committee evaluated performance of the operating divisions, saw that top management posts were properly staffed, and planned for anticipated needs. It employed a small staff for research and analysis of business problems.

Wright elevated the occasional meetings of the committee of divisional managers into regular monthly "management review meetings" attended not only by the division general managers, but also by TP's top corporate officers. The purpose of these meetings, he said, was threefold: "to analyze and discuss how we're doing so that all will understand how we're doing as a group; to make plans to meet the goals when figures show we're lagging behind; [and] to serve as an open forum in which all matters of general interest may be brought up." Livingstone recalls that the meetings were "very impressive and very well run." They were held in Crawford Hall, a big conference room at Tapco that was remodeled to include the latest in audiovisual aids.[64]

Other significant organization and policy changes followed during the early 1950s. With respect to new products, for example, Wright had long been concerned that TP's engineers were a fertile source of new ideas but lacked the financial discipline to abandon projects that had little hope of paying a return. He may have been thinking of products like the U-Flex piston ring and the Vitameter when he noted that "our managers would tend to think that a new product could be made cheaper later, then the profits would follow. But it often didn't work out that way. Our managers would be more interested in the product than the price."[65]

To remedy this tendency, early in 1950, Wright created a New Products Committee, which consisted of the senior technical personnel at both the corporate and division levels. Chaired by Colwell, the committee's mandate was "to screen ideas and determine whether they fit with TP lines." It was also charged to "conduct sales analyses to determine whether there is a good market for the product; cost analyses to determine the amount of capital investment required, and whether it would be profitable, and finally, decide in which division it logically belonged." The committee's tasks also included coordination of engineering work to eliminate duplication of effort, the improvement of staff engineering services, and the provision of specialist services to the divisions "on a proper charge basis." At the announcement introducing the committee, Wright called it "probably the most exciting development to date in perfecting and refining the recently evolved staff-divisional realignment of the company. It probably means more to the long-term health of the company than any other single step we have taken."[66]

Wright spoke frequently to employee audiences to explain the management changes at the company. In a 1950 speech, for example, he distilled the essence of TP's management philosophy into a few crisp paragraphs:

> We do not operate as most large companies with a large staff in a remote ivory tower. Neither do we have a staff that tries to run the business of the various divisions.
>
> Our philosophy is simply this: we are in business to make a profit—to make the greatest possible return on the investment entrusted to our care. We believe in decentralization. We believe that no man is smart enough to be a true expert on more than one related line of products. Accordingly, every major line of products is incorporated into separate divisions headed by a competent manager who is responsible for profit, volume and the welfare of his group. Every division manager has his own engineering, manufacturing, and selling. We believe in a small staff that may help—but never hinder the various divisions. As a matter of fact, their principal function is to look ahead—to make sure that we are going in the right direction—and that when it comes time for us to retire, our pensions will be paid, and our obligations to the community and all our people are continuously discharged. . . .
>
> Finally, we believe in the dignity of the individual. . . . It is a religion with us.[67]

In 1952, Wright standardized these views in an *Organization Guide* distributed to all senior managers in the company. The guide opened with a formal code of conduct for management, which Wright believed to be the first of its kind in the United States. He listed thirteen "responsibilities common to all members of management," beginning with three timeless maxims: "Live up to a high code of personal honor; follow the Golden Rule and obey the law." Responsibilities specific to business included "Understand and follow sound principles of organization" and "Fill all positions with the best qualified personnel; make promotions from within the organization whenever practicable, and maintain a sound replacement program." The code of conduct and other policies of the *Organization Guide* appeared deceptively simple and straightforward, but they were the product of long hours of thinking and writing. Composing the guide, said Wright, "was one of the hardest jobs of my life. I had to rewrite five pages of this 30 times before it came out like we wanted."[68]

Wright was also responsible for changing TP's management incentives. The new policy had two elements, both designed to reward improvements in profitability. A bonus system based primarily on profitability measures and the judgment of senior management could add between 30 and 40 percent to a manager's base salary. The second element was a stock option plan that enabled managers to acquire a significant stake in the company depending on its and their performance.[69]

In taking bold actions to reorganize the company and upgrade its management systems, Wright enjoyed the full confidence and support of Crawford. Only in one important respect did they differ. More than Crawford, Wright was concerned about management succession and the company's hiring practices. "To me, the number-one principle in business is to hire bright people," he said, continuing: "Crawford had a different idea. . . . He'd make speeches about how ordinary people can rise above the average to do great things. But I always thought that the way to build a business is to hire somebody bright. The bright ones aren't ordinary. All the important developments in the world are the result of the work of bright people."[70]

Wright acted on his concern for management succession in several ways, including the appointment of assistant general managers. He also started an informal training program for about thirty promising young managers across the company. This group met about once a month for dinner meetings and to hear speakers from inside and outside the company talk about key business issues. These occasions achieved simultaneous goals: they enabled the young managers to see different facets of TP, and they gave Wright and other senior managers further insights into the capabilities and ambitions of younger management personnel.[71]

Wright followed the example of other defense contractors and recruited management talent from the U.S. military. In 1951, he scored a coup by wooing thirty-eight-year-old Horace A. Shepard, who four years earlier had become the youngest general officer in the U.S. Air Force. Shepard joined TP as vice president and assistant to the general manager. For the Air Force, Shepard had served as chief of procurement at Wright Field and as chief of procurement and engineering at the Pentagon. He brought with him to TP not only considerable management skill and experience, but also a wealth of contacts in the Department of Defense and the defense industry. He remained with TP and its successors in senior management positions until he retired in 1977 as chairman and CEO. Other TP hires from the U.S. Air Force during the early 1950s included Col. Whitmell (Whit) T. Rison, who became general manager of the Replacement Division, a position in which he served until 1958, when he was killed in a tragic fishing accident; and Col. Stanley C. Pace, who rose through a series of general management positions to become vice chairman of TRW. He left the company in 1986 to become chairman and CEO of General Dynamics.[72]

Yet another step to upgrade the company's management involved the creation of an "executive inventory and development plan" administered by Livingstone and his top assistant, Stacy R. Black. This program entailed making "a careful inventory and analysis of all people with supervisory and related responsibilities, and a systematic review of the progress of each individual." The goal of the program was to "enable everyone in an executive or supervisory capacity to plan manpower development for his particular area in the same efficient manner that he now plans equipment and machinery requirements." The program included regular performance appraisals as well as long-term planning for the company's management needs.[73]

In July 1952, Crawford and Wright launched another management tradition by summoning TP's top ten officers to a week-long retreat at Old Home Crawford, a farm in northern Vermont that had been in Crawford's family since the eighteenth century. The occasion was an informal gathering to talk about the future of the company, and it confirmed Wright's sense that "it is not enough to let nature take its course as the orders come in, and merely to do today's job well." The session had two immediate outcomes. The first was a new charge to the division managers to develop annual plans focusing on improvements, "with particular emphasis on improvement of profit performance." The annual plans were to be presented to the policy group by the end of the year and to include discussion of basic business matters such as a sales forecast, shifts in the product mix, and pricing policies. The division managers were also required to present specific opportunities for cost reduction, to forecast and explain improvements in profit performance (expressed in dollars, return on sales, and return on investment), and to discuss management of inventories, capital spending needs, and R&D expenditures. The second outcome was to make the Vermont conferences an annual gathering of top corporate and division managers to consider the future of the company.[74]

THE WRIGHT "ERA OF CONSOLIDATION"

In the spring of 1949, when Crawford announced Wright's appointment as TP's general manager, he declared that "the Crawford era of expansion" had come to an end and that it would be replaced by "the Wright era of consolidating our gains and making the business more profitable."[75]

It did not take long for this prophecy to become dated. During the second half of 1949, automotive sales continued to rise, and even the replacement market showed signs of picking up. The latter improvement was reflected in TP's acquisition in

August 1950 of St. Louis-based Ramsey Corporation, a maker of piston rings and other products for the replacement market, for considerations worth about $1 million. Ramsey, which posted annual revenues of about $6 million and employed about 650 workers, had been founded in 1917 by J. A. Ramsey. The company had made its fortune on a simple principle: it manufactured tempered-steel piston rings that fit behind cast-iron rings to help keep them flexible and the piston from rocking. Later on, Ramsey developed a special type of inner ring that allowed older engines to be rebuilt without having to rebore the cylinders—resulting in a nice savings for owners of older cars who possessed neither the means nor the inclination to buy a new car. The Ramsey transaction brought to TP three manufacturing plants, an independent dealer network, and a well-established brand name in the replacement market. Under TP's ownership, Ramsey remained a separate subsidiary with its own management in place.[76]

TP's purchase of Ramsey nicely complemented its growing business in U-Flex piston rings. TP might have been even more successful and built a dominant position in piston rings much like its business in valves had it been able to complete a second acquisition in 1950. During the summer, TP announced agreement in principle to merge with Perfect Circle Corporation of Hagerstown, Indiana. Founded in 1895, Perfect Circle had grown to become a $13 million business employing about two thousand people in four factories in the United States and Canada. TP publications trumpeted the advantages of the proposed deal and carried news of get-togethers of TP and Perfect Circle managers, including a ballroom gala in October. By then, however, "disquieting rumors" had already begun to sprout. In fact, the Department of Justice announced early in 1951 that if the merger were consummated, it would institute litigation on the grounds that the combination of TP, Ramsey, and Perfect Circle would constitute a violation of the Sherman Antitrust Act. On January 31, 1951, the merger was quietly abandoned. Although TP briefly flirted with yet another producer, Muskegon Piston Ring Company, its hopes of becoming a major factor in the piston ring business were thwarted by government policy.[77]

The major engine of growth for TP was not the automotive or replacement markets, however. It was the third leg of the stool: the aircraft business. When Communist troops crossed the 38th parallel in Korea on the night of June 28, 1950, they set in motion a chain of events that would engage military forces from all over the world for more than three years, provide a crucial testing ground for the turbojet aircraft engine, and boost significantly the fortunes of U.S. defense contractors like TP.[78]

As a major producer of turbojet engine components before the war, TP was poised to profit from the surge in military orders after mid-1950. These orders came in rapid succession. On July 24, the board of directors approved $4 million for a major expansion to increase production of turbojet engine components at the Tapco plant. By the end of August, the company was hiring workers at a rate faster than during the peak months of World War II. This was only the beginning. During the next three years, the company added nearly two million square feet of manufacturing capacity by (1) acquiring an old steel mill in Danville, Pennsylvania, (2) leasing a plant nearby in Harrisburg, Pennsylvania, (3) leasing still another plant on Coit Road in East Cleveland and other smaller properties near Tapco, (4) building and leasing a new facility in

Willoughby, Ohio, and (5) expanding manufacturing capacity at its Canadian subsidiary in St. Catharines, Ontario. In 1952, employment soared to nearly twenty-six thousand people, a total nearly 25 percent higher than during World War II.[79]

In 1951, TP reported gross revenues of nearly $200 million, about 50 percent above its World War II peak. Sales to the aircraft industry more than doubled the previous year's total. That performance was repeated again in 1952, when total revenues hit $274 million, of which nearly three-fourths (about $200 million) represented sales of turbojet engine components. A reporter for the *Wall Street Journal* calculated that "as a big supplier of jet parts, Thompson [Products] has a much bigger niche in the aircraft industry than it ever had with piston engines. For a World War II fighter plane costing $56,000, Thompson might have supplied about $1,000 worth of valves and a pump or two. For today's F-86, costing $300,000, the TP contribution may run as high as 25 to 30 times that figure, for major parts for the motor and other accessories."[80]

The ultimate customer for turbojet engines took note of TP's technology leadership and its strategic role as the industry's largest supplier. "The Air Force thinks so well of Tapco," reported Harry Bubb, general manager of the Tapco plant, "that they regard us as a prime contractor, and as a result we are the only sub-contractor invited to sit in on Air Force conferences with its prime contractors."[81]

In addition to supplying components for turbojet engines, TP also manufactured many aircraft accessory products, such as high-altitude and high-pressure fuel pumps and specially designed "shallow-tank" booster pumps housed in the cramped quarters of the wings of jet fighters. Researchers at TP's fuel-system laboratory in Inglewood, California, developed several techniques that improved fuel utilization, including ways to control both the tendency of wax to form in fuels at low temperatures and the alarmingly high rate of evaporation during steep climbs at high altitude.[82]

Other unique requirements of jet-powered aircraft created new product opportunities for TP. Most electrical accessories in conventional aircraft, for example, drew surplus power from the reciprocating engine. In jet-powered aircraft, this proved difficult to do for technical reasons, and independent electrical systems were required to operate accessory products. Supplying these products brought TP into new areas of electrical engineering and power management. The company also investigated ways to tap compressed air from the jet engine to drive accessory equipment. The first such product was an air-driven after-burner pump that supplied power boosts to jet aircraft in emergency conditions.[83]

The growing complexity of the systems inside aircraft that controlled or assisted power, communications, navigation, and deployment of weapons provided another source of opportunity. In September 1950, TP announced its first electronic product, a coaxial switch used in radar and communications equipment in military aircraft. By moving the switch, a radar operator could select images on the radar screen from different antennas on the aircraft. As Ted Thoren, the TP development engineer responsible for the product, described it, the coaxial switch was essentially "an electronic selector cock very much like a fuel selector cock," enabling a user to switch between several electronic inputs and a receiving station. Manufacturing the switch posed unusual difficulties, "combining two different plastics and several alloys, all with different dielectric properties, in a mechanism that would operate only if made to inconceivably close tolerances." Indeed, the original developers of the switch, a Cleveland firm called Designers for Industry, approached TP because it could not fill an order for thirteen hundred units from the U.S. Navy's Bureau of Aeronautics.

During the summer of 1950, TP licensed patents from Designers for Industry and proceeded with a program to develop and manufacture the coaxial switch. The company organized a very high-frequency testing laboratory at the main plant and began recruiting electrical engineers. By November the work had gone so well that TP perceived "a diversification step of real magnitude" in making switches not only for the military applications but also for emerging markets in television and long-distance communications. Depending on their complexity, the switches fetched prices between $50 and $850. The company established an Electronics Division and announced "an aggressive sales program" to both military and civilian markets. By the spring of 1951, when the switch was ready for delivery, the division employed thirty-seven people, including eleven "electronic engineers." The switch itself was considered "only the first of a line of electronic accessories," and the company looked forward to entering "a rapidly expanding field" in electronics.[84]

In June 1951, TP made a related move into military electronics by acquiring Columbus, Ohio-based Antenna Research Laboratory (ARL) for about $120,000 in cash. This tiny and struggling firm was an offshoot of a government-funded R&D laboratory at Ohio State University. ARL had development contracts for several antenna designs, along with supporting equipment, for military aircraft. It also had a contract to manufacture a "dummy load," an electronic device to replace antennas in the field for testing purposes. ARL's leader, Robert Jacques, remained with TP, and he offered bullish projections for future growth. He pointed out that advanced military aircraft each used an average of thirty separate antennas, and he predicted "almost unlimited peacetime commercial possibilities" in communications and television.[85]

ADDING LEGS TO THE STOOL

In March 1953, TP made another important personnel announcement, this time a change of titles. The board of directors elected Crawford to the new position of chairman of the board and elected Wright as president. This action confirmed the reality, and Wright merely commented that "no changes in the character of the company" were contemplated. Speaking to the Cleveland Old Guard Association, however, he took great pains to emphasize that the company's "highly successful human relations policy" that evolved under Crawford's leadership would continue. Indeed, Wright viewed stable employee relations as TP's source of competitive advantage. "In a business like ours," he observed,

> the all important element is the people who make up the Thompson team. In the banking business, money is important. In the oil business it is oil wells. But Thompson is a highly technical business. Our business requires engineers, metallurgists, expert set-up men, skillful inspectors and machine operators, and many other technicians.[86]

During 1953, Wright focused on the challenges of the future. "Our program for 1953 is a simple one," he said. "There will be a tremendous emphasis on sales. Our salesmen are going to be awfully important." Wright's concern for growth reflected awareness of serious problems looming in two of TP's major lines of business. Despite Ramsey's contributions, the replacement business continued to struggle amid heated competition and chronic price wars. The impending decline of the aircraft business posed a much more difficult challenge. As Wright saw it, TP was "approaching a critical period, in some respects, similar to that existing in 1946 at the end of World War II." The new Eisenhower administration not only was eager to bring an end to the Korean War, but also planned other cuts to the defense budget. For the aircraft manufacturers, this meant both fewer orders and "stretch-outs," an industry term used to indicate that the government would take possession of aircraft a year or two later than it had originally contracted to do. Under the new budget, the USAF planned to shrink from 143 wings to 120. (A "wing" represents 65 to 80 aircraft, depending on whether the unit refers to fighters or bombers.)[87]

Appearing as the keynote speaker at the annual meeting of the Aircraft Industries Association, Crawford addressed the boom–bust nature of government orders and the havoc it wrought on defense contractors. Shepard, who was in the audience, recalls that Crawford captured the industry's frustrations—and created a stir—when he observed that "trying to do business with the government was like having a red-hot poker rammed up your rear end, immediately followed by an ice-cold douche. Repeatedly. He said a cycle like that was pretty rough on the patient."[88]

During 1953, TP could do little to influence the defense budget, but it could pursue other options. There was informal talk, for example, about selling TP to Westinghouse under an arrangement that would have placed Dave Wright in line to become Westinghouse's chief executive officer. TP's top executives also weighed a merger with Remington Rand, which was beginning its move away from traditional businesses in typewriters and electrical appliances into electronic computers. According to Crawford and Wright, these discussions ultimately came to naught because TP's leaders wanted TP to become a big company in its own right, without being swallowed up by a larger company.[89]

TP also tried to achieve growth by accelerating development of new products. Indeed, this approach was the theme of the second annual planning conference at Crawford's farm. In July 1953, the top twenty-five managerial and technical executives in the company gathered for a five-day, off-site meeting to review the product plans of each division. The forecasts were upbeat: each division reported that it had at least one product in development that might become a bigger sales item than anything currently made. The company's engineers were working on a rich variety of items, including gas meter housings, farm implement pumps, power-steering pumps, piston-type hydraulic pumps, high-temperature heat exchangers, new subassemblies for jet engines, new applications of powdered metal and liquid mercury casting technologies, and products made from new materials such as plastics, ceramics, and titanium alloys.[90]

This list of opportunities raised questions about the realism of the forecasts, as well as TP's financial capacity to fund every promising idea. In August, the board of directors met to consider these questions. Wright pointed out that a survey of "worth-while extraordinary capital expenditure projects," including some that would raise the level of automation in TP's factories, would entail $22 million in investment. As trea-surer, Coolidge stated that it wouldn't be prudent to pay for all of these projects at once, but that they might be funded over a three-year period without jeopardizing TP's financial health or requiring it to issue additional stock. In the end, the board voted to increase capital spending in 1953 from $10 million to $15 million.[91]

A third growth strategy was based on TP's engineering skills and capabilities. For example, early in the year, TP responded to a request from the U.S. Atomic Energy Commission (AEC) for an engineering contractor to build and operate a proposed new nuclear weapons processing plant at Spoon River, Illinois. TP assembled a project team and submitted a contract bid to the AEC. The company also reached agreement with the U.S. Navy's Bureau of Aeronautics to build and operate a turbojet engine test facility in Perry Township in northeastern Ohio. The assignment was a tribute to TP's strong position in turbojet engine components and gave the company the capability to test complete turbojet engines. To reassure its traditional aircraft engine customers, Colwell stressed that "we are parts makers. We intend to continue in that role." Added Ted Thoren, "TP is not going into the engine business, but the sooner we can subject a new material to the hard, hot facts of engine life the better . . . for the operating engine is always the final judge of what it likes in materials and designs."[92]

Still another growth alternative was to make a significant acquisition in another promising industry. The most desirable point of entry was the emerging electronics industry, in which TP, with the coaxial switch and experimental radar antennas, was already a fledgling participant. From the perspective of growth, the industry was cer-tainly attractive: between 1940 and 1945, electronics had grown from about $300 mil-lion in total revenues to $4.6 billion, virtually all from products for military applications; by 1953, the industry posted total revenues of $5.2 billion, of which nearly half represented civilian uses. Accordingly, TP pursued several acquisition opportunities in electronics.[93]

The possibility with the most immediate appeal was to acquire Hughes Aircraft, a division of the privately held Hughes Tool Company that had been on and off the auc-tion block for several years. Based in Culver City, California, Hughes Aircraft was an extremely attractive property, having grown from $2 million in sales to more than $200 million between 1947 and 1952. This performance reflected what *Fortune* magazine termed "a virtual monopoly of the Air Force's advanced electronic requirements," which consisted of electronic fire and navigational control systems for fighter aircraft and development and production contracts for the air-to-air Falcon guided missile. In all, Hughes Aircraft boasted a backlog of $600 million in government contracts.

But it was well known in industry circles that Hughes Aircraft was rife with dis-content, much of it due to the erratic behavior and highly publicized distractions of Howard Hughes, as well as to the tight financial controls imposed by his top deputy, Noah Dietrich. The key managerial and technical personnel at Hughes Aircraft all were eager to see the company find alternative ownership. This group included general managers (and former general officers of the Air Force) Ira Eaker and Harold George;

George's chief assistant, Charles B. "Tex" Thornton; vice president in charge of operations, Simon Ramo; and vice president of research and development, Dean Wooldridge. (The reasons for their unhappiness are discussed more fully in Chapter 7.)[94]

In 1953, TP joined a bevy of bidders for Hughes Aircraft, including Westinghouse, Lockheed, Convair, General Dynamics, Pennroad Corporation, and several other big companies. Hughes's asking price, which according to various reports ranged from $26 million to $50 million, was well beyond what TP was prepared—or could afford—to spend. Nonetheless, discussion proceeded far enough for Wright and Shepard to visit Hughes Aircraft, probably in early 1953, for informal talks. Shepard had served on the Air Force committee that had awarded the Falcon missile contract, and he already knew the Hughes Aircraft executives well. He arranged for Wright and himself to meet George, Thornton, Ramo, and Wooldridge for dinner in a private room at Romanoff's, a fashionable restaurant in Beverly Hills. As recalled by Wright, the occasion was "a very, very friendly get-together." The parties "spent the entire evening discussing [their respective] philosophies of business," and "it turned out that we were in almost unanimous agreement on the general objectives and philosophy of running a company." Wright also remembered that "the indications were that if we [TP] should be successful in acquiring Hughes that they [the key managerial and technical personnel at Hughes] would stay with us."[95]

TP's efforts to buy Hughes Aircraft broke off abruptly when it became apparent that Howard Hughes was reluctant to part with the unit and because TP executives had serious reservations about dealing with him in any event. The failure of this possibility left the company disappointed but not deterred. In July, just before the Vermont planning conference, the Atomic Energy Commission chose TP from more than a hundred bidders to operate its new Spoon River weapons plant. Outgoing AEC chairman Gordon Dean gave several reasons for the award, including TP's experience in taking plants "at point zero" and developing them into successful operations, the qualifications and track record of its administrative and technical staff, its decentralized organization and achievements in developing new products, and its long record of harmonious industrial relations.

Although not prone to enthusiastic outbursts, Wright appeared delighted to win the bid. The project seemed to him "a fine opportunity to make a further substantial contribution to national defense and at the same time to bring atomic know-how to some members of our organization against the time when this tremendous new source of power can be harnessed for peaceable use." He believed, moreover, that the project would place TP "in the forefront of all progressive developments in science and technology."[96]

During the spring of 1953, TP also opened negotiations to purchase Bell Sound Corporation of Columbus, Ohio, a maker of consumer electronics products such as high-fidelity speakers and tape recorders with annual sales "in the $1,500,000 range." William M. (Bill) Jones, the young general manager of TP's Electronics Division, had learned of the availability of Bell Sound at an electronics trade show. The company had been founded in the early 1930s by Floyd W. Bell. It had achieved its major growth as a maker of public address systems during World War II before developing other electronic products. By 1953, Floyd Bell was nearing retirement and willing to entertain offers for his company. Jones closed the deal on October 6. Terms called for Bell Sound to operate as a wholly owned subsidiary under TP's Electronics Division. It retained most of its management, its independent identity, and its manufacturing facility in Columbus. In a public announcement of the transaction, TP agreed to provide capital to expand Bell Sound's product lines and expected to introduce new products through its jobber organization.[97]

One other opportunity of the late summer of 1953 came as a surprise to Wright. In the wee hours of one mid-September night, Wright was awakened by a call from Harold George of Hughes Aircraft. George announced that he, Simon Ramo, and Dean Wooldridge had decided to resign from Hughes Aircraft. They planned to start their own company to develop electronic products for both military and commercial markets. George stated that the new company would need $450,000 in start-up capital—a sizable sum for a new venture. Finally, he asked whether TP would contribute that amount in return for 49 percent of the stock. "Yes," Wright said. "Call me in the morning and we'll work out the details." Then he went back to sleep.[98]

Chapter 7

Rocket Science

▶   ▶   ▶

1953–1957

W HEN HAROLD GEORGE OF HUGHES AIRCRAFT PHONED DAVE WRIGHT IN SEPTEMBER 1953 with his business proposition, he initiated a sequence of events that would eventually make Thompson Products into a different kind of company. To its traditional strengths in precision manufacturing of parts and components for the automobile and aircraft industries were soon added new lines of business in electronics, communications, computers, guided missiles, and even spacecraft. Just as important as these new lines was a new kind of management involving the engineering of complex technological systems. The capability to engineer such systems—as opposed to parts, components, subassemblies, and subsystems—was to have an enduring impact on TP, its new partner, the Ramo-Wooldridge Corporation (R-W), and the eventual combination of the two companies as Thompson Ramo Wooldridge (TRW).

The rise of R-W and the transformation of TP occurred against a backdrop of the maturing of the U.S. defense industry. The aftermath of the Korean War—unlike any prior postwar period in American history—brought no massive demobilization. Rather, it brought continuance of the Cold War—a term dating from these years—as the United States squared off against the Soviet Union in a geopolitical contest of superpowers. The Cold War was expensive—more expensive, in fact, than any "hot war" of modern times. In the United States, defense budgets throughout the 1950s ran at unusually high levels, accounting for more than half of all federal outlays and nearly 10 percent of GNP. Procurement awards, including R&D contracts, averaged more than $20 billion per year and absorbed about 5 percent of the nation's total output of goods and services.

This huge outlay of funds had enormous consequences for defense contractors like TP and R-W. For one thing, the defense industry took on aspects of permanence: as Fred Crawford and Dave Wright observed early in 1956, "We think that the defense industry is now to be counted with the other three basic industries which deal in the necessities of life—food, clothing and shelter." Weapons evolved from discrete devices into "weapon systems," in the process becoming more powerful and sophisticated, more likely to incorporate emerging and state-of-the-art technologies, and much more expensive.[1]

Big companies dominated the defense industry, as they had during the two world wars. As the industry evolved, however, it became more specialized. Industrial giants like AT&T, General Motors, Ford, Chrysler, General Electric, RCA, and Westinghouse continued to manufacture defense products, but they were eclipsed by other companies that focused narrowly on the U.S. Department of Defense (DOD) or on specific military services as their customer. During the 1950s, the largest share of defense procurement dollars flowed to the U.S. Air Force, which in turn passed them along to favored contractors such as Boeing, General Dynamics, and Douglas Aircraft. But the defense industry also gave birth to new companies and transformed others. Hughes Aircraft (in electronics), Raytheon, Litton, Varian Associates, Thiokol, Aerojet-General, and many others worked at the frontiers of science and technology, developing advanced electronics, guidance, and propulsion systems. These companies depended on R&D in the physical sciences, and their organizations prized scientists and engineers.[2]

Among these newer companies, one of the most impressive was R-W. Its spectacular performance as a pioneer in electronics and defense systems management became a major business story of the 1950s.

A Pair of Prodigies

Each forty years old in 1953, Simon Ramo and Dean E. Wooldridge made a remarkable pair. Both were brilliant and accomplished scientists and engineers with impeccable credentials. Born within a few weeks of each other in 1913, their lives and careers unfolded in parallel and at a rapid pace. Wooldridge graduated from high school at fourteen, earned a B.A. in physics at the University of Oklahoma at eighteen, and had his Ph.D. in physics summa cum laude from the California Institute of Technology (Caltech) by the time he was twenty-three. Ramo also skipped grades and breezed through school. An accomplished violinist, he had opportunities to pursue a career in music, but instead used a cash prize from a music contest to follow his other great love, engineering. After graduating from the University of Utah, Ramo moved to Caltech, where he took a Ph.D. in electrical engineering and physics, also at age twenty-three.[3]

At Caltech, Wooldridge and Ramo became friends, occasionally double-dating. After graduation, they went their separate ways but remained in touch. Ramo joined GE's R&D laboratories in Schenectady, where he worked on radar and microwave systems, assignments that eventually led him to coauthor what became the standard textbook in the field. Wooldridge moved to AT&T's Bell Laboratories, where he supervised research in physical electronics (including the creation of America's first airborne fire-control system) during World War II. After the war, Ramo developed a case of "California-itis," which prompted him in 1946 to join Hughes Aircraft to help build a business in military electronics. Soon thereafter, he enticed Wooldridge to join him, and the partnership proved immensely successful.

Although they shared similar backgrounds, interests, and achievements, and they could even have fit into each other's clothes—each was about 5'10" and weighed between 155 and 160 pounds—many people meeting them for the first time were struck by their dissimilarities. The bespectacled Wooldridge "looks and acts the part of a professor," noted a reporter for *Time,* adding that "he is calm, introspective, [and] plays the organ for relaxation." Ramo, on the other hand, "is flamboyant and mercurial, [and] takes mamba lessons for relaxation." The contrast extended to their manner of speaking: "Wooldridge marshals his thoughts carefully, is all business and lucidity, can make abstruse technical problems easily understandable to a layman; Ramo speaks impulsively, lets his thoughts bounce around like an errant light beam."[4]

Both men were friendly, amiable, and quick to smile, but Ramo possessed the sharper wit. Horace Shepard illustrates the point with a story: One time at a party attended by both Wooldridge and Ramo, a young man arrived late, explaining that his wife had just given birth to a baby boy. The man teased Ramo, saying that he didn't know whether to name the child Simon or Dean. "Quick as a wink," Shepard recalls, Ramo quipped, "Why don't you call him Demon!"[5]

In all important respects, the two men complemented each other well. "We were exactly alike in our way of thinking," notes Ramo, adding, "we could finish sentences for each other . . . we were so close together that we were like identical twins." A colleague went further: "Working together, they are not the equivalent of two men," he marveled, "but something a little closer to ten."[6]

At Hughes Aircraft, Ramo and Wooldridge presided over a talented team of scientists and engineers, and they managed a series of stunning technological breakthroughs. They developed the all-weather fire-control systems that became standard on the Air Force workhorses of the Korean War, the F-86 and F-94, as well as the miniature radar systems that fit in the needle noses of the Air Force's Century series of fighters, the F-100 through the F-108. Their most impressive technological achievement, however, was the Falcon air-to-air missile designed to defend against enemy bombers. The Hughes team took an unconventional approach to missile development, adopting a total systems approach. Competing antiaircraft weapons were based on World War II-vintage technologies such as radio proximity fuses; these weapons detonated warheads in the vicinity of enemy aircraft to knock them from the air. For such an approach to succeed, however, the weapons required big, heavy warheads, which in turn required big, heavy missiles that were all but impossible to launch from the air. Ramo was contemptuous of such tactics, which he believed typical of the airframe companies (which he disparaged as "Rosie-the-Riveter-type" operations) and of big, bureaucratic, overcautious electrical equipment companies such as GE and Westinghouse.[7]

The Hughes team sought to hit the enemy aircraft with a small, light missile carrying a small, light warhead. To accomplish this, Ramo and Wooldridge engineered a clever system that involved not only the missile itself, but also advanced electronics to provide guidance, navigation, and control. Fighters carrying the Falcon searched for targets using miniaturized microwave radar equipment, and the Hughes-developed "lead collision system" enabled them to approach enemy aircraft from any direction. Once the target was engaged, an airborne computer simultaneously launched the missile and steered the fighter out of harm's way. The missile itself homed in on its prey by coordinating its internal radar with that of the fighter, which remained locked on the target. All of this, notes Ramo, depended on "many ingenious things," including "use of precision circuitry and a steady group of inventions by our extremely brilliant staff."[8]

The feats of the Falcon and the systems approach behind it contributed to the growing reputations not only of Hughes Aircraft in general, but also of Ramo and Wooldridge in particular. By early 1953, when suitors for Hughes Aircraft began to appear, the two men were seen as essential to the unit's continued success. During the summer, however, as it became clear that Howard Hughes would neither sell the business nor address problems caused by conflicting lines of authority, as well as by his own public troubles and private eccentricities, Ramo and Wooldridge determined to leave. They had many options. Either man could have walked into a high-paying job in a dozen different companies, but they wanted to stay together and to control their own destinies. They evolved a general plan for a new business: specialists in military electronics, they would design and manufacture state-of-the-art components and equipment for the U.S. military; they would also attempt to transfer some military technologies into commercial markets.[9]

To establish a new company, Ramo and Wooldridge needed investment capital to lease space, hire people, buy equipment, and demonstrate the capability to manufacture advanced electronics hardware. The two men had each saved several thousand dollars, which they were prepared to pour into the business. Still, they needed a lot more money. They had several alternatives: they could borrow from a bank, raise funds from a venture capitalist, or affiliate with a big company in a related business. Behind each of these alternatives loomed a key question: which funding source would allow the two men maximum control over the new enterprise?

Ramo and Wooldridge were determined to avoid problems like those that had frustrated them at Hughes Aircraft. They ruled out borrowing from a bank or seeking funds from a venture capitalist. Both sources, they believed, would place too many restrictions on the way they expected to manage the company. That left the third alternative: an investment from a big company. But which big company? Again, the partners weighed several alternatives. From previous employment, they were familiar with corporate giants like GE and AT&T; from their work at Hughes, they had gained insights into their competitors in military electronics as well as into the aircraft manufacturers. They rejected most of these companies, however, believing them too bureaucratic or heavy-handed or simply lacking the key competencies necessary to help them succeed. Instead, they sought a big company with a good reputation for management, a decentralized organization, experience in manufacturing, and familiarity with government contracting.

The longer Ramo and Wooldridge pondered these criteria, the more attractive TP appeared as a potential backer. The two men were well aware of TP's reputation for progressive management and human relations; they admired and respected Horace Shepard from his days at Wright Field; and they liked what they saw of Dave Wright during TP's abortive attempt to buy Hughes Aircraft. They reasoned—correctly, as it turned out— that TP would be more than willing to provide them not only investment capital but also the freedom to develop and pursue their own strategy for the new business.[10]

This understanding was embodied in the legal documents that established the Ramo-Wooldridge Corporation (R-W), which was incorporated in Delaware on September 16, 1953, with TP as a major investor. R-W was capitalized at 54,000 shares, of which 4,000 consisted of preferred stock with a par value of $100 per share, and 50,000 were shares of common stock with a par value of $1 per share. The common stock divided into two classes: 49 percent of the total (24,500 shares) consisted of Class A stock, the holders of which as a class were entitled to elect three of the seven directors of R-W; 51 percent (25,500 shares) consisted of Class B stock, the holders of which as a class were entitled to elect four directors. TP held exclusive rights to the preferred stock and Class A shares, while Ramo and Wooldridge each held rights to 6,500 shares of the Class B stock—a majority interest in this class.

These arrangements gave Ramo and Wooldridge effective control of the company, because between them, they could elect a majority of the directors. (In the spring of 1954, Ramo and Wooldridge made Harold George an equal partner, so that the three men together effectively controlled R-W.) The remaining Class B shares were reserved for key employees of R-W. TP's initial stake consisted of 2,500 shares of the preferred stock and 7,500 shares of Class A common stock of R-W—an investment worth $265,000.[11]

The original working directors of R-W included the two founders, Harold George, and lawyer Samuel Gates, elected by the Class B stock, and Dave Wright, Horace Shepard, and Arch Colwell, elected on the basis of TP's Class A stock. To help cement relations between the two companies, Ramo and Wooldridge were elected directors of TP early in 1954. TP also agreed to retain R-W for "advisory services in the field of electronics" for a fee of $330,000 during its first year of business. During this time, R-W agreed "to cause periodic surveys to be made" of TP's electronics activities and submit written quarterly recommendations.[12]

The directors elected Wooldridge president of R-W, with Ramo as a vice president (and soon thereafter, an executive vice president). Neither their titles nor the order of names in the company indicated any sort of hierarchical ranking; rather, they reflected Wooldridge's greater willingness to shoulder an administrative load, as well as the sense that "Ramo-Wooldridge" seemed more euphonious than "Wooldridge-Ramo." In practice, the two men consulted with each other about all major decisions, and they regarded each other as equals. For its first home, R-W located in a former barbershop at 6316 W. 92nd Street in Los Angeles, California. The company started out with four employees, the two founders plus two associates from Hughes Aircraft, Anthony J. F.

"Frank" Clement, a young engineer who served as an administrative assistant, and Aimee Joy, who acted as secretary and accountant.[13]

A CUSTOMER-FUNDED COMPANY

At its founding, R-W possessed liquid assets of about $300,000—a sum that its founders believed would support the business for about a year. Wooldridge and Ramo expected the company to grow by obtaining R&D contracts from the government and other sources. These contracts would be used to hire employees, purchase equipment and supplies, and, as necessary, lease new space. By such arrangements, R-W's customers would finance the company's growth. Eventually, the founders hoped, some of the R&D contracts would lead to production contracts and expansion into manufacturing.[14]

During the fall of 1953, Ramo and Wooldridge planned to develop two general areas of business. The first was an outgrowth of their work on airborne fire-control systems at Hughes Aircraft, which all but monopolized the business. Sources high in the Pentagon had intimated that the Air Force would be pleased to consider additional suppliers, and Wooldridge thought that R-W had a good chance of becoming a second source. As a second business area, both founders believed that in the long run they could adapt some military electronics technologies such as digital computers and advanced communications to commercial applications.[15]

During the next several months, Ramo and Wooldridge recruited key personnel to direct the company's work. By January 1954, the initial assignments and appointments were in place. Joining Ramo and Wooldridge at the top were Ralph P. Johnson, director of research and development, and V. G. "Bud" Nielsen, controller and director of administration. A Ph.D. in physics from MIT, Johnson had served in senior staff roles for the Air Force, the Atomic Energy Commission, and most recently as director of R&D at Hughes Aircraft. Nielsen, a Harvard MBA, had held a comparable administrative position at Hughes Aircraft. In addition, Harold George served as executive consultant to R-W. A retired lieutenant-general of the Air Force, George focused on customer relations and occasional high-level administrative assignments.

At the same time, R-W borrowed funds from TP to finance a move into a new headquarters building on Bellanca Avenue near Los Angeles International Airport. The new facility housed the corporate offices and three operating divisions: Control Systems, Communications, and Computer Systems, headed respectively by Milton E. Mohr, Burton F. Miller, and William B. Hebenstreit.[16]

Mohr held a B.S. in electrical engineering from the University of Nebraska and had done graduate work in physics and mathematics at Stevens Institute of Technology. Later, he worked at Bell Labs and at Hughes Aircraft, where his experience included research in electronic communications technologies and integrated fire-control systems. At R-W, Mohr expected the Control Systems Division to grow rapidly as a developer and producer of fire-control systems. The division began with research and consulting studies for the Air Force in this area, as well as in electronic countermeasures and special weapons.[17]

Miller had earned all of his degrees in physics, including a Ph.D. at the University of Wisconsin. A veteran of the Manhattan Project, he brought an impressive background in large-scale research and development, especially of electronic communications systems. When he joined R-W, he held more than twenty patents, including several in motion-picture recording systems, for which he had won two Oscars from the Academy of Motion Picture Arts and Sciences. During the spring of 1954, the R-W Communications Division garnered its first R&D contract for a military project and expected to manufacture better, lighter, and smaller communications equipment for advanced military applications.[18]

The third division general manager, Hebenstreit, had earned a B.S. in applied physics at Caltech and had done graduate work in business at New York University. During World War II, he worked on many problems in electronics and communications at Bell Labs, where he specialized in vacuum tubes. He was credited as codiscoverer (with J. R. Pierce) of the principle of double-stream amplification. At Bell Labs, Hebenstreit became friendly with Wooldridge, and in 1947 followed him to Hughes Aircraft to work on advanced communications and data processing. In 1954, he joined Wooldridge again at R-W, adding considerable expertise in vacuum tubes, electron dynamics, microwave antenna theory, and other relevant technologies.

Under Hebenstreit, the R-W Computer Systems Division sought to apply "newer electronic techniques and procedures to the production control and business decision-making processes of major industrial organizations." Because it started with little capital, the division pursued study and research contracts to identify specific promising applications of computers. Its initial customer was TP, although the unit also assessed and organized the computing needs of R-W itself. Its first project involving construction of original equipment followed in October 1954 with an R&D contract with Westinghouse for an airborne digital computer for use in a new guided missile in development for the U.S. Army.[19]

During the first half of 1954, R-W indirectly entered another important line of business, the development and manufacture of semiconductors. Although its research lab and divisions all made use of semiconducting diodes and transistors, the company initially gave little thought to producing the devices itself. That began to change when Dr. Harper Q. North, who had been in charge of electronics R&D at Hughes Aircraft, approached Ramo and Wooldridge to gauge their interest in producing semiconductors. Neither man saw the business as essential to R-W's long-term success, and the level of investment needed to establish a credible presence in the business was far beyond their means. North was not to be deterred, however, and he announced that he would find investment capital elsewhere if he could not get it from R-W. At that point, Wooldridge and Ramo encouraged him to approach TP, which agreed to furnish up to $3 million—a significant sum, about ten times TP's original investment in R-W—to help start the business.

In June 1954, Pacific Semiconductors, Inc. (PSI) was incorporated as a subsidiary of R-W with Harper North as president. PSI used its capital to lease R&D and manufacturing facilities in Los Angeles and set about to design and develop semiconductors. The business did not expect to achieve profitability for several years, and it borrowed frequently from TP during this period in return for ceding increasing portions of its convertible preferred and common stock.[20]

A Different Kind of Company

Ramo's and Wooldridge's experiences at Hughes Aircraft exerted a strong influence on their plans for R-W. Resentful of the tight financial controls and administrative disorder that characterized Hughes in the early 1950s, Wooldridge and Ramo determined that R-W would be a different kind of company. Because its products featured "a high content of scientific and engineering newness," it would "assign to technically trained people more dominant roles in the management and control of the business than is customary or necessary in most industrial organizations." In fact, the scientists and engineers would not work for professional managers and administrators; rather, it would be the other way around. At R-W, the company's first official publication stated, "the combination of technical and administrative competence that is so frequently required is achieved by assigning top organizational responsibility to the scientist or engineer and providing him with the administrative and business-type assistants that he requires to carry out his organizational responsibilities."[21]

The operating managers of R-W were people much like Ramo and Wooldridge themselves. As an official publication put it, "All features of the organization and of the operational procedures of the company are designed to be as appropriate as possible to the special needs of the professional scientist and engineer." In many respects, the company in its earliest days more resembled a university or nonprofit think tank than a conventional commercial business—an image that would later haunt R-W. The similarities extended to architecture. At the new headquarters building occupied in the spring of 1954, for example, assignments diverged from the norms of most industrial contractors by giving private offices with windows to technical personnel and interior locations to administrative and support staff. As business expanded, the same principle was applied to additional office and laboratory buildings.

A Focus on Technology

As he had done at Hughes Aircraft, Ramo personally supervised the hiring of technical employees and sought out people with exceptionally strong records at the nation's best universities and engineering schools. During its first six months, R-W recruited more than forty accomplished scientists and engineers: Robert R. Bennett, Eugene M. Grabbe, James C. Fletcher (later head of NASA in two different stints), Jack H. Irving, John F. Mandrow, Robert B. Muchmore, and Albert D. "Bud" Wheelon (a future head of Hughes Aircraft), to name only a few. Many of these hires were veterans of Hughes Aircraft, although Wooldridge and Ramo avoided recruiting there, lest too many defections jeopardize vital projects for the Air Force.[22]

R-W rewarded its senior technical staff well, paying attractive salaries commensurate with achievements and experience. As an added incentive for some high-level employees, the company made them eligible to purchase Class B stock—a policy reflecting the founders' belief that scientists ought to be managers and owners. Ramo and Wooldridge also involved key employees in decision making. At least once a month, they met with senior staff to discuss the fortunes of the business.

R-W urged its technical staff to maintain close links with the nation's best research and engineering universities and to participate actively in professional scientific and technical associations. To the extent that available time and considerations of confidentiality permitted, technical staff members were encouraged to publish in scientific and technical journals. The company even established a regular lecture series and invited renowned scientists and figures from industry and government to speak on the latest developments in their areas.

As plans were taking shape during the months following the establishment of R-W, the future of the company veered suddenly in an unexpected direction. Within days of starting up the new company, Ramo and Wooldridge were summoned to Washington by Secretary of the Air Force Harold Talbott. In Talbott's office they were greeted by Trevor Gardner, a thirty-six-year-old assistant secretary for research and development, who presented them with a proposition. Gardner, who was an old friend of Ramo, described a high-level committee that he was assembling to review the Air Force's long-range ballistic missile programs. The committee would be headed by John von Neumann, the brilliant mathematician from Princeton University, and include many other senior scientists and engineers from industry and the academic community. Gardner invited Ramo and Wooldridge to serve on the committee and to direct the technical studies in support.

THE WEAPON OF THE CENTURY

Gardner's proposition was based on a history only partly known to Ramo and Wooldridge, and it concerned an issue of vital national importance: the development of an intercontinental ballistic missile (ICBM). (A *ballistic* missile is so named because, after an initial burst of propulsion, the missile, like a bullet, is launched on a predetermined course that it is powerless to affect; ballistic missiles should be distinguished from air-breathing *cruise* missiles, which fly under power and are maneuverable between launch and impact.)

Many people recognize that nuclear weapons transformed the nature of war and international politics during the second half of the twentieth century. Yet this transformation did not occur instantaneously in 1945, when the first atomic bombs devastated the Japanese cities Hiroshima and Nagasaki. Rather, it unfolded over a decade, as several nations acquired nuclear and thermonuclear weapons capability. What sealed the transformation was the development of a new and undefendable way to deliver these weapons. The first atomic bombs were dropped from airplanes, but by the 1950s, the major world powers could defend against air strikes. An ICBM was—and is—another matter. It can reach impact a quarter of the way around the world within thirty minutes of its launch. Flying through space, an ICBM attains unbelievable speeds—about five miles per second, or about twenty times the speed of sound. Only thirty seconds pass between the time it reenters the atmosphere above its target and the detonation of its warhead. There remains no proven defense against an ICBM after launch. With the development of this awesome technology, the nations of the world suddenly faced the prospect of obliteration at a moment's notice by a weapon they were powerless to intercept.

The race to develop the ICBM is comparable in many respects to the race to build the atomic bomb during World War II: any nation with ICBM capability would possess a weapon of frightening implications and enormous strategic significance. In the United States, the military, scientific, and technical communities were well aware of these issues. In 1953, however, few experts believed that the nation or any competing power possessed the ability or the resources—both scientific and financial—to make an ICBM operational within a decade.[23]

To begin with, building the ICBM posed extremely difficult technological challenges. It entailed, Ramo later observed, "a crash program of unprecedented size" and "marshaling the resources of industry, government, and science on a broader scale than had ever been previously attempted in peacetime." In fact, the developers of the ICBM considered the program more complex and ambitious than any attempted during World War II, including the atomic bomb. As one comparison of the 1950s put it, "the Manhattan Project in one way was a simple project. It involved only one new principle in physics." The missile programs, on the other hand, involved

> simultaneous advances on about ten different technical fronts. It means more thrust in propulsion than has ever been obtained before. It means less structural weight for the total weight of mass being flown and, hence, in a sense, stronger structures. It means the equipment must be able to withstand more severe environmental conditions of acceleration, temperature, and variations in speed and density of air. It means more severe temperature and materials problems. It means more accuracy in guidance. In every instance, the combination of basic science and difficult production engineering decisions must be made in a large number of technical fields all at one time and on an unprecedented schedule.

The goal of the Manhattan Project, the comparison continued, was to create "one component of a useful weapon system—namely, a bomb." The ICBM program, in contrast, sought to create "an entirely new way of providing a military capability. The military operations including all of the bases, launching equipment, equipment to insure readiness, training of special operators, must be combined with the research and development on every phase of the weapons system."[24]

In 1953, skeptics of the ICBM also pointed to the desultory progress of the Air Force's lone long-range ballistic missile program, which had proceeded in fits and starts since 1947 under the direction of the Consolidated Vultee Corporation (subsequently and hereafter known as Convair, which in 1954 merged with General Dynamics and became a division of that corporation). By mid-1953, specifications for that missile, now known as the Atlas, called for a colossal, one-and-a-half stage vehicle with a gross weight of 450,000 pounds. It would be launched by five separate engines combining into a total thrust of 600,000 pounds, and it would carry a payload weighing up to 7,000 pounds a total distance of 6,200 miles, landing within 1,500 feet of its target. The date of "initial operational capability" (IOC) was set for 1965. Several factors impeded the Atlas program, including technological uncertainties, limited budgets, and the reluctance of the USAF high command to push development of a weapon that would supersede the manned bomber. Some observers also doubted that Convair—or, for that matter, any airframe manufacturer of the time—possessed sufficient expertise in technologies such as electronics, thermodynamics, and rocket propulsion, which were deemed essential to missile development.[25]

Trevor Gardner's Mission

During late 1952 and early 1953, pressure built up to reassess the Atlas program. Breakthroughs in the design of thermonuclear weapons, intelligence suggesting a possible Soviet lead in missile technology, and the election of Dwight Eisenhower as president of the United States combined to support a thorough review of U.S. guided missile programs. The assignment was handed to Gardner. A former businessman whom admirers called "very bright and energetic," "a sparkplug," and "irrepressible," but whom detractors considered "sharp, abrupt, irascible, cold, unpleasant, and a bastard," he would play a key role in accelerating the ICBM program and encouraging new ways to organize and manage it.[26]

In April 1953, Gardner formed a joint services committee to study existing missile programs. He also hit the road himself to consult with leading technical and managerial personnel in the defense industry. On several occasions he visited Hughes Aircraft, where he became reacquainted with Ramo, a former colleague at GE, and met Wooldridge. Gardner's conversations with Ramo, Wooldridge, and others and his independent research convinced him that it was technically feasible to develop an ICBM much earlier than the Air Force planned. Gardner's sense of urgency increased sharply during the summer, when researchers at the government's Livermore Laboratory demonstrated the feasibility of producing small, light H-bombs—so light, in fact, that the gross weight of the Atlas ICBM could conceivably be cut in half and the missile would require appreciably lower thrust.

By the fall of 1953, Gardner and his superiors at DOD, especially Secretary Charles Wilson, his assistant secretary for research and development Donald Quarles, and Air Force Secretary Talbott, were all convinced of the compelling need to accelerate the ICBM program. The question was how best to proceed. To help determine an answer, in October Gardner assembled a high-powered group of scientists and engineers as the Strategic Missiles Evaluation Committee, with John von Neumann as chair. Better known by its code name, the Teapot Committee, it consisted of representatives from leading universities and several defense contractors—including both Ramo and Wooldridge, who promptly agreed to serve. The chief military officer attending the committee was Col. Bernard A. Schriever, assistant for development planning, office of the deputy chief of staff for development, and a brigadier-general designate.[27]

The composition of the Teapot Committee was noteworthy in many respects, not the least of which was the extraordinarily impressive credentials of its members. In addition to von Neumann, Schriever, Ramo, and Wooldridge, members included Clark B. Millikan, Charles C. Lauritsen, and Louis G. Dunn of Caltech; George B. Kistiakowsky of Harvard, (later) President Eisenhower's science adviser; Jerome B. Wiesner of MIT; Hendrik W. Bode of Bell Labs; Allen E. Puckett of Hughes Aircraft; and Lawrence A. "Pat" Hyland of Bendix Aviation (soon to become president of Hughes Aircraft). The group was tilted in favor of academic science, especially physics, while most of the industry representatives were experts in new and advanced technologies in electronics and communications. Although several members possessed a background in aeronautics or aeronautical engineering, none came from the airframe industry, which had served as prime contractors for most existing missile programs, including the Atlas. None of the committee members was wedded to past concepts or assumptions about the ICBM.[28]

Evaluating the Atlas

R-W's formal work on the ICBM began in October 1953 with the initial meeting of the Teapot Committee. Gardner arranged for the new company to provide administrative support to the committee under a letter contract entitled "Long-Range Analytical Studies of Weapons Systems." In addition, R-W was charged to conduct "a research study of certain means of delivering atomic warheads by intercontinental missiles and preparation of related recommendations of development programs." This assignment amounted to technical feasibility studies of the ICBM as a system, as well as of the major subsystems of propulsion, structure, guidance, and reentry.[29]

As a business proposition, the letter contract enabled R-W to start up and grow rapidly without drawing on its own capital. To carry out the work, Ramo and Wooldridge engaged about thirty high-level employees and university-based consultants. By early February, the contract had grown from an initial commitment of $25,000 for a four-month assignment to nearly $220,000 in reimbursable costs plus a fixed fee of 10 percent—standard for labor in study contracts—for a total engagement of eight months.

The Teapot Committee issued its final report on February 10, 1954. As principal author, Ramo had harsh words for the Atlas program:

> "It is the conviction of the Committee that a radical reorganization of the IBMS project considerably transcending the Convair framework is required if a militarily useful vehicle is to be had within a reasonable span of time. [IBMS was the original acronym for intercontinental ballistic missile system; later it was changed to ICBM to avoid visual confusion with the corporation IBM.] Specifically, the Committee believes that the design must be based on a new and comprehensive weapons system study, together with a thorough-going exploration of alternative approaches to several critical phases of the problem, adequately based on fundamental science.

The last point was crucial. The committee believed that building the ICBM was not an engineering problem, however complex; rather, it was a scientific problem. Accordingly, the committee not only advocated new specifications for the Atlas based on the likely availability of new warheads, but also recommended the formation of a new ICBM development group that would be given "directive responsibility for the entire project." During its first year, this group would carry out further technical studies of the ICBM before freezing a design. Notwithstanding this delay, the committee urged that the timetable for initial operational capability be compressed to within six to eight years. Acceleration of the Atlas program, the report concluded, could succeed only if entrusted to "an unusually competent group of scientists and engineers capable of making systems analyses, supervising the research phases and completely controlling the experimental and hardware phases of the program." This group, moreover, should be free "of excessive detailed regulation by existing government agencies."[30]

SETD CONTRACTOR

The Teapot Committee report left open many questions of just how its recommendations would be implemented. Indeed, the committee declined to specify who would carry out the research, analysis, and planning and who would be responsible for administering an accelerated program. During 1954, these questions were answered in ways that permanently altered R-W's future. Wooldridge and Ramo had certainly expected that R-W would continue to provide research and technical support to the government for an accelerated ICBM program. They did not anticipate, however, that the company's responsibility would expand far beyond research and advising to involve systems engineering and technical direction (SETD) for the entire program. Indeed, as the full dimensions of the new role became apparent, Ramo and Wooldridge were reluctant to take it on because of its implications for the company.

R-W's role as SETD contractor on the ICBM brought with it tremendous prestige, responsibility, and satisfaction. It also brought with it challenge, exposure, and discomfort, and it forced the fledgling company to divert from its original strategy. Eventually it became the focus of congressional hearings and in 1960 led the company to divest a significant part of its operations. For these reasons, it is worth pausing to consider just how the role came to be defined.[31]

Into Missile Management, Reluctantly

Even before the Teapot Committee finished its work, Gardner was urging the expansion and extension of R-W's contract to include provision of continuing technical assistance to the Air Force. He was also contemplating the creation of a new, centralized organization inside the Air Force to manage the Atlas program. He drew support from an independent study of the ICBM performed by the RAND Corporation, an independent organization of analysts specializing in issues in defense and technology.

Released two days before the Teapot Committee's report, the RAND document reached similar conclusions about the technical feasibility and strategic significance of a redesigned ICBM. Events also played into Gardner's hands: on March 1, the United States successfully detonated a lightweight H-bomb—the "Shrimp" shot—in the Marshall Islands, thereby validating proposals to shrink the Atlas dramatically.[32]

In rapid succession, Gardner obtained approvals from the secretary of the Air Force and the Air Force chief of staff to expedite the ICBM. In April, the Air Force took steps to form a new organization, subsequently named the Western Development Division (WDD) of the Air Research and Development Command (ARDC) in Los Angeles with "sole responsibility for the prosecution of research, development, test, and production leading to a successful intercontinental ballistic missile." Subsequent orders handed WDD the authority to develop the complete weapon system including ground support and operational, logistic, and personnel concepts. General Schriever was given command of the new unit.[33]

The forty-three-year-old Schriever proved an astute choice to lead the ballistic missile effort. He held engineering degrees from Texas A&M and Stanford. In 1938, while a pilot with the Reserve Air Corps of the U.S. Army, he married the daughter of a U.S. Army Air Corps general in a ceremony at the home of General "Hap" Arnold, who remained a longtime friend and mentor. Soon thereafter, Schriever accepted a commission as a regular second lieutenant and moved to Wright Field as a test pilot. During World War II, he flew more than sixty missions as a bomber pilot in the Pacific theater and rose to the rank of colonel. After the war, he held a series of assignments at the National War College and at the Pentagon, where he distinguished himself in several planning and development roles and helped organize the Air Research and Development Command after its creation in 1950. Tall, bright, energetic, and handsome, he was also a gifted athlete and a scratch golfer. Ramo, who first met him through the Teapot Committee, came away impressed. Schriever, he later wrote, possessed "determination, superb leadership and organizing talent, excellent grounding in science and engineering, intimate knowledge of the workings of the Pentagon, the Congress, and the government as a whole, and an uncanny sense for evaluating and managing people."[34]

While Schriever was organizing WDD, Gardner continued to push hard to make the ICBM a top national priority. In April, he persuaded most of the members of the Teapot Committee, including von Neumann, to reconstitute themselves as the Atlas [later ICBM] Scientific Advisory Committee. Ramo and Wooldridge did not join the new committee because by then they presumed that R-W would carry out the analytical work prescribed in the Teapot Committee's report. The presumption bore out: in early May, R-W received a new letter contract from the USAF to "perform technical services and furnish necessary personnel, facilities, and materials to conduct 'Long-Range Analytical Studies of Weapons Systems.'" The company was charged to "conduct research studies, experimental investigations, and consultations with others . . . as necessary to properly carry out technical evaluations and systems analysis in conjunction with conclusions and recommendations" of the Teapot Committee. The initial contract ran for six months at a budget of $500,000; soon thereafter it was augmented by funds for R-W to lease space in Inglewood, California, in a facility that would also house the headquarters of the WDD.[35]

During the spring and early summer, Ramo and Wooldridge had many discussions with government officials about ways to organize the new ICBM program. The two men were not eager to commit themselves wholly to the program for an indefinite period. In the first place, they had no wish to tie themselves exclusively to any single program, however big. They worried, moreover, about the impact of the ICBM program on R-W's other lines of business, recognizing that it would divert management attention and other resources. When Gardner and Talbott urged them to assume a long-term directive role on the ICBM, Wooldridge recalls, they turned the opportunity down "as politely as possible," preferring to concentrate on other lines of business. Not long afterward, however, the Air Force personnel who had previously encouraged R-W to bid to become a second source of fire-control systems for fighter aircraft "began to hedge a bit." "Pretty soon," adds Wooldridge,

> we came to the obvious conclusion that the Air Force wasn't going to give us this second source job unless we took over [the ballistic missile work] they wanted us to take over. . . . So pretty soon we got the idea . . . that we just weren't going to get much business from the Air Force unless we did it their way. . . . We were dragged kicking and screaming into the missile project.[36]

Still, Ramo and Wooldridge remained reluctant to commit themselves or their company too heavily to the ICBM program. In July 1954, when Ramo and Schriever appeared before the Atlas Scientific Advisory Committee to discuss the organization and management of the program, Ramo sought to limit R-W's role to the terms specified by the Teapot Committee. He stated that the company

> would have a small, but highly competent technical staff which would provide to General Schriever studies and advice on program planning and program direction. The actual development would be carried out by contractors, including one systems contractor who might presumedly be Convair or some other airframe manufacturer. After the initial systems studies that would determine some of the basic technical system engineering decisions and would set the basic approach to the problem, R-W's role would be then to support the systems contractor and to assist General Schriever in evaluating the work.

To many in attendance, flaws in the proposed arrangement seemed all too apparent. Assistant Secretary Quarles, for example, strongly criticized the plan. He focused on responsibility for systems engineering, where the relationship between R-W and the systems contractor seemed to him particularly unclear. If the responsibility were lodged in a systems contractor, he reasoned, there would be little continuing role for R-W. On the other hand, he shared the committee's view that neither Convair nor any other likely industrial company possessed the management strength or technical expertise to serve as systems contractor for the ICBM. This responsibility had to be fixed, he believed, at the earliest possible time. Other committee members concurred, concluding that the proposed plan of organization was "too awkward to achieve early attainment of this program."[37]

From Staff to Line

During the next few weeks, Schriever conducted a fresh review of approaches to managing complex programs such as the ICBM. He drew on the Teapot Committee report, Air Force directives, and interviews and discussions with key figures in industry, the scientific community, and the military. On August 18, he submitted to the ARDC his conclusions and recommendations. He laid out four factors that controlled the decision as to how best to fix authority for systems engineering: (1) the technical complexity represented by the ICBM system, which he considered to be "substantially greater than past development projects"; (2) the combination of the large numbers of specialized engineering skills with the short development time schedule; (3) the need for unusually strong support by university scientists; and (4) the unusually close and detailed integration that must exist between industry, the scientific body of the nation, and the Air Force, which "must of course retain over-all control."

In Schriever's mind, this constellation of factors militated against traditional ways of organizing weapon systems. For example, he quickly dismissed a suggestion that the Air Force itself manage development of the ICBM by attempting to use its development engineering organization at Wright Field as the basis of an arsenal modeled along the lines of the U.S. Army's Ballistic Missile Agency in Huntsville, Alabama, where Wernher von Braun directed the rocket program. Schriever apparently did not believe that the Air Force possessed the requisite technical capability to manage a program as complex as the ICBM, however, and he was well aware of the service's good experience with private industrial contractors.[38]

Schriever focused on three alternative models of program management. The first was the traditional vehicle of a prime contractor such as Convair. He rejected this approach for several reasons, the most compelling of which was that "existing industrial organizations generally lack the across-the-board competence in the physical sciences to [perform] the complex systems engineering job" required on the ICBM. The scientists he consulted, moreover, strongly believed that "the predominant technical aspects of the project have to do with systems engineering and with the close relationship of recent physics to all of the engineering"—both areas in which, as the scientists pointed out, the aircraft industry was "relatively weak." Schriever also argued that traditional industrial organizations "are not conducive to attracting or holding scientific personnel due to low-level positions within the organization and the effect which the predominant profit motive has on objective search for technical truths." Finally, he believed that an existing industrial company would find it difficult to hire the necessary scientific and engineering competence unless existing pay scales were exceeded.

Another alternative was to retain a university laboratory similar to those in place at Caltech, MIT, and other top scientific and technical universities. Schriever also rejected this approach, however, believing that it would be difficult for such an institution to manage and control a program as complex as the ICBM. In any event, he pointed out, "there is a very great reluctance on the part of universities to take upon themselves a responsibility for a development of so broad a scope as this."[39]

That left the third alternative: the U.S. Air Force, working in collaboration with a partner such as R-W. Clearly favoring this approach, Schriever advocated that "the senior technical executive of Ramo-Wooldridge would operate as the deputy for technical direction to the Commander, Western Development Division." R-W, in effect, would become "part of the Air Force family for this project" with "line responsibility and authority for technical direction." R-W would supply not only systems engineering, but also "the research and development technical planning, and the technical evaluation and supervision of the contractors." Associated industrial contractors would actually develop hardware for the missile. One—presumably Convair—would be responsible for "structure and physical system assembly," another for propulsion, another for guidance, and another for control.

Anticipating potential criticisms of these arrangements, Schriever noted that "in the persons of Ramo and Wooldridge," R-W possessed

> outstanding ability in systems management and engineering, and in addition, has a number of trained executives in this field. Its ability to attract top scientific people within its organization has already been demonstrated by the fact that several full professors and university department heads have already accepted leave-of-absence assignments to work for the Corporation on this project.

R-W could avoid charges of conflict of interest by agreeing to become ineligible for participation in either development or production contracts related to the program. He concluded by noting that R-W "appears to be in a unique position *timewise* [Schriever's emphasis] to fill this important Air Force need."[40]

Schriever's logic proved persuasive, not only to the Scientific Advisory Committee and the Air Force, but also to R-W and TP. On September 8, representatives of the Air Force met with Ramo, Wooldridge, Fred Crawford, and Dave Wright to revise R-W's May 1954 contract to recognize the company's expanded role. The group agreed on general terms, which were embodied in a definitive contract dated January 29, 1955. R-W's duties included the following: research studies and experimental investigations; maintenance of a development plan; preparation of systems specifications; technical direction of associated contractors; direction of the flight test program; investigation of alternative approaches; and general technical support to WDD. Ramo understood R-W's general role as carrying out technical analysis and making recommendations to the Air Force, which alone possessed the authority to set expenditure levels, authorize major procurement, and choose among alternative proposals and courses of action.

Because of its role in determining the technical specifications of the missile, as well as the intimate knowledge it would gain of the associated contractors' technical capabilities, R-W agreed to become ineligible to develop or manufacture any equipment for the program. To forestall the possibility that R-W could gain competitive advantage from its role in the missile program, it created a new Guided Missile

Research Division (GMRD) and segregated it from its other operating divisions. As R-W's chief financial backer, TP could bid on Air Force missile programs, but any contract award would require the express approval of the secretary of the Air Force. These terms were difficult to swallow, and Crawford and Wright bargained hard for R-W to receive an unusually high fixed fee as compensation for its contributions. The two sides eventually agreed on a fixed fee of 14.3 percent—about twice the customary level for government R&D contracts.[41]

Defining the Role

By the fall of 1954—a year after its incorporation—R-W had become through fits and starts the USAF's contractor for systems engineering and technical direction for the Atlas ICBM. The company's definition of its role reflected the growing complexity of weapon systems—as distinct from the weapon itself—the personal histories and careers of Ramo and Wooldridge, and the scientific biases of the Teapot Committee and its successors. The evolution of weapons into weapon systems reflected a general trend in the evolution of technology, as discrete inventions were incorporated into larger technological systems. The telephone, for example, is but one (and the most visible) part of a larger system of transmitters, receivers, electrical power sources, wires, switches, amplifiers, and repeaters necessary to complete a telephone call. The telephone system, moreover, extends beyond hardware and electromechanical and electronic processes to the personnel and organizations that manage them. Similarly, the advanced weaponry of the post–World War II period in the United States melded many different technologies and types of organization into a single functioning system. The Falcon missile system that Ramo and Wooldridge helped develop at Hughes Aircraft, for example, included not only the missile—itself a complex machine containing many subsystems—but also guidance, control, and communication systems inside the launching aircraft and ground support.[42]

The engineering of complex technological systems, or "systems engineering," as the term became popularized, posed technical and management challenges that were relatively new and evolving rapidly during the postwar era. Ramo, for example, acknowledged that systems engineering "is an old and always present part of practical engineering," but he also argued that the term was acquiring new meaning because "a typical, new, large engineering system depends much more than was the custom in the past on immediate exploitation of the newest discoveries in pure science." On the eve of his involvement with the ICBM program, Wooldridge defined a "systems development project" as "one in which a number of major complex components must simultaneously be developed to act together to perform some new or greatly improved operation, requiring that a considerable amount of development of various techniques beyond the present state of the art be accomplished in order to achieve the desired result."

What distinguished the ICBM from more conventional weapon systems was the variety and difficulty of the component problems and the necessity for unusually close technical coordination of the activities of the component groups. The work demanded a very high level of scientific expertise and analysis, especially in the physical sciences. "A major military systems project," Wooldridge argued, should

> achieve the required technical coordination primarily through the workings of a strong central group of competent analytical people, who at every stage perform the necessary calculations and analyses that are required to determine the design parameters of the various components of the system in such a way that the over-all objectives of the project can best be met.[43]

R-W put this understanding of systems engineering into practice on the Atlas in a series of overlapping phases defined in collaboration with WDD. The first phase was the period of evaluation and study that had started with the Teapot Committee. This lasted from the spring of 1954 until about the end of the year, when the configuration of the redesigned Atlas was frozen. The second phase was a brief period early in 1955 involving the selection of contractors and the awarding of contracts for major systems and subsystems. The third phase ran from the spring of 1955 for more than three years and entailed what Schriever called "the real development effort"—development, fabrication, and testing of the Atlas. The fourth phase was the operational phase, which began with deployment of the Atlas in the middle of 1958 and in which R-W played a lesser role.[44]

During the fall of 1954, as negotiations proceeded on the definitive contract, R-W divided its operations and responsibilities between Wooldridge and Ramo. Wooldridge took charge of the nonmissile businesses that were gathered together in the general electronics group. Ramo headed the GMRD, which in turn was organized into five separate departments for guidance and control, aerodynamics and structures, propulsion, flight test and instrumentation, and weapons system analysis.[45]

During the first phase of study and evaluation, R-W began to grow rapidly. On June 30, 1954, the company employed about 30 people on the ballistic missile program; six months later, the number had risen to 170. In addition to the staff already recruited, new personnel included Robert Bromberg, Milt Clauser, Paul Dergarabedian, Burton Fried, George Gleghorn, David Langmuir, Howard Siefert, George Solomon, and others who would make lasting contributions to the company. R-W achieved something of a coup by hiring Louis G. Dunn, a South African-born, Caltech-trained aeronautical engineer, director of Caltech's Jet Propulsion Laboratory (JPL), and a member of both the Teapot Committee and the Atlas Scientific Advisory Committee. As director of the GMRD, Dunn complemented Ramo in providing a high standard of leadership. He also brought with him or later recruited several JPL alumni, including Frank Lehan, Art Grant, and Gerry Elverum, who would make major contributions to R-W's work in propulsion.[46]

The strictly classified nature of GMRD's work imposed some unusual constraints on hiring. Most recruits lacked the necessary security clearances, and, during the wait for federal investigators to approve them, they were assigned to the Preliminary Studies Group (PSG). This unit, "affectionately known as the 'cooler' or the 'freezer,'" helped orient new employees to the company, provided them with nonclassified research projects, and brought them together with other new colleagues in frequent seminars and weekly town meetings. For many new hires, life in the cooler, which could last six months or more, seemed frustrating. As Bob Bromberg later noted, however, employees often looked back on the experience as one of their happiest times, because they had a freedom that disappeared once clearances came and they moved into the around-the-clock hothouse of missile work.[47]

Throughout 1954, GMRD scientists, engineers, and conscripts traveled extensively to meet with industrial contractors and government and university researchers. They also directed or commissioned research studies on various aspects of missile technology, including propulsion, guidance, digital computers, radio tracking, reentry, and many other areas. Many of these studies made intensive use of one of the first big digital computers, a Sperry-Rand UNIVAC, to model and simulate various scenarios.[48]

The most significant early systems study concerned the design and dimensions of the nose cone. Working jointly with representatives of the Atomic Energy Commission and the Sandia Corporation, R-W personnel examined trade-offs between warhead weight and yield, guidance accuracy, reentry speed and thermodynamics, nose-cone materials, and other variables. In December 1954, this study established the basic design and weight of the nose cone at a level about half of the original Convair design. This analysis, in turn, permitted scaling down of the gross weight of the Atlas from four hundred sixty thousand to two hundred forty thousand pounds and reduction of the propulsion system from five rocket motors to three. It is estimated that this analysis led to decisions that saved more than a year of development time and reduced the total cost of the missile by 25 percent.[49]

By early 1955, with the basic configuration of the Atlas settled, the Air Force was ready to let contracts for the structure and major subsystems. During this period, R-W evaluated contractor bids from a technical perspective and made its recommendations and conclusions available to the Air Force. R-W did not carry out cost analyses of technical alternatives, nor did it participate in the Air Force's final deliberations about which bids to accept. The ultimate winners were Convair for the structure and final physical assembly, GE for radio-inertial guidance, AC Spark Plug (later Delco) for all-inertial guidance, North American Aviation for the propulsion system, GE for the reentry vehicle (nose cone), and Burroughs for the on-board computer.

During the third phase of "real development," R-W's staff grew most rapidly. By the end of 1957, R-W had nearly two thousand employees assigned to the ballistic missile program and was commanding an annual budget of more than $30 million, including a fixed fee or guaranteed profit now set at 10 percent. Recruits were easy to come by. Although R-W could not advertise what it was doing, word spread rapidly through the scientific and technical communities that the company offered attractive opportunities for young scientists and engineers. "It was an unbelievably exciting time," recalls Budd Cohen, a young Princeton Ph.D. gas-dynamics specialist who joined the company in 1957. "Many of us were still in our twenties and thirties, yet we were handed very big responsibilities. The ICBM was the highest priority project in the country. We put in long hours and worked through weekends. And we enjoyed every minute of it."[50]

R-W's primary responsibility during this period involved technical direction of the associated contractors. This work entailed not only regular monitoring of contractors' performance and progress, but also occasional adjustments of requirements to take account of improvements or modifications to the overall system originating elsewhere. The decision to shrink the missile based on the availability of lighter warheads, for example, had enormous implications not only for Convair (the airframe and assembly) and Rocketdyne (the rocket motors), but also for contractors engaged in guidance and control, whose systems became smaller and lighter with new variables and magnitudes to monitor and control. R-W personnel were assigned full time to particular contractors and presided at technical direction meetings held frequently at the contractors' facilities. As the Air Force's technical representative, R-W had—and used—authority to order changes in specifications, schedules, and milestones.[51]

Propulsion was in many respects the simplest problem to solve. The rocket motor for the Atlas had been in development for many years as the booster engine for the more generously funded Navajo cruise missile. Built by the Rocketdyne Division of North American Aviation, the motor was a complex and sophisticated product that incorporated many advances over the German V-2 technology that had spawned other U.S. rocket programs. A key but poorly understood issue, however, was propellant utilization. Since large quantities of fuel and oxidizer were required, it was essential to use them efficiently and carry no more than necessary. In fact, R-W personnel calculated that if only 1 percent of the original propellant weight was not consumed by the time the engine shut off, the missile's range would be shortened by nearly six hundred nautical miles; at the same time, achieving maximum speed while carrying the extra 1 percent of fuel would require nearly twice as much fuel at liftoff.

To solve this problem, R-W led a series of research studies on the behavior of fluids as they drained, and on the design of fuel tanks. Dave Langmuir, for example, led recruits in the PSG (the cooler) in the Vortex Project, a theoretical inquiry into the laws that govern the formation of vortices in draining fluids. Milt Clauser headed another research team that studied the impact of "fuel sloshing" on the stability of an object in flight. The eventual solution to the problem was a redesigned fuel tank with baffles near the drain to direct and speed the flow of fuel from the tank. The new design both made for higher utilization of fuel and improved flight stability.[52]

Guidance posed stickier problems. R-W evaluated two system types—radio-inertial and inertial—and within each alternative, several different approaches. The radio-inertial system used more familiar technologies of ground-based radar installations to track and communicate with the missile from liftoff until its engines shut down, when it was no longer subject to control. In 1954, the technology had proven itself on tactical missiles such as the Corporal, and systems similar in concept worked well in other applications such as aircraft fire control.

Inertial guidance, in contrast, relied on a closed system of gyroscopes and accelerometers to sense the missile's position and orientation. All key components rode on board the missile. The German V-2s had used an inertial system, which the U.S. Army was also developing for its intermediate range ballistic missile (IRBM). Inertial systems had several attractive features: they were conceptually simple and invulnerable to enemy sabotage or jamming. In 1954, however, inertial systems suffered from poor accuracy, and the components were bulky and heavy. For these reasons, R-W preferred a radio-inertial system for the Atlas.[53]

Before 1954, Convair had pursued a radio-inertial system called Azuza, which relied on antennas arranged in a precise configuration near the launch site to triangulate on and communicate with the missile. In reviewing the Azuza system, R-W personnel noticed several significant weaknesses: limited accuracy because of the particular spacing of antennas; a substantial weight penalty because of reliance on particular types of heavy components; and reliability problems stemming from components containing more than three thousand vacuum tubes. R-W commissioned several scientific studies of poorly understood but ultimately significant phenomena such as irregularities in microwave propagation caused by atmospheric and tropospheric disturbances, and the attenuation caused by the rocket exhaust flames. In December 1954, R-W outlined a new approach to radio-inertial guidance that GE subsequently adopted. The new system used fewer downrange antennas, vacuum tubes, and other components, as well as a new digital computer designed and built by Burroughs for ground station control. The system proved simpler, lighter, more accurate, more reliable, and cheaper than the Azuza system.[54]

Perhaps the most complex problem involved the design of the nose cone or reentry vehicle. As with propellant utilization, weight was a critical factor. The less the nose cone weighed, the greater the payload it could carry, or the less fuel the missile could use, or the greater its range. But there were many unknowns about reentry. For example, the nose cone would encounter extreme temperatures and brutal stresses as it dived from space into the atmosphere. Indeed, it was not clear that there was any way to protect the warhead from destruction or to maintain its accuracy. As an R-W document put it, "theory for such conditions must be extrapolated beyond any previous experimental confirmations."[55]

The R-W/USAF team attacked the reentry problem in two ways. The first involved original research in aerodynamics and thermodynamics. In 1954, the best approach seemed to be to place the warhead inside a blunt copper shell with sufficient thickness in the hottest regions to absorb the heat during the short period between reentry and detonation of the warhead. The problem involved both design and weight reduction, since a large amount of copper was necessary for this heat-sink approach to succeed. In addition, the nose cone's blunt shape caused it to decelerate quickly at high altitudes and to descend slowly enough to cause it to be vulnerable to wind and other atmospheric disturbances that could make it drift well off course. Seeking to develop optimum designs for the copper heat-sink, as well as to consider alternative approaches, R-W engineer-scientists George Solomon, Bob Bromberg, and John Sellars directed many research and experimental studies on heat transfer (especially in the boundary layer) under turbulent conditions, on fluid dynamics, and on other related subjects.[56]

To test the reentry vehicle, the R-W/WDD team tried several approaches. For example, developers fabricated "shock tubes" containing instrumented scale models to simulate reentry conditions momentarily. The reentry vehicle could also be tested in the exhaust of rocket motors, although such temperatures were far below those it would actually encounter on reentry. Still another testing approach involved placing scaled-down models atop smaller rockets. In January 1955, the Air Force awarded a contract to Lockheed to develop a reentry test vehicle called the X-17. This vehicle consisted of several tactical missiles grouped together in three stages. The third stage was designed to fire in a downward direction and could attain speeds on the order of Mach 15—well below actual reentry speed but much closer than otherwise obtainable. The X-17 was no simple test vehicle. The first six launches resulted in catastrophic failures or loss of telemetry before meaningful data could be recovered. Finally, in July and August 1956, several X-17s hit Mach 12, allowing conclusive affirmation of the copper heat-sink approach.[57]

Methods of Missile Management

At the top of the U.S. Air Force–R–W partnership, Schriever and Ramo worked together extremely closely, "exchanging thoughts and ideas face to face virtually every day—for five years," as Ramo later wrote. Together, the two men developed most of the distinctive management practices of the ICBM programs: thorough and ongoing research and study of all major systems and components in the missile; dual sourcing of major system components; and "concurrent" or simultaneous development of major components and subsystems.[58]

At a meeting of the Atlas Scientific Advisory Committee in October 1954, for example, Schriever sketched out the dimensions of the problem graphically. He presented a chart—known as the window shade chart—that filled an entire wall of a large conference room with "all of the important elements in it. The R&D, then we had each one of the major subsystems, the logistics, the training, everything in a conceptual way with objective dates on the chart that we would have to achieve certain things in order to reach the end objective of having an initial operational capability." The chart was divided into six areas: nose cone, guidance and control, propulsion, engine-test vehicle, fully guided missile, and general, which included training programs, ground installations and handling equipment, determination of the location of the first operational base, and its construction.[59]

In the case of the nose cone, for example, decisions about gross weight and the design of a reentry test vehicle were made by the end of 1954. In January 1955, the test-vehicle contract was let to General Electric, with the design of the vehicle frozen in February. The design of the nose cone itself was frozen in October 1955, with flight testing scheduled for the middle of 1956 and final nose-cone design to be determined by the end of the year. As for guidance and control, the initial design study contracts were let in the final months of 1954, with detailed specifications ready by mid-1955. Tests of the radar-tracking system were scheduled to begin in mid-1956, with final design frozen soon thereafter, and first tests readied by January 1957.[60]

These "decision dates" were continually revised to reflect the situation as the program advanced. Every Saturday—an occasion soon dubbed "Black Saturday"—Schriever assembled a program review committee consisting of his top staff, Ramo and other top R-W scientists and engineers, and representatives of the major contractors for an all-day meeting to review progress and discuss interface issues.

Subsequent years brought additional management innovations pioneered by WDD and R-W: a configuration control board, which had responsibility for assuring that any necessary changes in component design would be immediately reflected throughout the total missile configuration; a production control board, which exercised complete control over allocation of equipment and resources with authority to move scarce items of equipment or to reprogram funds to that area most in need at a given point in time; a project control room, "to serve as a nerve center for all project information, including hardware delivery schedules, test schedules, and operational planning schedules (a graphical aid was a red flag pinned to any item that might lead to program delays); and sequence and flow charts or "bedsheets" that laid out goals, schedules, and tasks for each major component and subsystem as well as for the system as a whole.[61]

A related R-W responsibility was supervision of the testing of key components and subsystems produced by the associated contractors. These contractors performed the actual tests, subject to an overarching philosophy that R-W developed. The general goal was to minimize the number of factors that could be checked only during an actual flight test. Accordingly, R-W helped design and administer a hierarchy of tests, building up from components through assemblies and subsystems before the final systems test.[62]

AN EXPANDING AGENDA

The combination of urgent priority and the inherent technological risks of the Atlas missile stimulated many innovations and improvements in program management. One of the most important involved developing alternative approaches to the major subsystems so that the failure of any single approach would not paralyze the whole system. As Ramo put it, "It has been clear that more than one approach is technically and industrially feasible, but to predict which of these potential approaches would lead the others timewise is not always possible. Also, the importance of the program requires insurance against errors in human judgment." In addition, Ramo and Schriever believed that parallel development helped spread the immense burden of detailed design, testing, and production planning for the missile and its components and subsystems. During mid-1955, the Air Force awarded backup development contracts to Aerojet-General for propulsion; to Bell Labs, American Bosch Arma, and MIT for guidance; and to Avco for the nose cone.[63]

At the same time, the parallel development strategy provided an additional fringe benefit. With strong encouragement from the Atlas Scientific Advisory Committee, the Air Force directed R-W to analyze alternative approaches to the ICBM. The company complied, developing "missile optimization techniques" and computer software to examine the effects of key design variables such as the trajectories, first- and second-stage thrusts, distribution of weight between first and second stage, time of staging, fuel utilization rates, and many other factors. This analysis provided the Air Force and the Scientific Advisory Committee with the essential technical information they needed to justify development of an alternate ICBM.[64]

The justification for an alternate ICBM was also political and strategic. In February 1955, a scientific panel that President Eisenhower had commissioned to consider the vulnerability of the United States to surprise attack issued an alarming and influential report. The Killian Report—named after the panel's chairman, MIT President James R. Killian—warned of the rapid progress of Soviet rocketry and urged that the Air Force ICBM program, in response, should become "a nationally supported effort of the highest priority." The Killian Report played into the hands of missile advocates like Trevor Gardner and Sen. Henry Jackson (D-Washington), who lobbied hard for Eisenhower to declare the ICBM a top national priority as a means of further expediting development of the Atlas and creating additional missile programs. In July, Gardner, von Neumann, and Schriever briefed Eisenhower on the missile program and won their case. Six weeks later, after obtaining supporting opinions from the National Security Council and other agencies, Eisenhower issued a presidential directive establishing the ICBM as "a research program of the highest national priority, second to no others. . . ." The president pledged to use all available resources "to the end that nothing surmountable shall stand in the way of the most rapid progress of this program."[65]

The maximum urgency of the ICBM program prepared the way to move ahead with the alternate ICBM. For the Atlas, developers had traded off performance for the sake of earliest operational capability. The new missile, known later as the Titan, optimized the backup technologies for the Atlas into a new configuration that would become operational somewhat later. The Titan system included a different engine (but with similar size, weight, and performance specifications as the Atlas engine, should it be needed for that program); a monocoque airframe; both radio-inertial and complete inertial guidance systems; and an improved nose cone.

During the spring and summer of 1955, R-W personnel carried out analyses of each of the major subsystems and developed technical specifications for the contractors to meet. In October—less than a month after the presidential directive—Glenn L. Martin was awarded the contract for assembly and testing of the Titan. Bell Labs was chosen to develop an improved radio-inertial guidance system, with American Bosch Arma to develop an alternative inertial system. Avco won the contract for the nose cone.[66]

Once the Titan contracts were let, R-W vigorously carried out its SETD role. WDD and GMRD established separate project-management organizations for the Atlas and Titan programs. To head the Atlas program, Dunn appointed Edward Doll, a Caltech Ph.D. who had overlapped in graduate school with Ramo and Wooldridge. Doll's counterpart on the Titan was William "Will" Duke, a Ph.D. from UCLA and a veteran of Cornell's Aeronautical Research Laboratory, who joined R-W early in 1956.[67]

Duke's team directed many changes in the associate contractors' original designs for the Titan. For example, Martin had designed the first stage of the missile as a balloon structure similar to that of the Atlas; a combination of fuel and pressure would keep the structure stiff enough to support the second stage. R-W engineers questioned this approach, which it regarded as dangerous and unnecessarily difficult to engineer. They showed that the balloon structure gave no real weight advantage because it required a thick, heavy skin to contain sufficient pressure to support the weight of the second stage. R-W therefore directed that the Titan airframe be changed to a stiffened structure that could be completely loaded with propellant without any pressurization on the ground. "As a result," stated an official summary of the program, "the Martin missile was changed from one requiring the expensive tooling and complicated assembly procedures of balloon tanks to a type which is about as easy to build as conventional airplane structures, and which should be low in cost, simple to transport, and have maximum operational suitability."[68]

R-W personnel went on to identify many additional improvements to the Titan system. For example, they directed Martin to stiffen the airframe structure in a specific, novel way that both increased its strength and eliminated the need for spot welding; they designed a system using small solid-propellant rockets to separate the two stages of the missile prior to ignition of the main second-stage motor; they redesigned and simplified the propellant pumping system; they actually eliminated the propellant utilization system, which became unnecessary in a two-stage rocket; and they eliminated a heavy component in the Bell Labs radio-inertial guidance system. All of these contributions resulted in significant reductions of weight, simplification of design and manufacture, increases in reliability, and major savings in cost.[69]

Soon after assuming responsibility for the Titan missile, WDD took control of still another missile program, the Thor (whose descendant is today's "Delta" space booster) intermediate range ballistic missile. The Air Force had been reluctant to pursue an IRBM, which had a range of about 1,500 miles, about one-fourth that of the ICBM, in part because Schriever worried that doing so might dilute the priority given to the Atlas. By the middle of 1955, however, the Killian Report, the presidential directive, increasing demand for IRBMs to be based in Europe, and the gathering momentum of the Army and Navy IRBM programs drew the Air Force into the fray.[70]

The assignment to draft the initial specifications for the Thor fell to a recent recruit to R-W, Dr. Adolph K. (Dolph) Thiel. During World War II, the Vienna-born Thiel had worked on the secret German V-2 program at Peenemünde with Wernher von Braun. After the war, along with von Braun, he immigrated to the United States, where he helped develop the Redstone rocket and its successors for the U.S. Army. In 1955, Thiel saw that the future of American rocketry lay with the Air Force ICBM, and he determined to play a role. He made plans to join Convair, but changed his mind after receiving a phone call from Louis Dunn, who enticed him to R-W with the prospect of working on a family of missiles.[71]

In late November, the Department of Defense approved an Air Force crash program to develop the Thor at the earliest possible date, setting in motion a development competition with a similar missile, the Jupiter, pursued jointly by the Army and Navy. (The following year, the Navy abandoned the Jupiter program to focus on its own IRBM, the solid-fuel Polaris.) Although the government specified no rewards for winning—or penalties for losing—the rivalry among the service branches provided an additional spur to rush through an already compressed development schedule.[72]

R-W quickly assumed its by now customary role as SETD contractor for the Thor. The new program manager, Ruben F. Mettler, was a figure destined for a meteoric rise. The thirty-one-year-old Mettler had joined R-W just months earlier. He grew up on a farm in Shafter, California, a small town in the San Joaquin Valley. The eighth of ten children, his early life was disciplined by the dynamics of a large family as well as by the chores of the farm. An outstanding student, he received a scholarship to Stanford, where he matriculated in 1941, planning to prepare for the law. America's entry into World War II pushed him in new directions, however. He volunteered for the U.S. Navy, which saw in him an unusual aptitude for technical subjects and sent him to an accelerated program at Caltech, where he earned a B.S. in eighteen months. As a young midshipman, he moved next to radar training school at MIT. "I did well," Mettler recalls, "and I liked my Navy experience with radar and electronics. So after the war I decided to go back to Caltech to become a scientist or an engineer."[73]

Mettler earned a Ph.D. in electrical engineering at Caltech, graduating at the top of his class in 1949. One of his professors in graduate school was the moonlighting Wooldridge, who recruited him into Hughes Aircraft. Within a year, his work with Jack Irving at Hughes on the Falcon missile's lead collision system led to a significant expansion of business, and at twenty-six, Mettler became a project manager. When the Hughes exodus came, he moved to Washington as a senior analyst in the DOD, where he reported to, among others, Donald Quarles and Trevor Gardner. Major national recognition soon followed: in 1954, he received the Eta Kappa Nu Award as the nation's most outstanding young engineer; the following year, just after Wooldridge wooed him to R-W, he was named one of the ten outstanding young men in the United States by the U.S. Junior Chamber of Commerce. Extremely bright, with a cool analytical bent and a soft-spoken manner, Mettler proved a very capable program manager—just as later he would distinguish himself in a series of senior management positions at TRW, culminating as chairman and CEO for a decade before his retirement in 1988.[74]

Directed by Mettler and his Air Force counterpart, Col. Edward N. Hall, the Thor program embarked on an exceedingly ambitious, almost frenetic, schedule. WDD took control of the Thor program on November 28, 1955, with the goal of deploying the first squadron overseas within three years. The Thor development team wasted little time. To speed matters, the team made use of technologies already planned for the Atlas and Titan. Before Christmas, the major contracts were let: assembly and testing to Douglas Aircraft; propulsion to Rocketdyne (North American); a nose cone to GE. The program was the first Air Force missile to use inertial guidance, a system designed by the Instrumentation Laboratory at MIT (later Draper Labs) and built by AC Spark Plug. By January 16, the missile was sized and its basic configuration frozen.[75]

During the next few months, this breathless pace continued. In March 1956, the WDD received a directive to proceed to initial operational capability at the earliest possible time. Rocketdyne began engine testing in March 1956 and delivered its first flight engine in August. By then the first inertial guidance system was ready for installation. The government provided warhead data to GE in August, and in the next month the diameter of the nose cone was fixed.

Just thirteen months after the start of the program—and several months ahead of their counterparts on the Jupiter missile—the WDD/R-W team had the first Thor ready for flight testing. The first launch took place on January 25, 1957, and it proved a dramatic occasion. The countdown proceeded uneventfully and government officials, program managers, and engineers held their breath as the engine fired and the Thor readied to rise from its launch pad. Within seconds, however, the missile lost thrust. After climbing just a few inches, it fell back on its pad, broke up, and exploded. The failure devastated the morale of many people who had worked extraordinarily hard on the program for many months. Ramo, who was watching, lightened the mood by quipping, "Well, we've proven it can fly. Now we just need to work on the range!"[76]

During the next few months, the Thor team analyzed what had happened and attempted several more launches. Detailed review of films of the first test showed that a sloppy procedure in fueling had introduced a few grains of sand and dirt into the fuel system, causing a shut-off valve to fail at liftoff. The second flight test on April 19 proved even more frustrating. According to Mettler, who monitored the launch from the command center, the missile lifted off cleanly and all signs appeared positive, when suddenly, thirty-five seconds into the flight, the range safety officer pressed a button to abort the flight and destroy the missile. Apparently, however, the problem was not with the missile, but rather with the safety officer's assessment: his display of the missile track had been connected backwards and showed the missile apparently headed inland, perhaps to crash in a populated area rather than out to sea. This outcome proved costly to the Air Force's public image, for on May 31, the Army rocket team took credit for the first successful American IRBM launch when a Jupiter missile reached impact on a target sixteen hundred miles downrange.

Meanwhile, the Atlas was also being readied for flight tests at Cape Canaveral. On June 11, the first Atlas launch suffered a fate similar to that of the first Thor. The countdown proceeded uneventfully, and the missile appeared to lift off properly. Less than a minute into the flight, however, as it turned downrange over the Atlantic, the first sign of trouble appeared: "a sudden collapse of the columns of flame from the engines . . . as though a huge hand had closed over the apertures admitting propellants to the combustion chambers." Trailing smoke, the Atlas "fishtailed, performed a loop, and then started nosing to earth," and the range safety officer signaled its destruction.[77]

During the summer of 1957, two more Thors (including one that blew up on the launch pad four minutes before scheduled liftoff) and another Atlas test failed. The pressure on the R-W/Air Force team was intense, especially after several more productive Jupiter launches and the Soviet Union's stunning announcement on August 26 of a successful ICBM test flight. Finally, on September 20, a Thor completed a full range and duration flight, making impact thirteen hundred miles downrange from Cape Canaveral. A jubilant R-W/Air Force group rejoiced: the Air Force ballistic missile program was validated. Their triumphant mood proved short-lived, however. On October 3, another Thor collapsed within seconds of ignition and exploded on the launch pad. The next day brought disquieting news of another sort. The USSR announced the successful launch of *Sputnik,* the first satellite to orbit the earth. The Soviet feat demonstrated a shocking lead in space technology, and it hastened a fundamental review of American missile and space programs—a review fraught with implications for R-W and TP.

Chapter 8

The Making
of a Merger

▶   ▶   ▶

1953–1958

THE SOVIETS LAUNCHED *SPUTNIK* ON A FRIDAY EVENING, BUT SI RAMO LEARNED OF IT THE next morning. When word arrived, he was closeted with General Schriever and a host of Air Force, R-W, and missile-contracting personnel for a Black Saturday session. The mood of the meeting changed immediately, he recalls: suddenly it became "black-and-blue Saturday." Ramo's concern was not that the Soviets had achieved something beyond America's capability. As an artifact of technology, *Sputnik* (a Russian word meaning "companion" or "fellow traveler") was not particularly impressive. It resembled a medicine ball in size and weighed 184 pounds. Inside, it carried two radio transmitters that beeped methodically and continuously through each ninety-six-minute orbit for twenty-one days, when the satellite tumbled back to earth and burned up in the atmosphere.

Rather, Ramo writes, *Sputnik* "offended and alarmed us." This reaction reflected the satellite's symbolic value in the game of geopolitics as well as its sobering demonstration of Soviet launch capability. There could no longer be any doubt about Soviet claims to possess an operational ICBM. Thus the satellite not only ushered in the space race; it also suggested "a missile gap" in which the United States appeared to lag behind its principal rival on the world stage.[1]

For Ramo-Wooldridge and Thompson Products, the flight of *Sputnik* defined a turning point in their individual histories, as well as in the relationship between the two companies. The satellite precipitated a major shift in U.S. defense and national security policy and the development of new policies for the exploitation of space. It meant more missiles, fewer conventional aircraft, and opportunities to make wholly new products such as satellites and deep space communications networks. It also meant that the U.S. Air Force would jockey with other branches of the military and government agencies for jurisdiction in developing space, a contest the outcome of which would remain uncertain for nearly a year. These circumstances in turn raised questions about R-W's close relationship to the Air Force, especially its agreement not to make hardware for the missile programs. Would R-W continue to play its SETD role on the new weapons systems and space programs on the Air Force's drawing board? Would it be permitted to manufacture equipment for these programs? How would competitors respond? How would the Eisenhower administration and Congress resolve competing claims to develop space?

By October 1957, R-W was a far different company than it had been when Trevor Gardner recruited Si Ramo and Dean Wooldridge to serve on and support the Teapot Committee. The Guided Missile Research Division (GMRD) had proven itself on the Atlas, Titan, and Thor programs, and it was seeking other work. At the same time, a rapidly maturing General Electronics Group was making plans to move from customer-funded R&D contracts into production. Both parts of R-W, moreover, hoped for expanded roles in the Air Force's next-generation ICBM program, the Minuteman.

At TP, *Sputnik* accelerated an anticipated decline in the company's biggest business, making parts and components for turbojet engines. It also signaled an opportunity for TP to apply its skills in precision manufacturing for missiles and space programs. And once again, familiar questions surfaced: would the Air Force and public policy-makers permit TP to make parts and components for missiles and space hardware? Or would the restrictions placed on R-W also affect TP? If so, how would the company offset the decline of its jet engine components business?

During the year that followed the launch of *Sputnik*, its aftereffects rippled their way through R-W and TP, joining with other forces and pressures to build inexorably toward a redefinition of the relationship between the two companies. By the late spring of 1958, the leaders of TP proposed a merger with R-W, a solution that helped answer most, but not all, of the questions that plagued both companies after the fall of 1957.

INTO SPACE

In April 1957—six months before *Sputnik* and well before successful test flights of any ballistic missiles—*Time* magazine devoted two covers to the Air Force missile program, first profiling General Schriever and then Ramo and Wooldridge as prophets of a new era. Much of this interest reflected Americans' continuing wonderment at technology at its finest. Spin-off advances in electronics and communications from the missile program, moreover, promised to revolutionize the economy and, by extension, American society.[2]

By then a growing number of people recognized that the ICBM was more than an unstoppable weapon: the same technology could easily become a launch vehicle for space satellites. Indeed, Schriever stated as much in the first *Time* article. Away from public view, the Air Force was already exploring military uses of space. It had devoted more than two years of work, for example, to an advanced reconnaissance satellite system, a program designated Project WS-117L. As historian Walter McDougall has described it, "this was no 'quick and dirty' orbiting beeper" like the first satellites actually launched; rather, it was "a strategic satellite system" designed "to attain a precise, predicted orbit; to be stabilized on three axes with a 'high-pointing accuracy'; to maintain a given attitude for disturbing torques; to receive and execute commands sent from the ground; and to transmit information to ground stations." Although the program was still several years away from operational capability, the Air Force planned to launch the satellite using one of its own missiles as a booster.[3]

Lockheed served as the prime contractor for the reconnaissance satellite and its associated upper-stage vehicle for in-orbit propulsion and control, the Agena. R-W carried out some research studies and associated work on the program but resisted Air Force entreaties to play a more active systems engineering role after Lockheed experienced some delays. R-W adopted this stance because it sought to participate in developing hardware for the program. In fact, the Control Systems Division bid to develop and produce the intelligence data-handling system for Project WS-117L. Its proposal was judged the best on technical merit, but the contract was not awarded because of the hardware ban on the missile programs. As a consolation, Lockheed chose R-W to develop a small infrared system on the satellite.[4]

In addition to Project WS-117L, the Air Force had several other space programs in development before October 1957, and R-W was involved in long-range planning for many of them. Late in 1956, for example, the Air Force requested the company to study alternatives for organizing and managing space programs, including the possibility of establishing "a Ballistic Missile and Space Vehicle Center" at Hollomon Air Force Base (White Sands Proving Ground), near Albuquerque, New Mexico. In 1957, R-W's Jack Irving directed a multipart advanced weapons systems study to look at next-generation ICBMs, future military satellites for communications, reconnaissance, and surveillance, and long-range exploration of space. The latter sketched possibilities for human exploration of space, including development of more powerful booster rockets than the ICBMs, landing packages on the moon, orbiting Mars, and using nuclear propulsion for deep-space travel.[5]

The flight of *Sputnik* thus caught R-W and the Air Force by surprise, but not unprepared. In the short-term, in fact, *Sputnik*'s aftermath brought opportunity. While the other service branches and civilian agencies scrambled to develop policies and capabilities for space, the R-W/Air Force team could respond quickly with plans and hardware already in the pipeline. At the same time, increased funding poured into all missile development programs and eased some pressures and concerns. The Department of Defense, for example, decided to support both the Thor and Jupiter IRBMs, effectively ending the competition between those programs.

As the implications of the Soviet achievement began to sink in, however, the possibility of playing America's leading role in future space development receded from the Air Force's and R-W's grasp. In part, the problem reflected an angry and accusatory mood in Congress: in December 1957 and January 1958, when Ramo and Schriever testified before Senator Lyndon Johnson's Committee on Armed Services (then investigating the American space program), they appeared not as heralds of a new age but as defenders of a second-place finish. The stigma was of course unfair; the Air Force's primary mission was to develop the ICBM, not to launch a satellite, and part of the reason for the apparent U.S. lag in missile technology stemmed from underinvestment in the years before 1954. Nonetheless, the Air Force's Ballistic Missile Division (BMD, as the Western Development Division was renamed in June 1957) that Schriever headed was dealt a blow from which it never fully recovered. During 1958, sponsorship of many Air Force space initiatives—man in space, lunar probes, a million-pound-thrust rocket motor, and space exploration—passed from BMD first to a new agency in the Department of Defense, the Advanced Research Projects Agency (ARPA) and subsequently to the National Aeronautics and Space Administration (NASA), a new civilian agency created by statute at the end of July.[6]

From Reentry to the Moon

While decisions about the locus of authority to develop space hung in the balance, R-W and the Air Force responded swiftly to *Sputnik*. In November 1957, Ramo seized the initiative by renaming R-W's Guided Missile Research Division as Space Technology Laboratories (STL). Hoping to avoid controversies and potential conflict-of-interest charges such as had occurred on Project WS-117L, R-W established STL as an autonomous division, with Ramo as president, assisted by Louis Dunn as executive vice president and general manager.[7]

In pursuit of its primary objective, STL continued to push development of the Atlas, Thor, and Titan missiles. Flight tests of the Atlas and especially of the Thor late in 1957 and early the following year revealed a disturbing but irregular pattern of engine failure soon after launch. The Army's Jupiter IRBM, which featured a Rocketdyne engine much like that of the Atlas and Thor, encountered a similar problem. Some evidence pointed to a possible culprit: failure of the turbopump that forced fuel from the tanks into the combustion chamber. Under some circumstances, the bearings inside the turbopump casing appeared to "walk" out of alignment, with disastrous consequences. Yet the problem was difficult to diagnose, especially in the Thor, because Rocketdyne continued to refine and improve the engines for later test vehicles, some of which flight tested successfully.

Until the problem could be solved, therefore, each launch represented a calculated risk. Yet Schriever and STL managers Louis Dunn, Rube Mettler, and Dolph Thiel believed the gambles worthwhile because of the urgent need to meet goals for deployment. They also noted that even failed missions yielded valuable information about the performance of launch equipment, the guidance system, and other major subsystems and components of the missile. Slowly they began to isolate the bearing problem, and the summer of 1958 witnessed noteworthy Thor and Atlas engine tests, including the first long- (but not full-) range Atlas flight on August 2. By September 1958, the bearing problem was fully corrected, and during the following fifteen months, more than eighty Thor and Atlas launches proceeded without primary engine failure.[8]

Although STL focused most of its attention by far on ongoing work on the missile programs, the division also stepped up its long-range planning and research studies for the Air Force. As handled by Jack Irving, Al Donovan, and several other STL scientist engineers, the assignments not only expanded on earlier work on advanced weapons systems and satellites, but also opened entirely new areas ranging from the far-fetched (nuclear and thermonuclear propulsion) to concepts soon to become R&D programs (glide rockets, such as Boeing eventually proposed for a vehicle called Dyna-Soar, and an antiballistic missile system that would use satellites to detect launches).[9]

STL also began to play a more visible and ultimately more controversial role in public. The unit's work on problems of reentry, for example, led to its first big opportunity to make hardware for space. This story began in the middle of 1957, when R-W personnel George Solomon, Bob Bromberg, John Sellars, and Budd Cohen were conducting theoretical and research studies of advanced nose cones. The new approach abandoned the heavy copper heat-sink originally specified for the Atlas in favor of a material such as fiberglass or another composite that ablated (eroded away in layers) at reentry. The principle was "much like being sunburned at the beach," noted a popular writer, "with that top layer of skin peeling off to reveal a new layer underneath for the next exposure—but all happening within instants."[10]

The advantage of an ablative material was a substantial weight savings. The U.S. Army demonstrated an ablative nose cone on its Jupiter IRBM in August 1957, and the U.S. Navy intended to use an ablative nose cone on its Polaris IRBM. No one knew, however, whether an ablative material could survive the faster reentry speeds and higher temperatures of an ICBM. The first full-range flight of an Atlas was not scheduled until late in 1958.[11]

To test the ablative nose cone under ICBM reentry conditions, STL received permission in November 1957 to develop its first piece of hardware for the missile program. This was a new, two-stage test vehicle, cobbled together from a Thor IRBM, a second-stage propulsion system designed for another rocket (the civilian-sponsored Project Vanguard), and an ablative nose cone built by GE. The vehicle was given the code name Able, derived from Thor-A, using the World War II-era phonetic alphabet. STL engineers assembled the first Able rockets at Los Angeles International Airport in a hangar leased by R-W's Control Systems Division. For the first launch, they displayed a scientific bent, as well as a playful streak: in the space designed for the warhead, R-W engineers fashioned a special compartment containing a live mouse that was wired to test biomedical reaction to g-forces and weightlessness; they also planned to include a two-ounce container of Old Grandad bourbon, bearing the label, "Aged in Space." Neither the mouse nor the whiskey survived the first flight of what was now called the Able-0 program on April 23, 1958. During the countdown, the Air Force project manager found out about the whiskey; failing to see the humor, he ordered it removed. The mouse made it 146 seconds into the flight, when a turbopump failure aborted the mission in a fiery explosion.[12]

The first Able-0 launch failed to provide meaningful data on the ablative nose cone. The second, on July 9, was a full-range flight, with the missile soaring to a height of nearly a thousand miles before plunging down in the vicinity of its target in the South Atlantic. Although the nose cone—and a second mouse, named Mia II (for Mouse in Able and in memory of its predecessor)—could not be recovered, telemetry data appeared to validate the ablative nose cone. On July 23, the third and final Able-0 launch—in which an unfortunate Mia III or "Wickie" provided biomedical data—further validated the ablative approach.[13]

While the Able-0 program was getting under way, STL was readying itself to bid on a more ambitious space project: the country's first lunar probe. In 1956, analysts at the RAND Corporation had suggested to the Air Force that it would soon be feasible to land a package on the moon using an Atlas or Titan rocket as the booster, and some of R-W's long-range planning studies had also considered this possibility. The idea attracted little notice until *Sputnik*, when top U.S. officials believed that it was imperative not merely to duplicate the Soviet feat, but to surpass it as soon as possible, perhaps by becoming the first nation to land a package on the moon. During the next few months, more than three hundred proposals for a moon probe poured into the Department of Defense, including bids from Douglas, Convair, Martin, North American, Lockheed, and Caltech's Jet Propulsion Laboratory. In January 1958, STL joined the contest, when Paul Dergarabedian, a Caltech Ph.D. and propulsion specialist, prepared a moon-shot proposal. Designated Project Baker—suggesting that it was a logical extension of Project Able—the STL proposal called for adding a small solid-fuel rocket as a fourth stage to the Thor-Able configuration, as well as a small twenty-pound instrumentation payload. The proposal also involved building a network of ground stations to monitor the flight.

During subsequent weeks, the STL proposal won the enthusiastic backing of the Air Force. Col. Charles H. Terhune, one of Schriever's top deputies, pointed out that three Thor missiles allocated for Project Able-0 reentry tests could be reallocated and readied for a moon shot as early as August 1958. At the same time, STL engineers Dergarabedian, Dolph Thiel, and Al Donovan modified the mission from landing a package on the moon, which depended on unrealistic short-term advances in guidance technology, to an easier goal: placing a TV camera and other instruments into lunar orbit. In March, the newly formed ARPA awarded the first two lunar probe contracts to the Army Ballistic Missile Agency and to the Air Force Ballistic Missile Division. In the race to be first, BMD in turn chose STL to prepare a lunar probe, known as Able 1, as soon as possible.[14]

The Able 1 payload consisted of a laminated plastic shell containing five types of data-gathering instruments: an accelerometer, a narrow-band TV system, a micro-meteorite impact counter, a magnetometer, and temperature-variable resistors. In addition to assembling the launch vehicle and building the payload, STL also engineered the ground station network to track the vehicle in flight. The network consisted of a main tracking station in Hawaii where STL erected a sixty-foot parabolic antenna surrounded by four helical array antennas. To capture the TV broadcasts from the moon, STL and the Air Force arranged to use the recently built radio telescope at Jodrell Bank in the United Kingdom. The telescope included a two-hundred-foot antenna dish, which STL supplemented with special equipment and instruments. STL also borrowed or hastily built three other stations, at Cape Canaveral, on Millstone Hill in New Hampshire, and in Singapore, as well as a command center at its headquarters in Los Angeles.[15]

On August 17, 1958, the first lunar probe, STL's Able 1, soared off the launch pad at Cape Canaveral. The dignitaries in attendance, including Schriever and Roy Johnson, head of ARPA, and the STL representatives cheered and applauded the lift-off, which occurred without incident. Then, seventy-seven seconds into the flight, as the probe climbed past fifty thousand feet, a turbopump in the Thor engine failed, and the vehicle exploded. The mood of those present abruptly darkened. According to one eyewitness, Thiel put his head in his hands and wept.[16]

The next launch was scheduled for two months later. By then NASA had been established and the fledgling agency assumed nominal direction of the lunar probe program, now called Pioneer. On October 11, 1958, at 3:42 in the morning, Pioneer 1—the first launch in NASA history—lifted off for the moon. This time, all three stages fired according to plan, but the second stage veered off at a skewed angle and prevented the rocket from reaching full escape velocity. Although the mission failed in its objective to place an object in orbit around the moon, the eighty-four-pound payload nonetheless established a temporary record. It climbed to an altitude of nearly eighty thousand miles, well beyond the previous record of about twenty-five hundred miles achieved by a Vanguard satellite. Forty-three hours after liftoff, Pioneer 1 plunged to its destruction in the atmosphere above Papua New Guinea.[17]

STL's work on the reentry test and lunar probe programs was exhilarating, the failures notwithstanding. Employees worked tirelessly for long hours, and they were proud of the responsibility to advance America's capabilities in space. Outside the company, STL's aspirations to play a larger role in developing space proved controversial. Representatives of Douglas Aircraft and other aerospace contractors openly criticized the Air Force and STL for apparently violating the agreement that had placed R-W in the SETD role on the missile programs. These criticisms contributed to growing pressure on the leaders of R-W and TP to rethink the terms of their relationship.

BEYOND THE BRAIN FACTORY

The growth and aspirations of R-W's General Electronics Group and R-W's subsidiary, Pacific Semiconductors, Inc., provided another source of pressure on the leaders of R-W and TP. By 1958, the electronics group included four divisions (Computer, Control Systems, Communications, and Electronic Instrumentation), as well as separate laboratories for electronics and aeronautical research, and it believed itself poised on the threshold of rapid expansion. Key executives at PSI voiced similar optimism about their future in semiconductors.

Indeed, the growth rates of the General Electronics Group and PSI paled only in comparison to the mushrooming of the GMRD (see Table 8-1). At the the the end of 1957, the General Electronics Group accounted for about a quarter of R-W's total sales and more than a third of its employees. By the middle of 1958, the group included more than 350 technical and scientific personnel working on twenty-five prime contracts and more than a dozen significant subcontracts, with a total order backlog of $23.7 million.[18]

The performance of the General Electronics Group reflected steady progress in every division dating back to the organization of the company. Early in 1955, after barely a year in business, R-W boasted that a third of its dozen contracts involved "operations research, automation, and data processing" for nonmilitary customers. Its military contracts, moreover, included not only the work on the ballistic missile program, but also research and development contracts for aircraft fire-control systems and an airborne computer. Later in the year, when the U.S. government funded development of the secret U-2 reconnaissance aircraft, it chose R-W's General Electronics Group to produce advanced equipment for surveillance and electronic countermeasures.[19]

The company's quick start made it clear to Wooldridge, Ramo, and other senior staff that they would soon need to raise more capital to fund its expansion. By the end of 1954, the company had outgrown not only its new headquarters on Bellanca Avenue, but also the former church-school space in Inglewood that it cohabited with the Air Force. It sprawled into several office buildings on Arbor Vitae Street, around the corner from the Bellanca headquarters, and started construction of two new buildings using money borrowed from or through Thompson Products. These measures were mere palliatives. Less than a year later, R-W's plans included three more new buildings on Arbor Vitae Street, a flight-test facility on the grounds of Los Angeles International Airport, a forty-one-acre site nearby at the corner of El Segundo and Aviation boulevards that would house an R&D facility, and a one hundred forty thousand square-foot manufacturing plant in Denver capable of employing fifteen hundred people. (The Denver site was chosen in accordance with a DOD directive to disperse defense production facilities; the government worried that too much of its most advanced defense projects were situated within a few miles of each other in Los Angeles.)[20]

R-W's voracious appetite for capital shaped its future in ways that its founders probably failed to appreciate at the outset. In particular, once R-W began to grow, Wooldridge and Ramo had little choice but to involve TP in the quest for more money.

TABLE 8 - 1

THE GROWTH OF RAMO-WOOLDRIDGE, 1953–1958

YEAR	SALES	NET INCOME	TOTAL EMPLOYMENT	BALLISTIC MISSILE EMPLOYMENT
1953	$72,270	($1,132)	18	NA
1954	$2,217,454	$238,102	281	170
1955	$9,837,097	$812,892	1,156	760
1956	$28,945,405	$2,144,906	2,657	1,557
1957	$43,215,406	$2,077,129	3,269	1,961
1958*	$26,524,885	$996,558	NA	NA

SOURCE: Thompson Products, Inc., *Notice of Special Meeting of Shareholders Including Proxy Statement*, September 30, 1958, p. 5; U.S. Air Force, *Survey of Management of the Ballistic Missile Program*, 14 January–21 February 1958, p. 50.

*Totals for first six months.

In the process the two companies worked out a deal that all but guaranteed an eventual merger. In June 1955, TP agreed to provide R-W with a line of credit of up to $20 million. In exchange, TP received $4 million in a new issue of cumulative preference stock in R-W, as well as options and first refusal rights to acquire up to 70 percent of R-W's Class B common stock during stated periods between 1964 and 1966. This transaction meant, in other words, that by 1966 TP would own 84 percent of all of R-W's common stock.[21]

R-W required most of its new space for missile work for the Air Force, but it allocated a significant fraction to its mushrooming business in general electronics. Most of this work involved R&D contracts, but the company's avowed intent from the beginning was to move into production at the earliest possible time. The Denver facility, for example, was built to manufacture electronic instruments and equipment, including computers, for both military and commercial markets. The plant sat on a 640-acre site, and it was designed "in such a way as to facilitate rapid and economical expansion to several times" its original size.[22]

By 1958, the biggest unit in the General Electronics Group was the Control Systems Division. Although R-W failed to win an expected second-source contract to build fire-control systems—a situation that Wooldridge attributed to the Air Force's desire to keep the company focused on the ballistic missile program—the Control Systems Division grew rapidly by making electronic reconnaissance and countermeasures systems for use in aircraft, missiles, and (eventually) spacecraft. The reconnaissance systems were capable of covering and recording information from the entire radio-frequency spectrum from thirty to forty thousand megahertz and could operate unattended for up to 9.5 hours. The division also developed related technologies in signal scanning and direction finding, and it worked with R-W's Communications Division on techniques to ensure secure communications. Hardware included equipment to jam or confuse enemy radars. Devices designed to be carried aboard the Quail and Goose missiles, for example, made these small inexpensive projectiles appear to enemy radar as B-47 or B-52 bombers. The Control Systems Division also manufactured infrared equipment for such applications as aerial mapping, air traffic collision warning, and antiaircraft fire control.[23]

R-W's Communications Division worked on long-range air-to-ground communications and navigation systems. Details of most of these projects remain classified, but the division designed and built lightweight and compact systems for use in advanced aircraft and satellites. Because customers placed a premium on secure communications, R-W's systems made use of coded information, which entailed state-of-the-art work in data compression, encryption, and analysis. This work was the foundation of many subsequent "black" (classified) programs, as well as of projects involving communications between the earth and objects in space.[24]

The most visible projects of the General Electronics Group involved electronic instrumentation and computers. R-W established its Electronics Instrumentation Division in the summer of 1955, with George W. Fenimore as general manager. A graduate of Harvard Law School, Fenimore was an officer in the Air Force Reserve, and his management experience included stints at Ford, Hughes Aircraft, and Packard-Bell.

The new division sought to ensure that other R-W units would have advanced test equipment when they needed it. In the missile business, for example, development moved so quickly at the frontiers of knowledge that adequate testing was a constant problem. Early on, R-W began to fabricate its own specialized test equipment and soon realized that such tools would be valuable to other companies doing advanced research and development in aeronautics and electronics. In 1957, R-W moved manufacturing of test equipment from Los Angeles to Denver and projected sales of $2 million to $3 million in 1958. By then, the division was renamed the Electronic Instrumentation Company (EIC), a designation chosen to emphasize its separateness from R-W and hence its freedom to manufacture hardware.

EIC carried out research and development of many types of advanced electronic equipment that could be used either for testing or as components of other products such as computers. For example, it worked on transistorized power supplies and converters for airborne computers. It also built such specialized products as microwave test equipment, automatic and manual transistor test sets, transistorized telemetry subcarrier oscillators, telemetry signal generators and calibrators, variable function generators for analog computers and aircraft simulators, nuclear instrumentation, neutron detectors, control-rod position indicators for nuclear reactors, and guided missile test equipment. These products were fabricated as unique copies or in small batches at the Denver facility.[25]

R-W's Computer Systems Division designed, manufactured, and marketed computers for both military and commercial markets. The R-W 30, for example, an airborne computer developed under a subcontract to Westinghouse for the Army's LaCrosse tactical missile, was a fully transistorized digital computer capable of performing "essentially all of the computing and control tasks that arise in the control of weapons, bombing and navigation of interceptor or bomber aircraft." At 150 pounds, the R-W 30 fit snugly into a space measuring 3.5 cubic feet, yet it performed many calculations as quickly as the UNIVAC 1103 toiling in R-W's computing center. (That machine weighed nearly twenty tons and filled twenty-three hundred feet of cabinet space.) R-W applied similar technology to data processing equipment that it designed and built as a subcontractor to American Bosch Arma, which developed the guidance system for the Titan missile. This was the only time that the Air Force approved an R-W bid to make hardware for its missiles. Another related product was the R-W 3101 Telemetry Data Converter, which processed huge volumes of telemetry data from missiles and spacecraft.[26]

By 1957, R-W's early efforts to promote computer use in commercial markets were beginning to pay off. At the start, Wooldridge and Ramo had recognized that the company had little chance of competing head-on with IBM or Remington Rand in general-purpose computers. Instead, they targeted specialized uses where they hoped to find profitable niches. R-W's alliance with TP provided initial opportunities to develop computers for industrial automation. Applications included production scheduling, inventory control, and enhancing the capabilities of machine tools. The company also attempted to publicize uses of computers in industry in various ways. In 1957, for example, R-W's Eugene Grabbe, a Yale Ph.D. in physics, edited a textbook entitled *Automation in Industry* that was based on public and university lectures given by himself, Ramo, Wooldridge, and other R-W employees.[27]

R-W personnel also ranged farther afield in pursuit of opportunities. Soon after his arrival, Bill Hebenstreit, the general manager of the Computer Systems Division, commissioned study teams of R-W personnel and university-based consultants to investigate such areas as the handling of airline reservations, the monitoring of automobile traffic, and the processing of transactions in a bank. In 1956, for example, the company went public with news that it had carried out "a highly successful study" with Bankers Trust Company in New York. The study, whose results were not detailed, nonetheless apparently "proved that scientists can work in such areas of business and improve existing techniques." In November 1956, the Computer Systems Division accelerated this investigative work and established a new unit, the Industrial Control Systems Section. Led by Montgomery Phister, a Ph.D. from the University of Cambridge, the section focused on continuous process industries such as chemicals, petroleum, plastic, food, drugs, and paper.[28]

In July 1957, R-W was ready to introduce the R-W 300 Digital Control Computer, the first computer designed specifically for process control applications. The computer was one of the first completely solid-state computers ever built, and it featured a 7,936-word memory. It weighed about four hundred pounds and fit in a cabinet roughly the size of a desk. Company literature proclaimed that the machine could add a thousand numbers or carry out 350 multiplications per second. R-W conceived of the computer not as a stand-alone piece of hardware, but as the nerve center of a system that also included engineering studies, software, wiring, and monitoring and control devices, as well as installation and maintenance services. This conception positioned the company to capture not only income from the price of the computer—estimated at just $100,000—but as much as $250,000 from the entire system.[29]

To promote the R-W 300, the company joined with TP to establish the Thompson Ramo Wooldridge Products Company (TRWP) late in 1957. Headed by Joseph F. Manildi, a versatile manager whose background included graduate work at Harvard Business School, a Ph.D. in electrical engineering from Caltech, and more than a decade as a professor of engineering at the University of California at Berkeley, TRWP arranged its first installation at a Texaco petroleum refinery in Port Arthur, Texas. The terms of this deal reflected Texaco's power as a buyer, as well as R-W's predicament as a supplier of a wholly new service. Texaco agreed to pay $195,000 for the system, but only after a one-year trial period. In discussing this arrangement with R-W's board of directors, Wooldridge asserted that the risk involved "was well worth taking in the interest of promoting future sales of computers," and the Texaco deal went forward. During 1958, R-W personnel arranged trial demonstrations with other customers (including the military), worked the trade-show circuit, and cultivated opportunities wherever they could find them, especially in the continuous process industries. These demonstrations generally proved successful, although orders only trickled in.[30]

R-W's officers and directors also paid close attention to Pacific Semiconductors, Inc., a company with prospects both exhilarating and troubling. Exhilarating was the fact that PSI looked forward to tremendous growth opportunities as semiconductors began to supplant vacuum tubes and other clumsy components in electrical and electronic devices. The growth curve for PSI's principal market—the U.S. electronics industry, broadly defined—climbed steeply: between 1954 and 1960, total industry revenues were projected to double from about $8 billion to between $15 billion and $20 billion. PSI initially targeted a small piece of this huge market, and its first products were designed for specific and advanced military applications. In 1956, for example, the Army Signal Supply Agency purchased samples of a silicon diffused-junction, high-speed computer diode. Later on, PSI began to develop products with broader uses, such as voltage-variable capacitors (sold under the trade name Varicap) and very-high-voltage rectifiers used in commercial computers and television equipment.

The troubling aspect of PSI was its enormous appetite for capital (see Table 8-2). Unlike most of R-W's businesses, which started from research and development contracts funded by customers, semiconductor manufacture required significant investment capital. Money was needed not only to develop products, but also to buy the equipment to make the products. From the very beginning, PSI burned capital rapidly, and it returned periodically to R-W and TP for more money. The initial installment of $3 million, for example, was exhausted by 1956. PSI issued a new class of preferred stock to raise another $2.5 million. The company ran through this amount quickly and arranged additional short- and long-term borrowings from R-W and TP, including another $3.3 million in 1957. During its first four years of existence, PSI achieved total sales of $3.6 million, but recorded cumulative losses of more than $5 million. In 1958, however, PSI expected to turn a small profit on the basis of the Varicap and other new products. The company also saw a promising new opportunity to make advanced semiconductors to support an inertial guidance system for a new Air Force missile—if the government would permit and approve the bid.[31]

It was inevitable that the General Electronics Group and PSI, which manufactured hardware, would find themselves in tension with hardware restrictions placed on STL. The fate of the Control Systems Division's bid on the Air Force satellite system,

TABLE 8 - 2
THE GROWTH OF PACIFIC SEMICONDUCTORS, 1954–1958

Year	Sales	Net Income
1954	NA	($381,549)
1955	$30,803	($1,335,454)
1956	$396,867	($1,630,729)
1957	$1,585,142	($1,412,669)
1958*	$1,608,400	($322,800)

SOURCE: Thompson Products, Inc., *Notice of Special Meeting of Shareholders Including Proxy Statement,* September 30, 1958, p. 5.

*Totals for first six months.

Project WS-117L, proved a sign of things to come. In the summer of 1958, internal frictions at R-W contributed to the loss of several key personnel. Jim Fletcher and Frank Lehan, whose most recent assignments had involved engineering of the ground station network for the lunar probe programs, departed STL to establish their own electronics company. Among their reasons for going, recalls Lehan, was rivalry between the Control Systems and Communications Systems Divisions over the development of deep-space communications networks as well as continuing frustrations with the hardware ban on STL.[32]

The loss of Fletcher and Lehan was symptomatic of a growing debate inside R-W over priorities. On the one hand, STL was performing increasingly diverse tasks for the Air Force. On the other, Wooldridge and Ramo were publicly insisting that R-W was more than merely an R&D "brain factory" or an analytical "paper factory." Rather it was "an electronics corporation" that was "production-minded." As Ramo put it in the *Time* cover story, "You can't make money and you can't stay in business without production." But what role, then, should STL play inside R-W? Should it continue to accept the restrictions? Should it attempt to renegotiate them? Or should it be divested, leaving the other divisions free to compete for hardware contracts?[33]

As 1958 wore on, these questions grew increasingly pointed. Some top employees—reinforced by officers at TP—argued that because R-W had fulfilled its contract to provide the SETD role for the Atlas, Titan, and Thor missiles, then the original restrictions should no longer apply. The company should be allowed to revert to its original strategy and to grow as a producer of electronic systems for defense and commercial customers. Should the government not permit STL to manufacture, the argument ran, then it should be divested. Other officers warned of the risks of continued reliance on a few major Air Force contracts, pointing out that should one of these programs come to an end or a key contract be cancelled, the effect could prove devastating. Many recognized that the General Electronics Group and PSI would require management attention and capital investment and believed that R-W's work for the Air Force and attendant controversies represented time-consuming diversions.

Meanwhile, R-W faced a barrage of criticism from within the aerospace industry from competitors who alleged that the company enjoyed unfair advantages based on its intimate knowledge of the Air Force's future plans, as well as from the SETD role, which allowed it to scrutinize contractors' personnel, capabilities, and technologies. Others worried that STL was increasingly performing the functions of a captive arsenal for the Air Force; their concern was that the Air Force would entrust more and more work to its internal partner and contract less and less on the outside.

The establishment of STL as an autonomous division in 1957 did little to allay these fears, and R-W was obliged to consider more drastic measures. In July 1958, it announced plans to relocate its headquarters organization and the General Electronics Group to a new ninety-acre site in Canoga Park, about an hour north of the El Segundo and Arbor Vitae complexes that would continue as headquarters for STL. The Canoga Park facility was designed as a campus-style complex capable of housing about two thousand employees. The principal reason for the move was to underscore the independence of STL from the rest of R-W by establishing geographical distance between the two. At the same time, the move also emphasized the growth of the General Electronics Group and top management's sense of where its future really lay.[34]

Yet controversy continued to swirl within, among, and around R-W, STL, and TP, especially as the next-generation ICBM program appeared on the horizon.

The Second-Generation ICBM

Before 1957, the Atlas, Thor, and Titan programs occupied most but not all of the combined attention of R-W and the Air Force. As early as 1955, both parties were also thinking about the next generation of ballistic missiles and pursuing studies of solid-fuel rocket motors. A series of independent technical breakthroughs that year demonstrated the feasibility of solid-fuel motors powerful enough to propel a large missile. If the technology could be developed, these rockets had important advantages over their liquid-fueled counterparts: they would be simpler to manufacture, deploy, operate, and maintain in readiness. Late in the year, a team led by USAF Col. Edward N. Hall and including R-W's Dolph Thiel, Herbert Lawrence, and Barnet "Barney" Adelman outlined a long-term R&D plan for development of a solid-fuel IRBM. In February 1956, the ARDC approved the plan, but with a twist. Concerned that work on solid-fuel propulsion might detract from the higher priority Atlas, Titan, and Thor programs, the ARDC turned over responsibility for developing the new missile to another Air Force organization, the Wright Air Development Command. Schriever, Hall, and the R-W representatives were bitterly disappointed.[35]

During the next year and a half, work on the solid-fuel missile proceeded at a deliberate pace. By the middle of 1957, however, the potential advantages of solid-fuel rockets appeared increasingly attractive. The Air Force, for example, was pushing for a small, mobile IRBM for deployment in Europe, specifications best met with solid-fuel rockets. At the same time, the Air Force grew increasingly concerned about the Navy's lead in solid-fuel propulsion based on its high-priority and high-profile Polaris program. Key figures in the Department of Defense were lobbying the Air Force to abandon its work on solid-fuel propulsion and adapt Polaris technology to land-based use.

Concurrent with these events came several high-level reviews of U.S. defense policy, which concluded that the nation was vulnerable to a surprise attack and needed a major overhaul of its defense strategy. In particular, these reviews advanced the modern theory of deterrence: in a world of proliferating thermonuclear weapons that could fall anywhere on the planet within thirty minutes, the only safe course for the United States was to develop clear capabilities for a first strike as well as for massive retaliation. These capabilities would be based on deploying a large number of ICBMs that could be dispersed around the country and launched quickly from hardened silos that could survive a nuclear attack. Once again, these specifications appeared most likely to be met by solid-fuel rockets.[36]

Against this backdrop, Ramo suggested to Schriever that he commission a blue-ribbon task force to examine advanced weapons systems. Schriever duly appointed Caltech professor Robert Bacher to direct the review. In July 1957, R-W hosted several meetings of the Bacher panel, which endorsed the new concept of deterrence and stressed the immediate need to construct a missile force capable of surviving a surprise attack. This survivability, in turn, might depend on a small, simple, and reliable missile, possibly one compatible with mobile or semimobile bases. Such a missile, the panel reasoned, would probably be propelled by solid-fuel motors. The Bacher panel urged the Air Force either to accelerate its own solid-fuel program or to base a new missile on technology from the Polaris program.[37]

In August 1957, Schriever placed Col. Hall in charge of a special working group to design a new solid-fuel missile. The urgency of the program heightened after *Sputnik* removed all doubts about Soviet launch capabilities. By the end of the year, Hall was ready with a proposal for a new three-stage missile, code-named Weapon System Q. The new missile could be delivered in both IRBM and ICBM versions. It also represented a distinct departure from the Atlas, Thor, and Titan family: the new missile was specifically designed for low-cost, high-rate production; slow obsolescence; and quick reaction combined with maximum survivability in the face of a nuclear attack. Under these conditions, the advantages of solid-fuel propulsion proved decisive: the missiles were relatively small, relatively economical to manufacture in volume, and relatively simple in concept and operation.[38]

The Air Force high command approved Weapon System Q for accelerated development under Schriever's BMD in February 1958. By then, the missile's most prominent feature—its ability to launch within minutes of a decision—earned it the more familiar nickname, Minuteman. During the next several months, R-W and the BMD determined specifications, carried out background research studies, and evaluated contractors. The Minuteman was to have an inertial guidance system built by the Autonetics Division of North American Aviation, a nose cone by Avco, and rocket motors from Thiokol Chemical (first stage), and Aerojet (second and third stages), with Hercules Powder Company as a joint contractor on the third stage. In October, the Air Force awarded the final assembly and testing contract to Boeing. As with the earlier Air Force ballistic missiles, R-W provided the systems engineering and technical direction.[39]

The Minuteman program bristled with formidable technical challenges. It stretched the limits of solid-fuel propulsion technology. The first-stage motor, for example, required twenty-two tons of fuel. To ensure uniformity, this fuel had to be poured into the engine casing in a single batch. As of 1958, however, a single pouring of five hundred pounds was considered extraordinarily difficult. Major breakthroughs were necessary in solid-fuel chemistry and handling, the design of motor cases, ignition and thrust systems, and movable nozzles. The guidance and control systems also relied on technologies beyond the state of the art. The smaller lifting power of solid-fuel motors, for example, required major size and weight reductions in on-board computers. At the same time, these computers were expected to handle increased demands and to operate reliably under extremely hostile conditions.[40]

The larger system in which the Minuteman would operate also posed serious technical challenges. The ground support system (which also drew heavily on advanced computing technology) had to be designed from scratch. Hardened silos had to be developed, and many complicated problems associated with silo-based launching had to be solved.[41]

During 1958, Rube Mettler and Bob Bennett directed R-W's efforts to attack these challenges, working closely with Col. Hall. The relationship proved to be a constant source of friction and irritation. Part of the problem was an expanded SETD role for STL, which Louis Dunn described as including "experimental effort on certain supporting research and development programs, more direct participation in the design, assembly, and test of the missile system, and more detailed technical direction of the subsystem developments." To Hall, STL's calls for additional research represented unwarranted delay, while its elaborate systems planning seemed excessively complicated. In August 1958, when a panel of the President's Scientific Advisory Committee urged a cautious approach to the Minuteman while calling for more basic research on solid fuels, Hall was outraged. At about the same time, STL issued a technical report that agreed on the need for still more research. This only worsened the problem. During the fall, Hall's darkening mood prompted Schriever to remove him from the program; he was replaced by Col. Otto Glasser, a veteran leader of the Atlas program and an officer "noted for his technical, managerial, and interpersonal skills."[42]

The tension between R-W and the Air Force on the Minuteman was also structural. In 1954 and 1955, when the Atlas program had accelerated, the Air Force and major airframe contractors lacked expertise that only R-W (or one or two similar organizations) could supply. By 1958, however, matters had changed. The Air Force itself possessed a higher level of technical capability, and major contractors such as Glenn L. Martin, Douglas, and Boeing also had significantly upgraded their expertise in electronics and other advanced technologies. Indeed, Hall and other USAF officers joined with representatives of other aerospace contractors to question whether the Air Force still needed a separate organization like R-W to serve as SETD contractor.[43]

Within R-W itself, as well as within TP, concerns about STL's relationship to the Air Force also mounted. Several units of the General Electronics Group, for example, wanted to bid on subcontracts for the Minuteman. Although in 1958 the program was still in the research phase, it was apparent that many hundreds, perhaps thousands, of missiles would eventually be deployed. Such numbers contrasted sharply with the handfuls of Atlas, Thor, and Titan missiles scheduled for production. The likely scale of the Minuteman program also attracted units of TP, which sought volume opportunities in missiles to offset the likely decline of manned bomber production.

THE VIEW FROM THE TEPEE

"Business is like riding a bicycle," Fred Crawford observed in 1955. "You keep moving, or you fall down." The story of TP during the mid-1950s aptly illustrates Crawford's belief. The company continued evolving beyond its traditional business as a supplier of a few critical components for the automotive and aircraft industries in a restless search for new opportunities. It was fast becoming a diverse, decentralized, and dispersed corporation. It upgraded existing products, introduced new ones, and diversified into altogether new businesses such as consumer electronics, closed-circuit TV systems, and parts and components for the nuclear power industry. By 1958, TP had thirteen separate operating divisions (some of which included more than one distinct business), each working hard to grow fast (see Exhibit 8-1).[44]

Dave Wright's Company

Although Crawford remained a highly visible and active figure inside the company as well as outside, Dave Wright played an increasingly prominent role in presiding over TP's growth and change. He remained faithful to TP's core values and worked hard to communicate its principles and results to employees. As a speaker, he was far less entertaining than Crawford, but he was no less effective. As one employee put it in the mid-1950s, "I haven't heard a good story since [Crawford stepped down as president], but I sure know what's going on in this company."[45]

In October 1953, a few weeks after investing in the fledgling R-W, Wright described TP as "going through a rapid evolution from parts maker to the automotive and aircraft industries to the role of engineering specialist to the broad industries of the future." In practical terms, the company vigorously pursued the growth strategy laid out at its Vermont planning conference in 1953. Critical to the company's success, believed Wright, was its decentralized organization supported by strong central staff functions. TP's operating divisions remained responsible for meeting growth and profitability objectives, improving operations, renewing product lines, and developing new products. TP added new divisions when it became feasible for the engineering, production, and sales of a product line to be grouped under a single operating team. At the center, TP's corporate staff defined goals and objectives, developed common policies, and provided support in functional areas, including assistance with planning and research and development. The company as a whole also considered acquisitions as a way to diversify its business.[46]

Planning was a particularly important function. Top corporate management reviewed division plans each year prior to the annual summer conference at Crawford's Vermont farm. Beyond that, division managers were required to update their forecasts every quarter. As Wright explained to a group of analysts in 1957: "We look three years ahead. Actually, we plan farther ahead than that for some other purposes, but for routine forecasting we think that three years is as long as we can look ahead with any reasonable degree of accuracy. And, because conditions keep changing, we revise these forecasts [four] times per year." In the automotive businesses, for example, TP personnel talked to the principal automakers, economists, and other industry experts. Then, they applied "a little of our own judgement" to estimate the number of cars to be manufactured during the next three years and how many cars would be on the road. This information was then disseminated to the divisions, which used it to target market share and growth opportunities. "By and large," Wright noted, "as the years go by we seem to get better at this business of forecasting." On another occasion, however, he noted that "I'll never be satisfied until the forecasts can become the company's quarterly report."[47]

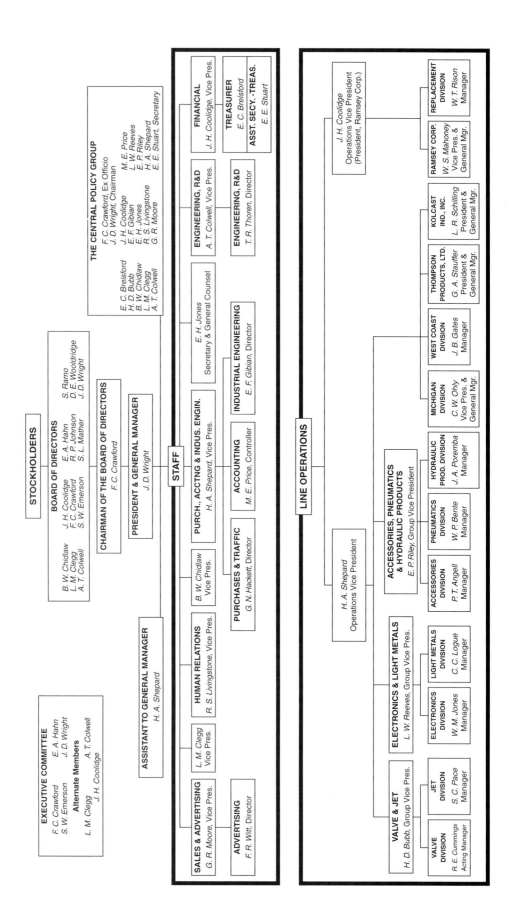

Another important central staff function was R&D, especially in areas and technologies such as advanced materials that were beyond the means of any single division to pursue. Early in 1955, TP announced plans for a new $5 million staff research center to be built on the grounds of the Tapco plant. Designed to be opened in stages between 1955 and 1958, the campus-like center was planned eventually to employ about three hundred engineers in four separate laboratories plus an administration building. TP broke ground for the first two labs—Automotive Development and Chemical and Metallurgy—in November 1955. The company planned to add separate labs for industrial engineering and new devices within several years.[48]

The Broad Industries of the Future

The industries of the future that Wright had in mind in October 1953 were nuclear energy and electronics. In both instances, TP quickly encountered obstacles. Entry into nuclear energy proved especially frustrating. In the summer of 1953, the U.S. Atomic Energy Commission had selected TP to operate a planned nuclear weapons processing facility in Spoon River, Illinois. Within weeks of finalizing the contract, however, the AEC abruptly canceled the facility as an economy measure. Because the termination came so swiftly, it meant "no more than minor inconveniences" to a handful of TP personnel assigned to the project. Nonetheless, it disappointed Wright. Subsequently, he admitted that nuclear energy was "not a major business for us, but it is a source of power, and we're in the power business, and we have to be alert to it."[49]

The passage of the Atomic Energy Act of 1954, which reduced government control over the development of nuclear power plants, provided another window of opportunity. Although TP remained reluctant to pour investment capital into nuclear power, it formed a small R&D lab at Tapco under engineer Andrew Pomeroy to investigate ways to enter the business. Lab personnel pursued three strategies. First, they looked for opportunities to adapt existing Tapco products such as quick-disconnect couplers, heat exchangers, and special ground-handling equipment for use in nuclear power plants. Second, TP sought to obtain customer-funded R&D contracts that might eventually lead to production. In August 1955, TP won its first development contract, an assignment from Westinghouse, which was bidding to build nuclear reactors for the U.S. Navy. The contract called for TP to assemble and test control-rod drive mechanisms. These "complex, high precision electro-mechanical devices" helped regulate the rate of chain reactions occurring in a nuclear reactor—and hence its power output—by raising, lowering, or holding control rods at an appropriate height inside the reactor core. Third, to help develop the business, TP engaged an expert in the field: Harry L. Browne, whose background included engineering work on the Manhattan Project and a stint as an associate director of the AEC. In September 1955, Browne joined TP as a member of Pomeroy's staff, and he began to work his contacts in the industry.[50]

Late in 1956, TP caught the break it had been seeking when the Westinghouse contract moved from development to production. The Accessories Division took on the job of fabricating the control-rod mechanisms for a reactor that would power the

USS *Skate*, a nuclear submarine. The project entailed precision machining of "the finest, high-alloy stainless steels" to "very close tolerances." TP manufactured parts and components including the rotor tube, the drip cover assembly, motor tube assembly, rotor segment arm, thermal barrier, and lead screw connection nut and locknut. Surviving records do not reveal the dollar value of the *Skate* contract, which could not have been very large. The Accessories Division nonetheless expected that the work would lead to other projects for Westinghouse and the Navy's Skipjack class of submarines.[51]

TP fared only marginally better in its electronics ventures outside Ramo-Wooldridge. Bell Sound Systems, a subsidiary acquired at about the same time as TP helped fund the start-up of R-W, made little headway in its consumer electronics business, despite investments from TP, including a new factory in Columbus, Ohio, and redesign of its product line. The unit consumed a lot of cash in developing an early model of tape cartridge that was prone to jamming and other problems and in tooling up to offer stereophonic equipment and its components in furniture cabinets.

In 1957, Ken Bishop, president of Bell Sound, and his boss, Bill Jones, general manager of TP's Electronics Division, made a controversial decision to change the unit's product and distribution strategy. Bell Sound components previously were sold by specialized hi-fi dealers who obtained the equipment through independent sales reps. Bishop and Jones saw greater opportunity in offering complete stereo systems through broader distribution channels and general retail outlets. The unit segmented its offerings into three product lines: Pacemaker, for the economy budget; Bell, for the discriminating music lover; and Carillon, for the audiophile. It also attempted to market these products through department stores and the general retail trade. "That was a mistake," admits Jones. "The dealers were not knowledgeable. They were not enthusiastic about promoting our systems. We also alienated the old people with whom we had been dealing." With annual sales under $5 million in 1958 and intensifying rivalry from big companies like RCA and Magnavox, Bell Sound did not have much margin for error.[52]

During the spring of 1954, TP augmented its small commercial electronics business by acquiring Dage Electronics Corporation. Based in Beach Grove, Indiana, Dage assembled closed-circuit TV equipment from purchased parts and components. It envisioned "a thousand and one potential uses" for its systems: in dental work, surgical operations, viewing of hazardous test operations, security, and underwater salvage. Dage even targeted the consumer market: "Imagine the peace-of-mind it would give to mother if she had one in the kitchen trained on the kids at play in the yard."[53]

Late in 1954, supported by TP funds, Dage moved from its outmoded facility into a new plant in Michigan City, Indiana. There, some of the "thousand and one uses" of closed-circuit TV systems began to materialize. In 1955, Dage introduced a color TV camera, and the following year it received favorable publicity by installing the world's largest closed-circuit TV system in New York's Pennsylvania Station. It also developed TV equipment to support a heart catheterization procedure at the Cleveland Clinic. These and other novel uses proved to be successes of a modest order, however. Like Bell Sound, Dage suffered from small scale and the need for huge investments to build a national presence against much bigger and wealthier competitors. In 1958, the business was losing money on sales of less than $2 million.[54]

A Changing Mix

Although TP devoted much of its publicity during the 1950s to its newer industries and diversification efforts, its performance depended far more on its traditional businesses in parts and accessories for the aircraft, automotive, and automotive replacement markets. In 1953, the company posted sales of $326 million, a record year based primarily on production for the Korean War, when shipments to the aircraft industry accounted for more than 70 percent of total revenues. The next year, revenues tumbled by $50 million before building gradually to another peak in 1957 of $413 million. This generally strong performance obscured major trends under way in each of TP's main businesses. The mix of its revenues was changing in fundamental ways (see exhibits in the introduction to Part II).

Although the conclusion of the Korean War brought a decline in the production of military aircraft, TP continued to fare well in manufacturing products for the aircraft industry. The main reasons for TP's success were the U.S. government's decision to maintain and continuously renew a strong Air Force, the company's continuing ability to fabricate complex structures from hard-to-work metals and materials, and its resourcefulness in finding new products to make.

During the first few years following the Korean War, the U.S. military succeeded in maintaining a high level of orders for aircraft—nearly three times the level before the conflict—and the Air Force actually planned to expand from 118 wings to 137. The new aircraft were bigger, more powerful, more sophisticated, and much more expensive than their predecessors. And almost all new military aircraft, including the B-52 and the KC-135 tanker (from which derived the Boeing 707 commercial jetliner) relied on a new generation of turbojet engines such as Pratt & Whitney's J-57 and GE's J-79. These engines developed between two and three times the thrust of their predecessors.[55]

TP's Jet Division took on the challenge of supplying parts and components for the new turbojet engines under new leadership. In 1955, Stan Pace succeeded Harry Bubb as head of the division, and he proved well suited to the task. During World War II, Pace had flown thirty-nine combat missions as a bomber pilot until he was shot down by enemy fighters. He spent the last nine months of the war in German hospitals and prison camps. After the war, he remained in the service, rising through a series of logistical assignments in the Air Force, where he worked closely with Horace Shepard. In 1954, he retired from the service and Shepard entreated him to join TP.[56]

For TP's Jet Division, supplying components for the J-57 and other big engines of the era meant mastering how to make buckets, blades, and other parts from such intractable metals as titanium and conducting ongoing research into new materials such as niobium (via a joint venture with Du Pont). Titanium, for example, is an extremely tough material with twice the strength of aluminum, 40 percent of the weight of steel, and a melting point of 3,270 degrees Fahrenheit. Learning to forge alloys of titanium to the exact tolerances required by advanced turbojet engines was a major accomplishment.[57]

TP also expanded its ability to fabricate complex structures by acquiring, in October 1954, Cleveland-based Kolcast Industries for considerations worth about $1.2 million. The company was a growing rival in frozen mercury casting techniques with a particular focus on bigger castings than TP itself made. In 1956, TP built a new seventy-five-thousand-square-foot manufacturing plant for Kolcast near Minerva, Ohio, designed specifically to turn out blades and buckets for big engines.[58]

Other TP divisions benefited from federal spending on aircraft. In May 1954, the Accessories Division won an important contest to produce alternator drive units for the B-52 bomber, at the time the largest aircraft ever built. In addition to its eight turbojet engines, the bomber required an enormous amount of power to drive its huge landing flaps, swiveling gun turrets, air conditioning system, and sophisticated electronics. Most aircraft dealt with auxiliary power needs through separate hydraulic and electrical systems. TP engineers believed that a single "pneumatic-mechanical" system could generate enough electrical power to satisfy all auxiliary power requirements. The TP system relied on four alternator drives—essentially high-speed turbines functioning with advanced lubricants—that were driven by heated compressed air from the turbojet engines. Instead of electric cables or hydraulic lines, the bomber's "main accessory power 'bloodstream'" was compressed air flowing through stainless steel pipes at high temperature and pressure. The system possessed many advantages besides simplicity: it was also smaller and lighter than competing technologies.[59]

The company's winning bid resulted from five months of intensive work during late 1953 and early 1954. Each B-52 carried four alternator drive units, each of which developed more than two hundred horsepower. In combination, the four devices helped generate enough electrical power to service a town of twenty-five hundred inhabitants. TP's business in alternator drives grew so big so quickly that the company created a new Pneumatics Division to oversee the business. In addition, TP's Electronics Division manufactured controls for the alternator drive units.[60]

The rapid growth of the Accessories and Pneumatics Divisions in mid-1956 led TP to acquire a thousand-acre tract in Franklin County, Virginia (near Roanoke), as the site of a new R&D center. The center was designed to develop and test fuel and auxiliary power systems for aircraft, rockets, and missiles. The company expected to spend as much as $10 million over five years to erect a complex of fourteen buildings that would house about five hundred people.[61]

Although more than two-thirds of TP's revenues reflected sales of aircraft engine parts and components and aircraft accessories to the military, most of the company's traditional automotive businesses also showed healthy growth during the mid-1950s, as the company refreshed its product line, revamped its facilities, opened new plants, and consolidated old operations. The market for automobiles in the United States during the mid-1950s was full of uncertainties, bouncing from peak to valley in short cycles. Coming off a weak year, for example, automakers produced nearly 8 million vehicles in 1955; by 1958, however, volume had plunged by nearly 50 percent to just over 4.2 million units. Such violent swings of fortune were hard on suppliers. Their difficulties were compounded by the backward integration strategy of the biggest auto companies, which raised the percentage of parts and components they manufactured themselves. The result was increased pressure on prices, and suppliers were obliged continually to drive costs down. For TP, this meant heavy investments to upgrade its factories and operations. As Wright put it, "our objective is to have facilities so efficient that the car companies just can't afford to take the business away from us."[62]

Fortunately, many of TP's newer products such as U-Flex piston rings, sodium-cooled valves for heavy-duty trucks, valve rotation devices, cast-aluminum pistons, and power-steering pumps proved to be hits. The company's most important new product, however, was the ball-joint suspension system developed jointly with Ford. Introduced on the Lincoln Continental in 1952, the ball-joint suspension quickly caught on. In December 1953, a Lincoln commercial on "The Ed Sullivan Show" credited the new system for the vehicle's improved handling and exceptionally smooth ride. The next year, the ball-joint suspension became a standard item on all Ford cars, and it soon spread to other car manufacturers. By early 1954, the plant at Fruitport, Michigan, where the ball joints were made, was operating three shifts, seven days a week, producing one hundred twenty thousand pairs a month, and still falling behind demand.[63]

In the mid-1950s, TP set new records for capital expenditure levels every year. In 1954, for example, the company allocated $6 million to build a new, state-of-the-art forging plant in Warren, Michigan (near Detroit), to house all of its chassis parts operations. After the 390,000-square-foot plant opened in January 1956, TP closed the Fruitport ball-joint plant and the old Conant Road facility that had been acquired by C. E. Thompson in 1916 and saved through Crawford's intervention in the following decade. The Michigan Division retained R&D activities in Detroit, where it focused on such promising new products as truck retarders (an auxiliary braking system) and suspension systems, power-steering cylinders, and permanently lubricated linkages.[64]

In the valve business, TP's traditional formula of investing to upgrade operations and ongoing research into new materials continued to pay dividends. In June 1955, TP allocated $5.4 million to acquire, expand, and upgrade a 370,000-square-foot manufacturing plant on E. 185th Street in Cleveland. The plant, built by GE during World War II, had later served the White Motor Company. Configured to accommodate all of TP's valve-manufacturing operations, the E. 185th Street plant began production in November 1955. TP also invested heavily to automate the plant. By the spring of 1957, when the new system was fully installed, a forging required no handling between the time it entered the production line and its shipment to a customer. The entire operation took about an hour, as compared to seven days in a conventional process. TP, its customers, and its rivals also continued to develop new, higher-performing materials. In 1956, for example, TP worked with Armco Steel to develop MS-201, a new steel alloy "vastly superior to any other valve material produced."[65]

During the mid-1950s, TP's capital spending extended to other lines of business. In 1954, for example, the company built a new plant for Ramsey in St. Louis, at a cost of more than $1 million. It even augmented the old Jadson plant in Bell, California, where TP made huge valves for marine diesel and railroad engines, as well as miscellaneous structural parts for aircraft. In July 1955, TP acquired Karl-Douglas Associates, Inc., and its subsidiary Tiger Tools in a stock transaction worth about $250,000. Based in Hawthorne, California, the operations of Karl-Douglas and Tiger Tools were consolidated into the Bell plant.[66]

Of TP's traditional businesses, only the automotive replacement business continued to disappoint during the mid-1950s. It could not escape the problem that had plagued it since shortly after World War II: little or no growth. In addition, under TP's decentralized, multidivisional organization, the Replacement Division no longer priced its goods at standard cost but on the basis of transfer prices negotiated with the manufacturing divisions. The result was a profit squeeze. The division's doldrums led TP's top management to cease viewing the replacement business as a growth area, and there was even talk of selling it.[67]

In December 1953, Wright placed the Replacement Division in the capable hands of Whit Rison, a young, energetic former Air Force officer, and a protégé of Horace Shepard. Rison immediately took bold steps to cut costs. First, he moved the offices of Toledo Steel Products from Toledo to Cleveland. Although Rison kept the Toledo brand name alive, the move suggested the eventual consolidation into a single replacement line. Rison also pursued other measures to improve the business. He sought, for example, to expand TP's product offerings in the replacement market, adding items such as "Sky-Ride" shock absorbers, some valve train parts, and other products not manufactured by TP. He also made plans to replace the labyrinthine parts warehouse in Cleveland—"a half a million square feet on 23 different levels," recalled Rison's colleague, George Poe—with a modern one-story distribution center south of Cleveland. The Replacement Division gradually returned to profitability, and in March 1957, Rison was promoted to vice president of TP. Tragically, he did not have long to enjoy his success. Eight months later, Rison's boat capsized and he drowned while on a fishing and hunting vacation in Canada. Carl Kahlert, a career manager with Toledo Steel Products, succeeded him as head of TP's Replacement Division.[68]

THE URGE TO MERGE

A merger between TP and R-W became inevitable after the summer of 1955, when TP had provided the $20 million line of credit to R-W in return for options to acquire more than 80 percent of R-W's common stock by the mid-1960s. The merger date was rushed forward, however, under mounting pressures on both partners. For R-W, the pressures reflected the need for additional capital for its commercial businesses, as well as the desire to produce hardware for emerging Air Force space programs and the Minuteman ICBM. For TP, the pressures resulted from dramatic shifts in U.S. defense policy and Air Force funding during 1957.

Several factors converged to change the picture for the aircraft industry and for key suppliers such as TP. The most important reflected a new understanding of warfare based on the availability of ballistic missiles. DOD analysts believed that future wars would be fought with missiles and short in duration. There would be no time for industrial buildups such as had occurred during the world wars and the Korean conflict. As a result, the government saw no need to continue traditional industrial preparedness and procurement policies, which had spread orders across many manufacturers so that their facilities would be available on short notice in the event of war. The flight of *Sputnik* further emphasized the future of rocketry at the expense of conventional aircraft technology.[69]

At the same time, the success of the ICBM and other advanced weapon systems validated new approaches to procurement. In the case of aircraft, this meant that the Air Force would no longer select the airframe of one manufacturer, the engines of another, the electronics equipment of a third, the armament of a fourth, and attempt to tie them together. Rather, the government believed that it would be more efficient and effective to hand complete systems responsibility to a single prime contractor and allow it to define specifications for subsystems and components and hire its own subcontractors. This change in policy particularly disadvantaged TP, which had enjoyed the status of a prime contractor in making turbojet engine components.[70]

Changing policies coincided with a recession in the United States that became noticeable late in 1957. The resulting drop in federal revenues prompted both President Eisenhower and Congress to look for ways to cut the budget. Air Force officials made it clear that they were no longer interested in new aircraft (and turbojet engines) that were "just a little faster or a little more maneuverable or [would] fly just a little higher" than current models.[71]

By then, more than half of the Air Force's procurement budget was earmarked for missiles. This factor, combined with all the others, led to sudden and sharp cutbacks, stretch-outs and hold orders for new aircraft, as well as outright cancellation of some programs during the spring and summer of 1957. The Snark cruise missile, for example, was canceled after more than a decade of investment. The B-58 medium-range bomber was put on hold. Soon thereafter, several turbojet engine manufacturers such as Ford—a big TP customer—announced plans to abandon the business. TP delayed completion of its Minerva casting plant and was forced to shutter two of the Korean War-era turbojet engine component plants. Rumors abounded that all aircraft engine production would be consolidated into the Tapco plant and even that Westinghouse would acquire TP.[72]

TP attempted to offset the sudden decline of the turbojet engine business by promoting its capability to manufacture hardware for missiles. (The company also noted that the coming of commercial jetliners during the 1960s would partly compensate for the drop in military jet production; as of late 1957, U.S. aircraft manufacturers had orders for about six hundred commercial jets.) The launch of *Sputnik* increased the urgency for the company to reposition itself. In November, for example, at the same time that R-W recast GMRD as STL, TP took out full-page advertisements in several national magazines and prepared a brochure citing its interests and abilities in fabricating missile structures, propulsion, guidance and control systems, and ground support equipment. And in fact, the company had development or small-scale production contracts to make auxiliary power units (APUs), turbo pumps, precision forgings, and ground support equipment of various kinds, including retractable roof panels and some mobile launch equipment, for twelve of the forty-three publicly acknowledged missile programs. TP made APUs for the Terrier missile, and it was experimenting with such items as fuel systems, new liquid monopropellants, and electronic controls for various missile subsystems. In a speech to employees, Wright noted that he expected the missile business to be important to TP, but he added that "the money will be smaller than [in] the manned aircraft business."[73]

In March 1958, TP gathered its Jet, Accessories, Pneumatic, and West Coast Divisions, as well as the military parts of its electronics divisions in Cleveland into a new "Tapco Group," with Ed Riley as general manager. At the same time, TP established a new customer requirements group headed by retired Air Force general Benjamin Chidlaw and G. R. "Dick" Moore to assess market opportunities. The Tapco Group created its own engineering organization to develop new products for a new era. Among the planned projects were ground-handling installations and equipment, titanium cases for solid-fuel rocket motors, titanium pressure vessels for the Atlas fuel system, and rocket motor nozzles and nose cones of advanced design. Although it was well aware of the hardware restrictions on R-W, the Tapco Group planned to bid on several subcontracts for the Minuteman missile—intentions that caused friction both between TP and R-W, and between the two companies and other defense contractors.[74]

The U.S. recession in 1958 worsened TP's short-term problems by softening its sales to the automakers. In these circumstances, the prospect of merger with R-W loomed increasingly attractive. "It is apparent that we must seek new types of business if we are to stop our downward trend and resume the growth trend we have enjoyed in recent years," Wright explained to the board of directors, adding:

> There is an ever-increasing emphasis on missiles and electronics in the national defense budget, and Ramo-Wooldridge is strongly entrenched in both of these fields. Consequently their organization can make a very important contribution to Thompson by creating new products and opening up new markets, and it seems desirable to obtain the benefits of such a combination at an early date. With the assistance of the Ramo-Wooldridge organization, we believe that combined sales can be brought to an annual level of $500 million or more within a few years.[75]

Two additional factors influencing the timing of the merger reflected TP's view of its own future. The decline of its major line of business occurred just after the company had arranged financing for a much higher level of activity. In 1958, TP was flush with cash and looking for places to put it. The company was also eager to bring R-W's managers into the fold. TP concluded—"rightly or wrongly," said Wooldridge—that R-W possessed considerable management strength to help lead the combined organization into the future.[76]

During the spring and summer of 1958, the terms of the deal were hammered out. As approved by shareholders of both corporations on September 30, 1958, the merger agreement called for R-W to exchange all of its outstanding common stock for 260,376 shares of TP common stock—a transaction worth about $15 million. The merged entity started business on October 31 as Thompson Ramo Wooldridge, Inc. (Although its name was not officially shortened into TRW Inc. until 1965, the company immediately became known by its initials, which is the convention used hereafter in this book.)[77]

In response to continuing scrutiny of public officials and competitors in the aerospace industry, STL was established as a separate subsidiary corporation with its own board of directors chaired by Jimmy Doolittle. An MIT-educated engineer, winner of the Thompson Trophy, World War II hero and holder of the Congressional Medal of Honor, retired Air Force general, and recently retired head of NACA (the core unit of the newly established NASA), Doolittle possessed impeccable credentials and unquestioned integrity. No member of TRW's board of directors or senior management served on STL's board. STL also featured an independent management team headed by Louis Dunn and Rube Mettler as president and executive vice president, respectively. All STL employees severed their employment relationship with TRW, divested any stock holdings, and accepted compensation and benefits unique to STL. At least part of the reason for organizing STL in this way—explicitly acknowledged in the merger documents—was to prepare the way for its eventual divestiture, should that step become necessary.[78]

PSI remained an independent subsidiary, now wholly owned by TRW. At the time of the deal, R-W (including PSI) had annual sales running at about $60 million and employed about thirty-nine hundred people, including more than eleven hundred scientists and engineers. TP had annual sales of about $300 million—a total down about 20 percent from the previous year as a result of declines in its aircraft and automotive markets.

On October 31, 1958, a new corporation was born: Thompson Ramo Wooldridge, Inc., with $340 million in sales and nearly twenty-three thousand employees. These totals do not include figures for STL, estimated at about $24 million in sales and about one thousand employees. The question facing the new TRW and its new, integrated management team: what kind of company would it be?

Epilogue: R-W's Record as SETD Contractor

From time to time since the 1950s, commentators have asked whether TRW's management of the ballistic missile program constituted an effective way to manage a complex weapon systems program. During the 1950s and 1960s, for example, in congressional hearings and in print, various parties charged that the Air Force/STL approach, using a separate, private SETD contractor and associate contractors, was inefficient, unwieldy, and prone to conflict of interest. These parties contended that alternative forms of management and organization could have yielded better outcomes, with the ICBM being developed more quickly, less expensively, or both. Some, for example, cite contrasts between development of the Air Force ballistic missiles and the Navy's Polaris program. Because it was launched from a mobile platform—a submarine—with severe space and weight constraints, Polaris was much more complex to develop than the ICBM. Yet it proceeded from go-ahead to operation at sea in just four years. Among their other achievements, the Polaris team pioneered the Program Review and Evaluation Technique (PERT) for scheduling, monitoring, and reviewing progress in complex projects—a technique widely adopted in aerospace companies and other organizations in the 1960s.[79]

Arguments about the comparative effectiveness of alternative approaches to managing complex programs are based on complicated issues that have been debated hotly for decades. The question whether the country would have been better off under another approach to developing the ICBM is, of course, hypothetical and cannot be answered authoritatively. We'll never know. Nor is it a straightforward matter to draw performance comparisons between ostensibly similar development efforts, such as the Air Force's Thor and the Army's Jupiter IRBMs, or the Air Force's Minuteman and the Navy's Polaris missiles. At first glance, it might seem that comparing, say, elapsed time between program authorization and initial operational capability or performance against budget would yield valuable insights. Such comparisons, however, are impossible to make given the vastly different assumptions, starting points, priorities, scales, and objectives of the programs concerned. Nonetheless, the following observations may shed some light on the quality of the Air Force/R-W approach.

First, given the imperative to develop an operational ICBM as soon as possible as a matter of the highest national priority, the Air Force and R-W succeeded. Atlas, which languished under low levels of funding until 1953, became operational in 1960, meeting the ambitious target that the Teapot Committee originally proposed. Moreover, evidence of a learning curve for subsequent Air Force missile programs is clear. In February 1959—about three and a half years after initial approval, the first Titan missile flew successfully. Owing to a somewhat relaxed schedule, the missile became operational in 1962. Thor, which used many elements of the Atlas program, proceeded from the drawing board to operational capability in fewer than three years, while Minuteman, which was based on a fundamentally different propulsion technology, also became operational in about three years. As a point of comparison, the development of a contemporaneous Air Force project, the B-58 bomber, a much less complex vehicle, consumed more than eleven years.[80]

Second, both the Air Force and TRW continued to use the SETD-associate contractors approach in subsequent missile and space programs, albeit with modifications. Throughout his career, General Schriever resolutely defended the Air Force's relationship with R-W and its successors. Even after government inquiries led TRW in 1960 to divest the part of STL concerned with advanced planning, including that for space-based weaponry, the Air Force continued to use a successor organization, the nonprofit Aerospace Corporation, in a similar role. For its part, TRW has served the Air Force as contractor for systems engineering and technical assistance on its ballistic missile programs continuously since 1954. In later years, TRW capitalized on its capabilities in systems engineering and technical management to work on other big programs for the Air Force and other customers. The company enjoyed an outstanding reputation for managing complex technological systems, and many customers sought to work with TRW for precisely this reason.

Third, the motives of the parties who questioned the effectiveness of the Air Force/R-W approach during the 1950s and early 1960s need to be examined. Much of the early criticism came from disgruntled associate or subcontractors and competitors such as Convair and Douglas Aircraft, or from proponents of rival approaches, such as the arsenal system used by the Army and later adopted by NASA. All of these parties had a vested interest in urging the superiority of alternative arrangements.

Finally, neither the Air Force nor R-W claimed that the management approach followed in developing the ICBM was the only suitable way to organize comparable programs. Rather, in 1954, it seemed to General Schriever, the Atlas Scientific Advisory Committee, and high-level officials in the Department of Defense to be the best approach under the circumstances. Given the need to manage an extraordinarily complex set of scientific and technical problems, shared concerns among DOD officials and prominent scientists about the capabilities of the airframe manufacturers, and the reluctance of other independent parties such as leading research universities to tackle the assignment, delegation of the SETD work to R-W seemed appropriate. On the other hand, the Air Force and TRW personnel acknowledged that other approaches could also be effective, as indeed they were in the cases of the Polaris missile and many other defense and NASA programs. Both the Air Force and TRW adopted techniques such as PERT developed elsewhere for use on their own projects.

In sum, what can be concluded about the Air Force/R-W approach to program management and systems engineering is that it worked, and that with many adjustments and improvements, it remains one of several viable approaches to developing complex systems still followed today.

Chapter 9

From Two
Companies to One

▶   ▶   ▶

1958–1965

THE MERGER THAT CREATED THOMPSON RAMO WOOLDRIDGE, INC., MADE AN UNUSUAL combination. The elder partner, Thompson Products, was by far the larger entity and well established in its major markets as a mass producer of parts and components to the automotive, automotive replacement, aircraft, and aircraft engine industries. TP had a proven management team, time-honored ways of organizing and conducting its business, and a formula for success that had worked for decades. The junior partner, however, was a strikingly different kind of entity: a specialized provider of scientific and engineering services with a small but growing business in the manufacture of electronics. Ramo-Wooldridge's top personnel were younger, better educated as a whole, and more comfortable in the fluid and pressurized environment of aerospace contracting.

In considering why and how to merge, neither of the parties apparently gave much thought to fashioning a single, homogeneous organization. Rather, they imagined that the erstwhile businesses of both TP and R-W would be left to their own devices, although some technology, management expertise, and personnel were expected to transfer across the company. At first, TRW even boasted of two "major offices" in Cleveland and Los Angeles—as opposed to a single-headquarters organization. The board of directors split overall management authority evenly between the two parties, with a gentle, genial recognition of TP's seniority. The geographical separation of the two pieces of the company reinforced their independence, as did stereotypical notions that each party held about the other: to the TP folk, R-W personnel seemed to be egg-heads, arrogant and condescending, more concerned about growth than making money, and addicted to sunshine, smog, and freeways; to R-W employees, the personnel at TP were "metalbenders," a bit old-fashioned, excessively concerned with doing things the way they had always done them, with a dour aspect reflecting patterns of life in an aging, cold-weather industrial city.

During the early months and years after the merger, the independence of the two major pieces of TRW and the attitudes thus engendered posed no particular problems to the company. More worrisome for the long term, however, was the question of just how TRW would be governed. Was it two companies, or one? If one, how would decisions be made to the benefit of the corporation as a whole? And who would make them? Further problems and questions, especially pertaining to the former R-W businesses, lurked a level down. Would the merger end concerns among aerospace industry competitors about STL's favored position in the Air Force? Would it be necessary to divest STL? If it should remain a part of TRW, how would STL cope with the inevitable eventual drop in revenues with the completion of work on the Air Force ICBM programs? Would R-W's computers and commercial electronics businesses and PSI finally take off? And for TP, would the merger solve the problems of heavy dependence on defense contracting and the decline of the aircraft engine business?

During the first seven years after the merger, these questions were answered in ways that transformed TRW from a loose federation of businesses to a more—but not fully—integrated corporation.

A Two-Headed Company

To employees in both organizations, as well as to the outside world, the merger between TP and R-W was portrayed as an alliance of equals, an impression supported by including the names of Ramo and Wooldridge in the new corporate name as well as by the decision to maintain separate "major offices" in Cleveland and Los Angeles. The primary beneficiaries of the setup, joked Dave Wright, would be the telephone and airlines companies.[1]

The merger, in fact, took place at the very top of the company, in the board of directors and the top management group, and it had little immediate effect at lower levels of the corporation. The merger triggered several significant changes in the board of directors, where sixty-seven-year-old Fred Crawford stepped down as chairman, although he remained a director and chairman of the board's executive committee. At the same time, four long-time TP directors—Lee Clegg, Sam Emerson, Edgar Hahn, and S. Livingston Mather—retired from the board, and they were not replaced. The new board was smaller, composed entirely of insiders, and slightly tilted in TP's favor.[2]

Wright assumed the mantle of chairman of the board and chief executive officer of TRW and maintained his primary office in Cleveland. (He also kept an apartment in Los Angeles, where he spent increasing amounts of time, especially during the winter months.) Dean Wooldridge became president, but he remained based on the West Coast, as did Ramo, who became executive vice president of the new company. Horace Shepard was elected vice president and executive assistant to the chairman, with responsibilities for the Thompson Division, which consisted of the former TP businesses.

Ralph Johnson moved up to become general manager of the Ramo-Wooldridge Division—successor to R-W's old General Electronics Group—in Canoga Park, but Johnson occupied a niche below the others: Wright, Shepard, Wooldridge, and Ramo constituted TRW's top "managing team." Any one of the four, said Wright, "can make a decision for the company and feel that it will get the support of the others." Of the four, only Shepard held operating responsibilities; the others, said Wright, were "free to study new fields and look ahead on a broad basis."[3]

This management structure signaled that for the short term, at least, the constituent pieces of TRW would remain autonomous. Division and group general managers continued to report to their existing bosses. The administrative staffs of TP and R-W remained intact. Veteran TP managers such as Arch Colwell and Ray Livingstone, both scheduled to retire in the mid-1960s, assumed nominal charge of technology and human relations for the entire company, but in practice neither man attempted to impose TP practices and culture on the former R-W businesses. As Wooldridge reassured employees at the Tapco plant, "There is no intention of interfering with the lines of activity of either company."[4]

TRW mounted modest efforts to bridge the two main parts of the company. Starting in 1959, for example, the division general managers and senior staff from the R-W divisions routinely attended the annual planning conference at Crawford's farm in Vermont. These arrangements represented less a departure than a continuation of a trend, however, since many senior R-W personnel had participated in earlier conferences to discuss the evolution of the defense industry, computers, electronics, and other businesses.

In efforts that continued experiments and activities begun before the merger, the company also attempted to transfer some personnel and technology between its two major parts, though with little success. In 1957, for example, Irwin Binder, a former manufacturing manager at Tapco, had moved to R-W as general manager of the electronic equipment factory in Denver. He did not survive a downturn in the business, however, and soon left the company. At about the same time, R&D personnel at R-W collaborated with their counterparts at TP to develop a "smog afterburner" to curtail emissions from automobile engines. This partnership met its technical objectives, but the device was "too large, too complicated and too expensive" to take to market. In 1960, TRW called a halt to the program, and it made no significant attempts to transfer West Coast technology to the automobile divisions for more than a decade.[5]

Establishing greater cooperation between STL and the emerging missile components business at Tapco was a more pressing need. Such efforts could be successful, however, only after TRW and the Air Force resolved whether to divest STL.

Spin-off at STL

Although TRW had organized STL as a completely separate subsidiary with its own independent board of directors (chaired by Jimmy Doolittle) and a strong management team (led by Louis Dunn and Rube Mettler), and although TRW had publicly announced that it would divest STL if the Air Force so wished, neither the company nor the Air Force proved eager or willing to take such a step. The stakeholders divided clearly: to TRW, STL represented important business, as well as a reservoir of outstanding managerial and technical talent; to the Air Force, STL was a proven and trusted resource essential both to operations support and to advanced planning; and to competitors, STL was a Trojan horse by which TRW, despite its protestations, could gain access to proprietary competitive secrets.

During the months following the merger, internal frustration at the continuing ban on manufacturing hardware continued to build, while outside criticism of STL's relationship with the Air Force continued to intensify. An escalation of missile development activity contributed to both problems. Testing continued on the Thor and Atlas missiles, with increasingly encouraging results. At the end of 1958, Thor was pronounced operational, and the government made plans to base squadrons in Europe and Turkey by 1960. In September 1959, the Air Force declared Atlas to be fully operational, and during the next several years 126 missiles were positioned at Air Force bases scattered throughout the United States.

As the Thor and Atlas programs moved into new phases, STL's role in missile development did not taper off, however, because other programs continued to grow. In mid-1959, concerned that the Soviet Union might have an operational missile force as early as 1960, the Air Force pushed up Minuteman's date of initial operational capability by a year, to no later than July 1962. The new deadline meant that an enormous amount of work had to be compressed into a short time. "It required moving heaven and earth," recalls Mettler, adding that "we just went into a frenzy" to meet the new goal. STL personnel made many contributions to the design of the solid-fuel rocket motors, the development of movable nozzles, a new inertial guidance system, the basing system and ground support, and many other areas. The facilities task was monumental, consuming billions of federal dollars, the organizational and management abilities of several thousand contractors, and the labor of tens of thousands of individuals for several years. During this hectic period, Mettler and program manager Bob Bennett worked closely and intensively with the Air Force program manager, Col. Samuel C. Phillips, to bring Minuteman to operational capability in short order.[6]

Also during 1959, the first Titan missiles began flight tests. The first three missiles launched successfully, a dazzling testimony to the value of missile program management concepts that also helped convince the Air Force to approve development of a second-generation Titan. The new Titan II incorporated many improvements over its predecessor. Among them were the use of noncryogenic storable liquid propellants, which gave the missile comparable response time to the Minuteman; a much more powerful second-stage motor that increased range and accommodated heavier payloads; and a fully inertial guidance system. Once again, STL personnel immersed themselves in the SETD role.[7]

The acceleration of Minuteman and the gathering momentum of Titan renewed old controversies for STL. Rather than watch its participation on Air Force programs wind down, it saw its role continue to expand. In these circumstances, the hardware ban loomed large, especially for TRW's Tapco divisions. To offset the decline of jet engine production, several Tapco units wanted to bid to fabricate components such as auxiliary power units, rocket motor nozzles, and equipment for basing systems for the Air Force missile programs. On several occasions, Tapco personnel received indications that they might win such bids—were it not for the hardware ban.[8]

STL's close relationship to the Air Force also remained a sore point for competitors in the aerospace industry. STL's ongoing role in several experimental, government-funded space programs fanned the criticism. On November 8, 1958, barely a week after the merger took effect, STL attempted for the third time to launch a lunar probe. This vehicle, known as Pioneer 2, fell well short of its objective when the third-stage rocket motor failed to ignite. Nonetheless, STL pressed ahead with participation in space programs in ways that raised questions about conflict of interest. In December, for example, STL carried out the mission and trajectory planning for Project SCORE, a satellite program funded by ARPA, the advanced R&D arm of the U.S. Department of Defense. To most observers, the launch appeared to be another full-range test of an Atlas missile. Only eighty-eight people, including more than a dozen top STL employees headed by Ed Doll, knew the real purpose of the mission, which was carried out under the extreme secrecy that ARPA mandated in case of failure. But the project did not fail, and it proved quite a boost to the U.S. space program, still reeling from *Sputnik*— though perhaps not, as proclaimed, "a master stroke in the space war."

Weighing in at more than four tons, Project SCORE consisted of the heaviest satellite placed in orbit to that time. In fact, the "satellite" consisted of an entire Atlas missile stripped of unnecessary components and instrumentation and minus the booster engines that peeled off in flight. Inside the special nose cone, which remained attached to the missile, sat a tape recorder that could be turned on and off from the ground to broadcast Christmas greetings to the world from President Eisenhower. As a vehicle for public relations, Project SCORE was a triumph. As a scientific or research mission, it had limited value. But it provided further proof of Atlas's boosting capability and demonstrated the feasibility of using a satellite to relay voice and radio signals between two earth stations. (In this sense, Project SCORE was the first communications satellite. The acronym stood for "Signal Communication by Orbiting Relay Equipment." Later, the founders of The 88 Club of SCORE, including many STL employees, revised it as "Society for the Correction of Russian Excesses.") After thirty-three days in orbit and a journey of 12.5 million miles, the "satellite" fell back into the atmosphere near Midway Island in the Pacific Ocean, burning up on reentry.[9]

The lunar probes and Project SCORE signaled an intensifying role for STL in government space programs. During 1959 and 1960, STL participated in more than a dozen programs for the Air Force, Army, Navy, ARPA, and NASA, including those for several early scientific, meteorological, navigation, and communications satellites boosted by configurations of Thor and Atlas missiles. STL's participation ranged from providing background analytical studies, to overall systems engineering services, to the engineering of subsystems and supply of components and instrumentation, to integration of stages, to fabrication of spacecraft, to launch supervision, to operation of ground systems and testing.[10]

Two remarkable successes from these years were the NASA-funded Explorer VI and Pioneer V spacecraft that STL designed, developed, fabricated, and instrumented.

Launched on August 7, 1959, the Explorer VI was a 143-pound earth-orbiting satellite that in space deployed four arms or "paddle wheels" fitted with more than eight thousand solar cells to generate electrical current. The satellite achieved an elongated elliptical orbit, and during its two months of operation it collected information about the Van Allen radiation belts, cosmic rays, and other characteristics of nearby space. Explorer VI also carried a television camera that transmitted the first picture ever made of earth from space. This was an impressive technological feat, although something of an anticlimax from an aesthetic point of view. Shot from an altitude of nearly two thousand miles, the image captured in crude and blurred fashion cloud cover over Mexico City.[11]

Like Explorer VI, Pioneer V was a paddlewheel satellite that generated its own electrical power. America's deepest space probe at the time, it roared into space in March 1960 and aimed to intersect the orbit of Venus and eventually achieve orbit around the sun. The satellite toiled for 107 days before contact was broken at a distance of 22.5 million miles, a little more than halfway to Venus's orbit. Along the way, it provided valuable data about the extent of earth's magnetic field, solar flares, and radiation levels in interplanetary space. Pioneer V also made an impressive demonstration of STL's capabilities in telemetry, tracking, and command (TT&C) systems. Engineers Bob Gottfried, Charlie Stephens, and Art Gold developed a digital telemetry system known as Telebit. The system featured the first digital transmitter to fly into space—a piece of hardware fabricated by STL—as well as tracking from STL's worldwide ground station network.[12]

STL's growing involvement in space programs collided with its ongoing role as SETD contractor for the ballistic missile programs and brought to a head the question of its continuing close relationship with the Air Force. During February and March 1959, the U.S. House of Representatives investigated the matter in a series of hearings chaired by Rep. Chet Holifield (D-California). A parade of witnesses from TRW, STL, the Air Force, and the aerospace industry testified. Charges and questions about the Air Force/STL relationship surfaced with new vehemence: that STL had "an intimate and privileged position" with its major customer, the Air Force; that the relationship inhibited Air Force efforts to upgrade its internal capability; that STL personnel commanded incomes well above industry norms; that STL seemed on its way to becoming a captive "arsenal" for the Air Force; that STL advantaged TRW in competitive bids; and that the company's rapid growth and profit orientation were inherently incompatible with the public interest in containing government spending. Although TRW and STL witnesses including Ramo, Dunn, and Fred Hesse vigorously disputed these charges, stoutly defended their behavior, sharply refuted any suggestions of impropriety, and openly restated a willingness to dispose of STL, neither they nor allies in the Air Force such as General Schriever could keep the controversy from spreading.[13]

Throughout much of 1959, representatives of TRW, STL, and the Air Force worked on a plan of divestiture that called for STL to be sold to the public. In August, the parties submitted the plan to James H. Douglas, secretary of the Air Force. Douglas rejected the proposal, however, arguing that it "was not a proper solution to the problem," because it merely substituted one set of private owners for another. This view was echoed by the formal report of the Holifield Committee, which appeared in September. The proposed sale might solve TRW's problem of eligibility for Air Force contracts, stated the report, but "the Air Force still would have to deal with STL as an investor-owned corporation committed to maximizing profits while occupying a privileged place" in the Air Force ballistic missile and space programs. The report went on to call for the conversion of STL into a nonprofit corporation "akin to the RAND Corp. and other private and university-sponsored organizations which serve the military departments and other agencies of the Federal Government on a stable and continuing basis."[14]

At first, TRW, STL, and General Schriever opposed establishing STL as a nonprofit, believing that many of its most talented personnel would elect to stay with TRW or simply leave. On September 3, however, Secretary Douglas appointed a high-level committee headed by Caltech professor Clark Millikan to investigate the Air Force's ballistic missile management organization. The Millikan committee, whose members included several people who had endorsed and applauded R-W's role in the ballistic missile program, issued its final report on January 29, 1960. The committee stopped short of calling for TRW to divest STL, but it urged that STL's role and mission be reoriented to focus on "its essential functions." By that statement, the committee evidently meant that STL should continue its SETD role on the ballistic missile programs, but that other activities such as designing or developing boosters, payloads, and other space machinery, and advanced planning and other administrative and technical work unrelated to the missile program ought to be transferred to other sources. Many of these activities could be carried out by "competitive industry," but the committee proposed that four functions—advanced planning and evaluation of new ideas, "broad-brush" initial system design, technical evaluation of contractors' proposals, and technical monitoring of program progress—should reside in "a civilian contractor organization" that was "basically noncompetitive."[15]

Representatives of TRW, STL, and the Air Force eventually embraced this position in modified form. The four functions that the Millikan committee earmarked for a noncompetitive organization were grouped into a new, independent nonprofit entity incorporated in California on June 4, 1960, as the Aerospace Corporation. The activities that the Millikan committee considered appropriate for private industry remained with STL, which continued as a wholly owned subsidiary of TRW. At the insistence of General Schriever, STL retained its SETD role on existing missile programs, leaving TRW under the ban against producing hardware for these programs, but allowing it to compete for full participation in space programs funded by the Air Force and other government agencies. In practical terms, the split meant that STL lost about $20 million in business—about a quarter of its total revenues—as well as roughly seventeen hundred employees, including many highly qualified technical staff. STL also agreed to sell at cost and vacate within eighteen months its recently finished R&D center on El Segundo Boulevard.[16]

The transfer of personnel from STL to Aerospace proved "a rather delicate and involved affair," in which outcomes involved balancing such factors as job assignments, salaries, career plans, individual preferences, inputs from the Air Force, and the need to ensure the viability of the new corporation. STL lost key personnel such as Jack Irving, Al Donovan, and Bud Nielsen, as well as many others who had contributed significantly to R-W's success.

Gamble on Space

The spin-off of Aerospace was a bittersweet experience. The whole episode was protracted and painful, putting STL on the defensive when its employees believed they had rendered an enormous, incalculable service to the nation. The loss of senior personnel and the attenuation of collegial relationships was also disheartening. The drain of time and energy on senior management was intense. It may even have aggravated Louis Dunn's heart condition, which in any event forced extended absences until his retirement in 1962 and left most key decisions in the hands of Rube Mettler.

The divestiture, ironically, left STL with significant continuing revenues as the SETD contractor on the Air Force ballistic missile programs. And once again, the expected outcome—that STL's role would eventually diminish and decline as the Minuteman and Titan squadrons became operational—failed to materialize. As the Air Force undertook planning for succeeding generations of ICBMs, it remained heavily dependent on STL. Developing advanced missiles continued to push the frontier into the unknown and untried, leaving a need for an outside technical organization to provide support. By virtue of its experience, track record, and intimate familiarity with ballistic missiles, the Air Force believed that STL was far better suited than Aerospace to offer such assistance. Finally, because the ballistic missiles of the 1960s—Minuteman II and Minuteman III—were derivatives of Minuteman I, for which STL had served as SETD contractor, STL remained the Air Force's preferred supplier.

In light of long-standing controversies, TRW made further concessions, evolving during the 1960s and 1970s into a provider of systems engineering and technical assistance (SETA) to the Air Force. In practice, the distinction between technical direction and technical assistance was largely semantic: it meant that TRW advised Air Force project officers on technical issues, and they in turn provided technical direction to the associated contractors. Another move that helped allay criticism was geographical: in 1962, TRW agreed to establish a separate organization at Norton AFB in San Bernardino (about ninety miles east of Los Angeles), headquarters of the USAF Ballistic Systems Division responsible for Titan and Minuteman operations. In December 1962, TRW transferred about five hundred technical and administrative personnel to the new location. The move achieved a symbolic effect, distancing the missile business from TRW's aggressive expansion in space and electronics systems at Space Park.[17]

At the time of the move Ed Doll, who had been R-W's program manager for the Atlas missile, served as STL's ballistic missile program management director. A few months later, Doll moved to Washington, D.C., to carry out a study for NASA on the applicability of TRW's program management techniques to the new manned space program. (At the same time, STL vice president for research and development George Mueller moved to NASA to head its manned space flight program—a position Mettler turned down, much to the relief of Wright and Ramo.) Doll's replacement at STL, Dick DeLauer, proved an extremely capable leader. A Caltech Ph.D. in mathematics and aeronautical engineering, DeLauer had joined STL in 1958 after a distinguished career that included work on Martin Aircraft's giant Mars seaplane, and on Northrop's Black Widow night fighter, and a fifteen-year stint in the U.S. Navy, where he helped develop aircraft as diverse as blimps and guided missiles. As director of STL's Vehicle Development Laboratory, he participated in the Explorer VI and Pioneer V triumphs. Later, he helped oversee the design of the structure of Minuteman and directed STL's program office for Titan. As head of STL's ballistic missile business, he presided over a major source of revenues and, eventually, a key platform for diversification.[18]

The divestiture of Aerospace finally liberated STL and TRW to compete in hardware for military and space applications. Looking ahead, STL could begin to shape its own future. The immediate questions it faced were daunting: What hardware should or could it make? Where? And could STL become a credible participant in an industry already populated by much larger competitors?

The divestiture agreement enabled TRW to treat STL as an operating unit like its other divisions. Accordingly, in August 1960, much of the military hardware business of the R-W Division (R-W's original Control Systems and Communications Systems Divisions) in Canoga Park was transferred to STL and placed under the charge of Will Duke. This work, which was seen as "broadly complementary to the technical role of STL," involved electronic warfare, antisubmarine and underseas warfare, reconnaissance systems, electro-optical systems, electromagnetic techniques, communications, and field service and support.[19]

Beyond these miscellaneous R&D programs and the ongoing SETD role on the Titan and Minuteman, the leaders of STL faced the challenge of finding new business. The problem, said Mettler, was that "we were a company that had not been in the competitive arena. We had no sales offices, no sales organization at all. And we had relatively few contracts." After the divestiture, he recalls, "Over the weekend I became the chief marketing person." STL had many highly qualified personnel coming off the Thor and Atlas programs, as well as ample experience in writing contract proposals. Mettler directed them to start bidding, fast. To gain still more experience and to advertise STL's capabilities, Mettler encouraged bids even for programs that STL had no chance of winning. As part of this effort, STL also produced two handsome and authoritative promotional publications.[20]

At the behest of Wooldridge and Ramo, TRW's corporate headquarters supplied help by commissioning a study team of eminent scientists and business leaders to advise STL. H. Guyford Stever, an MIT physicist, an occasional consultant to STL (and eventual director of TRW), and a member of many national scientific and technical panels and organizations, headed the group, which interviewed personnel inside STL, the Air Force, and across the industry before reporting back in late July.[21]

Stever summarized the problem crisply: "the uniqueness of the STL capability in the system engineering and space and ballistic missile fields is gone," and he listed several explanations:

. . . the field has lost some of its glamour; the very best of the STL people have gone on to other (usually higher) jobs in STL and TRW; some contractors really have some talent of their own in this field now; the whole technical fraternity of the country has learned a fantastic amount about ballistic missiles and space in the last few years; the Air Force generally has more capability now.[22]

Beyond that, Stever urged STL to avoid "flaunting" its SETD capability and to think of that capability more broadly than it had during the heyday of the ballistic missile programs. What STL had to sell, like some other aerospace contractors, was "a mature, experienced scientific and engineering capability in ballistic and space systems and components, both for military and civilian applications." Although some STL personnel believed that the unit could transfer its SETD capability directly to other branches of the military, federal agencies, and even local governments, Stever was skeptical. He argued that it would not be easy to win business "too far out of STL's ken" because competitors possessed better contacts and more experience.

Stever saw a brighter future for STL closer to home. He pointed out that the company enjoyed "real prestige and leadership" in Air Force and NASA circles, and he recommended that it join with other contractors to bid for some military and civilian space and missile programs. He was particularly bullish on communications satellites, where he thought STL could link up with a communications company such as AT&T, RCA, or ITT. He also encouraged STL to bid to participate in NASA's soft lunar landing program, which, he believed, "could be the forerunner of twenty years of business." More generally, he advised STL to focus explicitly on its future. He urged the unit to free up some of its top managerial and technical personnel who were buried in operations to concentrate on advanced planning and marketing.[23]

To Dunn and Mettler, this advice seemed sound, and they set about quickly to reorganize STL and to capitalize on its capabilities. They established five operating divisions: Fabrication, Integration, and Test (FIT); Physical Research; Systems Research and Analysis; Mechanics; and Electronics. They organized planning and marketing around three business areas: ballistic missiles, defense systems programs, and space systems programs. STL plunged into business planning and developed new policies to support sales and marketing. Although encouraged to hire specialists in these areas, Mettler preferred to equip existing personnel for the work. To support them, he backed a career development program designed by Jim Dunlap and Shel Davis of STL's industrial relations staff. This program entailed focused training in communications and interpersonal skills, business management skills, and technical skills.[24]

Dunn and Mettler also persuaded corporate management to place a big bet. To be a credible producer of aerospace hardware, STL required a manufacturing facility. Although it had produced small spacecraft such as Explorer VI and Pioneer V, STL lacked the capacity to build the bigger, more complex spacecraft on the horizon. This need, coupled with the imperative to vacate the El Segundo R&D facility that housed the Aerospace Corporation, meant that STL had to find new space, quickly.

Dunn and Mettler directed STL's administrative staff, including Fred Hesse, Ted Foley, and Bob Burgin to scout for a new home. By late summer, Burgin had located a promising site: a hundred-acre parcel of land owned by the Santa Fe Railroad along the northern edge of Redondo Beach, about a mile from the El Segundo R&D Center. By October, architects had prepared models for a ten-building complex to be known as the Redondo Beach Space Center. Like the Canoga Park facility, the Space Center would be laid out in the style of a campus, complete with a library, a cafeteria, and an auditorium. All technical personnel would have private offices and most would have windows unless they were engaged in classified work.[25]

STL's management chose deliberately to finance the entire complex privately— that is, to avoid using or relying on government support. This decision, Mettler believes, was critical to the unit's future. By controlling its real estate and facilities, STL took charge of its own fate. It would be free from government restrictions and close identification with the Air Force and able to bid for business with many government customers, both military and civilian. To finance the new complex, STL financial vice president Chuck Allen came up with a clever arrangement. He applied the proceeds from the sale of the El Segundo complex to cover the costs of the first three buildings and associated land. Next, Allen persuaded STL's banker—Mellon Bank— to treat the property as an industrial park, thereby assuring favorable interest rates. The land was divided by private streets and carved up into discrete lots with separate deeds. That way, should STL default or otherwise abandon the property, it could quickly be sold or leased to other businesses.

Accommodating the boom-bust nature of its business, STL also arranged to lease its buildings on a staggered basis. Each lease ran for ninety-nine years with ten-year review points. During a down cycle, then, STL would be able to relinquish leases quickly. Mettler recalls telling the TRW board that after ten years, the company could get out of 40 percent of its space within two years, saving millions of dollars on overhead. A third significant benefit of the financing was that government contracting rules of the time treated leases, including interest payments, as fully reimbursable costs. STL got the benefits of ownership and control of the property, yet it could pass most of the costs of operating the facility on to its customers.[26]

Ground was broken on December 7, 1960, for the first three buildings in the new complex, which quickly became known as Space Park: an engineering building (now E1) and two research labs (R1 and R2). Soon to be added, recalls Mettler, was another building that represented "a tremendous gamble": although STL had no major spacecraft contracts in hand, it planned to commit $7 million to construct a big, straight-line manufacturing facility designed specifically for building spacecraft. Known as M1, the building bore several distinctive features: a fifty-foot-high manufacturing bay and a ten-ton overhead crane; a thirty-foot spherical space simulator able to handle much bigger spacecraft than ever before built. The device could simulate temperature ranges from 275 degrees Fahrenheit to minus 325 degrees Fahrenheit under a nearly total vacuum. It used STL-designed carbon-arc lighting to simulate the sun. M1 also devoted seventeen thousand square feet to a "systems integration and test area," where spacecraft would be thoroughly and repeatedly checked out, and ninety-five hundred square feet to a structural test facility.[27]

STL highlighted its as-yet-nonexistent manufacturing facility in its first major proposal to design and build spacecraft. NASA's Orbiting Geophysical Observatory (OGO) program called for three satellites to serve as "streetcars": big, box-like vehicles, each capable of holding up to fifty different experiments as "passengers." The satellites would be launched between 1964 and 1966 into elliptical orbits, with experiments designed to investigate and measure conditions in, and characteristics of, surrounding space. NASA's Goddard Space Flight Center developed the specifications for OGO, calling for a stock model structure, basic power supply, attitude control, telemetry, and a command system.

STL's design, prepared in the fall of 1960 under the direction of Dolph Thiel and George Gleghorn, proposed a structure approximately six feet by three feet square (in launch configuration), weighing about one thousand pounds, and with room for about two hundred pounds of experiments—about ten times the capacity of Explorer VI. Festooned with folding booms and wings containing solar cells that would deploy in space, each OGO vehicle resembled, in the words of a contemporary press account, "a psychedelic dragonfly."[28]

On December 21, NASA Goddard chose STL from among eight finalists to design and build the first three OGO satellites. The initial contract was worth $23.5 million, and it included the possibility (subsequently realized) of building three additional satellites later in the decade. Thiel named Gleghorn as program director, and he assembled four teams—design and development; project control; fabrication, integration, and test; and experiments—to manage the project.[29]

In 1961, another big contract award helped assure STL's position as a major producer of spacecraft. The Air Force Space Systems Division chose the company to develop a satellite system to detect nuclear test explosions. The program, known as Project 823 or "Vela Hotel" (*vela* is Spanish for vigil), had its roots in disarmament talks during the Eisenhower administration, when representatives of the United States, the United Kingdom, and the Soviet Union agreed in principle on a control system to detect and identify clandestine nuclear explosions, including those in space.

The responsibility to implement U.S. detection systems fell to the Department of Defense, in cooperation with the Atomic Energy Commission. During the summer of 1960, the DOD assigned the problem of monitoring in space to the Air Force, which in turn awarded a feasibility study contract to STL. The following year, the Air Force sought proposals to design, develop, fabricate, and test prototype satellites, a competition that STL won in December 1961. The contract was structured in a novel way, with a cost-plus incentive fee (CPIF). The incentives applied both to production cost and spacecraft performance. Depending on its production expenses, STL could earn an incentive fee of between 3 and 15 percent of costs; successful operation of the spacecraft for a stated period could yield an additional 3 percent of costs to STL.[30]

Under the direction of program manager Dr. William J. Chalmers, STL designed the Vela satellites to be launched in tandem, separated in space, and ultimately positioned on opposite sides of the planet at an altitude of about sixty thousand miles. Each spacecraft was an icosahedron (a twenty-sided structure) about five feet in diameter and weighing nearly five hundred pounds. Solar cells mounted on eighteen of the twenty faces provided power to sensitive instruments capable of detecting X rays, neutrons, and gamma rays as far away as ten million miles. The first launch was scheduled for 1963.[31]

In winning the OGO and Vela bids, STL followed the conventional path to spacecraft development, responding to requests for proposals from government customers. During the early 1960s, STL also revealed an entrepreneurial bent. On its own, the company developed a series of tiny "environmental research satellites" that it sold to NASA, the Air Force, and other customers. Physicist Joseph M. Denney directed the program, which produced spacecraft designed in various polyhedral shapes as test vehicles to measure radiation, evaluate materials and welds, and calibrate communications equipment. These spacecraft measured from six to fifteen inches on edge and weighed as little as a few pounds. The satellites hitchhiked with other (mostly military) payloads, packed in crevices and dead space under the hoods that protected the satellites during launch. When the hoods opened in space, the tiny satellites were ejected to perform their missions. Between 1962 and 1969, thirty-two of these spacecraft were launched, including twenty-six that reached orbit.[32]

Programs such as OGO, Vela, and the environmental research satellites helped STL to build an early lead in the newly forming spacecraft industry. The company's achievements reinforced its promotional claim to be a unique source of capabilities. The unit could draw on a cadre of technical personnel still widely regarded as the best in the industry. Its experience and track record as SETD contractor on the ballistic missile program provided a head start in dealing with the advanced materials, power systems, electronics and miniaturized components, and other sophisticated requirements of spacecraft. The investment in Space Park enabled STL to reach beyond the Air Force to serve other military and civilian customers. At the same time, STL's work with launch vehicles, telemetry, tracking and command, and communications positioned the unit to engineer and manage spacecraft as a system that included not only fabrication, but also launching, deployment, operation, communications, and monitoring. As one of the most vertically integrated producers of spacecraft, STL enjoyed a major competitive advantage.

STL relied on the same set of capabilities to develop business in related areas such as classified programs, communications satellites and ground stations, and chemical propulsion. Classified work included several projects in electronic countermeasures begun in the 1950s by the R-W Communications and Control Divisions, as well as Project Windmill, an effort directed by Dr. William Carlson to interpret Russian communications and documents pertaining to missile launches. The dimensions of these programs, including their size, staffing levels, and achievements are known only to participants and their customers. Mettler, Carlson, and other STL executives, however, served on several high-level government committees dealing with intelligence, and classified work accounted for a growing fraction of STL's revenues later in the decade.

STL made more public progress by providing a variety of space-related services to government agencies and other aerospace companies. One of the most promising areas identified by the Stever committee, for example, involved communications satellites. As advised, STL traded on its missile experience to increase the scope of its participation in several programs of the early 1960s. It provided technical assistance and designed the booster configuration and trajectories for Courier IB, a military satellite built by Philco that, for two weeks in 1960, generated enough of its own power to qualify as an active communications relay station. Two years later, STL provided systems engineering services and built and operated several ground stations for NASA's Project Relay, which featured an active repeating satellite fabricated by RCA. Similarly, STL carried out "systems engineering and technical analysis" for the Advent program, an ambitious and ultimately ill-fated attempt managed by the U.S. Army to launch a series of active-repeating satellites into high altitude orbits.[33]

STL also pursued another recommendation of the Stever committee: space-borne propulsion. This opportunity reflected a shrewd appraisal of future needs for variable-thrust engines to help maneuver spacecraft in orbit or to negotiate soft landings on the moon or other planetary bodies. STL was also well positioned to respond. Although it lacked the capability to compete with Aerojet or Rocketdyne in making big rocket motors, it had gained considerable experience with propulsion systems for the Air Force missiles. As early as 1959, STL's Propulsion Laboratory had also investigated problems of firing liquid motors in the environment of space. Under the leadership of Bob Bromberg and Art Grant, engineers at the lab developed a set of tiny liquid rockets or thrusters capable of delivering a few pounds to help adjust the position of the Able 4, Able 5a, and Able 5b spacecraft. None of these small satellites belonging to the Explorer VI/Pioneer V family achieved orbit, although Able 5b, launched in December 1960, lasted long enough to test and validate the performance of the tiny thrusters. "Unfortunately," a sardonic STL reporter noted, "because of a failure in the second stage of the launch vehicle, the attitude of the spacecraft was such that the only contribution of the STL engine was to increase the velocity at which the spacecraft encountered the Atlantic Ocean."[33]

In 1960, the propulsion application on everyone's mind was the Surveyor program to soft-land a small unmanned spacecraft on the moon. STL's Propulsion Lab spent several years developing a five-hundred-pound thrust, mechanically throttleable engine for use in the program. Although it eventually lost the competition to Thiokol Corporation, a better-established maker of rocket engines, STL received a backup contract. It also demonstrated both the feasibility of its basic design and combustion efficiencies above 97 percent. These achievements helped ready STL to bid on the next big program in spaceborne propulsion: the landing engine for the manned Apollo lunar module.

For all of its success, STL did not become a prime participant in the biggest space bonanza of the era: NASA's manned space program. Although the company bid (sometimes in partnership) to build or integrate major components and systems for the Mercury, Gemini, and Apollo missions, NASA awarded the major contracts to other suppliers. Prime contracts for the space vehicles, for example, went to aircraft companies including North American, Boeing, General Dynamics, and Grumman, in part because of their experience in manufacturing, assembling, and integrating systems for large, complex aerospace vehicles. Before the opening of Space Park, moreover, lack of facilities affected the credibility of STL's bids, and even a state-of-the-art plant such as M1 was inadequate to the challenges of building and testing a space vehicle as large as the manned capsules.

Other factors limiting STL's prospects in manned space included NASA's wish to develop an expanded base of suppliers and to avoid dependence on contractors to the Air Force, as well as the Air Force's wish to keep its major contractors focused on its own business. The presence after 1962 of George Mueller, an STL alumnus, as NASA's director of manned spaceflight programs posed an additional complication, because he had to preempt any suspicion that he might favor his former employer. For all of NASA's manned space programs, however, STL engineered important subsystems, calculating guidance equations, lending expertise in long-range communications, and performing systems analyses.

Despite the disappointments in manned space, STL had plenty of work. Its wins on the OGO and Vela program and its myriad activities from fabricating small space-craft, to engineering tracking and control systems, to manufacturing small propulsion systems all contributed to rapid growth. Between June 1960 and June 1962, the unit expanded from serving 8 customers to serving 43, from managing 16 contracts to managing 103, from employing 3,860 employees to employing 5,440, and from achieving $63 million in annual sales to achieving $108 million. By then, STL was no longer dependent on the missile business or on any other single program or contract.[35]

Crises in Electronics

In the first years after the merger, much of TRW management's attention—especially that of Wooldridge—focused on TRW's younger electronics businesses. The company initially made little effort to combine the former TP military and consumer electronics operations with those of the R-W Division. And in fact, the types of businesses were so different that integration made little sense. For the short term, corporate management remained at a distance, although Wooldridge encouraged an independent acquisitions strategy as a complement to other TRW electronics ventures.

Wooldridge's plan was to acquire and develop small and medium-sized makers of electronics components and related items for military, industrial, and consumer products. Although such companies typically possessed a high degree of specialized capability, just as typically they lacked the scale and resources to maximize efficiency in manufacturing, technology, and distribution. In 1959, TRW made its first such acquisition: Radio Industries, Inc., a producer of transformers used extensively in radio and television equipment and capacitors for all kinds of electric circuitry, based in Des Plaines, Illinois.[36]

In 1960, TRW added Good-All Electric Manufacturing Company, based in Ogallala, Nebraska, a manufacturer of fixed capacitors, cathodic protection rectifiers, and industrial power supplies. It became the anchor unit of a new TRW Electronic Components Group, headed by Good-All's president, Warren Hayes. In rapid order, Hayes pursued and purchased other small and middle-sized electronics components companies, including the Radio Condenser Company of Camden, New Jersey (1960), a producer of variable condensers, radio tuning devices, and special-purpose precision capacitors, and Milam Electric Manufacturing Company of Providence, Rhode Island (1961), a maker of electrical insulation. Assisted by J. Sidney (Sid) Webb, a Wooldridge protégé from Canoga Park, Hayes began the process of integrating pieces of TRW's far-flung electronics operations by combining the Cleveland-based microwave antenna and switch business and Good-All's RF (radio frequency) connector and RF power switch lines into a new Microwave Division with headquarters in Los Angeles.[37]

In 1961, the young group's expansion plans were momentarily checked by troubles developing in Pacific Semiconductors, Inc. (PSI). Although the unit was growing rapidly, it continued to drain cash at an alarming rate. The recent development of integrated circuits was already transforming the industry and causing a shakeout. To keep pace with rapid technological change, demanding customers, and increasingly aggressive competitors, PSI required large investments in R&D and equipment. During 1959 TRW poured more than $5 million into PSI and provided an additional line of credit of $8 million above amounts previously committed; a year later, TRW's stake in PSI soared to more than $20 million. These investments helped sustain growth and enhanced PSI's capabilities. In 1959, for example, with the hardware ban still in effect, PSI won a key contract from the USAF to make high-reliability silicon diodes for the Minuteman guidance system. The principal contractor, North American Aviation, had pleaded with the secretary of the Air Force for a special exemption, arguing that no competitive products would do.[38]

PSI also continued to develop innovative products, such as a new line of micro-diodes, micro-transistors, and micro-assemblies. The unit also boasted an outstanding technical staff headed by Jim Buie. Buie obtained several key patents for "transistor-to-transistor logic" (TTL), the principle by which two transistors can be joined and one of the most powerful early ways to form integrated circuits—the microchips that began the vast improvement in the performance of digital computers during the 1960s. The unit also developed another major innovation, bipolar transistors.[39]

Despite its technical successes and achievements, PSI's crossover into profitability continued to hover at a distant and receding horizon. Late in 1960, matters took a sharp turn for the worse, when prices throughout the semiconductor industry began a steep and prolonged plunge. Components that once sold for between $60 and $80 traded for less than $10. The crisis compounded when, early the following year, the new U.S. secretary of Defense, Robert McNamara, canceled several big military programs and even ordered stretch-outs in deliveries of the Minuteman. PSI was caught with a big inventory and had little choice but to write it down at a cost of more than $3 million. To TRW, this was the last straw, and the company instituted a plan to reorganize, refinance, and recapitalize PSI, which became a unit of the Electronic Components Group. Thereafter, PSI abandoned hopes of competing in mass-market components but concentrated instead on becoming a specialty producer of high-reliability semiconductors and components of very advanced design, primarily for military customers. In 1962, PSI's sales rebounded, but it never fulfilled the hopes of its founders and investors for a big payback.[40]

The crisis at PSI rippled into the top ranks at TRW, where it affected the careers of several key managers, including Harper North, PSI's founder and leader, and Ralph Johnson. North left operating management to succeed the retiring Arch Colwell as TRW's vice president of research and development. The crisis also exacted a heavy toll on Johnson, who found the job of restructuring PSI distasteful. He disengaged from active management and soon afterward retired from TRW's board of directors. In his stead, Horace Shepard was elected vice president and general manager in charge of all TRW operations.

The crisis also contributed to Dean Wooldridge's decision to retire early. In 1961, many factors, including the electronics downturn, were weighing on his mind. "I was not doing an adequate job of 'presidenting,'" he admits, adding:

> There were certain aspects I knew that I should do differently to be a good president, such as spending more time in Cleveland, such as getting around to the various plants and facilities, such as making pep talks to employees, such as making myself more known internally and externally. These were important things, but they just didn't go with my personality. I didn't enjoy such things. Yet I realized that they were important and should be done. So I resigned.

Late in 1961, Wooldridge announced his retirement, effective January 1, 1962. He remained a director of TRW until 1969, but increasingly devoted his attention to writing and other scholarly pursuits as an adjunct professor at Caltech.[41]

To succeed Wooldridge as president, the board chose the forty-nine-year-old Shepard—known to everyone as "Shep." The choice was widely applauded inside the company, where for more than a decade he had held a series of increasingly responsible positions. An aeronautical engineer (trained at Auburn University), a survivor of Pearl Harbor, and once the youngest general officer in the U.S. Air Force, Shepard commanded thorough respect from the former R-W units as well as from the former TP divisions. His exterior was all affability and folksiness, a southern Fred Crawford without the flamboyance. Inside lay a core of steel, an impressive ability to assimilate detail and spot meaningful patterns, and a remarkable capacity for hard work. Observers who did not know him well sometimes remarked about his occasional tendency to knock off work early in good weather for a game of golf. They failed to realize that he routinely arrived at the office before 6 A.M., and often before 5.[42]

Shepard's management style complemented well those of Crawford and Wright, whom he admired and considered close friends. He shared Crawford's fondness for people as well as Wright's modesty and belief in delegation. In later years, when Shepard was chairman of TRW, a reporter asked him for a definition of his job: "That's easy," he replied. "I'm everybody's assistant." Behind the comment lay a basic approach to management: "It's principally the people [who are on the front lines] who come up with the ideas. From these the top-level people make choices. This company has never been operated by anybody who thought they had all the answers."[43]

When presented with options, Shepard did not shirk from making choices. Together with Wright, he closely scrutinized PSI and other fledgling electronic businesses. He quickly sized up Warren Hayes, head of the West Coast electronics components businesses, including PSI, as unsuitable for managing a turnaround and replaced him with Sid Webb. That proved an inspired choice, as Webb not only stopped the bleeding at PSI but also devised ways to implement Wooldridge's original strategy for TRW to become a leading producer of electronic components.

Shepard also took a hard look at the consumer electronics businesses nourished by the TP side of the company. Immediately after the merger, TRW had added two small acquisitions in consumer electronics: Bel Canto Stereophonic Recordings, a California-based producer of prerecorded tapes, stereophonic records, and stereo tape cartridges, and New York City-based Magnetic Recording Industries, a maker of electronic equipment for teaching languages that was subsequently renamed the Educational Electronics Division. In 1961, the latter effort was further expanded through the formation of a joint venture with McGraw-Hill to develop, produce, and market a wide range of teaching equipment and programs. In 1962, these units were combined with Bell Sound and Dage TV into a new Columbus Division, based in Columbus, Ohio.[44]

The Columbus Division continued to lose ground, however. Although Bell Sound finally delivered on its tape cartridge system, it failed to define a standard, and it fell farther behind bigger and better-financed makers of stereo equipment. At Dage TV signs of trouble were likewise apparent. The unit initially benefited from TRW's close association with the Air Force, winning the largest single contract in its history to provide remote viewing of fueling operations at Atlas missile installations. As an assembler of purchased components, however, Dage TV simply could not compete with bigger, vertically integrated rivals, and it scrambled to find new avenues of growth. The most promising opportunity involved making electronic controls for machine tools, including contouring controls for multiple-axis milling, grinding, and turning machines, as well as controls for flame cutting, filament winding, and drafting. The chronic problem Dage TV encountered, however, was lack of capital to get the business off the ground. Finally, in 1963, Shepard split off the part of Dage TV that manufactured numerical controls, combined it with the Computer Division, and sold the rest. The following year, he completed the divestiture by selling the Columbus Division to a group of its own managers.[45]

Shepard also had little patience for TRW's computer business, which encountered difficulties during the early 1960s, although it pioneered many new products, services, and applications. In 1959, for example, the R-W Division established an "Intellectronics" laboratory focused on the use of "electronic techniques to magnify and extend the capabilities of the unaided human intellect." Prodded by Ramo, the lab developed display devices and software to make computers easier to understand and operate for nontechnical users—a concept similar to today's Apple Macintosh personal computers.

The lab's approach proved so compelling inside the company that TRW soon merged the lab with the Computer Division and other nonmilitary parts of the R-W Division into an Intellectronics Group. The unit's second-generation computer, the RW-400, drew heavily on the lab's work. It used a variety of consoles and visual display devices to produce and manipulate diagrams, charts, and photographs, as well as printed words and numbers. The RW-400 also featured a modular design that allowed users to tailor systems to their particular needs by buying appropriate configurations and types of memory, input-output devices, and other components, including some available from other manufacturers. The RW-400 was also polymorphic: it was designed so that users could automatically link modules to form a single, very powerful computer, or they could, "a short time later," break the links to operate several smaller but completely independent computers.[46]

TRW promoted the RW-400 and other models heavily and formed joint-venture operations in the United Kingdom, France, and Japan to manufacture and sell equipment overseas. The company did not disclose the results of its computer operations after 1959, when it posted sales of about $25 million, although in 1963 sales apparently still hovered at about that level, and the business had yet to achieve profitability. Indeed, it continued to manifest disturbing signs. About four-fifths of sales went to the military, where the company had a strong track record and enjoyed good customer relations. On the commercial side, TRW computers made little headway. Although it was one of the first computer makers to target the automatic control of industrial processes, this market proved difficult to serve. For one thing, TRW lacked the internal expertise to make technical sales to particular companies in particular industries, and developing that skill consumed far more time and money than first anticipated. In addition, many customers proved skittish about relying so heavily on an unproven technology and an unproven computer company. To make matters worse, by the early 1960s, IBM, GE, Honeywell, and other better-funded rivals began to vie for business in the process-control industries.[47]

"It was obvious," Shepard recalls, "that as soon as companies like IBM really wanted to invade that particular niche . . . they had far more resources and a far better distribution system than we did. So we said to the West Coast, 'It's time to go out of this business now. Find a way to get out of it without costing us too much money.'" Soon enough, Ramo found an opportunity.[48]

During the fall of 1963, Martin Marietta had attracted notice in the business press for amassing a huge hoard of cash—about $150 million—from the sale of acquired assets. CEO George Bunker talked openly about using these funds to expand his company's position in computers and the automation of industrial processes. Bunker approached Sperry Rand but could not work out an acceptable deal. TRW watched this spectacle with more than passing interest. When Ramo and Bunker happened to cross paths at a management conference in October, there was a rapid exchange of thoughts and possibilities. On November 21, Wright met Bunker in New York to work out the details of a deal, which they accomplished "in a matter of days" to the satisfaction of their respective boards of directors.

The result was the establishment of a joint-venture company, the Bunker-Ramo Corporation, in which Martin Marietta held by far the bigger stake. In return for $17.4 million in cash and a 20 percent equity stake, TRW transferred to Bunker-Ramo its computer operations, including the facility at Canoga Park and the numerical control operations once part of Dage TV. Martin Marietta added its own military electronics operations and also arranged to acquire Teleregister, a stock quotation service, as part of the package. Bunker served as chairman of the new unit, with Ramo agreeing not only to lend his name, but also to serve as president for a period of at least two years. (During that time, Ramo remained vice chairman of TRW.) The new combination took with it several key managers, including Milt Mohr, Burt Miller, and Chuck Allen (temporarily), who had helped establish R-W in the 1950s.[49]

CONSUMMATING THE MERGER

The sale of TRW's Computer Division, the resolution of crises in its other electronics businesses, and the establishment of STL as a promising business provided answers to many of the biggest questions surrounding the merger between TP and R-W. In the mid-1960s, TRW was becoming one company rather than two, and taking on a single, unified outlook. The changes were apparent in many ways: in the retirements of Wooldridge and Johnson; in Shepard's decisive actions as president; in Ramo's divided responsibilities at TRW and Bunker-Ramo; and in the sale of the second "corporate" headquarters at Canoga Park. The final transformation of TP and R-W into a single organization—the consummation of the merger—awaited three further steps: the creation of consensus around goals and objectives for the corporation as a whole; additional changes in management and operating policies; and a new corporate identity campaign that emphasized one company with diverse capabilities.

Around broad goals and objectives for the company, consensus was easily reached: the company sought to grow rapidly and along the way to reduce its dependence on military business. At the annual planning conference at Fred Crawford's Vermont farm in July 1961, Dave Wright issued a major challenge to his troops: to achieve $1 billion in revenues before his scheduled retirement in 1970. Although TRW was coming off 1960 sales of about $400 million and staring at a down year—reflecting the crisis in electronics, a recession in the United States, and Kennedy-era defense cuts—the group endorsed the goal and set about figuring out systematically how to do it. And Wright added a kicker: a promise that, should the company hit $1 billion in sales before his scheduled retirement in the spring of 1970, he would step down early.[50]

Wright also sought to diversify the company's business, a goal widely shared inside the company. In the year of the merger, nearly three-quarters of the company's revenues had stemmed directly and indirectly from sales to the U.S. military. TRW strived to break this dependence on what it believed was a highly cyclical market in defense. It also aimed explicitly to reduce the company's reliance on any single line of business or contract, which had been major concerns in 1958, when so much of TP's fortune rode on jet aircraft engines and so much of R-W's depended on the Air Force ICBMs.[51]

In pursuing a strategy of diversification, TRW responded not only to its unique imperatives, but also to forces reshaping large American corporations as a whole. Between 1949 and 1969, the number of *Fortune* 500 companies that derived the majority of their revenues from a single or dominant business dropped by half (from about 70 percent to about 36 percent), whereas the number of companies that gleaned revenues from activities related and unrelated to their original core business more than doubled (from about 30 percent to about 64 percent). Several factors accounted for this trend, including the ease of making acquisitions, recent legislation, and judicial interpretations of federal antitrust law. In 1950, Congress had enacted the Celler-Kefauver Act, a tough statute that prohibited mergers that reduced competition "in any line of commerce," as well as mergers that "may substantially lessen competition." The statute had a chilling effect on mergers between companies in the same or closely related industries, outlawing not only horizontal combinations between competitors, but also vertical combinations of suppliers and their customers in the same industry. The decisive constitutional test of the statute came in 1962, when the U.S. Supreme Court overturned a merger between Brown Shoe (a manufacturer) and Kinney Shoe (a retailer). Soon thereafter, TRW's board met with Allen Holmes, managing partner of the Cleveland law firm Jones, Day and a leading antitrust lawyer. He advised that "any acquisitions of other concerns will ordinarily have to be limited to those whose products [TRW does] not now buy, make, or sell, and who do not now control a major portion of the market in their product lines."[52]

During 1963, TRW negotiated to make two big acquisitions of U.S.-based companies with the express intent of adding significantly to the total business of the corporation and "providing [an] entirely new line of products in the commercial rather than the military or defense areas, thereby reducing the Corporation's dependence on U.S. government business." Both deals were consummated on the same date in April 1964. The first involved the purchase of Marlin-Rockwell Corporation, a leading manufacturer of precision ball bearings and other types of bearings for transportation equipment and general industrial use. The company, which had grown by internal development as well as consolidations with other bearing companies, employed about thirty-two hundred people in three plants, including two in upstate New York and one in Connecticut. In 1963, coming off several years of struggle and flat performance, it posted sales of $44.2 million, with net income (after taxes) of $3.4 million. TRW's analysis showed "ample room" to improve profit margins, with products "open to technical improvements" well within TRW's capability to make.[53]

The second major acquisition of 1964 was Ross Gear and Tool Company, Inc., of Lafayette, Indiana. Since its founding in 1908, Ross Gear had become a leading supplier of manual and power-steering gears for vehicles of all types, with especially strong positions in steering gears for off-highway vehicles and heavy-duty trucks. At the time of the deal, Ross Gear posted annual revenues of about $32 million and employed roughly sixteen hundred people. It operated two manufacturing plants in the United States, owned subsidiaries in Brazil and Switzerland, and maintained "substantial investments" in foreign affiliates in England, Australia, France, and Canada.[54]

The acquisitions of Marlin-Rockwell and Ross Gear had the desired effect on TRW's revenues and sales mix. In 1964, revenues surpassed $500 million, and for the first time since before the Korean War, a majority of business originated as sales to commercial customers, with the amount based on defense contracts down to just over 30 percent.[55]

The company's success in meeting objectives for growth and diversification reflected the informal decision-making style at the top, the unusual role played by

Ramo, and the company's decentralized organization structure and policies. "Dave Wright and I worked smoothly together because we thought alike," recalls Shepard, adding,

> We both had the same ideas and the same understanding, and the same approach to working. . . . Dave Wright wasn't a boss; he was an associate. He didn't try to act like a boss any more than Fred [Crawford] or I did. He obviously had the final say on anything, but he conducted things so that it was a joint decision—not just with me, but with whomever he worked.

Shepard liked to kid Wright by noting that the president's job was to make money and the chairman's to spend it. In practice, each man participated in every key decision and, unless traveling or on vacation, in all key meetings of the company's management. When one was absent for an important occasion, the other took over. Each was comfortable with decisions made by the other.[56]

These arrangements also suited Ramo, who enjoyed a special status in the company after the merger, which made him a multimillionaire as well as one of the biggest stockholders. Although he served as a top officer for two decades (executive vice president from 1958 to 1961 and vice chairman from then until his retirement at age sixty-five in 1978), he had no direct operating responsibilities and seldom appeared at routine management meetings. He spoke frequently with Wright and Shepard and, in avuncular fashion, took special interest in the former R-W businesses. He spent most of his time, however, looking outward from the company. "Not with total facetiousness," he told an interviewer in 1984, "I really did my retiring in 1958, because I shifted to a pattern of activity which continues to this very moment." This pattern (which still holds in the mid-1990s) consisted of a whirlwind schedule of meetings, consulting projects, teaching assignments, and speaking engagements, plus cultural, educational, and philanthropic endeavors, and many other activities too numerous to mention.

For a time, he kept an office at Space Park but worked mostly out of a small office near his home in Beverly Hills. Between 1963 and 1967, his position as president of Bunker-Ramo occupied a good deal of his time, although, as a colleague noted, this responsibility did not indicate a lack of focus on TRW, but rather Ramo's capacity to hold down two full-time jobs. He served on many national advisory boards and councils, on several corporate boards, and as an adjunct professor at Caltech. He also became a frequent public speaker on subjects related to technology, and a prolific writer of books and articles on subjects ranging from the familiar (*Cure for Chaos,* a book for the general reader about systems approaches to technology and management) to the idiosyncratic (*Extraordinary Tennis for the Ordinary Player*). He moved in fast circles that did not often, except in his own person, overlap. He hobnobbed easily with CEOs, top academic scientists, senior government policymakers, Hollywood entertainers, and renowned classical musicians, on occasion playing violin duets with his neighbor, Jascha Heifetz.[57]

A reporter described Ramo's role at TRW in the 1960s as "a kind of self-monitored radar to anticipate coming perils or opportunities." He also served to uphold high standards and as an agent of change. Bob Burnett, who helped lead TRW's ongoing missile development work in the 1960s, recalls Ramo as being "very visible, and very interested in what we were doing. He's an unbelievably quick study, so within minutes of engaging a subject in a meeting, he was not only up to speed but ahead of most of us." He acted as an internal consultant, asking probing questions and penetrating through nonsensical, evasive, or insufficiently measured replies. A meeting with Ramo, says another associate, was like "taking a Ph.D. general exam." Ramo particularly concerned himself with recruiting, tracking how many of Caltech's top engineering and physics students joined TRW and demanding explanations for the candidates who went elsewhere.[58]

As vice chairman, Ramo paid close attention to TRW's planning processes and systems—a principal source of integration across the company's diverse businesses. In August 1962, he established planning teams to examine four areas defined to cross organizational boundaries where possible: space and missiles, automotive, advanced military products and services, and advanced electronics. Drawing on board members, operating personnel from the groups and divisions, and corporate staff, the planning teams were charged to study each area "in the broadest possible fashion," including "the national and, where pertinent, the international situation, the markets, the technology, the competition, and the present and future developments of the area as a profitable business venture."[59]

The informal and decentralized leadership style of Wright and Shepard and the visionary role of Ramo combined with TRW's organization and management policies to promote rapid growth. After the merger, the company effectively adopted a group structure, with divisions clustered together on the basis of similar markets served. The Automotive Group, headed by Ed Riley, included the engine and chassis parts and replacement parts operations, as well as the Canadian subsidiary, Thompson Products, Ltd., and a burgeoning portfolio of international operations and joint ventures. Pace's Tapco Group included the Jet, Accessories, Pneumatics, and Kolcast Divisions. The surviving members among the original R-W businesses were divided into two groups: STL, an entity unto itself under Mettler, and an Electronics Group made up of the remaining West Coast divisions and presided over by Sid Webb.

TRW's group executives enjoyed considerable autonomy. Explained Ramo:

> As to almost all basic operating decisions, our four group executives can commit to contracts, reorganize their operations, hire and assign executives, make acquisitions, spend internally generated funds for R and D, all with approximately the same freedom and the same minimum degree of need for prior approval on large issues as if they were heading separate companies. The TRW corporate management exerts no more "supervision" and is no more demanding of explanations or insistence on audit and approval than a sympathetic board of directors that these same chief executives might hope to deal with if they operated independent corporations.[60]

The group vice presidents met monthly with Wright, Shepard, and (sometimes) Ramo to form TRW's policy group. Division general managers, who possessed "complete bottom-line responsibility," as well as responsibility for meeting growth targets, met monthly with the group executives and Wright and Shepard for a management meeting or operating review. This system, says Shepard, "emphasized in the operating managers' minds that they had a considerable amount of power delegated to them. We tried to cultivate independence. We wanted [them] . . . to be able to call their own shots. That way, we thought, they'd perform better."[61]

As TRW added new divisions and subsidiaries in commercial areas, it found itself becoming a different kind of corporation—different not only from its predecessor companies, but also from the growing population of large, diversified companies elsewhere in the economy. The differences manifested themselves in the scale and scope of operations; the products and services rendered; the nature and competitive dynamics of the markets served; the background, experience, and expectations of employees; and the duties and interactions of managers. Although Wright, Shepard, and Ramo remained firmly in control at the top, the generation of managers below them came from different times and places, and the torch was beginning to pass. Among corporate officers, long-time TP executives Arch Colwell (R&D), Ray Livingstone (human relations), and Ernie Brelsford (finance) retired in the mid-1960s, and their replacements— Harper North, Jim Dunlap, and Chuck Allen—were all young and energetic, bearing advanced degrees in technical fields and/or business management, and schooled in the pressured environment of R-W's rapid growth. The general managers of the groups and of most of the divisions and subsidiaries were cut from the same cloth.

Looking outside, TRW faced new kinds of problems. For one thing, it was increasingly difficult to explain the company to important constituents. "During these recent years of change," the company acknowledged in its annual report for 1964,

> it has understandably been difficult to bring the new image of the company into focus. TRW cannot be categorized as an auto parts company, or an aerospace company, or as an electronics company. Rather TRW is a company of many specialties engaged in the development and practical application of advanced concepts to products and services for carefully selected segments of these and other major industries.[62]

At the same time, the company's leaders recognized the need for more aggressive public relations to increase name recognition, to inform investors about the company's distinctive strategy, and to bolster the value of its stock and its price-earnings ratio. Late in 1963, the company branded its groups and divisions, with the initials TRW forming an integral part of their names: STL became TRW Space Technologies Laboratories; the Automotive Group became TRW Automotive Group; the Electro-Mechanical Group (an interim name given to the Tapco Group) became TRW Equipment Group; and so on. Acquired divisions lost their founding names, as Kolcast Industries Division became TRW Metals Division, and the Good-All Division in the TRW Electronics Group split into two pieces, TRW Capacitor Division and TRW Rectifiers. Only subsidiaries such as Ramsey Corporation and foreign entities such as Thompson Products, Ltd. (Canada) retained their original names.[63]

The next step involved transforming the identity of the corporation. In May 1965, Thompson Ramo Wooldridge, Inc. became a more manageable TRW Inc. Shepard joked that the corporate name change was made to relieve weary travelers on company business from the burden of logging a long name in hotel registers. But the real motive was to imprint a new corporate image. That purpose was reaffirmed later in the year, when TRW-STL became TRW Systems Group. When the STL sign came down from E2, the tall administration building at Space Park, it marked the end of an era for many R-W veterans. As one of them put it, "That was the day the merger took effect."[64]

PART THREE

Diversified Corporation

▮　▮　　▮　　▮　　▮

1965–1996

DURING THE MID-1960S, MOST BIG AMERICAN CORPORATIONS ENTERED A PERIOD OF astonishing change. Consider the starting point. In 1965, U.S. manufacturers dominated both domestic and world markets in many industries. Imports accounted for less than 10 percent of U.S. purchases of automobiles, steel, machine tools, electrical equipment, and consumer electronics. The United States maintained a positive balance of trade. NASA's Apollo program proceeded at high levels of funding, and the U.S. defense budget consumed a growing share of federal expenditures. The dollar, with its value pegged to the price of gold, undergirded the nonsocialist economies. The Great Society programs of President Lyndon Johnson mobilized the power and resources of the federal government in an attempt to cure social ills. This was the heyday of the American empire, the apogee of American political, economic, and cultural influence around the world.

During the next three decades, the business environment altered dramatically. Imports, especially from Asia, claimed rising shares of most basic industries and nearly overwhelmed consumer electronics, as foreign producers offered goods with lower costs, higher quality, or, most compellingly, both. Trade accounts tipped strongly out of balance as the United States began a trend of importing far more than it exported. The federal government racked up sizable deficits and, cumulatively, a staggering amount of debt. Decoupled from the gold standard, the dollar fluctuated widely in value, alternately rewarding and penalizing American companies in ways hard to anticipate or control. The triumph of Apollo did not lead to comparable conquests in space. The defense budget swelled during the early phases of the Vietnam War, shrank after 1970, inflated again rapidly during the first years of the Reagan administration, and then in the mid-1980s began a prolonged contraction reflecting the end of the Cold War and the beginnings of a fundamentally new world order. In 1994, the Republican Party acquired control of both houses of the U.S. Congress and helped legislate significant reforms to many government programs and initiatives stretching back beyond the Great Society as far as the New Deal.

These changes carried profound consequences for most big American companies. During the late 1960s, most of these enterprises expanded and diversified rapidly, usually relying on acquisitions. This era came to a sudden halt in the early 1970s, as first a recession and a bear market, then worldwide energy shortages, the abandonment of the gold standard, and creeping inflation unsettled the world economy. Wild swings in energy prices, prolonged and deep recessions in the early 1980s and again in the early 1990s, and volatile securities markets further compounded problems. During these years, companies that once seemed invulnerable—GM, Ford, Chrysler, U.S. Steel, Bethlehem Steel, International Harvester, Caterpillar, Eastman Kodak, Xerox, IBM— reported record losses, endured crises (in some cases flirting with bankruptcy), changed management, and underwent restructurings that usually involved significant divestitures and downsizing.

In such an environment the work of the corporation also became more complex and demanding. To manage diverse businesses, large companies first followed a trend toward decentralization. These companies developed formal systems, processes, and procedures to track progress and aid decision making. Corporate executives also relied heavily on financial information and statistics as well as on new tools of portfolio analysis in making business decisions. Of necessity, senior managers delegated authority and responsibility to subordinate managers. The biggest companies built whole new layers of management to oversee groups and other agglomerations of business units. CEOs of diversified companies—even when assisted by colleagues in an "office of the chief executive"—typically spent little time on the concerns of any particular business unit unless a crisis compelled their attention. In the 1990s, however, the trend toward decentralization partly reversed under mounting cost pressure and more exacting standards of performance. As part of downsizing initiatives and corporate restructurings, for example, many big companies shortened reporting channels and abolished layers of management.[1]

Another major trend in big corporations was increasing specialization. New departments and functions appeared or acquired an elevated status in big companies: *public affairs*, to cope with increasing government regulation and intervention*; human resources*, to deal with the changing composition of the work force, new employment laws, and heightened need for training; *marketing*, to understand better the behavior of customers; *strategic planning*, to prepare for new competitive realities; *information systems*, to oversee the revolutionary impact of information technology on all aspects of business life; and *corporate communications*, to respond to new pressures from investors, financial analysts, and advocacy groups, as well as the insatiable appetite of the media.[2]

These patterns in corporate evolution occurred in a context of the rising speed and volume of information flow across corporate (and national) boundaries. Companies, business schools, the business press, and consulting firms promulgated and publicized new management concepts and tools. Joint ventures and strategic alliances between customers and suppliers and even between competitors proliferated and helped spread knowledge. The world of corporate management was transformed: the top executives of big companies now most likely held MBAs or other advanced degrees. They spent much of their time dealing with outside constituencies or, inside the company, reviewing abstract and aggregated information and managing managers.

Although top corporate executives apparently operated in a grayer, more constrained world than their predecessors, the stakes remained high. They continued to confront complex strategic decisions and the necessity of taking major (sometimes bet-the-company-sized) risks. In manufacturing companies, for instance, the outcome of choices to build a new plant, in what location, under what financial incentives and arrangements, with whom as partner, and under what economic scenarios could have enormous repercussions on the long-term viability of an enterprise.

All of these changes, trends, and issues affected TRW (see Exhibits III-1 to III-5). During the late 1960s, TRW fashioned itself into "a different kind of company" based on a set of particular "specialties" or capabilities in manufacturing and the management of complex projects and systems. The company also passed through a cycle of

---

EXHIBIT III - 1

TRW INC. NET REVENUES AND NET INCOME, 1965–1996

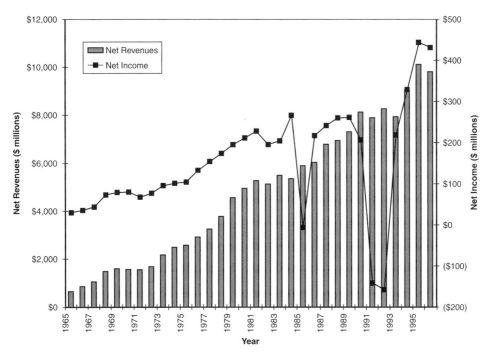

SOURCE: Annual reports.

expansion and diversification followed by retrenchment and regeneration. On its way up, TRW scored some major hits in new products (rack-and-pinion steering, occupant restraint systems, bigger and more complex spacecraft, new electronic systems), new markets (especially automotive supply in Europe), and new businesses (avionics, energy products, consumer and business credit reporting). The company's employment hit an all-time high in 1979 but almost immediately began to plunge, as TRW and many of the markets it served encountered turbulent times.

During the 1970s and 1980s, many of the company's businesses began to falter, and some (civil systems, energy systems, electronic equipment, and certain areas of automotive electronics) began to fail. TRW's strategy of diversification, which counted on upswings in some businesses to offset declines in others, apparently worked until the mid-1980s, although disquieting signs became apparent earlier. Management settled on strong medicine. In 1985, the company absorbed its first annual loss since the Great Depression and proceeded to divest many units, including such long-standing businesses as aircraft equipment and commercial electronic components, as well as more recent and profitable ventures in industrial and energy products. At the same time, it placed big bets by directing capital to newer businesses designed to carry the company forward into the twenty-first century: automotive electronics, information systems and services, and especially occupant restraint systems. A second restructuring—and two

EXHIBIT III - 2

TRW Inc. Measures of Profitability, 1965–1996

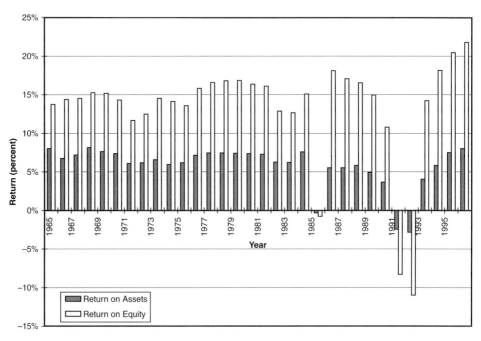

SOURCE: Annual reports.

more loss years—during the early 1990s cleansed the portfolio of problematical units and streamlined the corporation, positioning it for renewed growth in three core businesses: automotive supply, space and defense, and information systems and services.

TRW grew most rapidly (in real terms) between 1965 and 1969, when it burst ahead through every available means: extension of existing product lines, vertical integration, acquisition, geographical expansion, and new ventures (Chapter 10). The company obtained a valuable automotive steering technology from a foreign acquisition, and through acquisitions and joint ventures it gained significant business with foreign automakers, including the strongest in Europe. By 1969, the company conducted more automotive business overseas than in the United States. In space and defense markets, TRW Systems Group managed big, complex programs for defense and commercial communications, national security, and space exploration, including the Initial Defense Communications Satellite Program, the Defense Support Program, INTELSAT III, and the lunar module descent engine for the Apollo moon landings. Among many domestic acquisitions, four added promising new lines of business: United-Greenfield in tools and industrial equipment; United-Carr in fasteners and electrical controls; Reda Pump in energy products; and Credit Data Corporation in consumer credit reporting. In

EXHIBIT III - 3

TRW INC. EMPLOYMENT, 1965–1996

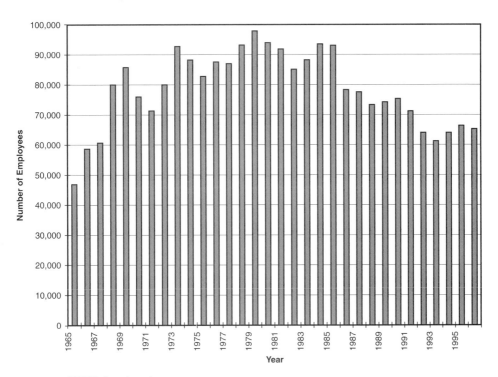

SOURCE: Annual reports.

1969, as Dave Wright handed the reins over to Horace Shepard, the company's future seemed extraordinarily bright.

During the early 1970s, however, significant changes in the business environment checked TRW's rapid growth and caused it to reassess its capabilities and strategy (Chapter 11). The first signs of a new era occurred in space and defense, where the completion of NASA's Apollo program and the winding down of U.S. involvement in the Vietnam War produced a deep recession in the aerospace industry. At Space Park, employment dropped by one-third, and the company scrambled to find new opportunities in spacecraft, electronic systems, software, civil systems, and energy systems. In climbing out of the aerospace recession, TRW was responsible for such notable technological achievements in spacecraft as *Pioneer 10* and *Pioneer 11,* which explored the outer planets of the solar system; the Viking biology instrument, which scratched for signs of life on Mars; the Defense Satellite Communications System II, which defined new standards for military communications; and several classified programs of significant size. TRW also expanded its business in electronic systems, developed new capabilities in software and large-scale integrated circuits, and made exploratory attempts to apply aerospace technology to commercial or nondefense government markets.

EXHIBIT III - 4

TRW INC. SALES BY LINE OF BUSINESS, 1968–1996

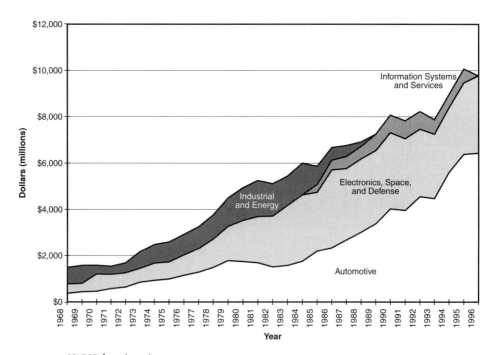

SOURCE: Annual reports.

NOTE: Categories adjusted for reporting changes in various years.

The company no sooner rebuilt its business in space and defense, however, than another blow struck (Chapter 12). The energy shock of 1974 triggered a deep world-wide recession that affected most of the company's businesses, especially automotive supply and industrial products such as bearings, tools, and fasteners. At the same time, promising new ventures in electronic equipment required significant capital invest-ments while continually delaying anticipated returns. That TRW outperformed the U.S. economy and most other manufacturing corporations bore testimony to the popu-larity of hot new products such as power rack-and-pinion steering systems, a new kind of seat belt for passenger cars, and hydrostatic steering for bigger vehicles, as well as to TRW's participation in major new defense programs such as the Fleet Satellite Communications System and NASA's Tracking and Data Relay Satellite System. Still, the severity of the crisis obliged management to reassess the growth strategy of the 1960s. A new management team headed by Rube Mettler, who succeeded Shepard as chairman and CEO at the end of 1977, took responsibility for this review and devel-oped new financial goals and corporate policies for the decade ahead.

The early 1980s marked a period of strategic reorientation and restructuring at TRW (Chapter 13). Troubles in the electronic equipment business could no longer be ignored, and the company took large write-offs in closing down several units. Amid

EXHIBIT III - 5

TRW INC. SALES MIX BY LINE OF BUSINESS, 1968–1996

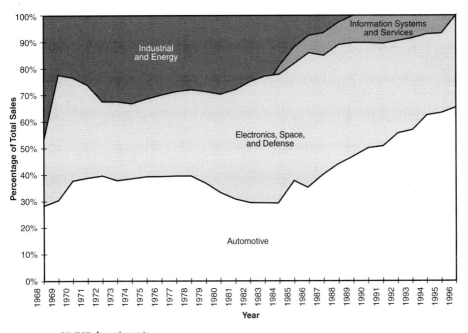

SOURCE: Annual reports.
NOTE: Categories adjusted for reporting changes in various years.

escalating global rivalry, U.S. automakers suffered huge losses and passed their misfortunes on to suppliers. TRW's geographical balance and the continuing popularity of its new steering and safety products partially offset these problems. Momentarily high energy prices and the Reagan defense buildup also helped. In the mid-1980s, however, energy prices plummeted and defense spending began a sustained decline. Mettler and TRW's new president, Joe Gorman, saw that funding TRW's best growth opportunities—occupant restraint systems, automotive electronics, and information systems and services—would necessitate a major restructuring. In 1985, the company began divesting "nonstrategic" businesses such as aircraft components, industrial and energy products, and commercial electronic equipment.

During the late 1980s and early 1990s, TRW entered another new era under a new management team (Chapter 14). Led by Gorman, who succeeded Mettler as chairman in 1988, the company continued to invest heavily to develop capabilities and capacity for its most promising businesses, especially occupant restraint systems. Although government space and defense budgets remained tight, TRW was positioned in relatively strong and stable segments in defense electronics, avionics, and software. The company continued its string of notable contributions to the American space program, building advanced scientific satellites such as the Gamma Ray Observatory and the Advanced X-ray Astrophysical Facility, as well as the latest Tracking and Data Relay Satellites and the next-generation communications payload aboard the Milstar satellites.

During the late 1980s and early 1990s, however, TRW once again confronted a severe worldwide recession that required significant changes in strategy and organization, including ultimately a second restructuring. To increase sales to Japanese automakers, it formed joint ventures with leading Japanese suppliers. It also paid down debt, abolished a layer of management, and divested still more operations, including the automotive aftermarket distribution business and marginal or struggling units in automotive supply and information systems and services.

By the mid-1990s, these measures appeared to be paying off, as TRW reported record peaks in sales and earnings. The company's management team blended experienced veterans such as Gorman with a younger generation led by new president and chief operating officer Peter Hellman (Chapter 15). During the previous three decades, the company traveled a full circle of expansion through diversification followed by contraction, divestitures, and renewed emphasis on core businesses. At the end of 1996, TRW remained a diversified and global high-technology corporation, a company of formidable capabilities, but it managed a streamlined portfolio of businesses that were operated to ensure not only sustained profitability but also renewed growth. Although its prospects appeared bright, TRW also looked forward to addressing major challenges in each of its key lines of business.

During the 1950s and 1960s, TRW's top brass assembled every summer at Fred Crawford's farm in Vermont to plan the future. Pictured here: Si Ramo addresses the group in 1967. The topic: diversification.

ACCURATE SPRING (founded 1930)

United-Greenfield Corporation's newest division is a manufacturer of springs, wire forms and metal stampings. Accurate Spring Manufacturing Company with its two subsidiaries was acquired in late 1967. Its three plants are located just west of Chicago. The complete story of Accurate Spring division is given on pages twelve and thirteen of this report.

J. H. WILLIAMS & CO. (founded 1882)

Drop forged hand tools such as wrenches, pliers and sockets, and commercial drop forgings comprise the Williams line. Some 4,500 standard catalog products are marketed through industrial distributors, many of whom also sell the products of other divisions. Over 1,000 stock forged items include eye bolts, hoist hooks, and the like. Other forged items are made to customers' specifications. The plant in Buffalo, N. Y., contains unique Williams-engineered equipment.

WHITMAN & BARNES (founded 1848)

Whitman & Barnes is one of the oldest quality names in twist drills, reamers and related products. These are distributed nationwide through "blue ribbon" distributors and tool specialists, some of whom have represented the company since the turn of the century. W & B's plant in Plymouth, Mich. is one of the most modern in the industry and is equipped for efficient output of both standard and special products for industrial users.

**U
GREE
CORPO
**
For the ben
stockholders, a
the memory of
ones, descriptions
Greenfield's opera
their products and
marks are again incl
annual report. The
products made by th
shown on page 16
most of the units
established a long
120 years, anothe
United-Greenfie
tion itself has
ten years, h
formed in
the
Un

WENDT-SONIS COMPANY (founded 1933)

Wendt-Sonis is a pioneer and acknowledged leader in production of carbides and carbide tipped tools. Tipped tools, many special solid carbide tools, and tool holders are volume items. In addition, Wendt-Sonis produces and sells basic carbide powder and inserts, blanks, and wear parts in a wide range of tungsten carbide grades. Production facilities are in Hannibal, Mo., Rogers, Ark. and Bentonville, Ark.

VULCAN TOOLS (founded 1960)

Some 3,000 items used in automobile service and related fields are marketed by Vulcan Tools. They include hand tools such as wrenches and pliers, and electric and pneumatic power tools. Wheel aligning equipment, battery chargers and similar heavy items are also in the Vulcan line. The division, based in Buffalo, N. Y., sells through franchised warehouses in major cities and direct-selling dealers who operate mobile vans.

UNIMET CARBIDES (founded 1955)

Carbide-tipped tools to cut the hardest steels and the new exotic alloys represent a fast growing field. Unimet offers an extensive line under its own name and also supplies the needs of other U-G divisions. This division manufactures its own basic carbide material, and also markets it in the form of carbide inserts and wear resistant parts for machinery. Plant and headquarters are in Chicago, adjacent to the Chicago-Latrobe facilities.

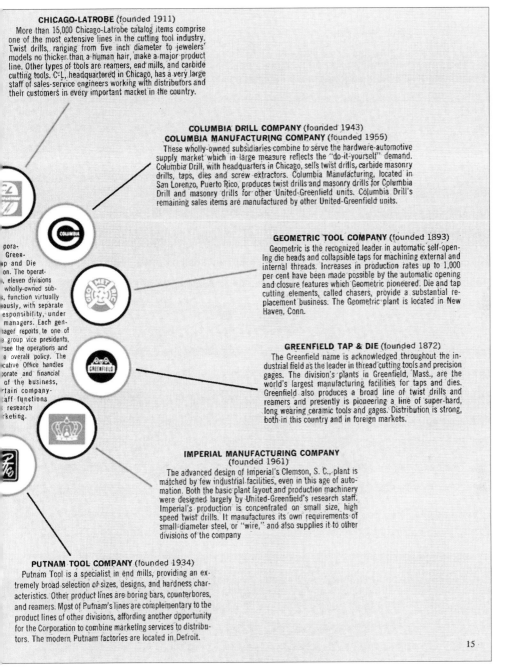

CHICAGO-LATROBE (founded 1911)

More than 15,000 Chicago-Latrobe catalog items comprise one of the most extensive lines in the cutting tool industry. Twist drills, ranging from five inch diameter to jewelers' models no thicker than a human hair, make a major product line. Other types of tools are reamers, end mills, and carbide cutting tools. C-L, headquartered in Chicago, has a very large staff of sales-service engineers working with distributors and their customers in every important market in the country.

COLUMBIA DRILL COMPANY (founded 1943)
COLUMBIA MANUFACTURING COMPANY (founded 1955)

These wholly-owned subsidiaries combine to serve the hardware-automotive supply market which in large measure reflects the "do-it-yourself" demand. Columbia Drill, with headquarters in Chicago, sells twist drills, carbide masonry drills, taps, dies and screw extractors. Columbia Manufacturing, located in San Lorenzo, Puerto Rico, produces twist drills and masonry drills for Columbia Drill and masonry drills for other United-Greenfield units. Columbia Drill's remaining sales items are manufactured by other United-Greenfield units.

GEOMETRIC TOOL COMPANY (founded 1893)

Geometric is the recognized leader in automatic self-opening die heads and collapsible taps for machining external and internal threads. Increases in production rates up to 1,000 per cent have been made possible by the automatic opening and closure features which Geometric pioneered. Die and tap cutting elements, called chasers, provide a substantial replacement business. The Geometric plant is located in New Haven, Conn.

GREENFIELD TAP & DIE (founded 1872)

The Greenfield name is acknowledged throughout the industrial field as the leader in thread cutting tools and precision gages. The division's plants in Greenfield, Mass., are the world's largest manufacturing facilities for taps and dies. Greenfield also produces a broad line of twist drills and reamers and presently is pioneering a line of super-hard, long wearing ceramic tools and gages. Distribution is strong, both in this country and in foreign markets.

IMPERIAL MANUFACTURING COMPANY
(founded 1961)

The advanced design of Imperial's Clemson, S. C., plant is matched by few industrial facilities, even in this age of automation. Both the basic plant layout and production machinery were designed largely by United-Greenfield's research staff. Imperial's production is concentrated on small size, high speed twist drills. It manufactures its own requirements of small-diameter steel, or "wire," and also supplies it to other divisions of the company

PUTNAM TOOL COMPANY (founded 1934)

Putnam Tool is a specialist in end mills, providing an extremely broad selection of sizes, designs, and hardness characteristics. Other product lines are boring bars, counterbores, and reamers. Most of Putnam's lines are complementary to the product lines of other divisions, affording another opportunity for the Corporation to combine marketing services to distributors. The modern Putnam factories are located in Detroit.

pora-
Green-
p and Die
on. The operat-
, eleven divisions
wholly-owned sub-
, function virtually
ously, with separate
esponsibility, under
managers. Each gen-
ager reports to one of
e group vice presidents,
see the operations and
e overall policy. The
cutive Office handles
porate and financial
of the business,
tain company-
aff functions
research
keting.

15

Already a diversified company, in the late 1960s TRW broadened its range further by acquiring diversified companies such as United-Greenfield and United-Carr. Pictured here: The dozen divisions of United-Greenfield.

Another acquisition from the late 1960s, Reda Pump, anchored the company's profitable Energy Products Group until it was sold off in the mid-1980s.

Two weeks before the first moon landing, TRW went public with its role. The lunar module descent engine performed perfectly on every Apollo mission, including Apollo 13, *when it substituted for the spacecraft's primary engine that was disabled in an explosion and brought the astronauts home safely.*

Above: *Introduced in 1972, the TRW Service Line, packaged and branded products for the automotive aftermarket, helped revive the company's struggling business in automotive replacement parts. A decade later, however, changes in distribution turned the Service Line into a business liability.*

Right: *TRW Equipment Group fabricated airfoils for the big turbojet engines of the 1970s and 1980s, but gradually lost ground as the number of customers dwindled and brought more work in-house. During the mid-1980s, TRW sold off its aircraft components business in pieces.*

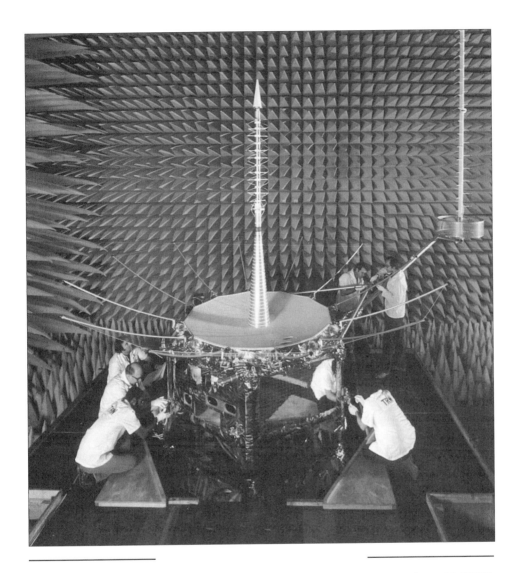

Left: *The Viking lander biological instrument was a marvel of miniaturization and one of the space program's major technological achievements in the 1970s. More than a thousand man-years of development poured into the instrument, which performed flawlessly on two missions, but uncovered no convincing evidence of life on Mars.*

Above: *Along with NASA's High Energy Astronomical Observatories, the Defense Satellite Communications System (DSCS-II), and the Defense Support Program, the Fleet Broadcast Satellite System (FLTSAT-COM) helped lift Space Park from the aerospace recession of 1970–1971.*

Above: *In 1983, TRW moved out of the Tapco complex to new headquarters in Lyndhurst, Ohio, on an estate formerly owned by U.S. Representatives Chester C. and Frances Payne Bolton.*

Above*: In 1977 and 1978, a new team of managers took over direction of the company. From left: Stan Pace, president; Rube Mettler, chairman and CEO; and Sid Webb, vice chairman.*

Pioneer 10 *and* Pioneer 11 *scored major triumphs in their voyages to the outer planets.* Pioneer 10 *returned the first close-ups of Jupiter in 1973 and ten years later became the first man-made object to leave the solar system.* Pioneer 11 *was the first probe to approach Saturn, returning this photograph six and one-half years after launch.*

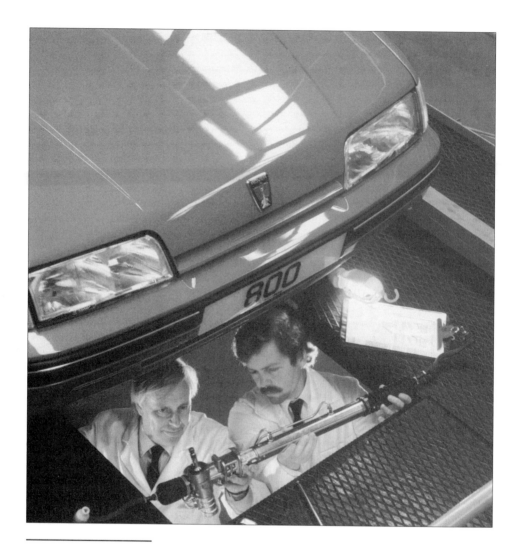

Among the company's hottest products during the past two decades have been rack-and-pinion steering systems, now standard on most passenger cars and light trucks around the world. The technology saves weight and space and provides superior feel. Pictured here: TRW engineers inspect a power rack-and-pinion steering system on a European luxury car.

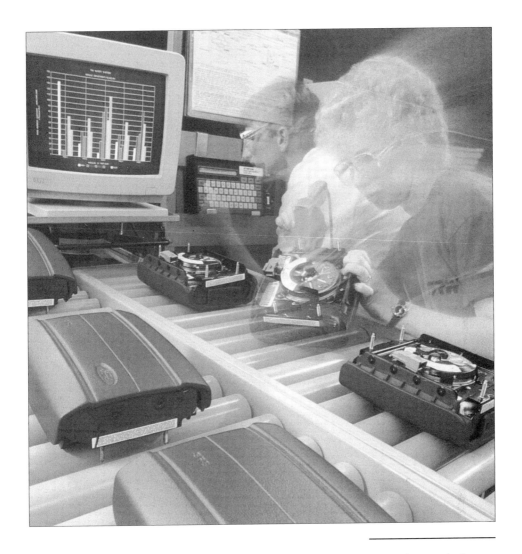

TRW's biggest single business today is occupant restraint systems, including air bag systems. Pictured here: Final assembly and inspection of air bag modules.

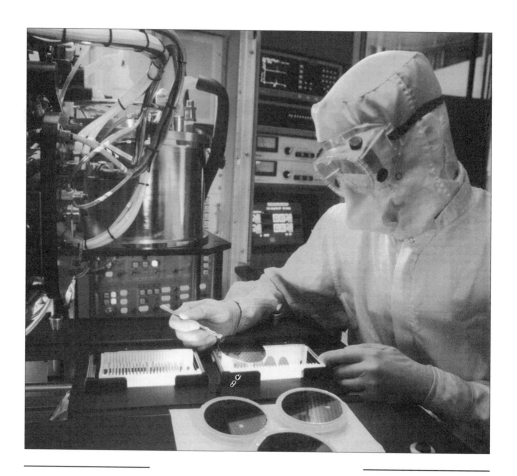

Above: *Long a pioneer in defense electronics, TRW continues to push the frontier into gallium-arsenide technology and other advanced technologies. Pictured here: Engineers handle gallium arsenide microwave/millimeter wave monolithic integrated circuits.*

Right: *For three decades, TRW has built satellites for the Defense Support Program. During the Gulf War of 1991, DSP satellites sensed Scud missile launches and helped protect United Nations troops on the ground.*

Right: *During the early 1990s, TRW maintained a consumer credit database containing 2.7 trillion pieces of information. To manage this vast resource, the company continually pioneered new software.*

Below: *The electronics payload aboard the Milstar satellites represents the biggest single contract in TRW's history. The satellites will support U.S. defense communications until well into the next century. Pictured here: TRW engineers test one of five extremely high frequency agile beam antennas launched with the spacecraft early in 1994.*

Facing page: *At thirty-five thousand pounds, NASA's* Gamma Ray Observatory *was the biggest and most complex satellite then placed in orbit. Since its launch in 1991, it has issued a stream of findings that challenge conventional theories about the origins and nature of the universe.*

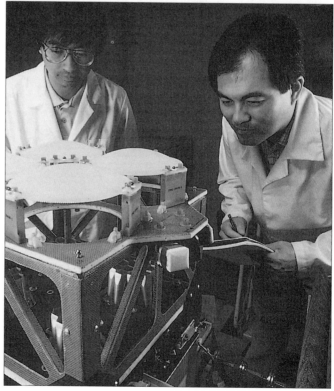

Above: *Leadership for the twenty-first century: Chairman and CEO since 1988, Joseph T. Gorman is joined in the office of chief executive by Peter Hellman, president and chief operating officer since 1995.*

Right: *TRW scored a major coup by becoming the prime contractor for the Tracking & Data Relay Satellites that provide continuous communications between the earth and objects such as the Space Shuttle in low-earth orbit, and freeing the United States from dependence on foreign space communication links.*

In the late 1970s, TRW was administered by the office of the chief executive and supported by a Management Committee that met monthly. Pictured: The Management Committee in 1997. Seated, from lower left (clockwise): Joseph T. Gorman, Peter S. Hellman, Ronald D. Sugar, Timothy W. Hannemann, Bernd Blankenstein, Carl G. Miller. Standing, from left to right: William B. Lawrence, Martin A. Coyle, John P. Stenbit, James S. Remick, Peter Staudhammer, Howard V. Knicely.

Chapter 10

A New Kind of Corporation

▶   ▶   ▶

1965–1969

THROUGHOUT THE LATE 1960S, TRW'S OVERARCHING OBJECTIVE REMAINED GROWTH. DAVE Wright, Horace Shepard, and Si Ramo sought to expand the company faster than the markets it served, and they endorsed all available means: improving operations, developing new products, opening new markets, increasing international sales, and making acquisitions.

The top management team unleashed every division in all four business areas—aerospace, automotive, equipment, and electronics—and most of them grew at a rapid clip. Public attention tended to focus on TRW Systems Group (née STL), which under Rube Mettler and Dick DeLauer expanded its lead in large and complex spacecraft, augmented its capabilities in related areas such as electronics systems and propulsion, and ventured into the unfamiliar terrain of community services, health care systems, industrial controls, and consumer credit reporting. Along the way, the company attracted flattering coverage in the business press, while popular magazines such as *Time, Life,* and *Look* admired its space-age management techniques. Yet a much bigger contributor to corporate performance during the 1960s was Ed Riley's Automotive Group: through internal development, acquisitions, and a rapid sequence of moves overseas, the company greatly enhanced its position as a major independent supplier and an emerging global competitor.

TRW Electronics Group grew the fastest, but started from the smallest base. Led by avid acquirer Sid Webb, TRW quickly gathered a mix of companies specializing in electronic components, controls, and switches. Only at TRW Equipment Group, where trends in the aircraft and aircraft engine industries constrained the core business during much of the decade, did sales rise at less than double-digit rates. Presided over by Stan Pace, the group nonetheless developed a diverse mix of precision-manufactured products for military, government, and industrial customers.[1]

TRW culminated a period of rapid growth by merging with two other sizable diversified companies during 1967 and 1968. United-Carr brought $120 million in sales, seven domestic divisions, and overseas operations in fasteners, switches, and electrical controls. United-Greenfield added another $90 million in sales from an even broader base of divisions that specialized in industrial and hand tools and industrial machinery and equipment.

By the close of the decade, TRW's activities had become extraordinarily diverse and complex. The company posted $1.6 billion in revenues and employed more than eighty-five thousand people around the world. It owned companies that owned companies that owned companies. Its businesses ranged from the traditional to the most contemporary and even to the exotic. It produced a bewildering assortment of products and services: valve train parts; forgings and castings; airfoils; pumps of all kinds and descriptions; motors of all sizes, shapes, and types; fasteners; hand tools and parts for machine tools; antifriction bearings; electronic components and systems; spacecraft and classified systems; plastics; industrial controls; biomedical testing equipment; and information packaged in various ways from management systems to computer software to consumer credit data. No single business accounted for as much as 10 percent of revenues, and it was no longer dependent on any major customer or segment of customers.

A Strategy of Growth and Diversification

Throughout its burst of growth, TRW acquired, merged with, or formed joint ventures with other companies at a dizzying pace, completing more than thirty deals and pursuing countless others (see the Appendix). Almost all of these transactions originated at the group level, where staff carried out analysis and negotiated terms with corporate support. TRW nonetheless imposed some general guidelines on acquisitions and mergers, and Wright spoke of "planned diversification" to maintain a healthy balance between commercial and government sales. "It is not our intention to go into many different businesses unrelated to our background," he stated, "but to stay within the technologies in which we have demonstrated competence, expanding the number of our customers and the variety of our products."

Or, as Ramo put it,

> TRW's acquisitions activity has been limited to product areas in which we are already strongly entrenched or which appear to be direct extensions in closely related fields. Consistent with this, we have defined the acquisitions of interest to be those which would not require a major redefinition of TRW's basic philosophy, which is that we are an operating corporation and not a holding company. Since TRW management cannot presume to be capable of operating well any and all kinds of business, this rule naturally translates into there being, of necessity, a great deal of similarity and integration potential between our existing product areas and any new acquisition.[2]

Like their counterparts at many other big American companies, TRW's leaders pursued a strategy of diversification partly in reaction to U.S. antitrust enforcement, which business leaders perceived as constraining opportunities to increase share in existing markets. In addition, Ramo cited the classical advantages of holding a portfolio of businesses: dampened effects of cyclicality; tax savings (applying credits from losses in one area against profits elsewhere); shared pools of capital; economies achieved by central provision of staff services such as planning, corporate law, accounting and auditing, public relations, and industrial relations; and the "free exchange of ideas and data" about technology, manufacturing, marketing, and finance.[3]

But other forces were also at work: during the late 1960s, "merger mania" was in the air, as the number and dollar value of deals soared to a record peak in 1968. Between 1965 and 1970, almost 10 percent of total manufacturing and mining assets in the United States changed hands. Conglomerate corporations such as Litton Industries, Gulf+Western, LTV Corporation, ITT, Textron, Teledyne, and others used acquisitions of unrelated businesses to grow at spectacular rates. (For example, TRW's 30 deals pale in comparison to the 125 mergers negotiated by Teledyne during the same period.)[4]

Companies completed so many mergers in part because these transactions were so easy to make during the bull market of the late 1960s. Even a big transaction, such as TRW's 1968 merger with United-Greenfield Corporation, which involved considerations worth about $180 million, was consummated quickly. Bill Reynolds, then a young manager who assisted with the acquisition analysis, later a TRW executive vice president, and later still chairman and CEO of Gencorp, recalls that when Shepard met with the investment bankers shopping United-Greenfield, the meeting lasted about five minutes. "Shep sat down and said, 'We think it's worth this [amount].' The bankers said okay, and they had a deal. That was it."[5] Deals also led to other deals in a kind of chain reaction. Many of the early mergers and acquisitions that composed TRW Electronics Group came about because executives in the acquired companies knew about other companies for sale. Accounting and investment conventions of the era also facilitated dealmaking. The critical measure to companies and investors was the price-earnings ratio (p/e), the market price of one share of a company's stock compared with its earnings per share over the previous four quarters. During the late 1960s, a ratio of ten to one was considered a sign of good financial health; companies with lower ratios were often considered "good buys" and targets for acquisition by companies with higher ratios. When big companies, like the conglomerates, possessed high p/e ratios—some ran into the thirties—they could acquire smaller companies with lower ratios by issuing new stock, in the process adding to earnings, raising the value of their stock, and increasing their p/e ratio. This virtuous cycle of "p/e magic" allowed any company with "a printing press and a reputation for success" expressed in a high p/e ratio to grow rapidly.[6]

Although TRW never enjoyed an unusually high p/e ratio, Wright and Shepard paid close attention to the measure, especially after the merger with Marlin-Rockwell resulted in a short-term drop in earnings per share. They also took steps to bolster the stock price, including the identity campaign around the new truncated corporate name in 1965. TRW followed up the name-change publicity with a clever institutional advertising campaign headed by Bob Burgin, who moved to Cleveland as Wright's assistant. New ads portrayed TRW as "an active but usually unseen force" in the economy, a billion-dollar high-tech growth corporation. A dazzling brochure prepared in 1967 emphasized that TRW was a company with "many facets," and "a new kind of corporation—a diversified technology company whose scientific and manufacturing talents contribute importantly to the growth of several major industries."[7]

Top executives also took to the road, not only visiting new operations and greeting new employees, but also meeting frequently with stock analysts. The executives took pains to describe TRW's strategy as "balanced" and "integrated" diversification and to distinguish the company from the conglomerates. TRW did not participate in wildly dissimilar industries, they noted. Rather, they pointed to an organic strategy of growth, where every new initiative or acquisition, at least in principle, built on or related to existing capabilities—especially given the broad definition that the company was to apply to such terms as systems engineering—and further embellished TRW's image as a technology leader.[8]

SPACE-AGE MANAGEMENT

During the late 1960s, TRW continued to provide systems engineering services to the Air Force ballistic missile program, maintained its early lead in advanced spacecraft, developed fledgling activities in propulsion and electronics systems into strong, independent businesses, and diversified into new areas. These activities thrived: between 1960 and 1969, revenues at STL and its successor, TRW Systems Group, soared from about $60 million to about $380 million, while employment climbed from about forty-three hundred to more than fifteen thousand. These totals reflected a dizzying array of programs, projects, and activities that ranged from the traditional to some that were only distantly related to TRW's historical strengths and areas of competence.[9]

To accommodate this growth and respond to important market trends, TRW Systems Group underwent a major reorganization during the fall of 1965. As Mettler explained, the central reason for change was "related to our growth—growth in sales volume, growth in number of employees, growth in capital investment and associated profit risks, product diversity, complexity of operations, and customer requirements." He was also concerned about "how to absorb growth, with all of the constraints it generates, without diminishing the innovating spirit, loyalty and dedication, high level of professional competence, and general resourcefulness which have been largely responsible for our success."[10]

Typical of Mettler's thoroughness—and reflecting the innate convictions of a systems engineering company—key executives and program managers devoted months to detailed planning, discussion, and analysis of various organizational alternatives. The structure that emerged from this process established five operating divisions: (1) Systems Engineering & Integration Division, responsible for applying program management and systems engineering skills to major programs and systems such as ballistic missiles, boost vehicles, general integration and test opportunities, and new business opportunities; (2) Space Vehicles Division, charged to develop and fabricate space-craft; (3) Electronic Systems Division, responsible for developing and manufacturing electronic hardware and systems; (4) Power Systems Division, charged to manage and pursue business in low-thrust engines and propulsion systems and related technologies; and (5) Systems Laboratories, a unit with the mission "to provide forward-looking research, analysis, and development support for existing product areas, to plan and develop new technical capabilities for new product areas and product lines, and to create and manage certain new projects."

Each division possessed its own staff for marketing (contracts and sales), personnel, and procurement and product assurance. In addition, all of them assumed responsibility, where appropriate, for manufacturing. In recognition that the production requirements for spacecraft, electronic systems and equipment, and rocket motors differed fundamentally, the old Fabrication, Integration and Test Division was dismantled, with various pieces and activities transferred to the new divisions.

To aid the divisions, the group-level staff provided central services in administrative operations, industrial relations, legal matters, marketing, materiel (purchasing), planning and control, and product assurance. Several small and anomalous units used unique reporting channels. "Special Projects," a euphemism for certain classified programs, reported to the top through its own vice president, Bill Carlson. Another unit, TRW Instruments Division (formerly STL Products, and before that R-W's Instrument Division), which produced commercial products, reported to Fred Hesse, a senior vice president, and a top assistant to Mettler. Hesse also looked after the group's international activities, which consisted of technical assistance agreements with several foreign aerospace companies and two joint ventures: MATREL S.A., a partnership with Engins-MATRA to bid on certain projects sponsored by the European Space Research Organization, and a teaming with Mitsubishi Electric to design, build, and operate ground stations for communicating with commercial satellites.[11]

Among the problems that the new structure addressed was a high level of operating conflict in the matrix organization. The matrix, it will be recalled, had evolved at Ramo-Wooldrige during the 1950s in response to the addition of the Titan and Thor programs to the Atlas. R-W created a program office for each missile; each program office, in turn, drew on a pool of scientists and engineers (called Members of the Technical Staff, or MTS) organized in functional labs for guidance, propulsion, electronics, and so on. Similar arrangements applied below the program level to discrete projects, subprojects, and subsystems. The managers of these projects and subprojects were responsible for planning and scheduling, budgeting, and accomplishing their assigned task. They thus had to recruit, coordinate, and motivate MTS personnel, but without much authority over them. The MTS personnel in turn worked for at least two bosses—their project manager and the head of their functional area—and often more, since it was common for MTS to be engaged on more than one project. These arrangements proved economical because they accommodated the episodic nature of aerospace contracting and enabled many MTS to work on problems when and as needed without incurring excessive overhead costs. At the same time, the arrangements created frictions and tensions at the intersections of reporting channels around issues of schedules, budgets, and availability of particular personnel. For project and subproject managers especially, the structure placed a premium on diplomacy and negotiation skills.[12]

A matrix structure, Mettler believed, was fundamental to the group's business and could not be abandoned: "Experience has shown us," he argued, "that the nature of the systems and subsystems business is such as to require an interdependent matrix of project and functional divisions." The challenge was to make it more effective and to strike the right balances among potentially conflicting objectives. To this end, the new structure was designed to distinguish between necessary and unnecessary interdependencies and to manage the latter at the appropriate levels—generally "deeper into the organization," so that the people encountering problems would also be responsible for solving them, rather than pursuing answers by reporting up through channels.

To help cope with the uncertainties and stresses of the matrix and accommodate rapid growth (by 1968, half of the employees at Space Park had been with the company for fewer than two years) the group relied on new approaches to management and human relations advocated in some leading universities and business schools such as MIT, the University of Michigan, Case Institute of Technology, and UCLA. The group also drew on the emerging field of organization development (OD), which used behavioral-science techniques such as sensitivity training, encounter groups, team-building exercises, and "deep sensing" to create a better work environment and improve organizational effectiveness.

TRW Systems Group's industrial relations staff, especially Jim Dunlap and Shel Davis, saw OD techniques as at least a partial solution to the problems of matrix management, a view shared by Mettler. As Davis put it, "no one can really get his job done in this kind of a system [i.e., TRW's matrix] without working with others. As a result, problems of relationships, of communication, of people being effectively able to problem-solve with one another are extremely critical." In the early 1960s, Dunlap and Davis had started a career development program that employed consultants to help provide sensitivity training, run off-site meetings, and lead team-building exercises for key executives and MTS. With the explosive growth of the group in the mid-1960s, these efforts broadened and intensified; by the end of the decade, more than eight thousand (out of a peak of sixteen thousand) employees had participated on some level, with intensive involvement by more than twelve hundred senior managers and MTS. A measure of the impact of the company's policies was a turnover rate about half of aerospace industry norms.[13]

TRW's commitment to the matrix and supporting OD techniques intrigued the business community and the general public. The fascination stemmed partly from a sense that the company was a new kind of organization and a model for other companies to follow. Davis reinforced this theme in speeches and articles, even speaking of the group's structure and policies as reflecting "a systems engineering approach" to human behavior in organizations. The group became the focus of a widely circulated set of Harvard Business School management cases, prompting a senior executive at Federated Department Stores to speculate, "Based on what we know today, TRW Systems may turn out to be one of the earliest complete models of the American business-industrial organization of the future."[14]

Mettler, Dunlap, Davis, and others always stated explicitly that the OD techniques were a means to an end—a higher-performing organization—but the public seemed most interested in the means. In 1968, a reporter from *Look* magazine attended a three-day off-site meeting of TRW personnel for sensitivity training. He emerged with an article bearing the provocative title, "It's OK to Cry in the Office." The reporter quoted Davis's set speech against the "soft, mushy, sweetness-and-light impressions" often associated with sensitivity training, as well as TRW's commitment to build "a more effective, efficient, problem-solving organization." The images that lingered, however, portrayed engineers and managers opening themselves up to frank interpersonal exchanges leading to a cathartic bonding experience. The article did little to quiet critics of OD techniques, who wondered how such an experience could translate into more productive work back at the office or otherwise achieve lasting effects. Even Dean Wooldridge entered the fray, calling Dunlap, who had not heard from him in a long time, to inquire about what was going on.[15]

Building Spacecraft

Through the end of 1964, TRW had participated in readying 218 of the 248 satellites orbited by the United States either through development of the space vehicle itself, integration and testing, or engineering of subsystems or through providing equipment in propulsion, electronic instrumentation, or communications. The company's reputation, capabilities, and facilities helped establish an early and enduring lead. In the mid-1960s, the business of building spacecraft changed in fundamental ways, however. In the early days of spaceflight, the principal technical challenges involved the launch, and participants in the industry focused on boosting objects successfully into orbit. With the coming of more reliable and more powerful boosters, the technical challenge shifted to the spacecraft themselves. Space vehicles became bigger, more sophisticated, capable of performing more and a wider variety of functions, more expensive, and fewer in number.[16]

At the same time, the number of viable competitors bidding for programs increased. The entrants included makers of aircraft such as Grumman Aerospace Engineering, North American Aviation, Boeing, and Lockheed, as well as manufacturers of electronic systems and equipment such as Hughes, RCA, Philco (later acquired by Ford Motor Company), Fairchild, GE, and Westinghouse. In scientific satellites, NASA added to the competition by forging a tight relationship with Caltech's Jet Propulsion Laboratory (JPL), which became virtually a captive supplier of unmanned spacecraft, including the ill-starred Ranger program and the acclaimed Mariner and Voyager series. JPL also developed a deep-space communications network that rivaled TRW's and became NASA's service of choice.[17]

Another key change involved pricing. Manufacturers had built the first satellites on contracts that reimbursed all costs and guaranteed a fixed return, whatever the outcome. In the early 1960s, most government agencies and all commercial customers for spacecraft adopted different arrangements, using fixed-price contracts with additional performance-based incentives. One of the first such deals involved STL's Vela satellites, which were used to monitor nuclear explosions. During the mid-1960s, as the

Velas were launched and met performance criteria, TRW earned nearly $1 million in incentives, including a short period in which it racked up a penny for every mile the satellites traveled in orbit.[18]

The Space Vehicles Division (SVD), headed by Dolph Thiel and George Gleghorn, responded to the technical and business challenges of the industry in various ways. In contrast to many of its rivals, because it could draw on the accumulated experience and expertise of the entire Systems Group, SVD could marshal strong teams of personnel in systems integration, propulsion, electronic equipment, and telemetry, tracking and command systems, as well as in spacecraft design and fabrication. These capabilities made SVD a particularly strong competitor for more complex and technically advanced systems, which also earned premium prices.

Like other Systems Group divisions, SVD also participated in several cost-reduction programs. The original impetus for these initiatives was to evaluate costs and lower them where possible. Over time, the emphasis shifted to ensuring that money was spent wisely. In June 1966, TRW Systems Group launched a program labeled The Right Way, playing off the corporation's name. This initiative anticipated quality management techniques that became fashionable across the industry decades later: its point was to organize to accomplish tasks the right way the *first* time to save on testing, inspection, and rework. The Right Way program not only improved quality, but also squeezed out costs, yielded new policies and procedures and ways of organizing tasks, and empowered employees to make critical decisions affecting their work. (Like the quality initiatives of the 1980s, The Right Way program crossed organizational boundaries to include suppliers and customers. TRW's habit of passing out pencils and other gift items bearing "The Right Way" slogan irritated some outsiders, who regarded it as a sign of the arrogance of "TR Wonderful," or, less charitably, "Turkeys Running Wild.")[19]

Intensifying competition led to a greatly reduced market share for SVD, although it had several notable successes during the mid- to late 1960s. For NASA, for example, TRW built a second successful series of orbiting geophysical observatories. It also manufactured five more satellites in the Pioneer series, a $15 million program directed by Dr. Aubrey Mickelwait. Although the last of the spacecraft was destroyed in a launch failure, the other four achieved remarkable successes. Launched between 1965 and 1968, *Pioneers* 6 to 9 continued NASA's exploration of the solar system, mapping out characteristics of space inside the earth's orbit. The satellites carried experiments designed to measure and monitor solar flares and other forms of solar radiation as well as magnetic phenomena in the inner solar system. *Pioneer 6,* boosted into solar orbit on December 16, 1965, by a Thor-Delta rocket, remains the oldest functioning satellite in space.[20]

Although TRW continued to engineer scientific research satellites with enormous success during the 1970s and 1980s, the size of the market and the presence of JPL and other competitors limited its prospects. SVD's future depended far more on commercial and especially military satellites. In the mid-1960s, by far the greatest opportunities involved communications satellites (comsats). The major technical challenge inhibiting development of comsats was the need to achieve higher orbit altitude. The near-earth orbits of early spacecraft such as *Relay* and its privately funded contemporary, AT&T's *Telstar*, severely limited their performance, because they revolved around the earth faster than the earth itself rotated. As a result, ground stations had to track moving targets that darted across the sky at speeds up to four miles per second, racing from horizon to horizon in a matter of minutes. Actually using the satellites for sustained communication proved a major headache: "About the time you got used to the high quality signal," wrote John McLucas, a participant in many early programs, "the satellite was gone again. It would be about two hours before it reappeared—only to go dashing off once more."[21]

The conventional solution to the tracking problem, favored by the military as well as by private companies like AT&T, was to design a network of at least a dozen satellites to permit continuous communication from the ground. A much simpler solution, conceptually, involved placing satellites in a much higher geosynchronous orbit: as they rotated at the same speed as the earth, they would hold a stationary position relative to the ground. Experts calculated that only three satellites in geosynchronous orbit could cover nearly the entire planet. The comsats of the Relay/Telstar generation, however, weighed far too much to boost into geosynchronous orbit—a problem that also plagued the U.S. Army's Advent program, for which STL had provided systems engineering services.

Only with the availability of more powerful boosters such as improved Delta systems (derived from the Thor IRBM) and of smaller satellites such as *Syncom* (engineered by a resourceful development team at Hughes Aircraft) did geosynchronous orbit become feasible. *Syncom* was "spin-stabilized"—using gyroscopic principles to maintain a constant orientation toward the earth—a lighter-weight, longer-lived, less complex, and more economical alternative to liquid-fuel attitude-control thrusters. Hughes also developed miniaturized electronics systems for the satellite, which weighed only seventy-nine pounds in orbit. Three successful test flights of *Syncom* in 1963 validated the feasibility of the approach.[22]

TRW designed and built a range of equipment for the *Syncom* program and continued to pursue ways to increase its participation in the development of high-altitude comsats. Its first big chance came in 1964, when it partnered with Philco-Ford on the Interim Defense Communications Satellite Program (IDCSP). The program entailed orbiting a constellation of small satellites to provide coverage twenty-four hours a day, worldwide, to military users. The satellites, designed to be launched eight at a time, were spin-stabilized and stationed at very high (but not geosynchronous) altitudes near the equator. TRW built the satellite frame structures, solar cell panels, electrical power subsystems, telemetry multiplexers and associated telemetry, tracking and command components, and booster-separation devices for thirty-two spacecraft launched between 1966 and 1968. During one particularly hectic period, the company had to deliver a new spacecraft every week for twenty-nine consecutive weeks, a requirement met through rigorous planning and scheduling, as well as by close cooperation with suppliers. In all, twenty-four spacecraft made it into space, where they provided the backbone for critical military communications during the Vietnam War. The satellites remained in service until more advanced systems superseded them in the 1970s.[23]

TRW's performance on IDCSP provided a point of entry into other comsat assignments. In March 1969, for example, the company became prime contractor on the next-generation Defense Satellite Communications System Phase II (DSCS-II). The new program took advantage of more powerful rocket boosters and other advances in spacecraft and electronics to provide a much simpler communications system. The DSCS-II satellites were much bigger than their predecessors, each measuring nine feet in diameter and ten feet in height, weighing about eleven hundred pounds, and managing a power output of up to 530 watts. Spin-stabilized and placed in geosynchronous orbit, four of them could handle traffic from around the planet. The satellites featured several significant innovations, including a wide bandwith, high performance communications repeater, steerable narrow beam antennas, and a clever control system that held the narrow beam antennas on target without burning fuel. SVD fabricated the satellites, and Electronic Systems Division produced the communications payload.[24]

TRW's work on defense comsats also helped reopen the way into commercial comsats, a market for which the company had high hopes that were eventually dashed. In December 1965, TRW scored a breakthrough when the private but highly regulated Communications Satellite Corporation (COMSAT) chose TRW over Hughes and RCA for a major program. The contract called for TRW to build a series of high-capacity comsats over three years for a fixed price of $32 million, with additional incentives based on performance. The satellites were designed as part of a global communications network developed for the International Telecommunications Satellite Consortium (INTELSAT), a partnership of about fifty nations that had agreed to own and operate a single system. This global network, designated INTELSAT III, was eventually expected to include as many as two dozen satellites (including replacements and upgrades) for positioning in geosynchronous orbit. Each satellite was designed to carry four TV channels simultaneously or twelve hundred first-class, two-way telephone circuits—about five times the capacity of the most powerful contemporary comsats—with an expected service life of five years. TRW's contract included assembly and testing of the first six units, as well as assembly of two additional engineering models and a prototype.[25]

INTELSAT III posed extremely difficult engineering challenges to the TRW program team led by Dr. Morris Feigen. To maintain stability, the satellites would spin at about 150 revolutions per minute. A ticklish problem not yet satisfactorily solved by any satellite builder involved how to "de-spin" an antenna from the spacecraft so that ground stations could lock onto it. TRW's initial design called for the antenna to be de-spun electronically, a technique yet untried. As work proceeded, however, Feigen's team ran into difficulties with the electronic system and began experimenting with a mechanical method that seemed to offer superior performance at lower cost—if it could be shown to be reliable under the extremely cold temperatures and zero gravity conditions of space.[26]

INTELSAT III proved to be a troubled program. Under the fixed-price contract, TRW was under constant pressure to contain costs, while delays and unexpected technical difficulties ate into margins. This squeeze was worsened by the failure to achieve many of the anticipated performance incentives. Three of the eight satellites never achieved orbit, and the five that were launched successfully did not meet full specifications. Designed for a service life of five years, the most successful of the satellites functioned for just forty-one months, and two failed in fewer than eighteen months. The mechanical systems for de-spinning the antenna worked, but they tended to freeze up when the spacecraft entered the earth's shadow. Every six months, the satellites had to be taken out of service and aimed at the sun, sometimes for as long as a month, before they could resume operation. Nonetheless, they racked up some significant achievements. At the end of 1968, for example, the first INTELSAT III satellite to reach orbit in position over the Atlantic Ocean brought live images to the United States of Pope Paul VI's Christmas message, and live TV coverage of the bombing of the Beirut airport. Europeans followed in real time the dramatic and uplifting flight of *Apollo 8,* the first mission to fly to the moon and back. Later satellites relayed coverage of the 1972 Olympic Games and many other newsworthy events, as well as countless telephone calls. But TRW's involvement in INTELSAT III did not extend beyond production of the first eight spacecraft.[27]

Lessons learned from the INTELSAT experience partly tempered its disappointments. During the late 1960s, TRW built geosynchronous satellites that proved highly successful for the Air Force and other customers. These programs remain partly or wholly classified, and only the skimpiest details have been revealed, often as a result of espionage trials. Under penalty of law, no one in the company can discuss or even confirm the existence of specific classified programs, but executives do acknowledge "major wins" and participation in "big, multiyear, multimillion-dollar programs" in the classified area starting in the mid-1960s.

One such program, for example, came to light in 1977 in a celebrated spy case involving a young TRW employee named Christopher Boyce and his boyhood friend, Andrew Daulton Lee. As reported in Robert Lindsey's popular book about the case, *The Falcon and the Snowman* (also a movie), Boyce worked in a "black vault" at TRW, where data from classified satellites were downloaded and processed on their way to the customer. Over a two-year period in the mid-1970s, Boyce and Lee sold classified information to agents of the Soviet secret intelligence agency KGB, to finance drug purchases and a faster lifestyle as well as an antiestablishment agenda characteristic of many young Americans who came of age during the Vietnam War.[28]

The program identified in this case involved "signal intelligence" or SIGINT reconnaissance and surveillance satellites that TRW built for the National Security Agency and the Central Intelligence Agency. Known in early versions under the code name Rhyolite, the SIGINT satellites were designed to intercept electromagnetic signals of all kinds, including telecommunications and radar, but especially telemetry data from Soviet and Chinese missile tests. (The code name is aptly metaphorical: rhyolite is a volcanic rock that consists largely of light gray ash. Embedded in the material, however, are small, colorful crystals of quartz and feldspar. The satellite's job was to sift through a huge volume of intercepted communications to find nuggets of useful information.)

According to Desmond Ball, an intrepid Australian researcher who has investigated the dark world of satellite reconnaissance systems, TRW received its first contract for a Rhyolite satellite in 1966 and delivered the first unit for launch four years later. Little has been revealed about the specifications and operating characteristics of the satellites, including their number, except that they were positioned at geosynchronous altitudes over their target areas. Obviously, the spacecraft contained sophisticated sensors and communications equipment, and they operated as part of an overall system, including antennas and ground stations, that TRW engineered.[29]

A classified program that the U.S. government and company have since publicly acknowledged began at about the same time. In 1967, the Air Force awarded a major contract to TRW and Aerojet Electrosystems to build a series of satellites to warn against hostile missile launches. Like their predecessors, the MIDAS early warning satellites that Lockheed had built with support from TRW as part of the WS-117L program, the Defense Support System (DSP) satellites used infrared sensors to detect the heat of missile plumes against the earth's background. By the mid-1960s, the availability of big, heavy-duty launch vehicles such as the Titan IIIC enabled bigger satellites to be boosted into geosynchronous orbit. The DSP satellites each weighed more than a ton and were the biggest and heaviest space vehicles that TRW had ever made. They used solar panels to generate about four hundred watts of power for thousands of sensor devices. The particular specifications and operating details of these satellites remain classified, although the series, including upgrades, provided a steady flow of business to TRW for more than a quarter-century.[30]

Electronic Systems—And More Black Programs

TRW's capabilities in designing and building spacecraft neatly complemented a burgeoning business in electronic equipment and systems. Indeed, among the motives for TRW Systems Group's reorganization in 1965 was the promise of an attractive business in this area. The new Electronic System Division (ESD), which Henry Samulon directed, was founded on the support that various parts of the Space Park organization had provided to its missile and spacecraft operations. The division also included remnants of the old R-W Communications and Control Divisions and PSI.[31]

Much of the division's work focused on tracking, telemetry, and command (TT&C), which involved integrating electronics equipment aboard missiles or spacecraft with ground station monitoring and control. TRW had participated in this business since the missile programs of the 1950s and it had expanded during the Able reentry vehicle tests. For these and other early satellite programs, the company cobbled together its own systems from purchased equipment. In 1965, Electronic Systems Division scored a major TT&C triumph by winning the design contract for the Air Force's Space Ground Link Subsystem (SGLS). The program addressed a nagging problem. The customary practice for communicating with satellites involved developing a unique TT&C system for each spacecraft. By the mid-1960s, with hundreds of satellites in orbit, such a practice had become wildly inefficient. The Air Force saw the solution as SGLS, a single, standardized system to talk to, control, track, and listen to its satellites.

ESD won SGLS with a design that featured a mix of standardized components with modules that could be added, depending on the requirements of particular missions.

The system used a single antenna for all TT&C functions and a single, compact flight package into which customized modules might fit. This basic concept proved successful and remained the standard TT&C approach for all U.S. military satellites for decades. Unfortunately for ESD, when the program moved from development to production in the late 1960s, the unit lost the follow-on contract on the basis of price.[32]

Despite this setback, ESD continued to expand its business. It took advantage of the trend toward more sophisticated spacecraft that could perform new and varied functions in flight. As SVD moved into new types of spacecraft during the later 1960s, ESD followed closely behind in support, often learning valuable lessons along the way. Although another contractor produced the communications payload for the INTELSAT III satellites, for example, "the support . . . rendered by ESD personnel provided valuable early insights into this emerging technology area." This new knowledge dovetailed with other lessons gleaned from the IDCSP military communications satellites (for which ESD built on-board transponders) to position ESD to engineer communications systems and to manufacture the payloads. These new capabilities, nurtured especially by Dick Booton, Charlie Stephens, and Bob Huang, served TRW well in the military communications satellite competitions of the 1970s and 1980s.[33]

R-W's communications experience combined with PSI's capability in microelectronics to help establish a more enduring business: secure communications, or COMSEC in the argot of the defense and security establishment. Canoga Park veterans such as Art Gold and Roger Trapp had garnered experience in electronic countermeasures and signal processing that became important to many ESD military programs of the 1960s. When TRW won a major classified spacecraft development program (presumably Rhyolite), for example, ESD could supply systems and equipment. New business opportunities in classified programs also emerged from ESD's unclassified work. For both IDSCP and SGLS, the Air Force required that communications be secure and mandated sophisticated techniques for encrypting and decoding data. This experience also linked ESD to the National Security Agency and led to a long-standing relationship in the COMSEC area.[34]

The arrival of personnel from PSI was an added boon. These veterans, especially a group led by Jim Buie, formed an important part of ESD's Microelectronics Center. The center had been established in 1964 to work on, among other activities, several military contracts that involved developing miniaturized amplifiers and receivers as well as new circuitry for signal conditioning and processing applications for COMSEC. Buie developed a critical technology (3D bipolar technology) that enabled the center to begin fabricating large-scale integrated circuits that provided "considerable benefit" to ESD's success rate in winning COMSEC business.[35]

To the Moon—And Beyond

Like SVD and ESD, TRW Systems Group's Power Systems Division (PSD), headed by Bob Bromberg and Art Grant, recorded notable successes during the late 1960s. PSD's work built on earlier contributions by STL's propulsion laboratory in the area of variable-thrust engines for maneuvering spacecraft. Development of the lunar excursion module descent engine (LEMDE) for the Apollo missions to the moon became the division's most significant contribution to NASA's manned space program and opened potential new lines of business in the process.

Each Apollo mission used two space vehicles, the command service module, in which the three astronauts spent most of the voyage and in which they returned to earth, and the lunar module, in which two astronauts separated from the command service module in orbit around the moon and descended to the lunar surface. The lunar module itself had two primary engines. The first, the LEMDE, powered the vehicle's transfer from lunar orbit to a soft landing on the moon, where it was abandoned. The second boosted the lunar module back into orbit for rendezvous with the command module.

The requirements for the descent engine were not only exacting, but also well beyond the state of the art in propulsion when the mission planning began in the early 1960s. Because the engine had to negotiate a soft landing—and even allow the spacecraft to hover for as long as a minute—it had to be throttleable; because it had to be throttleable, it had to use liquid fuels, which were extremely difficult to manage under the conditions of outer space; because it had to move a significant mass, even in low-gravity conditions, it had to be powerful; and because weight was carried at a huge premium on any space flight, it had to be extraordinarily efficient. As NASA's official history of the Apollo hardware puts it, the LEMDE "probably was the biggest challenge and the most outstanding technical development" of the entire program.[36]

Earlier, convinced that future programs for soft-landing packages on the moon and planets would require bigger and better engines, PSD personnel continued development of variable-thrust propulsion systems that had begun in 1959. Despite losing the competition to build the 5,000-pound-thrust Surveyor engine, which soft-landed an instrument package on the moon, PSD set its sights on the next prize: the 10,500-pound-thrust LEMDE. In the initial competition TRW suffered another disappointment when Grumman, the prime contractor for the lunar excursion module, chose Rocketdyne's proposal. Rocketdyne experienced development problems, however, and Grumman reopened the bidding. In May 1963, Grumman selected TRW to develop a parallel engine, with the final selection to be made by early 1965.

At this point, Mettler took a calculated risk, committing more than $2 million to build a rocket test facility in Rancho Mission Viejo, near San Juan Capistrano in Southern California. Construction of the twenty-seven-hundred-acre facility represented a gamble similar to that of building the first spacecraft manufactory at Space Park: the sense that new facilities would greatly enhance the company's credibility. When operation began in March 1964, the facility included six test stands for evaluating engines of varying sizes in different orientations and under varying conditions. It provided TRW with an immediate competitive advantage because it offered a proprietary location for testing and signaled the company's commitment to sustain a major presence in propulsion.[37]

Gerry Elverum led the LEMDE development team, which included Peter Staudhammer, a future corporate vice president for science and technology. Rocketdyne had sought to achieve throttleability by injecting helium, an inert gas, into the flow of propellants to decrease thrust while maintaining the same flow rate. Elverum's approach was less risky, although it involved many significant advances in engine design and mechanics. He proposed a mechanical throttling system that controlled thrust by adjusting the propellant flow rates and varying the area of the injection orifices—in concept, like a shower head—to regulate pressure, rate of propellant flow, and the pattern of the fuel mixture in the combustion chamber. Propellants were injected at the center of the engine in a precisely controlled fashion that could not only vary thrust but also prevent dangerous oscillation and instability.[38]

In practice, the development performance of the two competing engines was relatively close, and in January 1965 Grumman notified NASA that it wished to retain Rocketdyne, its original contractor. In an unusual move, however, a NASA review board overruled the decision, awarding the contract instead to TRW, citing the company's ability to supply "more management and superior resources to this program without interference of other similar programs . . . ." The verdict was both a compliment to TRW for its design and commitment and a slap at Rocketdyne, which was experiencing delays in developing reliable reentry engines for the Gemini program. The contract called for TRW to deliver fifteen flight engines to NASA, starting in 1967.[39]

Among the many technical challenges facing the LEMDE design team, propellant flow, injection, and combustion posed the greatest. The fuel had to be mixed and injected precisely under a wide range of operating conditions never before encountered except in theory. A host of smaller thorny problems also had to be addressed: the gimballing feature, which increased maneuverability, required extraordinarily precise engineering; the throttle actuator used an electromechanical system, including three redundant motors, to ensure reliability and extreme accuracy in the performance of the injector; a special ablative-cooled nozzle extension had to be strong enough to direct the flow of high-temperature, high-pressure gases, yet had to be crushable in case the lunar module should settle on a large rock.

Although TRW tested the LEMDE in many possible ways, including in earth and lunar orbits on early Apollo missions, the acid test would be the moon landing itself. As the time for the *Apollo 11* flight drew near, TRW took out some bold advertisements around the theme, "The last 10 miles are on us." (Late in the game, as the enormity of the LEMDE's role—and TRW's risk—became fully apparent, Dave Wright had called Rube Miller to ask only half facetiously whether the project was a risk TRW ought to bear; Mettler reassured him that it was.)[40]

On July 20, 1969, LEMDE performed perfectly as astronauts Neil Armstrong and Buzz Aldrin departed lunar orbit for the landing attempt in the moon's Sea of Tranquility. During the "powered descent initiation," which lasted just over twelve minutes, the astronauts spent most of their time monitoring instruments and coping with several nerve-wracking false alarms caused by computer overloads. With three minutes to go, at an altitude of about nineteen thousand feet, Armstrong noticed that a small crater and a field of boulders dominated the targeted landing site. He switched the landing sequence to manual control, throttled the engine up to 40 percent of rated thrust, and rotated the lunar module to get a better view. Moving laterally at nineteen thousand feet, he spotted a smoother area and maneuvered the module back into position to land. He throttled back again, and the module dropped toward the surface. During the last few seconds, while the world held its breath, dust kicked up from the surface to obscure Armstrong's view. He could not see the final landing site, although he could feel the module drifting backward and to the left, movements that he fought to counter. He was acutely aware of altitude and fuel measurements that Aldrin called out in a steady rhythm. In the final seconds, he concentrated so intensely on stabilizing the position of the module that he failed to notice the first touch or to hear Aldrin's call of "Light contact." A second later, the module was clearly down, and Armstrong shut the engine down. After another few seconds, the world heard the famous message: "Houston. Tranquility Base here. The Eagle has landed." The LEMDE had burned an extra thirty-two seconds during the manual landing. Only about 3 percent of the fuel remained in the tank—enough, had it been needed, for another twenty seconds of operation.[41]

At Space Park—and in Cleveland—relief was palpable, the first emotion before swelling pride. The lunar landing was a staggering technological feat in which TRW's LEMDE figured prominently. And the descent engine was only one of the company's significant contributions to Apollo: it also provided critical software for mission analysis and simulation, guidance and trajectory control, an abort guidance control, and a back-up communications system.

Although the LEMDE provided the biggest and most spectacular demonstration of its capabilities in propulsion during the 1960s, TRW also pursued many other projects in this area. For NASA and other customers, the company developed low-thrust attitude-control engines for the upper stages of the huge Saturn booster and investigated futuristic systems based on high-energy fuels such as radioisotopes and a cesium ion engine for interplanetary travel. These and other related studies of combustion and propulsion prepared the way for potential new lines of business ranging from gas dynamic lasers for military and industrial applications, to more efficient and cleaner processes for burning fossil fuels, to new composites and materials capable of withstanding extremely high temperatures.

Diversification, West Coast Style

At the reorganization of 1965, Mettler promoted Dick DeLauer to general manager of the Systems Engineering & Integration Division (SEID), which was primarily responsible for SETD/SETA support to the Air Force ballistic missile programs. The second and third generations of Minuteman continued to push the state of the art in virtually every area of missile technology. As the first Minuteman missiles became operational, for example, the Air Force's strategic concept for its ICBMs shifted from massive retaliation to controlled response. This shift meant that Minuteman II, which naturally would be bigger, more powerful, and longer-lived than Minuteman I, would also be more accurate and more flexible in its basing systems—innovations that called for creative technological responses from SEID personnel. Minuteman III, approved for development in 1965, was a still more powerful missile with the capability of launching three multiple, independently targetable reentry vehicles (MIRVs), which required major advances in guidance systems. The Air Force and SEID relied on proven techniques of organization and management to rush Minuteman II and Minuteman III successfully through development. By 1969 the U.S. arsenal of ICBMs included 500 Minuteman Is, 500 Minuteman IIs, as well as about 50 Titan IIs. (Minuteman III became operational in 1970, and eventually 550 missiles were built to replace all of the Minuteman Is and some Minuteman IIs in service.)[42]

Although the ballistic missile programs absorbed by far the greatest part of SEID's time, personnel, and budgets, DeLauer and Mettler remained partly concerned with a question that had plagued R-W since 1954: what would TRW do next? A very tempting answer was to apply SEID's formidable skills in systems engineering and program management in new areas, including in the service of nondefense government work and even commercial businesses. Several factors pushed and pulled TRW into these new areas.

One source of the push was the company's success at marketing. In the aftermath of the divestiture of Aerospace Corporation, as we have seen, STL used its skills in systems engineering and technical management to move into spacecraft, a business similar to missiles. This achievement became a form of advertisement and bred additional opportunities to sell and apply general capabilities. In 1963, Mettler appointed a vice president of marketing, and the effort intensified. The following December, the company landed its first significant systems engineering contract outside the aerospace industry with the U.S. Navy's Anti-Submarine Warfare (ASW) Program. The work entailed providing systems integration and test support—but no hardware—for the Navy's electronic surveillance, detection, location, and tracking systems used in shipboard, land-based, and airborne operations. The initial $6.1 million contract ran for ten months and eventually gave way to bigger and longer contracts starting in October 1965. In all, about 150 engineers and scientists, most of them recruited from the Minuteman office in San Bernardino, were involved in the program.[43]

Ramo provided another source of push. A fundamental problem facing society, he believed, was "the imbalance between accelerating technology and lagging social maturity"—the principal theme of his speeches from the mid-1960s on, as well as of his 1970 book, *Century of Mismatch.* He pointed to the major scientific breakthroughs of the mid-twentieth century—the harnessing of atomic energy, the cracking of the genetic code, the exploration of space, the coming of the computer—as signs of staggering technological progress. Yet at the same time problems abounded: unchecked population growth, crowded cities, an increasingly polluted environment, the apparent depletion of nonrenewable energy sources, and a fearsome struggle between decentralized and centralized economies for world dominance. The combination of these contrary trends added up to a "paradoxical hodgepodge of sophisticated technological progress and social primitivism."[44]

For Ramo, this paradox offered both social and political challenges as well as business opportunities. There was a prominent—and profitable—role, he declared, for companies that brought advanced technology and technical management to bear on social problems and concerns. He encouraged TRW to apply the skills, experience, and techniques proven on the ICBM and space programs of the 1950s and 1960s to a new order of business. He helped to popularize the term "civil systems" to refer to systems engineering and large-scale, technical project management approaches to challenges of natural resource development, environmental cleanup, mass transportation, housing, urban planning, and health care delivery—all of which he urged TRW to pursue.

In 1965, California's Democratic governor, Edmund G. "Pat" Brown, lent support to Ramo's vision by encouraging members of the aerospace industry to conduct "an examination and evaluation of the potential for the effective expansion of systems engineering methods and techniques to other government program [*sic*] encompassing socio-techno-economic areas." Needless to say, the studies, including several carried out by TRW engineers, concluded that techniques of systems engineering and program management were readily applicable outside the aerospace industry. These techniques included analyses to establish systems requirements and to break down complex problems into subsystems with interfaces, use of visual and graphic displays, and a host of specific measures for organizing, budgeting, monitoring, and reviewing performance.[45]

At the same time, TRW was pulled into civil systems as a consequence of its own historical successes. During the early 1960s, as details of the missile programs became public, the techniques of management and organization of large-scale projects rippled across to other aerospace companies and then into the economy generally. (TRW was by no means the only management pioneer in large-scale systems projects, and the ripples moved in all directions. The U.S. Navy team that developed the Polaris missile, for example, also became justly renowned. Government agencies and private corporations frequently invited Ramo, Mettler, DeLauer, Solomon, and other TRW missile pioneers to speak about systems engineering and program management and specific applications of computer modeling and graphical communications aids for planning, scheduling, and control. Inevitably, some of these invitations led to business opportunities, which ranged from pro bono work on community projects, to paid consulting assignments, to formal engagements to provide systems engineering services.[46]

The first true civil systems projects were direct outgrowths of missile management. During the site activation of a Minuteman wing near Grand Forks, North Dakota, a unit in SEID developed graphical techniques for scheduling and tracking projects. These techniques soon attracted notice in industry and government circles. As a result, TRW contracted with a consortium of oil companies to provide scheduling and task identification services and to help with automating some management tasks. At about the same time, TRW won a $200,000 contract from the State of California's Office of Planning to develop a regional land-use plan for portions of Santa Clara County. The North American Water and Power Alliance, an association of groups interested in redesigning the distribution of fresh water throughout the western regions of the United States and Canada, sought TRW's advice in planning what would have been, had it proceeded, a civil works project on a scale second in human history only to the Great Wall of China.

President Lyndon Johnson's War on Poverty program presented TRW with still more civil systems opportunities. In 1966, the federal Office of Economic Opportunity hired the company to provide training sessions on systems management for local governments and colleges and universities. TRW volunteered to test the approach in the San Bernardino office. From there, projects began to multiply: with the Federal Water Pollution Control Authority on systems approaches to water resource management; with the U.S. Department of Commerce, to investigate a new high-speed ground transportation system; and with the city of Redondo Beach, to analyze and improve the flow of automobile traffic in the South Bay area. Through one of Ramo's connections, the provincial government in Alberta, Canada, retained TRW to help design and plan a new $100 million medical center in Edmonton.[47]

TRW's initial civil systems contracts were small, although in 1969 they added up to about $10 million. The move into civil systems also initiated a modest shift in hiring practices in the Systems Group, as it recruited a handful of sociologists, economists, statisticians, and political scientists to its technical staff.[48]

Farther Afield

Among TRW's Space Park-based diversification efforts, civil systems appeared the most glamorous, but it was by no means the biggest. Ramo and Mettler also encouraged the Systems Group to enter new commercial businesses. After the divestiture of Bunker-Ramo, for example, Ramo continued to promote TRW's involvement in "intellectronics." He did not want or expect the company to reenter the computer hardware business. Rather, he saw many ways in which TRW could apply its expertise in communications, controls, software, and information processing and management in commercial settings. The control of industrial processes was one, and TRW continued to develop and market instrumentation and controls for industrial applications.

Early in 1961, STL had formed STL Products, a new organization under Fred Hesse. An MBA from Harvard Business School, Hesse had worked for Raytheon before joining R-W in its earliest days. He occupied several senior administrative positions and, along with Bob Burgin and Chuck Allen, played a key role in the building of Space Park. Hesse yearned for an operating assignment, however, and he welcomed the chance to run the new division. STL Products consisted of a motley assortment of units, including TRW Instruments Division—the descendant of an early R-W business—some parts of STL's R&D organization that sought commercial applications for high-speed image-converter cameras, an atomic clock and other products originally developed for scientific or military purposes, and a small factory in El Segundo, California. Hesse was bullish about the future, however, and projected a $2 billion market for TRW Instruments within five years.[49]

Such a scenario was one instance of Hesse's tendency to think big. Another was his long-term plan to make TRW Instruments the foundation for a bold strategy to become "the pre-eminent process controller" in industry. He believed that the only way to reach this goal was by acquiring expertise. With Ramo's support and encouragement, Hesse prevailed on his immediate bosses at Space Park, Mettler and DeLauer, to allow him to pursue acquisitions. His first deal, negotiated during the fall of 1967, involved the purchase of Mission Manufacturing Corporation, a Houston-based maker of valves and other products used in drilling for oil and gas, with annual sales of about $22 million. Although Hesse found Mission's involvement in the energy business appealing, he was principally interested in a subsidiary that made advanced instrumentation and supervisory control systems for the oil and gas industry. This unit, he believed, might facilitate TRW's entry into new kinds of instrumentation and remote metering.[50]

Hesse also arranged to acquire another business in 1967: Hazleton Laboratories, a small, twenty-year-old "life sciences research firm" based in Falls Church, Virginia. The company provided research, testing, and related services for several markets, including environmental protection and pollution control, ocean bioscience, and biomedical engineering and instrumentation. At the time of the deal, Hazleton Labs employed about six hundred people and posted sales of about $7 million. Official accounts of the acquisition touted the unit's "ability in utilizing the systems approach to problem solving in the civil market area," and Hesse expected it "to greatly extend TRW's capabilities in the fast-evolving and potentially large civil systems market." As with Mission's subsidiary, he was particularly interested in Hazleton's capabilities in testing and instrumentation.[51]

By combining these new units and some other pieces of TRW Systems Group, Hesse built the foundation of a sizable new operating group. Early in 1968, the arrangements were formalized with the establishment of TRW Industrial Operations Group, with Hesse as general manager. Soon thereafter, he negotiated his biggest deal: merger with Reda Pump of Bartlesville, Oklahoma, the leading American supplier of submergible electric motors and pumps for the petroleum industry, with a subsidiary that manufactured wire and cable for oilfield and general industrial use. By the late 1960s, Reda Pump had become the dominant maker of custom-built submergible pumps: huge units, twenty to forty feet long, outfitted with heavy-duty motors capable of lifting enormous quantities of oil or other fluids, and priced at tens of thousands of dollars each. The company posted annual sales of about $40 million and was Bartlesville's leading manufacturer and second-largest employer after Phillips.[52]

As Ramo inspired TRW's push into civil systems and industrial operations, so also he prodded the company into another area related to his long-standing interest in information technology. The new thrust reflected his vision of the coming "cashless society," in which computers and software would engineer a revolution in everyday finance. In 1964, he had predicted:

> Financial and accounting operations will be revolutionized by electronic information networks. Personal checks, and even currency and coin, will be delegated to a few rural areas or museums. When you buy a necktie or a house, your thumb print in front of the little machine will identify you, subtract from your account and put it on the seller's account; all through electrical signals and not by today's funny little pieces of paper with written words, or hieroglyphics.[53]

Ramo's prognostication meshed with Mettler's thinking about new applications for TRW Systems Group's formidable capabilities in software and data management and analysis. During the late 1960s, Mettler and several colleagues spent "at least a year" looking for information intensive industries that were not yet feeling the full impact of new electronic data processing technologies. Early in 1968, an opportunity surfaced in the form of a small acquisition candidate: Credit Data Corporation (CDC), a privately held San Francisco-based company that specialized in consumer credit reporting. TRW arranged to buy CDC, recalled Mettler, not because it wanted to own a credit bureau, but because it wanted "to learn the business and find out whether it was a vehicle for investment." Using CDC as a base, Mettler reasoned, it might be possible for TRW to create a big proprietary database and quickly establish a leading position in the industry.[54]

In the late 1960s, the credit-reporting industry was ripe for automation: it was something of a cottage industry, with many small, independent credit bureaus dotting the landscape. These small businesses tended to focus on local areas and seldom crossed state lines. They laboriously gathered information about the credit histories of individual consumers and recorded it by hand on small index cards, which were maintained in manual filing systems. Then they sold this information for a small fee to banks, credit-card companies, oil companies, retailers, and other customers for credit information. The data thus collected were subject to uneven quality and somewhat arbitrary classification depending on the experience, capabilities, and conscientiousness of the data-entry clerks. Routine consumer credit checks often took weeks, or even months.[55]

Founded in Detroit in 1930, CDC had established a leading position by 1968 based on a strategy of automation and geographical expansion. Under a youthful management team headed by the founder's son, H. C. "Bud" Jordan, the company branched into several states and formed relationships with ten of the top twelve banks in the United States, most of the major oil companies, the fledgling Master Charge system (forerunner of today's MasterCard network), and several national retail chains. Yet growth came with costs that proved too great for CDC to bear. It lacked cash to fund a new computer center and the software to make it work. When TRW came across it, CDC was not profitable and experiencing delays in bringing a new computer center onstream. Mettler, who pitched the acquisition to TRW's board, nonetheless saw "high growth and profit potential," including "almost explosive growth in certain portions of the business." He also conceded that "it was a high risk type of business." The terms of the deal were not disclosed, but TRW assumed bank loans and other liabilities totaling nearly $30 million. CDC became an autonomous subsidiary of TRW Systems Group, with its own independent board of directors, and Jordan continued as president.[56]

Several months later, TRW complemented CDC by acquiring for undisclosed terms Credifier Corporation, a Santa Monica, California-based company that produced charge authorization hardware (for credit-card approvals) compatible with NCR cash registers. Credifier had posted about $1 million in sales based on installations of equipment in some grocery stores in southern California.[57]

BECOMING A GLOBAL SUPPLIER

In covering TRW, the national media often portrayed the company as the result of a May-September marriage, and it tended to lavish attention on the junior partner. In so doing, they neglected an important story in the company's oldest business, automotive supply. Under Ed Riley's leadership, TRW Automotive Group grew rapidly during the 1960s, expanding its product line, increasing its market penetration, and extending its geographical reach to a global scale.

Riley's inconspicuous personality partly accounted for this oversight. A "sober and scrupulous" individual, Riley seemed older than his years, an impression reinforced by his apparent lack of a sense of humor and hard-nosed focus on operating results. Subordinates liked working for him, however. He was "just a nice guy and a very effective business manager," recalls Bill Reynolds, a young Stanford MBA who reported to Riley on several assignments. "Everyone who worked for Ed just thought the world of him."[58]

Trained as a chemical engineer, Riley had joined Thompson Products in 1933; he was the new employee who unwittingly voted himself a 10 percent cut in pay when Thompson Products was struggling to remain afloat. That momentary setback not-withstanding, he moved up through a series of technical and managerial assignments. During World War II, he served as a sales engineer in charge of aircraft accessories and led the development of aircraft booster pumps as a major product line. He spent the next fifteen years in the Accessories Division where, as general manager after 1950, he presided over a rapid expansion of business during the Korean War and the Cold War military buildup that followed. In the summer of 1958, Riley was named as a group vice president in charge of all the automotive manufacturing divisions and of sales to the original equipment manufacturers.

Under Riley, TRW followed its proven formula as a supplier to the automotive industry. In valves and piston rings, the company sought continually to improve manu-facturing efficiency, develop new materials and improved designs, and introduce closely related parts. In chassis components, TRW made continuing improvements to its suspension systems and redoubled efforts to increase penetration, especially at General Motors and Chrysler. In 1959, the Michigan Division introduced a hot new product, "greased-for-life," or permanently lubricated, steering linkages. By using new materials such as graphite (and later, Teflon™) and new types of seals, the division was able to guarantee that its steering linkages would never require routine service—a feature attractive to customers but regarded coolly by automotive dealers and service station owners. Developed by the same engineering team that had produced the ball-joint suspension, the new linkages quickly became standard throughout the industry and had "a lot to do with starting the extended warranty policies featured by U.S. car-makers" in the mid-1960s.[59]

The Michigan Division also fared well with another product of recent vintage. In 1957, TP had acquired Federal Industries, a small, privately held manufacturer of pumps for automatic transmissions. This acquisition not only complemented TP's business in hydraulic pumps, but it also led to another fast-growing market in power-steering pumps. By the early 1960s, pumps accounted for more than a fifth of the division's total sales.[60]

The Automotive Group also pursued acquisitions actively, although U.S. antitrust law constrained the kinds of companies it could buy in its home market. The purchases of Marlin-Rockwell and Ross Gear in 1964 typified the kind of deal TRW seemed comfortable making, bringing in new products, opening new niches, and adding new process technologies. Most of the company's domestic acquisitions were small, although it tried several times to land a big partner. In the mid-1960s, for example, TRW came close to consummating several large deals, including mergers with Akron-based McNeil Corporation, a supplier of tire-mold equipment and pumps for transportation equipment, and with Clevite Corporation, a Cleveland-based supplier of batteries and other auto parts, as well as of ordnance equipment. Both deals ultimately fell apart during final negotiations.[61]

During these years, however, TRW did merge with three companies that together enhanced its capabilities and position in industrial markets. Noblesville Casting, a small foundry operation in Noblesville, Indiana, that focused on "difficult, intricately cored, low volume castings" arrived in 1967. Two years later, TRW merged with Gregory Industries of Lorain, Ohio. The company's largest unit, Nelson Stud Welding, had pioneered a process for welding big pieces of metal used in shipbuilding, railroads, and automobile assembly.[62]

The third and by far the biggest merger occurred in 1968, when TRW joined with United-Greenfield Corporation, a diversified company that had itself grown via acquisition and merger. Headquartered near Chicago, United-Greenfield posted about $90 million in sales and had a net income after taxes of more than $10 million. The company employed about five thousand people in eleven autonomous divisions that manufactured carbide and high-speed cutting tools and wear parts, gauges, and other industrial products, as well as hand tools, including many sold under well-known trade names such as J. H. Williams and Vulcan. For many years, the company had been controlled by Edward B. Burling, cofounder of the prominent Washington, D.C., law firm Covington and Burling. Burling died in 1966, and United-Greenfield was put up for sale by investment bankers as part of the settlement of his estate. The prospect particularly interested Horace Shepard, who assigned Bill Reynolds to the pre-deal analysis. "It was an opportunistic acquisition," Reynolds recalls, adding that "it fit in with TRW's strategy to get big quick. It was a high-return, high-profit operation, a high-quality business with good brand names." The price was stock and other considerations worth about $180 million.[63]

The Automotive Group also negotiated a series of acquisitions and joint ventures that significantly expanded the company's position overseas. In the mid-1960s, annual production of automobiles outside the United States surpassed production inside the country, and manufacturers in several European nations were growing faster than the Big Three. In response, TRW accelerated plans to increase sales from abroad, especially in Latin America and Europe. These efforts had begun in the late 1950s with the formation of joint ventures in Mexico, Brazil, and Argentina to produce parts for local replacement markets and for American auto companies that were expanding production in these countries. In addition, in 1960, TRW had formed an International Division, and established a wholly owned subsidiary, TRW International S.A., in Geneva. This organization supported all of TRW's businesses, including electronics, computers, and even some space and defense projects but concentrated on automotive parts and components.[64]

By the mid-1960s, it was apparent to Wright, Shepard, and Riley that the company needed to pursue foreign opportunities more aggressively. The Big Three had each mounted significant efforts to expand into Europe, Latin America, Australia, and Japan, and they encouraged major suppliers such as TRW to follow suit.[65]

TRW's initial strategy involved acquiring its existing licensees. In 1961, the company purchased a half-interest in its West German automotive valve licensee, Teves & Co. GmbH, based in Barsinghausen. Over the next several years, TRW gradually acquired the remaining stock, and the unit became known as Teves-Thompson & Co. GmbH. In 1962, TRW took a 25 percent stake in Fuji Valve, Ltd., of Japan, and in France it acquired outright the Société Mécanique de Pringy, a maker of piston rings and other parts for the automotive aftermarket. Several years later, the company built a new plant to make automotive components at Vosges that subsequently became a separate operating division. In 1965, TRW and its subsidiary Ramsey Corporation established a 55 percent stake in a joint venture in South Africa to manufacture and distribute automotive parts. The corporate-level acquisition of Ross Gear further bolstered TRW's position overseas. With operations in Brazil, France, and Australia, Ross Gear "really enabled TRW to become a worldwide company," noted Chuck Ohly, head of the Michigan Division at the time.[66]

Accumulating momentum gathered behind more big moves. In 1965 TRW Automotive added another key international ingredient by acquiring a stake in Cam Gears, Ltd., of Birmingham, England, a company with major subsidiaries in Australia and Italy. Cam Gears was a leading producer of manual rack-and-pinion steering components, a lighter alternative to traditional integral steering gears that also supplied the tight handling characteristics and road feel that European drivers prized. Two other deals followed quickly to bolster TRW's position in the United Kingdom: Clifford Motor Components, a maker of valves and related engine parts and steering wheels, for about $28 million; and Engineering Productions, Ltd., of Clevedon, a maker of steering gears and components.[67]

By the mid-1960s, through its investments and subsidiaries, TRW had manufacturing facilities in all of the major automotive-producing countries of the Free World. In recognition of this rapid growth, Riley established the TRW Automotive International Division in 1965. Two years later, after a rocky process of integration, Shepard and Riley turned the division over to Bob Burgin, who brought to his first operating assignment a flair for marketing and communications, as well as the willingness and capacity to endure an exhausting travel schedule. (He flew roundtrip from Cleveland to Europe twice a month—with visits in between to such places as Australia, Japan,

South America, and South Africa—every month for about five years.) When he took the job, he recalls, his bosses were unhappy with the performance of the international automotive units.

> I think we had about $90 million in sales, but about $2 million in profit. It was hardly worth the effort. We had a lot of bad license agreements, including one with Fiat that gave them access to all of our products for a song. I think that they really would have liked me to figure out some way of maybe phasing out the business. There was certainly no charge to go out and build it up.[68]

Burgin started out by crafting a strategy to move beyond supplying the overseas operations of American automobile manufacturers to reach into the strongest European and (later) Asian producers. "It was clear that there was going to be a world-wide marketplace," he recalls. "The opportunities were tremendous." A key element of his strategy involved establishing TRW as the global leader in its strongest product lines, engine valves and steering and suspension systems. A simple matrix identified gaping holes. The antiquated license agreement with Fiat, for example, sorely constrained TRW's position in Italy until Burgin was able to renegotiate on more favorable terms.

A bigger problem involved the company's position in West Germany, home of Europe's strongest automobile industry. Although Teves-Thompson supplied valves locally to GM's Opel subsidiary, it had little success with Volkswagen or strong specialty producers such as Mercedes-Benz, BMW, and Audi. Worse, TRW lacked any capability to supply steering and suspension parts to German customers, a problem that Burgin believed could only be solved via acquisitions. His matrix chart not only identified the holes, but also listed the leading competitors in each market that TRW wanted to serve. Further analysis turned up several companies for sale, including Bayerisches Leichtmetallwerk KG (BLW), a small producer of engine valves, that TRW acquired in 1967. The following year, Burgin negotiated the purchase of a much bigger West German company, Ehrenreich & Cie. A major West German producer of steering systems and a key supplier to Volkswagen, Ehrenreich cost TRW considerations worth about $47 million.[69]

Elsewhere in Europe and Asia, Burgin used acquisitions and joint ventures to improve the company's position. In 1968, for example, TRW combined with the Australian subsidiary of Cam Gears to purchase Duly & Hansford, Ltd., for about $6 million Australian. This company manufactured engine valves, axle shafts, and other chassis parts for both the original equipment and replacement markets in Australia. Duly & Hansford was consolidated with other TRW operations in the country into a new subsidiary, TRW Australia, Ltd. In Japan, TRW was hindered by local regulations that restricted the amounts and types of foreign investment. Nonetheless, in 1969, TRW formed two joint ventures in Japan, holding 49 percent interests in each. The first consisted of a partnership with Koyo Seiko, Ltd., a leading supplier in the Toyota family, to manufacture and sell steering pumps and systems designed by Cam Gear. The second joint venture engaged TRW with Tokai Cold Forming Company to produce suspension ball joints and other chassis parts for Japanese automakers and the local replacement market. In both cases, TRW contributed an investment worth between $4 million and $6 million and know-how, while its Japanese partner managed the business.[70]

At the close of the decade, through the efforts of Riley, Ohly, Burgin, Reynolds, and others, TRW was a vastly bigger and stronger competitor in automotive supply than it had been at the time of the merger. It operated in every major automobile-producing nation in the West, and supplied most of the leading manufacturers in the world. And in the United States, the company bolstered its traditionally strong positions with the Big Three with new products such as integral steering gears for heavy-duty vehicles and rack-and-pinion steering systems for the smaller, lighter automobiles on the horizon.

THE TRAVAILS OF TRW EQUIPMENT GROUP

During the 1950s, several of the divisions that constituted TRW Equipment Group (formerly Tapco Group)—especially Jet, Accessories, and Pneumatics—had sustained the corporation, accounting for most of its growth and profitability and supporting the strategy of diversification into defense systems and electronics. During the following decade, the group faced significant internal and external challenges. The internal challenge involved accepting limits, as the corporate strategy favored opportunities in other areas. The external challenges included coping with wide swings in defense spending, changes in aircraft design, and the increasing sophistication of big customers in aircraft engines, as well as continuing to find opportunities to apply its expertise in precision manufacturing.

Stan Pace, who headed the Equipment Group for a dozen years after the merger, saw his plans to grow repeatedly bump up against corporate priorities to expand the commercial lines of the company. Wright and Shepard did not want to give up government business, Pace noted, but they "definitely didn't want me to make acquisitions in defense. We had already made the big acquisition in defense with Ramo-Wooldridge." Although Pace occasionally proposed acquisitions, Wright and Shepard turned him down each time. It was a frustrating position, he recalled, "but probably the right thing to do."[71]

The Equipment Group did include one anomalous unit acquired in 1959: Magna Products Corporation, a small company with big ambitions. Magna's founder, Dr. Gilson Rohrback, had built a promising business by developing specialty chemicals to facilitate pumping in oil wells. At the behest of Ramo and Wooldridge, TRW had invested $450,000 to acquire a 51 percent stake in Magna, taking an option to acquire up to 85 percent within ten years. According to one of his new colleagues, Rohrback "was an articulate son-of-a-gun, and bright as hell." A reporter from *Fortune* labeled him a genius and touted his work on a new technique for generating electricity through the action of bacteria from seawater on certain chemicals. The U.S. Navy expressed interest in the technique, which promised to generate enough power to operate radio beacons, buoys, and signals. The promise went unfulfilled, however, and in 1967 TRW divested Magna Products. That year, the unit earned just $38,000 on sales of about $4 million.[72]

After 1958, the group's core business—aircraft engine parts and aircraft accessories—faced a declining market. President Eisenhower's decision to shift defense funding from aircraft, especially long-range bombers, to ballistic missiles produced mixed effects at TRW—greatly benefiting STL but hurting Tapco Group. After the merger, TRW's sales to producers of jet engines and the makers of military aircraft dropped dramatically before beginning to rise again at mid-decade with increased procurement during the Vietnam War. Even then, production rates paled in comparison to the buildup during the Korean War fifteen years earlier. Production of commercial jet aircraft, beginning with the Boeing 707 in 1958, only partly offset the decline in production of military aircraft.[73]

TRW's problem involved not only decreased aircraft production, but also significant changes in the aircraft engine business. The coming of improved, bigger, and more powerful engines meant fewer engines per aircraft. The first commercial jetliners, for example, each had four engines. Their successors in the late 1960s more commonly had three or even two engines. During the 1950s, the company had accounted for more than half of the total value of a turbojet engine by producing air foils (buckets, blades, and vanes), the compressor disk, turbine wheels, shafts, and other precision-manufactured components. During the 1960s, this position proved impossible to sustain. The slowdown in production took its toll on turbojet engine manufacturers, and several of TRW's major customers, including Ford, Curtiss-Wright, and Lycoming, ceased building turbojets; the industry in the United States eventually narrowed down to a duopoly of Pratt & Whitney and General Electric. Decline in numbers of units and customers corresponded with a decrease in TRW's bargaining power as a supplier. The growing technological capabilities of the engine makers, who controlled the engine designs and sought to capture more of the total value of the product over time, further weakened TRW's position. "Strategically, we were vulnerable," says Pace. "As our customers matured, they started pulling production of key components in-house, piece by piece. The compressor disks and turbine wheels went first. Before long, we became an airfoil house. The next stage was that the customers started moving in on the airfoils. For a while, we managed to keep sales up, but our share of market kept declining."[74]

In these circumstances, Pace and his management team made some tough decisions. The company closed down the Accessories Division's R&D center near Roanoke, Virginia, and subsequently donated the campus to Virginia Polytechnic Institute. The Materials Division (originally Kolcast), which realized most of its sales to the Jet Division, suffered cutbacks and loss of employment. TRW also prospected vigorously for new markets where it could apply its skills in precision manufacturing, its knowledge of metallurgy, or its experience in subcontracting.

Many of the Equipment Group's opportunities grew out of development work and subcontracts that dated from the 1950s. For example, the company continued to produce fuel-rod mechanisms for the U.S. Navy's nuclear reactors, a business that generated annual revenues of about $15 million. Similarly, it maintained production of pumps and auxiliary power systems for aircraft and missiles. The group also won development and prototype contracts for several intriguing new products. During the early 1960s, TRW fabricated rocket motor nozzles for the Polaris ICBM and several smaller tactical missiles. The Tapco plants also turned out "transporter-erector-launcher" systems for the U.S. Army's mobile Pershing missile.

For NASA, the Equipment Group built experimental power conversion systems for deep-space probes. One of these, called Sunflower, unfolded like an umbrella in space to capture and concentrate solar radiation to boil liquid mercury and drive a turbine capable of generating up to three thousand watts of electric power continuously for at least a year. On some of these projects, the Equipment Group collaborated with the Systems Group, although their work never resulted in a major contract win or financial success. Indeed, the relationship between the Tapco facilities and Space Park was marked by rivalry and tension.[75]

Its miscellaneous projects pushed TRW Equipment Group in the direction of becoming a job shop in precision manufacturing. To balance these inherently lumpy revenue streams, Pace sought other opportunities in government contracting. Two major initiatives during the 1960s involved manufacture of the M-14 rifle and the propulsion system for the Mark 46 torpedo.

TRW's entry into ordnance followed a directive from the new Kennedy administration secretary of defense, Robert McNamara, who sought alternative sources to the traditional armsmakers, especially suppliers with proven high-quality mass-production capability. In 1961, the U.S. Army's Ordnance Department let bids for two five-year contracts to manufacture as many as 100,000 M-14 rifles. The contracts were potentially worth $15 million, and TRW won the competition against more than forty contestants with a bid based on amortizing the start-up costs over the full ten-year period. The company made a heavy investment in tooling and equipment at the Tapco plant and began manufacture early in 1962, delivering the first batch eight weeks ahead of schedule. Later that year, TRW took on an additional contract for 219,000 rifles, moving into position to become the potential prime source. The rifles had "outstanding quality," says Pace, adding, "the U.S. Army loved them." In due course, the second five-year contract kicked in. As the business approached breakeven, however, the government abruptly canceled the contract, leaving Tapco with "all of the expense and none of the production." "We lost several million dollars on that second contract," recalls Pace bitterly, "at a time when that was really a lot of money."[76]

The Equipment Group's experience with the Mark 46 torpedo proved happier. In 1965, the U.S. Navy selected a team of TRW and Honeywell as a second source to Aerojet General to build the Mark 46, the "the Navy's most up-to-date" antisubmarine torpedo, which could be launched from aircraft, helicopters, or surface ships. TRW manufactured the propulsion system, including the fuel section, engine pumps, accessories, and propeller assembly. Honeywell provided the guidance and control system, the warhead, and final assembly and test of the units. The initial contract was worth about $20 million over several years. Beyond that, it moved TRW into what proved to be an enduring and steady, if small, business in torpedo propulsion.[77]

The Vietnam buildup enabled the Equipment Group to close the decade on a high note, as production of jet engines for military aircraft rose by 50 percent between 1966 and 1969. The group's fundamental strategic problems remained unsolved, however, and it looked ahead to the 1970s as another decade of challenge.

Piecing Together Electronic Components

After the troubles at PSI, the Computer Division, and the Columbus Division, TRW Electronics Group also faced a future of challenge. The group consisted of a grab bag of small divisions, including pieces of PSI—now known as TRW Semiconductors— and several of the components companies acquired under Dean Wooldridge. The fate of the group lay in the hands of Sid Webb, an outgoing, outspoken, and occasionally outrageous manager with a fondness for fine wines and practical jokes.

Webb had joined Ramo-Wooldridge during the 1950s in an administrative position. He worked first for Bud Nielsen and Fred Hesse before assuming the job of vice president for administration and finance in R-W's Communications Division. In 1958, he took over planning for the Canoga Park facility and presided over the construction and move to that location, where he headed administration and finance for Ralph Johnson's R-W Division. Under Wooldridge's plan to expand commercial electronics, Webb became vice president for new enterprises, a job in which he worked closely with Wooldridge on the electronics ventures.[78]

As head of the Electronics Group, Webb first took a hard look at the viability of competing in electronic components. "I decided that we ought to get out of the business entirely or we ought to grow it and become better balanced," he recalls. A critical question involved how fast integrated circuits would erode the market for components. After studying the issue, Webb concluded that integrated circuits would not "wipe out components totally," but "that it was going to be a slow replacement process." There would be time to establish a major position in the industry, but success, Webb believed, required bigger scale. He wanted TRW to be able to offer its customers a full line of electronic components, including semiconductors, capacitors, resistors, coils, tuners, motors, and relays. He also believed that such scale was necessary to support the R&D investments necessary to remain an industry leader. Finally, he agreed with Wooldridge's original strategy, which rested on a view of the industry as being ripe for acquisitions: it remained populated by many small to middle-sized competitors, often privately held, that could benefit from professional management, new sources of capital, and other advantages possessed by bigger, more diversified, and more experienced companies like TRW.[79]

Webb pursued aggressive growth that involved unleashing each of the individual businesses to grow and adding to the total by making acquisitions. Dick Campbell, who worked hand in hand with Webb, recalls him predicting in 1962 that the group could hit $100 million in sales by the end of the decade: "God, that sounded exciting!" Webb started out by trimming a sizable staff that had grown up under his predecessor.

Campbell took over acquisitions, planning, R&D, and other functions, singlehandedly performing work previously assigned to eighteen staffers.[80]

Webb achieved further savings by combining several existing units that used a common channel of distribution into a new TRW Electronic Components Division. As a supplier to the burgeoning consumer electronics industry, the division enjoyed rapid growth as its components found their way into radios, television sets, and stereo equipment. TRW's "color convergence yokes," devices to control the electronic beams on color picture tubes, providing true color reproduction, were in particularly high demand during the 1960s, as color TV dazzled the American public, accounting for half of all consumer electronics sales. Industrial and military markets also absorbed enormous quantities of TRW components in computers, communications systems, and weapons systems. The market for electronic components was fiercely competitive and becoming global in scale. To help establish a low-cost manufacturing position, TRW established components plants in Mexico (in 1962, via joint venture) and Taiwan (in 1966).[81]

Webb also pursued acquisitions actively, with a sense of the costs as well as the benefits of buying growth. "I think acquisitions is a funny thing to try to strategize," he later mused, "because it very seldom happens that you get exactly what you want. I used to tell my people that you can list all the things you are looking for and why you want them. But then I'd cross all these things out and simply write 'availability.' In the end, that was what really mattered. It doesn't do you any good to find the ideal company if it's not for sale."[82]

The results of the acquisition spree were sometimes unexpected and often humorous. Early in 1964, Campbell met with a representative of Transco Products, a maker of components for microwave equipment, to discuss a deal that would add to TRW's Microwave Division. "He had a price on his business that was so wild," recalls Campbell, "that I said, 'God, if you think it's worth that kind of money, I think we're a seller instead of a buyer.'" Soon thereafter, Transco acquired TRW Microwave Division.

More typically, Webb and Campbell bought rather than sold, and TRW's electronics businesses accumulated rapidly. In 1966—by which time Webb had become a group vice president—TRW made two significant acquisitions. First, it purchased United Transformer Corporation, a privately held company with three small plants in the United States that manufactured small transformers, microminiature magnetic components, torodial coils and electric wave filters, as well as a line of high fidelity speaker systems. Second, TRW acquired Scientific Electronic Products, Inc., of Loveland, Colorado, a leading producer of metal- and glass-enclosed quartz crystals.[83]

The following year, Webb and Campbell arranged to buy three more companies and almost closed another. The first was Dayton, Ohio-based Globe Industries, a small producer of miniature precision electrical motors and related products acquired for considerations totaling about $8.5 million. Later in the year, Webb negotiated a merger agreement with Philadelphia-based International Resistance Company (IRC), a $50 million business that manufactured a broad line of resistors and other television and general electronic items, including semiconductors and wire and cable, in six U.S. plants. The cost of this transaction totaled about $25 million.[84]

The third deal of 1967 was even bigger and involved the acquisition of United-Carr Incorporated, a Boston-based diversified company that manufactured electronic controls, switches, and connectors, as well as fasteners and other industrial products, many of which found their way into the automobile industry. United-Carr's business included seven domestic operating divisions, a wholly owned U.S. subsidiary, and many foreign subsidiaries, joint ventures, and license agreements. In 1967, United-Carr posted annual sales of about $122 million. Webb was particularly interested in several divisions that produced electronic components, connectors, sockets, coaxial and RF connectors, and printed circuit boards. After the merger, these units became part of TRW's Electronics Group, while the other United-Carr divisions were transferred to the Automotive Group.[85]

TRW had cast covetous looks at United-Carr for years. The company was well known to Fred Crawford, who was a long-time friend of Sinclair Weeks, the business-man who created United-Carr in 1929 through the merger of two Boston-based fastener companies. (Later, Weeks became a U.S. senator from Massachusetts [Republican] and served as secretary of commerce under President Eisenhower.) In 1966, Crawford approached Weeks, then an honorary director of United-Carr, and Samuel Groves, the company's president, to explore the possibility of a merger. At that time, Weeks and Groves declined, although in the go-go years of the late 1960s, other suitors soon appeared. In April 1967, recognizing that its days of independence were past, United-Carr agreed in principle to merge with Boston-based United Shoe Machinery Corporation. As the deadline for approval approached, however, the directors of United Shoe Machinery voiced concerns, and rumors began to circulate that the deal was off. At that point, Crawford phoned Groves to inquire whether United-Carr might have "room on its dance card for TRW." Referring to his fiduciary responsibilities, the more formal Groves replied, "Of course, Fred. I would go to jail if I said no."[86]

Soon after merging with United-Carr, Webb sought unsuccessfully to merge with Mallory Industries, another sizable maker of components. The deal fell through when Mallory's board decided late in the game against selling. Nonetheless, by the close of 1968, TRW Electronics Group was approaching $150 million in sales and had set its sights on doubling itself within five years. In that year, Webb—now a corporate director—reshuffled his miscellaneous divisions into three subgroups around military, industrial, and commercial markets. He also began to entertain the possibility of pursuing really big acquisitions.[87]

INTEGRATING DIVERSITY

The decentralized organization structure and management policies that Thompson Products had adopted two decades before continued to govern TRW as it dramatically expanded its scale, scope, and reach during the late 1960s. Many analysts and observers found it difficult to understand the company and classified it as a conglomerate. That label smarted, and Wright, Shepard, Ramo, Mettler, and other senior managers tried hard to dispel it. In contrast to their counterparts at the conglomerates, TRW's senior executives emphasized that they were not merely or primarily interested in the financial performance of their divisions and subsidiaries. TRW was not simply a holding company, but an operating company whose top management attended to strategic and operating plans and decisions at the business unit level.

TRW relied heavily on its group and division general managers to make the system work. As head of the Electronics Group, for example, Webb participated in periodic meetings of the policy group—the group vice presidents and the top corporate officers and staff. But, he notes, he was free to run his group as he saw fit—provided that it stayed on course to meet targets. "I was left mostly to my own devices," he recalls.

> Every two or three months I met with Shepard for a half-day meeting to go over everything. But that was it. I was left alone a lot. [The company] really was a decentralized operation with centralized control, with lots of freedom and lots of accountability. I had to answer right away for any problems. But they didn't kill you if you made a mistake, unless you made the same mistake twice. I was able to learn and learn and learn.[88]

The group vice presidents, in turn, played the same role with their subordinates, the division general managers.

TRW extended this system to new arrivals via merger and acquisition. The company normally left intact the management teams at the companies it acquired. Recalls Shepard:

> In evaluating the value of a business, of a potential acquisition, I used certain criteria. Generally, I looked beyond just what the product was and what the industry was and what the growth potential theoretically might be. I looked at the *organization*, especially at the [management] team . . . because we had a practice of undertaking only friendly acquisitions, not takeovers. We wanted the people who came with the acquisitions to team up with us, just like we teamed up within the company.

TRW's decentralized organization and informal style proved attractive to employees in companies being considered for acquisition, and several, beginning with Ramo and Wooldridge, moved up into top management positions in the corporation. Vince Herterick and George Hart, two young managers at United-Carr, for example, were ticketed for general management positions in TRW soon after the merger. The arrangements also applied overseas, where the company avoided installing American citizens in general management positions. In most cases, the only Americans working overseas in TRW were accountants.[89]

To integrate its diverse operations, TRW continued to rely on its annual cycle of meetings. The company made only minor concessions to size, in mid-decade splitting the monthly operating meetings into two separate gatherings in Cleveland and Los Angeles. Thereafter, once a month, Wright, Shepard, and other corporate executives traveled cross-country for back-to-back all-day meetings. According to Stan Pace, the value of the monthly management meetings lay in the discipline they imposed. "The chairman, the president, and all your peers were there. The peer pressure was really great. You didn't want to look like a horse's ass to your peers. The chairman and president could be relatively benign in those meetings because we did our homework." The meetings also served, says Shepard, "to train and educate and develop our top operating and staff people faster than would have been possible otherwise. The meetings were valuable in helping managers do a good job of weeding out mediocre business and cultivating promising businesses." TRW supplemented the monthly meetings by requiring division managers to issue a three-year financial forecast, which was revised each quarter. The company also continued its annual planning conference at Fred Crawford's farm to provide additional opportunities to discuss prospects and plans for individual businesses as well as for the corporation as a whole.[90]

Although they regarded TRW as a technology-based company, top management bucked trends by deciding explicitly against establishing a central R&D facility. Rather, each group and division took responsibility for its own R&D needs. Corporate headquarters occasionally provided financial support to group and division projects but generally left managers at these levels to their own devices. Nonetheless, to help encourage technology transfer and improve the flow of technical information across the groups and divisions, in 1965 the company began requiring the divisions to participate in long-term "technology forecasts."

Harper North, corporate vice president for research and development, oversaw the forecasts, which adapted the Delphi method, a RAND Corporation technique for developing a consensus. TRW surveyed twenty-seven prominent scientists and engineers inside the company about the most probable "technological breakthroughs" in the next twenty years that could have an important impact on the company's business. The company also took note of some ideas contributed by Wernher von Braun. After synthesizing these data, North and his assistants prepared a fifty-page report listing 401 new technologies or technical developments ranging from the imminent (developments in red-hot dies, solid-state gyros), to the near future (3-D color TV by 1971), to the farfetched (air tents for ocean-bottom mining and farming by 1981 and commercial passenger rockets in service by 1985).

These studies, later referred to as "the Probe technique," were updated periodically to become, as Ramo put it, "a permanent component of our advanced planning." As such, the Probe studies provided "one more source of information" to product planners and market researchers in the operating divisions who were thinking about when and where the company could best invest its resources. The point was not to direct near-term investment in a particular direction, but rather to stimulate long-term thinking and cross-fertilization of ideas. In this sense, observed Pace, "the Probe becomes a prod."[91]

TRW's ability to manage growth and produce record earnings year after year attracted much attention in the national business press. In 1966, the company took the unusual step of inviting a reporter from *Fortune* to the annual planning conference to write about how the company went about its business. By that year, it was already apparent that Wright's ambitious $1 billion sales goal would be met well before 1970, and the company was beginning to focus on a new corporate objective for 1975. It seemed likely that at a minimum, the new target would fall between $2 billion and $3 billion in sales and possibly be considerably higher. Like all of its predecessors, the 1966 conference was informal and relaxed, yet also programmed to accomplish several purposes at once. In this case, the conference was designed to kick off a two-year process to identify a growth objective and plan how to achieve it. As such, the session was designed to "bring out pertinent issues and fork over the material out of which the ultimate [corporate] plan would be built and shaped."

The Vermont conference also enabled the participants to get to know one another better, an outcome achieved by structuring free time and meals to increase opportunities to mingle. As for formal business, the participants spent several days reviewing the forecasts of each major business group (Systems, Electronics, Automotive, and Equipment), the Probe technology forecasts, experts on defense policy, and reports from several corporate officers about financial strategy and organizational issues. At the end of the conference, Wright summed up the process by saying, "Setting a goal is not a game, but a way of maximizing our capabilities. Let's come back next year and hammer out a goal high enough to excite, and reasonable enough to attain."[92]

During 1966 and 1967, Ramo led an intensive effort involving staff and operating managers to plan the next phase of TRW's growth. The company aimed high: sales of $2.2 billion by 1970 and $4.5 billion five years later. To achieve these figures, TRW would have to grow at an annual rate of 20 percent, or "moderately higher" than its 18 percent annual rate of growth since the Great Depression. Using computer modeling, technology forecasting, and other advanced techniques pioneered in the company, the planners issued a printed plan of more than one hundred pages in June 1967. The plan projected the fortunes of the company's major business groups against analysis of competitors and a forecast of likely political and social changes around the world. TRW expected the greatest growth to come in Automotive, with additional overseas expansion and acquisitions, and in Systems, where TRW would continue to reach beyond defense contracting into civil systems and perhaps into new areas such as meteorological systems, information systems, and ocean systems. The plan went on to lay out and develop alternative projections of how revenues would divide should the business meet the target of $4.5 billion, a "probable" achievement of $3 billion, and a worst or "base" case of $1.5 billion.[93]

Many of these goals and plans were to prove unattainable, even fanciful, in the decade ahead, but the process of developing them, including the annual planning conference, played an important role in integrating TRW's diverse businesses and in instilling a sense of common purpose. That process received a further boost when, after the 1967 conference, Wright invited forty-five-year-old Rube Mettler to draft a set of corporate objectives to be included in the annual report. Mettler revised the internal financial goals for public consumption and listed six objectives that represented the company's plan for growth during the 1970s:

- To seek a balanced, interrelated form of diversification which provides maximum protection against cyclical changes in any of its major markets.

- To achieve an average compound annual growth rate in sales and pretax earnings of at least 10–15%, with appropriate improvement in earnings per share.

- To place the highest priority on internal growth, viewing selective acquisitions as a means of improving the base for future internal growth.

- To use technology in every possible way—improving present products and creating new ones, developing new methods and processes, analyzing new markets—to gain the competitive edge that leads to greater return on investment.

- To draw on the large cash flow generated by established businesses to finance unusual growth opportunities likely to provide the increase in profits tomorrow.

- To maintain a flexible, growth-oriented organization which will be able to attract and retain the creative, talented individuals who can keep TRW growing.[94]

That assignment, Mettler later believed, was pivotal in determining his future in the company. Indeed, not long after, Wright invited Mettler to lunch and asked him whether he would be interested in moving up the ladder. Because that would mean a move to Cleveland, Mettler asked for time to talk it over with his wife. When he got back to Wright a few days later, the answer was yes. In February 1968, TRW's board elected Mettler assistant president and Dick DeLauer his successor as head of TRW Systems Group. The expectation was that when Wright retired, Shepard would move up to become chairman and CEO, and Mettler would become president. Those changes followed in due course in December 1969, when Wright, true to his 1961 promise to retire early, stepped down about four months before his sixty-fifth birthday.[95]

Chapter 11

Testing Time

▶ ▶ ▶

1970–1974

TRW'S ACQUISITIVE BURST IN THE LATE 1960S DID NOT, AS PLANNED AND EXPECTED, HERALD a period of continuing rapid growth. Rather, the early 1970s provided the first stern test of the company's strategy of diversification. The decade opened with a recession in the United States. It continued with a period of wage and price controls, saw the end of the gold standard as the basis of Western currencies and a fundamental change in patterns of world trade, and witnessed a massive shock to the world's supply of fossil fuels that triggered a second and deeper recession.

These adversities rocked the U.S. economy, but TRW continued to prosper in spite of them. Although sales and earnings dipped in 1970 and 1971, they climbed back to record totals in 1974: net income of just over $100 million on revenues of about $2.5 billion. The company remained a darling of the business press, which admired its considerable accomplishments, especially in areas of high technology. TRW built space vehicles such as *Pioneer 10* and *Pioneer 11,* the extraordinary sojourners to the outer planets and beyond; three productive astrophysical observatories; and the ingenious biological instrument package for the Viking lander on Mars. For its customers in defense and national security, it continued work in comsats and classified areas. The growing scale and sophistication of payloads for such vehicles and advances in microelectronic circuitry for communications and signal processing helped build electronic hardware and systems into one of the biggest businesses based at Space Park. Large-scale software systems emerged as another business with an intriguing future.

Despite its growing reputation for tackling large, complex technical challenges, the company's financial performance depended on its more mundane operations. The big acquisitions of the late 1960s paid immediate dividends, and one of them, Reda Pump, became a cornerstone of a new strategic thrust in energy products. In automotive supply, TRW introduced a string of successful products, including manual and power rack-and-pinion steering systems for passenger cars, and hydrostatic steering systems and torque motors for heavy duty and off-highway vehicles and applications. The company also entered the emerging field of automotive safety products through a small German acquisition—a modest start to what would eventually become a multi-billion-dollar business in safety systems.

Yet for all its achievements, TRW's performance masked many changes and challenges inside the company and in the markets it served. This was a time of struggle, and progress did not come easily. Some acquisitions and new ventures failed to meet expectations or simply failed. Some technological triumphs—the Viking biology instrument, for example—were products of a painful birth. Many of the company's efforts to transfer technology from aerospace to commercial markets ended in retreat or defeat—a common outcome throughout the aerospace industry. A darkening climate threatened the aircraft components business and enduring success in commercial electronics remained at a tantalizing distance.

With the onset of the decade's second recession in 1974, TRW's top managers remained wedded to the strategy of diversification, but also showed increasing concern about its implementation. The struggles of many small divisions and projects consumed a disproportionate amount of management attention, highlighted problems of control, and taxed investors' patience. In an environment of slowing growth and scarce investment capital, some top managers began to wonder whether the company was pursuing too many activities that were too disparate in nature, and whether the occasion had arrived for a major correction in strategic direction. Not for the last time were these concerns raised.

A COMPANY OF COMPANIES

During 1969 and 1970, the transition to new leadership at the top of TRW proceeded smoothly, once more emphasizing continuities with the past. The members of the chief executive office—Horace Shepard, Rube Mettler, Si Ramo, and Ed Riley—had all grown up in the company and shared faith in its strategy of diversification, decentralized management, and informal style and manner of communication. Although all four men were involved in key decisions, Ramo remained on the West Coast and generally looked after the company's long-range planning and issues involving technology, and Riley principally attended to the automotive businesses until his retirement at the end of 1971. The smaller team of Shepard and Mettler focused on the company as a whole.[1]

Looking back on his tenure as CEO, Shepard recalls that his relationship with Mettler was exactly like his own relationship had been with Dave Wright. "When I was the chairman and [Mettler] was the president, we used to spend an awful lot of time together thinking out loud about where we stood and what we thought we ought to do. Invariably, we came to the same conclusions about what was important and what wasn't, what ought to be done and how." For his part, Mettler recalls that "Shep was a very organized manager, very efficient. He didn't spend a lot of time on nuances or details. . . . He delegated, and once a job or assignment was given, it was clear that he expected you to do it. So I had a very easy working relationship with Shep."[2]

In 1970, TRW's business groupings managed fifty-five separate divisions, and top executives were confident that this diversity would provide balanced and profitable growth. As Shepard argued, "We've spent the last few years trying to arrange a business plan sufficiently diversified to let us counter some of the economic cycles. We now have the whole business divided into a lot of relatively small increments so that if one segment has a 'bad year,' we are not particularly affected as a whole."[3]

At the same time, Shepard announced, "We don't have any deliberate plan to diversify much more broadly than we currently are." The company's impulse to acquire was checked by a recession in the United States, as well as by a new era of antitrust enforcement. The Federal Trade Commission's scrutiny, for example, led TRW in 1971 to call off a promising merger with General Battery that would have added new lines of automotive and industrial products to the fold. Although TRW completed some acquisitions during the early 1970s, these generally represented product line extensions of existing businesses and were negotiated at levels below corporate headquarters. The new deals were fewer in number and smaller in size than their predecessors in the mid- to late 1960s (see Appendix).[4]

TRW's senior executives were less concerned with accelerating growth than with developing new ways to manage the company's diverse and far-flung operations. By the time he ascended to the chief executive office, Rube Mettler had won many admirers for his systematic approach to management and his gentlemanly executive style. Colleagues invariably noted his intellect, thoroughness, rigor, and grasp of significant detail. He was also patient and reserved, almost to a fault. He was "almost totally unflappable," wrote one long-time associate. "The strongest words anyone has heard him say are, 'I am somewhat disappointed.' When he says that, you know you are in real trouble. Some of his associates have said that they wished on occasion he would really let fly. One said, 'Rube can really be chewing you out and you may not be fully aware of it.'"[5]

After Mettler moved to Cleveland in 1968 and during his first year as president, he traveled extensively to visit the company's operations. The purpose of these trips was to introduce himself around the company, to get to know people and operations, and to understand TRW's various businesses and customers. During the time he spent traveling, he thought long and hard about how TRW organized its businesses, and he shared his evolving ideas with Shepard, Ramo, and others. Mettler's review of the automotive area, for example, revealed several key points. First, the international automotive acquisitions of the 1960s had produced dramatic changes in the company's sales mix—in 1970, in fact, more of TRW's automotive revenues originated overseas than in the United States. Second, the automotive businesses included many diverse operations, including Marlin-Rockwell, United-Greenfield, and parts of United-Carr that served many markets besides motor vehicle manufacturers. The miscellaneous nature of these businesses threatened to divert attention from the company's most promising automotive businesses, especially in steering and chassis components.[6]

Mettler's thinking about the structure of TRW Automotive dovetailed with other concerns: the need to narrow spans of control of senior executives, for example, and to reorganize the business units around common characteristics, markets, and opportunities, as well as to open more pathways to develop senior managers. During the spring of 1971, Mettler announced a "rearrangement" of the company's operations, establishing three new organizations (later called sectors): Systems, under Dick DeLauer; Automotive Worldwide, under Vince Herterick; and Industrial and Replacement, under Bill Reynolds. The Systems organization included, somewhat confusingly, TRW Systems Group, headed after March 1971 by Dr. George Solomon; Industrial Operations, under Fred Hesse; and Systems Application Center, a small organization that focused primarily on data processing initiatives and some civil systems projects (see below). Automotive Worldwide combined three existing units: the engine components divisions, the chassis components divisions, and, for a transition period, the company's international automotive operations. TRW Industrial and Replacement included Marlin-Rockwell, several United-Carr divisions, United-Greenfield, and Aftermarket Operations (formerly the Replacement Division).[7]

The new organizations were headed by executive vice presidents, with Herterick and Reynolds elected to these positions and joining Sid Webb, head of TRW Electronics Group and Stan Pace, head of TRW Equipment Group, at that level. The new officers were highly talented. The hard-charging Herterick, forty-eight, had climbed swiftly through the ranks at United-Carr to become vice president and general manager when TRW acquired it. The thirty-seven-year-old Reynolds was on his second stint with TRW. He had begun his career with Thompson Products as an assistant to Ernie Brelsford, the company's chief financial officer, for whom he carried out some of the background financial analyses for the merger with Ramo-Wooldridge. Not long afterward, Fred Crawford tapped Reynolds to become president of Crawford Door, a job he held for seven years before returning in 1966 to TRW as an assistant to Ed Riley in the Automotive Group. He was later assigned to the Replacement Division and also worked on several corporate-level acquisitions, including United-Greenfield.[8]

On August 1, 1971, just as these changes were taking effect, Herterick died suddenly of a heart attack at his home in Lexington, Massachusetts. To replace him as head of Automotive Worldwide, Shepard and Mettler named Stan Pace and promoted Art Schweitzer, a veteran manager who had been running the Tapco operations, as head of TRW Equipment Group. Significantly, Schweitzer did not become an executive vice president, and TRW Equipment Group remained something of a weak sibling among stronger, more powerful units.[9]

Mettler also made significant changes in the corporate staff, bolstering traditional functions and adding officers to oversee new areas. In 1971, for example, he accepted the advice of Joe Gorman, TRW's brash young corporate secretary, to reorganize the corporate law department. The result was "a totally centralized" unit, with every lawyer in the company, regardless of business or location, reporting to the vice president and general counsel. Gorman's plan arose out of concerns about duplication of services and problems in the quality and consistency of the company's legal work. In approving the change, Mettler overrode the reservations of such entrenched powers as DeLauer, Solomon, and Webb and reversed TRW's long tradition of decentralized staff functions. The episode portended further changes in the role of corporate staff, as well as increasing responsibilities for Gorman during the 1970s.[10]

Late in 1972, Mettler recruited Lloyd Hand, a prominent Washington attorney and formerly a top aide to President Lyndon Johnson, to a new post as senior vice president and assistant to the president for communications. This move significantly increased TRW's role and visibility in public affairs management. Hand's organization included a new head of corporate communications, Bob Lundy, a veteran manager from Space Park, who soon afterward was named a corporate vice president for public relations and advertising. In November 1973, Mettler encouraged Chuck Allen, TRW's chief financial officer, to augment his staff to increase the company's focus on trends in the external environment. Allen duly appointed two new vice presidents, one in charge of corporate planning and development and the other as chief economist. Finally, in the area of human relations, Mettler initiated periodic formal reviews of the company's manpower development and succession planning programs so that future leaders in each business were identified and developed through appropriate assignments.[11]

Mettler next turned his attention to the governing procedures of the corporation. He made each executive vice president responsible for holding monthly operating reviews with management from the groups and divisions that reported to them, and he established quarterly reviews with the EVPs and the head of TRW Equipment Group. At the same time, Mettler created a policy group consisting of the members of the chief executive office, the EVPs, and senior staff officers. The policy group met four to six times each year to review the performance of the corporation as a whole. The annual planning conferences on Crawford's farm were replaced by gatherings every two or three years, often at or near TRW headquarters in Cleveland.[12]

Finally, to help monitor the company's performance, Mettler and Allen adopted a new measure, return on assets employed (ROAE). The company's traditional reports had emphasized return on sales, return on investment, asset utilization, and contributions to earnings per share, but Mettler preferred ROAE. Shepard became a convert, placing "great importance" on the new measure:

> It was a key yardstick in evaluating the performance of the businesses. It was the common denominator for us. . . . We had so many assets to deal with, and the decentralized managers always had more places to use the assets than we had assets available. Emphasizing return on assets employed was an obvious way to impress on them how choices should be made. After all, we were thinking in the final analysis about what's good for the shareholder.

Allen, who presided over the change in thinking, recalls that it took "a big education process" to wean operating managers away from the traditional measures. On the other hand, he says, understanding ROAE required management to focus on exceeding TRW's cost of capital as a true indication of long-term profitability. [13]

Phoenix at Space Park

TRW's new management structure and systems were soon put to the test. When the company reported its earnings for 1971, it marked the first time in eight years that it had failed to achieve a new record. In his annual report to stockholders, Shepard blamed a lingering recession in the United States and incipient inflation as the principal culprits. In fact, a major problem for the company was a deep recession in the aerospace industry, which posed the first real check on TRW's growth in this area in a decade.[14]

The aerospace recession began in the late 1960s with the convergence of several factors. Although the war in Vietnam lingered on until the mid-1970s, President Richard Nixon had won office in 1968 with a pledge to end it, and actual spending on defense had already begun to turn down. The spending cuts had an immediate impact on some Space Park activities, as well as on TRW Equipment Group in Cleveland. At the same time, despite the triumphs of the Apollo program, NASA's budget began to shrink, and future funding levels were uncertain. Finally and unluckily for TRW, these factors coincided with the conclusion of several big programs, including INTELSAT III, the Orbiting Geophysical Observatories, Vela, and some classified work, which did not lead to follow-on assignments.[15]

The aerospace recession devastated Space Park. Between February 1970 and October 1971, employment plunged from 15,500 to 9,500. (One of the casualties, chemist Jerry Buss, landed on his feet. A shrewd investor in real estate, he subsequently accumulated a fortune and became famous as the owner of the Los Angeles Lakers professional basketball team and the Inglewood Forum, the arena in which they play.)

TRW cut back sharply on internally financed activities and slashed overhead. It discontinued the technology forecasts, and Harper North and several other senior veterans left the company. The loss of so many jobs had an obvious depressing effect on morale. For many survivors, the downturn marked the first time since the founding of Ramo-Wooldridge that the future did not seem endlessly bright.[16]

Several factors helped ease the crisis. First, in April 1970, a dramatic space rescue mission boosted employee morale and the company's reputation for solving tough problems. Fifty-six hours into the flight of *Apollo 13*, as astronauts Jim Lovell, Jack Swigert, and Fred Haise approached the moon for the third lunar landing, they felt an unexpected jolt and shudder. An oxygen tank in the vehicle's service module had exploded, and within minutes the vehicle lost most of its breathable air and electrical power, including the ability to start the main propulsion system for the return voyage. There was no longer any question of continuing the mission. Indeed, the primary concern was whether the astronauts could make it home safely. Unless they could adjust their course, they would hurl around the moon and miss the earth by at least forty thousand miles on the voyage back. Their only hope of survival involved firing TRW's Lunar Excursion Module Descent Engine (LEMDE) as the spacecraft rounded the moon to boost it into a safe return trajectory. The problem was that no one had ever imagined such a contingency, least of all the designers and builders of the LEMDE.[17]

Apollo 13's predicament transfixed the American public for days—a circumstance later recreated in countless magazines, books, documentaries, and, after twenty-five years, a feature film starring two-time Academy Award–winner Tom Hanks. The three astronauts crowded into the lunar module, a space designed for two people, where they huddled amid freezing conditions and carefully husbanded their remaining oxygen and electrical power. Immediately after the accident, TRW personnel assigned to the Apollo program began working around the clock with colleagues at NASA and other aerospace contractors to develop new guidance and trajectory calculations based on the LEMDE's capabilities and prepare alternatives. About five hours after the accident, Lovell fired the engine for about thirty-two seconds to put the vehicle back on a free return trajectory. Some eighteen hours later, soon after the astronauts emerged from behind the moon and a nerve-racking communications blackout, Lovell fired LEMDE again for four minutes and twenty-one seconds. This burst lopped a day off of the return trip and positioned the astronauts for a landing in a Pacific Ocean recovery area. Used again a day later to provide a brief mid-course correction, the LEMDE once more worked perfectly.

On April 17, four days after the accident, the astronauts splashed down safely within four miles of a recovery vessel. Three weeks later, they visited Space Park to express their gratitude and bestow a commemorative plaque for TRW's contributions to the mission. Addressing a mass meeting of employees, Lovell won a loud ovation by suggesting that TRW change its advertising slogan to, "the last 300,000 miles are on us."[18]

Apollo 13 once more demonstrated TRW's formidable technological capabilities. As applied in continuing programs, including ballistic missiles, systems engineering for the U.S. Navy's Anti-Submarine Warfare Program, the second-generation Defense Satellite Communications System (DSCS-II), the Defense Support Program, and programs in classified areas, these capabilities provided the foundation for renewed growth. During the early 1970s, TRW also captured several significant spacecraft wins, including two Pioneer interplanetary space vehicles and the High Energy Astronomical Observatory (HEAO) program for NASA, and the Fleet Satellite Communications System for the U.S. military. In addition, TRW Systems launched many initiatives to win new business, expand on TRW's expertise in systems design, electronic systems and software, and diversify into new areas.[19]

A turnaround at TRW required the company first to contend with fundamental changes in the spacecraft industry, which was maturing at a rapid clip. During the early 1970s, satellites continued the trend of becoming bigger, more sophisticated, and much more expensive, with resulting contract awards dwindling in number. NASA's commitment to the space shuttle as the principal launch vehicle of the future had an enormous impact on satellite design. Most new satellites would fall within fixed dimensions of size and weight. Some scientific spacecraft were exempt from these requirements, but the drop in NASA's funding levels after Apollo diminished the appeal for manufacturers. During the early 1970s, TRW gained an acute understanding of the risks and rewards of the spacecraft business.

The first new space vehicle contract of the new decade began in February 1970, when TRW won a $38 million contract from NASA's Ames Research Center to design and build two unmanned vehicles, eventually known as *Pioneer 10* and *Pioneer 11,* to probe the outer reaches of the solar system. In 1965, a NASA scientist, building on a TRW analysis, had calculated that during the 1970s four of the outer planets (Jupiter, Saturn, Uranus, and Neptune) would be aligned so that a single spacecraft could pass near all of them—a configuration that occurs about every 175 years. To take advantage of this opportunity, NASA took few chances. Showing high regard for TRW, the agency bypassed the time-consuming process of soliciting requests for proposals and simply awarded the production contract to the company.[20]

Led by B. J. O'Brien and Herb Lassen (who was responsible for the design concept), and assisted by a team that included Ed Dunford, a young engineer who later became the company's president and chief operating officer, TRW built the spacecraft to meet extremely demanding specifications. The two vehicles would be the first spacecraft to fly through the asteroid belt. They would be the first exposed to the extremely high levels of radiation surrounding Jupiter and the other planets. And they would reach unprecedented speeds—over one hundred thousand miles per hour as the "gravity assist" from the giant planets hurled them from one trajectory to another. Because they would need to function so long while heading away from the sun, the spacecraft could not rely on solar collectors or batteries; rather, they needed an independent, long-lived source of power provided by radioisotope thermoelectric generators. At the same time, they also had to communicate reliably over vast distances from the earth—a requirement for significant advances in deep-space communications. One problem, for example, was the extremely low energy available for communications. The spacecraft carried eight-watt transmitters—a power level roughly equivalent to that of a child's night-light. At interplanetary distances, the signal was unbelievably faint: according to one calculation, from the vicinity of Jupiter it would take nineteen million years for the energy coming from the spacecraft to accumulate sufficiently to light a single Christmas-tree bulb for a thousandth of a second.[21]

Each *Pioneer* was essentially "a flying antenna." The spacecraft weighed 570 pounds including 65 pounds of scientific instruments and 60 pounds of propellant for attitude changes and course correction. The heart of each was a hexagonal bus that held the science packages, computers, guidance and communications systems, and propellant. Attached to the bus was a circular high-gain antenna nine feet in diameter. There were also three booms, one of which held a magnetometer, with the others supporting a pair of radioisotope thermoelectric generators. Each spacecraft carried equipment that would return the first real-time images of the outer planets. At the instigation of astronomer Carl Sagan, the *Pioneer* vehicles bore plaques bearing symbols of their earthly origins in the infinitesimal likelihood of a chance encounter with intelligent extraterrestrial life.[22]

Pioneer 10 and *Pioneer 11* proved astonishing successes. They were the first nuclear-powered spacecraft, first to cross the asteroid belt, first to Jupiter, first to Saturn, and first human-made objects to leave the solar system. They are the fastest spacecraft ever built and hold the record for communication over the farthest distance from earth. Launched in March 1972, *Pioneer 10* rendezvoused with Jupiter twenty months later, not only providing the richest scientific data ever collected about the planet but also returning the first real-time, close-up images. Among other achievements, *Pioneer 10* confirmed that the planet consists entirely of liquid and gas. *Pioneer 11* achieved comparable triumphs: launched in April 1973, it used Jupiter's gravity assist to slingshot to Saturn at speeds over 107,000 miles per hour. It arrived in the vicinity of Saturn in December 1979, returning the first close-up pictures of the planet, its rings, and moons, as well as invaluable scientific data.

Pioneer 10 and *Pioneer 11* reaffirmed TRW's leadership on the frontiers of aerospace technology and led to additional awards from NASA and other government agencies. In November 1971, TRW won a significantly bigger NASA program, a $70 million award to build the first two of four projected High Energy Astronomy Observatories (HEAOs) for launch later in the decade. The company's role was to design and develop the HEAO spacecraft, integrate the missions, support launch operations at the Kennedy Space Center, and perform flight operations of the in-orbit observatories in the mission control center. Herb Lassen led the initial design and development work, and Dick Whilden managed the program after NASA awarded the production contract.[23]

Like the Orbiting Geophysical Observatories and other early NASA scientific satellite programs, HEAO featured a modular design that called for TRW to fabricate the satellite bus and power and control systems to support a variety of experiments to be flown aboard different missions. In January 1973, with development work well under way, NASA reacted to budget pressures and suspended work on HEAO, threatening to cancel the program. To forestall this possibility, Whilden and NASA scientists swiftly restructured HEAO to proceed under a tighter budget. One of the planned missions was simply abandoned and many experiments were scaled back and reconceived. Whilden and his colleagues redesigned the spacecraft to make use of existing hardware and space-proven technology. This approach, later called the "protoflight" concept, eliminated the need for separate prototypes and achieved significant cost savings. Such measures so impressed NASA that in July 1974 it restored major funding to HEAO. Dick Halpern, the NASA program manager, gave high praise to Whilden and his "very, very classy team of engineers" for the comeback.[24]

During the mid-1970s TRW fabricated the three HEAO satellites with similar designs and subsystems. Each weighed about three tons and bore an octagonal shape about twenty feet long and eight feet in diameter. About 80 percent of the components came "off the shelf." Solar panels produced about four hundred watts of power to run the equipment and experiments on board each satellite. Launched late in the decade, all three satellites accounted for space spectaculars. HEAO-1 provided the first comprehensive mapping of the X-ray sky, discovering more than 1,500 new X-ray sources. Its successors returned X-ray images of quasars and studied gamma ray and cosmic ray phenomena and paved the way for the NASA's huge Gamma Ray Observatory program of the 1990s. "By all accounts, the performance of TRW was nothing short of outstanding," said Patrick Henry, a representative of the Smithsonian Observatory who worked on the program. "They were very good. I was amazed that a large company could do things so well."[25]

TRW's growing renown in microelectronics prepared the way for another major spacecraft program. Electronic Systems Division designed and fabricated integrated circuits and other hardware for classified programs and secure communications, landing several multimillion-dollar development and production contracts for encryptors and other devices and equipment. In 1970, the U.S. Navy awarded TRW a sole-source contract to develop a processing repeater for satellite communications. The device used TRW-developed large-scale integrated chips, and its successful performance helped position the company in November 1972 to obtain another major spacecraft program: the Fleet Satellite Communications System.[26]

The FLTSATCOM program entailed building an operational near-global satellite communications network to link naval aircraft, ships, submarines, ground stations, the Strategic Air Command, and the presidential command networks. The network consisted of five satellites (four in the operational configuration, with an extra as a spare) to be launched during the late 1970s and early 1980s. Each two-ton satellite would be stationed in geosynchronous orbit, be stabilized on three axes, and carry twenty-three channels in the ultra-high and super-high frequency bands.[27]

As the prime contractor for the FLTSATCOM satellites and electronics payload, TRW ran into a thicket of extremely difficult technical challenges, including many that resulted from inexact specifications. The most significant problem that project manager Emery Reeves and his team faced was completely unexpected, hitherto never experienced, and not discovered until well into the program. The initial design had called for a single parabolic antenna to receive and transmit signals. Although the power of the transmitter was one hundred billion billion times stronger than the signal received, experts believed that one antenna could handle two-way traffic because the send and receive channels were separated in frequency. Testing in 1974, however, uncovered crosstalk: intermodulation that caused interference in the receive channels.

TRW and Aerospace Corporation engineers applied themselves to this problem in an intense, around-the-clock effort for more than a year. The eventual solution involved adding a separate helical antenna for transmission. This in turn required "the most exquisite design and fabrication techniques" for the system finally to work. Although FLTSATCOM eventually was a technological tour de force and a business success, delays and cost overruns turned it into a troubled program during the middle of the decade.[28]

TRW's Applied Technology Division also encountered the challenges and risks of fabricating equipment for the specialized requirements of space missions. The division's biggest and most visible activity involved production of the biology instruments for two Viking spacecraft that would negotiate a soft landing on Mars. The initial contract awarded in September 1970 was worth $13.7 million, but it eventually ballooned to more than $59 million over five years, as TRW took on one of the most daunting technological challenges in the history of its aerospace operations.[29]

The Viking program represented one of NASA's biggest initiatives between Apollo and the space shuttle, and it eventually cost nearly $1 billion—more than $200 million above original estimates. The program involved sending two separate vehicles to land on Mars in 1974, although the landing finally took place two years later. The landers and the orbiters from which they separated were crammed with scientific and communications equipment designed to increase knowledge about the red planet. A primary scientific mission—and one that seized the public's imagination—was the search for life. That search was carried out by one of the most complex pieces of equipment ever assembled and a heroic feat of miniaturization: the Viking Lander Biology Instrument designed to test Martian soil for evidence of microorganisms.

TRW won the competition to produce the biology instrument as a subcontractor to Martin Marietta, the prime contractor for the Viking landers. The plan called for each lander to release a claw mechanism that would scoop up a bit of soil and place it inside the biology lab for analysis. Each lab included three separate experiments jammed inside a container about the size of a car battery, weighing about thirty-five pounds, and consuming the average power of a Christmas-tree bulb. The biology instrument contained more than four thousand components, including "tiny ovens to heat samples; ampules holding the broth that had to be broken on command; radioactive gases in tiny bottles; a xenon lamp to duplicate sunlight; Geiger counters and fifty separate valves." It had to withstand high-temperature sterilization to prevent earth organisms from contaminating results, the trauma of launch, the rigors of a one-year journey in the frigid environment of interplanetary space, and the shock of landing on Mars, where there was no guarantee that it would descend on level terrain. It then had to perform its experiments in controlled conditions in the unpredictable Martian climate, where temperatures could swing 120 degrees between night and day, and report its results back to earth, two hundred million miles away.[30]

Given these challenges, it is not surprising that building the instrument proved more difficult and expensive than originally imagined, as well as a continuing source of friction among TRW, Martin Marietta, and NASA. There was no room for error and little tolerance for delay because of limited launch opportunities when the orbits earth and Mars were suitably aligned. Part of the problem with the instrument—representing about one-third of the cost overrun—stemmed from NASA's shifting requirements and specifications as the dimensions and resources of the lander changed and testing mandated modifications. But most of the difficulties arose from the inherent and unprecedented complexity of the assignment, which stretched both TRW's technical and managerial capabilities to the fullest. It proved fiendishly difficult to control the weight of the package and to manage all planned activities given limited power available.[31]

Management challenges also bedeviled the project, which consumed more than a thousand person-years of TRW's resources, including at one point more than a thousand people. The project passed through the hands of four different project managers, with Eugene Noneman and Harold Adelson credited with extraordinary leadership to bring it to completion. (NASA awarded Noneman a Public Service Medal for his work on the project.) In late 1973, with progress lagging, TRW established a problem management center, following a model used by NASA and Martin Marietta elsewhere on the Viking program. When critical problems surfaced—there were eighty-six on the biology instrument—they were assigned to the center and a "tiger team" was set up with full responsibility for solving them. The team had to begin with a detailed plan of action that was subject to thorough scrutiny before the team was permitted to tackle the problem itself. From there, the team documented each step completely until the problem was solved, and no problem could be closed until the cause was determined and corrective action fully implemented. Once management committed the resources and personnel, the action plan was reviewed weekly and in some cases daily. The complete documentation proved an invaluable source of data that helped compress the preflight readiness reviews.[32]

TRW delivered three biology instruments to NASA in the summer of 1975. Two of them were launched with separate Viking spacecraft, on August 20 and September 9, respectively. *Viking 1* touched down on a stony area called the Chryse Plain near the Martian equator on July 20, 1976—the seventh anniversary of the first Apollo landing. On September 3, *Viking 2* landed about 4,600 miles to the north in an area called the Utopian Plain. In each instance, the biology instrument set about its tasks immediately and performed them flawlessly. The experiments found no conclusive evidence of life, although the results suggested an unusual soil chemistry on Mars in which microorganisms could possibly figure.[33]

Yet another strong contributor to Space Park's recovery was the Systems Engineering & Integration Division, which began to develop a major independent line of business in software to manage unusually complex problems. This business had its origins in Ramo-Wooldridge's original support to the ICBM, when the company developed software for guidance, reentry, and targeting, as well as for general program and project management. During the 1960s, the work continued and broadened as the company developed software for various space missions and ground station support, as well as signal and message processing.[34]

In 1972, TRW opened a major new area by teaming with McDonnell-Douglas on a $100 million program known as Site Defense. This program was a key part of U.S. efforts to defend missile sites with an antiballistic missile (ABM) defense system, and the software was needed to analyze the trajectories of incoming missiles and direct counterattack weaponry to knock them out. Given limited response time—less than thirty seconds between the time a ballistic missile enters the atmosphere and the detonation of its payload—there was no room for error. The software had to take account of an enormous number of variables and perform a sequence of extremely difficult calculations both to detect, acquire, and track the incoming missile, pinpoint the optimum point of intercept, and guide the defense weaponry. These requirements resulted in the biggest and most complex software system in history, a feat so daunting that many experts doubted whether it could be achieved at all. Bell Labs, the original contractor for the program, abandoned the challenge as not feasible under existing requirements.[35]

To develop the software, the TRW McDonnell-Douglas team pioneered many new techniques to ensure that the initial requirements were fully understood at all levels and that every piece of software met those requirements as they inevitably evolved during the project. The "waterfall" technique, for example, provided for comprehensive reviews at key points in the development of the software as it proceeded from requirements analysis and definition through coding to test and evaluation. Another technique called the Unit Development Folder required each software developer to document every step of his or her work so that anybody from any level of management or technical support could understand the goal of each piece of software and how it was being accomplished. The technique also proved invaluable in bringing new team members up to speed whenever the original programmers had to drop out.

Site Defense represented "a genuine landmark" in software history. Although the United States abandoned a full-blown ABM system, the software, which was developed on time and on budget, tested successfully against an actual ICBM in the Pacific Missile Range. The achievement sent shock waves through the software development community and helped position TRW for subsequent work in large-scale software projects.[36]

Prometheus Unbound

Although TRW rebounded from the aerospace recession on the basis of core capabilities in spacecraft, electronic systems, and systems engineering, DeLauer and Solomon—with corporate encouragement—accelerated attempts to diversify business at Space Park. Several factors added impetus: the wish to find productive employment for out-of-work engineers and scientists, the desire to reduce TRW's dependence on a handful of big government contracts, and the hope to develop profitable new businesses based on aerospace technology. New ventures emerged quickly from several different sources, including internal development, acquisitions, and joint ventures. By the mid-1970s, TRW was engaged in businesses as diverse as charge authorization systems for consumer credit, housing and real estate development, minerals exploration, construction engineering, and urban transportation systems (see Tables 11-1 and 11-2).

The Applied Technology Division (ATD) proved a particularly fertile source of ideas. One line of business emerged from propulsion technology originally developed for the LEMDE. As a rocket maker, however, TRW experienced limited success during the 1970s. The company adapted the LEMDE as the second-stage engine for NASA's Delta launch vehicle (a Thor missile derivative), a workhorse that achieved fifty launches without failure before the advent of the space shuttle. TRW lost its bid to develop the on-board rocket motors for the space shuttle, however, and its rocket-building business tapered off sharply later in the decade.[37]

TRW's expertise in high-temperature, high-pressure combustion soon found new applications, however. Most important were high-energy chemical lasers, which focus many thousands of watts of power instantaneously and had extraordinary potential as a weapon, perhaps in defending against missile attacks. In the 1960s, many aerospace companies and government laboratories pursued various ways to achieve high-energy lasers. One of the most promising emerged in 1969 at Aerospace Corporation, where a team of researchers demonstrated the first high-energy chemical laser using an electric arc to excite a mixture of hydrogen and fluorine gas as the medium in which to amplify a directed beam of light.[38]

The following year, TRW established a laboratory under Dr. John S. Martinez to investigate high-energy chemical lasers. Whereas Aerospace Corporation had relied on electrical power to excite the amplifying medium, TRW achieved a similar result with a high-temperature combustor. "This was an important development," noted one of the lab team, "since it eliminated the need for electrical power supplies and provided a laser in which chemical energy was transformed into coherent laser light simply, efficiently, and in a configuration that could be scaled up to thousands of watts." Among other implications, the TRW breakthrough meant that high-energy lasers in theory could be deployed in combat, on board ships, or even in space. These possibilities attracted high-level interest in the U.S. Department of Defense and the U.S. Navy, which funded TRW's continuing research generously throughout the 1970s and beyond.[39]

ATD also pursued opportunities in commercial areas, especially resulting from industry's need for clean combustion as a result of the Clean Air Act. Some projects again relied on the company's expertise in propulsion: a combustor based on LEMDE held promise reducing nitrogen oxide emissions from industrial processes by a factor of five or more; a device called a "charged droplet scrubber" used a technology derived from electrostatic colloid thrusters to control particulate emissions from industrial processes. ATD also made plans to exploit another proprietary technology. Dr. Robert Meyers and a team of assistants developed a process to treat coal before burning to remove sulfur, a source of noxious emissions. Early estimates suggested that the Meyers process could compete favorably with alternative scrubbing technologies.[40]

TABLE 11 - 1
TRW VENTURES IN CIVIL SYSTEMS, 1970–1975

NAME	DESCRIPTION
Canada Systems, Ltd.	Joint venture in 1971 between TRW, London Life Insurance, The T. Eaton Company, and The Steel Company of Canada, Ltd., to pool data processing capabilities and pursue civil systems opportunities in Canada. TRW sold its interest in the mid-1970s.
Community Technology Corporation	Start-up in 1971 to promote community planning and develop manufactured housing. Created two subsidiaries, Colorado Land Development, a joint venture with Mitsubishi, and Community Shelter Corporation. Built prototype housing in Sacramento and other locations and acquired land in Littleton, Colorado, for a model community. Sold at a loss in 1974.
International Decision Techniques	Joint venture between TRW and J.P. Morgan, Inc., to develop software to aid decision analysis for financial investment companies. Formed in 1969; discontinued in early 1970s.
OMAR Explorations, Ltd.	Joint venture between TRW, Barringer's Ltd., and two other parties to use TRW technology in airborne sensors for mineral exploration. Formed at Ramo's instigation—OMAR is Ramo spelled backward—in 1971; TRW sold its interest in 1975.

Other Space Park units joined in the quest for commercial applications of aerospace technology. The first formed in January 1970, when Mettler and Dick DeLauer established the Systems Application Center under Art Sommer. The center's initial mandate was to develop the company's businesses in credit reporting and credit authorization, but it was also charged to explore ways to "make systems technology available to various commercial markets." The foundation of the unit consisted of two acquisitions, Credit Data Corporation (renamed TRW Information Services), a consumer credit reporting operation, and the much smaller Credifier Corporation (renamed TRW Data Systems, Inc.), a Santa Monica, California-based company that produced charge authorization hardware (for credit-card approvals) compatible with NCR cash registers. [41]

TRW's immediate task was to make sense of these operations, install new management systems and cost controls, and develop formal plans for long-term growth. At TRW Information Systems, general manager Bud Jordan pruned unprofitable activities and sought to increase national coverage by all available methods, including direct investment, acquisition of existing credit bureaus, and cooperative arrangements. With the help of TRW software specialists and engineers, he instituted programs to improve the credit information itself, including tighter controls on data entry, standardization of formats, and new techniques for data compression, storage, transmission, and access. He also tapped TRW's financial resources to build a new national computer center in Anaheim, California. TRW's strategy involved considerable technological and financial risk. Although the unit increased sales rapidly, it lost about $30 million until the mid-1970s, when it turned the corner under the new leadership of Ed Brennan, a former bank executive. Throughout the dark days, Mettler remained steadfast in his conviction that credit reporting would evolve into a major business for TRW.[42]

TABLE 11 - 2
TRW VENTURES IN TRANSPORTATION AND ENVIRONMENTAL OPERATIONS, 1972–1977

NAME	DESCRIPTION
Civiltech Corporation	Joint venture (50/50) in 1972 with Mitsubishi to market TRW pollution control technology and research capabilities in Japan. Transferred to Energy Systems Group in 1976. Sold in 1985.
DeLeuw, Cather	Acquisition in 1972 of multinational architectural and engineering firm. Sold in 1977.
National Distribution Systems	Joint venture formed in 1971 between TRW, Eastern Airlines (majority stake), and Ralph M. Parsons Co. to establish a nationwide network of warehouses for use by a wide variety of customers. Dissolved soon after startup because of disagreements among the partners.
Traffic Control	Start-up at Space Park to apply systems engineering to problems of urban traffic control. Built traffic control systems south of Los Angeles, in Baltimore, Denver, and other communities. Discontinued in mid-1970s.
Transit Systems	Start-up at Space Park to apply systems engineering techniques to rail networks and public transit systems. Established the computer control systems for the Washington, D.C. METRO and other customers. Discontinued in mid-1970s.

At TRW Data Systems, TRW moved swiftly to upgrade Credifier's original product line, which used a primitive tape storage system that was slow in use and had to be replicated at each location. In November 1970, TRW aerospace engineer Donald Kovar led a crash program to develop a new programmable charge authorization system. Two months later, the company announced its System 4000, which included digital display terminals connected over telephone lines to a central minicomputer. The product proved an instant technical and marketing success, although problems in pricing and service and maintenance postponed crossover in profitability for several years. Nonetheless, System 4000 spawned several other similar—and marginal—businesses, including Validata, a charge authorization service sold to the airlines, and a security access control system for governmental agencies and defense contractors.[43]

In addition to credit reporting and authorization, the Systems Application Center engaged in many other commercial projects, most of which led brief, troubled lives. The fate of Community Technology Corporation, which TRW formed in June 1971 to develop manufactured housing and pursue land development, was typical. This entity spawned several subsidiaries, including Colorado Land Development, which partnered with Mitsubishi Corporation to acquire real estate for development in Littleton, Colorado, and Community Shelter Corporation (CSC), which planned to produce modular housing. In the summer of 1972, CSC obtained a contract from the U.S. Department of Housing and Urban Development to develop modular housing under a program called Operation Breakthrough. The contract called for CSC to build twenty prototype single-family houses near Sacramento. CSC licensed technology that Aerojet General had developed to wrap rocket motor cases from composite materials, announced a new product called Fiber-Shell, and poured about $5 million in equity and loans to build a small factory in Sacramento. The initial plan was to use the wrapping technology to fabricate cubical shapes that would serve as frames for entire rooms and that could be bolted together into housing units. CSC failed to get the process to work efficiently, however, and faced huge cost penalties. The government had set a target cost for manufactured housing at $9 per square foot; CSC's cubes exceeded the target by a factor of more than ten. Eventually CSC engineers abandoned the approach and got the costs down—but still far above the government target—by making prefabricated wall panels that could be stapled together.

Once the prototype houses were finished, CSC scrambled for orders and built a handful of houses in California and in New Mexico. The venture never came close to paying a return, however, and it was finally sold at a loss in the mid-1970s, when TRW also exited the community development business.[44]

TRW also pursued civil systems work through another Space Park organization, the Civil Systems Center. This organization took over some ATD projects and supervised projects in such areas as mass transportation systems, environmental systems, and general engineering services. One project, for example, involved an automated, computerized system for controlling the flow of automobile traffic in urban areas. The initial installation was in the South Bay area (including Redondo Beach, home of Space Park) near Los Angeles, where TRW obtained a $645,000 contract to develop a system called SAFER (Systematic Aid to Flow on Existing Roadways). The system employed a central computer system to monitor sensors placed at key intersections, but unfortunately, according to one of the project engineers, it had a lot of bugs in it. SAFER "actually screwed up traffic" for a while, he recalls, and it sparked "a lot of complaints from our own employees." Eventually, TRW ironed out the problems, and the system remained in service for many years. The company also bid successfully for installations on the East Coast between Washington, D.C., and Philadelphia.[45]

TRW knew that entry into this area would be expensive and was prepared to absorb losses to gain experience. The losses totaled more than expected, however, because of fierce price competition from low-cost rivals. In addition, unhappy memories of clashes with a multitude of local governments—hearings, delays, community protests, grandstanding, and contract discussions played out on the evening news and in local newspapers—lingered with Mettler. "Whatever our difficulties in dealing with the Defense Department or the Air Force," he recalls, "they were nothing compared to dealings with municipalities and local governments."[46]

The Civil Systems Center enjoyed better luck in related work. Early in 1972, the Washington Metropolitan Transit Authority awarded a $4.9 million contract to TRW to develop the Automatic Train Supervision System for the city's new subway system, the METRO. The METRO operated a 98-mile transit network, and the Transit Authority engaged TRW to design and build a dual computer complex, a display subsystem, and a manual control subsystem to be housed in a central control facility. The system included not only computerized control, but also a digital communications system. TRW not only made money on the deal but also acquired a partner on the project: The DeLeuw, Cather Company, an architectural and engineering consulting firm with headquarters in Chicago and about fourteen hundred employees in offices around the world.[47]

During the early 1970s, TRW's ventures in civil systems made slow headway as aerospace engineers scurried to transfer advanced technology and management practices into markets cool to such innovation. A few of these ventures paid modest returns but most lost money—a typical fate of start-ups—although none lost a lot. By the mid-1970s, most of them faced the same questions: Could they compete on cost? Could TRW develop the requisite marketing skills and understanding of customers? How long would it take before they made significant contributions to TRW's business? Would TRW have staying power, or would senior management pull the plug? As time wore on, the last of these questions loomed increasingly large.

Energy: A Growing Involvement

TRW Industrial Operations—the acquisitive group started by Fred Hesse—also attempted to apply Space Park-based expertise in new areas. Although Hesse had assembled a diverse portfolio of businesses, the strongest contributors were Reda Pump and Mission Manufacturing. As a result, he narrowed the group's focus to two areas, energy products and industrial controls, divesting Hazleton Laboratories, Inc., the biomedical testing business, and TRW Instruments, a small offshoot of Ramo-Wooldridge that had simply failed to grow.[48]

With these marginal units pruned, Hesse sought in various ways to strengthen the remaining product lines. The electronic remote control capabilities of a former subsidiary of Mission Manufacturing especially intrigued him, and he gathered a handful of key employees into a new unit called TRW Controls. The unit pursued two different lines of business. First, building on a relationship with Standard Oil of New Jersey (Exxon), it designed and developed an electrohydraulic remote control system to monitor and control deep-sea drilling operations—an alternative to the traditional platform-based control system. In 1974, this work seemed promising enough to become the basis of another independent unit, TRW Subsea Petroleum, Inc. The second thrust involved control systems for electric utilities to monitor and regulate distribution and transmission of electricity. In 1971, for example, TRW Controls provided "an advanced energy distribution and transmission management system" to Arkansas Power & Light Company, and later sold similar systems to many other electric utilities across the United States.[49]

Hesse also encouraged the expansion of the big units in Industrial Operations. Reda Pump drew on Space Park technology to develop polymer coatings for oilfield cable that could withstand the high temperatures and caustic environments of deep oil wells. TRW also strengthened Reda's service organization and built maintenance and support facilities in major oil-producing regions. Finally, Reda traded on the historical roots of its Russian founder, Armais Arutunoff. Early in 1973 the unit worked out a $20 million deal to supply pumps and associated equipment to the Soviet Union, one of the largest Soviet purchases of U.S. industrial goods in nearly a quarter century and a short but significant step on the road to détente.[50]

To increase business for the group as a whole, Hesse continued to prospect for acquisitions. In 1972, he negotiated three small deals, acquiring a minority stake in a French manufacturer of butterfly valves, an Australian manufacturer of valves and other equipment for the energy industry, and a West German builder of huge submersible pumps for high-volume water systems and maneuvering and thruster equipment for ships and offshore drilling rigs. The addition of the new pump lines complemented some of Reda's business and inspired Hesse to consider adding a new segment to Industrial Operations based on the concept of technology to transfer fluids—pumps, valves, controls, and even pipelines. This goal may have been in his mind in June 1974, when he agreed in principle to acquire three divisions of IU International Corporation that made valves and flow control systems, a combination that would have added $50 million in revenues to the Industrial Operations Group.[51]

The success of the Industrial Operations group contributed to a growing sense at Space Park that energy products and technology offered significant growth opportunities. To many observers, especially those who looked at trends in U.S. production and consumption of oil, the need to find alternative sources to petroleum seemed obvious. In 1972, DeLauer commissioned a study of the national energy situation in the United States. The study confirmed concerns about unsettled markets, as well as a sense that the U.S. government would mount a major institutional response and perhaps even form a new cabinet-level department.[52]

In September 1973, Mettler and DeLauer scored a coup by recruiting Dr. John S. Foster, a senior scientist and officer in the U.S. Department of Defense, to oversee a new thrust in energy-related research and development. Foster brought an impressive résumé along with a relaxed manner manifested in his usual nickname, "Johnny." A University of California, Berkeley, Ph.D. in physics, he spent more than a decade working on problems of nuclear energy and nuclear weapons at the Lawrence Radiation Laboratory, where he worked closely with Dr. Edward Teller on the development of the hydrogen bomb. In 1965, he moved to Washington as Director of Defense Research and Engineering. He was familiar with and well known to TRW, having worked on aspects of the ICBM while still at Lawrence-Livermore, and while at DOD, many projects that engaged TRW. In 1973, Foster let it be known that he was interested in moving to the private sector, and he was besieged with offers. Mettler and DeLauer wooed and won him with the opportunity to attack a number of energy problems, including new approaches to developing synthetic fuels.[53]

Foster's hiring proved extraordinarily prescient. A month after he joined TRW, war broke out between Israel and its Arab neighbors. The fighting ended in an inconclusive stalemate after a few weeks, but in the aftermath, the Arab members of the Organization of Petroleum Exporting Countries galvanized an ineffective multinational trade association into a militant cartel. During the next year and a half, OPEC initiated a series of price increases that tripled the price of crude oil, triggering a worldwide energy crisis and a deep recession in most of the developed world.

TRW could hardly afford to invest hundreds of millions of dollars in a major energy development initiative—the strategy that several big oil companies pursued. But the company could follow the tried and true path of performing customer-funded R&D work on specific energy-related problems, with reasonable expectation that commercial opportunities would eventually develop. Given Foster's connections with the Atomic Energy Commission and Ramo's prominent role in national science and technology affairs (early in 1974 he was named to the White House Advisory Council on Energy Research and Development, and he later worked closely with Vice President Nelson Rockefeller on the Ford administration's science and technology policies), such a course seemed natural. To highlight this new direction, in October 1973 the Systems sector acquired a new name: TRW Systems & Energy.[54]

The Big Contributors

TRW's steady corporate performance through the 1970–1971 recession plus its resumed growth reflected contributions from a variety of businesses, validating management's faith in the strategy of diversification. When aerospace went down, the company's other businesses picked up. Between 1970—a recession year in the United States—and 1974, TRW's automotive sales climbed by nearly $375 million, while pretax earnings almost doubled to more than $50 million. At the same time, the industrial and replacement businesses fared well. The segment identified in the company's annual reports as Fasteners, Tools, and Bearings, which included most of United-Carr and all of United-Greenfield and Marlin-Rockwell, grew 53 percent to reach annual sales of $357 million. Better still, margins were attractive: the segment contributed about 15 percent of the corporation's sales but more than 20 percent of its pretax margins. The automotive replacement business also enjoyed healthy and profitable growth, in 1974 reporting record earnings of $26.5 million on sales of $215 million.[55]

The strong results in TRW Automotive Worldwide reflected the success of its international strategy and organization, as well as popular new product lines. With Mettler's support, Stan Pace grouped TRW's major automotive businesses by product line on an international basis. Chuck Ohly, head of the Chassis Components Group, for example, assumed responsibility for all of the company's steering and suspension operations around the world, as did his counterpart in engine components. Mettler advocated such changes "because all the customers were organizing that way. It was also the only way we could coordinate our sales and marketing and transfer technology effectively."[56]

The transition to the new international structure unfolded over several years and varied by line of business and geographical market. The different requirements of American and foreign engine builders, for example, impeded close integration of R&D and product planning and allowed TRW's valve businesses to remain relatively decentralized. In contrast, the new structure facilitated international cooperation critical to the success of a new steering technology in the North American market. Different laws, regulations, and historical circumstances in some countries also presented barriers to cross-national integration. In Australia, for example, TRW manufactured engine components, as well as many other products for the local original equipment and replacement market through a national subsidiary.

Another factor that impeded the transition to a truly global organization by product line was the lingering presence of TRW Automotive International under Bob Burgin, who remained in the business of prospecting for acquisitions. In 1972, for example, Burgin bought two small West German companies: Werner Messmer KG and affiliates, a maker of electrical controls and switches for the German auto industry, and Repa Feinstanzwerk GmbH, a maker of seat belts for Volkswagen and other German automakers.[57]

The Repa deal, which involved an investment of about $8 million for a 70 percent interest and an option to acquire the rest, would eventually prove to be one of TRW's best. An entrepreneur named Erich Klink had founded Repa in 1961 in Lindach, West Germany, to make precision stampings of metal parts for the German automobile industry. In 1967, the company began assembling seat belts for Volkswagen and Porsche, acquiring a reputation for the quality and reliability of its products. Repa also featured an outstanding engineering staff and in 1971 pioneered the first "automatic" or "three-point" seat belts. The new design replaced separate lap and shoulder belts with a single seat belt connected to the automobile at three points: at the base of the seat, at the occupant's shoulder level, and, when closed, around the occupant. The system also included an automatic reel and locking device that made the seat belt easy and comfortable to use and kept it out of the way when people entered or exited a car. The Repa design, which was protected by several key patents, had other key advantages, including ease of manufacture and installation.[58]

Repa seat belts became standard equipment on virtually all German cars and the company quickly emerged as the market leader in all of Europe. In 1972, Repa made plans to build a second plant in Aldorf but was consuming capital so fast that to keep growing, the Klink family was willing to entertain offers to sell the company. TRW was interested because safety products would likely be a growth market as a result of regulation, few automakers were vertically integrated in this area, and the technology was bound to change—a situation ripe for independent suppliers. When Burgin learned through contacts at Ehrenreich that Repa might be available, he quickly struck a deal with the Klinks under terms that left Wolf-Dieter Klink, son of the founder, as general manager. Thus did TRW embark on a journey that two decades later would lead to a multibillion-dollar business in occupant restraints.[59]

The Messmer and Repa deals provided a grand finale for Automotive International, and in 1973 Pace dissolved the organization and assigned responsibility for overseas operations to the remaining group general managers. He also established a new General Components Group to oversee miscellaneous businesses such as Noblesville Casting in the United States, Repa and Bayerisches Leichtmetallwerk in West Germany, Clifford Components, a small British maker of steering wheels and other products that TRW had acquired during the 1960s, and TRW Australia.

Among its automotive product lines, TRW's steering systems for automobiles and commercial vehicles grew especially fast during the early 1970s. For automobiles, the company helped prompt the replacement of traditional steering systems that used worm gears or recirculating ball gears with rack-and-pinion systems. The advantages of rack-and-pinion systems—simplicity, light weight, small size, and precise feel— made them popular in small European automobiles and race cars, where TRW's subsidiary, Cam Gears, Ltd., held a leadership position. During the late 1960s and early 1970s, Cam Gears transferred its technology throughout TRW's worldwide organization, as TRW Italia and Gemmer do Brasil added capacity to serve Volkswagen. TRW also attempted to penetrate the Japanese automakers, and in 1969 formed a joint venture with Koyo Seiko, Ltd., a major supplier to Toyota, to produce rack-and-pinion systems in Japan. That relationship dissolved after several years, however, and TRW shifted its steering operations to another, smaller Japanese partner, Tokai-TRW, which had formed in 1970 to manufacture ball joints, tie rod ends, and steering linkages. (In 1988, TRW formed another and longer-lived joint venture with Koyo Seiko, as we will see in Chapter 14.)[60]

In the United States, rack-and-pinion steering was slower to catch on because U.S.-made cars were bigger and heavier than their European counterparts and roads in the United States were generally superior. The growing popularity of power (hydraulically assisted) steering during the 1950s and 1960s also tended to prolong conventional steering systems. This situation began to change during the early 1970s when small foreign cars started to capture an increasing share of the U.S. market. In response, the U.S. automakers sought to introduce their own small cars, a circumstance that reawakened interest in rack-and-pinion steering. In 1973, for example, the Ford Pinto subcompact became the first American model to feature rack-and-pinion steering as standard equipment. TRW initially supplied the Pinto's steering systems from Cam Gears. Soon thereafter, an engineering team at TRW's Michigan Division led by Rupert Atkin and supported by colleagues from Cam Gears and Ehrenreich made a bold advance by developing a power rack-and-pinion steering system for the Ford Mustang II. Ford subsequently adopted power rack-and-pinion for virtually all of its cars except big luxury models, as well as light trucks, and GM and Chrysler quickly followed suit. In anticipation of this surge in demand, TRW acquired a big manufacturing plant in Rogersville, Tennessee in 1973.[61]

Steering systems for commercial and off-highway vehicles also contributed strong growth and above-average returns. According to Ohly, this performance reflected the structure of the market, which was "not dominated by the Big Three." Rather, the industry featured scores of competitors, most of which relied on suppliers for engineering support, especially in the critical product lines in which TRW competed. When Ross Gear and its affiliated units developed new and more efficient power steering systems and hydraulic pumps and controls, these products proved immediate hits. Between 1971 and 1976, the percentage of medium- and heavy-duty trucks with power steering systems nearly doubled, from 37 percent to about 65 percent, with Ross Gear accounting for a major fraction of the increase. In 1973, Ross Gear added a new facility in Greeneville, Tennessee to manufacture heavy-duty power steering systems. At the same time, manufacturers of off-highway vehicles such as tractors and heavy-duty equipment such as farm implements, and marine and stationary equipment began replacing belt drives and mechanical linkages with complete hydraulic control systems. Sales of Ross Gear's hydraulic "Torquemotors" grew by 40 percent during the same five-year period.[62]

TRW Industrial & Replacement also made immediate and sizable contributions to corporate sales and earnings during the early 1970s. Although Bill Reynolds liked to joke that the sector "really ought to be called 'Everything Else'" because of its diverse and miscellaneous nature, Marlin-Rockwell, all of the United-Carr divisions, and most of the United-Greenfield divisions fared well. Under the leadership of George Poe, TRW's Aftermarket Operations staged its first strong surge in decades. These results partly reflected uncertain economic times in the United States, when car owners tended to maintain older cars rather than buy new ones. Poe also took several actions to improve profitability, successfully managing a price increase and also finding ways to increase volume. In 1971, the company spent $3.5 million to expand its main distribution center in Independence, Ohio. The following year, it introduced the TRW Service Line, a general line of car care and accessory products, and later added such items as hoists, wheel ramps, air tanks, and body repair supplies. By the middle of the decade, the company was distributing nearly two thousand catalog items under the TRW brand in the United States and making plans to develop a stronger replacement business in Europe.[63]

Problem Children

Although TRW's aerospace businesses rebounded swiftly from the recession and its automotive and industrial and energy businesses achieved strong growth, several other businesses, including TRW Electronics and TRW Equipment Group, struggled during the early 1970s. Shepard and Mettler nonetheless remained committed to these businesses, confident that TRW Electronics would later prove a growth engine for the company and that the Equipment Group would eventually return to health with the recovery of the aircraft and aircraft engine industries. The success of other businesses in TRW's diversified portfolio permitted such optimism.

At TRW Electronics, the first sign of trouble was inability to sustain momentum from the previous decade in part because of difficulty in consummating new acquisitions. During 1970 and 1971, two prospective deals that would have added significant new product lines and capabilities fell apart at the last minute. The first was Computer Terminal Corporation of San Antonio, better known subsequently (and referred to here) as Datapoint Corporation. A small publicly traded company, Datapoint had a hot product in the marketplace, another in the pipeline, and no money in the bank. The company pioneered cathode ray tube computer terminals and was working on an "intelligent" terminal (containing a microprocessor) that would make computer systems more efficient by decentralizing many functions previously carried out by big mainframe computers.

In the summer and fall of 1970, Datapoint was desperate for capital and eager to make a deal with TRW, whose technical capabilities it greatly admired. Webb negotiated an agreement in principle to acquire the company, but TRW's board of directors rejected the deal as too risky. Because talks had proceeded so far, however, TRW agreed to invest about $500,000 in stock and a note in return for international distribution rights to Datapoint's products for a period eventually settled as ten years. TRW's investments helped Datapoint remain independent while adding a profitable distribution business, called Datacom International, to TRW Electronics. Datapoint's new product line of intelligent terminals proved extraordinarily successful, and the company became one of the high flyers of the 1970s—unfortunately not under TRW's rubric.[64]

Another big disappointment to Webb was a near-miss merger with Collins Radio. Based in Cedar Rapids, Iowa, Collins was a leading supplier of airborne navigational and communications gear—what today is known as avionics equipment—with annual sales of about $150 million. The company's founder, Arthur Collins, was so committed to a big, cash-draining program to link up computers in networks—an idea at least a decade ahead of its time—that he was forced to seek outside capital. The prospect of acquiring Collins Radio appealed strongly to Webb, who especially wanted the company's core operations. The size of the transaction and the troubles of Collins Radio's computer business gave other TRW executives and directors pause, however. Finally, TRW's reluctance to guarantee a continuing executive role for Arthur Collins pushed him into a merger with North American Rockwell. This outcome frustrated Webb, who was unable subsequently to find a components business of comparable size or value to augment TRW's portfolio.[65]

The failure to find new partners proved the first of a series of challenges to TRW Electronics during the 1970s. The company's strategy to produce components, for example, had depended on the slow ramp-up of integrated circuits. During the early 1970s, however, these products caught on fast. Although TRW offered them, many customers fabricated their own or sourced them from low-cost producers overseas. TRW's cost structure represented another serious problem. Although the sector included assembly operations in Taiwan and Mexico (a joint venture), the vast majority of its output originated in the United States, where labor rates—a major driver of cost in electronic components—were relatively high. The situation was also troubling in Europe, where TRW's operations also struggled.[66]

A third serious problem was the declining fortunes of the U.S. consumer electronics industry—a major segment of TRW's customers. In the 1960s, for example, the company had built a profitable business in color convergence yokes for television sets. During the following decade, however, all but one U.S.-based TV manufacturer (Zenith) abandoned development of new models and either left the industry or sourced whole units abroad. The decline of U.S. production of radio and audio equipment was even more precipitous.[67]

These adverse trends were readily apparent during the early 1970s, leaving TRW Electronics to prospect for new market segments where it offered or could plausibly build expertise. With strong encouragement from Ramo and Mettler, Webb and his staff identified the intersection of the telephone and computer industries—what the company variously called "information handling" or "data communications"—as an area with enormous growth potential. Limited investment capital and the lessons of bitter experience in the computer business left TRW looking for the right niche. As Mettler later put it, "We decided we would *use* computers but would avoid any product remotely vulnerable to being integrated into the mainframe. We wanted something far enough away from the mainframe so that by no stretch of the imagination would IBM or anybody else say, 'I will make this now.' What we were interested in were end-user services." [68]

An apparent turnaround in the fortunes of the TRW's System 4000, its credit authorization system, partly influenced the company's thinking. When Dick Campbell took over the business in 1972, he initiated several measures that yielded immediate improvements. To save manufacturing costs, he had the system redesigned to accommodate large-scale integrated circuits and purchased key subsystems from outside contractors. Second, he changed contracting procedures to ensure a disciplined approach to pricing. Third, he recruited an experienced marketing executive from NCR. Almost immediately, J. C. Penney bought 13,000 terminals and 11 central processing systems to link up all of its retail outlets in the United States. The May Company made another large purchase, and by 1976, TRW had installed more than 70,000 systems. By then, sales had built up to about $30 million and the company was beginning to earn attractive returns. It was also thinking hard about new technology, such as point-of-sale terminals, that seemed likely to replace the System 4000 later in the decade.[69]

Signs of hope amid continuing struggles also characterized TRW Equipment Group during the early 1970s. As the only major business reporting to the chief executive office with a general manager ranked below executive vice president, the group occupied an anomalous position in the company. But Shepard, who had run the business during the 1950s, and Mettler were familiar with the group's operations, which were co-located with TRW's corporate headquarters. At the same time, the top officers had confidence in the leadership that veteran manager Art Schweitzer provided. During the aerospace recession of the early 1970s, that confidence was sorely tested as the group caught the down phase of a cyclical business.

Although the group manufactured power accessories such as aircraft fuel system pumps and propulsion systems for torpedoes and maintained a small but steady business in nuclear control rods for the U.S. Navy, more than four-fifths of its sales depended on the market for aircraft engines and parts. As aircraft production dropped off after peak funding during the Vietnam War, the group's sales plummeted from about $228 million in 1970 to $132 million in 1973, when it began a two-year string of losses. The group transferred its plant in Danville, Pennsylvania to the Automotive Sector, which converted it to produce automotive engine valves. Yet TRW also displayed willingness to invest in the business as it awaited the next uptick and orders for new commercial aircraft. In 1972, the Tapco plant acquired a twelve-hundred-ton forging press, the largest of its kind in the world. The group also completed an acquisition, purchasing a small company that manufactured ceramic cores for casting airfoils. Finally, TRW sought to offset the decline of the U.S. market by forming joint ventures with partners in Japan and Israel. At mid-decade, TRW Equipment Group seemed well positioned for renewed growth—when and if its principal market recovered.[70]

Warning Ahead

Horace Shepard began his letter to shareholders in TRW's annual report for 1974 by noting that it had been "the most successful year in TRW's history. Sales, net earnings and earnings per share all set records." He also noted that TRW's performance persisted through "a most difficult business environment" characterized by energy shortages, worrisome inflation, and generally deteriorating economic conditions. In short, the strategy of diversification appeared to be working exactly as its advocates had predicted.

What Shepard did not mention in his letter, although it was an enormous concern to him and other leaders of the company, was TRW's sagging stock price. After hitting a high of $43.25 during the first quarter of 1971, the company's shares tumbled to just over $10 during the latter half of 1974. Its price/earnings ratio fell to within a very low range of 3.6 to 5.3. At the same time, Standard & Poor's and Moody's threatened to downgrade TRW's historical "A" rating, a measure that would have significantly increased the company's cost of financing during an already difficult period.[71]

In these circumstances, TRW's leaders had little choice but to reassess the company's strategic direction and ways of doing business. The question at the beginning of 1975 was whether TRW needed to adjust to a curve in its path, or whether it had arrived at a crossroads.

Chapter 12

New Directions

▶   ▶   ▶

1975–1979

FROM THE EARLY 1960s FORWARD, TRW PURSUED GROWTH ENERGETICALLY, CHASING AFTER aggressive goals by every available means. Some of this growth was natural, resulting from enlarging markets or extending geographical reach. Some of it was organic, as existing technologies and capabilities begat new businesses. And some of TRW's growth was discontinuous, the product of acquisitions into unrelated or distantly related areas and ranging far afield from a well-understood technological base.

The recessions of the early and mid-1970s called all this expansion into question. With the company's stock price in the doldrums, TRW's leaders took strong measures to help restore investor confidence. Some actions were immediate. Early in 1975, TRW took steps to trim its proposed capital spending budget by $250 million over the next three years and implemented cost control measures across every business. It also called off Fred Hesse's impending deal to acquire a sizable valves and flow control systems business. It became clear, recalls Mettler, that "one of the things we had to do was make some choices. We could do a few things such as data communications, rack-and-pinion steering and international automotive, and we could support the growth in space and defense. But not all the children could go to college."[1]

Accordingly, TRW reassessed its priorities and took a hard look at unsuccessful or marginal operations. In January 1975, Dick DeLauer began to shut down many of TRW's ventures in civil systems, transportation systems, and engineering management. At TRW Electronics and TRW Industrial Operations, executives shed losing product lines, initiated management changes, and bore down on costs.[2]

The financial crisis of the mid-1970s also provoked new thinking about growth, diversification, and other elements of corporate strategy and policy. Horace Shepard,

Rube Mettler, and Si Ramo, chief financial officer Chuck Allen, and other top officers of the company hit the road to meet with institutional investors and financial analysts. These contacts fed into continuing internal discussions and analysis.

A companywide planning conference in June 1975 focused on new five-year goals for the corporation that would rebuild and sustain the value of its stock. Addressing the conference, Shepard outlined four new objectives. The first was a 30/70 debt-to-equity ratio, as opposed to TRW's recent 40/60 ratio, to upgrade the company's rating on debt securities from "A" to "AA." The second new objective was heightened emphasis on return on assets employed (ROAE), which TRW would strive to raise from historical levels of about 10 percent to a new target of 15 percent. This goal was "challenging," but also "realistic," because about three-fourths of the company's assets already passed the test. The implication, however, was not lost on managers throughout the company: in the future, Shepard stated, TRW would be "more choosy" about which businesses to expand, hold, or discontinue. The third objective was to maintain the company's historical dividend payout ratio of about 35 percent. Finally, Shepard announced a goal of $50 million of free cash flow by 1978 "to permit TRW to take advantage of unexpected opportunities, or provide for unexpected problems, without the *necessity* [emphasis in original] of raising new money in the capital markets."

TRW backed up the new objectives with several important changes in policy and organization. As Mettler put it at the conference, "Continuing emphasis on ROAE and cash flow as basic determinants of the desirability of TRW's businesses must become our way of life." That meant employing new management tools such as PIMS (Profit Impact of Market Strategy) to evaluate plans and performance market by market. It also meant "limiting further diversification to exceptional circumstances; evaluating acquisition proposals and new product development in the context of the new, higher ROAE goal; [and] developing a higher competence in divestment and in product line selection." Corporate management also imposed tighter controls on and allocations of working capital and increased the internal rate of return for new investments from 15 to 20 percent. Finally, it revised management compensation packages to reflect the new goals and mounted a major communications effort inside and outside the company to address the changes and the reasons for them.[3]

In December 1975, Mettler went public with the new objectives in a speech to institutional investors entitled "New Directions for TRW." He focused on the company's commitment to improve the "quality of earnings and quality and strength of [the] balance sheet" during the next "four, five, or six years." Pursuing the new objectives, Mettler argued, would produce "strong growth in earnings, earnings per share, and in sales—although sales growth, as such, is not a specific target." Rather, he noted, division general managers were told that "we are willing to exchange sales growth for higher profitability, as measured by return on investment.[4]

During the next several years, TRW reported each year in its annual report its progress against the new objectives. Within a year, the company had lowered its long-term debt and achieved the targeted 30/70 debt-to-equity ratio. Its performance against the ROAE target inched up past 12 percent as well, with return on equity over 16 percent. The stock price also manifested a healthy gain, returning to the mid-$30 range during the first quarter of 1976.

UP AND DOWN, DOWN AND UP

The energy crisis and the ensuing unsettled economic times affected TRW in mixed ways—yet more proof of the benefits of diversification. The most obvious beneficiaries were the energy-related units in Hesse's Industrial Operations Group and the energy R&D initiatives that Johnny Foster supervised. TRW's aerospace and defense operations focused on core capabilities and established momentum that offset the momentary declines of the automotive and industrial businesses and continued through the end of the decade. Even TRW Equipment Group mounted a comeback, while TRW Electronics produced impressive growth, but also manifested disturbing indications of declining profitability. The composite result was a quick recovery from the recession and strong performance during the late 1970s.

Between 1972 and 1976, TRW's sales of energy-related products and services more than doubled, soaring from $130 million to $286 million. Reda Pump's sales rose 21 percent in 1974 and 28 percent the next year. Mission Manufacturing did even better, recording increases of 46 percent and 38 percent, respectively. Unfortunately, Hesse could not fully enjoy this success: during 1973, he was diagnosed with pancreatic cancer, and after a prolonged battle he succumbed on Christmas Day 1975. He was 49 years old.[5]

Not long after Hesse's death, DeLauer renamed TRW Industrial Operations as TRW Energy Products Group and appointed Samuel Phillips, a retired Air Force general who had recently joined TRW, as vice president and general manager. A towering figure in the history of program management, Phillips bore a service record that included directing the Minuteman ICBM as it became operational, as well as directing NASA's Apollo program.[6]

During the second half of the decade, as energy markets settled down for a brief period, the growth rate of the Energy Products Group predictably slowed, although the biggest units, Reda Pump and Mission Manufacturing, remained profitable. Reda Pump's affiliated unit, Crescent Cable & Wire, however, struggled under the fluctuating costs of copper and intense competitive pressure. In 1978, TRW absorbed a $5 million after-tax loss in closing Crescent's plant in Trenton, New Jersey, while moving part of the business to another plant in Lawrence, Kansas. At the same time, management responsibility for the Energy Products Group shifted into the Industrial & Replacement sector in recognition of the commercial nature of its markets.[7]

TRW continued energy-related research and development work at Space Park through another new unit, Energy Systems Group, which formed early in 1976. Led by Foster, the group included three principal operations: the first focused on government-funded planning and analysis activities; the second performed similar work for the U.S. Environmental Protection Agency; and the third sought to commercialize technology developed in the other units. Space Park veterans directed most of the group's activities, although in 1976 Foster hired an executive from Shell Oil to assist with commercial development. Energy Systems Group devoted most of its attention to R&D projects, and it carried out many small studies and mounted several major projects, including several that had originated under the Applied Technology Division (see Table 12-1).[8]

The group's most successful effort involved isotope separation—an alternative way to enrich uranium for use in nuclear reactors. In the mid-1970s, Americans still held high hopes for nuclear power, although the industry continued to rely on the original process for enriching fuel developed in the Manhattan Project during World War II. This process involved separating the fissible isotope of uranium, U^{235}, from its far more common form as U^{238}. The traditional approach to separation consumed dollars and electricity extravagantly, however, accounting for a significant fraction of the total power output of the Tennessee Valley Authority. To explore alternatives, the U.S. Energy Research and Development Agency and its successor, the U.S. Department of Energy, started funding R&D studies of isotope separation.

TRW's interest in the field began in 1974, and it originated in work by Dr. John Dawson, a professor of physics at UCLA and a consultant to the company. Dawson proposed a plasma separation process that (crudely summarized) involved vaporizing uranium metal to form a plasma. Next, this plasma was subjected to a powerful electromagnetic field to control the flow of ions and an electric field to separate the U^{235} ions from U^{238} ions. Finally, "collectors" were spaced in such a way as to capture the U^{235} ions. TRW funded feasibility studies of the TRW/Dawson Process for several

TABLE 12 - 1
TRW VENTURES IN ENERGY SYSTEMS, 1973–1979

NAME	DESCRIPTION
Coal Combustion Systems	High-pressure coal combustion process using technology derived from Lunar Excursion Module Descent Engine. Product was a retrofit device to utility or industrial boilers that burn oil or gas.
Low NOx Burner	Clean-burning combustors for utilities and industry also using technology derived from Lunar Excursion Module Descent Engine. Combined with Civiltech Corporation (see Table 11-2).
Energy Engineering Services	Studies, planning, and analysis for the U.S. Department of Energy.
Environmental Services	Miscellaneous research and testing services for U.S. Environmental Protection Agency.
BEACON Process	New process for gasification of coal after mining. Marketed in partnership with Sohio.
TRW Carbon	Offshoot of the BEACON process resulting in a unique carbonaceous material for use as an additive in various industrial products.
Coalbed Methane Extraction	Proprietary process for gasifying coal *in situ*.
Gravimelt	Proprietary process for reducing the sulfur content of coal.
Hot Spot	Process for extraction of oil from tar sands.
Isotope Separation	New process for enriching uranium for nuclear power generation.
Ocean Thermal Energy Conversion	Tapping ocean thermal energy to generate electricity.

years until June 1976, when the Energy Research and Development Agency began supporting the work. Later in the decade, federal funding ranged between $20 million and $30 million per year.[9]

By the end of the decade, Energy Systems Group was reporting annual sales of about $50 million derived from a variety of projects. Most of these started with small steps, proceeded slowly and fitfully, and ended in frustration amid falling oil prices during the early 1980s. One of the first to fail under new market conditions was the Meyers process for coal desulfurization. In October 1975, the EPA awarded TRW a $2.4 million contract to test the Meyers process for removing pyritic sulfur in an eight-ton-per-day pilot plant at the company's Capistrano test site. The plant came onstream in April 1977, and after a brief shakedown, ran continuously for three months. The demonstration validated the technical feasibility of the process, but meanwhile, new and more stringent federal standards rendered it no longer suitable. As a result, TRW shelved the Meyers process, although it continued to investigate alternative approaches to desulfurization for much of the next decade.[10]

At Automotive Worldwide, the energy shock and ensuing recession produced mixed effects. The Engine Components Group, for example, now stared at a gloomy future, as U.S. automakers downsized engines from 8 to 6 or 4 cylinders. Bad news for one group, however, represented good news for another. The advent of smaller cars and front wheel drive vehicles offered bright prospects for rack-and-pinion steering in both manual and power versions. Indeed, recalled Chuck Ohly, who directed TRW's worldwide steering operations during the early and mid-1970s, "the business just kept growing and growing." TRW outgrew its plants in Michigan and Tennessee, and in 1979 acquired another facility in Greenville, North Carolina. The company also increased capacity to manufacture rack-and-pinion systems in Canada and throughout its European operations. Demand for TRW steering systems and torque motors also recovered quickly from the recession and remained strong during the late 1970s.[11]

The geographical diversity of TRW's automotive business helped ease the downturn in the United States. Although the energy crisis triggered recessions around the globe, they differed in timing, extent, and duration in various regions. Europe, for example, had a long history of high fuel prices, and the recession proved less damaging than in the United States. TRW's aggressive moves in the 1960s to open new markets and supply new customers thus served the company well, especially in steering systems and safety products. Repa's seat belt operation added a new product line in passive restraint seat belt systems and maintained rapid growth, quadrupling in size between the acquisition and the end of the decade. In 1979, the unit opened a new plant in Austria, its third manufacturing facility, and yet another indication of a bright future.[12]

During the 1970s, the automotive groups continued to invest overseas to support local investments by U.S. and European automakers, build relationships with new customers, and, in some cases, respond to local content rules. TRW added capacity in Brazil, Argentina, Germany, Spain, Australia, and other countries. It also responded to the growing power of Asian producers by forming a series of joint ventures with partners in Japan, Korea, and Taiwan (see Table 12-2).

During the late 1970s, the principal disappointment in TRW's automotive businesses was slow progress toward penetrating the fast developing market for automotive electronics. Although TRW Electronics had made electronic components for car radios for years, a newer and far bigger opportunity was taking shape, as electronic circuitry was applied to central automotive systems and functions, such as engine performance, fuel management, handling, and braking. During the 1970s, the electronics content of automobiles roughly tripled, reaching over $100 per vehicle. By 1980 it was expected that automotive electronics would constitute a $3.5 billion business worldwide.

Unfortunately, TRW encountered many obstacles in its path. The major automakers all regarded electronics as a strategic technology, and most of them possessed or quickly established strong internal capabilities. TRW's traditional automotive product line in engine and chassis components, moreover, did not immediately lend itself to electronic enhancements. Finally, interest in automotive electronics cut across organizational boundaries in the company and required a level of cooperation that proved difficult to achieve.[13]

TABLE 12 - 2
TRW'S FOREIGN AUTOMOTIVE VENTURES, 1969–1979

NAME	DESCRIPTION
TRW-Koyo Seiko	A 1969 joint venture with Koyo Seiko, Ltd., to produce rack-and-pinion steering gears in Japan. In 1973, TRW sold its stake to Koyo Seiko and transferred the steering business in Japan to TRW-Tokai.
TRW-Tokai	In 1970, formed a joint venture (49/51) with Tokai Seiatsu to manufacture ball joints and steering linkages in Japan. In 1977, Tokai Seiatsu was merged into TRW-Tokai and TRW gradually increased its stake.
Repa Feinstanzwerk GmbH	Acquisition in 1972 of German manufacturer of seat belts.
Werner Messmer KG	Acquisition in 1973 of German manufacturer of electrical switches and controls with an affiliate in Brazil. Organized as a subsidiary of Teves-Thompson. Later transferred to TRW Controls & Fasteners.
Motores y Refacciones, S.A. (MORESA)	In 1974, increased stake from 22.1 percent to 33 percent in Mexican operation to produce engine components.
Shin Han Valve, Ltd.	In 1972, acquired a stake in Korea-based producer of engine valves. TRW increased its stake in 1979.
Société Metallurgique G. Jeudy	In 1974, acquired 85 percent share of French maker of engine components.
Tornilleria Fina de Navarra, S.A. (TORFINASA)	In 1975, acquired a 50 percent stake in Spanish producer of steering and suspension components.
Wu Chou Valve Industrial Co.	In 1979 and 1980, acquired a minority position (8.3%) in Taiwan-based manufacturer of engine valves.

In 1973, the company created a new business unit, TRW Automotive Electronics, and placed it in the Electronic Components Group of TRW Electronics. This unit considered various points of entry, including "linking and diagnostic sensors, cruise and engine controls, transmission actuators, display and warning devices, safety systems and on-board data processing systems." The following year, the unit opened auto applications labs at its headquarters in Camden, New Jersey, and at another facility in Marshall, Illinois. By then the labs had narrowed their focus to "electronic ignition, low liquid-level warning systems for brake fluid and windshield washer fluid and other emission and safety related projects." That August, TRW Automotive Electronics announced its first major sale, when International Harvester (Navistar) placed an order "involving over $1 million per year" for an electronic speed switch "designed to provide effective emission control for gasoline-powered heavy trucks."

TRW Automotive Electronics made slow headway. In 1978, new Automotive Worldwide head Chuck Ohly recruited Trevor Jones from General Motors as vice president of engineering. Jones brought a background in aerospace and electronics at GM's Delco Division, and at TRW he gave special emphasis to automotive electronics. The following year, Ohly announced the establishment of "a multi-million dollar automotive systems laboratory" in Farmington Hills, Michigan, near Detroit as "the focal point for developing and evaluating electrical and electronic systems and components to serve the broad transportation electronics market."[14]

At TRW Industrial & Replacement, performance during the 1970s was generally encouraging, although troubling signs appeared in several businesses. The arrival of the Energy Products Group added about $250 million in sales and brought the sector's total to nearly $1 billion. Apart from the energy units, the fortunes of many divisions in the sector followed closely those of general industry in the United States—they dipped during the recession but recovered in the aftermath. The Fasteners, Tools, and Bearings segment, for example, reported sales of $364 million in 1975 and $558 million four years later. TRW continued to pour capital into these businesses, in mid-decade opening in Georgia new plants to make bearings and hand tools, and in Connecticut a new fasteners facility.[15]

Reynolds also focused on modernizing and streamlining operations in the United-Greenfield divisions, several of which began to struggle under increasing foreign competition and the declining fortunes of their customer base. In 1977, TRW sold off U.S. Diamond Wheel, one of the weakest of the United-Greenfield divisions. Two years later, Reynolds combined United-Greenfield with Marlin-Rockwell in a new Industrial Products Group. He then reorganized United-Greenfield, liquidating the headquarters organization in Northbrook, Illinois, trimming the staff, and reorganizing the divisions into four business areas: Carbide Tools, Drills & End Mills, Hand Tools, and Threading Tools.[16]

The automotive aftermarket business led by George Poe continued to thrive in the United States and showed encouraging signs of strength overseas. TRW's sales in this segment rose from $250 million in 1975 to $435 million at the end of the decade, with advances in Europe accounting for much of the gain. In 1975, Poe consolidated the aftermarket operations of the company's European subsidiaries into a single trans-national organization and invested in centralized warehouse facilities in Belgium and the United Kingdom. Although the company encountered significant national and cultural barriers, including a byzantine maze of distribution channels and strong resistance from automotive original equipment makers that sought to control the replacement market, TRW more than doubled its European revenues, reaching a total of about $130 million in 1979. In the U.S. market, Poe continued to refine the service line. In 1979, TRW added two new product lines by marketing hand tools from United-Greenfield's J. H. Williams Division and acquiring C. E. Niehoff & Co., a manufacturer and distributor of engine ignition and alternator parts.[17]

During the late 1970s, TRW Equipment Group staged an impressive comeback, resuming steady growth for the first time in nearly a decade. This progress came despite a difficult industry structure featuring a shrinking number of customers with a disturbing tendency to pull work in-house. TRW successfully retooled to make components for a new generation of giant turbojet engines designed to power wide-body aircraft such as the Boeing 747, the Lockheed Tristar, and the McDonnell-Douglas DC-10, as well as the newer Boeing 757 and 767. At the same time, TRW continued its work with advanced titanium alloys and experimented with powdered metals as materials for airfoils. By 1979, the group's sales had climbed back over $300 million, its highest level in more than a decade.[18]

NEW CAPABILITIES IN SPACE AND DEFENSE

During the second half of the decade, business boomed at TRW Defense & Space Systems Group (DSSG), the principal unit in TRW Systems and Energy. Between 1975 and 1979, DSSG's "delivered sales" rose from $443 million to $804 million, and employment at Space Park jumped from about 12,000 to about 15,500. This performance reflected significant progress in all of DSSG's major businesses, as well as careful diversification into related technologies and markets.[19]

Dick DeLauer, George Solomon, and the top officers in DSSG remained concerned by the group's dependence on big spacecraft programs, which had caused so much misery during the downturn at the start of the decade. The near cancellation of NASA's High Energy Astronomical Observatories (HEAO) and delays in FLTSATCOM underscored the inherent risks. At the same time, the government's plan to use the space shuttle as its principal launch vehicle in the 1980s meant that spacecraft programs would be bigger, fewer, and subject to more competition. In 1975, for example, TRW lost DSCS-III to General Electric and was also frustrated in a bid to reenter commercial communications satellites with the INTELSAT V program. Yet the ventures in civil systems had also taught lessons about the difficulties of transferring military technology to commercial markets. Accordingly, DSSG's leaders sought to apply the group's skills and capabilities in new or emerging government and defense markets for microelectronics, high energy lasers, large-scale software systems, and electronic warfare systems, including avionics.[20]

Meanwhile, ongoing work on programs such as the revived HEAO, DSCS-II, FLTSATCOM, the Defense Support Program, and classified work kept Space Park humming. In 1975, NASA chose TRW to design and build the primary communications system for the space shuttle. The initial contract for design, development, and testing of equipment and systems to handle voice, data, and television transmission was worth $10 million, but the involvement grew into steady business supporting the shuttle into the 1980s and beyond.[21]

TRW's work on the shuttle program prepared the way for much bigger and better opportunities in space communications. In January 1977, a partnership between Western Union Telegraph Company and TRW beat out RCA Global Communications for a huge contract to engineer NASA's Tracking and Data Relay Satellites (TDRS). TRW's share of the initial $800 million award was $309 million and called for the company to manufacture four satellites, components for additional satellites, and associated ground equipment. (TRW partnered with Harris Corporation to produce some antennas on the satellites, as well as some of the ground communication equipment.) The first satellite was projected to be ready for launch in 1980.[22]

NASA designed TDRS to solve one of the most frustrating problems in space communications: difficulty in maintaining space-to-ground contact with satellites, including the space shuttle, in low-earth orbit. The usual approach involved positioning ground stations at various locations around the earth that would track a satellite and communicate over ground networks to a command center. Ground stations typically could handle only one or two satellites at once, however, and they were in contact with these satellites only about 15 percent of the time. The spacing of ground stations also created significant communications gaps. During the Skylab missions of the 1970s, for instance, the satellite remained in contact with the earth less than twenty minutes during each ninety-minute orbit. The TDRS concept was to position above the equator at geosynchronous altitudes a series of satellites with the capability to switch transmission. In effect, said Ed Dunford, who managed the project during the late-1970s, each TDRS satellite is "like a telephone central office in space." Once all the satellites were deployed, three of them could track as many as twenty-six satellites at once and maintain contact at least 85 percent of the time with a single NASA ground station in White Sands, New Mexico. (The fourth satellite was kept in orbit as a spare and to handle peak demand loads.)

The TDRS satellites were the biggest and most complex telecommunications satellites ever launched. Designed to be carried aboard the space shuttle, each satellite weighed about two-and-a-half tons, with deployable solar panels with a total wingspan of nearly sixty feet. Described as "a veritable antenna farm," each satellite carried seven groups of antennas, one of which featured thirty elements in a phased array. A space first, the satellites could simultaneously offer service in the three frequency bands: S-band, C-band, and high-capacity Ku-band for rapid data transmission. (The Ku-band channel on *TDRS-1* could relay 300 million bits of digital information each second, about the same amount as crammed into ten, fourteen-volume sets of encyclopedias.) The TDRS satellites could thus handle voice, television, analog, and digital communications, and they were expected to have a service life of ten years.

The TDRS contract was a fixed-price arrangement that led TRW to modify its usual approach to program management. Solomon pointed out that the contract represented a trend and that "we need to demonstrate we can work under a fixed-price contract." To assist program manager Ed Noneman and top deputy Ed Dunford, Solomon appointed "a blue-ribbon" panel "to carefully assess the program from the beginning," "instead of waiting to assemble a review team downstream if problems develop." Chaired by Sam Phillips, the panel worked with program management to develop detailed technical specifications to reduce risks, as well as appropriate organizational arrangements to accomplish the work efficiently. The panel remained active for about six months through a development phase known as the preliminary design review that froze specifications for most aspects of the program. TRW also made a deliberate decision to contract out a relatively high proportion of the components to reduce its own exposure to a cancellation or significant program change.[23]

TRW's growing capabilities in electronic systems and microelectronics greatly enhanced its ability to manage programs such as TDRS. Led by general manager Charlie Stephens, the Electronic Systems Division capitalized on the trend of spacecraft payloads and ground support systems to become bigger and more sophisticated, while representing a bigger share of the total value of spacecraft programs. TRW produced the payloads and much of the ground equipment for TDRS and participated in many programs managed by other aerospace contractors. It also worked on many classified projects, especially in the areas of secure communications (COMSEC) and signal processing. The division's Communication and Antenna Laboratory carried out fundamental work on signal modulation and demodulation and signal processing, and developed extremely sensitive and accurate antennas and receivers. At the division's Microelectronics Center, TRW continued to build on the solid foundation that Jim Buie and others had provided. Key developments of the 1970s included very-large-scale integrated (VLSI) chips, which emerged from the requirements for high-speed logic in secure communications applications, and analog-to-digital converters, which had many uses in communications between space vehicles and the earth.[24]

VLSI chips represented the third generation of integrated circuits and could hold more than ten thousand components per chip. Led by Buie, TRW had fabricated the first VLSI chip in 1973 using a triple diffusion (3D) process also pioneered by the company. Continuing significant investments enabled TRW to put more than twenty thousand components on a chip by the end of the decade. The impressive capabilities, low cost, high reliability, and small size of these items had enormous appeal, and TRW earned a steady stream of awards for its work from the Department of Defense. The company's capability to design and fabricate these chips also proved crucial in certain key program wins, especially in the classified area. The business also showed commercial potential, and TRW was able to sell some items through mail order electronics catalogs. By 1978, sales were sufficiently large for a group of engineers to leave the Microelectronics Center at Space Park to form an independent business unit called TRW LSI Products. Headquartered near San Diego, the new unit achieved modest success marketing some versions of the company's multipliers, digital correlators, and analog-to-digital converters to makers of telecommunications and television equipment.[25]

Another intriguing growth area for DSSG was software, especially to manage large and complex tasks. To help realize this promise, Solomon split off general systems engineering development from ballistic missile support in the Systems Engineering and Integration Division. Solomon was also concerned by uncertainties about TRW's continuing role in the Air Force missile program. Although the company maintained a steady volume of business providing support for the Minuteman III program, during the mid-1970s there was considerable doubt about funding for the next-generation MX missile. TRW helped to develop the specifications for the new missile, eventually known as Peacekeeper, which was bigger, more powerful, and more accurate than its predecessors. It was also far more deadly, capable of carrying ten independently targeted reentry vehicles, compared with three on Minuteman III. The MX was also more controversial: a prolonged and spirited national debate on defense spending generally and on missile basing systems in particular delayed the program for several years. Finally, in September 1979, President Jimmy Carter approved engineering development of the MX and the Air Force ordered construction and flight tests of twenty missiles within five years.[26]

TRW's formidable capabilities in software systems also led to new business opportunities. The ground station software support for TDRS, for example, consisted of more than 750,000 lines of code on a system linking ten large computers. In 1978, TRW won two more sizable contracts in related areas. First, the company teamed with General Electric to win a significant part of NASA's Landsat D program, an earth observation satellite system. In awards totaling about $20 million over three years, Electronics Systems Division engineered X-band and Ku-band communications subsystems aboard the spacecraft, while Systems Engineering & Integration Division (SEID) provided the software for the real-time image processing system at NASA-Goddard in Maryland.[27]

The second big win of 1978 was a $33 million contract from the Air Force for SEID to engineer the Ground-based Electro-Optical Deep Space Surveillance System (GEODSS). One of the biggest competitive awards in the division's history, the program entailed building a global network of specialized ground stations to track satellites and other objects in space beyond reach of radar or conventional telescopes. The primary impetus for GEODSS was national security—the need to identify and track the growing population of satellites orbiting in so-called deep space—at an altitude of three thousand nautical miles and beyond. (By the early 1980s, estimates placed the number of such satellites at more than fifteen hundred.) The system worked by using sophisticated telescopes fitted with electro-optics and a very sensitive TV camera to capture the extremely faint reflected sunlight on objects in deep space. Computers and some 400,000 lines of code controlled the system, which eventually would include as many as five ground stations spaced around the globe. The software challenges were immense, ranging from mission planning to calibration of the equipment, to managing hundreds of interfaces between dissimilar subsystems and types of equipment.[28]

Avionics represented yet another promising area for TRW. Building on traditional capabilities in guidance, navigation, and control systems, in 1975 TRW won a small but significant contract to provide the Digital Avionics Information System for the U.S. Air Force. This software system supported and linked the Air Force's five logistics command centers in the United States and provided valuable experience and contacts for pursuing related business. The next step was to expand TRW's position in avionics hardware, which was closely related to its capabilities in electronic systems.[29]

TRW also pursued related opportunities in electronic warfare, including both tactical and strategic systems. In June 1978, DSSG made a significant move by merging with ESL Incorporated for considerations worth approximately $40 million. Based in Sunnyvale, California, ESL focused on defense electronics, producing both hardware and software for signal intelligence and tactical reconnaissance applications. Founded in 1964 by Dr. William J. Perry and other former employees of Sylvania's Electronic Defense Laboratories, ESL grew rapidly, especially in the mid-1970s. In 1977, the company reported net income of $3 million on sales of $68.4 million and employed about seventeen hundred people, nearly half of whom held advanced degrees. The company put itself up for sale when Perry moved to a high-level position in the U.S. Department of Defense. (Later he served as secretary of defense in the Clinton administration.) In explaining TRW's interest in the deal, DeLauer noted the financial attractions but stressed that "ESL is solidly established in rapidly growing markets which are complementary to those served by DSSG; and it services customer requirements which DSSG does not now address and which it could not otherwise effectively address in the foreseeable future." DeLauer particularly noted the deal "might create significant electronic warfare sales to expand our present EW penetration." [30]

The ESL merger paid quick returns. During its first full year (1979), sales increased 40 percent to surpass $100 million. Much of this performance reflected new business in electronic reconnaissance programs for the U.S. Army. The company also established a leading position in a new technology known as digital image enhancement—the use of computers to improve digital images and highlight specific features. The technology had obvious applications in reconnaissance and surveillance, as well as in commercial and scientific research. ESL also enabled TRW to expand its position in electronic warfare.

DSSG recorded another significant milestone in 1978 by winning the prime contract for a joint Army-Air Force program called Battlefield Exploitation and Target Acquisition. This was a three-year program "to integrate data from a wide array of battlefield sensors into a comprehensive picture of enemy activity," with TRW engaged to provide systems engineering and testing, software development, and field testing support. "This was the first time," recalled software engineer Jack Distaso, "that we moved from being a software subcontractor to being the prime. Rather than us working for hardware suppliers, they were working for us. It was also the first big command and control information processing contract that we had. It led to a lot of other business of a similar type and also enabled us to broaden our relationships in the U.S. military."[31]

EXPANDING TRW ELECTRONICS

Among TRW's main businesses, only TRW Electronics offered cause for serious concern during the late 1970s. The sector produced acceptable growth, but could not achieve attractive returns. As the decade wore on, the continuing struggle to establish secure and profitable niches became an increasing worry to TRW's senior management.

Part of the troubles at TRW Electronics stemmed from the ongoing investment needs of many of its newer businesses. At the same time, the older businesses in the Electronic Components Group contended with adverse market trends and proved unable to generate enough cash to assuage growing doubts about the fundamental health of TRW's commercial electronics ventures. The additions of LSI Products and a 1979 acquisition, Optron, Inc., a maker of electro-optical components, did little to allay these concerns.[32]

At TRW Credit Data, Ed Brennan persisted in the time-consuming strategy to increase geographical coverage and continually upgrade its consumer credit information database. TRW also set its sights on another extremely ambitious project: taking on Dun & Bradstreet in the big and profitable business credit reporting industry. With more than a century of experience—Abraham Lincoln was once an employee—Dun & Bradstreet all but monopolized the industry, accounting for more than 80 percent of the market. Nonetheless, in November 1974, Brennan found a point of entry: a relationship with the National Association of Credit Management (NACM), a confederation of sixty independent trade associations, which was seeking to automate its reporting system. To proceed with the new venture, Brennan created a new unit, TRW Business Credit Services.[33]

NACM's interest in TRW sprang from several sources, including the wish to provide better service to its member organizations, as well as long-standing resentment of Dun & Bradstreet's monopoly power manifested in high prices, slow service, and inclusion of information that some buyers deemed unnecessary. NACM could not compel its members to support TRW's efforts or supply information, but it could and did bestow a seal of approval on the company. TRW sought to deliver business credit information electronically in a statistical format, so that a credit manager could access needed information within minutes. This entailed developing a network of terminals linked to a central computer database—a challenge akin to the company's successful efforts in consumer credit reporting. But when TRW had acquired Credit Data, no rival dominated the industry. In the case of business credit reporting, Dun & Bradstreet enjoyed enormous entrenched advantages. In July 1976, for example, when TRW launched its National Credit Information Service, it had information supplied by 125 members of NACM, with commitments from another 275 members; at the same time, Dun & Bradstreet possessed historical information on four million companies. Against such odds, catching up was all but impossible except in the unlikely event that Dun & Bradstreet would stand still. Even to make a mark in the industry, TRW needed to spend a lot of money over a long period.[34]

TRW's position in an emerging electronic hardware market initially seemed more hopeful. The company proved especially eager to develop point-of-sale (POS) terminals, which were versatile machines that combined the functions of a cash register with credit authorization, inventory control, and other functions related to retail operations. In October 1974, The May Company abandoned plans to develop a proprietary POS system called Mark 2000, and it went looking for a more technologically sophisticated partner. Sid Webb regarded POS terminals as "a natural extension of our retail credit business," and agreed to take over manufacture of the Mark 2000 on a cost-plus basis. Webb handed responsibility for developing POS terminals to Dick Campbell.[35]

For the Mark 2000, TRW had a captive market in The May Company. To reach beyond a single customer, Campbell saw the need to develop a more sophisticated system. He launched another crash program to develop a next-generation POS terminal known as the TRW 2001. Unfortunately, difficulties in manufacturing and obtaining reliable components delayed the announced launch of the 2001 for more than a year and doubled cost of production. The system was riddled with "fundamental design errors," including many that stemmed from the early need to freeze dimensions so that plastic housings could be fabricated on time to meet delivery schedules. The tight dimensions of the housing meant that a custom printer would have to be designed and built. TRW cast about for suppliers, finally settling on a small company in Wyoming. This proved a disastrous mistake. The assignment far overstretched the supplier's capabilities: the printers cost much more than anticipated and were delivered more than a year late. Worse, when they finally arrived, they were prone to frequent breakdowns.[36]

The TRW 2001 finally made its debut in a May Company store in June 1976. The units were eventually made reliable, and they won a modest share of a market dominated by bigger and more established competitors. Sales peaked in 1978 at about $35 million, but the business never made money, losing about $40 million over its nine-year lifetime.[37]

TRW's situation in commercial electronic hardware might have been much worse but for a fortuitous acquisition. In May 1976, the company arranged to acquire the Customer Service Division of Singer Co. Like most participants in an overcrowded industry, Singer had encountered troubles in POS terminals. In December 1975, after trying in vain to find a buyer—including an approach to TRW—Singer made the extremely painful decision to exit and absorb a $385 million write-off. In addition to its hardware, Singer had built up a nationwide service and maintenance operation—the Consumer Service Division—with more than 2,000 employees to support the 65,000 terminals in use, including many at Sears. No longer a factor in POS terminals, Singer sought to exit the maintenance business, and it contacted more than 70 potential buyers. Increasingly desperate, it finally agreed to sell to TRW on a cost-plus fee basis that would permit TRW time to "restructure"—that is, raise prices on—Singer's existing customer service contracts. "In one fell stroke," Mettler noted, TRW gained "a distribution and sales organization of 2,000 people that would have taken us years to build," a profitable business, and a nationwide presence in repair and maintenance of electronic equipment. The business was added to Campbell's burgeoning operations, where it expanded quickly by negotiating third-party service deals with Docutel, Pitney Bowes, and other suppliers of terminals and office equipment.[38]

The Singer acquisition was one of the few 1970s deals in TRW Electronics that clicked. In 1973, concerned about struggles to grow, Mettler had asked Bob Burgin, whose International Automotive Division had disbanded, to work with Webb on acquisitions. During the late 1960s and early 1970s, Burgin had negotiated some of TRW's best deals, including Ehrenreich and Repa, as well as significant and valuable investments in Asia and South America. At TRW Electronics, the law of averages caught up with him. On the plus side, in 1976, he stanched a bleeding wound by arranging to sell some troubled components businesses in Europe. On the other side of the ledger, however, he was responsible for two electronics acquisitions that backfired.[39]

In the first deal, TRW acquired Orlando, Florida-based Financial Data Sciences, Inc. (FDS/i), early in 1974 in a stock transaction worth about $18 million. (In the down market of the time, this stock represented nearly 5 percent of TRW's total worth— a huge price for such a small business.) A closely held company, FDS/i produced specialized terminals for savings and loan associations, and had gained approximately 20 percent of the market in the United States, including a dominant position in the southeastern states. In 1974, it was also in the process of developing other equipment for commercial and retail banks, including automated teller machines (ATMs). TRW took over these efforts and almost immediately found itself in trouble, with products priced higher than the competition's, considerable delays in introducing new models, manufacturing and inventory problems, and money-losing service and maintenance agreements. Although TRW eventually introduced the products intended for the commercial banks and the ATMs, the business lost money steadily during an eight-year period.[40]

TRW's next deal turned out even worse. In July 1975, Burgin arranged for TRW finally to achieve entry into commercial telecommunications equipment by acquiring the assets of Vidar Corporation, a unit of Continental Telephone Company, for considerations worth approximately $14.2 million. Vidar manufactured digital transmission equipment for both voice and data communications, as well as systems to meter local messages for telephone companies and to enable private businesses to analyze and allocate calls made through their switchboards. At the time of the deal, Vidar employed about seven hundred people in two locations: a headquarters facility in Mountain View, California, and a manufacturing plant in San Luis Obispo. It became the anchor of a new organization that Burgin headed until he left early in 1978 to become chairman and CEO of Leaseway Corporation.[41]

To outward appearances, Vidar was a healthy company that was well positioned in an attractive market. However, serious problems lurked in the unit's new product plans. Vidar had launched a major initiative to develop a class 5 digital switch for the independent telephone companies, coming up with an extremely clever design. Unfortunately, neither Vidar's nor TRW's management fully understood the issues involved in manufacturing the switch, the fiercely competitive market for these products, and the investment requirements to remain viable in the long term. The switch turned into a nightmare. To ramp up for anticipated demand, TRW poured tens of millions of dollars into expanding the San Luis Obispo plant and opening another nearby. Problems continued to plague the project: Vidar promised deadlines it couldn't make and offered prices it couldn't afford. At the same time, the unit found itself in competition with bigger, wealthier, and more capable rivals such as Northern Telecom, ITT, and Rolm. By the late 1970s, the Vidar unit was losing between $10 million and $20 million per year. In these circumstances, both corporate and sector management wondered how much longer this performance could continue.[42]

THE RINGS OF SATURN

The varying fortunes of TRW's diverse operations in general and the troubles of TRW Electronics in particular became an increasing source of debate and concern at corporate headquarters as the 1970s drew to a close. A new team of leaders at the top of the corporation once more took a hard look at each of the company's businesses, as well as the company's overall strategy and management systems.

In July 1976—just after the bicentennial anniversary of the United States and coincident with the seventy-fifth anniversary of the start of operations at Cleveland Cap Screw—TRW staged yet another seamless transition in the chief executive office. The board of directors approved a plan that designated Mettler to succeed Shepard as chairman and CEO at the time of Shepard's scheduled retirement in December 1977. At the same time, the board chose Stan Pace to serve as assistant president until he would replace Mettler as president and chief operating officer. As time approached for these changes to take effect, TRW also announced that Si Ramo would retire on his sixty-fifth birthday in May 1978 and that Sid Webb would succeed him as vice chairman of the board and a member of the chief executive office.[43]

The members of the new chief executive office, like their predecessors, shared years of common experience and thorough commitment to TRW's broad strategy of diversification, corporate objectives and values, and approach to management. The fifty-three-year-old Mettler and Pace, his elder by three years, were friendly and worked together well. Mettler spent an increasing portion of his time dealing with outside constituencies. At the personal request of U.S. President Jimmy Carter, for example, he served for a year as chairman of the National Alliance of Business, which mounted a special effort to increase job opportunities for "the hard-to-employ." Pace attended to internal operations, while Webb, then fifty-seven, remained on the West Coast, where he continued to follow closely the fortunes of TRW Electronics and spent much of his time dealing with analysts and investors.[44]

Just as Mettler as president had injected systems thinking into TRW's approach to its business, so did Pace make distinctive contributions to the company's management. A hard-nosed, productive executive, he asked tough questions, bored in on significant details, and brooked no nonsense. One subordinate recalled that Pace kept a double-sided clock prominently displayed on his desk so that both he and visitors were visibly aware of the passage of time. Due to temperament, his long association with the "unglamorous" Thompson Products side of the business, and a history of competitive rivalry with his former peers, Pace took a skeptical view of the West Coast sectors. He showed little patience for the continuing struggles of the weaker businesses in TRW Electronics, for example, and he wondered whether TRW Systems & Energy's many efforts to transfer defense technology to commercial markets amounted to nothing more than "planting seedlings in the desert." Pace also worried about the concentration of employment at Space Park, which he thought increased risks and costs and tended to breed a technology-push rather than a market-pull outlook. His belief that some DSSG business units and activities should be moved to other locations such as Washington provoked notable clashes with DeLauer.[45]

Pace was "far more of a centralist than Shep or Rube had been," recalls Joe Gorman, who was TRW's vice president and general counsel after 1976. Pace sought to offset the independence of the sectors by bolstering the role of staff officers in meetings of the policy group. With Mettler's support and encouragement, he also helped recruit strong new additions to the corporate staff. In 1979, for example, Johnny Foster moved to Cleveland as vice president of science and technology, the first corporate officer in the position in nearly a decade and the most active since Arch Colwell. Pace went outside to obtain a new head of communications, wooing Tom Fay from Mobil Oil, where he had helped develop that company's famous "advertorials" and public policy white papers. To succeed the retiring Jim Dunlap as head of human relations, Pace brought in another outsider, Howard Knicely, a vigorous young executive with experience in such diverse businesses as Rockwell International and Hart, Schaffner & Marx. These appointments were clear signals of departure from past practices.[46]

Another potent force for change was Joe Gorman. He had joined TRW in 1968 after Yale Law School (where he recalls encountering the Fred Crawford–free speech case in a course in labor law) and a stint at Baker, Hostetler & Patterson, one of Cleveland's leading firms. Gene Ford, then TRW's vice president and general counsel, soon recognized Gorman's talents and assigned him to work on most of the company's acquisitions during that especially expansive era. He caught Shepard's eye and in 1970 succeeded Ford as corporate secretary. (When Shepard presented the offer, he noted that some members of the board had wondered whether Gorman, then thirty-two, was too young. Shepard's response to Gorman was, "I was made a general at your age, and I never thought I was too young. And I don't think you're too young. So come on in and do the job.") Two years later Gorman was named a corporate vice president and when Ford retired became vice president and general counsel. By then he had spent a brief tour of duty as a senior legal officer in Los Angeles to work both with TRW Systems and TRW Electronics, as well as a longer assignment as senior counsel in Automotive Worldwide, where he worked closely with Pace.

As evidenced by his role in the reorganization of the corporate law department in 1971, Gorman was acutely aware of the dangers of excessive decentralization. By the end of the decade, he was also redefining his role at TRW as something well beyond the company's chief lawyer. "From day one . . . I didn't limit myself to matters strictly of law," he recalls, adding:

I tended to take a broader view of my responsibilities and not only that, to offer ideas, possible solutions, suggestions on matters generally not law and that I understood weren't part of my responsibilities. And for some reason, they were well received generally. I did do my homework. I worked very hard. I did try to understand the businesses—more so, I think, than most staff officers.[47]

Both Mettler and Pace valued Gorman's unique role as part counselor, part consultant. Mettler relied on him to draft key statements and position papers—the role Mettler himself had played in support of Wright and Shepard a dozen years before. During 1978 and 1979, Gorman worked closely with Mettler to revise the company's goals and objectives, a document reviewed and revised over many months in planning conferences and small gatherings and eventually published as *TRW and the 80s.*

The document originated in Mettler's intention to update the five-year corporate goals announced in the Annual Report for 1975. This time, however, he followed a new process for arriving at them. He invited all members of the policy group to prepare a statement specifying the highest priorities for their business or organization, as well as for TRW as a whole, for the coming decade. At an offsite meeting, he then reviewed the goals with the group and found a strong consensus on priorities for the corporation. The top three involved significant improvements in quality, productivity, and management development. These found their way not only into the document but also into a major corporate initiative that Foster subsequently led (see Chapter 13).[48]

Although it displayed many affinities with earlier statements of corporate purpose, *TRW and the 80s* provided a much more comprehensive overview of management philosophy and a much more detailed exposition of how TRW planned to reach its goals. The document opened by spelling out four "fundamental objectives" for the corporation as "the starting point from which our more specific goals are derived." These included "the highest standards of conduct in all that the company does," "superior performance as an economic unit, with special emphasis on high-quality products and services," "high quality in . . . internal operations," and "participation in a wide range of community activities and communication programs." The document went on to list new financial goals appropriate to a more inflationary era to supersede those adopted in 1975: 10 percent real internal rate of return, 5 percent growth in earnings per share, 5 percent growth in real dividends per share, earnings providing a minimum of eight times interest coverage, and enough new high-return investments to yield 5 percent growth in real total assets. It then described in detail what TRW would do to reach these goals, emphasizing key words and phrases such as quality, productivity, innovation, meeting customer needs and requirements, establishing positions of market leadership, an "optimum level of . . . diversification," and developing "a superior level and depth of management talent."[49]

Mettler believed that such a strong and specific statement of the company's philosophy and objectives was necessary to counter the centrifugal pull of TRW's decentralized operations. "A strong central policy is the prerequisite of delegation of responsibility," he told a reporter, "because we at headquarters cannot lose control over the business." But whether statements such as *TRW and the 80s* constituted an effective control mechanism remained an open question. Indeed, some top officers at TRW were becoming increasingly restive about the company's future. These were years of double-digit inflation in the United States, an incipient revolution in Iran that threatened to disrupt world energy supplies again, and mounting concerns among many American manufacturers about the rising industrial power of Japan. Such concerns gave rise to what media commentators termed "a national malaise." At TRW, Webb fretted about "world ferment" and forecast the "the Eighties as a far harder time in which to manage than the Seventies." Some senior officers voiced concern that the company's management systems placed too much emphasis on bottom-line results, asset management, and meeting budgets and forecasts at the expense of long-term planning and investments. Others, including Gorman, worried that while the company held clear objectives, it lacked a clear strategy for reaching them.[50]

TRW's financial performance in the 1970s appeared to validate the strategy of diversification and the policy of decentralization. Looking back on the decade, Mettler ticked off impressive achievements: a sustained annual growth rate in nominal terms of 11.1 percent, with 85 percent of this growth generated internally; over 10 percent compounded growth in earnings; $1 billion in capital investment; $850 million for proprietary research and development and new product development; $3 billion in customer-funded R&D; and employment growth from 86,000 to 96,000, including 12,000 scientists and engineers.[51]

The 1970s concluded with a series of uplifting technological triumphs for TRW. The first two FLTSATCOM satellites were launched and performed exactly to specification. NASA's High Energy Astronomical Observatories carried out three dazzlingly successful missions. And in December 1979, *Pioneer 11* finally reached Saturn, six-and-one-half years after launch. The spacecraft performed flawlessly, returning the first close-up pictures of the planet and its spectacular rings, enabling the remarkable discovery of their layered and particulate structure. Like Saturn's rings, TRW itself presented one image when viewed from a distance and another when examined up close. In 1979, those closest to the company were increasingly concerned about what they saw: a view slipping out of focus. Events in the new decade would heighten these concerns and bring a significant change of perspective.

Chapter 13

From Policy to Strategy

▶   ▶   ▶

1980–1985

WHEN PIONEER 11 SOARED BY SATURN AT THE END OF 1979 AND VENTURED ON A NEW COURSE into outer space, TRW also embarked in new directions, starting down a path that would soon culminate in momentous changes. The new objectives and policies expressed in the planning document *TRW and the 80s* dovetailed with key executive changes, new management approaches, and fundamental shifts in the markets the company served to create a context for transformation.

The magnitude of the coming changes was not at first apparent. During the early 1980s, TRW survived the worst recession to strike the Western economies in a half century, thanks largely to its extensive diversity. When its automotive and industrial businesses turned down, in part because of the second big surge in oil prices in six years, its energy businesses picked up. The different timing of the recession around the world enabled the company's strong position in Europe to mitigate troubles in North America, and subsequently vice-versa. When commercial businesses faltered, defense operations boomed under the huge American defense buildup.

Although TRW's relative prosperity through lean times appeared to vindicate its diversity, the experience also inspired some executives, especially Joe Gorman, to raise tough questions about the company's priorities and its decentralized ways of management. Probing beneath the surface in the company's industrial and energy units, for example, Gorman discovered a hodgepodge of strong and attractive operations lumped together with many weak and declining businesses. He found a clear explanation for these differences in the structures of the industries in which TRW sought to compete as well as in the relative position of each unit within its industry. And he saw that the company's extreme diversity, organization and staffing policies, and management systems impeded deep understanding of its various businesses. As a result, he believed, it was unnecessarily difficult to make prudent investment decisions and to allocate capital where it would pay the best returns in the long run.

As Gorman began to sort, reorder, and reorganize the units in his care, Rube Mettler tapped him in 1984 to become the company's next president and heir apparent as chairman and CEO. Together, Mettler and Gorman extended the analysis from the industrial and energy units to the entire corporation. The result in 1985 was a new set of strategic priorities and a major restructuring of TRW's portfolio. To support its strongest businesses and nourish promising growth prospects in new areas such as occupant restraint systems, the company narrowed its focus to three areas: automotive supply, space and defense, and information systems and services. Within each area, it developed specific priorities, plans, and policies to achieve and sustain superior performance.

The cost of these changes was high: TRW's first annual loss since the Great Depression; the divestiture of many businesses, including long-standing contributors such as aircraft and aircraft engine components, as well as commercial electronics, industrial bearings and tools, and energy products and systems; and a steep drop in total employment. On the other hand, however, Mettler and Gorman were convinced that they were building a secure foundation for renewed growth and enduring profitability.

Changing of the Guard

To help achieve the ambitious targets set in *TRW and the 80s,* Rube Mettler and Stan Pace remade TRW's senior management team early in the new decade, along the way taking advantage of retirements and adapting to structural changes in several key businesses. Chuck Ohly's scheduled retirement at the end of 1980 created the first opening. In April, Mettler and Pace picked Bill Reynolds as the new head of Automotive Worldwide and, in view of emerging trends in the global automotive industry, agreed to shift the automotive aftermarket operations into the sector. At the same time, Joe Gorman was elected an executive vice president and moved into his first general management position as head of the newly named Industrial & Energy sector. This organization now included Energy Products Group, Industrial Products Group, and the United-Carr industrial divisions.[1]

A short while later, TRW Electronics merged with operations at Space Park in a new Electronics & Defense sector. At about the same time, Dick DeLauer resigned to become undersecretary of defense for research and engineering in the new Reagan administration. George Solomon was promoted to executive vice president and head of the new sector with Dick Campbell as his top deputy. For a brief period, TRW Equipment Group was orphaned once more, reporting directly to Stan Pace. In 1983, bearing the name Aircraft Components Group, it became part of the Industrial & Energy sector.[2]

Among all these organizational changes, the biggest involved the merger of two big organizations into the new Electronics & Defense sector. In explaining the move,

Mettler noted that much of the aerospace and commercial electronics businesses depended on similar technologies and that it made sense for them to share research and development activities. He also cited logistical factors, pointing out that both organizations were based in Los Angeles. Still another reason was the changing nature of the company's participation in several key commercial electronics businesses. In May 1980, for example, TRW founded a joint venture marketing company with Fujitsu Ltd., Japan's biggest computer manufacturer. The new entity distributed Fujitsu's small business computer systems in the United States, as well as TRW's POS terminals and ATMs. TRW announced the deal with fanfare, and *Business Week* hailed it as "the first full-scale invasion [of the U.S. market] by a Japanese computer maker."[3]

At the same time, other units of the old electronics sector were also winding down. Late in 1980, Datapoint Corporation, TRW's partner in Datacom International, announced that it would not renew its ten-year joint marketing agreement with TRW and would buy back its foreign distribution rights the following year. The terms provided TRW with a significant cash windfall, but at the cost of a thriving business. Other units in TRW Electronics posted mixed results. Vidar and the business credit reporting unit continued to record losses while several electronic components units also struggled. That left few healthy businesses in the sector, including consumer credit reporting, the equipment service and maintenance businesses acquired from Singer, and some components divisions.[4]

In practical terms, the formation of TRW-Fujitsu, the sale of Datacom International, and the increasing likelihood that Vidar would be sold or closed removed the bulk of TRW Electronics and eased the transition into the new Electronics & Defense sector. Not long after the reorganization, Sid Webb announced that he would take early retirement from TRW at the end of 1981 while continuing as chairman of TRW-Fujitsu. TRW's board elected not to replace Webb in the chief executive office, leaving Mettler and Pace, assisted by the policy committee, to guide the company. The policy committee now included many new faces in corporate staff roles, as well as the new constellation of executive vice presidents.

Following through on *TRW and the 80s,* the company launched a half-dozen corporate initiatives in such areas as quality, productivity, technology, manpower development, and management systems. Several new corporate officers led the initiatives, assisted by small staffs and charged to work with the operating units. As vice president of science and technology, for example, Johnny Foster took charge of the initiatives in quality, productivity, technical resources, manufacturing, and materiel. To direct these activities, he recruited several new vice presidents from the outside, including John Groocock, a renowned quality expert from ITT; Henry Conn, a leading authority on productivity with experience in senior line and staff roles; and Arden Bement, a distinguished engineer and former MIT professor who had held several senior positions in the U.S. Department of Defense, including deputy undersecretary for research and engineering.[5]

The quality and productivity initiatives assumed a similar shape. They began with written goals for each unit, proceeded to training programs to increase awareness and understanding, added new systems to measure and track progress, targeted specific areas for improvement, and established pilot programs to test new approaches. The company began measuring and reporting "quality cost," defined as "the cost of making defective products, including the cost of defective materials, scrap, rework, inspection, test, warranty, recall, retrofit, and so on." TRW announced a corporate goal of reducing its quality costs by 10 percent each year. To gain a better handle on productivity, the company developed a new measurement system that included separate ratios for each factor of production—capital, labor, material, energy—as well as a weighted composite ratio for the whole. TRW tracked these results quarterly and began to compare its performance to that of peer companies and key competitors. Both corporate initiatives were guided by a steering committee of senior corporate and operating executives that was assisted by companywide councils of about two hundred division employees actively involved in quality and productivity issues. As these corporate initiatives took hold, TRW recorded significant gains in competitive performance, especially in its automotive and industrial businesses.[6]

During the early 1980s TRW also mounted new efforts in corporate communications and human resources led by senior executives recruited from the outside. As head of communications, Tom Fay led an effort to enhance the company's image as a progressive, high-tech company in the minds of investors, customers, employees, and the general public. The effort took several forms, including a new corporate logo and corporate image campaign, as well as a new series of annual meetings with financial analysts that became more formal and scripted and shifted around the company to show off its principal operations. Fay also beefed up TRW's office in Washington, D.C. Finally, he initiated the slow process of branding the company's subsidiaries and divisions with the TRW initials. Although many division managers saw the wisdom of leveraging TRW's name and experience, some, especially in Europe, resisted the change for several years, citing local laws and strong customer identification with traditional brand names. Corporate persistence eventually paid off, and by the early 1990s, all of the company's operations around the world bore the TRW logo.[7]

As corporate vice president of human relations (HR), Howard Knicely was charged to upgrade the company's manpower planning systems. The challenge had both political and technical dimensions. The political part involved ongoing attempts to bridge continuing cultural gaps between the aerospace and commercial operations, and between corporate headquarters and the operating units. It was no accident, Knicely believes, that this assignment fell to an outsider without ties to any of the business areas. "When I arrived here," he recalls, "it was very clear to me that the organization was fragmented. Consequently we were losing a lot of efficiency and effectiveness. I was brought in to develop a human resource strategy that was closely tied to the business strategy—something that hadn't been done here before."[8]

Knicely sought to preserve the informality and friendly feel of the company while combining it with more rigorous systems for training and developing employees at all levels—the technical part of his challenge. With the backing of Pace and Mettler, he developed policies to make operating managers accountable for performance in the area of human relations. In 1981, he presided over a conference of the company's top

HR personnel from around the world that identified six specific issues to work on: organizational structure and management succession; development of people; productivity; compensation; cost management; and employee relations. During the next several years, TRW managers across the company made significant progress in all of these areas, improving relations with universities and business schools where TRW recruited, developing programs to identify and train promising managers, adjusting compensation and benefit systems to reflect new competitive realities and new corporate objectives, and supporting the corporate initiatives in quality and productivity while adding a focus on employee involvement.[9]

A final corporate initiative of the early 1980s was architectural: to help draw the company closer together, TRW made plans for a new headquarters complex. The facility on the grounds at Tapco was bursting at the seams, with many Automotive Worldwide and Industrial & Energy executives scattered in other locations, including some near Cleveland. Although TRW considered relocating to another city, it also recognized its long-standing involvement in Cleveland, as well as the potential costs of uprooting many employees. In 1980, the company settled the matter by acquiring "Franchester," a 135-acre estate formerly belonging to U.S. Representatives Chester and Frances Payne Bolton. (Recall from Chapter 3 that in 1934, the Boltons, as owners of a significant holding of preferred stock in Thompson Products, had rallied to Fred Crawford's banner in his proxy fight with Ed Thompson for control of the company.) Located in Lyndhurst, an eastern suburb of Cleveland, "Franchester" would be the site of a new facility.

In July 1981, TRW retained Fujikawa Conterato Lohan and Associates of Chicago to design the new facility. A year later, ground was broken for a four-story structure featuring a central atrium from which radiated four long office wings. The facility, which eventually cost about $100 million, was designed to house 700 employees. It offered 460,000 square feet of office space and two underground levels for parking. It also boasted many amenities, as well as the latest information technology, video-conferencing facilities, ample meeting and conference rooms, a 237-seat auditorium, and a cafeteria. Raised flooring, movable walls, and modular furniture were designed to accommodate growth and change. The main structure was set far back from the entrance road, well screened from the surrounding community. The building occupied less than 10 percent of the carefully groomed estate, which featured trails for walkers and joggers. TRW moved into its new headquarters in July 1985.[10]

DIVERSIFICATION AT WORK

TRW's management changes and corporate initiatives occurred during the worst recession in the United States in fifty years. Starting in 1979, the recession hammered the company's automotive and industrial businesses and exposed fundamental competitive problems. Automotive Worldwide, for example, experienced a double hit: its primary North American customers suffered staggering losses, and Chrysler staved off bankruptcy only by obtaining a last-minute loan guarantee from the U.S. government.

The Big Three ceded big shares of the North American market to Japanese competitors, the new global industry leaders, that it would not recover when the economy bounced back. Similar problems became apparent in electronic components and industrial operations such as bearings and tools, where foreign competitors established new competitive benchmarks in cost and quality far more demanding than the company's traditional standards.

Once more, TRW was able to ride out the recession during the early 1980s as sales dipped but the company reported positive earnings and steady cash flow—a performance that Mettler believed proved "that our diversification really is working." More specifically, huge increases in federal spending on defense and technology benefited the Electronics & Defense sector, while temporarily high oil prices enabled the energy businesses in Industrial & Energy to record strong contributions, and the different timing of the downturn in Europe offset Automotive Worldwide's problems in North America. Meanwhile, TRW continued to follow the growth strategy it had pursued since the mid-1960s, encouraging the sector and group heads to expand business via internal development and acquisitions. The company's portfolio of businesses continued to churn as new partners were added and marginal performers dropped (see Appendix).[11]

Electronics & Defense: Big Buildup and Little Letdowns

TRW's defense businesses contributed by far the biggest share of corporate growth and earnings during the early 1980s. Between 1979 and 1984, sales in this segment nearly doubled from $1.5 billion to $2.9 billion, and operating profit exactly tripled, from $89 million to $267 million. Massive increases in defense spending under the new administration helped propel this growth. In October 1981, President Ronald Reagan announced a major commitment to upgrading U.S. strategic forces, opting to deploy the B-1 bomber and the Peacekeeper (MX) ICBM, as well as funding development of a new generation of military satellites. Two years later, Reagan provided another enormous boost to the aerospace industry by outlining the Strategic Defense Initiative (SDI), a set of programs designed to defend the nation and ultimately the planet from ICBM attacks. Known popularly as the Star Wars program, SDI would rely on extremely advanced sensing and information processing capabilities, as well as laser weapons to destroy missiles in flight, preferably in space. All of this added up to a bonanza for defense contractors. Between 1981 and 1987, the Department of Defense doubled its annual spending on research, development, test, and evaluation—an area in which TRW was ideally positioned.[12]

The Reagan buildup benefited all of TRW's defense operations, which recorded significant new business in ballistic missiles, high-energy lasers, spacecraft, electronic systems, and software. The decision to deploy the Peacekeeper ICBM, for example, brought in steady revenues worth about $200 million per year. Between 1978 and 1981, funding for the government's high-energy laser program nearly doubled from $150 million to $275 million, with TRW capturing a significant fraction. Generous funding, which surged again after the announcement of the Strategic Defense Initiative, enabled the company to extend research on chemical lasers and investigate other types of high-energy lasers. The company also expanded its old rocket motor proving grounds near San Juan Capistrano as a laser test site.[13]

These were also heady times in the spacecraft business. In 1981, TRW booked orders for three additional FLTSATCOM satellites, with the expectation of still more to follow later in the decade. The Air Force poured funds into the Defense Support Program, all but guaranteeing TRW continuing work until at least the end of the decade. The company also scored well with NASA, winning contracts for additional Tracking and Data Relay Satellites (TDRS), and some preliminary research and design contracts for the space station. In 1983, NASA's Goddard Space Flight Center awarded TRW a $250 million contract to build the Gamma Ray Observatory, a sister to the *Hubble Space Telescope* and one of the biggest and most sophisticated spacecraft programs ever attempted.

Unfortunately, TRW lost out in its bid to become prime contractor on the era's biggest spacecraft: the Milstar military communications satellite program. This program had originated in the same October 1981 speech in which President Reagan authorized deployment of the Peacekeeper ICBM and development of the B-1 bomber. The Milstar system represented the most ambitious space-based communications system in history. Its payload, like its counterpart on the Tracking and Data Relay Satellites, acted a switchboard in space and was a marvel of electronic engineering. But the Milstar payload was far more capable. It was designed to configure instantaneously voice and data networks among users around the globe, relay messages via crosslinks to other Milstar satellites (thereby eliminating the need for a network of ground stations), resist enemy signal jamming, and even survive radiation from a nearby nuclear blast. It also enabled all three branches of the U.S. military to communicate on the same network regardless of their geographical location and independent of their position on land or aboard ships, submarines, or aircraft.

Solomon reckoned that Milstar would be worth between $2 billion and $3 billion over the next decade, and TRW teamed with Hughes Aircraft to form what he called "an unbeatable team" for the prime contract. TRW's decision to partner with Hughes led the Air Force to separate the payload and space vehicle contractor selections. Early in 1983, the Air Force chose Lockheed as prime contractor for the spacecraft. The following year, this bad news was mitigated when the TRW-Hughes team won the payload contract, which it performed as a subcontractor to Lockheed. Directed by TRW's Daniel Goldin—later head of NASA—the payload contract engaged more than a thousand employees for several years and was valued at $1.3 billion.[14]

TRW's ability to win the Milstar payload partly reflected greatly enhanced capabilities in microelectronics. In 1979, concerned that most research in the field applied only to commercial business, the U.S. Department of Defense announced a competition to develop very-high-speed integrated circuits (VHSIC) for use in advanced communications equipment and "smart" or "brilliant" weapon systems. Total funding of VHSIC was expected to reach about $1 billion during the decade, as the government sought to produce "a dramatic forward leap" in technology—posing a technical challenge that rivaled the Apollo program in complexity—and to develop an industrial base to produce it. During the first phase, for example, each VHSIC chip was to include at least 100,000 semiconducting devices and operate at a clock speed of twenty-five megahertz—about twenty-five times faster than a typical personal computer of the era. During the second phase, the bar was raised to five hundred thousand devices on a single chip and a clock speed of one hundred megahertz.

Under Charlie Stephens, general manager of the Electronic Systems Division, TRW joined with Motorola and Sperry to bid, and in 1981 the team was selected as a principal contractor, with TRW's share of the award totaling $34 million to begin the first phase of the program. The company's participation in this phase eventually swelled to revenues worth about $125 million over a four-year period. Along the way, the TRW-Motorola team (Sperry dropped out) racked up notable achievements, including in February 1983, the first fully functional VHSIC chip. The following year, the company managed the first insertion of VHSIC technology into an operational avionic system, the electronic countermeasures pod carried aboard the F-16 fighter. During the first phase, the TRW-Motorola team produced eight distinct VHSIC chips, more than any other team, and inserted VHSIC chips into several other military electronic systems. In 1984, TRW was selected to work on the second phase of the program, with an initial award of about $30 million. Not satisfied to meet the five-hundred-thousand-component government specification, the team proposed to fabricate relatively large wafers (1.5 inches square) that would each contain as many as twenty *million* components. To support this and other work, the company spent nearly $70 million to build and equip a new state-of-the-art microelectronics center at Space Park.[15]

Other TRW defense businesses notched significant achievements during the early 1980s. ESL built up a backlog in strategic and tactical reconnaissance systems and equipment of more than $200 million. In 1983, the Military Electronics Division set up its headquarters near San Diego and opened a $100 million facility for research and development, design, and fabrication of integrated avionics systems. Most aircraft typically maintained separate systems for command and control, guidance and navigation, communications, and electronic countermeasures. For next-generation aircraft, TRW sought to provide a single, coordinated system to manage all of these functions and activities. In 1983, the company won its first significant business in this area with the advanced development model programs for the Integrated Communications Navigation Identification Avionics and the Integrated Electronic Warfare System for the Air Force's Advanced Tactical Fighter. As with the Milstar payload win, TRW's VHSIC capabilities proved instrumental in securing these contracts.[16]

TRW's software business also boomed. A $70 million program called Support Analysis File Environment (SAFE) for "a Washington customer" (i.e., a national security organization) established an early form of networking capability to link as many as three thousand on-line users and provide them with the ability to share data and documents. To speed development, TRW pioneered a new technique called "rapid prototyping," which enabled programmers to build graphic displays early in the design process and involve users in setting up a system's "man-machine" interface. TRW even developed hardware for SAFE, including a bus interface unit that enabled "desktop computers" to connect in a distributed data processing network.[17]

Other big software challenges of the early 1980s included the Science Operations Ground System for NASA's *Hubble Space Telescope*. TRW's first prime installation of a complex ground station, the system was designed "to command and control *Hubble* in orbit as well as to acquire and calibrate its captured data on the ground." In all, the system featured about four million lines of code, representing "almost 2,000 man-years of computer programming." This work led to other major ground station projects, including the Consolidated Space Operations Center in Colorado Springs, an Air Force installation similar to NASA's Mission Control Center in Houston, and the Space Defense Operations Center, in which TRW subcontracted to Ford Aerospace to develop software to control the Air Force's central command and control facility for space warning and defense and antisatellite operational control activities. TRW software teams also developed significant systems in avionics, electronic warfare, strategic defense, and many classified programs in signal processing and communications and message processing.[18]

The remarkable performance of TRW's defense portfolio far overshadowed the company's efforts in commercial electronics. The Electronic Components Group proved sensitive to the recession and vulnerable to foreign competition and the ongoing tendency of customers to integrate components on to chips. Even LSI Products began to founder as military microelectronics technology grew more highly specialized and the transfer of people, technology, and ideas from Space Park to commercial markets slowed to a trickle.[19]

TRW Vidar also continued to disappoint. In December 1981, after a prolonged and futile search for a buyer, TRW finally cut its losses, announcing the decisions to liquidate the unit and absorb a $34 million write-off. (Throughout the long period the unit was on the block, TRW worked hard to turn it around while attempting to put the best face on a tough situation. In routine communications with the press and financial community, the company mentioned in three successive years that Vidar was turning the corner. That prompted Bill Lawrence of TRW's Law Department to quip: "If we've turned the corner three times, I guess that means we're back where we started.") When added to the acquisition cost and annual losses during the late 1970s and early 1980s, however, the total cost of the venture exceeded $100 million. Sale of assets later lowered the damage somewhat, but the episode reverberated in TRW's culture as an example of poor planning, misunderstood markets, and organizational barriers to technology transfer. The liquidation of TRW Vidar also caused some senior TRW executives to reassess the company's organization structure, planning, and reporting systems.[20]

The marriage between TRW and Fujitsu also failed to click. Although the joint venture made progress in marketing POS terminals, it encountered stiff resistance in selling ATMs and Fujitsu's line of computers. In May 1983, less than three years after the joint venture formed, Fujitsu arranged to buy out TRW's interest while admitting that its original strategy did not work.[21]

The lone bright spots in TRW's commercial electronics portfolio were the consumer credit reporting operations and the computer equipment repair business. In 1984, TRW combined these with the still-struggling initiative in business credit reporting into a new Information Systems Group under Dick Whilden as vice president and general manager. A veteran aerospace engineer who had helped save NASA's High Energy Astronomical Observatory program from the scrap heap during the 1970s, Whilden plunged into his new assignment, armed with an impressive industry study prepared by McKinsey & Co. and the full backing of senior management to pursue aggressive growth.[22]

Automotive: The Benefits of Balance

During the early 1980s, the fortunes of TRW's automotive businesses proved decidedly mixed. Automotive Worldwide's sales dipped from a peak of $1.8 billion in 1979 to $1.5 billion in 1982 before climbing to a new peak of $2.2 billion in 1985. Operating profits followed a similar trajectory, but the company, in contrast to many of its customers and competitors, did not lose money in the period. Automotive Worldwide's product and geographical diversification contributed to this balanced performance. When the original equipment market went down, for example, the aftermarket picked up, and vice-versa. When the U.S. automotive market collapsed, markets in Europe partly compensated, and vice-versa. When passenger car sales tumbled, the market for heavy duty and off-highway vehicles fared better, and vice-versa.

Nonetheless, the early 1980s represented a time of contraction and cautious diversification for Automotive Worldwide. Under Reynolds' leadership, the sector embraced the corporate initiatives in quality and productivity and emphasized improving operating performance. The groups and divisions adopted—or rediscovered—techniques such as statistical process control that simultaneously improved quality and lowered costs. At the same time, Automotive Worldwide rationalized and combined operations; applied new shop-floor techniques such as manufacturing cells, computer integrated manufacturing, and quality circles; improved purchasing and inventory management; and made better use of information technology throughout the production process from design to distribution. Automotive Worldwide also abandoned marginal operations such as Clifford Components, a small unit in the United Kingdom that produced steering wheels and other components, and Thompson Ramco Argentina, which faltered in a volatile local economy.[23]

Automotive Worldwide approached new investments warily. To reach toward the corporate goals for return on assets employed and real internal rate of return, Reynolds noted that the sector would "avoid major programs that would produce large negative cash flows." Rather, he said, "our goal is a moderate, sustained, positive cash flow." This attitude also reflected the sustained investment that the company had made in capacity to make rack-and-pinion steering gears. This became a hot product line after 1979, when the Iranian revolution triggered another big surge in oil prices and accelerated the U.S. automakers' shift to smaller cars with front-wheel drive. Nonetheless, the business did not turn profitable until 1982, and TRW was unwilling to consider investing on a comparable scale until it had a better sense of technology and market trends.[24]

Automotive Worldwide did invest to grow some of its smaller but most promising businesses, however. Reynolds took a tentative approach to automotive electronics. In

1981, he formed a Transportation Electrical & Electronics operation to focus on developing microprocessor-based engine and vehicle control systems, primarily for heavy duty trucks and off-highway vehicles such as tractors—areas in which TRW's customers lacked significant electronics capabilities. The new unit pursued a variety of approaches to growth including internal development, joint ventures, and small acquisitions. These provided low-cost entry and a means of gaining experience and testing ideas in a market with enormous potential. Progress remained maddeningly slow, however, and automotive electronics accounted for less than 1 percent of TRW's total automotive revenues.[25]

Safety products offered more immediate, less threatening, and ultimately far bigger opportunities to Automotive Worldwide. By 1980, Repa had established itself as a significant force in the European auto industry, racking up more than $100 million in profitable sales while supplying most leading automakers in the region. Under Wolf-Dieter Klink, the company developed a steady stream of new products, including a proprietary pretensioner device that used an electronic sensor to activate a seat belt retractor and snug the belt around passengers in the vehicle. With the support of his immediate boss, Chuck Miller, head of Automotive Worldwide's General Components Group, and Reynolds at the sector level, Klink also negotiated several key acquisitions in Europe, between 1983 and 1985 adding seat belt companies in France, Spain, and Italy. In the United States, Miller followed suit by arranging during the summer of 1984 to acquire the Hamill Division of Firestone Tire & Rubber, then undergoing a restructuring, for considerations valued at about $50 million. These acquisitions and natural growth propelled TRW's seat belt business to more that $400 million in sales and made it the leading independent supplier in the world, with operations in nine countries and strong relationships with all leading North American and European automakers.[26]

Industrial & Energy: The Coming of Strategic Management

TRW's third business segment, the Industrial & Energy sector, also posted mixed results during the early 1980s. Sales climbed during the recession, peaking at about $1.6 billion in 1981 before dropping to $1.3 billion in 1984. Operating profit followed a similar pattern, with the boom in energy prices following the Iranian revolution pushing the sector to record earnings. In 1981, for example, the sector accounted for 30 percent of the corporation's sales but 45 percent of its profits. Yet this situation soon reversed, as oil prices began a steady decline and units such as the Aircraft Components Group encountered a sharp reversal of fortune. By 1984, the sector accounted for 24 percent of TRW's sales and 23 percent of its profits.[27]

During his first few months on the job, Joe Gorman traveled widely to visit operations and develop a clearer understanding of each business in the portfolio. Along the way, he formed a small team of key operating and staff executives, including Adi Mueller, Van Skilling, and Bill Lawrence. Together, the team discovered some similarities and commonalities across the sector. The strongest units, for example, held leading market positions, enjoyed a reputation for producing high-quality products and services, and featured high engineering content in both products and processes. But there were many more differences. Some businesses, such as the main units in the Energy Products Group and United-Carr, were global; others, such as the tools and bearings operations, focused primarily on the U.S. market. Some units—Energy Products Group and Aircraft Components Group (which reported its results in the Industrial & Energy segment, although it did not become part of the sector until 1983)—tracked specific industrial or market indicators closely; others, such as the United-Carr and tools and bearings operations, sold into a broad range of industries. Some units, such as Reda Pump, earned valuable premiums for after-sales service and support; others, such as most of the industrial products divisions, created value by offering superior product features. Some units, such as the Aircraft Components Group, depended on a very small number of buyers; others, such as the fastener units, sold to hundreds of different customers.[28]

To make sense of all these businesses, Gorman relied heavily on his own study and analysis, the strong support of his management team, and emerging techniques of strategic planning and management. He found concepts becoming popularized by Harvard Business School Professor Michael Porter particularly helpful. In a series of influential books and articles, Porter showed that competitive performance depended on two principal factors: the structure of the industry in which a company competed and the company's relative position within that industry. This approach led to techniques for a particular business to identify the drivers of profitability and sources and sustainability of competitive advantage. At Industrial & Energy, these proved essential to understanding how businesses create value and enabled top management to make appropriate investment decisions and determine future courses of action.[29]

In 1983, Joe Gorman outlined his philosophy for managing the Industrial & Energy businesses in a speech to investment analysts. His views anticipated a new approach to managing the corporation as a whole later in the decade:

> More than anything else, we have endeavored to convince our key managers that we can't afford a "business as usual" attitude; that we must avoid steadfastly a "me-too" approach; that there is no single solution, nor any single set of solutions; that each of our many and diverse product lines is different and requires different actions; that in every case we must understand and even anticipate the critical factors that are affecting our customers, end-users, and competitors; that in every case we must identify a range of strategic and tactical alternatives from which to choose; that we must focus our key resources on those issues and actions offering the highest leverage; and that in doing so, our central focus must be on comparative advantage—developing or enhancing some significant edge over the competition.[30]

At Industrial & Energy, strategic management enabled TRW to decide where and when to push ahead or pull back. In the early 1980s, for example, Gorman and Sam Phillips, head of the Energy Products Group, sought to augment TRW's business by acquiring The Brandt Company, a maker of solids control equipment for mud systems that are used on drilling rigs, and by taking an equity position in Trico Industries, a manufacturer of sucker rod pumping systems, well-completion equipment, and storage tanks. The following year, TRW approved plans to build a major new facility in Singapore to build submergible pumping systems.[31]

Just as TRW was completing these measures, however, petroleum prices hit a peak and began a prolonged period of decline. This trend had an obvious adverse impact on TRW's energy businesses, although the full magnitude of the problem did not become apparent for several years. Most of these businesses were tied to exploration and secondary and tertiary recovery—getting hard-to-pump oil from the bottom of old wells, for example. In an era of excess capacity and tumbling prices, these businesses remained profitable, but they faced limited prospects for growth. Although sales picked up slightly in 1984, in part due to a significant contract for Reda Pump to supply pumping systems to China, TRW abandoned plans to complete the acquisition of Trico Industries, and held off making additional energy investments. Falling oil prices also curtailed activities in energy research and development at Space Park, where funding sources, customers, and joint venture partners began to lose interest in alternative energy projects. Another factor was the Reagan administration's decision in 1981 to cut spending on R&D through the U.S. Department of Energy. Although TRW continued to promote its coal combustion technology and a few other energy-related projects, most of the initiatives that the company's Energy Systems Group had launched during the 1970s slowly ground to a halt.[32]

Strategic analysis of the fasteners, tools, and bearings businesses revealed contrasting patterns and prospects. The tools and bearings operations generally suffered from relatively weak market positions in the United States and faced serious threats from low-cost imports. Gorman concluded early on that TRW would probably have to find a way out of bearings and hand tools. Initially, he had higher hopes for industrial cutting tools. He prodded managers at the group and division levels to pursue a strategy based on developing smart tools and bundling TRW products with other products and services into components, systems, and services for advanced manufacturing applications. Management also launched programs to upgrade cost accounting and reporting systems and made plans to invest in process improvements and new procedures to bring costs into line.

Unfortunately, high costs continued to plague the industrial tools business, a problem that Gorman attributed partly to a mistaken decision in the 1970s to relocate production from Chicago to a new nonunion facility in Georgia. The rationale for the move had been to contain labor costs, but Gorman pointed out that the loss of "the black magic" possessed by the old work force, which was intimately familiar with the production process, more than offset the payroll savings. High scrap rates and low yields made the new facility noncompetitive.[33]

The fasteners and controls units in the old United-Carr divisions and Nelson Stud Welding offered more promise. Although Gorman believed that these businesses had been milked for a long period, certain structural features were attractive: the products were highly engineered and valued in the marketplace; the company's cost position was not out of line with global standards; the products sold in diverse markets, with the auto industry the biggest single customer; brand names had established value and the divisions enjoyed good reputations with customers; the threat of backward integration by customers was negligible; TRW held leading positions in many market segments and in many geographical regions; opportunities existed to transfer technology across the operations; manufacturing processes could be significantly improved with CAD/CAM and other advanced techniques; and there was potential to add—and capture—value by providing fastening systems to customers to help improve their productivity and operations. Accordingly, TRW invested to improve operations and expand the business by adding new products and pursuing new markets. Along the way, the business continued to achieve attractive returns.

The Aircraft Components Group became Gorman's responsibility early in 1983 and presented special complications. For about five years the group had ridden on a wave of expansion. As record orders flowed in, the group added new capacity in Georgia, North Carolina, and Singapore. It also announced plans to develop new materials and casting and forging technologies, and it extended its product line by acquiring Hartzell Propeller Products, a small company that served the general aviation market. In 1982, however, the recession caught up with the group, and sales declined more than 10 percent and remained flat for several years.[34]

The business faced several significant challenges, including, in Gorman's distinctive phrasing, "the unrelenting combination of structural and cyclical factors and near-suicidal competitive practices [that] have dealt the major airlines one devastating blow after another" and all but stopped commercial aircraft purchases. Another serious problem that strategic analysis exposed was the increasingly unattractive structure of the aircraft engine industry: the dwindling number of customers exerted enormous power in bargaining for prices and other terms; these customers all had—or could readily obtain—capabilities comparable to TRW's; and overbuilding during the late 1970s and early 1980s had created excess capacity. In 1985, Pratt & Whitney, a major customer for TRW's compressor fan blades, invested to equip a new, highly automated facility to make fan blades in Georgia.[35]

In these circumstances, "vigorous cost-reduction programs" and other measures at TRW represented temporary palliatives, and serious questions about the timing and extent of a recovery remained.

Momentous Changes

TRW's steady performance through the recession of the early 1980s earned it many admirers in the American business community. In 1982, *The Wall Street Transcript* named Mettler best chief executive in the category of "Auto Parts/Diversified Original Equipment," and quoted many tributes. One analyst, for example, noted that "the record of the company over the past dozen or so years is just very superior. . . . It's just been good management of assets and very efficient utilization of both financial and human resources. I don't think anybody can touch TRW's management." Mettler also made the cover of *Business Week* and, as elected chairman of the Business Roundtable, became a national spokesman on issues of industrial competitiveness. The crowning achievement was an extraordinarily flattering profile of the company in *Forbes* under the title "A Paragon Called TRW." The editors set up the article by describing the company as "unapologetically conglomerate, unashamedly asset-managed, aggressively multinational as well," before asking, "How unfashionable, and how well managed, can a company possibly get?"[36]

Although appreciative of—and a bit embarrassed by—such acclaim, TRW executives wondered how much longer the company could sustain its performance. To some, the Vidar episode and other problems in commercial electronics appeared to expose serious weaknesses in planning and management systems and to call into question TRW's ability to transfer military technology to commercial markets. Others remained concerned with the more general issue of the company's diverse and decentralized operations.

In 1982, for example, Pace asked Gorman to draft a memorandum on TRW's staffing and organization. The result echoed themes Gorman had stressed for years and included a withering criticism of the status quo. In a section entitled "Observations on Some Troublesome Trends in the Company," for example, he identified a dozen "syndromes" that afflicted TRW. These included the "more is better" syndrome, in which the company tended to attack problems by hiring more people; the "counterpart at every level" syndrome that caused staffs to multiply at every level; the "review upon review" syndrome that created layers of superficial reviews and paralyzed decision making; the "failure to establish or understand priorities" syndrome that impeded focus on critical issues; and the "form (or process) over substance" syndrome that bred mediocrity. In sum, Gorman called for a comprehensive review of TRW's staffing policies to identify functions that needed to be performed and make appropriate decisions regarding how and by whom they should be performed. Clearly, he believed that TRW's staffs had become too big, and decision making too dispersed and diffused.[37]

Internal concerns also reflected turbulent times. TRW's leaders were well aware of changes sweeping across the American economy. Hostile takeovers, leveraged buyouts, and huge mergers and acquisitions were in the air. During the decade, 37 percent of companies on the *Fortune* 500 list disappeared or reorganized in ways that rendered them unrecognizable. Stretching back to 1970, 60 percent of companies on the *Fortune* 500 list experienced a similar fate. Big companies such as Gulf Oil, Beatrice, Bendix, Hughes Aircraft, and RCA disappeared in a climate characterized by a bull market, cheap debt, and the virtual collapse of antitrust enforcement. Voluntary asset restructurings were also commonplace among highly diversified companies such as Litton Industries, Textron, and United Technologies. In such an environment, TRW had to calculate, constantly, its breakup value. After all, other parties, including investment bankers, were surely doing the same.[38]

Another increasingly important consideration was TRW's ability to fund the future it sought. To develop or acquire expertise to become a major factor in automotive electronics, occupant restraint systems, and information systems and services would be expensive and consume more capital than the company normally allocated to just a few businesses. If TRW were to take these risks, it would have to change its priorities and the way it managed itself.

These issues provided the backdrop for another transition in the chief executive office. In February 1984, TRW's board announced a new management succession plan that named Gorman, forty-seven, assistant president. The announcement indicated that he would succeed Pace as president on January 1, 1985, when the latter was expected to become vice chairman. In light of TRW's traditions, the announcement of Gorman's election also signaled that he would in all likelihood become chairman after Mettler's scheduled retirement in 1988. In 1985, for reasons unrelated to these changes, Pace moved to General Dynamics as chairman and CEO. He was not replaced in the chief executive office at TRW.

Gorman's election reflected the sense of Mettler, Pace, and the board that the company needed a new strategist to chart the waters ahead. At the Industrial & Energy sector, Gorman had demonstrated a probing intellect and the capacity to master the details of many disparate operations. Throughout his career, he had also displayed a penchant for hard work: "time on task is important," became a favorite saying. All of these qualities were required in his new assignment, which empowered Gorman to pursue plans to reorganize the company and overhaul its management systems. The needs, he believed, were urgent. At a management conference in Scottsdale in the fall of 1984, he reviewed the company's recent performance relative to a group of "investment peers"—similar big, diversified corporations. TRW sought to hold a position in the middle of the top third of this group, but during recent years had fallen back into the pack. Extrapolating from the stock price, he calculated that investors anticipated that the company would earn real returns significantly below the corporate forecast of more than 10 percent. The corporate forecast went on to predict that by 1989 sales would grow at a compound annual growth rate of 14 percent, assets at 10 percent, and profits at "a 'whopping' 21 percent," with most of the growth occurring in the last two years of the forecast—the classic "hockey stick" projection of future gains trending up sharply after an interim period of flat performance.

Gorman argued that TRW's only hope of reaching these "highly optimistic" goals depended on its willingness to undertake radical change, especially in the area of "systematic, urgent, and substantial cost reduction." He also urged the company to place greater stress on "strategic management," and he outlined five tests by which the chief executive office would evaluate future plans. First, TRW must have a sound basis for choosing to compete in given markets; second, the company must develop and consider alternative strategies and from among them select the one likely to produce the greatest value; third, strategies and action plans must display "sufficient clarity"; fourth, TRW must possess adequate organizational capability to implement the strategies; and finally, all management actions must be driven by or linked to the chosen strategies.[39]

Gorman worked with Mettler and Pace to develop new criteria for TRW's plans. He also revamped the company's management systems, streamlining reporting requirements to emphasize clear and concise communications and tying routine activities such as forecasting, capital budgeting and spending, management information systems, and compensation and reward systems to new strategic objectives. He instituted a companywide "cost effectiveness plan" that subsumed the corporate initiatives of the early 1980s and challenged management at each level to set priorities for spending and examined all management systems, structures, and practices. Finally, he commissioned a series of strategic management seminars, multiday offsite training sessions for division managers across the company to highlight the company's new approach to its business.[40]

As he had done in the Industrial & Energy sector, Gorman urged general managers to evaluate their businesses in terms of market attractiveness and relative market position, consider options and alternatives, and finally select the strategy of highest value. This course, he suggested, could entail "major change in direction, including significant scaling-back or restructuring."

This was prophetic advice, for major changes at TRW were in the offing. In 1984, corporate analysis showed that 59 percent of TRW's assets fell in units that would not meet the company's financial objectives in five years. At the same time, it was clear that the company would fall far short of reaching its goals for the 1980s. Of the targets set in 1979—5 percent real growth in earnings and assets, return on equity of over 20 percent, debt leverage in the range between 25 and 35 percent with a single "A" bond rating, and a targeted dividend payment between 30 and 40 percent—the company was able to meet only its dividend payment objectives. Finally, the company's sales mix had shifted dramatically since 1980, and its various businesses faced sharply different outlooks. The most promising of all—automotive occupant restraint systems—had just received an immense boost from a new U.S. federal regulation that required automakers to provide "automatic occupant protection" or "passive restraint systems" in all models by 1990. For TRW to seize this opportunity would require hundreds of millions of dollars and possibly more than $1 billion in capital investment. This total dwarfed any comparable investments in TRW's history and could be afforded only with a drastic reordering of corporate priorities.[41]

With these issues in mind, in September 1985—just two months after moving into its new headquarters facility—TRW announced a major restructuring. As outlined by Mettler, the restructuring included four steps: an increase in the company's bank lines from $750 million to $1.5 billion; a plan to divest the Industrial Products and Aircraft Components Groups and some units of the Electronic Components Group, representing combined annual sales of about $700 million; the establishment of a $170 million reserve related to the restructuring—also the source of the company's first annual loss in fifty years; and a plan to buy back between 5 million and 8 million shares of common stock in a Dutch Auction Tender Offer (a technique that uses sealed bids to set the lowest price at which a transaction may occur). The buyback offer expired on October 15, when the company announced the purchase of 7.7 million shares—about one-fifth of all shares outstanding—for a total of about $625 million.[42]

Dick Campbell, who had succeeded Gorman as head of the Industrial & Energy sector, took charge of dismantling his organization. He retained several investment bankers and put his properties on the block. Most of them sold within eighteen months. During the next several years, the continuing struggles of many of the commercial electronics businesses led TRW to divest many divisions in the Electronic Components Group and fold others back into the defense operations. At the same time, the continued slump of oil prices rendered TRW's energy businesses less attractive, and they too went on the block (see Appendix).[43]

Looking back on the restructuring from a distance of a half-dozen years and the perspective in the interim as chairman and CEO of General Dynamics, Stan Pace saw a certain inevitability to the changes:

> I must say that the business had become so diverse that the top management of the company was not in a position to work in detail on specific problems. Let me contrast TRW with General Dynamics, which is a $10 billion company with 15 major programs. With only fifteen major programs I could really know a great deal about each of them and make inputs on them. At TRW, when I left [just before the restructuring] I had eighty-five divisions, and multiple products in each of those divisions.
>
> . . . There was no effective way for a president to look after all of those unless there was a raging inferno of some sort. . . . So there is a question when does diversification become too broad for truly effective management? I don't know the answer to the question, but I think there is a diminishing effectiveness with size and diversification."[44]

The restructuring marked a watershed in TRW's history, as the company abandoned the decentralized management policies that Thompson Products had instituted in the immediate postwar era and ceased depending on the diversity of its businesses to carry it forward through good times and bad. New challenges called for new approaches and new solutions. With the pain of restructuring behind it, TRW looked forward to competing in a more focused and disciplined manner in markets where it held leading positions and possessed deep understanding. The company recognized obstacles ahead, but believed it could now more easily avoid them. It also saw big opportunities and believed it could now more easily pursue them.

Chapter 14

Refocus and Renewal

▶   ▶   ▶

1986–1996

Rube Mettler and Joe Gorman designed the restructuring of 1985 to prepare TRW for an era of renewed growth in its core automotive and space and defense businesses. At the same time, they expected to pursue exciting new opportunities in automotive safety systems and information systems and services—the umbrella name given to credit reporting and related businesses.

As this strategy took shape, however, TRW once again confronted a host of difficult challenges. While the company poured investment capital into the growth businesses of the future, it also was forced to cope with yet another deep worldwide recession. At the same time, the structure of global politics underwent a shift of seismic proportions. Eastern Europe broke free of Soviet domination. The Berlin Wall tumbled and the two Germanys reunited. The Soviet Union collapsed and shattered into a dozen new pieces. Around the world, centrally planned economies gave way to fledgling market-based economies. The assumptions under which the United States invested so heavily in defense technology for nearly four decades suddenly became obsolete. Although TRW's livelihood depended on the research and development part of the defense budget—as opposed to big hardware programs—the new world order had far-reaching implications for every defense contractor.

In 1988, when Gorman succeeded Mettler as chairman in another of TRW's orderly transitions at the top, TRW was about to face a string of dark years as it poured investment capital into its most promising new businesses while simultaneously adapting to the sea change in world politics and the restructuring of the U.S. aerospace industry. In 1991, the company restructured for the second time in six years to rid itself of marginal contributors (including, eventually, the information systems and services unit), refocus on its best performers, and improve operations.

In the mid-1990s, however, TRW's perseverance finally paid big dividends. The company's rewards for rebalancing its portfolio, investing more than $1 billion to become a world leader in air bags, and consolidating and diversifying its aerospace operations began flowing in. Between 1994 and 1996, TRW notched the best financial performance in its history, with record sales and earnings based on positions of strength in all of its core operations.

Rebalancing Act

In the aftermath of the 1985–1986 restructuring, TRW refocused on its core businesses and new prospects for resuming growth. And there it faced a host of challenges. One of the biggest had a familiar look about it: just as in the late 1950s, the company had become uncomfortably reliant on the defense business, which accounted for nearly 60 percent of corporate sales. As also happened back then, the company had to contend with major changes in the U.S. defense market, albeit of a quantum difference in scale. Although federal spending on defense remained at a high level in 1985, aerospace industry leaders knew that it couldn't last much longer. Signs of change were already evident in policies of glasnost and perestroika that were warming relations between the superpowers, as well as in increasing concern in the United States about the size of the federal deficit. The key questions in the industry were how far and how fast defense spending would drop.

In such circumstances TRW aggressively sought to rebalance its portfolio. That meant that leaders in the company's aerospace operations once again began to pursue opportunities outside of traditional military and national security customers. Even more, it meant that TRW's corporate management was eager to improve and expand its automotive businesses and to explore building the information systems and services into a sizable independent operation.

A Fading Boom

In the mid-1980s, Rube Mettler and Joe Gorman were acutely aware of the need to reduce TRW's dependence on the U.S. defense budget. They recognized that the boom in defense spending would soon fade, but they believed the company would be shielded from the worst effects. They expected that defense R&D spending would escape the biggest budgetary cuts and that the sheer diversity of TRW's activities—in any given year, it performed work on more than twenty-five hundred contracts ranging from bench-scale studies to massive programs like the Milstar payload—would help buy time to rebalance its portfolio of businesses.

Accordingly, under George Solomon and his successor in 1987, Ed Dunford, TRW's Space & Defense sector (so named when Dunford took over) continued to build on its foundation in software and analysis, avionics, electronic warfare, high-energy lasers, microelectronics, and space technologies. In addition to Milstar, the company's most visible defense programs during the second half of the 1980s included a new $743 million contract to build another round of Defense Support Program satellites (TRW attributed this win to a bold bid to deliver five satellites for the price of four); the Army's Worldwide Military Command and Control Information System and Forward Area Air Defense System Command and Control; the Navy's Ocean Surveillance Information System; ongoing development of high-energy lasers as antimissile weapon systems; and many tactical electronic warfare programs. And of course, the company still participated in classified programs whose nature and scale have not been disclosed.

TRW also made significant progress in the multibillion-dollar very-high-speed integrated circuit (VHSIC) program, including insertions of Phase 1 technology into military programs and research and development on Phase 2. In 1988, a team consisting of TRW, Honeywell, Hittite, and General Dynamics won a $57 million award to develop gallium arsenide microwave/millimeter wave monolithic integrated circuits. The program, known as MIMIC, was designed to achieve "the same dramatic advances in sensor systems" as VHSIC achieved in signal processing. The new gallium arsenide chips were expected to be significantly lighter and faster than traditional silicon-based integrated circuits. They were expected to find applications in advanced electronic systems, especially in contexts where portability was important—the electronic battlefield, for example. Some experts believed that the new chips would also find uses in wireless communications systems including, eventually, cellular telephony.[1]

TRW won several major NASA awards during the late 1980s, while work continued on the Gamma Ray Observatory and the TDRS satellites. Both programs were delayed, however, in the aftermath of the space shuttle *Challenger* disaster in January 1986. (When it blew up, *Challenger* was carrying the second TDRS satellite.) Later that year, NASA chose TRW as prime contractor to build the first Orbital Maneuvering Vehicle, a kind of space tug designed to ferry payloads from the space shuttle's low-earth orbit to higher altitudes. The initial contract was valued at $214 million. In 1988, TRW won an $800 million competition to become prime contractor for the Advanced X-Ray Astrophysics Facility, the third of NASA's four Great Observatories.[2]

For all of these achievements and contract wins, however, Dunford was well aware of the sensitivity of TRW's business to the federal spending on defense and space. In an era of shrinking resources, competition was bound to heat up. And in fact TRW lost bids that it might well have won in earlier times, including the ultra-high-frequency communications satellite system to replace FLTSATCOM and key subsystems for NASA's space station. At the same time, other programs encountered difficulties and did not lead to renewals. In 1984, for example, TRW had won a five-year development contract worth $107 million for the payload on NASA's Advanced Communications Technology Satellite (ACTS). Working as a subcontractor to RCA, TRW met the technical specifications for the payload but ran over budget. That caused RCA to pull the contract in-house—one more frustration in TRW's attempts to penetrate the market for commercial comsats.

In addition to grappling with structural change in its space and defense markets during the 1980s, TRW had to deal with another unpleasant matter: the discovery of improper and in some cases criminal behavior in four different defense-related operations in separate incidents between 1984 and 1986. Although the company eventually emerged from these episodes chastened and more careful, they helped trigger changes in federal contracting procedures that subjected suppliers to more paperwork and increased public oversight.

The company's first and most serious problem became apparent after an internal audit at the Compressor Components Division—part of the old aircraft engine components business, for which TRW was still legally responsible despite its divestiture—revealed that several finance managers had certified inaccurate cost data and had overcharged the government for certain activities over a six-year period. Several months later, another internal audit uncovered problems at an electronic systems plant in Colorado, including mischarging contract labor costs to overhead accounts. Still later, TRW found similar improprieties at two more electronics divisions. The latter three incidents reflected problems and confusions in contracting procedures rather than criminal behavior, but each case led to overcharging the government.[3]

As soon as he learned of the problems in the aircraft engine components business, Mettler mobilized an investigation that resulted in the firing of the individuals involved. Once the facts were in, he flew to Washington, D.C., to meet personally with senior officials in the U.S. Department of Defense and disclose the problem. This proved to be the first of many voluntary disclosures in the U.S. defense industry that involved virtually all major contractors. These incidents prompted congressional investigations and prepared the way for legislation to establish new contracting rules and guidelines. TRW also immediately disclosed the other incidents as soon as it verified them and fired the general managers of the units involved. In September 1987, the company settled all four cases with the government, paying $17 million in restitution. The following August, the company settled criminal charges stemming from the Compressor Components Division case by pleading guilty to three counts of conspiracy to defraud the government and paying criminal fines and penalties of $3 million.[4]

The impact of these incidents on TRW hurt far worse than on the bottom line. The company's reputation was tarnished, and as the first defense contractor to come forward with a voluntary disclosure, it drew particularly intense scrutiny from the government and national media. Mettler, who had long prided the company on good corporate citizenship, was visibly distraught. In the aftermath, TRW redoubled efforts to promote ethical behavior and improved awareness and understanding of contracting procedures among employees. "We embarked upon an extremely ambitious communications and educational training program," says Bill Lawrence, then a company lawyer who worked on all four cases, adding that TRW also changed reporting relationships, modified its internal controls, beefed up its audit staff, established advisory review boards and committees, and opened an 800-number hot line for employees to report any improprieties. In 1989, the company drew some solace when an independent government review found no evidence of additional problems and acknowledged the company's improved reporting and contracting procedures.[5]

Such incidents, combined with the cancellation and downsizing of government programs and escalating price competition, portended a harsh environment for government contractors in space and defense. In response, Dunford undertook the unhappy task of thinning the ranks and streamlining operations at Space Park. And for the first time since it had pursued energy systems research during the 1970s, TRW began to consider seriously diversification outside of its traditional space and defense markets. Given the fate of its earlier ventures in civil systems, the company approached this subject with some trepidation. In 1986, the first step was to establish a new unit, eventually named TRW Systems Integration Group, which was housed in a new 45-acre complex near Washington, D.C. The unit took oversight of the company's existing systems engineering projects for the U.S. military, including decades-old assignments for the Air Force and Navy. At the same time, it began to explore potential business with the Federal Aviation Administration and the U.S. Departments of Energy, the Interior, and the Treasury.[6]

Determined to avoid earlier misadventures, Dunford also commissioned a review of TRW's initiatives in civil systems during the 1960s and 1970s. The study reached few definite conclusions, noting that the company had achieved the best results when entering commercial markets through acquisition rather than through start-ups and when these ventures had been led by experienced commercial managers rather than by aerospace engineers. Any new civil systems programs would play to TRW's traditional strengths in managing "nationally important and technically challenging problems."[7]

Automotive Renaissance

In the decade following the restructuring, TRW bet its long-term future on its oldest business, automotive supply. It faced several big challenges: to make its existing operations more focused and competitive; to develop a new, highly risky and highly promising business in automotive safety products; and to increase penetration of the new industry leaders, the Japanese automakers. TRW rose successfully to all three challenges. Along the way, it took advantage of the increasing concentration of the automotive supply industry and the growing willingness of automakers to share the risks and rewards of design and development with their most capable, first-tier suppliers.[8]

In the mid-1980s, Gorman believed that TRW needed to take strong actions to improve the competitiveness of its automotive businesses. As he reviewed the portfolio of automotive operations, he saw weaknesses similar to those he had encountered in the old Industrial & Energy sector: a set of businesses that were highly diverse, serving a wide variety of customers, and facing much different prospects. The steering and new occupant restraints businesses were poised on the threshold of rapid growth. The engine valve business appeared mired in a prolonged period of stagnation. The aftermarket operations had slowed down because of high costs, the growing number of Asian vehicles in the used-car park, and structural changes in distribution channels that shifted power away from parts makers to big retailers such as Pep Boys and Autozone. And the fasteners and controls unit operated as a miniconglomerate, overseeing a varied mix of rising (electronic) and declining (mechanical and electromechanical) businesses.

Early in 1987, Mettler appointed Gorman to take over leadership of the Automotive Sector for an indefinite period while the search was under way for a new general manager from the outside. During this period TRW experienced considerable turnover among general management personnel in the automotive units—"certainly over 50 percent," Gorman later acknowledged. Change continued with increased emphasis on programs to improve cost and quality and to prune marginal product lines and operations. The company sold off its Ramsey division, the piston ring manufacturer that Thompson Products had acquired in 1950, as well as the heavy-duty suspension business. TRW also took a hard look at its aftermarket operations to evaluate the investments needed to restore competitiveness against alternative uses of capital.[9]

In the remaining automotive businesses, TRW addressed a host of changes and concerns. In engine components, for example, the company suddenly rediscovered new opportunities for growth. Some new engine designs called for four valves per cylinder, a trend that portended a pronounced surge in volume. At the same time, lower gasoline prices helped revive the market for six- and even eight-cylinder engines. The quest for ever higher performance and lighter weight also provided openings for suppliers with the expertise and capability to take advantage of them. TRW stepped up its research on new alloys and materials. To gain insight into emerging technologies, TRW entered joint ventures to study making valves and other engine parts from advanced materials such as ceramics and powdered metals. Partly offsetting these opportunities, however, were new problems. With its fortunes tied closely to General Motors, which endured heavy losses and ceded market share in North America during much of the decade, TRW was bound to suffer, too. At the same time, the company's old crosstown rival, Eaton Corporation, capitalized on two modern valve plants in low-cost areas to gain a temporary cost advantage in the North American market.[10]

In the steering business, TRW addressed the challenge to manage the continuing transition to power rack-and-pinion steering systems in North America and to prepare for a similar rapid conversion in Europe during the early 1990s. Although European drivers had long preferred manual steering systems, the advantages of the latest generation of power rack-and-pinion systems were coming to the fore—as evidenced by adoption rates above 90 percent in North America and Asia. These advantages included improved feel, less cost and weight, and superior compatibility with new front-wheel-drive power trains. To meet the anticipated demand, TRW invested nearly $500 million to build new plants in the United States, Germany, France, Italy, and Spain and to expand capacity in England and Brazil. The company expected these investments to raise its worldwide market share in steering systems from about 20 percent to more than 30 percent by 1995.[11]

TRW also spoke openly about plans to develop electronically controlled, electrically assisted steering systems as a future replacement for power rack-and-pinion systems. The new technology came in a multitude of configurations, including hybrids with hydraulic systems, but the basic approach involved using electronic sensors in the steering gear to gauge position and resistance. This information was relayed to a control computer, which in turn controlled an electric motor to assist turning when appropriate. The new technology opened up a multitude of possibilities, since it was lighter, smaller, simpler, and more efficient than hydraulic systems and was said to provide superior responsiveness and feel. The electronic sensors and controls, moreover, could be linked easily to other control systems in the vehicle such as active suspensions.[12]

In the mid-1980s, TRW had raised hopes for electrical and electronic steering systems and announced that they would be available as an option before the end of the decade. After Gorman took charge of the automotive businesses, however, he pushed back the time horizon so that management would concentrate on the rapid scale up of the power rack-and-pinion business. At the same time, TRW shifted the focus of development of the new technology from a replacement for conventional systems to an enhancement of them. In particular, the company targeted the market for lightweight vehicles such as those popular in Europe and Asia. These vehicles did not ordinarily feature power steering systems but could use electrically assisted systems to help realize fuel savings and while also easing parallel parking.

TRW's drive to supply modules and systems, rather than parts and components, to its customers reflected major changes under way in the world auto industry. Many experts noted that the success of Japanese automakers depended partly on close interdependencies with their major first-tier suppliers. A supplier such as Nippondenso, for example, participated in design and development work and furnished complete subsystems to Toyota. Both parties benefited: Toyota shared its development costs and risks with Nippondenso, which in turn shared in the rewards. Such a relationship offered powerful competitive advantages such as lower transaction costs, compatible incentives, and other factors. The Japanese automakers that set up assembly operations in North America expected to replicate the supply system that worked so well in Japan. To TRW's senior management, it seemed inevitable that similar relationships would have to flourish between automakers and key suppliers in North America and Europe. And TRW intended to be a first-tier systems supplier to its customers.[13]

TRW's best opportunity to test this premise arose in one of its younger businesses: automotive occupant restraint systems. In July 1984, at a moment almost exactly coincident with the company's acquisition of Firestone's seat belt business, U.S. Secretary of Transportation Elizabeth Hanford Dole announced a highly significant new automotive safety regulation. Known as Federal Motor Vehicle Safety Standard (FMVSS) No. 208, the ruling mandated use of "automatic occupant protection" or "passive restraint systems" in passenger cars to protect the driver and a front-seat passenger in the event of a 30 mile-per-hour barrier (head-on) crash. The new standard did not specify any particular technology to meet this requirement and allowed the automakers to phase in systems of their choice over a three-year period starting with the 1987 model year. The regulation carried teeth: starting in the 1990 model year, no new car could be sold in the United States without a passive restraint on the driver's side; by the 1993 model year, passive restraints would have to appear also on the passenger's side. The regulation was later amended to delay compliance for the passenger's side of vehicles until the 1995 model year and also extended to cover minivans and light trucks.[14]

FMVSS-208 opened an enormous opportunity for independent suppliers because few auto companies had internal capabilities to produce passive restraints. The alternative approaches were automatic shoulder belts, which relied on electric motors to wrap a seat belt around a driver or passenger after entering a vehicle and closing the door, and air bag systems, which were less obtrusive to consumers but raised more complex technical problems, especially on the passenger's side. Several leading automakers and suppliers had experimented with air bags during the 1970s, for example, and most had lost a fortune. In the early 1980s, only Talley Industries continued to produce driver's side air bags, supplying a handful of units to General Motors and Ford, which offered them as an option on some luxury models. Part of the resistance to air bag systems reflected high cost: Talley's systems, for example, were priced at about $800 each. There were also many unanswered questions about the reliability of air bag systems, the feasibility of manufacturing them in volume, and consumer acceptance.[15]

When FMVSS 208 was enacted, TRW was well equipped by virtue of Repa's growth and the Hamill (Firestone) acquisition to supply active and passive seat belt systems. The company had essentially no capability to produce air bag systems, however. Then again, very few companies did. During the next several years, Chuck Miller led a determined effort to leap to the front in what promised to be an extremely expensive but potentially highly rewarding race. Miller pursued a systems approach, building on TRW's existing capabilities at Repa and the operations acquired from Firestone, where it already possessed research and testing facilities and considerable expertise in crash dynamics. At the same time, TRW drew selectively on its aerospace scientists and engineers for insights into systems engineering, electronic sensing and diagnostic devices, and pyrotechnics and propellants. To gain further advantage, TRW licensed key patents held by Eaton, which had abandoned air bag development during the 1970s after posting $20 million in losses.[16]

During 1986 and 1987, TRW moved rapidly to augment its growing capabilities in safety systems. In October 1986 the company paid $13.2 million for an 85 percent stake in Technar, Inc., a California-based supplier of electromechanical sensors for air bag restraint systems. Although a small company, Technar had development and production contracts with many leading automotive manufacturers, including the Big Three, Honda, Mitsubishi, BMW, Porsche, Saab, and "even Rolls Royce," and it was poised on the verge of skyrocketing growth. Also in 1986, TRW negotiated a joint venture with C-I-L (subsequently Imperial Chemical Industries, the global chemicals giant) called Sabag, Inc. to manufacture gas generant for passenger's side air bags at a facility near Montreal. The Technar acquisition and the Sabag deal made TRW the only supplier with capabilities in all key technologies of air bag systems.[17]

From there the company pushed forward aggressively. In April 1987, TRW achieved an American auto industry breakthrough by persuading Ford to allow it to design and supply virtually all of the automaker's occupant restraint requirements in North America. The arrangement took the form of a joint venture company based on TRW's assets and Ford's commitment to purchase its output. To help secure this deal, TRW itself arranged a sole source contract with Talley for driver's side air bag modules. At the same time, TRW negotiated to supply most of Chrysler's and about one-third of GM's requirements. During the summer, Gorman established a separate occupant restraint systems unit that reported directly to the chief executive office and named Miller as general manager.[18]

The next step was to scale up to satisfy the enormous demand for air bag systems beginning to materialize. In 1988, Miller projected that the worldwide market for occupant restraints would double in five years to hit $4.4 billion, and he estimated that

TRW would get about one-third of this total. To help realize these projections, in 1989 TRW paid approximately $100 million to acquire Talley's air bag business, including its manufacturing facility in Mesa, Arizona. The deal included an unusual arrangement whereby Talley would collect royalties for a dozen years on every air bag TRW sold anywhere in the world, as well as for any air bag sold in North America regardless of source. This arrangement pushed the estimated cost of the deal to about $200 million.[19]

An added, intended benefit of the enormous sums TRW poured into its steering and occupant restraints businesses was enhancement of the company's ability to penetrate the leading Japanese automakers, especially those unaffiliated with American partners. By virtue of Ford's relationship with Mazda, GM's with Isuzu, and Chrysler's with Mitsubishi, TRW supplied some parts and components to these Japanese companies. Earlier investments in Fuji Valve and Tokai Cold Forming, moreover, enabled TRW to supply some parts and components to Nissan and Mazda. But it had much weaker relationships with two of the most powerful producers, Toyota and Honda. This was a source of increasing concern as both companies announced plans to build assembly plants in the United States. Accordingly, Gorman made it a top priority to increase investments in Asian facilities and joint ventures and form alliances and joint ventures with Japanese manufacturers that set up operations in the United States (see Table 14-1). The company pushed ahead in all of its product lines, but enjoyed particular

TABLE 14 - 1
TRW INC. SELECTED AUTOMOTIVE INVESTMENTS AND JOINT VENTURES, 1985–1989

YEAR	NAME	DESCRIPTION
1985	TRW Steering Co., Ltd.	Joint venture with Kia Machine Tool Ltd., subsidiary of Kia Industrial Co., Korean maker of steering systems.
	AAE-TRW Components SDN.BHD	Share of 27 percent in ASEAN industrial joint venture to sell ball joints and steering linkages. Increased to majority ownership in 1989.
1986	Quality Safety Systems Co. (TRW Canada and Tokai Rika)	Production of seat belts in Windsor, Ontario.
	Fuji Serena	Additional investment.
	Direcciones y Suspensiones Automotrices S.A. de C.V. (DIRECSA)	Mexican venture to make manual rack-and-pinion steering gears for Japanese-designed automobiles made in Mexico.
	Tokai TRW & Co., Ltd.	Additional investment.
1987	TRW-Fuji Valve, Inc.	Engine valves for Japanese transplants. Plant in Sevierville, Tennessee.
	Wu Chou Valve Industrial Co.	Additional investment.
1988	TRW-Koyo Steering Systems Co.	Joint venture with Koyo Seiko to manufacture rack-and-pinion steering gears. Facility in Vonore, Tennessee.
1989	TRW-Toyoda Machine Works	Manufacture power steering pumps for Toyota U.S.A.

success in steering systems and occupant restraints, where it capitalized on technological leadership and modern facilities. TRW also targeted Toyota and Honda for special emphasis.[20]

In 1986, TRW scored a breakthrough by joining with Tokai Rika, a supplier in the Toyota family, to build and operate a seat belt plant in Canada to serve Toyota's North American operations, as well as a joint Mazda-Ford facility in Michigan. TRW held a 60 percent interest in the joint venture, called Quality Safety Systems Company, which invested $2.8 million in a new facility in Windsor, Ontario. Early in 1988, TRW followed up by renewing ties to Koyo Seiko, a particularly powerful member of the Toyota family and a former partner for a brief period in the early 1970s. The new joint venture, TRW-Koyo Steering Systems Co., operated a plant in Tennessee to manufacture rack-and-pinion steering gears for Toyota and other Asian automakers with assembly operations in North America. Finally, TRW's investments to serve the Japanese transplants included two additional facilities in Tennessee: a new valve plant jointly owned and operated with its Japanese equity partner, Fuji Valve Co., Ltd., and a joint-venture operation shared with Toyoda Machine Works to produce power steering pumps and hoses.[21]

These investments and ventures paved the way for TRW to gain virtually all of the North American requirements for steering and occupant restraint systems of the Japanese automakers. They also helped the company slowly increase its market position in Japan.

The Vicissitudes of Information Systems and Services

During the late 1980s, TRW's automotive businesses in general, and occupant restraints in particular, accounted for the company's biggest opportunities by far. Mettler also remained committed to another burgeoning business, information systems, which he predicted would reach $1 billion in sales by the end of the decade. He anticipated that much of this growth would be generated internally, but also acknowledged that a significant portion would come from acquisitions. In Dick Whilden, general manager of the Information Systems Group, TRW had its most active acquirer since the heydays of Sid Webb, Fred Hesse, and Bob Burgin fifteen years before.

With strong support from the chief executive office, Whilden embarked on an ambitious growth strategy that included expanding existing operations and opening new and related areas. He continued the slow and piecemeal process of acquiring local credit bureaus and computer equipment maintenance and repair businesses. He also expanded the Customer Service Division's line by acquiring a series of small companies that specialized in repair and service of medical equipment such as X-ray machines, CAT scanners, and similar products.

Whilden's plans for growing the consumer credit reporting business included developing additional services for the retail banks and credit-card companies that bought and supplied basic credit data, as well as a novel attempt to cultivate the consumer market. By the mid-1980s, TRW's consumer credit data base had swelled to enormous proportions, with credit profiles of 140 million individuals. Whilden was eager to find ways to leverage that resource. Federal law placed strict limits on the use of credit information, but TRW's database included some information not subject to such controls—name and address, for example—as well as data gleaned from public sources such as tax records and court documents that could be used for any lawful purpose. In 1985, TRW launched a target marketing service that supplied mailing lists to customers such as banks looking to identify likely prospects whom they might approach with credit-card offers. The lists were compiled in a new and separate database that could be cross-checked with the credit database to verify names and addresses. TRW's ability to model the data in many different ways also promised to add value to the business.[22]

Another start-up launched in 1986, a new consumer service called TRW Credentials, almost immediately revealed limits to any attempt to leverage the company's database of credit information. The concept was to sell individuals access to their credit histories plus additional "personal information" convenience services. In the original California test market, for example, TRW charged consumers an annual $30 fee for an unlimited number of credit reports, timely notification of inquiries into their credit history, the convenience of maintaining on file a "universal loan application" for use whenever the consumer sought credit at a bank or store, and a registry of credit cards in case any should be lost or stolen. Later, TRW added a change-of-address notification service, and Whilden also talked of creating a centralized file of personal information that would help consumers to manage such tasks as financial and estate planning. In addition to the fee income, the benefit to TRW was additional and valuable information to support its target marketing business, as well as potential new customers from among market research firms and direct-mail merchandising companies.

The troubles with TRW Credentials, however, included wary regulators, a skeptical business press, and an apathetic public. Under federal law, many consumers could obtain their credit histories for free if they had been denied credit within the past thirty days, or for a modest charge any time that they wanted it. "I'm astounded that there are people out there who want to pay for this," observed one Federal Trade Commission staffer responsible for policing the credit reporting industry. Reporters marveled at TRW's "chutzpah" and "nerve to sell consumers something they can get for free." *Forbes* derided the "marketing aces" who dreamed up the service, in which "customers will pay $35 a year, first for a service they could get for less elsewhere and in some cases for free; and second, for the privilege of giving the company information that is so valuable that it can be resold at a profit. That's creative marketing for you."

Although generally greeted with skepticism bordering on cynicism, TRW ran a second test of the credentials service in New York in 1987, and two years later claimed 650,000 customers. The fine print, however, noted that this total included spouses—indication of a lukewarm consumer response.[23]

Whilden also sought new market niches similar to consumer credit reporting where no big competitors dominated and where TRW's expertise in systems engineering, software, and database management would confer competitive advantage. The unit's long-term goal was to become "a broad-based information supplier, particularly in the financial services marketplace." During 1985, TRW moved into new segments of this marketplace by acquiring two small companies that supplied "a comprehensive package of services to the home equity lending industry," including "nearly all the information and documentation necessary to create a new loan." Customers included banks, savings and loan institutions, and consumer finance and financial services companies. TRW projected a rosy future—a 35 percent compound annual growth rate and 12 percent pretax profit by 1987.[24]

These purchases sparked a furious buying spree of small companies specializing in information and services for the real estate industry. Between 1985 and 1989, TRW completed more than thirty acquisitions in selected markets such as California, Florida, Arizona, and Missouri. The new partners added title, property, and tax information, as well as appraisal and closing services. Whilden sorted these businesses into two new divisions: Real Estate Information Services, which maintained a database that could be accessed in various ways, with information modeled to match specific customer needs; and Real Estate Loan Services, which combined information in the database with mortgage credit reports, appraisals, title insurance, and loan documentation—a one-stop shop for real estate lenders.[25]

TRW also branched out in other new areas. In 1986, for example, the Information Systems Group established a new Technology Systems Division to transfer technology from the company's aerospace operations to information systems markets. The technology transfer involved both hardware and software and included networking systems and a security algorithm to thwart unlawful entry into TRW's files on consumer credit. Another new venture arrived via acquisition in 1986, when TRW paid about $200 million for Teknekron Financial Systems, Inc. This unit, which was renamed TRW Financial Services, produced systems based on proprietary cameras and software to scan hard copy records at very high speeds and convert them into digital form. Banks, credit-card companies, financial services companies, and other high volume processors of paper used the systems to scan transaction slips, checks, and similar records for storage, retrieval, and manipulation. The systems made it possible, for example, for users to provide clear and legible copies of transactions to consumers without sorting and keeping track of millions of pieces of paper.[26]

Whilden's next move was a blockbuster acquisition, the biggest in TRW's history. In the spring of 1988, TRW agreed in principle to acquire Chilton Corporation, a Dallas-based subsidiary of Borg-Warner, for considerations worth about $330 million. Roughly the same size as TRW in consumer credit reporting, Chilton became available after Borg-Warner restructured under a leveraged buyout and announced plans to sell off several businesses to reduce the acquisition debt. When Whilden learned that Borg-Warner was talking with Equifax, another big competitor in consumer credit reporting, he launched a preemptive strike, within a week negotiating a deal to acquire Chilton.[27]

On the face of it, the deal made a lot of sense for TRW beyond its value in preempting a competitor. By combining two of the industry's biggest rivals, TRW could break ahead of the pack to become by far the biggest supplier of consumer credit information in the country. Second, although both TRW and Chilton maintained full national files on consumers from the major national lenders, at the local level they offered complementary coverage. TRW's local files were more complete on the two coasts, with significant gaps in the center of the United States. Chilton's strengths were apparently just the reverse.

Unfortunately, the U.S. Department of Justice prevented TRW from closing the deal quickly and cleanly and finally approved it under terms that offset its principal advantages. In many locations where both TRW and Chilton had operations, for example, the Justice Department ruled that files could not be combined and that one or the other local bureau would have to be sold to a competitor. Meeting these requirements took almost a year, during which Equifax merged with another competitor to rival the scale and scope of services TRW provided.[28]

Whilden's acquisitions, including Chilton, helped TRW's information systems and services business grow rapidly. Revenues soared from $270.8 million in 1984 to $705 million five years later. The latter number proved to be a peak, however, and profitability problems curtailed top management's appetite for additional expansion. The problems surfaced in various ways, including-higher-than anticipated costs associated with integrating acquisitions and the technical incompatibility of systems and information in many of the acquired units.

Other difficulties arose in the Customer Service Division. Many of the division's acquisitions in the 1980s consisted of "salvage" operations in which TRW assumed service responsibility for manufacturers that wanted to abandon service contracts for older, obsolete equipment or had even gone into bankruptcy. At first, like the Singer deal that started TRW in the customer service business (see Chapter 12), the arrangements were extremely profitable, as the parties abandoning service obligations paid handsomely for TRW to take over the business. By the late 1980s, however, salvage deals became much harder to find, and TRW was forced to buy additional business, often taking on big inventories in the process. In 1988, TRW's operating profit in information systems and services plunged from $68.4 million to $22.6 million, a performance attributable mostly to the crisis in the Customer Service Division.[29]

DOING THINGS DIFFERENTLY

In December 1988, Mettler reached TRW's mandatory retirement age of sixty-five and stepped down as chairman and CEO. During his two decades in the chief executive office he presided over enormous changes in the company, including its rapid expansion and painful restructuring. TRW's long-standing faith in diversification, which emphasized different parts of the business at different times and enabled the corporation as a whole to ride through cycles and recessions, guided many of these changes. As Mettler had put it in 1983, two years before the restructuring, "We should grow the high-return parts of our business by allocating more resources to them. At the same time we should make hard decisions about units with poor histories, poor trends, poor market positions." He went on to add, "We don't think of TRW as a static sort of business. We have to adapt and change."[30]

Adapt and change TRW did under Mettler. He led the company in many new directions and at the end of his tenure pushed it into new areas such as occupant restraint systems and information systems that he believed would secure its future. He also did not shrink from making tough choices, such as the decisions to restructure and pick a successor, Joe Gorman, who would surely pursue new and different ways of leading the company. "I think Joe was picked because in Rube's mind he had the best strategic vision of where TRW ought to go," reflected Howard Knicely, the head of the company's human resource function. "I believe Rube recognized that Joe would not be wedded to how the company had operated in the past and that we needed a fresh take on the future."[31]

Atop the corporation, Gorman maintained the strategic course set after the restructuring. He departed from TRW conventions, however, by continuing to hold for an indefinite period the combined responsibilities of chairman and CEO and president and chief operating officer. For the first time since the early tenure of Fred Crawford, TRW had all of its leadership authority invested in a single individual. Although reluctant to continue this arrangement for long, Gorman wanted time to groom candidates for the number-two job and weigh alternatives. He also sought to signal to the operating managers that "we're going to do things differently . . . and I'm going to be close enough and understand enough [about the business units] to know whether things are getting done."[32]

Gorman introduced many changes to TRW's governing structure and policies. Under Shepard and Mettler, the chief executive office had separated operating reviews from policy discussions. The president and the sector and group heads met periodically to review performance, while the senior operating and corporate staff executives met four to six times a year with members of the chief executive office as the policy group to consider more general matters. Gorman combined the two types of meetings into one, creating a new management committee that consisted of both operating and staff executives as "an extension of the chief executive office." The committee met about ten times a year to consider all key issues facing the company. He also enlarged the jobs of four corporate staff officers by combining functions and promoting them to the same rank as the senior operating managers—executive vice president—to minimize turf battles and status differentials based on traditional line and staff distinctions. The four new EVPs assumed responsibility for law; finance and investor relations; human resources, communications, and information resources (management information systems, or MIS); and planning, technology, and government affairs.[33]

Shortly before assuming the top office, Gorman assembled the company's senior executives for a two-and-a-half-day off-site meeting. There was no specific agenda; rather he wanted the participants to "candidly discuss their concerns and priorities." The discussions soon began to overlap and converge on the need for a new and unifying statement of purpose to guide the company in the years ahead. The group toiled many hours over a crisp, one-page statement of mission and values in draft form that was later circulated to hundreds of employees across the company for discussion and comment. A graceful writer—and, some would say, compulsive editor—himself, Gorman labored over draft after draft. Finally, in May 1989, TRW's statement of mission and values was ready. It boiled down TRW's mission to three sentences and offered a pointed contrast to the prolix objectives and ambitious and specific financial targets in *TRW and the 80s.* As such, the document also proved emblematic of Gorman's approach to leading the company. He wanted shorter reporting channels, less formality, less detailed (but still rigorous) analysis, less paper.[34]

RESTRUCTURING, PART TWO

The transition at the top of TRW occurred at a difficult time for all of its major businesses. The booming stock market of the mid-1980s performed a spectacular nose dive in October 1987. Although the indexes quickly recovered, the crash foreshadowed a prolonged period of unsettled markets and a deep and sustained worldwide recession in the early 1990s. TRW's automotive businesses suffered particularly, with problems compounded by huge investments to establish the air bag business and expand capacity in power rack-and-pinion steering systems.

Ramping up a steep growth curve, TRW's occupant restraints business suffered predictable and costly growing pains. By the end of 1990, TRW had invested about $500 million to acquire its leadership position in air bags, and sales surpassed $1 billion; still, crossover into profitability remained several years out. More big investments, including an expansion of the erstwhile Talley facility in Arizona, a second and much bigger plant nearby to make both air bag modules and gas generant, and a new module facility in Tennessee, were in the offing, bringing the total to nearly $1 billion at risk.

In March 1990, TRW suffered a serious setback when a fire shut down Sabag, Inc.'s Canadian gas generant facility. Restoring the facility took nearly a year, causing extensive delays in shipments to the automakers. In addition, quality problems at the Talley facility in Arizona led Ford in the fall of 1990 to recall 165,000 vehicles because of potentially faulty air bags that TRW had produced. This incident sparked litigation between TRW and Talley and temporarily strained relations between TRW and Ford. In March 1991, the two companies agreed to restructure their deal, with Ford reducing its commitment to purchase all of its occupant restraint requirements in North America from TRW and arranging to buy up to 20 percent from other sources.[35]

At the same time, the astonishing collapse of the Soviet empire and eventually the Soviet Union itself ushered in a new era in U.S. defense spending, while concerns about the national deficit led to additional spending cutbacks across the board. The "peace dividend" produced a major restructuring of the U.S. aerospace industry. Although a few opportunistic companies such as Loral Corporation initially found ways to grow via acquisition, a far more common response was retrenchment. Longtime participants such as Ford, General Electric, and Emerson Electric abandoned the business. Other leading competitors such as Grumman and Northrop, Lockheed and Martin Marietta, Boeing and McDonnell-Douglas, and Raytheon and Hughes Electronics resorted to blockbuster mergers in the pursuit of scale and efficiency.

Facing an environment characterized by cancellations, stretch-outs, scaled-back programs, and fierce cost competition, TRW certainly felt the pain. In 1990, NASA abruptly canceled the Orbital Maneuvering Vehicle program. Although the Gamma Ray Observatory functioned smoothly after its April 1991 launch, managers at Space Park voiced concern that the Advanced X-Ray Astrophysics Facility program would be downsized—and ultimately, it was. Other spacecraft customers also canceled orders, including a $100 million design contract for a major element of the Strategic Defense Initiative and some classified business. Total employment in Space and Defense plunged from about thirty thousand in 1988 to about twenty-four thousand in 1991, and TRW closed several small operations, including an avionics facility in San Luis Obispo.[36]

The information systems and services operations also continued to suffer due to slumping sales during the recession, poor operating performance in the maintenance business, and much higher than anticipated costs associated with the integration of Chilton and other acquisitions into the company. Late in 1989, Gorman installed Van Skilling as the new general manager of IS&S. Skilling acted swiftly to improve the business mix and reduce costs. He sold off the medical equipment maintenance and repair business and announced plans to sell the rest of the service operation. He also put the real estate loan services business on the block, consolidated eight operating units into five, and cut the group's headquarters staff from eighty-six to twenty-six.[37]

Amid these changes, TRW found itself in the center of a firestorm of bad publicity and litigation resulting from actual and alleged quality problems in the company's consumer credit database. The company received an embarrassing black eye when a part-time contractor that it had retained mistakenly identified fourteen hundred citizens of Norwich, Vermont—virtually every adult in the community—as bad credit risks. Working through public records, the contractor misconstrued a list of taxpayers as a list of tax delinquents. The episode played out in nightmarish fashion for Norwich citizens, who suddenly found their credit cards worthless, loans impossible to obtain, and their credit histories stained. Although TRW soon cleared up the matter, considerable damage was done. The company faced lawsuits in fourteen states, while both it and the credit reporting industry generally absorbed a barrage of criticism.[38]

TRW recovered from the Norwich gaffe by making changes in management, strategy, and operations, and after waging expensive legal fights and a public relations campaign to rehabilitate its reputation. The company abandoned the credentials service and agreed to furnish one free credit report per year to any customer who asked. It also redesigned the format and language of the reports to make them accessible to nonspecialists. It took a leading position in the industry in favor of legislation to protect consumer interests. And it invested more than $30 million during a three-year period to upgrade its software and records. The new Copernicus System designed to come onstream in the mid-1990s, for example, used very advanced hardware and software to manage and update continuously a database with a capacity of *four trillion* pieces of information. Despite these measures, TRW continued to walk a tightrope between competing consumer interests in privacy and speedy credit checks. Privately,

TRW's leaders determined to sell off the remaining information systems and services business as soon as the unit could be restored to health.[39]

To help contain costs and improve operations across the corporation, TRW mounted a major effort to overhaul its operations, adopting total quality management (TQM) techniques that stressed continuous process improvement, reduced bureaucracy, and increased employee involvement throughout all operations. Gorman also initiated several management changes. When Skilling took over IS&S, for example, Bill Lawrence succeeded him as head of corporate planning, technology, and government affairs. Not long after, Gorman installed Peter Hellman, a recent star recruit from BP America, as executive vice president and chief financial officer.

In September 1990, after consulting with the management committee, Gorman abolished the sector layer of management in the automotive businesses and began a gradual reorganization that left three separate businesses reporting directly to corporate headquarters: Occupant Restraints & Controls, Steering & Suspension, and Engine Components. The following April, the board of directors elected Ed Dunford as president and chief operating officer. After an interim period, Gorman and Dunford liquidated the sector layer of management in Space & Defense, and they eventually reorganized operations into two separate groups: Space & Electronics, based in Space Park, and Systems Integration Group based near Washington, D.C.[40]

At the end of 1991, TRW announced its second restructuring plan in a half-dozen years. The plan included the divestitures of businesses worth $400 million to $500 million, a $100 million cut in capital spending—about 16 percent of the total—and layoffs of twenty-five hundred employees. TRW also took a $250 million after-tax charge during the fourth quarter, which led to a loss for the year of approximately $150 million, much of which traced to problems in the information systems and services unit. The operations publicly earmarked for divestiture included units already up for sale, as well as a receivables management business that had been part of Chilton, the automotive aftermarket business, and several other marginal units (see Appendix).[41]

Payoff

During 1992, the restructuring began to take effect, although TRW reported a second consecutive annual loss of $156 million on sales of $8.3 billion. These results reflected a one-time charge associated with an accounting change, as well as the lingering effects of the restructuring. Behind the scenes, however, encouraging signs were already apparent: excluding the accounting charge, operating profit for the year hit $194 million, and excluding the restructuring charge, it reached $547 million. From there, the company's momentum began to accumulate: by 1994, the company reported record totals in sales and profits, the beginning of a string of strong results that continued through 1996.

These results reflected significant progress in improving the company's cost position and operating performance in every area of the corporation, as well as the happy effects of the crossover of the air bag business into profitability. TRW produced its first air bag systems for the driver's side in 1991; five years later, it delivered more than 13 million units for both driver's and passenger's sides. The company expected this volume to rise unabated through the early years of the twenty-first century. It also forecast rapid growth for new related technologies such as side-impact air bags and smart occupant restraint systems.[42]

In the mid-1990s, TRW responded to the continuing globalization of the automotive industry by spawning operations and joint ventures throughout the developing world. Between 1993 and 1996 it moved into seven new countries, including China, the Czech Republic, Poland, India, Thailand, and Turkey. As a result, the company's leaders believe that TRW can not only tap vast new markets, but also remain in position to serve vehicle manufacturers in any area of the planet.

Meanwhile, TRW made headway in several problem areas. Although the defense operations lost more jobs and sales continued to dip, operating margins held steady and productivity soared. TRW scored several notable wins, including the avionics package to integrate communications, navigation, and identification systems for a new Air Force advanced tactical fighter, and a similar program for the RAH-66 Comanche helicopter; the Short-Range Unmanned Aerial Vehicle; and continuing work on the MIMIC program and Strategic Defense Initiative programs such as the Alpha high-energy laser (tested successfully in April 1989 and demonstrated to the public two years later), the Brilliant Eyes space-based early warning system, and the Brilliant Pebbles space-based missile defense system.[43]

TRW Space & Defense also continued the quest for business outside of its traditional markets. In contrast to the diversification efforts of the civil systems era (see Chapters 10 and 11), the approach this time was judicious: new programs played to TRW's traditional strengths in managing large-scale, complex problems and appeared to provide a foundation on which it could continue to build. Between 1987 and 1996, the company's share of sales to military agencies dropped from 92 percent to about 65 percent of the total Space & Defense portfolio. Some of the new business was with government or quasi-public customers outside the military: a contract potentially worth $1 billion over ten years to support the Department of Energy to help manage the problem of nuclear waste disposal; a $138 million contract from the Federal Aviation Administration to assist in improving the nation's air traffic control systems; a contract worth potentially $450 million to manage the U.S. Treasury Department's nonvoice communications systems (on top of an older $300 million deal to help modernize the computer systems at the Internal Revenue Service); a $180 million contract to engineer an "intelligent transportation system" to handle the massive influx of visitors to the 1996 Olympic Games in Atlanta; and a $243 million contract to integrate the information technology requirements of the Centers for Disease Control.

TRW also sought new commercial customers for aerospace technology. For example, the company pushed development of small, inexpensive satellites for research and communications purposes in both domestic and foreign markets. TRW also adapted other defense technologies such as lasers and high-performance communications hardware for commercial applications and reengineered equipment developed in military avionics for ground-based transportation systems.[44]

The outcome of the company's most ambitious attempt at technology transfer would not be known for several years. In alliance with Canada's Teleglobe, Inc., and other partners, TRW sought to raise more than $2 billion to engineer a space-based global communications network called Odyssey. The system would rely on a network of a dozen satellites in medium earth orbit to provide wireless communications services to customers virtually anywhere on the planet—an elegant and theoretically more cost effective alternative to satellite networks being built by competitors. TRW obtained key patents on the Odyssey system architecture and, if enough capital is raised, the company will fabricate the satellites, electronic payloads, and ground stations and will engineer the integration of the entire system.[45]

During the early 1990s, TRW also saw encouraging signs that several other long-standing problems were coming to favorable resolution. First, its work on occupant restraint systems finally propelled the company into the front ranks of the automotive electronics market. TRW added to the business by acquiring several small companies that made promising products such as keyless entry systems and remote convenience systems. In 1993, Gorman noted that TRW's combined automotive electronics operations, including the traditional business in controls, was approaching $1 billion in sales. The following year, TRW grouped these operations into a new automotive electronics organization.[46]

The company also approached the problem of transferring technology from aerospace to commercial markets in a novel manner. Gorman and Dunford established the Center for Automotive Technology (CAT) at Space Park under Peter Staudhammer, a storied veteran of such programs as the Lunar Excursion Module Descent Engine and the Viking biological instrument package, as well as many classified projects. Staudhammer set up CAT with corporate funding to provide support to automotive projects already in progress or on the drawing board. In contrast to past technology transfer efforts, CAT did not seek to invent new products or systems and push them on its customers; rather it focused on meeting the specific requirements of TRW's automotive project engineers.

In the past, the incentives for California-based aerospace scientists and engineers to apply themselves to automobiles were never sufficiently compelling: the technical challenges appeared unenthralling, the economics of mass production unappealing, and job assignments in the Midwest unattractive. In view of the downturn in space and defense markets, however, many Space Park engineers eagerly participated in CAT projects. The unit's staff was small, and it operated with a total annual budget of about $3 million, not including contributions from the divisions on specific projects. CAT personnel participated in work long under development, such as side-impact restraint systems, and wholly new products such as collision-avoidance systems that used advanced sensors and diagnostics based on radar systems that will anticipate and help avoid crashes. Other projects in development included "intelligent" cruise control to automatically adjust speeds and maintain proper spacing between vehicles on highways; "smart" struts that employed the piezoceramic wafers used to help dampen vibration in spacecraft; new shock absorbers using electro-rheological magnetic fluids to yield dramatic improvements in the smoothness of ride; electronic lane-change aids to compensate for the blind spots not covered by rearview mirrors; and advanced keyless entry systems that remember the preferences of individual drivers and automatically adjust seat position and angle, mirror angles, climate control, and radio station. In the mid-1990s, Staudhammer was promoted to corporate vice president for science and technology, while CAT remained a productive contributor to TRW's automotive operations.[47]

The company's strong performance in the mid-1990s provided the backdrop to another set of changes to the company's chief executive office. In 1994, Dunford chose to take early retirement and return to California at the end of the year. To succeed him, the board elected Peter Hellman, who, as chief financial officer, had been one of the architects of the second restructuring. Although Gorman would not reach the company's mandatory retirement age until 2002, most observers expected that Hellman would be his eventual successor.

Meanwhile, in 1996, the second restructuring culminated in its final act: the sale of the information systems and services unit to a buyout group for considerations worth approximately $1 billion. The business had resumed growing in a controlled fashion but it was no longer deemed central to TRW's strategy. "Bear in mind," said Gorman, "the consumer credit side of that business represented only four percent of our total sales. Good or bad it gave us a third of our headaches." The chairman added that gains in automotive and the rebound in space and defense meant that TRW simply no longer needed a third line of business, especially when it could earn better returns in its core operations.[48]

Given the company's global leadership position and geographical balance, the future looked rosy indeed. As Gorman put it, "TRW is positioned for sustainable, significant increases in both sales and earnings. In this regard, we have taken major steps toward becoming a truly superior-performing company." He also noted "a sense of renewed pride within the company" as well as the emergence of "more and more admirers outside the company" who "see us fulfilling our expectations and doing what we said we would do."[49]

Chapter 15

Epilogue: The Next Era

▶   ▶   ▶

THIS BOOK HAS BEEN DIVIDED INTO THREE PARTS: THE STORY OF TRW AND ITS PREDECESSORS as a supplier to the automotive industry before World War II, as a defense contractor between 1939 and the mid-1960s, and as a diversified corporation during the past three decades.

If there were to be a fourth part of this book, it would begin in the mid-1990s. The divestiture of TRW's information systems and services unit signaled another major transition in the company's evolution. It had traveled full circle from the expansive era of diversification into a new era in which the core businesses in automotive (still including fasteners, the original business of Cleveland Cap Screw) and space and defense were expected to provide attractive and profitable opportunities for growth and renewal.

The key strategic question facing TRW's leaders in this new phase of its history is how the company will build on its existing capabilities and prosper in the twenty-first century. At the end of a long book, it seems appropriate to invite these leaders to comment on the challenges ahead. In 1997, Joe Gorman and Peter Hellman accepted the invitation, pausing to reflect on TRW's prospects in light of its history. Gorman sounded a cautionary note, however, paraphrasing Mark Twain: "It's a good idea to look ahead," he says, "but not farther than the eye can see."[1]

LESSONS OF EXPERIENCE

A word that comes up frequently in conversation with Gorman and Hellman is "focus." As they reflect on TRW's modern history, they believe that during the period of expansion and diversification the company lost its focus. Says Gorman:

> As happened to many companies in the late 1960s and early 1970s, we got caught up in merger mania. We acquired a bunch of businesses, many of them unrelated. In my view, many of these deals were not very well thought out from a long-term, strategic-positioning point of view. At the time, they apparently made sense financially. You'll recall that if you had a pooling of interest and you did a stock-for-stock deal, in general TRW's multiple was higher than the company acquired, and therefore there was a flow through in earnings per share. That was the game.

> The problem was that many of the businesses we acquired were not leaders in their industries. Many were facing, or about to face, very strong and aggressive foreign competition. Some had no chance of survival as part of TRW or of any other conglomerate, for that matter. Their only hope was to become part of a broader, global, highly focused business.

> Take Marlin-Rockwell, the bearing business that we were in. It was facing stiff Japanese and European competition. It was relatively isolated in terms of applications and product niches. In my view that business was doomed unless it was acquired by a global bearing company that had sufficient critical mass to support R&D and invest capital in new processes and improved distribution. TRW couldn't afford to keep it going given all our other investment needs. That's why we sold it. And that's why we divested many other businesses.

Although TRW's diversity enabled it to ride out several recessions in the 1970s and early 1980s, when some financial analysts believed the company performed "relatively well" under the circumstances, Gorman considered this performance unacceptable. "We weren't earning the cost of capital year in and year out," he maintains. "That's not performing relatively well. Generally 75 percent of our businesses were earning, at any given point in time, above the cost of capital. The other 25 percent were dragging down the overall margins." As a result, he points out, "if you're diverse enough to ride out the downward part of the cycles, you don't take full advantage of the up cycles either. What it amounted to in our case was averaging down."

In sum, Gorman concedes that TRW may have done "a better job of diversification than many of the conglomerates of the day":

> But our performance was mostly aimed at smoothing out financial results rather than building upon the strategic position of the company and the businesses that we acquired. In some of these businesses, we did not manage well: we had no domain knowledge, or we weren't the best at process manufacturing, or we didn't do enough R&D or do it well enough.

Gorman also believes that TRW's management systems hindered its performance during the diversified era:

You can succeed as a conglomerate, but you've got to manage very differently than we did. You have to have managers who know the business. Their compensation must be tied totally to the success of that particular business in that marketplace. We did just the opposite. Everybody's compensation was tied to the performance of the company as a whole. At the same time, a big component of management compensation was highly subjective. It didn't vary much year to year, and it was not dependent upon success.

In hindsight, our general management systems were flawed. We did forecasting quarterly, for example. We always had the hockey stick forecast—the hockey stick going up in terms of profits; the hockey stick going down in terms of assets required to produce those profits. Of course, both projections were almost always wrong. Growth took more assets than we predicted and produced less return on the investment. In addition, our strategic planning was fundamentally a joke. Every year we would have a climactic meeting around the plans and then the binders we produced would be put back on the shelf until the next year. Another problem was that our short-term operating plans bore little resemblance often to the long-term strategic plan.

Gorman sums up by returning to the concept of focus, a preoccupation since he accepted his first general management assignment in 1979. In that job and later in the chief executive office, he stresses, his sense was of a need to focus:

> We needed to understand our key businesses far better than we had previously. To make significant progress, we had to change our culture, way of thinking, general management systems and compensation schemes.

> We began that painful, difficult process in the first restructuring of the 1980s. At the time, I didn't think it was going to be as painful or difficult as it proved to be. We had to change out a lot of managers. We had to get rid of a number of businesses. We had to cause our people to think differently. We've been on that path for a number of years now.

Although Hellman did not rise to the top of TRW until after most of these changes had occurred, he agrees that the company lacked focus during most of the 1980s. And that, to him, was the point of both restructurings: the first one involved "sorting through of the key industries we wanted to be in"; the premise of the second was, "within those industries, which businesses were most strategic to us. That's what left us, at least for now, in two industries: the aerospace industry and the automotive industry."

In Search of the Next Air Bag

Like most big companies in the mid-1990s, TRW emerged from a decade of restructuring, downsizing, and streamlining with an emphasis on renewed growth. In recent speeches, Gorman spelled out ambitious goals for the next seven years: doubling the company's revenues and market capitalization while maintaining a premium price-earnings ratio in the vicinity of twenty. To achieve such goals, he acknowledges, "we've got to find another major engine for growth—the next air bag investment, if you will."

One area already targeted is telecommunications. Despite historical frustrations, both Gorman and Hellman remain convinced that TRW will at last become a major player in this mammoth industry. "We've been a leader in defense communications for a long time," says Hellman:

> Because of our streamlining and downsizing in the past decade, we can take advantage of this technology as it moves into the commercial sector. We're no longer a high-cost producer. Besides, the traditional differences between defense and commercial technologies are beginning to blur as the military worries more about cost-effective solutions than pushing the state of the art. That can only help us in the commercial sector.

Hellman also notes that other TRW businesses contribute to its expanding position in telecommunications. In 1996, for example, the company began commercial production of gallium arsenide chips, a key technology in wireless communications, a business projected to explode in the coming decade. In addition, several of TRW's big contract wins in civil systems—the $425 million program for the U.S. Treasury, for example—are essentially projects in telecommunications.

Whether telecommunications should become "the next air bag" or replace the divested credit reporting unit as a third leg of the corporation, both Gorman and Hellman project that TRW's core businesses will continue to generate rapid and profitable growth.

The Future of Automotive

"I have no doubt," Gorman says, "that we will be able to grow our automotive businesses fairly dramatically, on a regular basis, both organically and by acquisition." This faith reflects the strong global positions attained by most of the company's operations and continuing high expectations for performance. As he puts it, "We set—and are meeting—key strategic goals for global leadership in each of the automotive businesses in terms of market share, technology, and value, which is the combination of quality and price. We have also diversified our geographical position and customer base so that we are not overly dependent on any one region or customer."

Underscoring the point, Gorman emphasizes that TRW is bigger in most of its businesses than any of its customers. Citing 1996 figures, for example, Gorman notes that General Motors, the biggest vehicle manufacturer, has a worldwide market share of about 20 percent, and it is followed by Ford, Toyota, and Volkswagen at shares of 12, 10, and 6 percent, respectively. In contrast, TRW and its affiliates accounted for about half of the worldwide market for engine valves, more than a third of the market for occupant restraints, and more than a quarter of the market for power steering gears. The scale of TRW's global operations, argues Gorman, is significant for several reasons. First, it helps shield the company from swings in the fortunes of any of its customers. Second, it translates into cost advantages that no competitor can match. And third, it helps to minimize the threat that any of its customers will integrate backward to manufacture products that TRW makes.

Looking ahead, Gorman and Hellman project that TRW will continue to expand the occupant restraints and steering systems businesses at a rapid clip. During the next ten years, for example, business in side-impact air bags and smart occupant-restraint systems (in which air bags will deploy in customized ways, depending on the dynamics of a crash, the configuration of the seating area, and the size and location of passengers) is expected to mushroom. At the same time, orders are at last pouring in for electrically assisted steering systems, based on their ability to improve fuel efficiency and aid parallel parking in small vehicles, such as those popular in the huge markets of Asia, Europe, and the developing world.

TRW is also exploring ways to extend and expand its existing businesses, perhaps even linking them together. The 1996 acquisition of the steering wheel and air bag cover business of Izumi Corporation positions TRW to offer modular steering wheel packages including air bags. At the other end of the steering column, the company already makes key components, so it could soon conceivably supply a complete steering and air bag assembly as a single package.

Early in 1997, TRW acquired two European operations of Magna International, a leading supplier of parts and components of automotive interiors, suggesting another avenue of growth. The transaction included an agreement to cosponsor research and development activity. The deal prompted Gorman to ask, "Do we think of ourselves as being in the occupant restraint business or in the passenger safety business?" If the latter, then TRW (in partnership or on its own) could accelerate development of smart protective interiors, collision avoidance systems, and other new products.

To Hellman, prospects in automotive were all the more appealing because TRW is one of a handful of industrial competitors "on the verge of becoming a global company." By that, Hellman means being able "to operate without the barriers or impediments that boundaries cause . . . where the definition of countries is lost, where there is no flagpole, where your management is a global team and your products are produced globally and supplied to global customers."[2] He explains:

> Globalization requires a total reexamination of the way we do things, driving it toward standardization. When our customers are making the same vehicle around the world, they want the same part made the same way. We don't necessarily do that yet. Right now our German designs might be different than our Chinese designs that might be different than our Brazilian designs. But if we're supporting Volkswagen in China, Brazil, and Germany, and they want the same gear made the same way, we've got to get our designs and processes the same.

Hellman argues that globalization in this sense will yield significant benefits for TRW. For one thing, he notes, the company's geographical balance will help to moderate the auto industry's periodic ups and downs:

> Due to cyclicality, volume in any particular region might vary twenty-five percent from boom to bust. The period between cycles averages about seven years. But worldwide vehicle production is not nearly as volatile, and that's because as one economy or region is in expansion, another is in recession, and they offset each other. If we can use these offsetting cycles to our advantage, then we'll be a much stronger competitor.

In the last recovery in North America, for example, we downsized our work force. As we expanded, we were paying overtime to make ball joints. At the same time we were going into recession in Spain, and we were laying off Spaniards who make ball joints. That doesn't make any sense. We were also paying the Spaniards two years' severance pay. Why can't Spaniards make ball joints for North America? If you do that, you can stabilize the work flow. When you talk to employees, stability of employment is their number-one priority. They hate lay-offs, and they also find long stretches of overtime to be oppressive. If we can create stability of employment, we will become a more attractive employer.

Globalization also means that we will need less plant, because we don't need to hold peak capacity in reserve in each part of the world. Instead, we can manage ourselves more like a public utility where we're managing a load, and paying some transportation costs.

New Frontiers in Space and Defense

In 1995, TRW finally arrested the decade-long decline of its space and defense businesses by increasing its market share in traditional lines and diversifying aggressively into civil systems. Although the company's automotive businesses dominate the corporate portfolio, Gorman and Hellman believe that it will not take long for the space and defense businesses to swing back into balance.

In support, they tick off a list of recent developments and contract wins that suggest burgeoning growth: the promising business in gallium arsenide chips, the high-energy laser programs, NASA's Advanced X-Ray Astrophysics Facility and Earth Observation System satellites, and new ventures in the civil systems area. By emphasizing capabilities in engineering and integrating complex systems, the company is attracting a growing volume of business with civilian government agencies in the United States and elsewhere. Gorman estimates that TRW's civil systems sales, presently in the $1 billion range, could triple and may even grow faster in the next five years.

TRW's leaders also continue to assert that the company will not only be shielded from future cuts in the U.S. defense budget, but also resume growth in this area. Gorman cites national security estimates that during the next twenty years, perhaps twelve to fifteen nations that do not presently have ICBM capability will acquire it. For the United States, that threat will probably translate into increased demand for TRW's electronic reconnaissance and surveillance systems and antimissile weapon systems such as high-energy lasers. At the same time, the coming of the "electronic battlefield" should also benefit TRW, which is involved not only in the key technologies of reconnaissance and communications, but also in systems integration, simulations, and training.[3]

GLOBAL REACH, LOCAL TOUCH

In pursuing growth, TRW's leaders do not intend to expand the company's lean organization structure or increase the degree of decentralization. Another lesson of experience is an aversion to adding layers of management or tolerating too much decentralization. If current plans are followed, the management of growth in the late 1990s and the early years of the next century will scarcely resemble patterns from TRW's past.

As chief operating officer, Hellman makes it a priority to produce growth without causing attendant expansion of overhead. That requires what he calls a "seamless management process" that minimizes internal friction, enhances cooperation (as, for example, the Center for Automotive Technology does), and takes advantage of the company's global scale and scope. "We used to manage TRW with a great number of fairly autonomous business units," Hellman says.

> In automotive we may have maintained thirty or forty plants or groups of plants, and they managed themselves with their own overheads. They were like separate business units. That was fine as we grew out and expanded both our product lines and our geographical presence. But now that we're in those markets, we need to integrate these units much better. As we become more global, we have to put more windows in the walls and communicate. I use an example of buying steel. We buy about $700 million of steel a year. In the old days, each of our thirty or forty units would place a separate order. We now coordinate all of that.

> By the way, when we were growing out geographically, our approach typically was to acquire strong companies in foreign markets and retain local management. Sometimes we even allowed local management to retain partial ownership of the business. We wanted these people to run their "own" company in the way they believed best—not necessarily in the way TRW would have run it. We got exactly the behavior we wanted.

> Now we want a balance between "global reach and local touch," to borrow a phrase from Joe Gorman. The idea is to get the best of both worlds. We don't want to be fully centralized because we need to be close to our market and close to our customers, but we want to get the leverage of a very large, global company. That's the balancing act and our new management tenet.

Hellman acknowledges that managing the company in this way requires special sensitivity to TRW values and traditions. "The very notions of centralization and standardization are anathema to a proud engineering culture such as we have here. That's why we talk about the need to 'commonize' activities."

Gorman credits modifications of TRW's executive compensation system for driving stronger performance and a new way of managing:

> One of the most helpful tools in engineering change is the compensation schemes that we created, both short term and long term. Sixty percent of our compensation is based on the company's financial performance. The measures are similar to those in place in many other companies. But the other forty percent, which obviously is a big factor, is tied to specific objectives of the job in question. These are very clearly linked to customer satisfaction, quality, market share, and other appropriate priorities. The point is that the compensation scheme both rewards performance and helps reinforce superior strategic positioning. As a result, it has accounted as much as any other factor for our success.

Finally, in looking forward, Hellman emphasizes not only changes, but also continuities with TRW's past. The 1995 annual report attempted to distill the company's mission in few words: "performance and growth through people and technology."[4] Between the 1958 merger of Thompson Products and Ramo-Wooldridge and about 1985, the company had pursued growth avidly. Then, during the decade of restructurings, TRW's focus shifted to performance. And then in the mid-1990s, the pendulum swung back once more. "That's why we emphasized performance and growth," says Hellman.

> The words "through people and technology" came about because the company had always emphasized both, going back to Fred Crawford and Si Ramo. But in more recent times, we were talking so much about performance and downsizing that we placed too little emphasis on people. If we're going to double the size of the company through organic, internally generated growth, then we need to expand the breadth and depth and diversity of our people.

> I think that the real breakthrough in the company's history, the real way in which TRW was ahead of its time, was understanding the power of its people. That probably is the company's fundamental long-term contribution and value. Yes, we produce really good products, and we're very innovative. We pioneer new technology. But it's the people that develop the technology, and it's the people who produce the high value products. Who knows what we'll be doing as a company a hundred years from now, but I hope and imagine TRW will consist of highly motivated, productive, talented people, doing whatever it is the company is doing, serving the markets of the twenty-second century.

For his part, Gorman also seeks to reassure employees, investors, and the interested public that TRW has established a secure foundation on which to grow:

> We really believe we've learned how to manage a large global company in current times and for the foreseeable future. I believe that we can continue to grow and grow profitably. We can continue to create value for the shareholder, and we will. We know how to do that now. We've accomplished a series of strategic moves that make sense. We have an extremely strong balance sheet. In fact, it may be underutilized in terms of our financial capability, potential strength. We will create our future in a proactive way, not just in an opportunistic way. We're working hard to bring that about.

APPENDIX: TRW INC.—PRINCIPAL ACQUISITIONS AND MERGERS, JOINT VENTURES, AND DIVESTITURES, 1959–1996

YEAR	ACQUISITION	JOINT VENTURES	DIVESTITURES	DESCRIPTION
1959	Bel Canto Stereophonic Recordings			Educational recordings
	Magna Products Corporation			Chemical products; power generation
	Magnetic Recording Industries, Ltd.			Consumer electronics
	Radio Industries, Inc.			Electronic components
		Productos Thompson de Mexico		Automotive aftermarket (Mexico)
		Thompson-Cofab-Companhia Fabricadora		Automotive aftermarket (Brazil)
1960	Good-All Electric Manufacturing Co.			Electronic components
	Radio Condenser Co.			Electronic components
			Aerospace Corporation	Systems engineering, long-range planning for U.S. Air Force
		Anillos Ramco S.A. de C.V.		Automotive aftermarket (Mexico)
		Auto Partes Mexicanes S.A.		Automotive aftermarket (Mexico)
		Compagnie Européene D'Automatisme Electronique		Factory automation (France)

SOURCE: TRW Inc., board minutes, annual reports, and press releases, 1959–1996.

NOTES: 1. Table does not include small asset purchases or dispositions.

2. In many joint ventures and foreign investments, TRW's changed over time. The dates in this table refer to the initial investment only.

3. Table does not account for consolidations and liquidations unless otherwise noted.

4. Table does not include the acquisitions and subsequent divestitures of more than thirty small companies specializing in information services for the real estate lending industry. These deals occurred in the late 1980s and early 1990s (see Chapter 14).

YEAR	ACQUISITION	JOINT VENTURES	DIVESTITURES	DESCRIPTION
		Productos Thompson Argentina S.A.		Automotive aftermarket
		Thompson Ramco Argentina S.A.		Automotive aftermarket (piston rings)
1961	Milam Electric Manufacturing Co.			Electronic components
	Teves-Thompson & Co. GmbH			Engine valves (Germany)
		Ayrola Radio (Mexico)		Electronic components
		International Systems Control Ltd.		Factory automation
1962	Fuji Valve, Ltd. (minority)			Engine valves (Japan)
	Société Mécanique de Pringy			Automotive aftermarket (France)
		Elementos Electronicos Mexicanos, S.A.		Electronic components
		Mitsubishi-TRW Co., Ltd.		Electronic components
1963			Dage Division	Commercial electronics
			Mitsubishi-TRW Co., Ltd.	Electronic components
1964	Marlin-Rockwell Corporation			Bearings
	Ross Gear and Tool Co., Inc.			Steering components (heavy duty)
	Industrias Gemmer do Brasil S.A.			Steering components
		Bunker-Ramo Corporation		Computers
			Columbus Division	Consumer electronics
			Microwave Division	Commercial electronics
			TRW Rectifiers	Electronic components

YEAR	ACQUISITION	JOINT VENTURES	DIVESTITURES	DESCRIPTION
1965	Cam Gears, Ltd.			Steering components (United Kingdom)
	Steerings Pty., Ltd.			Steering components (Australia)
		MATREL S.A.		Aerospace (France)
		Thompson Ramco South Africa (Pty.) Ltd.		Automotive aftermarket (South Africa)
		TRW-Hawker-Siddeley		Aerospace (United Kingdom)
1966	Clifford Motor Components			Steering components (United Kingdom)
	Engineering Productions, Ltd.			Steering components
	Scientific Electronic Products, Inc.			Electronic components
	United Transformer Corporation			Electronic components
		TRW Electronic Components		Electronic components (Taiwan)
1967	Globe Industries			Electronic components
	Hazleton Laboratories, Inc.			Biomedical testing
	Mission Manufacturing Co.			Energy products
	Noblesville Casting			Metals foundry
	Société Usinages des Vosges			Engine components (France)
	United-Carr Incorporated			Diversified manufacturer of fasteners and controls
		Mitsubishi-TRW		Aerospace (Japan)
		TRW-Saab		Aerospace (Sweden)
			Bunker-Ramo Corporation	Computers

YEAR	ACQUISITION	JOINT VENTURES	DIVESTITURES	DESCRIPTION
			Electro-Insulation Division (Milam Electric Manufacturing Co.)	Electronic components
			Structures Division	Aerospace
1968	Bayerisches Leichtmetallwerk KG			Metals foundry (Germany)
	Credit Data Corporation			Consumer credit reporting
	Duly & Hansford, Ltd.			Automotive components (Australia)
	Hobson Brothers, Inc.			Industrial machinery and equipment
	International Resistance Company			Electronic components
	Reda Pump			Energy products
	Rhoden Manufacturing Company			Industrial equipment
	United-Greenfield Corporation			Diversified manufacturer of tools and equipment
		HYSTL (TRW-Commonwealth Oil Refining Co.)		Polymers
			Magna Products Corporation	Chemical products; power generation
1969	Credifier Corporation			Credit authorization equipment
	Ehrenreich & Cie			Steering components (Germany)
	Gregory Industries			Fastening systems
		Thompson Ramco S.A. de C.V.		Automotive aftermarket (Mexico)

YEAR	ACQUISITION	JOINT VENTURES	DIVESTITURES	DESCRIPTION
		International Decision Techniques		Decision analysis software
		TRW-Koyo Seiko		Steering components (Japan)
1970		TRW-Tokai Cold Forming, Ltd.		Suspension components (Japan)
1971		Canada Systems, Ltd.		Civil systems (Canada)
		OMAR Explorations, Ltd.		Minerals exploration (Canada)
1972	Applications Méchaniques et Robinetterie Industrielle			Energy products (France)
	The DeLeuw, Cather Company			Engineering and architectural services
	Pleuger Unter-wasserpumpen GmbH			Energy products
	Repa Feinstanzwerk GmbH			Automotive safety products
		Datacom International		International distribution of terminals and electronic equipment
		Shin Han Valve, Ltd.		Engine components (Korea)
1973	Dreadnought Equipment Division of Bell's Asbestos and Engineering Pty., Ltd.			Energy products (Australia)
	Werner Messmer KG			Electrical switches and controls
1974	Aertech Inc.			Commercial electronics (microwave equipment)
	Financial Data Sciences, Inc.			Data-entry terminals
	Mialbras, S.A.			Electronic components (Brazil)

YEAR	ACQUISITION	JOINT VENTURES	DIVESTITURES	DESCRIPTION
	Sherwood Refractories, Inc.			Ceramic molds
	Société Metallurgique G. Jeudy			Engine components (France)
		International Ceramics Ltd.		Ceramic molds (United Kingdom)
1975	Vidar Division of Continental Telephone			Digital transmission equipment
		Tornilleria Fina de Navarra S.A. (TORFINASA)		Steering and suspension components (Spain)
			Canada Systems, Ltd.	Civil systems
			OMAR Explorations, Ltd.	Minerals exploration
1976	North American Maintenance Division of Singer Co.			Service and maintenance of terminals and computer equipment
1977			The DeLeuw, Cather Company	Engineering and architectural services
1978	Control Concepts, Inc.			Steering components (heavy duty)
	ESL Inc.			Electronic surveillance and reconnaissance systems
1979	C. E. Niehoff & Co.			Automotive aftermarket
	Optron, Inc.			Electro-optical devices
		Wu Chou Valve Industrial Co.		Engine components (Taiwan)
1980	Stanley Spring Works			Suspension components (heavy duty)
		Fuji Serena Valve Co. Ltd.		Engine components (Taiwan)
		TRW-Fujitsu Co.		Distribution of terminals and small computers

YEAR	ACQUISITION	JOINT VENTURES	DIVESTITURES	DESCRIPTION
			Cam-TRW	Automotive aftermarket
			Cinch-Monadnock	Fasteners and electrical hardware
			Holyoke Wire and Cable	Industrial products
1981	Eagle Controls			Electronic controls for heavy-duty engines
	Hartzell Propeller Products			Aircraft products
		Koa-TRW Inc.		Electronic components (Japan)
			Bayerisches Leichtmetall-werk KG	Metals foundry (Germany)
			Butterfly valve business of Mission Manufacturing	Energy products
			Clifford Ltd.	Steering components (United Kingdom)
			Datacom International	International distribution of terminals and electronic equipment
1982	The Brandt Company			Energy products
	Daut + Rietz			Automotive controls (Germany)
	Dynalco Corporation			Automotive electronics (engine instruments and controls)
	Erni Elektro-Apparate GmbH			Fasteners and controls (Germany)
	Probe Engineering Company, Ltd.			Electronic controls (United Kingdom)
		Trico Industries		Energy products and equipment
			TRW Vidar	Digital transmission equipment (liquidation)

YEAR	ACQUISITION	JOINT VENTURES	DIVESTITURES	DESCRIPTION
1983	Securaiglon S.A.			Automotive safety products (France)
			Noblesville Casting	Metals foundry
			TRW-Fujitsu Co.	Distribution of terminals and small computers
1984	Decor Products			Automotive safety products (Canada)
	Hamill Division of Firestone Tire and Rubber			Automotive safety products
	H. W. Systems			Information systems for title insurance industry and lending institutions
	Irvin-Securaiglon S.A.			Automotive safety products (Spain)
	Theta J			Automotive electronics (switch-mode power supplies)
			Casting operations of Mission Manufacturing	Energy products and equipment
			Hand Tools Division	Originally part of United-Greenfield
			La Zincocelere S.p.A.	Electronic components; originally part of United-Carr
			Niehoff Alternator Products	Automotive aftermarket
			Printed Circuit Division	Electronic components
			TRW Controls	Energy products
1985	Etablissements Torrix S.A.			Automotive switches (France)
	Pressure Systems, Inc.			Aerospace products
	Record Data, Inc.			Information systems for home equity industry

YEAR	ACQUISITION	JOINT VENTURES	DIVESTITURES	DESCRIPTION
	Sabelt S.p.A.			Automotive safety products (Italy)
	Sybase, Inc.			Database management systems (affiliate)
	Trans Tech Services, Inc.			Information systems
		TRW-Norton		Engine components (ceramics)
		TRW-Steering Co., Ltd.		Steering components (Korea)
		AAE-TRW components SDN.BHD		Steering and suspension (Malaysia)
			Aviation Product Support Division	Aircraft products
			Iscar Blades	Aircraft products
			Niehoff Automotive Products	Automotive aftermarket
1986	Revere Mold and Engineering			Controls and fasteners
	Technar			Automotive safety systems (electromechanical sensors)
	Teknekron Financial Services			Information systems and scanning equipment for financial services
		Quality Safety Systems Co. (TRW Canada and Tokai Rika)		Automotive safety products (to serve Asian manufacturers in North America)
		Direcciones y Suspensiones Automotrices S.A. de C.V. (DIRECSA)		Steering components (Mexico)
		TRW-Calzoni S.p.A.		Steering systems (Italy)
			Bearings business	Originally Marlin-Rockwell

YEAR	ACQUISITION	JOINT VENTURES	DIVESTITURES	DESCRIPTION
			Capacitor business	Electronic components
			Castings business	Aircraft products
			Compressor components business	Aircraft products
			Cutting tools business	Originally part of United-Greenfield
			Hartzell Propeller Products	Aircraft products
			Power accessories business	Aircraft products
			Resistor business	Electronic components
			Turbine components business	Aircraft products
			TRW Subsea Petroleum	Energy products (liquidation)
1987		Sabag, Inc.		Gas generant for air bags
		TRW-Fuji Valve, Inc.		Engine valves (to serve Asian manufacturers in North America)
			Connective components business	Electronic components
			Microwave business	Electronic components
			Electric Motors	Electronic components
			Pleuger Unter-wasserpumpen	Energy products
			Ramsey Corporation	Engine components (piston rings)
			Trico Industries	Energy products and equipment
1988		TRW-Koyo Steering Systems Co.		Steering systems (to serve Asian manufacturers in North America)

YEAR	ACQUISITION	JOINT VENTURES	DIVESTITURES	DESCRIPTION
			Dynalco Controls	Controls and fasteners
			Heavy-duty parts business	Steering and suspension products (heavy duty)
			Industrial duo-check valves business	Energy products
			Mission drilling business	Energy products
			Optoelectronics business	Electronic products
			Reda Pump	Energy products
			RF Devices	Electronic products
			Oilwell cable business	Energy products
			Koa-TRW	Electronic components (Japan)
1989	Active Control Systems			Fasteners and controls
	Automotive Products Division of Talley Industries			Automotive safety products
	Chilton Corporation, Subsidiary of Borg-Warner Corporation			Consumer credit reporting
	Industrias Pobesa S.A.			Automotive electrical products (Spain)
		TRW-Toyoda Machine Works		Steering products (to serve Asian manufacturers in North America)
			Brandt Solids Controls	Energy products
			Gemmer France (Suresnes)	Suspension products (heavy duty)
1990	Electrical Division of Wickes Manufacturing			Automotive electrical controls

YEAR	ACQUISITION	JOINT VENTURES	DIVESTITURES	DESCRIPTION
	Electro-Automation			Automotive switches and controls (Germany)
	National Module Systems			Automotive electronics
	Reliable Rack & Pinion			Steering components
		TRW-Fabryka samochdow Mazolitrazowych		Automotive safety products (Poland)
			Medical Electronics Division	Information systems and services
1991		TRW-REDI		Real estate information services
			DOT brand product line	Fasteners; originally part of United-Carr
			European piston ring/ cylinder sleeve business	Engine components
			Image processing services	Information systems and services (originally Teknekron)
			Switch-mode power supply business	Automotive electronics (originally Theta J)
			Sybase Inc.	Database management (affiliate)
			TRW Thompson KG	Foundry products (Germany)
1992		Benesov		Automotive switches and controls (Czech Republic)
			Aftermarket business	Automotive aftermarket products and distribution
			Computer-output microfiche business	Information systems and services

YEAR	ACQUISITION	JOINT VENTURES	DIVESTITURES	DESCRIPTION
			Customer Service Division	Information systems and services
			Daut + Rietz connectors	Automotive electronics
			Decor Products	Automotive safety systems (Canada)
			DOT brand industrial fasteners business	Fasteners (originally part of United-Carr)
			Fax encryption technology business	Aerospace electronics
			LSI Products	Commercial electronics
			Receivables management business	Information systems and services
			TRW-Calzoni S.p.A.	Steering systems (Italy)
			TRW Pressure Systems, Inc.	Aerospace products
1993	James M. Kirby Products Pty. Limited			Steering systems (Australia)
			Environmental services business	Environmental services
			Fasteners Division (Palnut)	Fasteners
			Real Estate Loan Services	Information systems and services
			Ross Hydraulic Motor/ Hydrostatic Steering Controls	Steering components (heavy duty)
			TRW-Norton	Engine components (ceramics)
1994	Dacicke Strojirny S.P.			Steering, suspension, and engine components (Czech Republic)

YEAR	ACQUISITION	JOINT VENTURES	DIVESTITURES	DESCRIPTION
	Satip Plastic			Molded fasteners and assemblies (Italy)
1995		TRW Rane Occupant Restraints Ltd.		Automotive safety systems (India)
1996	FIAT steering gear factory in Poland			Steering components
	Steering wheel and air bag cover business of Izumi Corporation			Steering components
		Hema/TRW Otomotiv Steering Systems A.S.		Automotive safety systems (Turkey)
		Jinan TRW Engine Valve Co. Ltd.		Engine components (China)
		TRW Endiksan Automotive Safety Systems A.S.		Automotive safety systems (Turkey)
		TRW Suzhou Automotive Electronics Co., Ltd.		Steering components (China)
			TRW Information Systems and Services	Information systems, including consumer credit reporting

NOTE ON SOURCES

The history of Thompson Products and its forebears is well documented in several accessions of company papers housed in the library of the Western Reserve Historical Society (WRHS) in Cleveland, including the main collection gathered by William Crowell of TRW's public relations department during the 1960s and several additional collections donated by Fred Crawford. The main collection includes board minutes and account books for the early years of the company and associated ventures of C. E. Thompson and his family. It also includes general correspondence, biographical information about key executives, advertising and publicity materials, clippings, and company and employee publications, such as the invaluable *Friendly Forum,* the employee newspaper started in 1934. Other TRW collections at WRHS include oral history interviews with Crawford, Livingstone, and Arch Colwell in the 1960s, as well as a more recent set of oral history interviews with company leaders including Crawford, Dave Wright, Horace Shepard, Simon Ramo, and Dean Wooldridge done in the late 1980s.

A major part of the TRW holdings at WRHS pertain to labor relations at TP during the 1930s and 1940s. A duplicate set of these materials is housed in the archives at Harvard Business School, with similar materials in the Raymond S. Livingstone collection at Florida Atlantic University in Boca Raton.

The documentary record for TRW since 1958 is incomplete and scattered. The board minutes for the years since 1916 are kept in the Law Department library at TRW headquarters in Cleveland. Official records of acquisitions, mergers, and joint ventures are also maintained in the Law Department library. There is no central repository of other key historical records, however. Some documents pertaining to planning, finances, and public relations are available in various departments at corporate headquarters or housed in a nearby warehouse. Others have been lost—or at least I have been unable to locate them.

As the company diversified, it made little effort to centralize information. As a result, each constituent part of the company maintains its own records, and the status of these is very uneven. There is an incipient archive of materials relating to the history of Ramo-Wooldridge and TRW's operations in space and defense at Space Park. Maintained by members of the TRW Retirees Association, this archive includes several valuable holdings, including Ruben Mettler's voluminous, meticulously organized correspondence from the 1950s and 1960s and a much less extensive but nonetheless valuable set of papers from the office of George Solomon, who headed TRW's Space & Defense sector between 1981 and 1986. The Mettler papers shed light on virtually every aspect of the company's business; the other collections at Space Park feature administrative bulletins and printed accounts such as press materials pertaining to major, nonclassified space programs. The Public Relations Department at Space Park maintains bound copies of employee newsletters since 1955 and some other key publications.

Outside the company, major collections pertaining to TRW's space and defense business are available in the U.S. Air Force History Office, which maintains collections at various locations around the country. Papers related to the development of the ICBM are housed at Norton Air Force Base near San Bernardino, California; papers pertinent to USAF space programs are at Los Angeles Air Force Base. Transcripts from the Air Force's extensive oral history program are available at Bolling AFB in Washington, D.C. Simon Ramo's personal papers are deposited at his *alma mater*, the University of Utah. The National Air and Space Museum at the Smithsonian Institution has started to build what promises to be a valuable oral history collection to document the development of the American space program. Several retired TRW executives, including Rube Mettler, Ed Doll, and George Mueller, have participated in these interviews.

The following people participated in oral history interviews for this book. It is expected that transcripts of these interviews will be placed in the archive at Space Park.

ORAL HISTORY INTERVIEWS

ALLEN, CHARLES	*November 12, 1990*
ARMBRUSTER, JOHN	*April 7, 1990*
BARTER, NEVILLE	*November 14, 1990*
BOOTON, RICHARD	*June 17, 1992*
BRADBURN, DAVID	*October 8, 1991*
BROMBERG, ROBERT	*November 14, 1990*
BURGIN, ROBERT	*October 10, 1991*
BURNETT, J. ROBERT	*November 14, 1990*
CAMPBELL, RICHARD	*February 12, 1991*
COHEN, C. BUDD	*March 4, 1992*

CORPENING, ROBERT	*June 19, 1991*
COYLE, MARTIN	*April 17, 1990*
CRAWFORD, FREDERICK	*November 29, 1989*
	January 8, 1990
	August 8–9, 1990
	September 12–14, 1990
	October 15, 1990
	June 27, 1991
	August 27, 1991
	February 12, 1992
DERGARABEDIAN, PAUL	*March 3, 1992*
DISTASO, JACK	*November 15, 1990*
DOLL, EDWARD	*February 15, 1991*
DONOVAN, ALLEN	*October 9, 1991*
	March 4, 1992
DUKE, WILLIAM	*October 8, 1991*
DUNFORD, EDSEL	*September 24, 1991*
DUNLAP, JAMES	*June 26, 1991*
DUNN, JAMES	*October 6, 1991*
ELVERUM, GERALD	*June 17, 1991*
FOSTER, JOHN	*February 12, 1991*
FRAZIER, MONTGOMERY	*April 16, 1990*
GLEGHORN, GEORGE	*November 11, 1990*
GOLDIN, DANIEL	*October 8, 1991*
GORMAN, JOSEPH	*April 17, 1990*
	February 15, 1991
	April 17, 1991
	March 4, 1997
GRANT, ARTHUR	*June 18, 1991*
HALL, EDWARD N.	*June 2, 1993*
HANNEMANN, TIMOTHY	*October 9, 1991*
	June 3, 1993
HARTER, GEORGE	*October 10, 1991*
HAYES, HARRY	*June 19, 1991*
HELLMAN, PETER	*February 6, 1997*
HIRSCH, HAROLD	*June 19, 1991*

IRVING, JACK	*June 16 and 17, 1992*
JONES, WILLIAM M.	*September 23, 1992*
KNICELY, HOWARD	*April 17, 1991*
	July 9, 1991
KOVAR, DONALD	*November 16, 1991*
LANGMUIR, DAVID	*June 18, 1992*
LAWRENCE, WILLIAM	*March 11, 1991*
	May 9, 1991
LEHAN, FRANK	*June 20, 1991*
LIVINGSTONE, RAYMOND	*February 6–7, 1991*
LOEFFLER, DAVID	*April 17, 1991*
LUNDY, ROBERT	*April 16, 1990*
MACEY, CHESTER	*April 18, 1991*
MANDROW, JOHN	*November 13, 1991*
METTLER, RUBEN	*March 6, 1990*
	June 18, 1991
	June 16, 1992
	May 11, 1994
MILLER, CHARLES	*September 4, 1991*
MOHR, MILTON	*March 3, 1992*
MUELLER, GEORGE	*June 4, 1992*
OHLY, CHARLES	*February 1, 1994*
PACE, STANLEY	*February 11, 1991*
POE, GEORGE	*April 30, 1991*
RAMO, SIMON	*March 6, 1990*
	March 5, 1992
	June 16, 1992
REYNOLDS, A. WILLIAM	*September 1, 1992*
SAMULON, HENRY	*March 3, 1992*
SELLARS, JOHN	*November 15, 1990*
SHADER, MELVIN	*June 18, 1991*
SHEPARD, HORACE	*September 25, 1990*
SKILLING, D. VAN	*May 9, 1991*
	June 25, 1991
SOLOMON, GEORGE	*February 13, 1991*
STAUDHAMMER, PETER	*June 2 and 4, 1993*

THIEL, ADOLPH	*November 16, 1990*
TREMBATH, NATHANIEL	*November 13, 1990*
WAHLQUIST, ROBERT	*June 18, 1991*
WEBB, J. SIDNEY	*February 14, 1991*
WOOLDRIDGE, DEAN	*October 11, 1991*
WRIGHT, J. DAVID	*August 27, 1990*

INTERVIEWS BY OTHER SOURCES CONSULTED

COLWELL, ARCH	*WRHS, 1967*
CRAWFORD, FREDERICK	*WRHS, 1967*
	TRW-C, 1988–1989
DAVIS, LT. GEN. W. AUSTIN	*USAF, 1973*
DOOLITTLE, LT. GEN. JAMES	*USAF, 1969*
ESTES, GEN. HOWELL M., JR.	*USAF, 1973*
LIVINGSTONE, RAYMOND	*WRHS, 1967*
METTLER, RUBEN	*TRW-C, 1989*
PUTT, LT. GEN. DONALD	*USAF, 1974*
RAMO, SIMON	*UCLA, 1983–1984*
	TRW-C, 1988–1989
SCHRIEVER, GEN. BERNARD	*USAF, 1973*
	USAF, 1977
SOPER, COL. RAY E.	*USAF, 1966*
SHEPARD, HORACE	*TRW-C, 1988–1989*
WOOLDRIDGE, DEAN	*TRW-C, 1988–1989*
WRIGHT, J. DAVID	*TRW-C, 1988–1989*

KEY

TRW-C	TRW Communications Staff
UCLA	University of California at Los Angeles, Entrepreneurs of the West Oral History Program; copy in PR Department at TRW in Space Park
USAF	Office of Air Force History, Bolling AFB, Washington, D.C., and Maxwell AFB, Montgomery, Alabama
WRHS	Western Reserve Historical Society, Cleveland, Ohio

Notes

Preface

[1] This collection is Accession 3942 in the manuscript collection of the library of the Western Reserve Historical Society in Cleveland, Ohio.

[2] A former TRW employee, Bruce Zewe, conducted all but one of these interviews, and the transcripts are housed at the Western Reserve Historical Society as Accession 88-088. The exception is the Mettler interview, which another former TRW employee, Michael L. Johnson, conducted but did not complete. I am grateful to Mr. Johnson for furnishing a copy of the tape, which I had transcribed for this project.

[3] William Oliver of public relations served on the committee until he left the company in 1993.

[4] In 1984, Crawford was elected to the National Business Hall of Fame, where Simon Ramo later joined him. TRW is one of a handful of companies and the only one of its size or nature with more than a single leader honored in this way.

[5] See Alfred D. Chandler, Jr., "The Competitive Performance of U.S. Industrial Enterprise since the Second World War," *Business History Review* 68, no. 1 (Spring 1994): 1–72, and George David Smith and Davis Dyer, "The Rise and Transformation of the American Corporation," in *The American Corporation Today,* Carl Kaysen, ed. (New York: Oxford University Press, 1996), 28–73.

Chapter 1

[1] TRW Inc., Annual Report for 1996.

[2] TRW Inc., Annual Report for 1996. The employment figure given in the report is 65,218. That total does not include about 3,000 people who joined early in 1997 through acquisitions.

[3] *Business Week,* March 24, 1997, 170; *Industry Week,* August 19, 1996, cover story.

[4] The sale was closed on September 19. TRW retained 16 percent of the equity in the new entity, which was renamed Experian Corp. In a windfall transaction several weeks later,

the new owners sold Experian, including TRW's remaining interest, to another party for $1.7 billion.

5 TRW Inc., Annual Report for 1996.

CHAPTER 2

1 The standard history of the internal combustion engine is C. Lyle Cummins, Jr., *Internal Fire: The Internal Combustion Engine, 1673–1900,* rev. ed. (1976; Warrendale, Pa.: Society of Automotive Engineers, 1989). See esp. chaps. 8–9 and 12. See also Lynwood Bryant, "The Beginnings of the Internal Combustion Engine," in Melvin Kranzberg and Carroll W. Pursell, Jr., eds., *Technology in Western Civilization,* vol. 1 (New York: Oxford University Press, 1967), 648–664.

2 Cleveland (and Northeast Ohio) is well served by local historians who have produced work of extremely high quality in recent years. The following two paragraphs are based on information gleaned from Thomas F. Campbell and Edward M. Miggins, eds., *The Birth of Modern Cleveland, 1865–1930* (Cleveland, Ohio: Western Reserve Historical Society, 1988), chaps. 1–3, esp. pp. 38–49; David D. Van Tassell and John J. Grabowski, eds., *The Encyclopedia of Cleveland History* (Bloomington, Ind.: Indiana University Press, 1987); Carol Poh Miller and Robert Wheeler, *Cleveland: A Concise History* (Bloomington, Ind.: Indiana University Press, 1990), chaps. 7–8; and the marvelous chronicle of William Ganson Rose, *Cleveland: The Making of a City,* reprint ed. (Kent, Ohio: Kent State University Press, 1990), chaps. 12–13.

3 The minutes of the Cleveland Cap Screw Company and its successors through 1916 are housed in the library of the Western Reserve Historical Society in Cleveland, Accession 3942, vol. 1. [Hereafter cited as TRW, WRHS 3942, with volume or box number.]

4 For Morley's biography, see Albert Borowitz, *Jones, Day, Reavis & Pogue: The First Century* (Cleveland, Ohio: Jones, Day, 1993), 22–23, 41–42. For Frederick Bright, see Hudson T. Morton, *Anti-Friction Bearings,* 2d ed. (Ann Arbor, Mich.: n.p., 1965), 451.

5 Kurtz's father-in-law, Servetus W. Park, is the subject of a brief biography in Joseph G. Butler, *History of Youngstown and the Mahoning Valley, Ohio* (Chicago: American Historical Society, 1921), 2: 11–12. Kurtz's career and movements can be followed in various annual city directories of Cleveland, which are available on microfilm at the library of the Western Reserve Historical Society.

6 TRW, WRHS 3942, vol. 1, January 11, 1901; TRW, WRHS 3942, vol. 3.

7 "The First 50 Years at TP," *Friendly Forum,* January 1951, 3–4. Elsewhere, the business definition was more precise: "screw machine products, including 'hexagon and square head cap screws of superior quality, irregular and large heads, a specialty filister head, and coupling bolts and studs.'" See Frank K. Dossett, A Chronological Record of the Physical and Economic Development of Thompson Products, Inc. (typescript, May 1951), TRW, WRHS 3942, box 21. This source is useful for establishing basic chronology and because Dossett had access to documents that apparently no longer exist. It contains many minor factual mistakes, however, and it should be used with caution.

8 Omission as Deduction for All Periods of Depreciation on Cost of Patents Acquired on June 1, 1916, Exhibit A, p. 1. This document, prepared in 1933 by Thompson Products lawyer J. David Wright, a future CEO of TRW, is housed in TRW, WRHS 3942, box 2. On the importance of the Franklin Institute Standards, see Bruce Sinclair, "The Direction of Technology," in *Technology and Social Change in America,* Edwin T. Layton, Jr., ed. (New York: Harper & Row, 1973), 65–78. (This article appeared originally under the

title, "At the Turn of a Screw: William Sellers, the Franklin Institute, and a Standard American Thread," *Technology and Culture* 10 [January 1969]: 20–34.)

9 W. Bingham & Co., *Illustrated and Descriptive Catalogue of Hardware* (Cleveland, Ohio: January 1894), p. 376; Omission as Deduction, Exhibit A, pp. 1–2. A cap screw of the dimensions described cost $2.45 at a True Value hardware store in 1994.

10 David B. Hounshell, *From the American System to Mass Production: The Development of Manufacturing Technology in the United States* (Baltimore, Md.: Johns Hopkins University Press, 1984), 149, 200–201. See also Howard B. Cary, *Modern Welding Technology*, 2d ed. (Englewood Cliffs, N.J.: Prentice Hall, 1989), 6, 24, 239–242, 250–252. For a thorough discussion of the origins of electrical resistance welding, see John B. Schmitt, "The Invention of Electric Resistance Welding: Elihu Thomson as Pioneer Innovator," unpublished paper, The Smithsonian Institution, August 30, 1974. I am grateful to David Hounshell for providing me a copy of this paper.

11 Frederick C. Crawford interview, January 1967, WRHS, Accession 963. For a description of the Thomson process, see "A New Welder," *Iron Age* 46 (December 4, 1890): 988.

12 Omission as Deduction, Exhibit A, p. 2; Exhibit C, pp. 1–3, Part 2, p. 2.

13 TRW, WRHS 3942, vol. 1.

14 Ibid., vol. 3.

15 Dossett, Chronological Record, May 1, July 15, and September 2, 1901. Frederick Bright may have had an interest in the Grant Ball or Grant Tool properties; since his initial stake in Cleveland Cap Screw was $40,000 in stock—the amount represented by the value of the Clarkwood Avenue property.

16 According to his birth certificate, Thompson's full name was Charles Frederick Thompson. Throughout his career, however, he used "E" as a middle initial, standing variously for Edwin or Edward. Early in life he apparently went by "Charlie," but he later told Fred Crawford that he needed a middle initial for some occasion and simply chose the letter "E." From the 1920s onward he was known to friends as "C. E."

Another anomaly concerns Thompson's date of birth, which he observed as July 16, despite the record of his birth certificate, which states August 9. WRHS, Accession 983, Ctr 1. See also Carle Robbins, "They Changed the Future of Aviation," *The Bystander of Cleveland*, August 17, 1929, 7–9.

17 Crawford interview, January 1967.

18 "Cleveland Cap Screw Co.'s Cap Screws and Bolts," *Journal of the Franklin Institute*, 160 (July–December 1905): 182, 185–186.

19 Points two and three on this list are inferences drawn from a letter of Frederick Bright to Kurtz on June 14, 1905, during negotiations to combine Cleveland Cap Screw and Russell-Burdsall & Ward. TRW, WRHS 3942, vol. 1, June 26, 1905.

20 TRW, WRHS 3941, vol. 4, August 21, 1903; vol. 1, January 30, 1904.

21 W. D. Fraser, an associate who helped Winton build his first gasoline engine, quoted in *Cleveland Press*, September 24, 1934 (unpaginated clipping).

Winton has no biographer, although he surely deserves one. The most complete accounts of his public career are Richard Wager, *Golden Wheels: The Story of the Automobiles Made in Cleveland and Northeastern Ohio, 1892–1932*, 2d ed. (Cleveland, Ohio: Western Reserve Historical Society, 1975; reprint, with corrections, Cleveland: J. T. Zubal with the cooperation of the Western Reserve Historical Society, 1986), 3–24; Walter E. Gosden, "Winton: The Man and His Motorcars," *Automobile Quarterly* 22

(1984): 306–329; and a series of four articles by Menno Duerksen published in *Cars & Parts*: "Your Winton Waits," October 1979, 22–31; "Two Men, a Mutt and a Car That Made History," November 1979, 34–46; "Tragedy Strikes at San Francisco and Wintons Rumble to the Rescue," December 1979, 36–42; and "The Final Years," January 1980, 12–16. See also James Dalton, "He Sold the First Car," *MoToR*, January 1927, 114–115, 124, 126; William G. Keener, "Ohio's Pioneer Auto Maker: Alexander Winton," *Museum Echoes,* March 1955, 19–22.

    The story about Ford's job application appears in Wager, *Golden Wheels*, 5. See also Gosden, "Winton," 309.

[22] Dalton, "He Made the First Car," 124.

[23] This vehicle is on display at the Frederick C. Crawford Auto-Aviation Museum of the Western Reserve Historical Society in Cleveland. According to Duerksen, "Your Winton Waits," p. 25, Winton's claim to have sold the first car is exaggerated. Apparently Charles Duryea sold at least thirteen vehicles during 1898.

[24] Duerksen, "Your Winton Waits," 26.

[25] Winton lived at 37 Bolton Place in the Hough neighborhood; Kurtz at 290 Bolton Avenue, south of Hough. For Winton's connections to Lindsay Wire Weaving, see Van Tassell and Grabowski, eds., *Encyclopedia of Cleveland History*, 633.

[26] TRW, WHRS 3942, vol. 1, April 6, July 14, and August 10, 1904.

[27] The account of these events is based on TRW, WRHS 3942, vol. 1, April 8, May 13, and June 26, 1905.

[28] Ibid., June 26 and July 21, 1904.

[29] Ibid., September 21, 1905.

[30] Wager, *Golden Wheels*, 115; Robbins, "They Changed the Future of Aviation," 9.

    After the collapse of his automobile company, Russell launched another venture, Industrial Engineering Company, for which Thompson served as treasurer. Thompson and Russell continued to share a residence until 1909 or 1910, when Russell and his company disappeared from Cleveland directories. According to Robbins, Thompson lived during this period with his brother-in-law, who may have been Russell.

    In other versions of these events, Thompson's insight into the connection between cap screws and valves may have been helped by an acquaintance (Russell? Verner Bright?) who had worked as a mechanic for Otto Konigslow, a Cleveland bicycle maker who diversified into producing automobiles. See *Fortnightly Telephone Engineer*, February 1, 1949, 34.

[31] Omission as Deduction, Exhibit A, pp. 3–4; Exhibit D, p. 2; Robbins, "They Changed the Future of Aviation," 9.

[32] Ben G. Elliott, *Automobile Power Plants* (New York: McGraw-Hill, 1923), 69; Victor W. Page, *The Modern Gasoline Automobile* (New York: Henley Publishing Co., 1924), 248.

[33] Omission as Deduction, Exhibit D.

[34] TRW, WRHS 3942, vol. 1, September 7, 1906.

[35] Ibid., March 14, 1908; Omission as Deduction, Exhibit A, p. 4.

[36] "The First 50 Years at TP," 4; TRW, WRHS 3942, vol. 1: Thompson salary (February 8, 1909, and February 5, 1911); expansion (October 22, 1909; March 16, 1910; September 30, 1912; February 4 and August 6, 1914; March 20, August 30, September 14, and November 10, 1915); retirement of Cleveland Cap Screw bonds, June 20, 1913; dividends (September 14, 1911; March 25 and August 30, 1912; March 6 and September 22, 1913; February 4, 1914); stock split (February 24, 1915).

37 Omission as Deduction, 5, and Exhibit A, p. 9.

38 Crawford interviews, January 1967, 1988 (WRHS Accession 88-088), and interview with author, September 12, 1990, Cotuit, Mass.

39 Crawford interview, 1988. Ray Livingstone, who knew Krider starting in the late 1920s, remembers him as "a gentle, smiling man" regarded in the company as "a financial genius." Raymond S. Livingstone, telephone conversation with the author, November 24, 1992.

40 Crawford interview, 1988.

41 Omission as Deduction, 6–7 and Exhibit A, pp. 5–6. The key patents were U.S. Patent No. 915,249 (March 16, 1909) for the clamp device, supplemented by U.S. Patent No. 1,048,642 (December 31, 1912), which extended the earlier patent specifically to the manufacture of valves.

42 Omission as Deduction, 6–7 and Exhibit A, pp. 5–6. This patent was U.S. Patent No. 910,434 (June 19, 1909) for welding two-piece valves of dissimilar metals. U.S. Patent No. 1,106,064 (August 4, 1914) covered improvements to the process for welding two-piece valves of dissimilar metals.

43 See Omission as Deduction, Exhibit E, for engineer William H. Spire's affidavit on the cost advantages of the Electric Welding Products Company's process.

44 John B. Rae, *The American Automobile Industry* (Boston: Twayne Publishers, 1984), 17, 180; Robert Paul Thomas, *An Analysis of the Pattern of Growth of the Automobile Industry, 1895–1930* (New York: Arno Press, 1977), 324; Wager, *Golden Wheels*, xiii.

45 George V. Thompson, "Intercompany Technical Standardization in the Early American Automobile Industry," *Journal of Economic History* 14 (Winter 1954): 5–7; James Read Doolittle, ed., *The Romance of the Automobile Industry* (New York: Klebold Press, 1916), 189–190; Lawrence H. Seltzer, *A Financial History of the American Automobile Industry* (Boston: Houghton Mifflin, 1928), 42–43, 48.

46 Wager, *Golden Wheels*, 20. See TRW, WRHS 3942, vols. 28 and 29, for sales journals from 1915 and 1916.

47 Crawford interview, January 1967.

48 Dossett, Chronological Record, April 30, 1910.

49 Agnew's patent was U.S. Patent No. 1,160,557, issued November 16, 1915.

50 Crawford interview, January 1967.

51 Omission as Deduction, Exhibit A, p. 7.

52 TRW, WRHS 3942, vol. 38.

53 Crawford interview, January 1967; TRW, WRHS 3942, vol. 38.

54 The $2,500 fee is cited in Thompson's deposition, Omission as Deduction, Exhibit A, p. 7. Elsewhere, the terms are described differently, though not necessarily incompatibly: see Omission as Deduction, Exhibit B, p. 1, for a copy of an agreement between Electric Welding Products and Thomson Electric Welding, dated October 29, 1912. This document terminates the license agreement of 1902 for "a consideration of one dollar and other valuable considerations paid by Electric Welding Products Company."

55 Omission as Deduction, Exhibit A, pp. 7–8; Exhibit F; TRW, WRHS 3942, vol. 38, p. 91.

56 TRW, WRHS 3942, vol. 1, February 24, 1915.

57 Dossett, Chronological Record, February 2, 1914. This entry is probably misdated by a year, since the minutes of Electric Welding Products record the sale of its 102 shares of Michigan Electric Welding on May 28, 1915. TRW, WRHS, vol. 1, May 28, 1915. See

also Dossett, Chronological Record, February 24, 1915, and TRW, WRHS 3942, vol. 1, February 7, 1916.

[58] Deposition of Charles E. Thompson, Washington, D.C., March 16, 1923, p. 3. Signed by Winton, Henderson, and Brown in Cleveland on March 15, 1923. TRW, WRHS 3942, box 2.

[59] Wager, *Golden Wheels*, 22–24; Duerksen, "The Final Years," 12–16; Gosden, "Winton," 318–319.

[60] Crawford interview, January 1967; TRW, WHRS 3942, vol. 1, June 27, 1916.

[61] Steel Products Company, Board Minutes, vol. 1, 1916–1935, Meeting of June 27, 1916. Volume in Law Department Library at TRW Headquarters in Cleveland. (A duplicate is in TRW, WHRS 3942, vol. 2.)

[62] TRW, WRHS 3942, vol. 1; Steel Products Company, Board Minutes, June 27, 1916.

[63] Information on Kurtz was gleaned from Cleveland city directories. In some earlier histories of TRW, Kurtz is identified as an automotive entrepreneur who "had been known to tinker with gasoline engines, and was the designer of a new type of transmission for 'horseless carriages.'" (See, for example, "The First 50 Years at TP," 4.) Such accounts confuse David Kurtz with Cyrus B. Kurtz, whose Kurtz Motor Company in Cleveland produced cars with an early form of automatic transmission. See Wager, *Golden Wheels*, 183–186.

[64] Duerksen, "The Final Years," 12–16; Wager, *Golden Wheels*, 22–24; McKinstry, "Alexander Winton," 10–11; Jim and Susan Borchert, *Lakewood: The First Hundred Years* (Norfolk, Va.: Donning Co., 1989), 87.

CHAPTER 3

[1] Frederick C. Crawford dictation, tape no. 9, transcript in possession of the author; see also Frederick C. Crawford interviews, January 1967, WRHS, Accession 983, and 1988 WRHS Accession 88-088; interview with the author, September 12–14, 1990, Cotuit, Mass.; and J. David Wright interview, 1988, WRHS, Accession 88-088. Others had nice things to say about Thompson, too. See Arch T. Colwell interview, 1967, and Raymond S. Livingstone interview, 1967, both in WRHS, Accession 983; and Livingstone interview with the author, February 6–7, 1991, Boca Raton, Fla.

[2] Crawford interviews, January 1967, 1988, and September 12–14, 1990. The quotations are drawn from the 1988 interview.

A brief article in the fiftieth anniversary edition of the company magazine recounts this story slightly differently: "Crawford landed a job in the shop and one day admired a curious inkwell on the desk of C. E. Thompson, then president. 'The day you are made general manager,' Mr. Thompson said in a half-joking manner, 'I'll give you that inkwell.' Years passed. In 1929 Mr. Crawford was made general manager. He claimed the inkwell. It is now one of his most prized possessions." See "Inkwell a Symbol of Crawford Rise," *Friendly Forum,* January 1951, 48.

[3] For Thompson's connections to Glenn L. Martin, see Frederick C. Crawford, "Aviation Pioneers," in *Selected Speeches of Frederick Coolidge Crawford*, Christopher Johnston, ed. (Cleveland, Ohio: privately published, 1993), 158–174.

[4] Frank K. Dossett, A Chronological Record of the Physical and Economic Development of Thompson Products, Inc. and Subsidiaries (typescript, May 1951), TRW, WRHS 3942, ctr. 21, entries for May 23, 1913; June 12, 1917; October 16, 1919; and December

10, 1935. See also "Small Storeroom on Cherry Street Was Toledo Steel Products Cradle," *Friendly Forum*, January 1951, 40.

5 On Clarke's falling out with Thompson, see Crawford interviews, 1988 and September 12–14, 1990. On Reader's departure, see Dossett, Chronological Record, April 18, 1918, May 15 and June 6, 1919. The sale of the gas welding business netted Steel Products $70,000.

6 U.S. Bureau of the Census, Department of Commerce, *Historical Statistics of the United States, Colonial Times to 1970* (Washington, D.C.: GPO; 1975), 224; John B. Rae, *The American Automobile: A Brief History* (Chicago: University of Chicago Press, 1965), 70–71.

7 U.S. Bureau of the Census, *Historical Statistics of the United States*, 126, 199; Robert Paul Thomas, *An Analysis of the Pattern of Growth in the Automobile Industry, 1895–1930* (New York: Arno Press, 1977), 324; Richard S. Tedlow, *New and Improved: The Story of Mass Marketing in America* (New York: Basic Books, 1990), 161–162.

8 In 1916, poppet valves accounted for 50 percent of Steel Products' revenues. See Omission as Deduction for All Periods of Depreciation on Cost of Patents Acquired on June 1, 1916, p. 10, TRW, WRHS 3942, box 2.

9 A handy, nontechnical explanation of how intake and exhaust valves differ appears in *Firewall Forward—Top End*, vol. 1 of *The Light Plane Maintenance Library* (Riverside, Conn., n.d.), 70–71. This series is published by the editors of *Light Plane Maintenance* magazine.

10 A brief history of Rich Tool appears in *The History of Eaton Corporation, 1911–1985* (Cleveland, Ohio: Eaton Corp., 1986), 71; Omission as Deduction, 8–9.

11 "The First 50 Years at TP," *Friendly Forum*, January 1951, 4; C. Fayette Taylor, "Aircraft Propulsion: A Review of the Evolution of Aircraft Powerplants," *Smithsonian Report*, no. 4546 (Washington, D.C., 1962), 262–263; Wayne Biddle, *Barons of the Sky* (New York: Simon & Schuster, 1991), 94; Crawford interview, 1988.

12 Philip S. Dickey III, *The Liberty Engine, 1918–1942* (Washington, D.C.: Smithsonian Institution Press, 1968), 39–40; Taylor, "Aircraft Propulsion," 275–276; Sam D. Heron, *History of the Aircraft Piston Engine* (Detroit: Ethyl Corp., 1961), 26, 106–107; Steel Products Company, Minutes of the Board of Directors, February 6 and June 29, 1917; June 27, October 1, and November 25, 1918; March 31, 1919. Copy in Law Department Library at TRW Headquarters.

13 The Bartlett-gathering process is described in F. L. Prentiss, "Photo-Electric Tubes Used in Making Automobile Valves," *Iron Age* 129, no. 6 (February 11, 1932): 381–382.

14 U.S. District Court, Northern District of New York, *Ludlum Steel Company vs. Daniel F. Terry*, n.d. [1927?], 6–8, TRW, WRHS 3942, box 2; Crawford interview, 1988.

15 *Ludlum Steel vs. Daniel F. Terry*, p. 14; Crawford interview, January 1967; Dossett, Chronological Record, September 11, 1923. The formula for Silcrome No. 1 was about 3.7 percent silicon, about 8.9 percent chromium, and about .46 percent carbon.

16 "The 'Devil Steel' That Turned Saint," *Steel Horizons*, October 4, 1939, 6, 11; Colwell interview, 1967; Crawford interviews, January 1967, 1988, and September 12–14, 1990.

17 "The 'Devil Steel' That Turned Saint," 6; Crawford interview, 1988.

18 *Ludlum Steel Company vs. Daniel F. Terry*, 14; "The 'Devil Steel' That Turned Saint," 6 and 11; "Silcrome Valves," *Aviation* 14, no. 15 (April 1923): 400; A. H. Allen, "Alloy Steels Important in Valve Manufacture," *Iron Trade Review* 86, no. 8 (February 20, 1930): 40; Crawford interviews, January 1967, 1988, and September 12, 1990.

[19] "Silcrome Valves" *(Aviation)*, 400.

[20] Crawford interview, January 1967. Bissell's reservations may have reflected concerns about the weakness of valve stems made from silcrome. For an illustration of this problem, see J. B. Johnson and S. A. Christiansen, "Characteristics of Material for Valves Operating at High Temperatures," *Proceedings of the American Society for Testing Materials* (Philadelphia, 1924), pt. 2, pp. 395, 399–400.

[21] Crawford interview, January 1967; Colwell interview, 1967; Board Minutes, September 11, 1923 and February 7, 1924.

[22] "The First 50 Years at TP," 4.

[23] Colwell interview, 1967; *History of Eaton Corporation*, 71.

[24] Omission as Deduction, p. 10. The evolution of steering linkages is discussed briefly in T. P. Newcomb and R. T. Spurr, *A Technical History of the Motor Car* (Philadelphia: A. Hilger, 1989), 320–321, 325–326.

[25] This account is based on two documents in TRW, WRHS 3942, box 2. The first is an unsigned and undated affidavit. The second is a copy of an affidavit of Frederick C. Crawford that is unsigned but dated 1934. The two accounts conflict in many details but agree in essential points. In instances of conflict, I have relied on the Crawford affidavit, which is corroborated by his interviews in January 1967, 1988, and September 12–14, 1990.

[26] Affidavit of Frederick C. Crawford, 1934. Cf. Crawford interview, January 1967: "The Schweppe & Wilt Co. people brought parts to the little Michigan plant to be welded, and seeing it was a good business they began to take orders for themselves for drag links. Then followed some patent disputes with Schweppe & Wilt, which claimed we had stolen their stuff. Which probably was true."

[27] Affidavit of Frederick C. Crawford, 1934; Board Minutes, June 6, 1919. The other account in box 2 does not mention a license agreement and states that the conflict was resolved only after Schweppe & Wilt approached Steel Products' customers with the threat of liability. These customers, including Buick, then threatened Steel Products with loss of business unless the conflict was resolved immediately. This triggered the negotiations leading to Steel Product's purchase of the assets of Schweppe & Wilt.

[28] Board Minutes, August 5, 1919.

[29] "Told to Close Detroit Factory, Fred Crawford Revived It," *Friendly Forum*, January 1951, 34; Crawford interviews, January 1967, 1989, and September 12–14, 1990; Davis Dyer, "A Voice of Experience: An Interview with TRW's Frederick C. Crawford," *Harvard Business Review* 69 (November–December 1991): 116–118. The HBR article is a compilation of the many versions of this story and is followed here.

[30] Crawford dictation, tape no. 14; "Told to Close the Detroit Factory," 34; "With Matt Graham at Helm, Michigan Operation Prospers," *Friendly Forum*, January 1951, 37; Crawford to the author, December 12, 1990, and July 12, 1994.

[31] "Told to Close the Detroit Factory," 34; Dyer, "A Voice of Experience," 117.

[32] "Detroit Plant Leads the World," *Friendly Forum*, January 1951, 34, 37; A. T. Colwell, "Good Engineering Gave Impetus to Company's Growth," *Friendly Forum*, January 1951, 20; Colwell interview, 1967.

[33] "Told to Close the Detroit Factory," 34; Fred Crawford to Charles E. Thompson, September 8, 1928, TRW, WRHS 983, box 2; Crawford interview, September 12–14, 1990.

[34] Crawford interview, 1988.

[35] John B. Rae, *The American Automobile Industry* (Boston: Twayne Publishers, 1984), 180; U.S. Bureau of the Census, *Historical Statistics of the United States*, 716; Tedlow, *New and Improved*, 155–156.

[36] Dossett, Chronological Record, June 15, 1915, and October 22, 1919; Jim Syvertsen, "Service Salesman Had to Have Long Legs in Early Days," *Friendly Forum*, January 1951, 31; Russ Riley, "Merchandising Plays Large Role in Building of TP Service Sales," ibid., 32. The organizers of Ford-Clark included the incorporators of the new Steel Products Company in 1916.

[37] Dossett, Chronological Record, October 22, 1919; "Some of the Men and Women Who Helped Build Thompson Products," *Friendly Forum*, January 1951, 11; Syvertsen, "Service Salesman," 31; Riley, "Merchandising Plays Large Role," 32.

[38] Dossett, Chronological Record, October 12, 1922; September 11, December 4, and December 14, 1923; Syvertsen, "Service Salesman," 31; Riley, "Merchandising," 32.

[39] Dossett, Chronological Record, April 11 and December 3, 1924; February 17 and May 13, 1925.

[40] Colwell interview, 1967; Lee M. Clegg, "TP Sales Record Mirrors Half Century of Advancement," *Friendly Forum*, January 1951, 18

[41] Clegg, "TP Sales Record," 18; Crawford interviews, 1988 and September 12–14, 1990.

[42] Syvertsen, "Service Salesman," 31; Riley, "Merchandising," 32; "A Starting Crank Was Sheer Necessity When Mom Was Dancing the Charleston," *Friendly Forum*, January 1951, 32.

[43] Dossett, Chronological Record, April 8 and 15 and May 18, 1926; "The First 50 Years at TP," 4; Clegg, "TP Sales Record," 18.

[44] Board Minutes, May 18 and July 7, 1926.

[45] Board Minutes, September 15, 1926, and June 18 and July 1, 1927; Crawford interviews, January 1967, 1988, and September 12–14, 1990.

[46] Crawford interview, 1988.

[47] Board Minutes, November 5, 1925, June 7, 1926, and January 19, 1934; Dossett, Chronological Record, entries of same dates; Crawford to the author, January 20, 1992.

[48] Crawford interview, January 1967; Board Minutes, December 3, 1924. Thompson told Crawford that he contracted syphilis from a college classmate of Alexander Winton's daughter. Thompson met the young woman at a party at Winton's home.

[49] Crawford interview, January 1967.

[50] The saga (and soap opera) of Thompson's life with Gloria Hopkins is told in great detail by Crawford and Livingstone in their 1967 interviews.

[51] Crawford interview, January 1967; Livingstone interview, 1967, WRHS Accession 983, box 1; Crawford to the author, July 12, 1994. Livingstone provides a hilarious account of driving the Duesenberg from Cleveland to New York in 1929, as well as of the bizarre dynamics of Thompson's household. This container also includes a file of pictures of Chateau Gloria.

[52] Lawrence H. Seltzer, *A Financial History of the American Automobile Industry* (Boston: Houghton Mifflin, 1928), 42–45, 52, 55–57; James Rood Doolittle, ed., *The Romance of the Automobile Industry* (New York: Klebold Press, 1916), 189–190, 196, 207; George V. Thompson, "Intercompany Technical Standardization in the Early American Automobile Industry," *Journal of Economic History* 14 (Winter 1954): 6–9, 12; John K. Barnes, "The Men Who 'Standardized' Automobile Parts," *World's Work* 42 (1921): 207.

53 Thompson, "Standardization in the Automobile Industry," 6.

54 Crawford interview, 1988. The story appears in similar form in other Crawford interviews and reminiscences. According to Ray Livingstone, telephone conversation with the author, November 24, 1992, C. E. Thompson frequented the Pontchartrain Hotel, where he loved to sing until the wee hours of the morning.

55 Affidavit of Frederick C. Crawford, 1934; Seltzer, *Financial History of the American Automobile Industry*, 52–55, 57.

56 "The First 50 Years at TP," 4; Clegg, "TP Sales Record," 19.

57 Board Minutes, November 17, 1925; December 13, 1926; August 14, 1928; and March 29, 1929.

58 Board Minutes, September 12, 1927.

59 Board Minutes, May 8, 1928; "Thompson Acquires French Valve Firm," *Automotive Industries*, October 5, 1929, 503.

60 Crawford interviews, January 1967, 1988, and September 12–14, 1990; Board Minutes, February 4, 1926; July 26 and November 14, 1927; and May 8, 1928.

61 Syvertsen, "Service Salesman," p. 32; "TP Branches Now Span U.S. as Sales Volume Runs into Millions," *Friendly Forum*, January 1951, 51; "Caswell Builds TP Name in Far Lands," ibid., 33; Edwin G. Thompson to G. R. Moore, February 21, 1933, TRW, WRHS 3942, box 18. According to George Poe, who spent many decades in the automotive replacement business for Toledo Steel Products, TP, and TRW, TP acquired fourteen warehouses from "a company called Republic Gear" in 1927 or 1928. If so, the transaction was sufficiently small as to escape notice in the board minutes. See George Poe, interview with the author, April 30, 1991, Cleveland, Ohio.

62 Board Minutes, January 18 and February 20, 1929.

63 "Cox Learned Business from All Angles," *Friendly Forum*, July 3, 1935; Dossett, Chronological Record, May 22, 1922, May 31, 1926, and February 20, 1929; Crawford interviews, 1988 and September 12–14, 1990.

64 Crawford interview, 1988.

65 U.S. Bureau of the Census, *Historical Statistics of the United States*, 768; John B. Rae, *Climb to Greatness: The American Aircraft Industry, 1920–1960* (Cambridge, Mass.: MIT Press, 1968), 49; Taylor, "Aircraft Propulsion," 267–276.

66 Taylor, "Aircraft Propulsion," 269; Reminiscences of Heron by Thomas T. Neill and Raymond W. Young, from a file on Heron at the Library of the Smithsonian Institution; Joseph C. Robert, *Ethyl: A History of the Corporation and the People Who Made It* (Charlottesville, Va.: University Press of Virginia, 1983), 153. See also Colwell interview, 1967, for his impressions of Heron, with whom he was friendly.

67 Robert Schlaifer and S. D. Heron, *The Development of Aircraft Engines and Fuels* (Boston: Division of Research, Harvard Graduate School of Business Administration, 1950), 196–198; Heron, *History of the Aircraft Piston Engine*, 26, 108; Taylor, "Aircraft Propulsion," 269, 275–276; Eaton Manufacturing Co., Wilcox-Rich Division, *The Sodium-Cooled Valve* (Detroit, n.d.), 1; Colwell interview, 1967; Colwell, "Recent Developments in Poppet Valves," Society of Automotive Engineers, *Transactions* 26 (1931): 358.

68 Schlaifer and Heron, *Development of Aircraft Engines and Fuels*, 198; Heron, *History of the Aircraft Piston Engine*, 26, 108; Colwell, "Recent Developments in Poppet Valves," 358–359; Colwell interview, 1967; Allen, "Alloy Steels Important in Valve Manufacture," 41.

69 Schlaifer and Heron, *Development of Aircraft Engines and Fuels*, 198; Colwell, "Recent Developments in Poppet Valves," 358–359; Allen, "Alloy Steels Important in Valve Manufacture," 42, 47.

70 "Manufacturing Precision and Evolution of Thompson Aircraft Valves Pictured," *Friendly Forum*, September 21, 1934, 5; A. T. Colwell, "Modern Aircraft Valves," *S.A.E. Journal* 46, no. 4 (April 1940): 147–148; Colwell, "Recent Developments in Poppet Valves," 358–359; *Firewall Forward—Top End*, 72.

71 "Lee Clegg Believes Success Key Is Plain Hard Work," *Friendly Forum*, January 1951, 19; Crawford interviews, 1988 and September 12–14, 1990; Livingstone interview, February 6, 1991, and telephone conversation, November 24, 1992; Wright interview, 1988. According to Livingstone, Clegg did not own the hunting lodge in Quebec but belonged to a club that owned it.

72 Clegg, "TP Sales Record Mirrors Half Century of Advancement," 18; Clegg, Speech to Conference Group on Management Practices, August 29, 1960, TRW, WRHS 3942, box 10; Taylor, "Aircraft Propulsion," 270; Rae, *Climb to Greatness*, 238n.

73 Crawford interview, September 12–14, 1990.

74 Fred Witt to William Kaiser, June 9, 1955; and Fred Witt to Paul Mantz, May 25, 1955. Both letters are in WRHS, Accession 87-052, box 36. Witt obtained the blueprint from Ryan Aeronautical when the movie *The Spirit of St. Louis* was being made.

75 Wilcox-Rich, *The Sodium-Cooled Valve*, 2; Livingstone interview, February 6, 1991; "Love for People Is Spark That Fires Ray Livingstone," *Friendly Forum*, January 1951, 24.

76 Roger Huntington, *Thompson Trophy Racers: The Pilots and Planes of America's Air Racing Glory Days, 1929–1949* (Osceola, Wis.: Motorbooks International, 1989), 10–14.

77 "Thompson Trophy Symbolizes Speed Supremacy in Skies," *Friendly Forum*, January 1951, 50; Livingstone interview, February 6, 1991.

78 "Thompson Trophy Symbolizes Speed Supremacy in Skies," 50; Livingstone interview, February 6, 1991, and telephone conversation, November 24, 1992. Livingstone recalls lining up a photographer from the *Cleveland Plain Dealer* and tipping him $10 for the job.

79 Huntington, *Thompson Trophy Racers*, 14; "Thompson Trophy Symbolizes Speed Supremacy in Skies," 50; Livingstone interview, February 6, 1991; Crawford interview, 1988.

80 Crawford interview, 1988.

81 E. G. Thompson to G. R. Moore, February 21, 1933. See also Allen, "Alloy Steels Important in Valve Manufacture," 39, for a statement that TP manufactured "a large majority" of aircraft engine valves.

82 Board Minutes, September 29, November 21, and December 24, 1929; February 25, 1930.

83 Board Minutes, September 29, 1929; Ralph L. Nelson, *Merger Movements in American Industry, 1895–1956* (Princeton, N.J.: Princeton University Press, 1959), 121–122.

84 Crawford to the author, July 12, 1994. A merger between Eaton and TP in 1929, Crawford said, "would have been like two drunks leaning on each other."

85 F. C. Crawford to C. E. Thompson, May 1, 1930, TRW, WRHS Accession 983, ctr. 1; Board Minutes, October 31, 1929; *The History of Eaton Corporation*, 10–12.

86 In 1929, C. E. Thompson may not have regarded his son as a serious candidate to become general manager. Ed had opposed his father's marriage to Gloria Hopkins, and

relations between the two men eventually deteriorated to the point where the father dis-inherited the son.

87 Crawford interview, 1988; Board Minutes, November 6, 1929. The day of Crawford's chat with Thompson may have been Friday, November 1. Crawford recalls the meeting as being the Friday after the stock-market crash, referring to the forty-three-point plunge on Tuesday, the 29th. On Thursday, October 31, the Thompson board of directors met, with no hint of any executive changes, except that a newly created finance committee included Crawford but not Miller. Crawford's appointment was confirmed officially on Thursday, November 6. For an alternative version of the inkwell story, see note 2 and the *Friendly Forum* article cited there.

88 Rae, *American Automobile Industry*, 180; U.S. Bureau of the Census, *Historical Statistics of the United States*, 768.

89 Crawford to C. E. Thompson, July 18, 1931, WRHS, Accession 983, box 2.

90 Thompson Products, Inc., *Background for Tomorrow* (Cleveland, Ohio, 1951), 29; E. G. Thompson to G. R. Moore, February 21, 1933; Crawford to C. E. Thompson, July 18, 1931, WRHS, Accession 983, box 2; Fred Witt, "The Story of TP—A Picture History, No. 21," *Friendly Forum*, May 25, 1945, 5.

91 Thompson Products, Inc., Annual Reports for 1930–1933; "Canadian Subsidiary Is Rated High in Automotive Field," *Friendly Forum*, January 1951, 38. The progress of TP's merger talks can be followed in Crawford's letters to C. E. Thompson between 1929 and 1931, which are in WRHS, Accession 983, box 2. The deal that came closest to consummation was a merger with Columbus Auto Parts, a small and struggling maker of shock absorbers and other suspension parts, under terms that would have left TP's management in control. Crawford's correspondence gives no reasons why the merger failed to go through, however.

92 Board Minutes, August 17, 1932; Dossett, Chronological Record, August 17, 1932; Crawford dictation, tape no. 6 (copy in possession of the author); E. G. Thompson to G. R. Moore, February 21, 1933.

93 F. C. Crawford to C. E. Thompson, April 15, 1930, WRHS, Accession 983, ctr. 1; Crawford interview with the author, October 15, 1990, Guildhall, Vt.

94 R&D expenditures declined from a peak of just over $1 million in 1929 to just under $800,000 in 1932.

On the Cleveland Clinic Disaster, which occurred on May 15, 1929, see David D. Van Tassel and John J. Grabowski, eds., *Encyclopedia of Cleveland History* (Bloomington, Ind.: Indiana University Press, 1987), 223.

On Colwell: "Fame as Engineer Followed Arch Colwell's Army Career," *Friendly Forum*, January 1951, 21; "Colwell, Soldier-Engineer, Learned Golf from a Book," ibid., July 19, 1935; Crawford interview, 1988; Wright interview, 1988; Livingstone interview, February 6, 1991. Colwell published at least thirty-six articles in SAE journals. These are indexed in *Cumulative Index of SAE Technical Papers, 1906–1964* (Warrendale, Pa.: Society of Automotive Engineers, 1990).

95 F. C. Crawford to C. E. Thompson, July 11 and July 20, 1931, WRHS, Accession 983, box 1, Thompson Family Files; Prentiss, "Photo-Electric Tubes Used in Making Automobile Valves," 381–384.

96 Colwell interview, 1967; Colwell, "Good Engineering Gave Impetus to Company's Growth," 20.

97 Colwell, "Recent Developments in Poppet Valves," 359–360; "Copper-Cooled Valves Are Introduced by Thompson," *Automotive Industries*, August 22, 1931, 281; "Forges

Exhaust Valve of Alloy Steel with Copper Cores for Cooling," *Steel*, September 10, 1931, 42; Dossett, Chronological Record, January 13, 1932; Colwell interview, 1967.

[98] Crawford interview, September 12–14, 1990; "Early History, Crawford Door Company," TRW, WRHS 3942, box 7.

[99] Crawford interview, September 12–14, 1990.

[100] "Early History, Crawford Door Company."

[101] The information about traffic markers is from Livingstone interview, February 6, 1991; and "TP Traffic Markers Still Adorn Streets of U.S. and Mexico," *Friendly Forum*, January 1951, 48. The company's promotional literature claimed that its markers achieved savings of nearly $50,000 versus painting over a five-year period. Thompson Products, Inc., Traffic Marker Division, *Thompson Traffic Markers* (promotional brochure, n.d.), copy in author's possession.

[102] Board Minutes, April 6 and September 25, 1933; Crawford interview, 1988; Wright interview, 1988.

[103] F. C. Crawford to C. E. Thompson, July 31, 1931, WRHS, Accession 983, box 1; Colwell interview, 1967; Wright interviews, 1988 and with the author, August 27, 1990, Cleveland, Ohio.

[104] Livingstone telephone conversation, November 24, 1992.

[105] Crawford dictation, tape no. 14; Crawford interview, September 12–14, 1990; Livingstone interview, February 6, 1991, and telephone conversation, November 24, 1992. Livingstone remembers the day of Thompson's funeral as being so overcast that it was impossible to see the Union Trust building. The plane was moving so fast, moreover, that there was little hope of depositing the ashes where they were supposed to go.

CHAPTER 4

[1] Frederick C. Crawford interview, 1988, WRHS 88-088.

[2] Thompson Products, Inc., Minutes of the Board of Directors, November 29, 1933. Copy in Law Department Library at TRW headquarters. One other director, S. Livingston Mather, left the meeting before the critical vote. Crawford does not recall why Mather left but notes that he was a good friend and strong supporter. Frederick C. Crawford interview with the author, October 15, 1990, Guildhall, Vt.

[3] Frederick C. Crawford interview with the author, February 12, 1992, Cleveland, Ohio; J. David Wright interview, 1988, WRHS 88-088, recalls Thompson's stake as 30,000 shares. Wright was executor of C. E. Thompson's estate.

[4] Board Minutes, vol. 1, 1916–1935, unnumbered pages at the front of the volume.

[5] Crawford to Ambrose Bowyer, December 30, 1933, TRW WRHS 3942, box 2.

[6] Frederick C. Crawford interview with the author, September 12–14, 1990, Cotuit, Mass. J. David Wright interview with Robert D. Lundy, 1983, copy in the possession of the author.

[7] On Ginn, see Albert Borowitz, *Jones, Day, Reavis & Pogue: The First Century* (Cleveland, Ohio: Jones, Day, Reavis & Pogue, 1993), chap. 3, esp. pp. 46–47.

[8] "Death Keeps Its Date on the Dude Ranch," undated clipping, American Weekly, Inc., 1935, in TRW WRHS 3942, box 3; WRHS Accession 983, box 1.

[9] On Rev. Breed, see David D. Van Tassel and John J. Grabowski, eds., *The Encyclopedia of Cleveland History* (Bloomington and Indianapolis, Ind.: Indiana University Press, 1987), 121. Breed's philosophy for a long, successful ministerial tenure was "Take long

vacations and keep sermons short." Bill Breed, incidentally, later became president of United Parts Company, a Cleveland-based auto parts company. See Crawford correspondence in WRHS 87-052, box 16.

Dave Wright has an interesting and credible speculation about Thompson's reasons for hiring Crawford: he wanted a tutor for his son Edwin. See Wright interview with Lundy, 1983. Crawford does not agree, however: Crawford to the author, June 28, 1994.

[10] Biographical information from *Friendly Forum*, January 1951, various articles; average age from J. H. Coolidge, "Finances—Sales—Earnings," in Thompson Products, Inc., *A Decade of Achievement* (Cleveland, Ohio: Thompson Products, Inc., 1944), 29.

[11] See Davis Dyer, "A Voice of Experience: An Interview with TRW's Frederick C. Crawford," *Harvard Business Review* 69 (November–December 1991): 126.

[12] Crawford interview, 1988. This story is corroborated by Raymond S. Livingstone interview with the author, February 6 and 7, 1991, Boca Raton, Fla.

[13] Crawford interviews, 1988, September 12–14, 1990, and October 15, 1990.

[14] Kay Crawford, comment to the author, September 12, 1991, Cotuit, Mass.; Wright interview, 1988; Fred Witt, "Mosaics of a Personality," typescript, July 14, 1941, TRW WRHS 3942, box 16.

[15] Crawford interview, 1988.

[16] Witt, "Mosaics of a Personality"; F. C. Crawford to M. P. Graham, Inter-Office Letter, June 10, 1937, in TRW WRHS 3942, box 1. I am indebted to Joseph T. Gorman, chairman and CEO of TRW, for calling my attention to the latter memo, copies of which have circulated among the company's top management for years.

[17] Crawford interview, 1988; Witt, "Mosaics of a Personality."

[18] Wright interview, 1988.

[19] Crawford interview, 1988.

[20] Board Minutes, November 29, 1933; January 19 and March 9, 1934. I have not found a copy of the Ernst & Ernst report; its contents are inferred from comments in the Board Minutes.

[21] Copies of monthly financial statements from 1930 through 1934 are housed in box 43412 of TRW records at an independent warehouse in Cleveland.

[22] Board Minutes, May 29, 1935; J. D. Wright, "A Ten-Year Summary," in Thompson Products, Inc., *A Decade of Achievement*, 10.

[23] Executive Committee Minutes, February 1, 1935; Board Minutes, March 9, April 25, June 22, December 5, and December 19, 1935. Wright mentions the importance of the National City Bank loan in both interviews, 1983 with Lundy, and 1988. Wright particularly credits banker Sidney Condon with having faith in TP when other lenders were skeptical of the company's future.

[24] Board Minutes, August 8 and December 24, 1935, and May 8, 1936; Executive Committee Minutes, December 24, 1935.

[25] Board Minutes, December 5, 1935; Wright, "A Ten-Year Summary," 10; Crawford interviews, 1988 and September 12–14 and October 15, 1990.

[26] Thompson Products, Inc., Annual Report for 1938.

[27] For statistics on the motor vehicle industry: U.S. Bureau of the Census, *Historical Statistics of the United States* (Washington, D.C., 1976), 716. For improvements in valve technology during the 1930s: Colwell, "The Trend in Poppet Valves," *SAE Journal (Transactions)* 45, no. 1 (July 1939): esp. pp. 298–304; and H. E. Blank, Jr., "Valve Materials," *Automotive Industries*, November 19, 1938, 673–676.

28 Crawford interview, 1988. On valve rotation, see Colwell, "The Trend in Poppet Valves," 301–302; A.T. Colwell, "Wear Reduction of Valves and Valve Gear," *SAE Journal (Transactions)* 43, no. 3 (September 1938): 370; Colwell, "Good Engineering Gave Impetus to Company Growth," *Friendly Forum,* January 1951, 20; Colwell, "Speaking of the Future," in Thompson Products, Inc., *A Decade of Achievement*, 35; Thompson Products, Inc., *Background for Tomorrow* (Cleveland, Ohio: Thompson Products, Inc., 1952), 7; and A. T. Colwell interview, 1967, WRHS Accession 983.

29 Board Minutes, March 10 and 30, 1937; "Jadsons, Forerunner of West Coast TP, Was Started in 1898 by Stalwart Smithy of Traver, California," *Friendly Forum*, January 1951, 42; Paul Hileman, "Plant Also Major Supplier of Auto and Airframe Parts," *Friendly Forum*, January 1951, 42; *Cleveland Plain Dealer*, April 22, 1937, unpaginated clipping.

30 Crawford interviews, September 12–14 and October 15, 1990.

31 "Caswell Builds TP Name in Far Lands," *Friendly Forum*, January 1951, 33.

32 Russ Riley, "Merchandising Plays Large Role in Building of TP Service Sales," *Friendly Forum*, January 1951, 32; "Fred Crawford's Company," *Fortune*, December 1946, 148–149; George Poe interview with the author, April 30, 1991, Cleveland, Ohio. During the 1930s, the service division published a magazine for jobbers called *TP Tips*. A few copies survive in WRHS 87-052, box 16.

33 Board Minutes, November 8, December 5 and 10, 1935.

34 J. E. Adams, "'Toledo'—A Pioneer Name in Replacement Parts," in Thompson Products, Inc., *A Decade of Achievement*, 21; "Small Storeroom on Cherry Street Was Toledo Steel Products Cradle," *Friendly Forum*, January 1951, 40; H. K. Lang, "Toledo Steel Products Enjoys Steady Growth as Service Parts Lines Expand," *Friendly Forum*, January 1951, 52

35 John B. Rae, *Climb to Greatness: The American Aircraft Industry, 1920–1960* (Cambridge, Mass.: MIT Press, 1968), 49, 81; Thompson Products, Inc., Financial Statements, Month of November 1934, p. 14 in box 43412 of TRW warehouse records; Thompson Products, Inc., *A Decade of Achievement*, 30. One index of the relative insignificance of aircraft engine valves is that the company did not publicly report sales in this segment until 1937.

36 Fred Witt, "Hubbell Aircraft Paintings Make Thompson Calendar Widely Sought," *Friendly Forum*, January 1951, 54.

37 "Thompson Trophy Symbolizes Speed Supremacy in the Skies," *Friendly Forum*, January 1951, 50; "Crawford, Frederick Coolidge," in *The National Cyclopedia of American Biography* (New York: J. T. White, 1938), 522–523.

38 Rae, *Climb to Greatness*, 74–75, 81–82, 94–98; Thompson Products, Inc., *A Decade of Achievement*, 11. See also Robert Schlaifer, *Development of Aircraft Engines* (Boston: Division of Research, Graduate School of Business Administration, 1950), chaps. IX–XI; Colwell, "The Trend in Poppet Valves," 298.

39 A. T. Colwell, "Modern Aircraft Valves," *SAE Journal* 46, no. 4 (April 1940): 147–149, 151; "Fred Crawford's Company," 150.

40 Colwell, "Modern Aircraft Valves," 149.

41 Schlaifer, *Development of Aircraft Engines*, 285–293; Edward W. Constant II, *The Origins of the Turbojet Revolution* (Baltimore: Johns Hopkins University Press, 1980), 126–127.

42 Crawford interviews, 1988 and September 12–14, 1990; Colwell, "Good Engineering Gave Impetus," 20.

[43] Crawford interview, 1988; Wright interview, 1988.

[44] The remainder of this chapter and much of the next is based on interviews with Crawford, Ray Livingstone, and J. D. Wright, as well as on voluminous records documenting personnel policies at TP between 1934 and 1946. These records, which include articles, speeches, and published materials as well as corporate documents, are housed in overlapping collections at the Western Reserve Historical Society in Cleveland (especially in TRW WRHS 3942, Series III, but also in other accessions) and at Harvard Business School in Boston (Thompson Products Collection). Also useful are the Livingstone Historic Collection at the College of Business, Florida Atlantic University in Boca Raton. Helpful secondary sources include Harvey Shore, "A Historical Analysis of Thompson Products' Successful Program to Discourage Employee Acceptance of Outside Unions" (DBA diss., Harvard, 1966); Sanford M. Jacoby, "Reckoning with Company Unions: The Case of Thompson Products, 1934–1964," *Industrial and Labor Relations Review* 43, no. 1 (October 1989): 19–40; and a lengthy chronicle and digest prepared by Frank K. Dossett, Thompson Products: A Study in New Deal Legislation (typescript, 1947), TRW WRHS 3942, boxes 19 and 20.

[45] Between 1933 and 1936, the number of people employed in the executive branch climbed from about 591,000 to more than 850,000, an increase of 44 percent. During the same period, federal budget expenditures soared from $4.6 billion to $8.4 billion, an increase of more than 80 percent. The national debt soared from $2.7 billion in 1932 (an unusually high total caused by the depression) to $4.4 billion in 1936, a total high by design. See U.S. Bureau of the Census, *Historical Statistics of the United States,* 1102, 1104–1105.

[46] Foster Rhea Dulles and Melvyn Dubovsky, *Labor in America: A History,* 4th ed. (Arlington Heights, Ill.: Harlan Davidson, 1984), 260.

[47] Dulles and Dubovsky, *Labor in America,* 262.

[48] Crawford's contempt for FDR is evident in all of his interview transcripts; for the FDR picture story, see Witt, "Mosaics of a Personality." Crawford voiced his views on the New Deal in hundreds of speeches and articles. For a particularly clear, forceful, and succinct critique, see Crawford, "Our National Government: Director or Umpire of Business," *The Clevelander,* April 1940, 4, 63.

[49] F. C. Crawford to Earl Harding, assistant to the president, Remington Rand, Inc., May 17, 1937, TRW WRHS 3942, box 28.

[50] The speech was printed in its entirety in a special four-page issue of *Friendly Forum,* April 8, 1935.

[51] See Dyer, "A Voice of Experience," 116; Frederick C. Crawford, "The Cruelty of Administrative Law," *Cleveland Enterprise* (Spring 1992): 8–9.

[52] Communication from the Old Guard Committee, January 13, 1934; Constitution of Thompson Products, Inc. Employees' Association, February 23, 1934, p. 1; Minutes of the First Meeting [of the Joint Council] of the Thompson Products Employees Association, February 19, 1934; Frank K. Dossett, Physical and Economic History Highlights. A Chronological Record of the Physical and Economic Development of Thompson Products, Inc. (typescript, May 1951; WRHS 3942, Ctr. 21); Board Minutes, March 6, 1934.

Jacoby, "Reckoning with Company Unions," p. 21, states that Ray Livingstone served as secretary to the Old Guard Association, that he conceived the idea of the TPEA, and that loyal Old Guard members carried it out. However, in January 1934, Livingstone was not yet engaged in any way with personnel matters. He also lacked five years of service with the company and would not have been eligible for membership even in the expanded Old Guard.

53 Shore, "Historical Analysis," 55–59, 67–69, 124–131, 140–155; *Friendly Forum*, May 10, 1934, 1, 4. See also n. 43 above.

54 Michigan plant: Shore, "Historical Analysis," 102–104, and Livingstone interview, February 6 and 7, 1991. Pin plant strike: Shore, "Historical Analysis," 115–124; Livingstone interview, February 6 and 7, 1991; and Board Minutes, August 8, 1935. The passage of the National Labor Relations Act (the Wagner Act) on July 5 may also have lent impetus to the strike. The statute prompted an increase in organizing activity throughout midwestern manufacturing industries. For the impact of the Wagner Act on TP, see text below.

55 Livingstone interview, February 6 and 7, 1991.

56 Livingstone interview, February 6 and 7, 1991; Crawford interview, September 12–14, 1990. A short time later, Cox left TP for reasons that apparently had little to do with the strike. Crawford recalls that the bank for the Cleveland-based Weatherhead Company approached him to find "a good factory man" as a vice president for manufacturing. Crawford recommended Cox for the job; Cox accepted and helped guide Weatherhead back to prosperity. Crawford to the author, June 28, 1994; also, Livingstone telephone conversation with the author, November 24, 1992.

Cox apparently enjoyed the full support of his bosses during the strike, and both Crawford and Livingstone recount the story in approving terms. At one point during the strike, Crawford recalls, the IAM—or possibly another, more militant union—claimed to have signed up a majority of the plant's workers. The union submitted the cards to the U.S. Department of Labor, and Crawford soon heard from Frances Perkins, President Roosevelt's Secretary of Labor, who ordered him to recognize the union. Advised that as many as two-thirds of the signatures were counterfeits, Crawford shot back a letter to Perkins that read, "Dear Mrs. Perkins: I received your letter, and I must advise you that your information is incorrect. The union has just deceived you. And incidentally, if you tend to your business, I'll tend to mine, and we'll get along very well." See Dyer, "Voice of Experience," 120, and Borowitz, *Jones, Day, Reavis & Pogue*, 47. I have not been able to locate the original correspondence.

57 See Crawford to Harding, May 17, 1937 for Crawford's reasons for starting *Friendly Forum*. These reasons included educating employees about the company and presenting management's view of the labor situation.

58 The timing of Livingstone's appointment is a bit confusing in surviving records. His appointment was announced in late January 1935, by which time the Personnel Division, the creation of which was announced along with Livingstone's appointment, had already published its *Industrial Relations Manual*. In 1951, Livingstone recalled that Crawford gave him the personnel assignment in 1934, but that description, as well as his oral history interview in 1991, reads as though Livingstone is confusing his appointment as executive secretary to the TPEA joint council with his appointment as head of the personnel division.

What is clear is that before the spring of 1934 Livingstone had nothing to do with personnel. As a former journalist, he may have been involved in the start-up of *Friendly Forum*. His first official appointment in a personnel-related job was his supporting role with the TPEA joint council. It seems likely that as he grew more absorbed by the work of the association, he assumed more responsibility over personnel matters. For example, the joint council discussed early in 1935 a wage survey of Cleveland area employers that must have taken some time to produce, and Livingstone probably was responsible for it. Livingstone probably also had a hand in the November 1934 launching of the foreman's training program, and he surely worked on the *Industrial Relations Manual* before his appointment.

In sum, what probably happened is that at some time in mid to late 1934, Livingstone was appointed head of personnel and that for some reason the company chose not to announce it until early in 1935.

59 R. S. Livingstone, "Good Human Relations Contribute to Company's Success," *Friendly Forum*, January 1951, 24; Livingstone interview, February 6 and 7, 1991. Livingstone's appointment as personnel director was announced in late January 1935. See *Friendly Forum*, February 1, 1935, 1.

60 Livingstone interview, February 6 and 7, 1991; Livingstone, "Good Human Relations," 24–25; Jacoby, "Reckoning with Company Unions," 22. The first survey I've discovered pertained to the "average married factory worker" and is dated January 11, 1935. Livingstone Collection, Florida Atlantic University, section IX.

61 Livingstone interview, February 6 and 7, 1991; Livingstone, "Good Human Relations," 24–25; Dossett, Physical and Economic History, November 12, 1934; Jacoby, *Employing Bureaucracy*, 229–232.

62 Livingstone interview, February 6 and 7, 1991; Livingstone, Memo to Mr. Clegg, February 14, 1936, in Thompson Products Papers, Harvard Business School.

63 Livingstone, "Good Human Relations," 25; Livingstone, Speech to the Foreman's Club, September 12, 1935, as reported in Dossett, Physical and Economic History, September 12, 1935.

64 "Apprentice Program Draws Praise from State, Nation," *Friendly Forum*, January 1951, p. 48; Dossett, Physical and Economic History, September 5, 1935, and January 3, 1936.

65 Dossett, Physical and Economic History, March 2, 1936; Shore, "Historical Analysis," 132–133 and 135; Livingstone, "Good Human Relations," 25. Livingstone borrowed the final quotation from Whiting Williams, a labor authority whom he admired.

66 *Friendly Forum*, December 7, 1934, 1, 3; Shore, "Historical Analysis," 124–130; Thompson Products, Inc., *Employee's Handbook* (March 12, 1935), 3.

67 *Friendly Forum*, February 15, 1935, 3; *Friendly Forum*, August 16, 1935, 1, 4.
   Both Shore ("Historical Analysis," 124–130) and Jacoby ("Reckoning with Company Unions," 24) argue that the TPEA was dominated by management or otherwise proved ineffectual in negotiating wages. The evidence for domination is clear enough but the second charge is questionable. Indeed, the evidence suggests the contrary. Each time that employee representatives pushed for pay increases, management responded by working with employee representatives to study the issue and determine appropriate pay levels. The result in each year after the formation of the TPEA was a wage increase (at least for some classes of work) that kept the company's pay in line with other Cleveland-area manufacturers, including some that were unionized. It is true that the TPEA did not demand pay increases under threat of dispute and that management reserved the final say. It is also true that management directed the entire process of pay negotiations. The important point, however, is that when employees sought increases or clarifications of policy, they participated in finding the answers. They received good information and prompt answers to requests, and they often benefited from favorable decisions.

68 Thompson Products, Inc., *Industrial Relations Manual*, January 1, 1935, 8–9, 16, 18–19; Shore, "Historical Analysis," 85–95.

69 Thompson Products, Inc., *Employee's Handbook* (March 12, 1935), 1–3; Shore, "Historical Analysis," 96–101.

70 *Friendly Forum*, February 15, 1935, 1–2.

71 *Friendly Forum*, April 12, 1935, 2; *Friendly Forum*, November 20, 1936, 1–2. The first separately printed Annual Report to Employees appeared in 1941. For a lengthy explanation of why and how TP issued these reports, see Livingstone interview, February 6 and 7, 1991, and correspondence between Livingstone and John Jennings in June 1978 in the Livingstone Papers at Florida Atlantic University, section V.

72 Jacoby, *Employing Bureaucracy*, 232–239, esp. Table 7.2 on p. 233.

73 *Friendly Forum*, May 24, 1935, 3; Shore, "Historical Analysis," 106–107, 170.

74 The UAW-CIO's victory at the Michigan plant proved fleeting anyway. During the ensuing months, the union's local organization fell apart amid internal strife, inability to collect dues, and problems signing up many employees who refused to join them. These challenges were compounded by a sharp recession in the auto industry, which resulted in layoffs that the union was powerless to prevent. When the contract expired in September, it was already a dead document. *Friendly Forum*, May 7, 1937, 1; *Friendly Forum*, May 21, 1937, 1; Shore, "Historical Analysis," 158n, 166–169; Crawford interview, 1988; Crawford letter to the author, April 30, 1991; Livingstone interview, February 6 and 7, 1991; Jacoby, "Reckoning with Company Unions," 24–25.

75 Shore, "Historical Analysis," 165–166; *Friendly Forum*, April 9, 1937, 1; Dossett, Physical and Economic History, April 12, 1937. Cochran later became scholar at Columbia University, where he wrote several books about American politics, including *Labor and Communism: The Conflict That Shaped American Unions* (Princeton, N.J.: Princeton University Press, 1977). None of his works that I have seen mentions his experiences at Thompson Products.

76 Shore, "Historical Analysis," 174–177; Jacoby, "Reckoning with Company Unions," pp. 25–26. For the organizations of independent unions in Toledo and Bell, see Shore, "Historical Analysis," 181–188; for the independent union in Detroit, see *Friendly Forum*, April 1, 1938, 3.

77 The information in this paragraph is drawn from Shore, "Historical Analysis," 188–193.

CHAPTER 5

1 "Fred Crawford's Company," *Fortune* 34, no. 6 (December 1946): 146ff.

2 Thompson Products, Inc., *Now It Can Be Told* (Cleveland, Ohio: Thompson Products, Inc., 1945), passim. A copy of this publication is in WRHS 87-055, box 6. See also Thompson Products, Inc., *A Decade of Achievement* (Cleveland, Ohio: Thompson Products, Inc., 1944), 40–45; and Bert Titley, "Canadian Subsidiary Is Rated High in Automotive Field," *Friendly Forum*, January 1951, 38.

3 Thompson Products, Inc., *A Decade of Achievement*, 10, 13, 35; Thompson Products, Inc., *Background for Tomorrow* (Cleveland, Ohio: Thompson Products, Inc., 1951), 29.

4 T. O. Duggan, "'Thompson Merchandising and Service,'" in Thompson Products, Inc., *A Decade of Achievement*, 20–21; "Fred Crawford's Company," 148–49; WRHS 87-052, box 16.

5 John B. Rae, *Climb to Greatness: The American Aircraft Industry, 1920–1960* (Cambridge, Mass.: MIT Press, 1968), 81, 107; I. B. Holley, *Buying Aircraft: Material Procurement for the Army Air Forces, The United States Army in World War II*, Special Studies, no. 7 (Washington, D.C.: U.S. Government Printing Office, 1964), 201; Board Minutes, January 13, October 20, and December 5, 1939.

[6] Rae, *Climb to Greatness*, 81, 107, 113–115, 142.

[7] Holley, *Buying Aircraft*, 299.

[8] Frederick C. Crawford interview with Bruce Zewe, TRW Inc., 1988, WRHS 88-088; J. David Wright interview with Bruce Zewe, TRW Inc., 1988, WRHS 88-088; Thompson Products, Inc., *A Decade of Achievement*, 11.

[9] Wright interview with Zewe, 1988; Crawford interview with Zewe, 1988.

[10] Board Minutes, January 22, 1941; *Friendly Forum*, February 7, 1941, 1; "Thompson Aircraft Products Company," in Thompson Products, Inc., *A Decade of Achievement*, 46–48; "Factory Dedicated to Service of U.S.," *Cleveland Press*, March 18, 1942, 27; Wright interview with Zewe, 1988; Crawford interview with Zewe, 1988.

[11] "Thompson Aircraft Products Company," in *A Decade of Achievement*, 46–49.

[12] A. T. Colwell interview, 1967, WRHS 983; A. T. Colwell, "Good Engineering Gave Impetus to Company Growth," *Friendly Forum*, January 1951, 21. The 90 percent figure is mentioned in Crawford interview, 1988, and in "A Tribute to John David Wright," *Friendly Forum* (Tapco edition), September 8, 1963, 1. Other sources say that between them, the Tapco and Bell, California, plants accounted for 83 percent of total U.S. valve production. See Thompson Products, Inc., Annual Report for 1943.

[13] Colwell interview, 1967.

[14] "For Meritorious, Distinguished Service, Dependability, TP Men and Women Won Army-Navy 'E' Award Three Times," *Friendly Forum*, January 1951, 12–13. The other "E" awards were presented to the Jadson plant on September 1, 1943, and to the Toledo plant on January 5, 1945. See "The Story of TP—A Picture History, No. 31" *Friendly Forum*, September 13, 1946, 5.

According to Crawford, the "E" Award almost did not happen: "We never got an 'E' till I went to Washington and found that the granting of an 'E' required a union labor approval. I called on War Secretary Patterson and said I was going to blast the 'E' as a disgrace. Charlie Wilson (Electric) got me an 'E' by signing up an old labor leader as his deputy and ordering him to approve [it]. I had to blackmail the War Department to get it." Crawford to the author, June 28, 1994.

[15] J. David Wright interview with Robert D. Lundy, TRW Inc.,1983, copy in the possession of the author; Board Minutes, January 23 and March 21, 1942.

[16] Colwell interview, 1967; Frank K. Dossett, A Chronological Record of the Physical and Economic History of Thompson Products, Inc., July 1, 1941 (typescript, May 1951), TRW, WRHS 3942, boxes 20–21.

According to Crawford (letter to the author, July 20, 1993), TP wanted to acquire Curtis's business, but Curtis wanted to remain independent. The booster pump posed such challenges, however, that Curtis needed extraordinary support, which he got from TP. Colwell agreed to finance Curtis's work and pay a small royalty on orders produced. Later, the Department of Defense set limits on the size of the royalty and ordered further that the royalties be placed in escrow for later review. After the war, Curtis received about $700,000 for his work. Says Crawford: "This proved a mistake for Bill because he spent the money for a California lemon grove that never did well."

[17] Dossett, Chronological Record, July 1, 1941, and March 30, 1943; Colwell, "Good Engineering Gave Impetus," 20; L. M. Clegg, "1,400 Precision Products," in Thompson Products, Inc., *A Decade of Achievement*, 13; Crawford interview with Zewe, 1988; Ben M. Marino, "Power for Peace," *Friendly Forum* (Tapco edition), September 8, 1963, 3.

[18] Board Minutes, March 30, 1943; *Friendly Forum*, April 4, 1947, 4.

[19] Andrew L. Pomeroy, "Task of Development Staff Is to Make New Ideas into Top Products," *Friendly Forum*, January 1951, 54; Colwell, "Good Engineering Gave Impetus," 21.

[20] S. D. Heron, *Development of Aviation Fuels* (Boston: 1950), 646–651.

[21] Heron, *Development of Aviation Fuels*, 649–650; Colwell, "Speaking of the Future . . . ," in *A Decade of Achievement*, 36–37; Colwell, R. E. Cummings, and D. E. Anderson, "Alcohol-Water Injection," *SAE Journal (Transactions)* 53, no. 6 (June 1945): 358–370; Colwell interview, 1967.

[22] Colwell, "Good Engineering Gave Impetus," 21; Colwell interview, 1967; Leslie E. Neville and Nathaniel F. Silsbee, *Jet Propulsion Progress: The Development of Aircraft Gas Turbines* (New York: McGraw-Hill, 1948), chap. 4, esp. pp. 98–101; Robert Schlaifer, *Development of Aircraft Engines* (Boston: Division of Research, Graduate School of Business Administration, Harvard University, 1950), 328–329, 440–441, 494–500; Rae, *Climb to Greatness*, 163–67; Edward W. Constant II, *The Origins of the Turbojet Revolution* (Baltimore: Johns Hopkins University Press, 1980), 122–124; Virginia P. Dawson, *Engines and Innovation: Lewis Laboratory and American Propulsion Technology* (Washington, D.C.: National Aeronautics and Space Administration, Office of Management, Scientific and Technical Information Division, 1991), 42–45. TP may also have been an attractive supplier to make superchargers because of its expertise in water pumps, which turbines resembled conceptually. See Heron, *Development of Aviation Fuels*, 627n.

[23] For an excellent brief description of the principles of the turbojet engine, see Alex Roland, *Model Research: The National Advisory Committee for Aeronautics, 1915–1958* (Washington, D.C.: Scientific and Technical Information Branch, National Aeronautics and Space Administration, 1985), vol. I, p. 187. See also Constant, *The Origins of the Turbojet Revolution*, passim.

[24] For an excellent general history of the turbojet, see Dawson, *Engines and Innovation*, chap. 3. See also Holley, *Buying Aircraft*, 549; also reproduced in Rae, *Climb to Greatness*, 169.

[25] Neville and Silsbee, *Jet Propulsion Progress*, 110, 122–135; Schlaifer, *Development of Aircraft Engines*, chap. XVI, esp. pp. 462–466; Rae, *Climb to Greatness*, 163–167; Constant, *The Origins of the Turbojet Revolution*, 218–226; William R. Travers, *The General Electric Aircraft Engine Story* (n.p., General Electric Company, 1978), 1-6–1-26; General Electric Company, *Seven Decades of Progress: A Heritage of Aircraft Turbine Technology* (Fallbrook, Calif.: General Electric Co., 1979), 51–57; Daniel Ford, "Gentlemen, I Give You the Whittle Engine," *Air & Space*, October–November 1992, 88–98; Colwell interview, 1967. Unfortunately, Colwell did not recall the name of his classmate.

   GE delivered 241 I-16s to the U.S. Army Air Force during the war. Travers, *General Electric Aircraft Engine Story*, I-12; *Seven Decades of Progress*, 52. Since GE made some—probably a majority—of its own turbine wheels, TP's contribution to this program was modest.

[26] For the J33 and J35 engines, see Travers, *General Electric Aircraft Engine Story*, I-20 to I-26; *Seven Decades of Progress*, 54–56; and Paul Sonnenberg and William A. Schoneberger, *Allison: The Power of Excellence, 1915–1990* (Malibu, Calif.: Coastline Publishers, 1990), 92–96.

[27] Wright interview with Zewe, 1988; Wright interview with Lundy, 1983; Colwell interview, 1967; Crawford interview with Zewe, 1988.

[28] *Friendly Forum*, February 2, 1945, 1. See also the correspondence between various TP executives and GM in TRW WRHS 3942, box 1, 1937–1945. TP contracted to supply

components not only for the TG-180 (J35) but also for the TG-100, a hybrid turboprop engine for the U.S. Navy.

29 *Foremen's Bulletin*, February 1, 1941. Copies of this series are in TRW WRHS 3942, boxes 156 and 157.

30 *Foreman's Bulletin*, December 1, 1939; Raymond S. Livingstone, "Recruiting and Selecting Employees," in *Discussion before the 11th Annual Conference on Industrial Relations at the University of Michigan*, April 17 and 18, 1941. The first *Foreman's Bulletin* was issued on January 27, 1939.

31 *Foremen's Bulletin*, September 1, 1941. See also R. S. Livingstone, "Policies for Promotion, Transfer, Demotion and Discharge," *Supervision*, December 1941, 6–9.

32 *Foreman's Bulletin*, November 1, 1940; Livingstone, "How 20,000 People Work Together," in Thompson Products, Inc., *A Decade of Achievement*, 23–24.

33 *Friendly Forum*, January 12, 1940, 6; Raymond S. Livingstone interview with the author, February 6 and 7, 1991, Boca Raton, Fla.; Livingstone telephone conversation with the author, November 24, 1992. The formal responsibilities of the personnel supervisors covered "all matters pertaining to employment, safety, accidents, workmen's compensation, employee relations, and company policies."

34 *Friendly Forum*, January 12, 1940, 6; Livingstone interview, February 6 and 7, 1991; Livingstone to Fred Crawford, August 20, 1940; *Employee Bulletin*, May 10, 1941; Livingstone, "Good Human Relations Contribute to Company's Success," *Friendly Forum*, January 1951, 25.

35 Thompson Aircraft Products Company, *Employee Handbook, 1943*, 29–33; Harvey Shore, "A Historical Analysis of Thompson Products' Successful Program to Discourage Employee Acceptance of Outside Unions" (DBA diss., Harvard, 1966), 430–432; *Foreman's Bulletin*, June 1, 1941; *Business Week*, May 9, 1942, pp. 70–71; Ray Livingstone to Negro Members of Thompson Products, Inc., October 18, 1945. According to an employee survey published in August 1944, 12 percent of employees at the Main and Tapco plants were black. See Thompson Products, Inc., and Thompson Aircraft Products Co., *We Led with Our Chin!* (Cleveland, Ohio: Thompson Products, Inc., 1944), 4.

36 *Friendly Forum*, October 16, 1943, 3; Shore, "Historical Analysis," 428–430; Thompson Products, Inc. and Thompson Aircraft Products Co., *We Led with Our Chin!*, 4.

37 *Friendly Forum*, January 9, 1942, 8; R. E. Bender, "Learner Training," a manual describing the program in TRW WRHS 3942, box 24.

38 *Friendly Forum*, May 31, 1940, 6, and June 27, 1941, 1; Livingstone, "How 20,000 People Work Together," 24–25.

39 Livingstone interview, February 6 and 7, 1991. TP's communications strategy and tactics are sketched in "Two-Way Information Flow Pays Off," *Factory Management and Maintenance*, May 1946, unpaginated reprint; and Dossett, Chronological Record, November 21, 1941.

40 Thompson Products, Inc., *Employees' Handbook, 1940*. The company and Tapco issued annual editions of this publication throughout the war. The script for "Men, Management, and Production" is in the Thompson Products Collection at Harvard Business School.

41 R. S. Livingstone, "Duties of Personnel Supervisors," mimeographed bulletin, February 17, 1943.

42 *Time*, February 16, 1942; *Friendly Forum*, April 3, 1942, 5.

43 Thompson Products, Inc., *A Decade of Achievement*, 10.

44 R. S. Livingstone, "Personnel Direction: Dynamic Function of Business," unpaginated reprint from *The Clevelander* (October 1943).

45 Crawford, "A Business Advances," in Thompson Products, Inc., *A Decade of Achievement*, 6.

46 Crawford interview with Zewe, 1988.

47 *National Cyclopedia of American Biography* (1938), 523; "Awards, Citations, Etc.—F. C. Crawford" (typescript, 1989); Dawson, *Engines and Innovation*, 10–15; "Boundless Crawford Energy Tapped for Tapco and U.S.," in *Boys Grown Tall: A Story of American Initiative*, a special publication of the *Cleveland Plain Dealer* (Cleveland, 1944), 32.

48 "TP Auto Album Retains Spirit and Skill of Past," *Friendly Forum*, January 1951, 15; Thompson Products, Inc., Annual Report for 1943.

49 *Investment Banking*, November 15, 1938; Crawford interview, September 12–14, 1990. Crawford recalls that he began working on the basic ideas of the triangle of industry during the 1920s as a factory manager in Detroit. Crawford to the author, July 20, 1993.

50 F. C. Crawford, "The Triangle of Industry and the Production of Wealth," address at the National Association of Manufacturers 45th Annual Convention, December 13, 1940, reprinted from *Steel*, November 1940. A number of Crawford's most important speeches, including this one, have recently been reprinted privately in Christopher Johnston, ed., *Selected Speeches of Frederick Coolidge Crawford* (Cleveland, Ohio: privately printed, 1992).

51 Crawford interview, September 12–14, 1990; *Friendly Forum*, January 9, 1942, 1; "N.A.M. Raises Sights to Victory—with Crawford," *Business Week*, December 5, 1942, 16; Howell John Harris, *The Right to Manage: Industrial Relations Policies of American Business in the 1940s* (Madison, Wis.: University of Wisconsin Press, 1982), 108.

 The speech that S. S. McClure so admired was reprinted as a pamphlet: Crawford, *Plowshares into Swords*, An Address before the Academy of Political Science, Hotel Astor, New York City, November 12, 1941. Crawford proclaimed that "by far the greatest uncertainty, which hinders and often completely stops the wheels of production, is the complete confusion in the labor field," which he attributed to New Deal labor policy. See pp. 11–14 of the speech.

52 "Boundless Crawford Energy," 32.

53 Crawford, *Free Competitive Enterprise and the Common Man*, a speech before the Economic Club of Detroit, February 15, 1943; Crawford interview, September 12–14, 1990; Crawford, "The American Triangle of Plenty," *Reader's Digest*, April 1943.

54 The quotation is from an account of the exchange in Ed Hall's letter to President Roosevelt, December 17, 1941. The letter is reproduced in Shore, "Historical Analysis," 420–422. For Crawford's wartime activities, see the biographical file in TRW WRHS 3942, box 10.

55 For a useful survey of labor history in Cleveland, see David D. Van Tassell and John J. Grabowski, eds., *Encyclopedia of Cleveland History* (Bloomington, Ind.: Indiana University Press, 1987), 604–606. This subject deserves much fuller treatment. The most extensive secondary source I've seen is Raymond Boryczka and Lorin Lee Cary, *No Strength without Union: An Illustrated History of Ohio Workers, 1803–1980* (Columbus, Ohio: Ohio Historical Society, 1982). This book contains useful information but is not analytical in its approach.

 In 1944, at Crawford's initiative, Long became active in the War Labor Board, a position in which he helped employers regain the initiative against the national industrial unions. See Harris, *The Right to Manage*, 108.

56 33 NLRB 1033; quotations from Shore, "Historical Analysis," 374–375.

    The earlier propaganda war can be followed in materials from UAW Local 300 and TP in TRW WRHS 3942, Series III. See also Shore, "Historical Analysis," 299–322, 371–375.

57 On Hall and especially Mortimer, see Roger Keeran, *The Communist Party and the Auto Workers Unions* (Bloomington, Ind.: Indiana University Press, 1980), chap. 9, and Mortimer's autobiography: *Organize! My Life as a Union Man* (Boston: Beacon Press, 1971), esp. pp. 150–158.

58 Shore, "Historical Analysis," 399–403, 432. The UAW-CIO's amended petitions to the NLRB were dated January 12 (combine Main and Tapco into a single unit) and February 10 (disestablish the AWA).

    TP's first *Let's Have the Truth* bulletin had appeared in February 1941 during the initial war of propaganda.

59 *Cleveland Union Leader*, October 17, 1941, 1; *Cleveland Plain Dealer*, November 28, 1941, 1.

60 *Cleveland Union Leader*, October 17, 1941, 1; *Cleveland Press*, February 23, 1942, 1. See also Shore, "Historical Analysis," 418–422; Minutes of the Labor Relations Council Meeting, January 26, 1942; and *Friendly Forum*, March 6, 1942, 10.

61 *Cleveland Press*, January 30, 1942; Sanford M. Jacoby, "Reckoning with Company Unions: The Case of Thompson Products, 1934–1964," *Industrial and Labor Relations Review* 43, no. 1 (October 1989): 27.

62 Crawford interview, September 12–14, 1990; Livingstone interview, February 6 and 7, 1991; Jacoby, "Reckoning with Company Unions," p. 27. Quotations are taken from an undated memorandum of the meeting prepared by Livingstone and given to the author and from a letter from Livingstone to Crawford, May 10, 1989.

63 *Statement of Raymond S. Livingstone to the Committee on Education and Labor of the House of Representatives, February 24, 1947* (TRW headquarters), 7; Shore, Historical Analysis, pp. 466–482.

64 The details of the campaign can be followed in TRW WRHS 3942, Series III, and in Shore, "Historical Analysis," 432–487.

65 *Cleveland News*, May 2, 1941, 1. The totals at the Main Plant were 1288 for UAW, 87 for IAM, and 2519 for Neither; at Tapco the totals were 1203 for UAW, 2249 for AWA, and 134 for no union. See *Business Week*, May 8, 1942, 72.

66 Shore, "Historical Analysis," 507n, 513; Livingstone interview, February 6 and 7, 1991.

67 *Friendly Forum*, April 30, 1943, special second section, 1.

68 The findings and orders are reprinted in Shore, "Historical Analysis," 527–535.

69 Thompson Products, Inc., and Thompson Aircraft Products Co., *We Led with Our Chin!*, esp. pp. 36–37. The published results of the survey claim that it was "conducted in accordance with tested, scientific principles," but provide no information about the size of the sample or other tests of the data. The booklet mentioned that the full report and recommendations from Fenn College were available in TP's business reference library, but I have been unable to locate these documents.

70 *Let's Have the Truth*, August 21 and 29, 1944.

71 Several of these speeches were taped. The original recordings are available at the Western Reserve Historical Society. Transcripts of the tapes are included in research materials gathered for this history. Crawford's speech to the third shift at the main plant on August 24, which is quoted here, is excerpted in Davis Dyer, "A Voice of Experience: An

Interview with TRW's Frederick C. Crawford," *Harvard Business Review* 69 (November–December 1991): 118–119.

72 *Cleveland News*, August 31, 1944, 1. The totals at the main plant were 1291 for the UAW-CIO, 256 for the IAM-AFL, and 2033 for neither; at Tapco, the totals were 1276 for the UAW-CIO and 4582 for no union.

73 *Cleveland Press*, October 18, 1945.

74 *Cleveland Plain Dealer*, October 23, 1945: "Fred Crawford's Company," 208; *Statement of Raymond S. Livingstone to The Committee on Education and Labor*, 12; Livingstone interview, February 6 and 7, 1991. The vote at the main plant on October 23 was 929 for the UAW-CIO, 55 for the IAM-AFL, and 1,707 for neither.

75 *Cleveland Plain Dealer*, October 20, 1945; Crawford to Fellow Members of the Thompson Organization, November 5, 1945.

76 Harris, *The Right to Manage*, chap. 5. See also Harry A. Millis and Emily Clark Brown, *From the Wagner Act to Taft-Hartley* (Chicago: University of Chicago Press, 1950), passim.

77 The principal secondary sources on the TP case are Jacoby, "Reckoning with Company Unions," and Shore, "Historical Analysis." See also Sanford M. Jacoby and Anil Verma, "Enterprise Unions in the United States," *Industrial Relations* 31, no. 1 (Winter 1992): 137–158, and Robert N. McMurray, "War and Peace in Labor Relations," *Harvard Business Review* (November–December 1955): 48–60. Note: Jacoby's book, *Modern Manors: Welfare Capitalism Since the New Deal* (Princeton, N.J.: Princeton University Press, 1997), which includes new material on TRW, appeared too late for me to consider here.

All of these accounts focus on TP's relations with independent and national unions and pay scant attention to the impact of Crawford's beliefs, the role of TP's personnel department, and the business and production challenges that the company faced in shaping its policies and activities.

78 During the 1940s Cleveland-area and national media focused frequently and extensively on human relations at TP. In general, coverage reflected the editorial biases of the publications, with perspectives divided along ideological lines.

The question of whether TP resorted to "questionable" tactics lingered into the secondary literature. For example, both Shore and Jacoby (see n. 77) suggest that TP may have overstepped boundaries in some instances during the fight with the national unions. In equivocal language, Shore writes that the company apparently sanctioned "the use of questionable methods if (and only if) necessary to sustain healthy labor relations" (35, 173). He cites a single example—conflicting testimony in the NLRB hearings that suggest management may have involved itself illegally in the establishment of the A&AWA in 1937—a charge that "if conclusively proven, would constitute the one unsavory aspect of Crawfordism." Jacoby (29) states that "some of the tactics the company pursued were more clearly coercive than captive audience speeches. Dismissals of UAW activists were a regular occurrence during each of the UAW's organizing drives at Thompson."

79 Crawford conversation with the author, January 8, 1990.

80 When I put this question to Ray Livingstone, he nodded and smiled before saying it was hypothetical, wasn't it? He then went on to acknowledge that both the activities of national unions and the need to scale up production during World War II were important factors in shaping TP's personnel policies. See Livingstone interview, February 6 and 7, 1991.

[81] In this context, TP's experience is exceptional. See Daniel Nelson, "The Company Union Movement, 1900–1937: A Reexamination," *Business History Review* 56 (Autumn 1982): 335–357; Stuart Brandes, *American Welfare Capitalism, 1880–1940* (Chicago: University of Chicago Press, 1976); and David Brody, *Workers in Industrial America* (New York: Oxford University Press, 1980), esp. chap. 2.

   Note: TP's history points up another confusion apparent in many secondary accounts of industrial relations in the United States. Many authors use the term "company union" to refer both to employee representation plans like the TPEA, which were often dominated by management representatives, and to independent unions like the AWA, which were independent from management and not affiliated with national unions or the biggest national labor federations. The two sorts of organization were vastly different. The Wagner Act outlawed employer-dominated employee representation plans, but independent unions remain legal to this day. Recent statistics are not available, but in 1983, some 479,000 workers in the United States were members of independent labor unions. This total represents about 3 percent of total U.S. union membership for that year. See Jacoby and Verma, "Enterprise Unions," 140.

[82] Dyer, "A Voice of Experience," 120.

[83] TRW was considered a model nonunion employer. See Jacoby and Verma, "Enterprise Unions," 142. See also Fred K. Foulkes, *Personnel Policies in Large Nonunion Companies* (Englewood Cliffs, N.J.: Prentice-Hall, 1980); and Thomas A. Kochan, Harry C. Katz, and Robert B. McKersie, *The Transformation of American Industrial Relations,* rev. ed., (Ithaca, N.Y.: IRL Press, 1994).

[84] See also Livingstone interview, February 6 and 7, 1991, and James Dunlap interview with the author, June 26, 1991, Cleveland, Ohio.

[85] Jacoby and Verma, "Enterprise Unions," 145–146.

CHAPTER 6

[1] Raymond S. Livingstone interview with the author, February 6–7, 1991, Boca Raton, Fla. Livingstone's account of this meeting is the most detailed of several. See also Frederick C. Crawford interview with the author, September 12–14, 1990, Cotuit, Mass., and J. David Wright interview with Bruce Zewe, TRW Inc., 1988, TRW WRHS 88-088.

   None of the participants is very exact on the timing of the meeting. Livingstone, for example, thought it happened in 1945 or 1946. I date it to 1944 because by November of that year, TP had already announced plans to buy the Tapco plant. *Friendly Forum,* November 10, 1944, 2. There is also ample evidence in executives' speeches and TP's product literature that the company was planning for the end of the war as early as 1943.

[2] Wright interview with Zewe,1988.

[3] John Kenneth Galbraith, *American Capitalism* (Boston: Houghton Mifflin, 1952), 63–83.

[4] Thompson Products, Inc., Annual Report for 1945.

[5] J. D. Wright, A Message to All Tapco Employees, August 20, 1945; copy at TRW WRHS 3942, box 156; *Friendly Forum,* September 14, 1945, 1; TP, Inc., Annual Report for 1945.

   In September 1945, Crawford forecast a demand "sharply higher than anything ever experienced in pre-war years," and he predicted that "the ten years directly ahead . . . would be the greatest in company history, with employment ranging from 8,000 to 10,000 men and women." (*Employee Bulletin,* September 25, 1945; TRW WRHS, box 156.)

In a letter to all employees, Livingstone was especially bullish on the automotive and replacement markets, forecasting "about eight straight years of terrific automobile production," and pointing out that "although we have had an 82% increase in our service business since 1941, *during the war we filled only 47% of our orders!*" (R. S. Livingstone, "To Members of the Thompson Organization," August 20, 1945, TRW WRHS, box 156.)

[Bound copies of TP's newsletters and administrative bulletins from 1945 to 1957 are in TRW WRHS 3942, box 156. Unless otherwise specified, this reference applies generally to such sources in the notes below. Because many of these documents are not paginated, or are paginated irregularly, I cite them by date only.]

6 *Cleveland Plain Dealer,* September 20, 1945, unpaginated clipping; Davis Dyer, "A Voice of Experience: An Interview with TRW's Frederick C. Crawford," *Harvard Business Review* 69 (November–December 1991): 123.

   Crawford's story makes good reading, but two points should be remembered. First, most of TP's directors were insiders who were already intimately familiar with Tapco. Second, although the government disposed of some machinery and equipment after the war, virtually all of it was still in place when the company bought it.

7 Board Minutes, September 17, 1945; "Five New Divisions Set Up for Improved Operations," *Friendly Forum,* October 12, 1945, 1; *Foremen's Bulletin,* September 20, 1945; TP, Inc., Annual Report for 1945.

8 *Employee Bulletin,* September 25, 1945.

9 J. David Wright interview with Robert D. Lundy, 1983, copy in the possession of the author; Wright interview with Zewe, 1988; Crawford interview, September 12–14, 1990; and Frederick C. Crawford interview with Bruce Zewe, TRW Inc., 1988, WRHS 88-088.

   In 1944, Lee Clegg defined the company's products as having four common characteristics: "1. They serve exacting uses and must be designed to endure unimagined punishment by heat, friction, motion, wear, and stress. 2. They are fabricated out of high-alloy steels which are difficult to handle. 3. They must be made to the closest possible tolerances. 4. They are made in large quantities." Clegg, "1,400 Precision Products," in Thompson Products, Inc., *A Decade of Achievement* (Cleveland, Ohio: Thompson Products, Inc., 1944), p 12.

10 Wright interview with Zewe, 1988.

11 Wright interview with Zewe, 1988; Thompson Products, Inc., *Newsletter to Supervision,* July 18, 1952, TRW WRHS 3942, box 156.

12 *Toledo Blade,* November 26, 1945, clipping in TRW WRHS 3942, box 16, Toledo file.

13 Crawford's activities are drawn from a vita prepared during the early 1950s in TRW WRHS 3942, box 10.

14 Elizabeth Hawes, *Hurry Up, Please, It's Time* (New York: Reynal & Hitchcock, 1946), 182, 187–191.

   Crawford considered suing Hawes for libel. He rejected the idea both because he thought it would be difficult to win and because he thought a suit would give the book more publicity than it deserved. He did have an amusingly pointed correspondence with Hawes. He sent her his copy of the book with a request for her to sign it, suggesting several possible inscriptions: "'To Harvard from Vassar'; or maybe 'To a hopeless capitalist from a hopeful socialist'; or perhaps 'To one of the country's dangerous nazi-fascists from a charming communist'; or better still, just 'To a bastard from a bitch.'"

   Crawford concluded the letter by adding, "Whatever you are prompted to write will add to my ego, which has already been inflated by receiving so much attention in your book. I do hope you will receive this letter in the spirit in which it is written."

After an extended delay and prodding by Crawford, Hawes eventually returned the book with the following inscription: "To Fred Crawford: The man who writes that this book has inflated his ego—an interesting character: one whose ego expands under proof that he breaks laws and falsifies figures."

Crawford to Hawes, December 2, 1946; Crawford to Paul Garrett, January 27, 1947, in TRW WRHS 3942, box 1.

15 National Industrial Conference Board, *Organization of Personnel Administration,* Studies in Personnel Policy, no. 73 (New York: National Industrial Conference Board, 1946), 76–84; quotations from 80.

Livingstone also became something of a management guru in the postwar years. Before the war, he had been a novice in personnel management, a student sitting at the feet of his elders in big companies and experts at the American Management Association. After 1945, big companies and national management organizations often sought him out for advice on industrial relations. See Livingstone's articles "Labor Relations in a Non-Unionized Company," notes transcribed from an extemporaneous talk to the American Management Association, 1947; "Two-Way Information Flow Pays Off," *Factory Management and Maintenance* (May 1946); and "The Changing Concept of the Personnel Function," in *Industrial Applications of Medicine and Psychiatry: Personnel Series No. 130* (New York: American Management Association, 1949), 18–31.

16 *Newsletter to Supervision,* May 18, 1951; Robert N. McMurray, "War and Peace in Labor Relations," *Harvard Business Review* 33 (November–December 1955): 48–60; cf. Crawford, "Creating the Proper Climate," in Edward C. Bursk, ed., *How to Increase Executive Effectiveness* (Cambridge, Mass.: Harvard University Press, 1953), 7–22.

17 Horace A. Shepard interview with Bruce Zewe, TRW Inc., 1988, TRW WRHS 88-088; Fred Crawford, "A Good Place to Work," *Friendly Forum,* January 1951, 1; TP, Inc., Annual Report for 1952. According to Ray Livingstone, the Tapco plant was also known as "the country club." Livingstone telephone conversation with the author, November 24, 1992.

Crawford responded to the gift of the scroll by writing a letter to all TP employees: "If I live to be a hundred I shall never forget the moment . . . when the parchment was unrolled. You were more than generous in what you said on it. I can only repeat what I told those of you who were present: Anything I am, the men and women of Thompson Products have made me." See Crawford, "To Members of the Thompson Organization," April 11, 1952.

18 Lee M. Clegg, A. T. Colwell, J. D. Wright, J. H. Coolidge, and Ray Livingstone, "A Report to Employees on the Business Outlook," May 30, 1947, 3; *Friendly Forum,* August 22, 1947, 1, and March 5, 1948, 3; George Poe interview with the author, April 30, 1991, Cleveland, Ohio.

19 I have seen no comprehensive or authoritative history of the automobile or aircraft supplier industries, although there is at least one promising start by a young economist: see Susan Helper, "Strategy and Irreversibility in Supplier Relations: The Case of the U.S. Automobile Industry," *Business History Review* 65, no. 4 (Winter 1991): 781–824.

20 *Newsletter to Supervision,* April 20, 1950.

21 Davis Dyer, "A Voice of Experience: An Interview with TRW's Frederick C. Crawford," *Harvard Business Review* 69 (November–December 1991): 125. After a year or so, TP was able to raise its prices and improve its margins. See the correspondence between TP and GM on this subject in TRW WRHS 3942, box 1.

22 Lee M. Clegg, "TP Sales Record Mirrors Half Century of Advancement," *Friendly Forum,* January 1951, 18–19; Thompson Products, Inc., *A Decade of Achievement,* 12; Wright interview with Zewe, 1988.

23 Dyer, "A Voice of Experience," 120.

24 *Newsletter to Supervision,* April 21 and June 16, 1950; Crawford interview with Zewe, 1988; Wright interview with Zewe, 1988.

25 Wright interview with Zewe, 1988; *Newsletter to Supervision,* April 29, 1946.

26 Emil Gibian, "The Industrial Engineering Department" (typescript, December 5, 1945) (copy in the possession of the author); and Gibian, "Industrial Engineers Bring Order to Complex Operations," *Friendly Forum,* January 1951, 49. See also Gibian, "Management Control through Industrial Engineering," *SAE Quarterly Transactions* 1, no. 2 (April 1947): 192–203; and Gilbert P. Muir, "Thompson Products, Inc.: Engineering Is Their Business," *The Tool Engineer* (June 1951), 55–63

27 Gibian, "Industrial Engineers Bring Order," 49; Gibian, "The Industrial Engineering Department," 4; Gibian, "Management Control," 193, 202.

28 Gibian, "Industrial Engineers Bring Order," 49; Gibian, "Management Control," 203; and Gilbert P. Muir, "Thompson Products, Inc.: Engineering Is Their Business," *The Tool Engineer* (June 1951), 59, 61.

29 Muir, "Thompson Products," 55.

30 Colwell, "Good Engineering Gave Impetus," 20–21; Thompson Products, Inc., *Background for Tomorrow* (Cleveland, Ohio: Thompson Products, Inc., 1952), 13–14, 19; and Muir, "Thompson Products," 59–61.

31 Colwell, "Good Engineering Gave Impetus to Company's Growth," *Friendly Forum* (January 1951), 20.

32 Muir, "Thompson Products," 60–61.

33 *Friendly Forum,* December 23, 1949, 3.

34 Ibid.; *Newsletter to Supervision,* September 28, 1945; Crawford interview with Zewe, 1988.

35 Colwell, "Good Engineering Gave Impetus," 20; Thompson Products, Inc., *Background for Tomorrow,* 7–8; Thompson Products, Annual Report for 1949. Also *Friendly Forum,* February 4, 1949, 1; September 30, 1949, 1; December 23, 1949, 3; and November 24, 1950, 1.

36 *Friendly Forum* (Detroit edition), February 1, 1952, 1, 3; *Newsletter to Supervision,* January 18, 1952; TP, Inc., Annual Reports for 1951 and 1952.

37 James H. Booth, "Application of Ball Joints to Front Suspensions," *SAE Quarterly Transactions* 6, no. 4 (October 1952): 710–722; *Friendly Forum* (Detroit edition), February 1, 1952, 1, 3.

38 Booth, "Application of Ball Joints," 710–722.

39 *Newsletter to Supervision,* September 19, 1952, and March 13 and December 11, 1953; *Friendly Forum,* October 10, 1952, 8.

40 "Thompson Vita Meter Promises That Added 'Lift' in Postwar Cars; Invites Use of Low Octane Gas," *Friendly Forum,* February 1, 1945, 2; "Vita Meter to Be Produced by AA Division," *Friendly Forum,* April 27, 1945, 1–2.

41 Muir, "Thompson Products, Inc.," 60–61; *Friendly Forum,* January 10, 1947, 3.

[42] Arch T. Colwell interview, 1967, WRHS 983; *Newsletter to Supervision,* September 15, 1948; *Friendly Forum,* September 17, 1948, 1–2; Thompson Products, Inc., *The Vitameter Gives Your Car a Helping Hand,* product brochure, 1948.

[43] Colwell interview, 1967; *Friendly Forum,* November 24, 1950, 2, and April 4, 1952, 2.

[44] Colwell reported the $4.25 billion figure in a paper to the SAE early in 1947. See *Friendly Forum,* April 2, 1948, p. 4, for an account of his speech.

[45] Colwell interview, 1967.

[46] John B. Rae, *Climb to Greatness: The American Aircraft Industry, 1920–1960* (Cambridge, Mass.: MIT Press, 1968), 169, 174–192, 202. Rae quotes J. H. "Dutch" Kindleberger, president of North American Aviation, as saying that the aircraft of 1950 were about four times as complicated as the aircraft of 1940 (see p. 198). See also Charles D. Bright, *The Jet Makers: The Aerospace Industry from 1945 to 1972* (Lawrence, Kan.: Regents Press of Kansas, 1978), 9, 16–17.

[47] Paul Y. Hammond, *Organizing for Defense: The American Military Establishment in the Twentieth Century* (Princeton, N.J.: 1961), chaps. 8 and 9; Rae, *Climb to Greatness,* 192–197; G. R. Simonson, "The Demand for Aircraft and the Aircraft Industry, 1907–1958," *Journal of Economic History* 20, no. 3 (September 1960): 378–379; TP, Inc., Annual Report for 1947.

[48] "Fred Crawford's Company," *Fortune,* December 1946, 203.

[49] Thompson Products, Inc., *Background for Tomorrow,* 10; A. T. Colwell, "Manufacture of Blades, Buckets, and Vanes for Turbine Engines," *SAE Transactions* 63 (1955): 492; Thompson Products, Inc., *Newsletter to Supervision,* September 7, 1951. According to the last source, other turbojet engine components were similarly high priced: compressor rotors cost about $4,200; impellers, more than $1,000; and nozzle diaphragms, about $1,300.

[50] "Jet Propulsion and TP," *Friendly Forum,* June 21, 1946, 2; Thompson Products, Inc., *Background for Tomorrow,* 10–11.

[51] Doyle F. Smee, "Thompson Products in 51 Years Has Become $290 Million Auto, Aircraft Parts Maker," *Wall Street Journal,* July 7, 1952, 16; Virginia P. Dawson, *Engines and Innovation: Lewis Laboratory and American Propulsion Technology* (Washington, D.C.: NASA, 1991), 139–140; Colwell, "Good Engineering Gave Impetus," 21.

[52] Colwell, "Manufacture of Blades, Buckets, and Vanes," 496–497; Colwell, "Good Engineering Gave Impetus," 21; Thompson Products, Inc., *Background for Tomorrow,* 19.

[53] Board Minutes, February 4, 1947; Colwell, "Good Engineering Gave Impetus," 21; Colwell, "Manufacture of Blades, Buckets, and Vanes," 496–497; *Friendly Forum,* August 24, 1951, 4.

[54] A. T. Colwell and R. E. Cummings, "Turbine Engine Blading: Manufacturing Techniques and Fastening Methods," *SAE Quarterly Transactions* 2, no. 3 (July 1948): 424.

[55] Colwell, "Manufacture of Blades, Buckets, and Vanes," 500–501; Colwell, "Good Engineering Gave Impetus," 21; Thompson Products, Inc., *Background for Tomorrow,* 15, 18; "Iced Mercury Opens Fields for Casting," *Business Week,* November 11, 1950, unpaginated reprint.

[56] Board Minutes, March 29, 1949; "Spirit of Teamwork Makes Dave Wright's Job 'Fun,'" *Friendly Forum,* January 1951, 15.

Crawford's recollections of this appointment are interesting, especially with regard to the reactions of other senior managers in the company. Lee Clegg was apparently bitterly disappointed at being passed over, while Arch Colwell had also considered himself a candidate to succeed Crawford. See Crawford interview, September 12–14, 1990.

57 Crawford interview with Zewe, 1988.

58 A William Reynolds interview with the author, September 1, 1992, Fairlawn, Ohio.

59 Wright interview with Zewe, 1988.

60 Crawford interview with Zewe, 1988; Wright interview with Zewe, 1988; Raymond S. Livingstone telephone conversations with the author, February 15, 1991, and November 24, 1992. Livingstone also admired Wright's "genius for brevity," citing his ability to communicate in letters of just a paragraph or two in length.

61 "Notes—Management Review Meeting, December 23, 1949," in TRW WRHS 3942, box 12.

62 Wright interview with Zewe, 1988; "Notes—Staff Meeting, December 22, 1949"; TP, Inc., Annual Report for 1949.

63 *Friendly Forum,* April 1, 1949, 1.

64 "Notes—Staff Meeting, December 22, 1949"; J. D. Wright, draft typescript of speech to the management of Perfect Circle Corporation, 1950; and "Notes on Management Review Meeting, July 25, 1949," in TRW WRHS 3942, box 12.

65 Wright interview with Zewe, 1988.

66 Wright interview with Zewe, 1988; *Letter to Supervisors,* March 17, 1950.

67 Wright, Speech at Perfect Circle, 1950.

68 I have not found an original edition of this manual, although a related document from 1954, *Manual of Organization,* is in TRW WRHS 3942, box 149. "Responsibilities Common to All Members of Management" is reproduced in the company's annual report for 1952. The quotation "one of the hardest jobs" is from "Thompson Head Does Job Well," *Cleveland Plain Dealer,* October 4, 1953, 10-C.

69 Wright interview with Zewe, 1988; Board Minutes, December 18, 1950, and March 27, 1951.

70 Wright interview with Zewe, 1988. Crawford brushes aside this difference as unimportant, noting that the views expressed applied primarily to "my pet subject, the blue collar worker." Crawford to the author, June 28, 1994.

71 William M. Jones interview with the author, September 23, 1992, Independence, Ohio. In addition to Jones, the group included Chuck Ohly, Art Schweitzer, Bob Paetz, Bill Angst, Bill Bente, Pierce Angell, and others who eventually became department or division general managers. Ohly rose the highest, retiring in 1980 as an executive vice president of TRW.

72 Wright interview with Zewe, 1988; Shepard interview with Zewe, 1988; Stanley C. Pace interview with the author, February 15, 1991, Indian Wells, Calif.

Incidentally, Shepard recalls that Crawford and Wright were considering buying Cleveland-based Parker Appliance Co. (forerunner of today's Parker-Hannifan) as a sideline investment under arrangements similar to their ownership of Crawford Door. Shepard was recruited with the idea that he would become head of Parker Appliance. When that deal fell through, he joined TP as Wright's assistant. Wright recalls that Shepard had three goals in leaving the military. "He wanted a good job. He wanted to have fun. And he wanted to make a million dollars." Wright added, "I think he achieved all three."

73 *Newsletter to Supervisors,* February 15, 1952.

74 Frederick C. Crawford Papers, Group 4, Daily Diaries, July 1952, WRHS 90-010; Shepard interview with Zewe, 1988; Wright interview with Zewe, 1988; Crawford interviews with Zewe, 1988, and with the author September 12–14, 1990, and October 15, 1990, Guildhall, Vermont; *Newsletter to Supervision,* September 12, 1952.

[75] "Spirit of Teamwork Makes Dave Wright's Job 'Fun,'" *Friendly Forum,* January 1951, 14.

[76] Board Minutes, May 22, 1950; Crawford interview with Zewe, 1988; TP, Inc., Annual Report for 1950; *Newsletter to Supervision,* September 1, 1950; *Friendly Forum,* September 1, 1950, 2; "Ramsey Corp., Top Ring Maker Is Recent Addition to TP Family," *Friendly Forum,* January 1951, 52.

[77] Board Minutes, August 8 and 31, 1950; TP, Inc., Annual Report for 1950; *Foreman's Bulletin,* September 22 and October 27, 1950, and February 2, 1951. On the proposed deal with Muskegon Piston Ring Company, see Board Minutes, August 27, 1951, and *Newsletter to Supervision,* April 4, 1952.

[78] Rae, *Climb to Greatness,* 197–200, 205–206; Bright, *The Jet Makers,* 15. According to the latter, more than half of engines produced during 1950 were reciprocating; by 1953, more than half were jets.

[79] Board Minutes, July 24 and October 6, 1950; *Newsletter to Supervision,* September 1, 1950, and December 12, 1952; TP, Inc., Annual Reports for 1950–1953.

[80] TP, Inc., Annual Reports for 1951 and 1952; "Thompson Products in 51 Years Has Become $290 Million Auto, Aircraft Parts Maker," *Wall Street Journal,* July 7, 1952, 16.

[81] *Friendly Forum,* December 21, 1951, 8.

[82] Thompson Products, Inc., *Background for Tomorrow,* 11; Colwell, "Good Engineering Gave Impetus," 21; *Friendly Forum,* April 4, 1947, 4.

[83] Thompson Products, Inc., *Background for Tomorrow,* 11–12.

[84] *Newsletter to Supervision,* October 6 and November 17, 1950, and March 23, 1951; Thompson Products, Inc., *Background for Tomorrow,* 14; Colwell interview, 1967; TP, Inc., Annual Report for 1953.

[85] Board Minutes, June 25, 1951; Thompson Products, Inc., *Newsletter to Supervision,* September 25, 1951; *Friendly Forum,* October 5, 1951; Jones interview, September 23, 1992.

[86] *Newsletter to Supervision,* April 1, 1953.

[87] Board Minutes, August 24, 1953; Thompson Products, Inc., *Newsletter to Supervision,* April 3, 1953.

[88] *Newsletter to Supervision,* May 29, 1953; Shepard interview with Zewe, 1988. Cf. Lon C. Kappel, "How to Get Modern Air Power Cheaper," *Aviation Age,* November 1953, 21–23; this article is based on a long interview with Crawford.

According to Shepard, at the AIA meeting Crawford "had the entire audience just rolling on the floor. They couldn't control themselves. No one was offended or angered by his explanation. It didn't upset the customers. It delighted the industry people. It was just typical of his gift for saying and making a very fundamental point in a very dramatic way. Shepard repeated this story in a background interview he gave to *Fortune* magazine in 1980, when Crawford was inducted into the National Business Hall of Fame. A transcript of this interview is in the possession of the author. Crawford also remembers the story: see Crawford interview, September 12–14, 1990.

[89] Wright interview with Lundy, 1983; Wright interview with Zewe, 1988; Shepard interview with Zewe, 1988; Crawford interviews with Zewe, 1988, and with the author, September 12–14, 1990.

[90] *Newsletter to Supervision,* August 14, 1953; Dyer, "A Voice of Experience," 123; Crawford interviews, September 12–14 and October 15, 1990.

[91] Board Minutes, August 24, 1953.

92 Thompson Products, Inc., *Newsletter to Supervision,* August 21, 1953; *Friendly Forum,* September 17, 1954, 1.

93 TP, Inc., Annual Report for 1953.

94 *Business Week,* October 3, 1953, 61–63; Charles J.V. Murphy, "The Blowup at Hughes Aircraft," *Fortune* (February 1954), 116–118, 188–200; Simon Ramo, *The Business of Science: Winning and Losing in the High-Tech Age* (New York: Hill and Wang, 1988), chap. 2; Simon Ramo, interview with Christian G. Pease, UCLA Oral History Program, 1984; James Parton, *"Air Force Spoken Here": General Ira Eaker and the Command of the Air* (Bethesda, Md.: Adler & Adler, 1986), part 6.

The reporting relationships at Hughes Aircraft were deliberately unclear because Howard Hughes liked checks and balances and did not want to groom a strong number-two executive. As vice president of Hughes Tool Company, Eaker first reported to Hughes, then to Dietrich. Eaker was based in Culver City and responsible for relations between Hughes Aircraft and Hughes Tool. George was vice president and general manager of Hughes Aircraft. He apparently reported to Eaker (who had outranked him in the Air Force), but also to Dietrich and, when he could get to him, to Hughes.

TP executives became aware of the possible availability of Hughes Aircraft in several different ways: Wright through his cousin General Putt; Shepard, through his contacts in the Air Force; and Crawford, apparently, directly from a telephone conversation with Howard Hughes, whom he knew from the National Air Races. See Wright, Shepard, and Crawford interviews with Zewe, 1988 and Wright interview with Lundy, 1983.

95 Wright interview with Lundy, 1983; Wright interview with Zewe, 1988; Shepard interview with Zewe, 1988. Wright recalls that TP offered $20 million for Hughes Aircraft.

Accounts of the dinner meeting by Ramo and Wooldridge square with Wright's recollections. See Simon Ramo interview with the author, March 6, 1990, Beverly Hills, Calif., and *The Business of Science,* 76n; and Dean E. Wooldridge interview with Bruce Zewe, TRW Inc., 1988, WRHS 88-088.

96 *Newsletter to Supervision,* July 20, 1953.

97 "Thompson Products Buys Bell Sound of Columbus," *Cleveland Plain Dealer,* October 8, 1953, 14; *Newsletter to Supervision,* October 9, 1953; Board Minutes, October 19, 1953; Jones interview, September 23, 1992. The price of the transaction is not mentioned in any of these sources, but it was probably well below $1 million.

98 Wright interview with Lundy, 1983; Wright interview with Zewe, 1988; Crawford interview with Zewe, 1988.

CHAPTER 7

1 Thompson Products, Inc., Annual Report for 1955.

2 William L. Baldwin, *The Structure of the Defense Market 1955–1964* (Durham, N.C.: Duke University Press, 1967), 6; Margaret B.W. Graham, "Industrial Research in the Age of Big Science," *Research on Technological Innovation, Management and Policy* 2 (1985): 47–79.

Helpful studies of the defense industry generally during this period include Baldwin plus Merton J. Peck and Frederick M. Scherer, *The Weapons Acquisition Process: An Economic Analysis* (Boston: Division of Research, Graduate School of Business Administration, Harvard University, 1962); and Herman O. Stekeler, *The Structure and Performance of the Aerospace Industry* (Berkeley, Calif.: University of California Press, 1965).

[3] Simon Ramo, *The Business of Science: Winning and Losing in the High-Tech Age* (New York: Hill and Wang, 1988), 9–11.

[4] "Electronics: The New Age," *Time,* April 29, 1957, 86.

[5] Horace Shepard interview with Bruce Zewe, TRW Inc., 1988, WRHS 88-088.

[6] "Electronics: The New Age," 86; Simon Ramo interview with Christian G. Pease, Oral History Program, University of California at Los Angeles, 1984, 272–273.

[7] James Parton, *"Air Force Spoken Here": General Ira Eaker and the Command of the Air* (Bethesda, Md.: Adler & Adler, 1986), 459–461.

[8] Ramo interview with Pease, 1984, 247, 299–300. Wooldridge gives his views of guided missile development in "Some Characteristics of Military Research and Development," *American Journal of Physics* 22, no. 2 (February 1954): 62–68. Also Ruben F. Mettler, telephone conversation with the author, September 15, 1993, and Jack Irving interviews with the author, June 16 and 17, 1992.

[9] Simon Ramo interview with the author, March 5, 1992, Beverly Hills, Calif.; Dean E. Wooldridge interview with the author, October 11, 1991, Santa Barbara, Calif.

[10] Simon Ramo interview with the author, March 6, 1990, Beverly Hills, Calif. Ramo also had met and liked Arch Colwell on a government advisory panel evaluating a potential big investment in wind tunnels. As early as the fall of 1954, Wooldridge considered approaching TP to be "probably the smartest thing we ever did." See Philip Klass, "New Avionics Team Makes Fast Start," *Aviation Week,* October 11, 1954, 53.

[11] The minute book of The Ramo-Wooldridge Corporation is in the Law Department Library at TRW headquarters in Cleveland. At the time of incorporation, Ramo and Wooldridge each bought 3,375 shares of Class B stock for $2 per share, and held options to buy an additional 3,125 at the same price. In March 1954, to lure George into the business on equal terms, Ramo and Wooldridge each sold him some of their shares at cost. After that transaction, each man held 2,125 shares, with the option to buy an additional 2,082 shares. Thereafter, the company sold additional Class B stock to Samuel Gates, their lawyer, as well as to key employees like Milt Mohr, Burt Miller, and V. G. "Bud" Nielsen.

   TP's holdings included $250,000 (2,500 shares of the preferred stock at $100 per share) worth of preferred stock and $15,000 for 7,500 shares of Class A common stock at $2 per share.

[12] R-W, Board Minutes, September 1953.

[13] Dean E. Wooldridge interview with Bruce Zewe, TRW Inc., 1988, WRHS 88-088. R-W continued to use the barbershop location until 1957.

[14] In pursuing a strategy of customer-funded growth, R-W was unusual (although hardly alone) among new entrants into the defense industry. Most start-ups depended upon the personal funds of owners, the sale of stock, or bank loans to get started. See Peck and Scherer, *The Weapons Acquisition Process,* 627.

[15] Wooldridge interview, October 11, 1991; Ramo interview, March 5, 1992; Ramo interview with Pease, 1984, 305–306.

[16] The Ramo-Wooldridge Corporation, *An Introduction to The Ramo-Wooldridge Corporation,* May 1954. The new headquarters address was 8820 Bellanca Avenue.

[17] Milt Mohr interview with the author, March 3, 1992, Malibu, Calif.

[18] R-W, *An Introduction to The Ramo-Wooldridge Corporation,* May 1954; *RevieW,* August 31, 1955, 2–3.

[19] R-W, *An Introduction to the Ramo-Wooldridge Corporation;* The Ramo-Wooldridge Corporation, *RevieW,* August 31, 1955, 2–3; *RevieW,* April 4, 1957, 3–4.

[20] The Ramo-Wooldridge Corporation, news release, June 22, 1954; Thompson Products, Inc., Minutes of the Executive Committee, June 22, 1954.

The financing of PSI was broadly similar to that of R-W. The North group held rights to a convertible preferred stock that would eventually make them substantial owners not only of PSI but also of R-W. TP anted up most of the $3 million in the form of loan credits and purchases of preferred stock, with rights to convert its preferred stock into common stock.

[21] All quotations are from R-W, *An Introduction to The Ramo-Wooldridge Corporation,* May 1954. The same or similar language appeared in subsequent editions of this pamphlet in 1955, 1956, and 1958.

[22] Wooldridge interview, October 11, 1991. According to the head of Hughes Aircraft in 1954, Wooldridge agreed to a three-month moratorium on hiring from Hughes to help it return to equilibrium. See L. A. "Pat" Hyland, *Call Me Pat,* ed. William A. Schoneberger (Virginia Beach, Va.: The Donning Company, 1993), 219.

[23] The most noteworthy skeptic of the ICBM was Dr. Vannevar Bush, the MIT engineering professor who headed the U.S. Office of Scientific Research and Development during World War II, and who participated in or led many national scientific and technical organizations thereafter. In 1945, Bush told a congressional hearing that the ICBM "is impossible and will be impossible for many years," chiefly because of limitations in guidance. In 1949, he qualified his skepticism by noting that an ICBM would be uneconomical, even if technologically feasible. See Vannevar Bush, *Modern Arms and Free Men* (New York: Simon & Schuster, 1949), 85, and Edmund Beard, *Developing the ICBM: A Study in Bureaucratic Politics* (New York: Columbia University Press, 1976), 69–71.

[24] Simon Ramo, "We *Now* Have a Manhattan Project," *Life* 43, no. 22, November 25, 1957, 35; The Ramo-Wooldridge Corporation, "Ramo-Wooldridge Role in Air Force Ballistic Missile Program," March 5, 1957, copy in WRHS 3942, box 15.

[25] The historical literature on the USAF ballistic missile program is extensive. The most authoritative sources are Jacob Neufeld, *The Development of Ballistic Missiles in the United States Air Force* (Washington, D.C.: Office of Air Force History, 1990); Beard, *Developing the ICBM;* and Ernest G. Schwiebert, *History of the United States Air Force Ballistic Missiles* (New York: Praeger, 1965). A journalistic account, John L. Chapman, *Atlas: The Story of a Missile* (New York: Harper & Brothers, 1960), is also useful but tells the story almost entirely from Convair's point of view.

[26] Ramo, *The Business of Science,* 82, 109; Neufeld, *The Development of Ballistic Missiles,* 96.

[27] On the origin of the committee's nickname, see Simon Ramo interview with the author, June 16, 1992, Redondo Beach, California. According to Ramo, the code name "Teapot" was a play on Trevor Gardner's name. Ramo originally proposed to call the Committee the "Tea Garden" Committee, but the idea was rejected because it was hardly a disguise. The group kept the basic notion, however, by choosing "Teapot." For a different version, see Chapman, *Atlas,* 73. According to this source, Gardner and Ramo were having lunch one day when they decided that the committee needed a name. A teapot sitting between them provided the inspiration.

[28] Robert L. Perry, *The Ballistic Missile Decisions* (Santa Monica, Calif.: The RAND Corporation, 1967), 12.

[29] Letter Contract AF 18(600)-1002, dated October 15, 1953. Copy at U.S. Air Force, Ballistic Missile Organization, History Office, Norton Air Force Base, San Bernardino, Calif. [Hereafter cited as BMO Norton.]

[30] The report is excerpted in Neufeld, *The Development of Ballistic Missiles,* 249–265. quotation from p. 259.

[31] See Davis Dyer, "Necessity as the Mother of Convention: Developing the ICBM, 1954–1958," *Business and Economic History* 22, no. 1 (Fall 1993): 194–209.

[32] In early February, Gardner urged that R-W's contract be expanded yet again so that it could "perform further technical studies with the object of determining realizable performance parameters leading toward an optimum" ICBM. Gardner believed that this additional work could be funded for about $100,000. See "Chronology. Sequence of Events. Participation of Ramo-Wooldridge in the Air Force Guided Missile Program" (typescript, BMO Norton), 1–4.

  The RAND report was Bruno Augenstein, *A Revised Development Program for Ballistic Missiles of Intercontinental Range* (Santa Monica, Calif.: The RAND Corporation, February 8, 1954).

[33] Memo from ARDC to AMC [Air Materiel Command], April 21, 1954, at BMO Norton; Beard, *Developing the ICBM,* 170–171.

[34] Schwiebert, *History of the United States Air Force Ballistic Missiles,* 76–78; Ramo, *The Business of Science,* 101.

[35] The contract was signed on May 17 as USAF 18(600)-1190. "Chronology. Sequence of Events," 5; Schwiebert, *History of the United States Air Force Ballistic Missiles,* 80–81.

  On April 15, R-W had proposed to undertake this work for an annual budget of $1.2 million.

[36] Wooldridge interview, October 11, 1991; Wooldridge interview with Zewe, 1988; Ramo, *The Business of Science,* 77, 83–85; Ramo interview with Pease, 1984, 328–329, 338–339.

[37] Minutes of the Scientific Advisory Committee Meeting, July 20 and 21, 1954, at BMO Norton.

[38] For Air Force criticisms of the arsenal approach, see Michael H. Armacost, *The Politics of Weapons Innovation: The Thor-Jupiter Controversy* (New York: Columbia University Press, 1969), 153–163. (Interestingly, Armacost, a noted political scientist, was elected a director of TRW Inc. in 1993.)

[39] According to one source, Caltech, MIT, and Bell Labs were discussed as candidates for the job but "some who were approached did not want to be considered for the role." Gerald W. Siegel, "The Atlas Case Study: A High Priority Long-Range Ballistic Missile Development" (typescript, Harvard Business School, n.d.), 18. See also Chapman, *Atlas,* 74–75.

[40] U.S. Air Force, Western Development Division, "Study of the Development Management Organization for the Atlas Program," at BMO Norton. Cf. Beard, *Developing the ICBM,* 172–177; Neufeld, *Development of Ballistic Missiles,* 111; Schwiebert, *History of the United States Air Force Ballistic Missiles,* 84–85.

[41] Letter Contract AF 18(600)-1190, January 29, 1955, at BMO Norton; Roger Lewis, Memorandum for the Record, September 8, 1954, at BMO Norton. In July 1956, the financial terms were modified to reduce R-W's fixed fee to a more conventional 10 percent.

  The Scientific Advisory Committee approved the arrangements at its meeting in October, but there was one dissenter: Franklin R. Collbohm, president of RAND Corporation. He believed that the arrangements would separate responsibility and authority in the program, that R-W had not yet demonstrated strong capability in SETD, and that several "old-line reliable" contractors, though perhaps not Convair, could handle the job. To answer these objections and meet again with Collbohm, von Neumann established a subcommittee consisting of Charles A. Lindbergh, MIT President Jerome Wiesner, and Harvard Professor George Kistiakowsky.

The subcommittee reported back in early December, when Collbohm stated once more his opinion that "too much time was being devoted by the present Atlas management complex toward optimizing the intercontinental ballistic missile rather than getting into design and production on a system which would give an early operational capability. He implied that the job to be done is one requiring a top-flight engineering organization experienced in product design, development, and production, not one requiring the talents of basic scientists."

Ramo answered Collbohm point by point. He noted that R-W personnel had considerable experience in product design and development, as well as complex systems engineering. He pointed out "that it is one thing to establish technical feasibility but quite another to take two or more pieces of complex equipment which might be available on the shelf and put them together and make them work as a system." At this point, several members of Schriever's staff jumped in and noted that to date the Navajo program had slipped a total of 8.3 years; that the Snark program had slipped 4 years; and that the Matador missile had slipped 4.5 years. "All of these programs, when initiated, were considered to be technically feasible, requiring only straight-forward product design, development, and production engineering." The officers conceded that the delays were due to many factors, including those beyond the control of the contractors, but concluded nonetheless that "industry's past record and demonstrated competence in the field of missiles is not good."

By such reasoning, Collbohm was evidently persuaded, and he "agreed that at the present date the management structure and concept as now established with Ramo-Wooldridge should remain unchanged." He strongly urged that a parallel development effort should be started at the earliest possible time for a second ICBM and/or an intermediate range ballistic missile (IRBM).

[42] Thomas P. Hughes, *American Genesis: A Century of American Invention and Technological Enthusiasm* (New York: Viking, 1989), introduction and chap. 5.

[43] Simon Ramo, "The Guided Missile as a Systems Engineering Problem," *Canadian Aeronautical Journal* 3, nos. 1 and 2 (January and February 1957): 3; Dean Wooldridge, "Some Characteristics of Military Research and Development," unpaginated reprint.

Wooldridge believed that systems engineering as a distinctive management approach had originated at Bell Labs and that it was working its way into military research and development as weapon systems grew more complex. At Hughes Aircraft, for example, he and Ramo practiced systems engineering in the development of the Falcon missile system, and they brought those techniques with them to R-W. Wooldridge interview, October 11, 1991; Wooldridge interview with Zewe, 1988.

[44] Major General Bernard A. Schriever, "The USAF Ballistic Missile Program," *Air University Quarterly Review* 9, no. 3 (Summer 1957): 11–12; "The Ballistic Missile Challenge . . . As Seen by Major General Bernard A. Schriever," *Missiles and Rockets* 2, no. 4 (April 1957): unpaginated reprint edition.

[45] Lt. Col. J. C. Bogert, Memorandum for the Record, 26 October 1956, at BMO Norton; Neufeld, *The Development of Ballistic Missiles,* 181; Minutes of the ICBM Scientific Advisory Committee Meeting, October 15, 1954, at BMO Norton.

[46] R-W, News Release, September 28, 1954. For Dunn's career at JPL, where he directed work on the Corporal and Sergeant tactical missiles, see Clayton R. Koppes, *JPL and the American Space Program: A History of the Jet Propulsion Laboratory* (New Haven, Conn.: Yale University Press, 1982), esp. pp. 31–32, 64–65.

[47] "PSG Provides Interesting Study, Fruitful Research," *RevieW,* December 22, 1955, 4–5; C. Budd Cohen interview with the author, March 4, 1992, Redondo Beach, Calif.

[48] The Minutes of ICBM Scientific Advisory Committee Meeting, 15 October 1954, include a listing of several studies carried out by industrial contractors under R-W's "study contract program." As for the UNIVAC, in 1984 Ramo joked that "we'd still be working on the ICBM" if not for the computer's ability to simulate conditions otherwise obtainable only on test flights. Ramo interview with Pease, 1984, 346–347.

[49] The Atlas nose-cone story is described in a USAF Staff Study by Lt. Col. Bogert in 1956, Tab S, at BMO, Norton.

[50] C. Budd Cohen, comment to the author, May 10, 1994.

[51] U.S. Air Force, *Survey of Management of the Ballistic Missile Program,* 14 January–21 February 1958, copy at BMO Norton, pp. 14, 50; Weapons System Engineering of the USAF Ballistic Missile Programs—The Ramo-Wooldridge Responsibility, undated document at BMO Norton, pp. 2–3; Irwin Stambler, "Scientific Management of Ballistic Missile Systems," *Aviation Age* 29, no. 4 (April 1958): 18–19, 190–200.

[52] Ramo-Wooldridge, "Notes on Technical Aspects," 51; David Langmuir, interview with the author, June 18, 1992, Redondo Beach, Calif.; "PSG Provides Interesting, Fruitful Research," 4–5.

According to Wooldridge, Clauser's group also investigated and disproved the myth that vortices spiral in opposite directions depending on whether they occur in the northern or southern hemispheres. Wooldridge interview, October 11, 1991.

[53] Donald MacKenzie, *Inventing Accuracy: A Historical Sociology of Nuclear Missile Guidance* (Cambridge, Mass.: MIT Press, 1990), 117–118.

[54] Bogert Study, Tab R; Ramo-Wooldridge, "Notes on the Technical Aspects of Ballistic Missiles," 39–40; Chapman, *Atlas,* 81–82. For an excellent history of guidance generally, see MacKenzie, *Inventing Accuracy,* esp. chap. 3; and D.G. Hoag, "Ballistic-missile Guidance," in B. T. Feld et al., eds., *Impact of New Technologies on the Arms Race* (Cambridge, Mass.: MIT Press, 1971), 19–108.

[55] Ramo-Wooldridge, "Notes on Technical Aspects," 53.

[56] Robert Bromberg interview with the author, November 14, 1990, Redondo Beach, Calif.; Cohen interview, March 4, 1992; John Sellars interview with the author, November 15, 1990, Redondo Beach, Calif.

[57] "The Spectacular X-17," *Missiles and Rockets* 2, no. 4 (April 1957): unpaginated reprint; Chronology of Significant Technical Accomplishments and Major Milestones Passed in the Air Force Ballistic Missiles Program (1955–1956), document in Ruben F. Mettler papers, TRW Inc., Redondo Beach, Calif.

[58] Ramo, *The Business of Science,* 93.

[59] Gen. Bernard A. Schriever, oral history interview with Dr. Edgar F. Puryear, June 29, 1977, copy at U.S. Air Force History Office, Bolling AFB, Washington, D.C.; Schwiebert, *History of the United States Air Force Ballistic Missiles,* 96.

[60] For an excellent detailed case history of the evolution of guidance systems, see MacKenzie, *Inventing Accuracy,* passim.

[61] Schwiebert, *History of the United States Air Force Ballistic Missiles,* 96–99.

62 Bogert Staff Study, Tab E, at BMO Norton; Edwin A. Swanke and Richard K. Jacobson, "The Ballistic Missile Test Program," *Air University Quarterly Review* 9, no. 2 (Summer 1957): 108–120.

63 Ramo, "The ICBM Program—Its Relation to Past and Future Developments," 10.

64 Bogert Study, Tab T: "Ramo-Wooldridge's Contribution to the Titan Missile."

65 Neufeld, *The Development of Ballistic Missiles,* 132–137. The presidential directive, dated September 13, 1955, also triggered administrative reforms inside DOD and the Air Force to streamline decision making. The reforms, known as the Gillette Procedures after their principal author, Air Force Deputy for Budget Hyde Gillette, slashed the number of reviewing authorities in the missile program from 42 to 10.

66 "Chronology of Significant Technical Accomplishments and Major Milestones Passed in the Air Force Ballistic Missile Program (1955–1956)," BMO Norton; Robert L. Perry, "The Atlas, Thor, Titan, and Minuteman," in Eugene M. Emme, ed., *The History of Rocket Technology* (Detroit: Wayne State University Press, 1964), 145.

67 Edward Doll interview with the author, February 15, 1991, Santa Barbara, Calif.; William Duke interview with the author, October 8, 1991, Newport Beach, Calif.

68 Bogert Study, Tab T; Duke interview, October 8, 1991.

69 Bogert Study, Tab T.

70 For background on the Thor, see Julian Hartt, *The Mighty Thor: Missile in Readiness* (New York: Duell, Sloan and Pearce, 1961); and Armacost, *The Politics of Weapons Innovation,* passim. Hartt offers a useful chronology of key milestones in the development and testing of the Thor.

71 Adolph K. Thiel interview with the author, November 19, 1990, Redondo Beach, Calif.

72 Perry, "The Atlas, Titan, Thor, and Minuteman Missiles," 150–151; Armacost, *The Politics of Weapons Innovation,* chaps. 2 and 3.

73 Bruce A. Jacobs, "Dr. Ruben F. Mettler: Prudent Adventurer in the Worlds of Science and Business," unidentified and unpaginated reprint in PR files at TRW Inc.; Ruben F. Mettler, interviews with the author, March 6, 1990, June 18, 1991, and June 16, 1992, all in Los Angeles.

74 Jacobs, "Dr. Ruben F. Mettler"; Mettler interview, June 18, 1991.

75 *Survey of Management of the Ballistic Missile Program,* 14 January–21 February 1958, Tab B, p. 20; MacKenzie, *Inventing Accuracy,* 120–122. For Hall's account of the Thor—which is highly critical of R-W—see Edward N. Hall interview with the author, June 2, 1993, Palos Verdes, Calif.; Edward N. Hall, *The Art of Destructive Management: What Hath Man Wrought?* (New York: Vantage Press, 1994), esp. chap. 4; and Edward N. Hall, Narrative of Air Force Engineering (typescript, 1993).

76 Mettler interview, July 18, 1991; Thiel interview, November 16, 1990. Another version of the story has it that Ramo said (or also said), "O.K. We've got a missile with a 5,000 mile CEP [circular error probability—a term of the trade to indicate guidance accuracy]. Now we just need to work on the accuracy." Jack Bromberg, the program director from Douglas Aircraft, noted that the flight achieved "the lowest apogee of any trajectory in history." Hartt, *Mighty Thor,* 104.

77 Chapman, *Atlas,* 127.

CHAPTER 8

1 Simon Ramo, *The Business of Science: Winning and Losing in the High-Tech Age* (New York: Hill and Wang, 1988), 117–119. To those in the know, including Ramo, the surprise

was not that the Soviets possessed an operational ICBM—which they had announced in August 1957—but rather the spectacular, worldwide nature of the *Sputnik* demonstration.

2 "Armed Forces: The Bird and the Watcher," *Time,* April 1, 1957, 16–20; "Electronics: The New Age," *Time,* April 29, 1957, 84–90.

The first public mention of R-W's role in the Air Force missile programs had come in March 1956 from Donald Quarles, who had succeeded Harold Talbott as secretary of the Air Force. Quarles described R-W's role in a press conference that also listed the major contractors for the Atlas, Thor, and Titan missiles. The first public statement from the Air Force followed in July in a speech by Gen. Don R. Ostrander. See the *RevieW,* issues of March 22 and August 2, 1956.

3 Gen. Bernard A. Schriever, Interview with Dr. Edgar F. Puryear, June 29, 1977, copy at U.S. Air Force History Office, Bolling AFB, Washington, D.C.; Walter A. McDougall, *. . . the Heavens and the Earth: A Political History of the Space Age* (New York: Basic Books, 1985), 111; William E. Burrows, *Deep Black: Space Espionage and National Security* (New York: Random House, 1986), 80–82, 86–87; Jeffrey T. Richelson, *America's Secret Eyes in Space* (New York: Harper & Row, 1990), chaps. 1 and 2; Curtis Peebles, *Guardians: Strategic Reconnaissance Satellites* (Novato, Calif.: Presidio Press, 1987), chaps. 3, 4 and 17.

Between 1959 and 1964, the WS-117L space vehicles and their close relatives served as platforms for three different kinds of missions: Discoverer satellites tested and pursued an approach to photographic reconnaissance using recoverable film canisters; MIDAS satellites used infrared detection to serve as an early warning system; and SAMOS satellites were part of an Air Force reconnaissance system that radioed real-time data to ground stations. More than eighty of these various satellites were launched, with predictably mixed results. The WS-117L program spawned later generations of reconnaissance satellites that proved important to TRW and other defense contractors.

4 U.S. Air Force, *Survey of Management of the Ballistic Missile Program,* 14 January–21 February 1958, 23–24, 52; 1958 Separation Study (typescript). Copies of both documents are available at the U.S. Air Force, Ballistic Missile Organization, History Office, Norton AFB, San Bernardino, Calif. [hereafter cited as BMO Norton].

5 Jack Irving interviews with the author, June 16 and 17, 1992, Los Angeles; Allen F. Donovan interviews with the author, October 9, 1991 and March 4, 1992, Los Angeles. I am grateful to Dr. Irving for showing me copies of some of the documents described here.

6 U.S. Senate, Committee on Armed Services, *Inquiry into Satellite and Missile Programs. Hearings Before the Preparedness Investigating Subcommittee,* 85th Cong., 1st and 2nd sess. (Washington, D.C., 1958).

7 Ramo, *The Business of Science,* 120–121.

8 Michael H. Armacost, *The Politics of Weapons Innovation: The Thor-Jupiter Controversy* (New York: Columbia University Press, 1969), 138–143; Julian Hartt, *Mighty Thor: Missile in Readiness* (New York: Duell, Sloan and Pearce, 1961), 129–130, 164–169; Ruben F. Mettler comment to the author, October 27, 1993; G. Harry Stine, *ICBM: The Making of the Weapon That Changed the World* (New York: Orion Books, 1991), 222.

9 Jack Irving interviews, June 16 and 17, 1992. Many of STL's projects are summarized in STL, *The Astronautics Outlook,* July 15, 1958, a document prepared for the Air Technical Intelligence Center, copy in the possession of Jack Irving.

[10] Hartt, *Mighty Thor,* 142; George Solomon interview with the author, February 13, 1991, Santa Barbara, Calif.; Robert Bromberg interview with the author, November 14, 1990; John Sellars interview with the author, November 15, 1990; Budd Cohen interview with the author, March 4, 1992 (all three interviews conducted in Redondo Beach, Calif.).

[11] George Gleghorn, "Able Zero-Pioneer I," speech to TRW Forum, October 21, 1988; George Gleghorn interview with the author, November 11, 1990, Redondo Beach, Calif.

[12] Hartt, *Mighty Thor,* 166–167.

[13] Ibid., 193–194.

[14] Craig B. Waff, "A History of the Deep Space Network" (working draft, 1991), chap. 1, esp. pp. 10–15, 21–27. I am grateful to Dr. Waff for furnishing a copy of this typescript to my colleague, Virginia Dawson. Donovan interview, October 9, 1991; Paul Dergarabedian interview with the author, March 3, 1992, Redondo Beach, Calif.

[15] STL, *The Astronautics Outlook,* July 15, 1958, pp. 20–21; TRW Space & Technology Group, *We've Proven It Can Fly* (Los Angeles: TRW Space & Technology Group, 1986), 8; Waff, *Deep Space Network,* chap. 1, esp. pp. 6–18; Frank Lehan interview with the author, June 20, 1991, Santa Barbara, Calif.

[16] Hartt, *Mighty Thor,* 198–200; Waff, "Deep Space Network," chap. 1, pp. 51–53.

[17] Hartt, *Mighty Thor,* 201–204.

[18] Thompson Products, Inc., Notice of Special Meeting of Shareholders Including Proxy Statement, September 30, 1958, 9.

[19] Dean E. Wooldridge interview with the author, October 1991, Santa Barbara, Calif.; R-W, untitled newsletter (subsequently the *RevieW*), July 29, 1955, 1. The details of R-W's work on the U-2 program remain classified.

[20] See "Company to Observe Fifth Birthday on September 16," *RevieW,* September 11, 1958, 1–2, for a helpful review of building expansion.

[21] The Ramo-Wooldridge Corporation, Minutes of the Board of Directors, May 31, 1955 (copy in the Law Department Library at TRW Inc.); Thompson Products, Inc., Board Minutes, June 20, 1955.

This transaction apparently caused momentary discomfort at R-W and may have been the occasion when Ramo and Wooldridge gave up any thoughts that their company would ever be independent. As recounted by Fred Crawford, when Ramo and Wooldridge described their plan to raise money to TP's officers—it is not clear whether this occurred at a board meeting of R-W or of TP—they first proposed that R-W would sell additional stock to the public. At that point, Dave Wright piped up, "Great. We'll take our 49 percent of the new offering." Ramo and Wooldridge looked at one another for a moment, and there was an uncomfortable silence. Then Wooldridge agreed, admitting that R-W had needed TP at the start and that it was only fair that the relationship remain close. Thereafter, the two sides worked out the terms that made a merger inevitable. Frederick C. Crawford interview with the author, September 12–14, 1990, Cotuit, Mass.

The news of the eventual merger also raised consternation among R-W's senior staff, who were concerned about the potential loss of their independence. At a meeting to discuss the terms of the 1955 loan, Wooldridge and Ramo fielded pointed questions about R-W's future. In typical fashion, Ramo mollified the staff with a display of wit. He speculated that if he were to die young, his widow, bless her heart, might marry a man who looked like Clark Gable. He then said that if he were an R-W employee, he'd rather have Thompson Products running the company than a man who looked like Clark Gable! Robert Corpening interview with the author, June 19, 1991, Redondo Beach, Calif.

22 Philip Klass, "New Avionics Team Makes Fast Start," *Aviation Week,* October 11, 1954, 48; The Ramo-Wooldridge Corporation (General Electronics Group), Progress Report, January 1958, p. 2-1. A copy of this document is at WRHS 3942, box 15.

23 R-W, Progress Report, January 1958, sections 3 and 5.

24 R-W, Progress Report, January 1958, section 6.

25 R-W, *An Introduction to the Ramo-Wooldridge Corporation* (Los Angeles: Ramo-Wooldridge Corporation, October 1955); R-W, Board Minutes, July 1955 and September 1957; "EIC Operating R-Ws Primary Production Facility," *RevieW,* January 2, 1958, 3; "EIC in Denver Explains Role in Development, Marketing," *RevieW,* April 24, 1958, 3.

26 R-W, Progress Report, January 1958, Section 4; "Airborne Computer Model Ready for Fall Test," *RevieW,* May 17, 1956; U.S. Air Force, *Survey of Management of the Ballistic Missile Program,* 14 January–21 February 1958, 52.

27 "Cleveland Group Undertakes Hike in Commercial Activity," *RevieW,* December 22, 1955, 8; Eugene M. Grabbe, ed., *Automation in Business and Industry* (New York: Wiley, 1957), passim. See "R-W Founders Aid in Automation Book Edited by Grabbe," *RevieW,* April 4, 1957, 2. Grabbe spoke widely on the subject of automation including at TP's Vermont Planning Conference in 1957. In the spring of 1956, he achieved some notoriety by winning a $1,500 jackpot on Groucho Marx's TV show, "You Bet Your Life." *RevieW,* July 11, 1957, 5.

28 "R-W to Double Size, Sales in 1956," *RevieW,* February 23, 1956, 6; R-W, Progress Report, January 1958, section 4; *RevieW,* November 15, 1956, 1; Philip Klass, "New Avionics Team Makes Fast Start," *Aviation Week,* October 11, 1954, 50.

29 "RW-300 Computer Seen Major Step in Industry Automation," *RevieW,* July 11, 1957, 1, 3; "RW Unveils New Desk-Size Computer," *RevieW,* September 19, 1957, 1, 3; *Mechanical Engineering,* March 1958, cover story; "Missile Architect Digs into Production," *Business Week,* December 28, 1957, 112.

30 For Manildi, see *RevieW,* May 2, 1957, 2. On the establishment of TRWP and the Texaco deal, see R-W, Board Minutes, September 23 and November 18, 1957; and *RevieW,* December 12, 1957, and January 2, 1958.

31 Thompson Products, Inc., Annual Reports for 1955 and 1956; R-W, Board Minutes, April 10, 1956, and March 27, 1957; Thompson Products, Inc., Notice of Special Meeting of Shareholders including Proxy Statement, September 30, 1958, 5, 10; *RevieW,* November 28, 1957, and April 10 and May 8, 1958.

32 Lehan interview, June 20, 1991.

33 "Missile Architect Digs into Production," *Business Week,* December 28, 1957, 110–111; "Electronics: The New Age," *Time,* April 29, 1957, 87.

34 "R-W to Build New Facility on Valley Property," *RevieW,* July 31, 1958, 1, 6; Thompson Ramo Wooldridge Inc., *Ramo-Wooldridge Laboratories* (pamphlet) (n.p., n.d.).

35 On Minuteman, see Robert L. Perry, "The Atlas, Thor, Titan, and Minuteman," in Eugene M. Emme, ed., *The History of Rocket Technology* (Detroit: Wayne State University Press, 1964), 155–159; Roy Neal, *Ace in the Hole: The Story of the Minuteman Missile* (Garden City, N.Y.: Doubleday, 1962); and George A. Reed, "U.S. Defense Policy, U.S. Air Force Doctrine and Strategic Nuclear Weapon Systems, 1958–1964: The Case of the Minuteman ICBM" (Ph.D. dissertation, Duke University, 1986), 51–52 See also R-W, *Consideration of Operational Aspects for the Solid Propellant IRBM* (technical paper, December 1956), passim, copy at TRW archives at Space Park.

36 Reed, "U.S. Defense Policy," 43–46.

37 Irving interviews, June 16 and 17, 1992; Reed, "U.S. Defense Policy," 50; *RevieW,* July 11, 1957, 11. The panel included Drs. Clark Millikan (Caltech); Wolfgang Panofsky (Stanford); Walker Bleakney (Princeton); Otto Laporte (Michigan); Francis Clauser (Johns Hopkins); John Whinnery (Berkeley); John R. Ragazzini (Columbia); Hans Bethe and Dale Corson (Cornell); Gordon Brown and Guyford Stever (MIT); George Kistiakowsky (Harvard).

38 Perry, "The Atlas, Thor, Titan, and Minuteman," 158.

39 Reed, "U.S. Defense Policy," 85–87.

40 Reed, "U.S. Defense Policy," 84–85.

41 These issues are outlined in Space Technology Laboratories, *Solid Propellant ICBM Ground Support System* (technical paper, February 1958), copy at TRW archives at Space Park.

42 Louis G. Dunn, "Solid Propellant ICBM Program—Management Concepts," January 29, 1958, copy at BMO Norton; Neal, *Ace in the Hole,* 98–99; Reed, "U.S. Defense Policy," 81–82.

43 For Hall's criticisms of R-W, see Edward N. Hall interview with the author, June 2, 1993, Palos Verdes, Calif. See also Hall's book, *The Art of Destructive Management: What Hath Man Wrought* (New York: Vantage Press, 1984), esp. pp. 53–73; and two typescripts: "Epitaph" (August 29, 1958), copy at BMO Norton, and "Engineering in the United States Air Force" (1993), chap. 7, copies in the possession of the author.

44 TP, Annual Report for 1955.

45 TP, Annual Report for 1955; "Tapco Learns How to Change," *Business Week,* October 23, 1954, 184.

46 *Newsletter to Supervision,* October 16, 1953, TRW WRHS 3942, box 156; "Tapco Learns How to Change," 184.

47 J. D. Wright, Speech to Delegates Visiting Tapco During the Annual Convention in Cleveland of the National Federation of Financial Analysts, May 21, 1957, TRW WRHS 3942, box 12. Note the bracketed number [four] reads three in the original, but that number is either a mistake or a change in policy. See "Tapco Learns How to Change," 186.

48 *Friendly Forum,* February 11, 1955, 1.

49 *Newsletter to Supervision,* November 13, 1953. The contract between TP and the AEC had been finalized in late September or early October. Wright, Speech to Delegates Visiting Tapco, May 21, 1957.

50 *Newsletter to Supervision,* August 19 and September 9, 1955, and February 17, 1956. *Friendly Forum,* April 15, 1955, 8; September 16, 1955, 1; November 11, 1955, 8; March 16, 1956, 3; and May 18, 1956, 6. TP, Annual Report for 1956.

51 *Newsletter to Supervision,* January 4, 1957. *Friendly Forum,* January 18, 1957, 3; March 14, 1958, 3; October 18, 1957, 2. TP, Annual Report for 1957.

52 William M. Jones interview with the author, September 23, 1992, Independence, Ohio; TP, Annual Report for 1958; J. D. Wright Scrapbook, TRW WRHS 3942, vol. 83, pp. 140, 157.

53 *Friendly Forum,* May 14, 1954, 1.

54 *Friendly Forum,* January 14, 1955, 1; March 16, 1956, 2; December 14, 1956, 5. Wright scrapbook, pp. 140, 157; TP, Annual Report for 1957; *Newsletter to Supervision,* October 22, 1954.

55 TP, Annual Report for 1954; *Newsweek,* December 20, 1954, unpaginated reprint; John B. Rae, *Climb to Greatness: The American Aircraft Industry, 1920–1960* (Cambridge, Mass.: MIT Press, 1968), 202. Crawford applauded the Air Force's long-range plan, which he had long advocated. See Lon C. Kappel, "How to Get Modern Air Power Cheaper," *Aviation Age,* November 1953, 21–23.

56 Stanley C. Pace interview with the author, February 11, 1991, Indian Wells, Calif.

57 Pace interview, February 11, 1991; *Friendly Forum,* June 15, 1956, 3.

58 Board Minutes, October 26, 1954; *Friendly Forum,* December 16, 1955, 1, and July 13, 1956, 2; TP, Annual Reports for 1956 and 1958.

59 *Newsletter to Supervision,* October 21, 1955.

60 TP, Annual Report for 1954; Jones interview, September 23, 1992.

61 *Friendly Forum,* October 12, 1956, 1; TP, Annual Report for 1956.

62 John B. Rae, *The American Automobile Industry* (Boston: Twayne Publishing, 1984), 180–181; Wright, Speech to Delegates of the National Federation of Financial Analyst Societies, May 21, 1957.

63 *Newsletter to Supervision,* December 11, 1953, and March 19, 1954.

64 TP, Annual Reports for 1955 and 1956; *Friendly Forum,* January 13, 1956, 5, and November 16, 1956, 5.

65 Board Minutes, June 20, 1955; *Friendly Forum,* December 16, 1955, 8, and November 16, 1956, 5; and May 17, 1957, 5; David Loeffler interview with the author, April 17, 1991, Cleveland, Ohio.

66 Board Minutes, July 18, 1955.

67 George Poe interview with the author, April 30, 1991, Cleveland, Ohio.

68 Board Minutes, November 19, 1957; *Friendly Forum,* November 15, 1957, 1.

69 Charles D. Bright, *The Jet Makers: The Aerospace Industry, 1945–1972* (Lawrence, Kan.: University of Kansas Press, 1972), 66; G. R. Simonson, "Missiles and Creative Destruction in the American Aircraft Industry," *Business History Review* 38, no. 3 (1964): 302–314.

70 *Newsletter to Supervision,* August 15, 1957, 1.

71 Ibid.

72 J. D. Wright, Speech at Coit Road Plant, November 5, 1957, copy in TRW WRHS 3942, box 12; TP, Annual Report for 1957; *Newsletter to Supervision,* November 8, 1957.

73 *Newsletter to Supervision,* November 22, 1957; Wright, Speech at Coit Road Plant, November 5, 1957; TP, Annual Report for 1957; *Friendly Forum,* July 11, 1958, 6; "Thompson Products Is Working on Space Platform Power Unit," *Wall Street Journal,* March 17, 1958, unpaginated clipping.

74 *Newsletter to Supervision,* March 31 and June 3, 1958; *Friendly Forum,* July 12, 1957, 8, and April 11, 1958, 1; Pace interview, February 11, 1991; Jones interview, September 23, 1992.

75 Board Minutes, June 30, 1958.

76 Dean E. Wooldridge, Draft Memorandum to General Schriever, July 21, 1958, BMO Norton. According to Bill Reynolds, who as a young TP manager helped prepare financial analysis of the merger, TP managers were also impressed with prospects for PSI. A. William Reynolds interview with the author, September 1, 1992.

77 Thompson Products, Inc., Notice of Special Meeting of Shareholders Including Proxy Statement, September 30, 1958; Thompson Ramo Wooldridge Inc., Annual Report for 1958.

78 TP, Notice of Special Meeting, September 30, 1958, 9; Space Technology Laboratories, Inc., Annual Report for 1958.

79 See, for example, U.S. House of Representatives, Committee on Government Operations, *Organization and Management of Missile Programs* (Washington, D.C.: U.S. Government Printing Office, 1959); U.S. Senate, Committee on Aeronautical and Space Sciences, *Government Organization for Space Activities Hearings* (Washington, D.C.: U.S. Government Printing Office, 1959), and Armacost, *Politics of Weapons Innovation,* 153–163. See also Glenn Bugos and Thomas P. Hughes, "Systems Engineering and Program Management: Post-Scientific Management," draft paper, July 1993. I am grateful to Dr. Bugos for lending me a copy of this paper.

80 See Davis Dyer, "Necessity as the Mother of Convention: Developing the ICBM, 1954–1958," *Business and Economic History* 22, no. 1 (Fall 1993): 194–209.

CHAPTER 9

1 "Teamwork across 2,000 Miles," *Business Week,* November 29, 1958, 54.

Ramo cites these arrangements in making an argument that the merger created an entirely new company. "One day there was Ramo-Wooldridge and Thompson Products, and the next day there was TRW." He thus considers himself a cofounder of TRW. Simon Ramo interview with the author, March 6, 1990; Simon Ramo, *The Business of Science* (New York: Hill and Wang, 1988), dust jacket.

Horace A. Shepard interview with Bruce Zewe, TRW Inc., 1988, WRHS 88-088, raises an interesting point about the corporate name. He points out that including the names of Ramo and Wooldridge was an inducement to the two men to support the merger earlier than planned in the 1955 loan agreement. See Chapters 7 and 8.

2 The board of directors included Crawford, Wright, Shepard, Coolidge, and Colwell from TP and Ramo, Wooldridge, Johnson, and General George from R-W. All but Johnson had been directors of TP prior to the merger.

3 "Teamwork across 2,000 Miles," 54; Thompson Ramo Wooldridge, Inc., Annual Report for 1958.

4 "Drs. Ramo, Wooldridge Visit TP-Cleveland," *Friendly Forum,* September 12, 1958, 1. For a short time, the West Coast businesses followed Livingstone's lead in producing employee manuals and other personnel policies but apparently paid little attention to these.

5 J. F. Mandrow, R. A. Campbell, M. J. Tauschek, and J. E. Coppage, "Internal Development Programs," 23 August 1968, 12; David Langmuir interview with the author, June 18, 1992, Redondo Beach, Calif.

6 Ruben F. Mettler interview with Michael L. Johnson, TRW Inc., 1988, copy in the possession of the author; W. S. Kennedy, S. M. Kovacic, and E. C. Rea, "Solid Rocket History at TRW Ballistic Missile Division." Paper for the American Institute of Aeronautics and Astronautics, Nashville, Tenn., July 6–8, 1992, 14, 16–17; Roy Neal, *Ace in the Hole* (Garden City, N.Y.: Doubleday, 1962), esp. chap. 7; Ernest G. Schwiebert, *A History of the United States Air Force Ballistic Missiles* (New York: Praeger, 1965), esp. pp. 131–141.

[7] Schwiebert, *A History of the United States Air Force Ballistic Missiles,* 118–123; G. Harry Stine, *ICBM: The Making of the Weapon That Changed the World* (New York: Orion Books, 1991), 229–230.

[8] Stanley C. Pace interview with the author, February 11, 1991, Indian Wells, Calif.

[9] On Project Score, see "Project Score Made History 4 Years Ago" *Cocoa Tribune,* December 18, 1962, 1–2; Irving Stone, "STL Integrates Space Probe Payloads" (last of a three-part series on STL) in *Aviation Week including Space Technology,* June 1, 1959, unpaginated reprint; and John L. Chapman, *Atlas: The Story of a Missile* (New York: Harper & Brothers, 1960), 152–165.

[10] The failure rate of these early programs was distressingly high; only about half fully achieved mission objectives. Although each failure represented the loss of millions of dollars and proved immensely frustrating and disappointing, STL and its sponsors recognized these unhappy outcomes as the price of learning. Only so much of a spacecraft-booster system could be tested on the ground. After each launch, study teams reviewed the results, and in the case of failures, carried out exhaustive investigations to determine the cause. The explanation usually proved difficult to isolate, and often resulted from multiple factors such as aerodynamic instabilities resulting from sudden crosscurrents of air, overstressed components such as pumps, a materials failure, and occasionally a design flaw or human error. The lessons from these experiences were used to improve the odds for the next launch. See Mettler interview with Johnson, 1989.

[11] STL's capabilities are described in two company publications: *An Introduction to Space Technology Laboratories* (Los Angeles: Space Technology Laboratories, 1961) and *The Capabilities of Space Technology Laboratories, Inc.* (typescript, Los Angeles, 1961). Convenient summaries of STL's early space programs are available in a special edition of *SenTineL:* "Able Program—Nation's 'First' in Space," undated, 1962; and *TRW Space Technology Laboratories . . . Roles in Space,* a public relations pamphlet published in 1964. For information on failure rates, see TRW Space and Technology Group, *Space Log, 1957–1987,* vol. 23 (Los Angeles, 1988), 30.

[12] Space Technology Laboratories, undated slide presentation circa 1962; "TRW Spacecraft Programs," *SenTineL,* April 4, 1975, 4; TRW Space & Technology Group, *We've Proven It Can Fly* (Los Angeles: TRW Space & Technology Group, 1986), 10–12.

[13] U.S. House of Representatives, Committee on Government Operations, *Organization and Management of Missile Programs,* H. Rept. No. 1121, 86th Cong., 1st sess., September 2, 1959.

[14] H. Rept. 1121, 97; U.S. House of Representatives, Committee on Government Operations, *Air Force Ballistic Missile Management (Formation of Aerospace Corporation),* H. Rept. 324, 87th Cong., 1st sess., May 1, 1961, 8–9.

[15] H. Rept. 324, 11–14.

[16] H. Rept. 324, 14. See also The Aerospace Corporation, *The Aerospace Corporation: Its Work: 1960–1980* (Los Angeles: The Aerospace Corporation, 1980), 15–19; Robert Sheehan, "Thompson Ramo Wooldridge: Two Wings in Space," *Fortune* (February 1963), 140.

[17] TRW Ballistic Missiles Division, "TRW SE/TA Support: A Summary History of the TRW Systems Engineering and Technical Assistance Support Provided to the U.S. Air Force—1954–1985," undated typescript at TRW BMD headquarters in San Bernardino, Calif.; "Company Operation Closely Supports USAF in Systems Engineering, Technical Direction," *SenTineL,* December 3, 1962, 4.

[18] "Profile: Dr. Richard D. DeLauer," *SenTineL,* July 14, 1960, 2, 4; "DeLauer Named Director of Ballistic Missile Program," *SenTineL,* August 5, 1963, 1.

[19] "Dr. Duke to Head STL Canoga Park Division," *SenTineL,* August 4, 1960, 1; William C. Duke interview with the author, October 8, 1991, Newport Beach, Calif.; Thompson Ramo Wooldridge, Inc., Annual Report for 1960.

[20] Willard E. Wilks, "STL Drives for Hardware Business," *missiles and rockets,* March 19, 1962, 28, 31–32; Mettler interview with Johnson, 1989.

[21] Records of this study group are sparse, but Rube Mettler recalls that it also included Samuel Gates, a lawyer with the New York firm Debevoise & Plimpton. In 1953, Gates had done the legal work connected with the founding of Ramo-Wooldridge, a company that he continued to advise from time to time. Ruben F. Mettler interview with the author, June 18, 1991, Los Angeles.

[22] H. G. Stever, "Some Notes on Question 'What Is the Future of Systems Engineering/ Technical Direction and Similar Activities for STL?'" memorandum for STL executives, July 22, 1960. I am grateful to Dr. Stever for furnishing a copy of this document, the original of which is included with his papers at the Gerald R. Ford Library at the University of Michigan, to Dr. Mettler, who passed it along to me.

[23] Stever memo, pp. 7–8.

[24] Mettler interview, June 18, 1991; James Dunlap interview with the author, June 26, 1991, Cleveland, Ohio; *TRW Systems Group (A and B Condensed)* (Boston: Harvard Business School Case Services, 9-476-117), 8–10; "Teamwork Through Conflict," *Business Week,* March 20, 1971, 44–46.

[25] "STL Planning New 10-Building Complex in Airport Vicinity," *SenTineL,* October 6, 1960, 1; Bob Burgin interview, October 10, 1991, La Jolla, Calif.

[26] Chuck Allen interview with the author, November 12, 1990, San Diego, Calif; Burgin interview, October 10, 1991; Mettler interview, June 18, 1991.

[27] Wilks, "STL Drives for Hardware Business," 32; Mettler interview, June 18, 1991.

[28] "NASA Names STL for OGO: Releases News of Project," *SenTineL,* January 9, 1961, 1, 5; TRW News (press release), July 21, 1967. On OGO generally, see John E. Jackson and James I. Vette, *OGO Program Summary* (NASA SP-7601, December 1975).

[29] George Gleghorn interview with the author, November 11, 1990; "OGO Project Personnel Organization Described," *SenTineL,* February 6, 1961; Wilks, "STL Drives for Hardware Business," 31.

[30] "Nuclear Detection Satellite, Program Milestones," TRW News Release, April 25, 1967; "STL Begins Production of Flight Spacecraft for AF 823 Program," *SenTineL,* May 6, 1963, 8; "Backgrounder on Incentive Fee Contract for Nuclear Detection (Vela) Satellites," TRW News Release, April 25, 1967; William E. Burrows, *Deep Black: Space Espionage and National Security* (New York: Random House, 1986), 176–177.

[31] "STL Begins Production of Flight Spacecraft for AF 823 Program"; TRW Space and Technology Group, *We've Proven It Can Fly,* 18.

[32] "Tiny STL Spacecraft Offers Materials Test Economies," *SenTineL,* August 6, 1962, 6; "ERS Program Provides Timely Test Capabilities," *SenTineL,* January 7, 1966, 6; TRW Space and Technology Group, *We've Proven It Can Fly,* 14.

[33] The early history of commercial communications satellites is well told by NASA expert Burton I. Edelson, "The Experimental Years," in Joel Alper and Joseph N. Pelton, eds., *The INTELSAT Global Satellite System* (New York: American Institute of Aeronautics and Astronautics, 1984), 39–54, and by John L. McLucas, *Space Commerce* (Cambridge, Mass.: Harvard University Press, 1991), chap. 1. For TRW's involvement in Relay and Advent, see "Company Integrates, Mans Project Relay Test Stations," *SenTineL,* October 1, 1962, 1, 6; and "Advent Program Outlined; STL Technical Staff Named,"

SenTineL, August 7, 1961, 1, 5. See also Ivan A. Getting, *All in a Lifetime: Science in the Defense of Democracy* (New York: Vantage Press, 1989), 554–559; and TRW Systems Group, *Spacecraft Systems,* unpaginated brochure, Los Angeles, 1967.

34 "A Capsule History of STL Propulsion," *SenTineL,* March 5, 1965, 4; TRW Space and Technology Group, *We've Proven It Can Fly,* 22; C. Budd Cohen, The Evolution of TRW Defense Business Lines from Ramo-Wooldridge Guided Missiles Research Division (GMRD) (typescript, Los Angeles, March 26, 1986), 81; Robert Bromberg interview with the author, November 14, 1990, Redondo Beach, Calif.; Arthur Grant interview with the author, June 18, 1991, Redondo Beach, Calif.

35 George Mueller interview with the author, June 4, 1992, Boston; TRW Systems Group, Capabilities Briefing, Summer 1966; Wilks, "STL Drives for Hardware Business," 31; cf. *TRW Systems Group (A and B Condensed),* 2.

36 Dean E. Wooldridge interview with Bruce Zewe, TRW Inc., 1988, WRHS 88-088; William M. Jones interview with the author, September 23, 1992, Independence, Ohio.

37 Thompson Ramo Wooldridge, Inc., Annual Report for 1960.

38 Board Minutes, September 23 and November 16, 1959, and November 14, 1960; Sheehan, "Thompson Ramo Wooldridge," 145.

39 Richard A. Campbell interview with the author, February 12, 1991, Los Angeles; TRW Electronic Systems Group, *The First 35 Years* (Los Angeles: TRW Electronic Systems Group, 1989), 8; Arden L. Bement comment to the author, October 26, 1993.

40 Board Minutes, January 17, June 13, September 26, October 24, and November 13, 1960; Thompson Ramo Wooldridge, Inc., Annual Report for 1961. On the crisis in the semiconductor industry, see Ernest Braun and Stuart Macdonald, *Revolution in Miniature: The History and Impact of Semiconductor Electronics,* 2d ed. (New York: Cambridge University Press, 1982), 86–87.

41 Board Minutes, September 26, 1961, and April 24, 1962; Wooldridge interview with Zewe, 1988; Dean E. Wooldridge interview with the author, October 11, 1991, Santa Barbara, Calif.

42 Joseph T. Gorman interview with the author, February 15, 1991, Cleveland, Ohio.

43 Horace A. Shepard interview with the author, September 25, 1990, Cleveland, Ohio; Ruben F. Mettler, *The Little Brown Hen That Could: The Growth Story of TRW Inc.* (New York: The Newcomen Society in North America, 1982), 18.

44 Thompson Ramo Wooldridge, Inc., Annual Report for 1959.

45 Thompson Ramo Wooldridge, Inc., Annual Report for 1961.

46 Other new models introduced during the early 1960s included the TRW-330, featuring "high flexibility, medium speed, [and] expandable memory," the TRW-340, a similar machine with faster memory, and the TRW-530, "a high speed core memory" computer. Both were designed for applications in continuous process industries such as chemicals, petroleum, steel, and cement. For military uses, the company developed the TRW-130 (AN/UYK), a minicomputer designed for shipboard operations of the U.S. Navy.

47 Thompson Ramo Wooldridge, Inc., Annual Report for 1959; Sheehan, "Thompson Ramo Wooldridge: Two Wings in Space," 145.

48 Shepard interview with Zewe, 1988.

49 "The Millions under Martin Marietta's Mattress," *Fortune* (November 1963); "Bunker-Ramo: From under That Mattress," *Fortune* (February 1964), 76, 78; Milt Mohr interview with the author, March 3, 1992, Malibu, Calif.; Allen interview, November 12, 1990; J. Sidney Webb interview with the author, February 14, 1991, Los Angeles.

50 Mettler interview, March 6, 1990.

51 Webb interview, February 14, 1991.

52 Richard P. Rumelt, *Strategy, Structure, and Economic Performance* (Boston: Harvard Graduate School of Business Administration, 1974), 50–51; Board Minutes, December 18, 1962; Kenneth M. Davidson, *Megamergers: Corporate America's Billion-Dollar Takeovers* (Cambridge, Mass.: Ballinger, 1985), 110–111; Kathleen McDermott, *Retail Revolutionary: Kinney Shoe's First Century, 1894–1994* (Cambridge, Mass.: The Winthrop Group, 1994), 66.

53 Board Minutes, December 17, 1963, March 31 and April 28, 1964. On the last occasion, lawyer Holmes opined that the Marlin-Rockwell and Ross Gear transactions did not carry risks of antitrust violations. See also Thompson Ramo Wooldridge, Inc., Proxy Statement, March 31, 1964, for the specific terms of the deals.

54 Thompson Ramo Wooldridge, Inc., Proxy Statement, March 31, 1964.

55 Thompson Ramo Wooldridge, Inc., Annual Report for 1964.

56 Shepard interview with Zewe, 1988.

57 Webb interview, February 14, 1991. See also Walter McQuade, "Caution! Si Ramo at Work," *Fortune* (November 1970), 105–107, 185–192.

58 J. Robert Burnett interview with the author, November 14, 1990, Redondo Beach, Calif.

59 "Establishment of TRW Corporate Planning Effort Told by Dr. Ramo," *SenTineL,* September 4, 1962, 2, 6.

60 Simon Ramo, "TRW and Diversification." Essay prepared for the Vermont '67 Planning Conference, June 1967, 7.

61 Shepard interview with Zewe, 1988.

62 Thompson Ramo Wooldridge, Inc., Annual Report for 1964.

63 "Company Trademark, Streamlined Division Names to Build TRW Identification," *SenTineL,* December 2, 1963, 8.

64 Shepard interview with Zewe, 1988; Dolph Thiel interview with the author, November 14, 1990, Redondo Beach, Calif.

Part III

1 Alfred D. Chandler, Jr., "The Competitive Performance of U.S. Industrial Enterprise since the Second World War," *Business History Review* 68 (Spring 1994): 1–72, esp. 18–23; George David Smith and Davis Dyer, "The Rise and Transformation of the American Corporation," in Carl Kaysen, ed., *The American Corporation Today* (New York: Oxford University Press, 1996), 28–73.

2 Smith and Dyer, "The Rise and Transformation," esp. 57–64.

Chapter 10

1 See TRW Inc., Five-Year Plan, 1970–1974, February 6, 1970, section III, p. 1.

2 Thompson Ramo Wooldridge, Inc., Annual Report for 1964; Simon Ramo, "TRW and Diversification," Essay Prepared for the Vermont '67 Planning Conference, June 1967, 12. Wright later described TRW's acquisition screens as being consistent with those of Crawford at TP in the 1930s: "One, we'd look for a product that was hard to make. Two, we'd look for a product [that wouldn't have us] competing with one company that had an overwhelming market share. And three, we'd look for a product in which we could gain an edge—make it better or offer it at a better price." J. David Wright interview with Bruce Zewe, TRW Inc., 1988, WRHS 88-088.

[3] Ramo, "TRW and Diversification," 1–4. Ramo's essay also considered disadvantages of diversification, such as potential bureaucratic delays, increased risk of making suboptimal decisions (from the vantage point of any single business), lack of focus, and potential confusion and criss-crossing of signals with customers. He concluded, however, that for TRW the advantages of diversification far outweighed the disadvantages.

[4] Norman A. Berg, *General Management: An Analytical Approach* (Homewood, Ill.: Richard D. Irwin, Inc., 1984), 123–125; Kenneth W. Davidson, *Megamergers: Corporate America's Billion Dollar Takeovers* (Cambridge, Mass.: Ballinger, 1985), 138–143.

[5] A. William Reynolds interview with the author, September 1, 1992, Fairlawn, Ohio; J. Sidney Webb interview with the author, February 14, 1991, Los Angeles.

[6] The result of p/e magic was that most takeovers in the era took the form of mergers or an exchange of stock, rather than acquisitions or an exchange of cash. Davidson, *Megamergers,* 139–140, 145.

[7] TRW Inc., *Preliminary Prospectus Dated October 18, 1968,* 10; Board Minutes, March 31, 1964; Robert Burgin interview with the author, October 10, 1991, San Diego; Horace A. Shepard interview with Bruce Zewe, TRW Inc., 1988; TRW Inc., *This Is TRW,* June 1967, 1.

[8] TRW Inc., Annual Report for 1964.

[9] "Systems Group Employment History," *SenTineL,* September 23, 1967, 8; C. Budd Cohen, The Evolution of TRW Defense Business Lines from Ramo-Wooldridge Guided Missiles Research Division (GMRD) (typescript, Los Angeles, March 26, 1986), 10.

[10] R. F. Mettler, "Organizational Trends and Changes," Interoffice Memo, October 13, 1965; "Systems Group Organized into Five Operating Divisions; Seven Supporting Staff Functions," *SenTineL,* September 23, 1967, 5.

[11] F. W. Hesse and R. F. Mettler, "TRW Systems International Activities," Interoffice Memorandum, December 6, 1966; "International Ops Broadens Base in Foreign Markets," *SenTineL,* September 23, 1967, 5–6; TRW Inc., News Release, January 13, 1967.

[12] The operation of TRW's matrix is described in a famous business school teaching case, which exists in many different versions. I've relied on *TRW Systems Group (A and B Condensed)* (Boston: Harvard Business School Case Services, 9-476-117). See also Stanley M. Davis and Paul R. Lawrence, *Matrix* (Reading, Mass.: Addison-Wesley, 1977); and James Dunlap interview with the author, June 26, 1991, Cleveland, Ohio.

[13] Sheldon A. Davis, "An Organic Problem-Solving Method of Organizational Change," *Journal of Applied Behavioral Science* 3, no. 1 (1967): 3–21; *TRW Systems Group (A and B Condensed);* John Poppy, "It's OK to Cry in the Office," *Look,* July 9, 1968, 64–76; "New Concept Aims at Keeping Communication Flowing Upward," *SenTineL,* December 2, 1966, 5; "Teamwork Through Conflict," *Business Week,* March 20, 1971, 44–46.

[14] Poppy, "It's OK to Cry in the Office," p. 66.

[15] Ibid., 75; Dunlap interview, June 26, 1991.

[16] Thompson Ramo Wooldridge, Inc., Annual Report for 1964; Cohen, Evolution of TRW Defense Business, 89, 119–122.

[17] For competitive dynamics in scientific satellites, see Clayton R. Koppes, *JPL and the American Space Program: A History of the Jet Propulsion Laboratory, 1936–1976* (New Haven, Ct.: Yale University Press, 1982), esp. chaps. 9–11; and William E. Burrows, *Exploring Space: Voyages in the Solar System and Beyond* (New York: Random House, 1991), esp. chaps. 5 and 6. For the development of deep space networks, see Craig Waff, "The Road to the Deep Space Network," *IEEE Spectrum,* April 1993, 50–57.

[18] For changes in government procurement, see Herman O. Stekeler, *The Structure and Performance of the Aerospace Industry* (Berkeley, Calif.: University of California Press, 1965), 67–70, 80–84; and William L. Baldwin, *The Structure of the Defense Market, 1955–1964* (Durham, N.C.: Duke University Press, 1967), 125–134. On the Vela incentives, see TRW News Release, April 25, 1967.

[19] "Highlights of The Right Way Program Illustrate Results," *SenTineL,* February 3, 1967, 4; Ruben F. Mettler interview with the author, March 6, 1990, Los Angeles; Lawrence J. Reeves, President, Systems Research Associates, Los Altos, Calif., letter to the author, September 7, 1993. For STL's earlier attempts at cost reduction, see Ruben F. Mettler, "STL Cost Reduction Program," Interoffice Memorandum, October 5, 1964.

[20] TRW Systems Group, *Spacecraft Systems,* unpaginated brochure, Los Angeles, 1967; TRW Space & Technology Group, *We've Proven It Can Fly* (Los Angeles: TRW Space & Technology Group, 1987), 14, 20; TRW Inc., "Pioneer 6, Oldest Living Spacecraft, Celebrates Silver Anniversary in Space on December 16," News Release, December 16, 1990; Burrows, *Exploring Space,* 264–265.

[21] John L. McLucas, *Space Commerce* (Cambridge, Mass.: Harvard University Press, 1991), 26.

[22] On satellites in geosynchronous orbit, see McLucas, *Space Commerce,* 26–36; Burton I. Edelson, "Global Satellite Communications," *Scientific American,* February 1977; Burton I. Edelson, "The Experimental Years," in Joel Alper and Joseph N. Pelton, eds., *The INTELSAT Global Satellite System* (New York: American Institute of Aeronautics and Astronautics, 1984), 39–54; and L. A. "Pat" Hyland, *Call Me Pat* (Virginia Beach, Va.: The Donning Company, 1993), 312–320.

[23] "Orbiting of Military ComSats Adds Final Touch to Successful IDCSP," *SenTineL,* July 5, 1966, 1–2; Cohen, Evolution of TRW Defense Business, 95; A.T. Finney, "A Phase II Satellite for the Defense Satellite Communications Systems," in Nathaniel E. Feldman and Charles M. Kelly, eds., *Communications Satellites for the 70s: Systems* (Cambridge, Mass.: MIT Press, 1971), 363–364; comments from Lawrence J. Reeves, Systems Research Associates, June 1994.

[24] U.S. Department of Defense, Defense Communications Agency, *The Defense Satellite Communications System* (Washington, D.C.: U.S. Government Printing Office, August 1970), 2–3, 10–11; Finney, "A Phase II Satellite for Defense Satellite Communications Systems," 363–374; Aerospace Corporation, *The Aerospace Corporation: Its Work, 1960–1980* (Los Angeles: Aerospace Corporation, 1980), chap. 6, esp. pp. 55–57; TRW Space and Technology Group, *We've Proven It Can Fly,* 30–31.

[25] Emeric Podraczky and Joseph N. Pelton, "INTELSAT Satellites," in Alper and Pelton, *The INTELSAT Global Satellite System,* chap. 6, esp. pp. 103–109; "TRW Systems Wins Comsat Nod," *missiles and rockets,* December 20, 1965, 19; "COMSAT," *SenTineL,* May 6, 1966, 1, 8; TRW Space and Technology Group, *We've Proven It Can Fly,* 24.

[26] "COMSAT Program," *SenTineL,* February 3, 1967, 1, 8; "Communications Capability Increased by Design Change on INTELSAT III," *SenTineL,* June 2, 1967, 1.

[27] Cohen, *Evolution of TRW Defense Business,* 93; "INTELSAT III F-2 Earns First Incentive Pay by Completing First 30 Days over Atlantic," *SenTineL,* February 7, 1969, 1.

[28] Robert Lindsey, *The Falcon and the Snowman* (New York: Simon and Schuster, 1979), 61–62; William E. Burrows, *Deep Black: Space Espionage and National Security* (New York: Random House, 1986),183–185; Curtis Peebles, *Guardians: Strategic Reconnaissance Satellites* (Novato, Calif.: Presidio Press, 1987), 199–204.

[29] Desmond Ball, *Pine Gap: Australia and the U.S. Geostationary Signals Intelligence Satellite Program* (Sydney, Australia, and Boston: Allen & Unwin, 1988), esp. chap. 2. Ball, a Ph.D., is head of the Strategic and Defense Studies Center at the Australian National University of Canberra. The remote interior of Australia is home to several satellite ground stations used for military and security purposes.

[30] About all that TRW personnel will or can reveal about DSP is contained in TRW Space and Technology Group, *We've Proven It Can Fly,* 26, and an undated fact sheet, "DSP Satellites: America's Orbiting Sentries," issued in the late 1980s. For many years, the company did no more than acknowledge the existence of the program. For accounts of DSP, see Daniel Ford, *The Button* (New York: Simon and Schuster, 1985), 58–68; Ivan A. Getting, *All in a Lifetime: Science in the Defense of Democracy* (New York: Vantage Press, 1989), 540–541; and a crisp scholarly summary: Paul B. Stares, *Space and National Security* (Washington, D.C.: Brookings Institution, 1987), 24–26. Stares provides a map of the globe describing the views of the three primary satellites. He also speculates (25n47) that at any given time, several spares may be in orbit.

[31] This section is based primarily on John Mandrow and Richard Booton, TRW Electronics Systems Group: The First 35 Years (typescript, Los Angeles, June 1989). The authors of this internal report to management were longtime veterans with the company who retired during the 1980s. The section also draws on interviews by the author with Booton (June 17, 1992), Ed Dunford (September 24, 1991), Tim Hanneman (October 9, 1991), Harry Hayes (June 19, 1991), David Langmuir (June 18, 1992), Mandrow (November 13, 1990), Henry Samulon (March 3, 1992), and Nat Trembath (November 13, 1990). All of these interviews save Dunford's took place in Redondo Beach, Calif.; the interview with Dunford took place in Cleveland, Ohio. See also Cohen, Evolution of TRW Defense Business, esp. pp. 111–122.

[32] Cohen, Evolution of TRW Defense Business, 113–114; Mandrow and Booton, TRW Electronics Systems Group, 4; "SGLS Provides Standard Package for Satellite TT&C," *SenTineL,* September 3, 1965, 5.

[33] Mandrow and Booton, TRW Electronics Systems Group, 5; TRW Inc., TRW 1972 Plan, p. IV-35.

[34] Cohen, Evolution of TRW Defense Business, 113–114; Mandrow and Booton, TRW Electronics Systems Group, 3–4.

[35] Mandrow and Booton, TRW Electronics Systems Group, 8; Cohen, Evolution of TRW Defense Business, 117–118; "Microelectronics Center Dedicated," *SenTineL,* September 4, 1964, 3; TRW Systems Group, *Spacecraft Systems,* unpaginated brochure, 1967.

[36] Courtney G. Brooks, James M. Grimwood, and Loyd S. Swenson, Jr., *Chariots for Apollo: A History of Manned Lunar Spacecraft* (Washington, D.C.: NASA, 1979), 155.

[37] Board Minutes, October 22, 1963; "Work to Start on Propulsion Site This Fall," *SenTineL,* August 5, 1963, 1, 8; "Ground-Breaking Starts New STL Propulsion Test Facility," *SenTineL,* November 4, 1963, 1, 5.

[38] R. G. Gilroy and R. L. Sackheim, "The Lunar Module Descent Engine—A Historical Summary," American Institute of Aeronautics and Astronautics, no. 89 (1989), 4, 6; Brooks, Grimwood, and Swenson, *Chariots for Apollo,* 155–156; TRW Space & Technology Group, *We've Proven It Can Fly,* 22.

Subsequent paragraphs also draw on the following: G. Elverum, Jr., P. Staudhammer, J. Miller, A. Hoffman, and R. Rockow, "The Descent Engine for the Lunar Module," American Institute of Aeronautics and Astronautics, no. 69-452 (1969); Gerald

Elverum, Jr., interview with the author, June 17, 1991; Arthur Grant interview with the author, June 18, 1991; and Peter Staudhammer, interviews with the author, June 2 and 4, 1993. All of these interviews were conducted in Redondo Beach, Calif.

[39] Brooks, Grimwood, and Swenson, *Chariots for Apollo,* 155–156.

[40] Gilroy and Sackheim, "Lunar Module Descent Engine," 1; Ruben F. Mettler interview with the author, June 16, 1992, Los Angeles.

[41] Brooks, Grimwood, and Swenson, *Chariots for Apollo,* 343–344; Gilroy and Sackheim, "The Lunar Module Descent Engine," 2; "Lunar Module Descent Engine Lands Eagle Gently on Moon," *SenTineL,* August 8, 1969, 1, 8.

[42] W. S. Kennedy, S. M. Kovacic, and E. C. Rea, "Solid Rocket History at TRW Ballistic Missiles Division," AIAA/SAE/ASME/ASEE 28th Joint Propulsion Conference, Nashville, Tenn., July 6–8, 1992, esp. pp. 14–20.

[43] R. F. Mettler to S. Ramo, H. A. Shepard, and J. D. Wright, "Anti-Submarine Warfare" (memo, May 11, 1964); "Systems Integration Contract Forbids Firm from Bidding on Hardware," *missiles and rockets,* November 1965, 16; "Berry Heads ASW Program from Washington Office," *SenTineL,* January 8, 1965, 1; "Negotiations Completed on $12 Million ASW Contract," *SenTineL,* August 5, 1966, 1. On STL's marketing, see "Marketing at STL," *SenTineL,* February 5, 1965, 3.

[44] Copies of many of Ramo's speeches from the 1950s through the 1970s are warehoused in TRW's records storage area, file boxes 40,228 and 40,895. The quotation is from "Mobilizing Science for Society," The Charles M. Schwab Memorial Lecture, delivered at New York City, May 22, 1968. See also Simon Ramo interview with Christian G. Pease, UCLA, 1984.

[45] Robert W. Hovey, "History and Trends of Systems Engineering" (unpaginated typescript, April 1970); K. H. Borchers, C. S. Lightfoot, and R. W. Hovey, "Translation and Application of Aerospace Management Technology to Socio-Economic Problems," *AIAA Journal of Spacecraft and Rockets* 5, no. 4 (April 1968): 467–471.

[46] Glenn E. Bugos, "Programming the American Aerospace Industry, 1954–1964: The Business Structures of Technical Transactions," *Business and Economic History* 22, no. 1 (Fall 1993): 210–222 ; "PERT! New Space-Age Management Control Tool at STL," *SenTineL,* November 6, 1961, 3; Arch R. Dooley, "Interpretations of PERT," *Harvard Business Review* 42 (March–April 1964): 160–172.

[47] "Civil Systems Grow in SEID Management Systems Section," *SenTineL,* October 7, 1966, 2; "TRW's Civil Systems Work Discussed on 'Today' Show," *SenTineL,* March 4, 1967, 3; "TRW to Study Land-Use Planning," *Technology Week,* June 6, 1966, unpaginated reprint. See also the North American Water and Power Alliance advertisement that ran in *Scientific American* (September 1965) and was duplicated in *SenTineL,* September 3, 1965, 4.

[48] "Civil Systems Grow in SEID Management Systems Section," *SenTineL,* October 7, 1966, 2; Walter McQuade, "Caution! Si Ramo at Work," *Fortune,* November 1970, 184.

[49] "F. W. Hesse, D. G. Fladlein to Head New Company Unit, 'STL Products,'" *SenTineL,* February 6, 1961, 1, 8; Van Skilling interview with the author, May 9, 1991, Cleveland, Ohio; James Dunn interview with the author, October 5, 1991, Bedford, Mass. Space Technology Laboratories, *A Brief History of STL* (unpaginated, undated brochure, Los Angeles, circa 1962); "TRW Instruments Eyes Two-Billion Dollar Market," *SenTineL,* August 6, 1965, 2.

[50] TRW Inc., News Release, September 26, 1967.

51 TRW Inc., News Release, October 17, 1967; "TRW, Hazleton Reach Agreement to Combine Firms," *SenTineL,* November 3, 1967, 3, 5; TRW Inc., Annual Report for 1967; Dunn interview, October 5, 1991.

52 TRW Reda Pump Division, *Memories: A Story of People and a Company Called TRW Reda* (Bartlesville, Okla.: TRW Reda Pump Division, 1980), 19–33; Dunn interview, October 5, 1991.

53 Ramo, "The Coming Technological Society," address delivered at a luncheon meeting of the Los Angeles Town Hall, Tuesday, November 10, 1964. The speech was printed in modified form in *NATO's Fifteen Nations,* December 1964–January 1965, 66–73. The quotation about the revolution in finance and accounting was picked up by *Time* in its issue of November 27, 1964.

54 Ruben F. Mettler interview with Michael L. Johnson, TRW Inc., 1989, copy in the possession of the author; Mettler interview, June 16, 1992.

55 TRW Inc., News Release, May 13, 1968; Skilling interview, May 9, 1991.

56 Board Minutes, February 14, April 30, and October 22, 1968.

57 Donald Kovar interview with the author, November 16, 1990, Redondo Beach, Calif.; TRW Inc., Five Year Plan, February 6, 1970, section VIII.

58 For Riley's biography, see "Accessories Division Proud of Aircraft Fuel Pumps and Parts," *Friendly Forum,* January 1951, 47; Reynolds interview, September 1, 1992. See also Charles Ohly telephone interview with the author, February 1, 1994.

59 Robert Sheahan, "Thompson Ramo Wooldridge: Two Wings in Space," *Fortune,* February 1963, 145.

60 Thompson Ramo Wooldridge, Inc., Annual Report for 1961.

61 Board Minutes, October 5 and 11 and November 15, 1965. The Clevite saga can be followed in the Board Minutes entries from March through October 1968, when U.S. Smelting and Refining, which owned a significant stake in Clevite, increased its holdings and terminated merger talks with TRW. See TRW Inc., News Release, October 22, 1968.

62 For Noblesville Casting, see Board Minutes, April 25 and June 28, 1967, plus TRW Inc., TRW 1972 Plan, September 1968, section IV, p. 9. For Gregory Industries, see Board Minutes, October 30, 1968, and News Release, January 31, 1969.

63 Board Minutes, April 30, June 11, and October 4, 1968; United-Greenfield Corporation, Annual Reports for 1966 and 1967; TRW Inc., News Release, September 20, 1968; Reynolds interview, September 1, 1992.

64 Thompson Ramo Wooldridge, Inc., Annual Report for 1960 and 1961.

65 Mira Wilkins, *The Maturing of Multinational Enterprise: American Business Abroad from 1914 to 1970* (Cambridge, Mass.: Harvard University Press, 1974), 377. See also Wilkins and Frank E. Hill, *American Business Abroad: Ford on Six Continents* (New York: Scribner's, 1964), for a discussion of Ford's investments overseas during the late 1950s and early 1960s.

66 Board Minutes, December 15, 1964; Thompson Ramo Wooldridge Inc., Proxy Statement, March 31, 1964, 8, 16–18; Ohly interview, February 1, 1994.

67 Board Minutes, October 5 and December 17, 1965 and April 26, 1966; News Releases, December 20, 1965, and January 12 and May 9, 1966.

68 Burgin interview, October 10, 1991.

69 For the BLW deal, see Board Minutes, December 19, 1967, and News Release, February 6, 1968; For Ehrenreich, see Board Minutes, April 29, 1969; Burgin interview, October 10, 1991.

70 For Duly & Hansford, see Board Minutes, April 20 and June 25, 1968, and News Release, June 11, 1968. For the founding of TRW Australia, see News Release, October 8, 1968. For the deals in Japan, see Board Minutes, April 29, July 22, and December 11, 1969; News Releases May 1 and December 8, 1969; Burgin interview, October 10, 1991.

71 Stanley C. Pace interview with the author, February 11, 1991, Indian Wells, Calif.

72 Webb interview, February 14, 1991; Sheahan, "Thompson Ramo Wooldridge," p. 146; Board Minutes, March 25, 1959; Thompson Ramo Wooldridge, Annual Report for 1961. Magna Products's financial performance is recorded in a notebook in box 44,249 at TRW's records storage warehouse in Cleveland.

In 1965, Magna Corporation's Research Department was transferred to TRW Systems Group to become part of the Chemical Sciences Department in the Physical Research Division. *SenTineL,* April 2, 1965, 1, 6.

73 Aerospace Industries Association, *Aerospace Facts and Figures* (Washington, D.C.: Aerospace Industries Association, 1973 edition).

74 Pace interview, February 11, 1991.

75 Board Minutes, October 25, 1966; Sheahan, "Thompson Ramo Wooldridge," 95, 145–146; Dunn interview, October 5, 1991.

76 Thompson Ramo Wooldridge, Annual Report for 1961; Pace interview, February 11, 1991.

77 TRW Inc., News Release, January 5, 1966; Pace interview, February 11, 1991.

78 Webb interview, February 14, 1991.

79 Ibid.

80 Richard A. Campbell interview with the author, February 12, 1991, Redondo Beach, Calif.

81 TRW Inc., TRW 1972 Plan, September 1968, section IV, pp. 20–31.

82 Webb interview, February 14, 1991.

83 TRW Inc., *This Is TRW,* June 1967; TRW Inc., News Releases, June 28 and September 26, 1966; Campbell interview, February 12, 1991; Board Minutes, March 31, 1964.

84 Press Releases, October 3, 1967, and January 19, 1968; IRC, Inc., TRW Inc., Annual Report for 1966. The cost of the merger was 409,885 shares of $4.40 serial preference stock II and 546,514 shares of TRW common stock.

85 United-Carr Incorporated, Annual Report for 1967; C. Loring Hall, *The History of United-Carr* (privately printed, 1986), passim; Samuel Groves conversation with the author, February 7, 1991.

86 Shepard interview with Zewe, 1989; Hall, *The History of United-Carr,* 90–93.

87 TRW Inc., TRW 1972 Plan, September 1968, section IV, p. 20; TRW Inc., News Release, December 9, 1968; Campbell interview, February 12, 1991.

88 Webb interview, February 14, 1991.

89 Shepard interview with Zewe, 1989; Burgin interview, October 10, 1991.

90 Pace interview, February 11, 1991; Shepard interview with Zewe, 1989; "Where Diversity Is the Tie That Binds," *Business Week,* September 24, 1966, 95.

91 TRW Inc., *A Probe of TRW's Future: The Next 20 Years,* July 5, 1966; "Probe Technique Used as Planning Tool for TRW," *SenTineL,* August 4, 1967, 3, 8; "Probe II Predicts Future Technological Innovations," *SenTineL,* November 3, 1967, 8; TRW Inc., Annual Report for 1969; "Setting a Timetable," *Business Week,* May 27, 1967, 52–61; Robert Sheahan, "The Way They Think at TRW," *Fortune,* October 1966, 155–156, 194, 196.

The 1966 *Probe* also included several predictions from Wernher von Braun pertaining to developments in aerospace systems.

92 Robert Sheahan, "The Way They Think at TRW," *Fortune,* October 1966, 153–157, 194, 196. See also "Where Diversity Is the Tie That Binds," *Business Week,* September 24, 1966, 88–96; and "Audacious TRW," *Time,* July 21, 1967, 69.

93 TRW Inc., TRW 1975 Plan, June 15, 1967. The company's annual report for 1967 includes a long description with highlights of the 1967 planning conference.

94 TRW Inc., Annual Report for 1968.

95 Mettler, Interview with Johnson, 1989; Wright interview with Zewe, 1989; Board Minutes, February 18, 1968.

CHAPTER 11

1 Horace A. Shepard interview with Bruce Zewe, TRW Inc., 1988, WRHS 88-088; Ruben F. Mettler interview with the author, May 11, 1994, Los Angeles; Ruben F. Mettler interview with Michael L. Johnson, TRW Inc., 1989; TRW Memo to Managers, January 28, 1970.

   Behind the scenes, Ed Riley was known to be disappointed that he reported to a much younger man (Mettler). He was also unhappy with the 1971 reorganizations that among other things significantly restructured TRW's automotive business. By all accounts, Riley did not let his feelings affect his professional duties on the job, although he took early retirement in October 1971. See Richard A. Campbell interview with the author, February 12, 1991, Redondo Beach, Calif.; J. Sidney Webb interview with the author, February 14, 1991, Los Angeles; Joseph T. Gorman interview with the author, February 15, 1991; A. William Reynolds interview with the author, September 1, 1992, Fairlawn, Ohio.

2 Shepard interview with Zewe, 1988; Mettler interview with Johnson, 1989. For corroborating descriptions of the relationship between Shepard and Mettler, see Stanley C. Pace interview with the author, February 11, 1991, Indian Wells, Calif.; Webb interview, February 14, 1991; and Reynolds interview, September 1, 1992.

3 TRW Memo to Managers, January 28, 1970, copy at Space Park Archives. See also "It Can't Happen Here," 19–20 and "The Growth Management of TRW," *Dun's Review,* December 1968, 30–34, 71, 73. In 1973, Ramo explored the concept of selective diversification in a speech to TRW managers. A copy of the speech is included in George Solomon's papers at the TRW archives at Space Park.

4 TRW Memo to Managers, January 28, 1970. For General Battery, see Board Minutes, February 17 through October 20, 1971.

5 Nathaniel Trembath interview with the author, November 30, 1990, Redondo Beach, Calif.; Reynolds interview, September 1, 1992; Michael J. Jablonski to William B. Van Buren, April 10, 1979. Copy in Mettler papers at TRW headquarters.

6 Metter interview, May 11, 1994; Mettler interview with Johnson, 1989.

7 TRW Interoffice Correspondence, March 12, 1971; Board Minutes, April 28, 1971; Mettler interview, May 11, 1994. At the time of the change, TRW had agreed in principle to merge with General Battery, although concerns about possible antitrust actions later led TRW to call the deal off. Had it proceeded, General Battery would have been added to Reynolds's Industrial and Replacement Division. The reorganization included several other minor changes. United-Carr's Cinch Connector unit moved to Sid Webb's Electronics Group, and Noblesville Casting, formerly a part of the Replacement Division, moved to the Engine Components Group.

8 Reynolds interview, September 1, 1992; "Herterick, Reynolds Named Executive Vice Presidents," *Sentinel,* April 2, 1971, 1, 8.

9 TRW Memo to Managers, October 4, 1971.

10 J. T. Gorman to R. F. Mettler and E. E. Ford, "Organization and Operation of the Legal Function," October 13, 1971. I am grateful to Mr. Gorman for furnishing me a copy of this document, which he recalls staying up all night to draft in preparation for a hastily scheduled meeting with Mettler. The willingness of Shepard and Mettler to assent to Gorman's plan was influenced partly by their desire to keep the young lawyer from accepting a senior position at another company. See Gorman interview, February 15, 1991.

11 TRW Memo to Managers, June 21 and December 18, 1972, November 7, 1973, and February 4, 1974; Mettler interview, May 11, 1994; Robert Lundy interview with the author, April 16, 1990, Solon, Ohio; Board Minutes, December 13, 1972; James E. Dunlap interview with the author, June 26, 1991, Cleveland, Ohio; Charles R. Allen interview with the author, November 12, 1990, San Diego, Calif.; Reynolds interview, September 1, 1992.

12 Allen interview, November 12, 1990; Dunlap interview, June 26, 1991.

13 Shepard interview with Zewe, 1988; Allen interview, November 12, 1990.

14 TRW Inc., Annual Report for 1971.

15 George Solomon interview with the author, February 13, 1991, Santa Barbara, Calif.

16 Solomon interview, February 13, 1991; Trembath interview, November 13, 1990; Mettler interview, May 11, 1994.

17 For an account of this mission by one of the main actors, see Jim Lovell and Jeffrey Kluger, *Apollo 13* (New York: Pocket Books, 1995), passim. (This book was originally published in 1994 under the title *Lost Moon: The Perilous Voyage of Apollo 13.*)

18 Ben M. Gillespie, "TRW's LM Descent Engine Lauded for Role in Apollo 13 Lifeboat," *Sentinel,* May 8, 1970, 1, 7; "Hundreds of TRW Employees Greet Astronauts with Roaring Welcome," *Sentinel,* June 5, 1970, 4; TRW Space & Technology Group, *We've Proven It Can Fly* (Los Angeles: TRW Space & Technology Group, 1987), 22. See also Ben M. Gillespie, "Apollo's 'Big Bang' Changed Routine Evening in Houston," *Sentinel,* May 8, 1970, 4, for a list of TRW personnel involved in the rescue.

19 TRW personnel do not discuss classified work, even to the extent of confirming or denying such published accounts as the well documented Christopher Boyce espionage case (see Chapter 10). Authors who have written widely about the classified satellite programs of the 1970s and 1980s link TRW with signal intelligence satellites, as well as with other types of spy satellites, including the KH-11 series. These satellites were the first to use a digital imaging system to return real-time images of the ground. This represented a major advance over earlier spy satellites that returned canisters of film to earth for processing. The KH-11 program is further described as a breakthrough contract for TRW, which supposedly dislodged Lockheed from the favored position it had occupied since the 1950s. Senior TRW personnel state flatly that such reports are incorrect. See William E. Burrows, *Deep Black: Space Espionage and National Security* (New York: Random House, 1986), 235–240; Curtis Peebles, *Guardians: Strategic Reconnaissance Satellites* (Novato, Calif.: Presidio Press, 1987), 118–127; and Jeffrey T. Richelson, *America's Secret Eyes in Space* (New York: Harper & Row, 1990), esp. chap. 6.

20 William E. Burrows, *Exploring Space: Voyages in the Solar System and Beyond* (New York: Random House, 1990), chap. 10, esp. pp. 264–268, 271–272; C. Budd Cohen, The Evolution of TRW Defense Business Lines from Ramo-Wooldridge Guided Missile Research Division (transcript, Los Angeles, March 26, 1986), 85; "Pioneers F and G Being Readied for Deep Space Probes to Planet Jupiter," *Sentinel,* July 2, 1970, pp. 1 and 3; TRW Space & Technology Group, *We've Proven It Can Fly,* 28–29.

[21] Burrows, *Exploring Space,* 261.

[22] Burrows, *Exploring Space,* 271; TRW Space & Technology Group, *We've Proven It Can Fly,* 28.

[23] "NASA Announces Details on Observatory Satellite," *Sentinel,* July 2, 1970, 8.

[24] Wallace H. Tucker, *The Star Splitters: The High Energy Astronomy Observatories* (Washington, D.C.: Scientific and Technical Information Branch, National Aeronautics and Space Administration, 1984), 26, 29–32; TRW Space & Technology Group, *We've Proven It Can Fly,* 34. The original HEAO contract was for about $70 million. In July 1972, the size of the contract was increased to $83.6 million. *Wall Street Journal,* November 24, 1971, 9, and July 3, 1972, 8.

[25] Tucker, *The Star Splitters,* 29–30.

[26] John Mandrow and Richard Booton, TRW Electronic Systems Group: The First 35 Years (transcript, Los Angeles, 1989), 9–15: Cohen, Evolution of TRW Defense Lines, 123–132.

[27] TRW Inc., News Release, February 1978. U.S. Air Force, *Fleet Satellite Communications (FLTSATCOM) System,* undated fact sheet; TRW Space & Technology Group, *We've Proven It Can Fly,* 32–33. The initial contract for FLTSATCOM totaled $35.9 million. TRW Inc., News Release, November 15, 1972.

[28] George Harter, interview with the author, October 10, 1991, Palm Desert, Calif.; Timothy Hannemann, interview with the author, October 9, 1991; Harry Hayes, interview with the author, June 19, 1991, Redondo Beach, Calif.; Aerospace Corporation, *The Aerospace Corporation* (El Segundo, Calif.: Aerospace Corporation, 1980), 60–61; Ivan A. Getting, *All in a Lifetime: Science in the Defense of Democracy* (New York: Vintage Press, 1989), 568–571.

[29] Edward Clinton Ezell and Linda Neuman Ezell, *On Mars: Exploration of the Red Planet* (Washington, D.C.: NASA SP-4212, 1984), esp. chaps. 6–11; cost figures on pp. 229, 251, and 269. See also Burrows, *Exploring Space,* chap. 8; Don Bane, *Viking and the Search for Life on Mars* (Los Angeles: TRW Systems and Energy, 1976); Harold E. Adelson, Frederick S. Brown, and Ronald I. Gilje, "Looking for Life on Mars," *Quest* (a TRW publication) 1, no. 2 (Autumn 1977): 28–51; Peter Staudhammer interview with the author, June 2, 1993, Redondo Beach, Calif.; Arthur Grant interview with the author, June 18, 1991, Redondo Beach, Calif.; Robert Bromberg interview with the author, November 14, 1990.

[30] The quotation is from Burrows, *Exploring Space,* 215; see also Ezell and Ezell, *On Mars,* 229.

[31] Ezell and Ezell, *On Mars,* 229–242; Staudhammer interview, June 2, 1993.

[32] Adelson, Brown, and Gilje, "Looking for Life on Mars," 37. These authors provide a list of credits of key personnel assigned to the project on p. 51.

[33] Ezell and Ezell, *On Mars,* 398–414; Adelson, Brown, and Gilje, "Looking for Life on Mars," 49–50; Burrows, *Exploring Space,* 226–228.

[34] Cohen, Evolution of TRW Defense Lines, 145–166; Jack Distaso interview with the author, November 15, 1990, Redondo Beach, Calif.

[35] Cohen, Evolution of TRW Defense Lines, 145, 153–154.

[36] "Software Performs Well in First Full-Scale Test," *Sentinel,* July 1, 1977, 4. TRW subsequently remained a pioneer in structured programming techniques, in part through the efforts of Dr. Barry W. Boehm, who served as chief scientist in the Defense Systems Group between 1973 and 1989.

[37] TRW organizational announcement, March 9, 1971; Grant interview, June 18, 1991; Bromberg interview, November 14, 1990; Staudhammer interview, June 2, 1993; Gerald Elverum interview with the author, June 17, 1991.

[38] Joseph Miller, "Chemical Lasers," *Quest,* 4, no. 1 (Spring 1980): 2–21. This article is a revised version of one that appeared earlier, "High Energy Lasers," *Quest* 1, no. 2 (Summer 1977): 52–72; Grant interview, June 18, 1991; Elverum interview, June 17, 1991; *The Aerospace Corporation,* 170–171.

[39] Miller, "Chemical Lasers," 11.

[40] "STD Develops Combustor to Help Combat Air Pollution," *Sentinel,* December 18, 1970, 2; "Japanese, TRW in Joint Venture," *Sentinel,* February 4, 1972, 2; "Space Science Invention Fights Industrial Pollution," *Sentinel,* December 13, 1974, 2; "Meyers Process Bathes Coal, Reduces Pollution," *Sentinel,* July 12, 1974, 6; R. F. Mettler Interview, January 13, 1977, with William Reddig of *Forbes,* transcript at TRW Inc.; Robert A. Meyers, Leslie J. Van Nice, and Myrrl J. Santy, "Coal Desulfurization," *Quest* 3, no. 1 (Spring 1979): 32–51, esp. 41–43.

[41] TRW Memo to Managers, January 12, 1970; "New TRW Operating Unit Formed for Commercial Market Systems," *Sentinel,* February 6, 1970, 1; "Sommer, Burnett Named to New Top Posts," *Sentinel,* October 2, 1970, 1; Donald Kovar interview with the author, November 16, 1990, Redondo Beach, Calif.; TRW Inc., Five Year Plan, February 6, 1970, section VIII.

[42] TRW Inc., Five Year Plan, February 6, 1970, section VIII; TRW Inc., 1975 Plan, April 1971, section VIII; John E. Davis, "Commercial Electronic Equipment at TRW: An Historical Analysis," TRW Inc., March 1984; Mettler interview, May 11, 1994; Webb interview, February 14, 1991, and Campbell interview, February 12, 1991.

[43] "New Credit Authorization System Introduced by TRW Data Systems," *Sentinel,* June 4, 1971, 1, 5; Webb and Campbell interviews, as well as Kovar interview, November 16, 1990; Melvin Shader interview with the author, June 18, 1991, Redondo Beach, Calif.; and Davis, "Commercial Electronic Equipment."

[44] For a general overview and inventory of TRW's many civil systems projects and other attempts to transfer aerospace technology to commercial markets in the early 1970s, see H. H. Rosen, *Technology Transfer in the Service of Mankind* (Redondo Beach, Calif.: TRW Systems Group, circa 1971). This report was also serialized in the *Sentinel* during 1970 and 1971.

For TRW's venture into manufactured housing, see Board Minutes, July 21, 1971, and April 12, July 19, and December 13, 1972; TRW Inc., News Release, June 21, 1971, and August 4, 1972; Harold Hirsch interview with the author, June 19, 1991, Redondo Beach, Calif.; TRW Inc., Annual Reports for 1972 and 1974; "TRW Selected for Operation Breakthrough," *Sentinel,* March 6, 1970, 8. According to Tom Harrington, whom Peter Stenzel interviewed in 1990, the entrepreneur who bought TRW's assets in Sacramento eventually did quite well by selling modular housing in Saudi Arabia. Peter D. Stenzel, Lessons Learned: A Study of TRW Space & Defense Sector's Civil and Energy Business (typescript, TRW Inc., Space & Defense Planning Department, 1990), 34. See also Stenzel's interview with Dean Lowrey in Lessons Learned, 53–56. Incidentally, TRW's approach to modular housing, as well as its ultimate fate in the business, followed closely that of Hercules Incorporated. See Davis Dyer and David B. Sicilia, *Labors of a Modern Hercules: The Evolution of a Chemical Company* (Boston: Harvard Business School Press, 1990), 369–370.

45 "County Supervisors Select TRW for Computerized Traffic Control," *Sentinel,* July 2, 1991, 2; Tom Harrington interview in Stenzel, Lessons Learned, 35–38; Mettler interview, May 11, 1994.

46 "County Supervisors Select TRW"; Tom Harrington interview in Stenzel, Lessons Learned, 35–38; Mettler interview, May 11, 1994.

47 "TRW Will Provide Supervision System for Washington, D.C. Transit Authority," *Sentinel,* April 7, 1972, 6; Board Minutes, April 26, 1972; Tom Harrington interview in Stenzel, Lessons Learned, 46–47; "DeLeuw, Cather—It's Part of TRW," *Sentinel,* April 2, 1976, 5; *Wall Street Journal,* October 11, 1977, 21.

48 Board Minutes, February 15, 1972; *Wall Street Journal,* February 14, 1972, 4.

49 Dunn interview, October 6, 1991; Van Skilling interview with the author, May 9, 1991, Cleveland, Ohio; Davis, "Commercial Electronic Equipment," 33–38; "Arkansas Power Company Orders TRW Controls Management System," *Sentinel,* June 4, 1971, 1.

50 James Dunn interview with the author, October 6, 1991, Bedford, Mass.; Wilson interview in Stenzel, "Lessons Learned," 107; *Wall Street Journal,* January 18, 1973, 7. In 1975, Reda negotiated a similar contract for $27.5 million with the Soviets. See *Wall Street Journal,* May 29, 1975, 17.

51 TRW Inc., Annual Report for 1976. For Dreadnought, see Board Minutes, December 1, 1972; for Applications Mécaniques et Robinetterie Industrielle, see Board Minutes, October 18, 1972, and July 19, 1977; for Pleuger, see Board Minutes, April 26, 1972. See also Dunn interview, October 6, 1991; TRW Memo to Managers, June 10, 1974.

52 See Richard H. K. Vietor, *Energy Policy in America since 1945: A Study of Business-Government Relations* (New York: Cambridge University Press, 1984), esp. pp. 314–315, for a discussion of national energy policy before the first oil shock. See also Ruben F. Mettler interview with the author, March 6, 1990; and Milt Kirkpatrick interview in Stenzel, Lessons Learned, 67.

53 TRW Memo to Managers, September 10, 1973; "Foster Joins TRW Energy Research and Development," *Sentinel,* September 14, 1973, 1; John Foster interview with the author, February 12, 1991.

54 Foster interview, February 12, 1991; TRW Interoffice Correspondence, November 12, 1973; Simon Ramo, *The Business of Science: Winning and Losing in the High-Tech Age* (New York: Hill and Wang, 1988), chaps. 5 and 6, esp. pp. 212–217. Ramo dealt with U.S. science, technology, and energy policy in many writings of the 1970s and 1980s.

55 Financial performance by line of business is drawn from TRW Inc., Annual Report for 1976.

56 Mettler interview, May 11, 1994; Gorman interview, February 15, 1991.

57 For Tokai Cold Forming, see Board Minutes, July 22, 1969, and October 21, 1970. TRW invested about $9 million in Messmer. Board Minutes, December 13, 1972.

58 Board Minutes, October 18, 1972. The value of TRW's option was about $3.5 million, although it later increased. In April 1979, TRW acquired an additional 20 percent of Repa for $3.8 million. Board Minutes, April 25, 1979.

59 *Repa: Precision and Safety* (Lindach, West Germany: Repa, 1975); Mettler interview, May 11, 1994; Robert Burgin interview with the author, October 10, 1991, La Jolla, Calif.; and Charles Miller interview with the author, September 4, 1991, Cleveland, Ohio.

60 For the new capacity in Italy and Brazil, see TRW Inc., 1975 Plan, April 1971, p. IV-11. For TRW's relationship with Koyo-Seiko, see Board Minutes, October 17, 1973. Accord-

ing to Ches Macey, the joint venture fell apart because of disputes about royalty payments. Macey interview, April 18, 1991.

61 TRW Inc., Five Year Plan, February 6, 1970, p. IV-11; Macey interview, April 18, 1991; Charles Ohly, telephone interview with the author, February 1, 1994; TRW Inc., Annual Report for 1973.

62 TRW Inc., Data Book for 1976; TRW Inc., Annual Report for 1976; Board Minutes, December 15, 1972; C. W. Ohly Remarks to Security Analysts, Los Angeles, January 18, 1977, unpaginated document.

63 TRW Inc., Annual Report for 1973; George Poe interview with the author, April 24, 1991, Cleveland, Ohio; Reynolds interview, September 1, 1992.

64 Webb interview, February 14, 1991, Los Angeles; Campbell interview, February 12, 1991; Shader interview, June 18, 1991, Redondo Beach, Calif. According to these interviews, Shepard told Webb he would approve the deal if TRW Electronics set aside a reserve equal to the purchase price. Such an act would have seriously compromised margins and management incentives, however, and Webb declined the suggestion.

For Datacom International, see Davis, "Commercial Electronic Equipment," 38–42.

65 Webb interview, February 14, 1991; Campbell interview, February 12, 1991; Henry Samulon interview with the author, March 3, 1992, Redondo Beach, Calif. TRW's talks with Collins Radio were covered in the media. See *Wall Street Journal,* March 26, 1971, 2, and May 19, 1971, 38.

66 For TRW Composants Electronique, see Board Minutes, December 18, 1970, and October 20, 1971. For Mialbras, see Board Minutes, October 17, 1973, and Burgin interview, October 10, 1991.

67 Mettler interview, May 11, 1994. For the fate of the U.S. consumer electronics industry, see Michael L. Dertouzos, Richard K. Lester, and Robert M. Solow, *Made in America: Regaining the Productive Edge* (Cambridge, Mass.: MIT Press, 1989), 12–14, 217–231.

68 Campbell interview, February 12, 1991; TRW Inc., TRW 1975 Plan, April 1971, p. VI-5; "From Auto Cranks to Space Age," *Forbes,* March 15, 1977, 31–32.

69 Campbell interview, February 12, 1991; Kovar interview, November 16, 1990; Davis, "Commercial Electronic Equipment," 8–11.

70 TRW Inc., TRW 1975 Plan, section V; TRW Inc., Data Book for 1979; *Wall Street Journal,* January 19, 1972, 36; TRW Inc., Annual Report for 1972; Board Minutes, July 17, 1974; Stanley C. Pace interview with the author, February 11, 1991, Indian Wells, Calif.; George Harter interview with the author, October 10, 1991, Palm Desert, Calif. For the joint venture with Mitsubishi, see Board Minutes, February 17, 1971 and April 28, 1976; for the joint venture in Israel, see Board Minutes, December 13, 1972.

71 TRW Inc., Annual Report for 1974; TRW Inc., Data Book, 1970–1974. Taking a longer view of the company's performance, the value of TRW's common stock had been subject to a sustained decline since the middle of 1968.

CHAPTER 12

1 TRW Memo to Managers, October 8, 1974; Board Minutes, October 16, 1974; Mettler interview, May 11, 1994.

2 For the fate of the civil systems businesses, see Stenzel, Lessons Learned: A Study of TRW Space & Defense Sector's Civil and Energy Business (typescript, TRW Inc., Space & Defense Planning Department, 1990), passim; for DeLeuw, Cather, see Board Min-

utes, October 12, 1977; for TRW Electronics and TRW Controls, see TRW Inc., Annual Report for 1976.

3 TRW Interoffice Correspondence, August 7, 1975, "Some Highlights of the 1975 Corporate Planning Conference." See also Charles Allen interview with the author, November 12, 1990.

4 The speech is reprinted in TRW Inc., Annual Report for 1976. Starting in the fall of 1975, TRW also began publishing an annual data or fact book aimed at making the task of analyzing the company easier.

5 Results from TRW Data Book, 1976; "Fred Hesse," *Sentinel,* February 6, 1976, 4; Skilling interview, May 9, 1991. See also TRW Inc., Annual Report for 1975, which includes a long section on TRW's energy-related businesses and activities.

6 TRW Interoffice Correspondence, January 6, 1975; TRW Organizational Announcement, December 29, 1975, and January 13, 1976; TRW Memo to Managers, January 23, 1976; TRW Organizational Announcement, April 27, 1976; "Phillips Joins Systems and Energy Staff," *Sentinel,* November 7, 1975, 1; David Bradburn interview with the author, October 8, 1991, Redondo Beach, Calif.

7 An Address by Ruben F. Mettler before New York Society of Security Analysts, September 28, 1978; Interview with Peter Wilson in Stenzel, "Lessons Learned," 25.

8 TRW organizational announcement, December 29, 1975. Originally Sam Phillips headed Energy Systems Management Division, which was charged with "identifying, securing, and executing major energy management and implementation programs of national significance," and Development and Applications Division, which focused on commercial development. When Phillips moved to Energy Products Group, the two divisions merged under Bob Meeker. At its formation, Energy Systems Group also included DeLeuw, Cather until its divestiture in 1977. See also Davis, "Commercial Electronic Equipment," 49; Interview with Milt Kirkpatrick in Stenzel, Lessons Learned, 67–84; and Interview with Whit Wilson in Stenzel, Lessons Learned, 85–108.

9 "ERDA Funds Development of TRW Dawson Process," *Sentinel,* October 1, 1976, 1, 4; and Steve L. Korn, Laurence N. Harnett, Thomas E. Romesser, and Sol R. Rocklin, "PSP: The Plasma Separation Process for Isotope Separation," *Quest* 6, no. 1 (Winter 1982–1983): 3–23.

10 "TRW to Build Coal Test Plant at Capistrano," *Sentinel,* October 3, 1975, 1, 4; "Plant to Wash Coal Opens at Capistrano," *Sentinel,* May 6, 1977, 1; Robert A. Meyers, Leslie J. Van Nice and Myrrl J. Santy, "Coal Desulfurization," *Quest* 3, no. 1 (Spring 1979): 33–51; Robert A. Meyers, "Gravimelt: A New Process for Ultra-Clean Coal," *Quest* 7, no. 1 (Autumn 1984): 20–23.

11 Ohly telephone interview, February 1, 1994; *Wall Street Journal,* March 6, 1979, 44.

12 Miller interview, September 4, 1991; TRW Annual Report for 1979; C.W. Ohly, presentation to 1979 planning conference.

13 TRW Inc., Five Year Plan, February 6, 1970, pp. VI-11 and VI-12; "Electronics Helping Solve Energy-Related Problems," *Sentinel,* October 1, 1976, 3; TRW Memo to Managers, August 29, 1972, August 27, 1973, August 20, 1974, undated [April or May 1978], October 11, 1978, and May 2, 1979.

14 TRW Memo to Managers, undated [April or May 1978], October 11, 1978, and May 2, 1979.

15 TRW invested $16.3 million for the new bearings plant and $8 million for a new hand tools plant. See *Wall Street Journal,* August 15, 1974, 19, and April 4, 1975, 7.

16 For U.S. Diamond Wheel, see Board Minutes, December 14, 1977; Reynolds interview, September 1, 1992; for the Industrial Products Group and changes at United-Greenfield, see TRW Memo to Managers, January 9, 1979, and October 17, 1979.

17 For Niehoff, see Board Minutes, April 25, 1979. The acquisition price was $29 million, plus the assumption of $6.25 million in debts. Financial information is derived from TRW Inc., Annual Report for 1976, and TRW Inc., Data Books, various years. See also Poe interview, April 30, 1991.

18 Stanley C. Pace interview with the author, February 11, 1991, Indian Wells Calif.; George Harter interview with the author, October 10, 1991, Palm Desert, Calif.; TRW Inc., Data Book for 1980; Douglas H. Maxwell and Thomas A. Kolakowski, "The Crystallography of Cast Turbine Airfoils," *Quest* 4, no. 2 (Autumn, 1980): 50–73, esp. pp. 69, 72.

19 "79 Annual Report to Employees," *Sentinel,* undated issue, early 1980, 1.

20 TRW Interoffice Correspondence, October 12, 1976; "Midyear 1977—A Report to Employees," *Sentinel,* July 1, 1977, 3; George Solomon interview with the author, February 13, 1991, Santa Barbara, Calif.; F. Robert Burnett interview with the author, November 14, 1990, Redondo Beach, Calif.; Harter interview, October 10, 1991.

21 TRW Memo to Managers, April 4, 1975.

22 TRW Memo to Managers, January 6, 1977; TRW Inc., TDRSS-1 Press Kit (January 1983); TRW Space & Technology Group, *We've Proven It Can Fly* (Los Angeles: TRW Space & Technology Group, 1987), 36–37; Harter interview, October 10, 1991; Edsel Dunford interview with the author, September 24, 1991, Cleveland, Ohio.

Western Union operated the Westar satellite system, the first domestic communications satellite system, which NASA used as a backup. Western Union later added American Satellite Co. as a partner in the TDRSS prime contract. The combination was a venture called Space Communications Company (Spacecom). American Satellite itself was a partnership between Fairchild Industries and Continental Telephone Company.

23 David Bradburn interview with the author, October 8, 1991, Redondo Beach, Calif.; Dunford interview, September 24, 1991; "Midyear 1977—A Report to Employees," *Sentinel,* July 1, 1977, 3–4; "TDRSS Changes Approved," *Sentinel,* August 5, 1977, 1. The panel consisted of Phillips as chair, Gene Armstrong, O. R. Baisden, Bob Bennett, Dave Bradburn, Frank Lehan, Eberhardt Rechtin, John Stenbit, Zack Taylor, and Bob Williams.

24 John Mandrow and Richard Booton, TRW Electronics Systems Group: The First 35 Years (typescript, Los Angeles, 1989), 11 and 15; C. Budd Cohen, The Evolution of TRW Defense Business Lines from Ramo-Wooldridge Guided Missiles Research Division (GMRD) (typescript, Los Angeles, March 26, 1986), 123–128, 140; Richard L. Booton interview, June 17, 1992; Redondo Beach, Calif.; Harry Hayes interview with the author, June 19, 1992, Redondo Beach, Calif;. James L. Buie, "VLSI: Very Large-Scale Integration," *Quest* 2, no. 1 (Spring 1978): 22–41; "Two TRW LSI Circuits Receive DOD Awards," *Sentinel,* March 4, 1977, 1.

25 TRW Inc., Annual Report for 1978; Nat Trembath interview with the author, November 13, 1990, Redondo Beach, Calif.; J. Sidney Webb interview with the author, February 14, 1991, Los Angeles; Booton interview, June 17, 1992; Buie, "VLSI," 36–37.

26 Trembath interview, November 13, 1990; Burnett interview with the author, November 14, 1990; W. S. Kennedy, S. M. Kovacic, and E. C. Rea, "Solid Rocket History at TRW Ballistic Missiles Division," American Institute of Aeronautics and Astronautics, AIAA-92-3614 (July 1992), 20–23.

27 TRW Inc., TDRSS-1 Press Kit; Cohen, The Evolution of TRW Defense Business, 155; TRW Inc., Memo to Managers, July 25, 1978.

28 "SEID Awarded $33 Million GEODSS Contract," *Sentinel,* June 9, 1978, 1; David D. Otten, Elliot I. Bailis, and Jerry G. Klayman, "GEODSS: Heavenly Chronicler," *Quest* 4, no. 2 (Autumn 1980): 2–23. GEODSS also had commercial and scientific import. In 1979, earth tracking stations "lost" a big and expensive RCA communications satellite, which the system could help find. In addition, astronomers believed the system could help track comets and other faint objects in space.

29 Cohen, The Evolution of TRW Defense Business, 145, 151–152.

30 R. D. DeLauer to R. F. Mettler and S. C. Pace, March 31, 1978; TRW DSSG, "Pre-Merger Evaluation of ESL, Inc.," March 31, 1978. Copies of both documents are included in George Solomon's papers at Space Park archives. See also Board Minutes, December 14, 1977, and February 15 and April 26, 1978; and "ESL: TRW's New Addition," *Sentinel,* July 7, 1978, 3.

31 "79 Annual Report to Employees," 3; "DOD Awards BETA to TRW," *Sentinel,* June 9, 1978, 1; Alexander W. Dobieski, "Modeling Tactical Military Operations," *Quest* 3, no. 1 (Spring 1979): 52–77: Jack Distaso interview with the author, November 15, 1990, Redondo Beach, Calif.

32 Board Minutes, February 14, 1979. $16.8 million; Webb interview, February 14, 1991.

33 TRW Credit Data, Organizational Announcement, November 10, 1972; TRW Memo to Managers, November 8, 1974; Van Skilling interviews with the author, May 29 and June 25, 1991, Cleveland, Ohio; Peter Nulty, "An Upstart Takes on Dun & Bradstreet," *Fortune,* April 9, 1979, 98–100.

34 Nulty, "An Upstart Takes on Dun & Bradstreet," 99.

35 TRW Memo to Managers, October 8, 1974; Donald Kovar interview with the author, November 16, 1990; Davis, "Commercial Electronic Equipment," 14–19; "TRW Tests Its Luck in a Tricky Market," *Business Week,* May 31, 1976, 24–25; "From Auto Cranks to Space Age," *Forbes,* March 15, 1977, 31–32. Interestingly, Credifier had also had limited and unfortunate experience with point-of-sale systems, including a money-losing system marketed to fast-food restaurant chains.

36 Kovar interview, November 16, 1990; Melvin Shader interview with the author, June 18, 1991, Redondo Beach, Calif.; Davis, "Commercial Electronic Equipment," 15. For trivia buffs, LRC stands for "Longitudinal Redundancy Check," a term of art in electronic data transmission.

37 John E. Davis, Commercial Electronic Equipment at TRW: An Historical Analysis (typescript, TRW Inc., Space & Defense Planning Department, March 1984), 16.

38 Board Minutes, July 14, 1976; Kovar interview, November 16, 1990; Shader interview, June 18, 1991; "TRW Tests Its Luck," 24; "See How She Runs," *Forbes,* June 1, 1976, 53; Jeannette M. Reddish, "People of the Financial World," *Financial World,* July 1, 1977, 24; TRW Inc., Annual Reports for 1976 and 1977. According to Campbell, TRW looked at buying all of Singer but did not want to get back into the computer business.

39 Robert Burgin interview with the author, October 10, 1991, La Jolla, Calif.; Board Minutes, April 28, 1976.

40 *Wall Street Journal,* April 17, 1974, 24; Kovar interview, November 16, 1990; Shader interview, June 18, 1991; Richard Campbell interview with the author, February 12, 1991, Redondo Beach, Calif.; Davis, Commercial Electronic Equipment, 20–25. In

1978, TRW acquired certain assets of Mosler Safe Co., a unit of American Standard, that added two ATM product lines to the mix.

41 Board Minutes, April 30 and July 16, 1975; TRW Memo to Managers, June 13, 1975; *Wall Street Journal,* May 5, 1975, 19.

42 Davis, Commercial Electronic Equipment, 26–28; Joseph T. Gorman interview with the author, April 17, 1991, Cleveland, Ohio.

43 Board Minutes, July 14, 1976; TRW Annual Report for 1976.

44 Mettler interview with Johnson, 1989; Pace interview, February 11, 1991; Webb interview, February 14, 1991.

45 This portrait of Pace is a composite drawn from Allen interview, November 12, 1990; Campbell interview, February 12, 1990; Foster interview, February 12, 1991; Gorman interviews, February 15 and April 17, 1991; Harter interview, October 10, 1991; Howard Knicely interviews with the author, April 17 and July 9, 1991, Cleveland, Ohio; Robert Lundy interview with the author, April 16, 1990, Solon, Ohio; Charles Ohly telephone interview with the author, February 1, 1994; Pace interview, February 11, 1991; George Poe interview with the author, April 30, 1991, Cleveland, Ohio; A. Williams Reynolds interview with the author, September 1, 1992, Fairlawn, Ohio; and Webb interview, February 14, 1991.

46 Gorman interview, April 17, 1991; Knicely interviews, April 17 and July 9, 1991. For the staff appointments, see TRW Memo to Managers, May 7 (Fay), June 6 (Foster), and December 14, 1979 (Knicely).

47 Joseph Gorman interview with the author, February 15, 1991, Cleveland, Ohio; Gorman interview, April 17, 1991. In 1976, for example, Gorman drafted a memo to Mettler that sought to redefine the traditional relationship between corporate staff and the operating sectors by identifying tasks and functions clearly belonging to one party or the other and outlining ways to resolve tensions that cropped up in areas of overlapping responsibilities. Too many disputes ended up in the chief executive office, he believed, resulting in burdensome and inefficient decision making and inhibiting teamwork. He argued that traditional line/staff distinctions failed to account for the interdependent nature of most modern executive tasks and, at their worst, tended to brand corporate staff as second-class citizens. Accordingly, he urged the development of "lean, capable, and leadership-oriented corporate staff" and a structure and policies designed to make it clear that "all top level, key players have *equal* responsibility for those tasks clearly assigned them" [emphasis in original]. Gorman, "Outline for Mtg w/ Mettler on Organization," hand-written memo, June 18, 1976.

48 Mettler interview with the author, March 6, 1990, Los Angeles; Mettler interview with Johnson, 1989; John Foster interview with the author, February 12, 1991, Redondo Beach, Calif.

49 TRW Inc., *TRW and the 80s* (n.d.), esp. pp. 5, 8–21.

50 John Thackray, "TRW Tries to Turn," *Management Today,* June 1980, 100–191; Gorman interview, April 17, 1991; E. M. Foley to R. F. Mettler and S. C. Pace, Draft Memorandum, March 28, 1978. Copy at TRW headquarters. I am grateful to John Armbruster for making these files available to me.

51 Dr. Ruben F. Mettler, Concluding Remarks, TRW Inc., 1980 Annual Analyst Meeting, San Francisco, March 27–28, 1980.

CHAPTER 13

1 TRW Memo to Managers, April 6, 1980, and January 19, 1981.

2 Ruben F. Mettler presentation in TRW Inc., 1981 Annual Analyst Meeting, Chicago, April 1–2, 1981, 4–5; Joseph Gorman interview with the author, February 15, 1991, Cleveland, Ohio; J. Sidney Webb interview with the author, February 14, 1991, Los Angeles; Richard Campbell interview with the author, February 12, 1991, Redondo Beach, Calif.; George Harter interview with the author, October 10, 1991, Palm Desert, Calif.; A. William Reynolds interview with the author, September 1, 1992, Fairlawn, Ohio.

3 TRW Electronics, Compass Business Plan, vol. 1 (1980), Executive Summary; Board Minutes, April 30, 1980; "TRW: Fujitsu's Key to the U.S.," *Business Week,* May 19, 1980, 118–119; Webb interview, February 14, 1991; Campbell interview, February 12, 1991; Melvin Shader interview with the author, June 18, 1991, Redondo Beach, Calif.

4 Larry Marion, "It's Working," *Forbes,* December 22, 1980, unpaginated reprint; Board Minutes, February 18, 1981.

5 John Foster interview with the author, February 12, 1991, Redondo Beach, Calif.; Ruben F. Mettler interview with the author, May 11, 1994, Los Angeles. Groocock later described his work at TRW in a book: *The Chain of Quality* (New York: Wiley, 1986).

6 Stanley C. Pace presentation in TRW Inc., *Annual Analysts Meeting,* Dallas, Texas, April 22, 1982, 7–9; TRW Inc., Annual Report for 1981, Conference section at back; "TRW Leads a Revolution in Managing Technology," *Business Week,* November 15, 1982, unpaginated reprint.

7 Mettler interview, May 11, 1994; Howard Knicely interview with the author, July 9, 1991, Cleveland, Ohio. At Mobil, Fay had worked on the company's famous "advertorials," which staked out positions in public policy areas. At TRW, Fay was aided by another recruit, Pat Choate, who published extensively on U.S. economic and industrial policy. Choate left the company in 1990 and subsequently earned brief notoriety as Ross Perot's running mate in the 1996 presidential election.

8 Howard Knicely interview with the author, April 17, 1991, Cleveland, Ohio.

9 Knicely interview, April 17, 1991; TRW Inc., *In Retrospect: Achievements in Human Relations, 1982–1994* (Cleveland, Ohio: TRW Inc., 1985), passim.

10 Board Minutes, October 17, 1979, and July 15, 1981; TRW Memo to Managers, July 15, 1981; TRW Inc., News Release, July 11, 1982; TRW Inc., *TRW Headquarters* (pamphlet) (TRW, n.d. [circa 1985]), passim; Gorman interview, April 17, 1991.

11 Quoted in Larry Marion, "It's Working," *Forbes,* December 22, 1980, unpaginated reprint.

12 TRW Inc., Annual Report for 1984 and Data Book for 1984; George Solomon presentation in TRW Inc., *1981 Annual Analyst Meeting,* 14.

13 Solomon presentation in TRW Inc., *1981 Annual Analyst Meeting,* 14; John Waypa, "High-Energy Laser Update," *Quest* 8, no. 1 (Summer 1985): 44–47.

14 George Solomon interview with the author, February 13, 1991, Santa Barbara, Calif.; Edsel Dunford interview with the author, September 24, 1991, Cleveland, Ohio; Timothy Hannemann interview with the author, October 9, 1991, Redondo Beach, Calif.; Daniel Goldin interview with the author, October 8, 1991; John Mandrow and Richard Booton, TRW Electronics Systems Group: The First 35 Years (typescript, Los Angeles, 1989), 17.

15 Charles W. Stephens, "VHSIC: DOD's Very High Speed Integrated Circuit. A Pivotal Technology for TRW," speech, April 15, 1985, copy in Stephens files at TRW archives at Space Park; "TRW's Superchip Passes First Milestone," *Electronics,* July 10, 1986, 49–54; William J. Broad, "The First of the 'Superchips' Arrive," *New York Times,* July 23, 1985, 17, 20; Hannemann interview, October 9, 1991.

16 Mandrow and Booton, TRW Electronics Systems Group, 16; Gorman presentation in TRW Inc., *Annual Analysts Meeting,* Los Angeles, April 17, 1985, 7; Timothy Hanneman interview with the author, June 3, 1993, Redondo Beach, Calif.

17 C. Budd Cohen, The Evolution of TRW Defense Business Lines from Ramo-Wooldridge Guided Missile Research Division (GMRD) (typescript, March 26, 1986), 147–148; Jack Distaso interview with the author, November 15, 1990, Redondo Beach, Calif.; Solomon presentation in TRW Inc., *1981 Annual Analyst Meeting,* 14.

18 Eric J. Chaisson, *The Hubble Wars: Astrophysics Meets Astropolitics in the Two-Billion-Dollar Struggle over the Hubble Space Telescope* (New York: HarperCollins Publishers, 1994), 59; Cohen, Evolution of TRW Defense Business Lines, 145–166; Distaso interview, November 15, 1990.

19 Richard Booton interview with the author, June 17, 1992, Redondo Beach, Calif.; Gorman interview, February 15, 1991.

20 TRW Inc., Annual Report for 1981; Lawrence interview, March 11, 1991; Shader interview, June 18, 1991; Booton interview, June 17, 1992.

21 "Fujitsu Backs out of Its Deal with TRW," *Business Week,* March 14, 1983, 27.

22 "TRW: Digging Even Deeper into Data Services," *Business Week,* July 1, 1985, 80.

23 Reynolds interview, September 1, 1991; Reynolds presentation in TRW Inc., *Annual Analysts Meeting,* Dallas, Tex., April 22, 1982, 15–16.

24 Reynolds presentation in TRW Inc., *Annual Analysts Meeting,* Los Angeles, April 19, 1983, 12.

25 Trevor O. Jones presentation in TRW Inc., *1981 Annual Analyst Meeting*, Chicago, April 1–2, 1981, 17–19; Reynolds presentation in TRW Inc., *Annual Analysts Meeting,* Dallas, Tex., April 22, 1982, 15–17; TRW Transportation Electrical & Electronics Operations, *Quality Electronics,* n.d. [circa 1983], passim.

26 Charles Miller interview with the author, September 4, 1991, Cleveland, Ohio. For the European acquisitions, see Table 12.2. For Hamill, see Board Minutes, July 25, 1984.

27 TRW Inc., Annual Report for 1981; Mettler presentation in TRW Inc., *Annual Analysts Meeting,* Washington D.C., May 9, 1984, 4.

28 Gorman interview, April 17, 1991; William Lawrence interview with the author, May 5, 1991, Cleveland, Ohio.

29 Gorman interview, April 17, 1991. For Porter's early work on strategy see his book, *Competitive Strategy: Techniques for Analyzing Industries and Competitors* (New York: The Free Press, 1980), passim.

30 Gorman presentation in TRW Inc., *Annual Analysts Meeting,* Los Angeles, April 19, 1983, 18.

31 Board Minutes, Octobert 27, 1982.

32 TRW Inc., 1984 Data Book, 19; Melvin Shader interview with the author, June 18, 1991, Redondo Beach, Calif.

33 Gorman interview, April 17, 1991.

34 TRW Inc., 1984 Data Book, 19.

[35] Gorman presentation in TRW Inc., *Annual Analysts Meeting,* Los Angeles, April 19, 1983, 16; Gorman interview, April 17, 1991; William H. Gregory, "TRW Reorganizes to Emphasize High Technology," *Aviation Week & Space Technology,* January 6, 1986, 78–79.

[36] "TWST Names Mettler Best Chief Executive Auto Parts/Diversified Original Equipment," *The Wall Street Transcript,* October 4, 1982, unpaginated reprint; "TRW Leads a Revolution in Managing Technology," *Business Week,* November 15, 1982, 124–128; James Cook, "A Paragon Called TRW," *Forbes,* July 18, 1983, 102–107. During these years TRW also ranked as one of the most admired corporations in the country. See *Wall Street Journal,* July 23, 1985, 1, 5.

   According to Gorman, the *Forbes* article was less a commentary on TRW than a reflection of Malcolm Forbes's desire to defend conglomerates from criticism. Gorman interview, April 17, 1991.

   Interestingly, TRW was not one of the field sites in the famous McKinsey study of excellent companies, though its approach to planning received favorable notice. See Thomas J. Peters and Robert H. Waterman, Jr., *In Search of Excellence: Lessons from America's Best-Run Companies* (New York: Harper & Row, 1982), 40.

[37] J. T. Gorman to S. C. Pace, "'Staffing' Memorandum," July 16, 1982. I am grateful to Mr. Gorman for providing me a copy of this memorandum. See also Stanley C. Pace interview with the author, February 11, 1991, Indian Wells, Calif.

[38] *TRW: 1985* (Boston: Harvard Business School Case Services, 9-288-047), 1–3. For the general subject of restructuring during the 1980s, a valuable guide is Gordon Donaldson, *Corporate Restructuring: Managing the Change Process from Within* (Boston: Harvard Business School Press, 1994), esp. chaps. 1, 3, and 9.

[39] J. T. Gorman, speech at Scottsdale Management Conference, October 7–11, 1984. Mettler endorsed these measures soon thereafter. See R. F. Mettler, Memo to Policy Group, Group Executives, Division Managers, Company & Sector and Group Staff, and Scottsdale Conference Attendees, November 27, 1984.

[40] The strategic management seminars were developed by Monitor Company, a strategy consulting firm associated with the work of Michael Porter.

[41] Gorman, speech at Scottsdale, October 7–11, 1984; Dr. Ruben F. Mettler, Presentation to Security Analysts, New York, N.Y., November 12, 1985; *TRW: 1985,* 6.

[42] Mettler, presentation to Security Analysts, November 12, 1985; "TRW Casts Off the Burdens of the Past," *Business Week,* October 7, 1985, 36–37; Charles Allen interview with the author, November 12, 1990, San Diego, Calif.; Campbell interview, February 12, 1991; Van Skilling interview with the author, May 9, 1991, Cleveland, Ohio.

[43] Mettler, presentation to Security Analysts, November 12, 1985; "TRW's 'Dutch Auction': I Have 88! Do I Hear 87? . . . ," *Business Week,* October 7, 1985, 37; Lawrence interview, April 17, 1991.

[44] Pace interview, February 11, 1991. See also Gorman interview, February 15, 1991.

CHAPTER **14**

[1] Edsel Dunford presentation in TRW Inc., *Remarks from the Annual Analysts & Bankers Meeting,* Detroit, May 18, 1988, 33–39. See also TRW Inc., 1986 Data Book, 8–11, for a partial listing of principal defense and space contracts.

[2] For a description of the Orbital Maneuvering Vehicle, see TRW Inc., 1988 Data Book, inside back cover; and TRW Space & Technology Group, *We've Proven It Can Fly* (Los Angeles: TRW Space & Technology Group, 1986), 40.

3 U.S. General Accounting Office, Report to the Chairman, Subcommittee on Oversight and Investigations, Committee on Energy and Commerce, House of Representatives, *Government Contractors: Internal Controls and Charging Practices at TRW Inc.* (Washington, D.C.: U.S. Government Printing Office, July 1989), 3; William Lawrence interview with the author, March 11, 1991.

4 "TRW Discloses Cost Estimate Overcharges," *Aviation Week & Space Technology,* November 26, 1984, 25. In 1994, TRW settled a civil lawsuit from the cases that added another $12.6 million to the total paid to the government. TRW Inc., News Release, April 15, 1994.

5 U.S. General Accounting Office, *Government Contractors,* 14–15; Lawrence interview, March 11, 1991.

6 John Mandrow and Richard Booton, TRW Electronics Systems Group: The First 35 Years, (typescript, Los Angeles, 1989), 17–18; Dunford presentation in TRW Inc., *Remarks from the Annual Analysts Meeting,* Arlington, Va., May 18, 1989, 28, 37.

7 TRW Inc., Space and Defense Planning Department, "Summary of TRW Ventures," May 18, 1990, copy at TRW archives at Space Park; Davis Dyer, "The Limits of Technology Transfer: Civil Systems at TRW, 1965–1975," in Thomas P. Hughes and Agatha Hughes, eds., *Systems, Experts, and Computers, 1939–1970* (in press), a book based on a conference sponsored by MIT's Dibner Institute and scheduled for publication in 1998.

8 For accounts of structural changes in the relationship between the automakers and their suppliers, see James P. Womack, Daniel T. Jones, and Daniel Roos, *The Machine That Changed the World: The Story of Lean Production* (Cambridge, Mass.: MIT Press, 1991), esp. chap. 6; and Susan Helper, "Strategy and Irreversibility in Supplier Relations: The Case of the U.S. Automobile Industry," *Business History Review* 65, no. 4 (Winter 1991): 781–824, esp. 811–822.

9 Dana Milbank, "Air-Bag Woes Knock Wind out of TRW," *Wall Street Journal,* March 12, 1991, unpaginated clipping. Others who the reporter interviewed claimed that turnover exceeded 80 percent.

10 David Loeffler interview with the author, April 17, 1991, Cleveland, Ohio; Chester Macey interview with the author, April 18, 1991, Cleveland, Ohio.

11 Chester O. Macey in TRW Inc., *Remarks from the Annual Analysts Meeting,* May 21, 1991, Cleveland, Ohio, 46.

12 Jack Keebler, "So Long, Hydraulics—The Electronic Revolution in Power Steering," *Popular Science,* May 1968, 50–56; Mike Knepper, "Electronic Steering: TRW's Fluid-Free Rack and Pinion," *Motor Trend,* June 1986, 83, 137; Macey interview, April 18, 1991; Robert M. Lynas in TRW Inc., *Prepared Remarks from the Annual Analysts Meeting,* May 15, 1986, Cleveland, Ohio.

13 Monitor Company, AWW Sector Strategy: Environmental Analysis (consulting report, 1986; copy at TRW headquarters), Part I, 35–40; Myers presentation in TRW Inc., *Remarks from The Annual Analysts & Bankers Meeting,* Detroit, May 18, 1988; Joseph T. Gorman, speech to Chrysler Corporation Board of Directors, April 5, 1990; remarks by Joseph T. Gorman, Automotive News World Congress, Detroit, January 13, 1991.

14 U.S. Department of Transportation, National Highway Traffic Safety Administration, *Facts You Should Know about Air Bags,* rev., October 1986, unpaginated pamphlet; Charles L. Miller presentation in TRW Inc., *Remarks from the Annual Analysts Meeting,* May 16, 1990.

15 Charles Miller interview with the author, September 4, 1991, Cleveland, Ohio; William Lawrence interview with the author, May 9, 1991, Cleveland, Ohio; Thomas H. Vos and George W. Goetz, "Inflatable Restraint Systems: Helping Save Lives on the Road,"

Quest (Winter 1989–1990): 3–18; TRW Inc., "Backgrounder: How the Automotive Air Bag System Works," News Release, January 1990. For a recent survey of the early development of air bag systems, see Don Sherman, "The Rough Road to Air Bags," *American Heritage of Invention & Technology* 11, no. 1 (Summer 1995): 48–56.

16 Milbank, "Air-Bag Woes Knock Wind out of TRW"; "TRW's Air-Bag Business Looks Ready to Balloon," *Business Week,* November 2, 1987, 74–75.

17 Board Minutes, October 22, 1986; Joseph T. Gorman, *Remarks from the Annual Analysts & Bankers Meeting,* April 22, 1987, Los Angeles.

18 Board Minutes, April 29 and July 22, 1987, and April 27, 1988.

19 Board Minutes, October 25, 1989; Marcia Berss, "Nothing Is in the Bag," *Forbes,* March 4, 1991, 97.

20 During 1986 and 1987, Automotive Worldwide commissioned Monitor Company to help prepare a global automotive strategy. The author was part of that consulting team.

21 Charles L. Miller in *Remarks from the Annual Analysts & Bankers Meeting,* May 18, 1988, Detroit.

22 Whilden presentation in TRW Inc., *Prepared Remarks from the Annual Analysts Meeting,* May 15, 1986; Van Skilling interview with the author, June 25, 1991, Cleveland, Ohio. In the fall of 1987, ISG added to its business by acquiring Executive Services, a Texas-based supplier of target marketing data and services, for $13.2 million. See Board Minutes, October 28, 1987.

23 "The Loan Game," *Newsweek,* January 27, 1986, 46; Adam Snitzer, "Money for Nothing," *Forbes,* May 18, 1987, 212–213; "TRW Takes Credit out of the Closet," *Sales & Marketing Management,* June 1987, 34; Whilden presentation in TRW Inc., *Remarks from the Annual Analysts Meeting,* May 18, 1989, Arlington, Va.

24 Board Minutes, October 26 and December 14, 1984, and April 24, 1985; Whilden presentation in TRW Inc., *Prepared Remarks from the Annual Analysts Meeting,* May 15, 1986, Cleveland, Ohio.

25 Whilden presentation in TRW Inc., *Remarks from the Annual Analysts Meeting,* Arlington, Va., May 18, 1989.

26 Whilden presentation in TRW Inc., *Remarks from the Annual Analysts & Bankers Meeting,* April 22, 1987, Los Angeles; Board Minutes, October 22, 1986; Skilling interview, June 25, 1991.

27 Board Minutes, April 26, 1989; Ruben F. Mettler interview with the author, May 11, 1994, Los Angeles; Skilling interview, June 25, 1991.

28 Mettler interview, May 11, 1994; Skilling interview, June 25, 1991.

29 Whilden presentation in TRW Inc., *Remarks from the Annual Analysts Meeting,* May 18, 1989, Arlington, Va.; Skilling interview, June 25, 1991.

30 Quoted in Cook, "A Paragon Called TRW," *Forbes,* July 18, 1983, 103–104.

31 Howard Knicely interview with the author, October 1995, Cleveland, Ohio.

32 Joseph Gorman interview with the author, April 17, 1991, Cleveland, Ohio; Knicely interview, April 17, 1991.

33 Gorman interview, April 17, 1991; Knicely interview, April 17, 1991; Skilling interview, June 25, 1991; TRW Inc., Annual Report for 1988.

34 TRW Inc., *A Special Report for Managers: Mission and Values Defined* (1989).

35 Milbank, "Air-Bag Woes," unpaginated clipping.

36 Gorman and Dunford presentations in TRW Inc., *Remarks from The Annual Analysts Meeting,* Cleveland, Ohio, May 21, 1991, 1, 13–14, 18.

37 Skilling presentation in TRW Inc., *Remarks from the Annual Analysts Meeting,* May 21, 1991, Cleveland, Ohio; Skilling presentation in TRW Inc., *Remarks from the Annual Analysts Meeting,* May 19, 1992, Mesa, Ariz.; Skilling interview, June 25, 1991; Mettler interview, May 11, 1994.

38 Michael W. Miller, "Credit-Report Firms Face Greater Pressure; Ask Norwich, Vt., Why," *Wall Street Journal,* September 23, 1991, 1, A6.

39 "Attack of the Cyber Snoopers," *Business Week,* May 18, 1994, unpaginated online version; Peter Hellman interview with the author, February 6, 1997, Cleveland, Ohio.

40 Knicely interview, April 17, 1991.

41 "TRW Tries to Shape Up," *New York Times,* December 15, 1991; TRW Inc., Annual Report for 1991; Skilling interview, June 25, 1991.

42 TRW Annual Reports for 1991, 1995, and 1996.

43 See Dunford, Timothy W. Hanneman, John P. Stenbit, and Robert J. Kohler presentations in *Remarks from the Annual Analysts Meeting,* Cleveland, Ohio, May, 19, 1993.

44 TRW Inc., News Releases, March 2, 1990, and February 13, May 20, and December 12, 1991.

45 Jeff Cole, "Star Wars: In New Space Race, Companies Are Seeking Dollars from Heaven," *Wall Street Journal,* October 10, 1995, 1; Gary Samuels, "Crowded Skies," *Forbes,* May 22, 1995, 99–100.

46 Gorman presentation in TRW Inc., *The Annual Analysts Meeting,* Cleveland, Ohio, May 19, 1993, 2; Jerry K. Myers presentation in TRW Inc., *The Annual Analysts Meeting,* May 16, 1990, 39; Peter S. Hellman presentation to Annual Analysts Meeting, 1994, unpaginated slide.

47 Gorman interview, April 17, 1991; Peter Staudhammer interviews with the author, June 2 and 4, 1993, Redondo Beach, Calif.

48 Joseph T. Gorman interview with the author, March 4, 1997, Cleveland, Ohio.

49 TRW Inc., Annual Report for 1994; *TRW Leader,* November 1994, 1.

Chapter 15

1 The remainder of this chapter is based on Joseph T. Gorman interview with the author, March 4, 1997, and Peter Hellman interview with the author, February 6, 1997. Both interviews took place in Cleveland, Ohio.

2 Peter Hellman, Speech to Cleveland Engineering Society, November 7, 1996.

3 Gen. William W. Hartzog and Susan Canedy, "The 21st Century Army," *Army,* February 1997, 22–28.

4 TRW Inc., Annual Report for 1995.

INDEX

ABOUT THE AUTHOR

Davis Dyer is managing director of the Winthrop Group, a firm in Cambridge, Massachusetts, that specializes in business and technology history. He is the co-author of many publications, including (with David Sicilia) *Labors of a Modern Hercules: The Evolution of a Chemical Company* (HBS Press, 1990), and the co-editor (with Alan Brinkley) of *The Reader's Companion to the American Presidency* (Houghton Mifflin, forthcoming).